THE

THEOLOGICAL WORKS

OF THE

REV. JOHN JOHNSON, M.A.,

VICAR OF CRANBROOK IN THE DIOCESE OF CANTERBURY.

VOLUME I.

WIPF & STOCK · Eugene, Oregon

Wipf and Stock Publishers
199 W 8th Ave, Suite 3
Eugene, OR 97401

The Unbloody Sacrifice and Altar, Unvailed and Supported
In Which the nature of the Eucharist is explained according to the
sentiments of the Christian Church in the four first centuries. Vol. 1
By Johnson, John, M. A.
ISBN 13: 978-1-62032-672-5
Publication date 12/15/2012
Previously published by John Henry Parker, 1847

THE
UNBLOODY SACRIFICE,

AND

A L T A R,

UNVAILED and SUPPORTED,

IN WHICH

The nature of the Eucharist is explained according to the sentiments of the Christian Church in the four first centuries;

PROVING,

That the Eucharist is a proper material Sacrifice,
That it is both Eucharistic, and propitiatory,
That it is to be offered by proper officers,
That the Oblation is to be made on a proper Altar,
That it is properly consumed by manducation :

To which is added,

A Proof, that what our Saviour speaks concerning eating His Flesh, and drinking His Blood, in the vith Chapter of St. *John's* Gospel, is principally meant of the Eucharist,

With a Prefatory Epistle to the Lord Bishop of NORWICH;

Animadversions on the Reverend Dr. *Wise's* Book, which he calls *The Christian Eucharist rightly stated :*

And some reflections on a stitched book, entituled, *An Answer to the exceptions made against the Lord Bishop of* OXFORD's *Charge.*

Nil adeò quod obduret mentes hominum, quàm simplicitas Divinorum operum, i. e. Sacramentorum, quæ in actu videtur; & magnificentia, quæ in effectu repromittitur.
Tertullian, *De Baptismo, mox ab initio.*

Κρατοῦμεν τὴν ΟΜΟΛΟΓΙΑΝ ἕως ἂν ζήσομεν [ζῶμεν. Ed. Ben.]
Origen. contra Celsum, Lib. 8.

By *JOHN JOHNSON*, M.A. Vicar of Cranbrook in
the Diocese of *Canterbury.*

EDITOR'S PREFACE.

CONSIDERABLE delay has occurred in the publication of this Volume, from accidental circumstances. Owing to the difficulty of obtaining a copy of the Second Edition, (which came out in 1724, in the Author's life-time, and which is now become extremely rare,) it was found necessary to begin working with the First Edition, (that of 1714;) and the Volume had been completely prepared for the press as early as July last, before a copy of the Second Edition was obtained; which, of course, involved a thorough examination *de novo*. For the loan of that copy, the Committee is indebted to the courtesy of the Rev. C. L. Cornish, M.A. of Exeter College. All the passages, inserted by the Author in his Second Edition, have been distinguished in the present by being inclosed in brackets; only it must be observed, that where instances occur of *single* words bracketted, they have been put in by the Editor on his own responsibility; and he trusts that it will clearly appear from the context, that in the very few instances of their occurrence such a course was necessary. There are several passages in the text of the First Edition, which the Author has entirely omitted in the Second; these it has been thought advisable to retain in the present Edition in the shape of notes. The reader will thence have an opportunity of discriminating the shades of theological difference (if any such really exist,) to which Johnson's mind was subject in a decade of years; and the Editor is thereby spared the invidious task of assuming their arbitration. A few sentences only have been entirely omitted, which the Author has withdrawn in his Second Edition, and wherein he had been betrayed, by the heat of controversy, into an undue asperity of expression.

It may be as well to remark, that wherever the word 'Sacrifice' is here employed to designate the mysterious oblation in the Christian Eucharist, it is marked by a capital initial; whereas the 'sacrifices' of the Elder Dispensation, and their heathen counterfeits, are left in small letter. The same rule obtains with regard to 'Blood,' when applied to the adorable and spiritual Mystery of our Saviour's Presence; 'Bread and Wine,' when they signify the Sacramental symbols; and generally all specific terms of the Catholic Ritual and Theology are so marked. It might have been expected, that according to the usual custom, this work should have opened with a Memoir of the Author; but the bulk of the present Volume has necessarily precluded it. A biographical notice at considerable length has been prefixed to a posthumous Edition of his Sermons; which may on a future occasion be published. It will then be necessary to give some account of the various adversaries, with whom our Author broke a lance in the polemical lists; Dr. Hancock, Dr. Pelling, Dr. Whitby the Commentator, Dr. Henry More of Cambridge (of Platonic celebrity,) Mr. Lewis of Margate, and Dr. Thomas Wise, are among the opponents to whom we are introduced in this Volume. It has been a subject of regret with the Editor, that he has been unable to verify the references to Dr. Wise's pamphlet; and the urgency, with which this long-delayed, long-promised Volume has been called for, admitted not of further investigation. It is consoling, however, to reflect, that the omission is not of material importance to the elucidation of the important subject of the present work, it being simply a record of contemporary controversy; and it may be allowed

$$————————— \text{καὶ ὑπὸ στέγῃ} \ ^a$$
$$\text{Πυκνᾶς ἀκούειν ψεκάδος εὐδούσῃ φρενί.}$$

In verifying the references to the works of the Fathers and other writers, the best Editions have been used by the Editor, without confining himself to those employed by the Author, as will be seen by the following List.

R. O.

Jesus Coll.
Feb. 19, 1847.

ᵃ [Sophocles apud Ciceronis Epp. ad Att., Lib. ii. Ep. 7.]

LIST OF EDITIONS EMPLOYED IN VERIFYING
THE PRESENT VOLUME.

Ambrosius, S. Paris. 1686.
Aquinas, S. Thomas, Summa Theologica, Duaci, 1614.
Athanasius, S. Paris. 1698.
Athenagoras, Oxon. 1706.
Augustinus, S. Bened. 1679.
Barclay, Apology, 1736.
Barnabas, S. Hefele, 1842.
Basilius, S. Paris. 1721.
Bellarminus, De Missa, 1601.
Bennet, Rights of the Clergy, 1711.
Beveregii Synodicum, Oxon. 1672.
Beza, In Nov. Testamentum, Cantabrigiæ, 1642.
Bibliotheca Veterum Patrum, Galland. 1770.
———————————————— Colon. 1618.
———————————————— Paris. 1624.
Bingham's Works, London, 1840.
Binius, 1636.
Calepine, Dictionarium, Lugd. 1681.
Calvini Institutiones, Lugd. 1654.
——— Harmonia Evang. Genevæ, 1595.
Canus, Melchior, Colon. Agripp. 1605.
Catena PP. Græcorum, Corderio.
Chrysostomus, S. Joh. Savil. 1612.
Clarke's, Dr. Samuel, Works, 1738.
Clemens Alexandrinus, S. Potter, Oxon. 1715.
Clemens Romanus, S. Hefele, 1842.
Codex Canonum Eccles. Africanæ, Justelli.
Concilia, Labbe. et Cossart. 1728.
Confessio Waldensium, Basil. 1568.
Cowell's Law-Interpreter, Cambridge, 1607.
Cyprianus, S. Paris. 1726.
Cyrillus Alexandrinus, S. Paris. 1638.
Cyrillus Hierosolym. S. Paris. 1720.
Ephrem Syrus, S. Romæ, 1732.
Epiphanius, S. Paris. 1622.

Eusebius, De Præparatione Evang. Paris. 1628.
——— De Demonstratione Evang. Paris. 1628.
——— Hist. Eccles. Zimmerman, 1822.
Eustathius, Romæ, 1551.
Fasciculus Rerum, Brown, Lond. 1690.
Fulgentius, S. Lugd. 1633.
Gerhard, 1657.
Gregorius Magnus, S. Sacrament. Par. 1642.
Gregorius Nazianzenus, S. Paris. 1778.
Gregorius Nyssenus, S. Paris. 1638.
Grotii Opera, Amstelodami, 1679.
Hakewell, Dr. Dissertation with Dr. Heylyn, 1641.
Hammond, On the New Testament, 1659.
Hancock, Dr. Patres Vindicati, 1709.
Heroldi Hæresiologia, Basil. 1556.
Hieronymus, S. Paris. 1706.
Hilarius Pictaviensis, S. Paris. 1693.
Ignatius, S. Hefele, 1842.
Irenæus, S. Paris. 1710.
Isidorus Hispalensis, S. Colon. Agr. 1617.
Justin Martyr, S. Paris. 1742.
Larroque, Histoire d'Eucharistie, Amsterdam, 1671.
Lightfoot, Synopsis Critic. Cant. 1674.
Maximus, Contra Marcionitas, Wetsten. 1673.
Mede's Works, 1664.
Melanchthon. Explic. in Mal. Witeberg. 1601.
Optatus, S. Paris. 1679.
Origenes, Paris. 1733.
Outram, De Sacrificiis, 1677.
Pearson, Annotationes in D. Ignatium, Oxon. 1709.
Philo Judæus, Mangey, 1742.

Plutarchus, Francofurti, 1599.
Socini Opera, 1656.
Sozomenus, Valesio, Paris. 1668.
Spencer, De Legibus Hebræis, Cantab. 1685.
Surii Sanctorum Historiæ, Col. Agripp. 1576—81.
Tertullianus, Paris. 1664.
Theodoretus, Paris, 1642.

Theodori Archiep. Cant. Pœnitentiale, Paris. 1677.
Theophylactus, Lindsell. Londini, 1636.
Thuanus, London, 1733.
Vitringa, Observationes Sacræ, Franequer, 1689.
Voigtus, Gothofred. Thysiasteriologia sive De Altaribus Veterum Christianorum, Hamburg. 1709.

PREFATORY EPISTLE

TO THE RIGHT REVEREND

THE LORD BISHOP OF NORWICH,

AFTERWARDS OF WINCHESTER.

My Lord,

With all the submission and deference that is due from a Priest to a Bishop, I crave leave to inscribe your name to these papers; not that I think your Lordship disposed to patronise them, but because you have been pleased to shew your inclination to be a judge in this dispute, to whom therefore I, as an humble advocate, have thought fit to address myself.

And, my Lord, I have just reason to expect that you should not discountenance my plea, as you are one of that Right Reverend Order which has always been esteemed, till now of very late, to have had the guardianship of the Altar in an especial manner committed to it by Christ Jesus Himself.

"One Bishop, and one Altar," has been looked upon as the distinguishing motto of the Apostolical Church ever since the time of St. Ignatius, and to contend *pro Aris*, 'for the Altars,' has ever been thought honourable in all men, but especially in those whose business it is continually to attend them.

Some may suggest to your Lordship, that several of our Bishops since the Reformation have declared against the doctrine for which I plead, but I am persuaded that this is all mistake. Our Protestant Bishops have indeed with good

JOHNSON.   B

reason pronounced judgment against the Sacrifice of the
Popish Mass, and we all unanimously and heartily concur in
subscribing to their determinations in this particular; but,
my Lord, it is the Sacrifice of St. Cyprian, Irenæus, Justin
Martyr, Ignatius, Clement of Rome, the Apostles, and Christ
Jesus Himself, for which we now contend; that sacrifice
which Archbishop Laud and his most learned and pious
chaplain Mr. Mede asserted in the last age, and which no
Bishop before your Lordship had ever disapproved. The
only person of your venerable order who may seem to have
shewed his dislike of it, was he whose name rather glares than
shines in our English history, I mean Archbishop Williams,
and yet it is well known that he rather opposed his rival and
superior Archbishop Laud, than the Altar and Sacrifice itself.
[And indeed the Altar against which he particularly expressed
his indignation and resentment, was literally a Popish Altar,
on which the sacrifice of the Mass had formerly been offered,
and which a private vicar had re-erected in his church[a]:] so
that I must, till better informed, consider your Lordship as
the first Christian Bishop that ever yet openly declared
against that Sacrifice for which we now plead; but heavens
forbid that you should finally persist in your hostility against
so primitive and Divine an institution.

Some may think that your Lordship has already passed a
definitive sentence against it, or that you are gone too far to
retreat; but, my Lord, I have seen a very learned and
upright temporal judge sitting upon the bench, who upon
the first opening of the cause has with some degree of vehemence espoused the plaintiff's plea, and yet upon hearing
the adverse counsel and evidence has finally pronounced
sentence for the defendant. And, my Lord, that candour and
impartiality, by which your Lordship stands distinguished in
the opinion of those who pretend best to know you, give me
reason to hope that you will upon a full hearing be convinced
that Dr. Hancock (of whose learning and judgment you had
entertained so favourable an opinion) has imperfectly and
falsely represented the case now in dispute: and, my Lord,
the whole learned world can look upon what you have
hitherto said on this subject as no more than the propensities

[a] The words between brackets are not in the edition of 1724.

of a judge to one side of a cause, before the witnesses have
been thoroughly examined, and the arguments of each side
laid in an equal balance; and all reasonable men will allow
that it is very consistent with the integrity and ability of the
greatest human judges to pass final sentence against that
side which they themselves favoured during the trial. And,
my Lord, it is the design of these papers to take off those
false colours which our adversaries have endeavoured to lay
upon their errors, and to state and clear the notions of the
ancients upon this weighty subject according to the best
light I had from Scripture, and the most early monuments
of primitive antiquity.

Further, my Lord, the censure you was pleased to pass
upon somewhat that I had said upon this subject in the
Second Part of The Clergyman's *Vade Mecum*[b], gives me a
right to say something in my own defence. I did indeed
in the postscript to The Propitiatory Oblation, consider the
most specious appearance of argument which your Lordship
had urged against that passage in the *Vade* so far as the
doctrine itself was concerned, but I was not so solicitous for
the reputation of that book or the author of it, as for what
concerned the Oblation itself, and therefore deferred the vindication of them till some further opportunity should offer
itself, as now it does.

And I choose to make my defence by way of Prefatory
Epistle, because I desire to convince your Lordship and the
world that I make a great distinction between you and those
who pass under the name of adversaries in the following
book; for, my Lord, I abhor the thoughts of being an adversary to a Bishop. I thank God I was always bred under an
awe and reverence of the Episcopal character, and I hope I
shall never so far forget myself as to be guilty of any insolence or contempt toward the persons that are invested with
it, whatever treatment I receive from any of that bench.

My conscience bears me witness that the book (I mean
the Second Part of the *Vade Mecum*) which has fallen under
your Lordship's displeasure, was compiled from one end to
the other with a sincere design of serving the Established
Church, and especially the Bishops themselves, and all things

[b] Part II. first ed.

that bore any relation to them, of which I esteemed the Altar and Sacrifice not the least; and he who when I published that book should have told me that one of those Bishops, and particularly your Lordship would be the first, and in effect the only man that would condemn it, I should have looked upon as a person that either did not understand your Lordship's temper, or was disposed to misrepresent it; for I could not believe that any of our English Bishops were for obliging enemies and giving up friends, a counsel which is believed to have undermined and shaken the royal throne and can never support the episcopal.

My Lord, I shall use a true English freedom throughout this whole book, and particularly this epistle, and therefore think necessary to bespeak your Lordship's patience and good temper. For I am one that have always studied truth much more than complaisance, and I think it my duty in this case, which I take to be of great moment, not to suppress my sentiments. If I had not been fully persuaded of the justice of my cause, I would never have so heartily espoused it, and he who is in earnest convinced of any Divine truth, and of the great moment and consequence of it, cannot but think that he has a right to speak what he believes, and that those arguments which have determined his own judgment, will have the same power in determining the judgments of others when duly considered and applied. Your Lordship will give me leave to speak with competent assurance of the truth of the doctrine for which I am now pleading, if I may be believed when I do most solemnly declare that if I had had any the least doubts or mistrusts either of the certainty of the doctrine, or my own integrity and disinterested zeal for it without any sinister or indirect view, I would never have troubled the world with a new book upon this subject.

But there are several topics made use of by those that are adversaries of the Sacrifice, to inflame the minds of men against the thing itself and the assertors of it, which it will be very proper for me briefly to consider, and humbly to lay before your Lordship my thoughts upon every one of them. Whatever concerns the merits of the cause is, I hope, fully treated of in the following book; but there are objections which do not at all affect the cause itself, but the reputation only of those who write for it, and these I have reserved for this place; and I will not omit any that I have hitherto met with, either in the books that have been written, or in the conversation I have had with others upon this subject.

1. The first and capital objection of this sort is, that the Sacrifice of the Eucharist is right down Popery; if by Sacrifice be meant a material proper Sacrifice, which is what I have asserted in this treatise. And this indeed is a very terrible objection if it were a true one. If any of us asserted the Sacrifice of the Mass, I would readily grant that no reproaches were too hard, no censures too severe against them, who were guilty of attempting to introduce so abominable a corruption. But, my Lord, it is evident to any man that is not exceedingly prejudiced, that the Sacrifice of the Primitive Church, for which we plead, and that of the Church of Rome, are substantially and essentially distinct. The Sacrifice of the Primitive Church consists of bread and wine, consecrated into the Sacramental Body and Blood of Christ by the secret operation of the Holy Spirit. The Sacrifice of the Church of Rome consists (if we may believe the Papists) of the very substantial Body and Blood of Christ, together with His human soul and Divine nature, or, in a word, of the one very true Christ, both God and man. And what necessarily follows from hence is, that the Sacrifice of the Primitive Church was thought to be effectual and prevalent, in virtue of the grand Personal Sacrifice, but the Sacrifice of the Church of Rome is affirmed to be the very same in substance that was made on the cross, and therefore of itself expiatory and satisfactory; and I am very sure that to all impartial inquirers this is a sufficient compurgation of the crime objected against us.

I confess, my Lord, it is one thing for men to answer and confute any criminous objection laid against them, and it is another thing to free themselves from all suspicions of it. And it fares with us as it does with many other honest men, our own consciences acquit us, and we can abundantly refel all the arguments brought against us, but we cannot cure the jealous heads, or silence the reproachful tongues and pens of our adversaries; and whether this be our fault or theirs I submit to your Lordship's judgment.

Popery has ever been the watchword of the enemies of the Church of England, whereby they have alarmed the people to the destruction of those that have stood in their way, and opposed their assaults upon the constitution; within these hundred years it was Popery with some, nay and is so to this day, to assert the co-operation of the will of man with the grace of God, or to contradict those notions of predestination or reprobation, which Mr. Calvin and his followers had made the fundamental article of religion. The Solifidians and Antinomians have produced as plausible allegations from some of the first reformers in behalf of their execrable opinions, as our adversaries can now pretend to bring from the same writers against us. Episcopacy and Liturgy, and all those particular doctrines and practices by which the Church of England is happily distinguished from the several sorts of dissenters, are to this day cried out upon as rank Popery by the main body of those who separate from us; they have indeed been taught better manners by those who have of late had the management of them, than to beard or insult our prelates with this sort of rhetoric; but those of the clergy whose duty requires them frequently to converse with these dissenting brethren on the level, know full well the truth of what I say by daily experience. And sure we have no just reason to be concerned, that the very same artillery is now employed against us which was formerly made use of against the whole constitution of our Church, and especially the defenders of it. There is indeed one consideration that does very much sharpen the edge of this objection, which is, that it comes from the tongues or pens of those of our own communion. This is a demonstration that our adversaries do too much symbolise with the hot bigoted fanatics, and are learning their language and logic; and I must have leave to say, that this reproach does no more affect the assertors of the Sacrifice, than the assertors of Episcopacy and Liturgy; and I have reason to expect that all impartial men should believe what I now say, till our opponents can produce a proof of a Bishop without an Altar, or a Liturgy without a proper Sacrifice, from the remains of genuine antiquity.

Therefore I am heartily sorry that my Lord Bishop of

Oxford in his last year's Charge[c], should say of this among other doctrines, "that it savours too much of Popery." By this his Lordship gives countenance to our adversaries in their most unmanly and unchristian revilings, and it is certain that by this means his Lordship has done more injury to his own reputation than to ours in the judgment of all discerning men; for persons of dignity cannot more degrade themselves, than by stooping down so low as to take up a vulgar reproach against any man, or body of men, especially when this reproach must at last fall, not only upon Archbishop Laud, and some of the most valuable of our English prelates and divines, but upon the whole race of the Primitive Bishops, and 'the whole Church of the first-born,' and of the most pure and uncorrupted ages. I cannot but say that his Lordship had much better consulted his own honour, by leaving this dirty work to Dr. Hancock and Dr. Wise. In the sequel of the Charge, he is pleased to say a great many sweet things, to persuade both sides to peace and mutual forbearance; and having observed[d] that "some of each party accuse the other as betraying the Church, one side to Popery, the other to Presbytery;" he adds, "Hard censures, and such as will one day be severely accounted for, if they are groundless, as I trust they are in the main on both sides. I do hope there are very few on either that are justly liable to them." Now certainly the most prevailing argument that my Lord could have used to them who charge some of the Church with a design of betraying us to Presbytery, was to have given an example in his own person of laying aside all suspicions of Popery in the doctrines there mentioned, and which are now asserted by those against whom this part of his Charge is directed, and such a pattern might have been very influential and powerful; and if there were any on that side who charge the other with betraying us to Presbytery, that proceeded to calumniate the Bishop or any of his side for the future, they would have been more inexcusable. As for myself, I solemnly declare that I do not believe any one of our English Bishops disposed to betray us to Presbytery[e], much less is it credible that his Lordship should have so ill

[c] Page 10.　　　　[d] Page 21.
[e] This was written by me A.D. 1713. [Author's note, 2nd ed.]

an opinion of his own friends, though he knows them much better than I can pretend to do. And I cannot conceive what his Lordship intended by seeming to give it for granted that a few on both sides might be justly liable to these censures, unless it were that he found it convenient for his hypothesis to have it believed that some few of the writers on our side were disposed to betray us to Popery, and then for a proof of his own impartiality, thought it but reasonable to give up a few of the other side, as willing to betray us to Presbytery. And by the few who would betray us to Popery, it is obvious to suppose, that he by a usual figure of rhetoric meant one single man, for it is very hard for a successor to forget his ejected living predecessor.

You, my Lord, are pleased to begin your arguings on this head with the same reflection; for you were truly sensible that there was no proof that could be thought of any force against this doctrine, but what had a spice of the same sort of logic. You do not " wonder that priests of the Church of Rome, but that presbyters of a Reformed Church should lay claim to a Sacrifice;" and are pleased to add that " it is pretty new, and somewhat unaccountable^f." Now, my Lord, with submission, the sturdy dissenters from our Church are much fuller of admiration at all who believe that Episcopacy is of Divine or Apostolical institution, or that we can pray spiritually by a form, than your Lordship can be at us for affirming the Eucharist to be a Sacrifice. And it is certain that the Sacrifice of the Primitive Church, explained in the following book, differs as widely from that of the Papists as our Episcopacy and Liturgy does from theirs. As to the newness of it, your Lordship will give me leave to wonder that it should be an objection against the Sacrifice, since it is very evident (not to mention Mr. Perkins the rigid Calvinist's known opinion in this point) that Mr. Mede publicly declared for the Altar and Sacrifice in Cambridge, A.D. 1635; whereas there is a doctrine openly espoused by several leading men of late, that is younger than this by six years, and when it was first started was universally dis-avowed by all the sound clergy and laity of the Church of England, and yet is now the darling notion of some that

^f Page 13.

boast themselves your Lordship's friends, against which you have not cautioned your clergy in your Charge; nay, of which your Lordship is believed to be a fautor. And I must add, that whereas the doctrine of the Sacrifice is truly primitive and Apostolical, this latter is destitute of all authority from the writings and practice of the first and purest ages, and was always by our Protestant divines of the Church of England represented as an invention of the Hildebrandine Papists, until now of late days. I need not tell you that I mean the doctrine of Resistance.

Your Lordship is willing to have it believed that Archbishop Laud was of a different sentiment from us, when he wrote his Conference with the Jesuit; and to prove it, you observe that he calls it 'The Memory of a Sacrifice;' and so did the Fathers,. my Lord, and so do we, who yet believe it to be a real Sacrifice, as will appear by this book. You are pleased farther to cite that blessed martyr, for asserting "three Sacrifices[g], one by the priest, i. e. the commemorative sacrifice of Christ's death, represented in bread and wine; another by the priest and people, i. e. the sacrifice of praise; the third, by every particular man, i. e. the sacrifice of body and soul." Upon these words your Lordship is pleased to remark, " this enumeration of sacrifices, without putting any distinction between them, is a plain sign he thought none of them proper." I submit it to your Lordship's second thoughts, whether the enumeration do not necessarily imply a distinction; or how it can in common equity be supposed that so excellent a writer should say, first, second, third, and yet mean one and the same. If the first be not a proper sacrifice, I must confess I am wholly mistaken in my reasonings on this subject. Your Lordship spends two or three pages more on this subject, but I hope you will excuse me if I wholly omit the consideration of them, since you are not pleased to mention any authority of the ancient Church, except only that of St. Chrysostom, on the Epistle to the Hebrews, which I have considered Chap. II. Sect. 1, nor to offer at any argument from Scripture or reason. And as to what concerns the author of the *Vade*, I shall briefly speak to it before I conclude this epistle. But when your Lordship

[g] § 35. p. 199.

had been pleased in your Charge to intimate that "it was more fit for Romish priests than English presbyters" to plead for the Sacrifice, I cannot but think that you too much lessen your performance in your preface, when you speak of those paragraphs which were intended against the Sacrifice, and call them the "little you have said" on that subject; for, my Lord, I am perfectly of opinion that your Lordship has used the strongest, I may say, the only argument against it, by intimating, though in a more gentle and tender manner than others, that it is a Popish doctrine : for this little is the sum and substance of all that has been said to purpose in the writings of Dr. Hancock, and others. They may outdo your Lordship in multiplicity of words and pages, but not in true and solid argument; and your Lordship has said all that in a line or two, which others have been able to say in their larger writings ; for if I know any thing of the matter, I must profess that I am fully of opinion that nothing great can be said against the Sacrifice.

There is another writer, whose style speaks him a gentleman of polite learning, and distinguishes him from our adversaries of the coarser sort, though he is pleased to conceal his name and character, who in a small book[h], which he calls A Defence of the Doctrine and Practice of the Church of England, is "at a loss how Dr. Hickes will distinguish his propitiatory Sacrifice of the Eucharist, from the propitiatory Sacrifice of the Mass[i]," though Dr. Hickes expressly calls it "an oblation of bread and wine," in the words cited by this ingenious author : and one would think this made an essential difference between the Sacrifice of Dr. Hickes and of the Papists: by this you may measure the impartiality of this writer.

And I am of opinion that his politeness, and other good qualities, cannot make amends for his want of faithfulness in representing the opinion of the most excellent Mede ; for this author would persuade us that "Mr. Mede, from first to last, resolves all into an oblation of prayer and thanksgiving to God the Father, through Jesus Christ[k]." Again, "Mr. Mede owns that here is nothing offered in this Sacrament, but

[h] I had been falsely informed that Bishop Fleetwood was the author of this book, whereas I am since assured that it was Dr. Turner of Greenwich.

[Author's note, 2nd ed.]
[i] Page 10.
[k] Page 7.

prayer and thanksgiving, and these made acceptable to God, by the Sacrifice of Christ on the cross, commemorated and represented by the bread and wine;" and in the next page, "though he carries this notion of a Sacrifice much higher than any Protestant writer before him; yet while nothing was in reality pretended to be offered, but only prayer and thanksgiving, and those only in commemoration of the real Sacrifice of the death of Christ, and not otherwise; this has been looked upon as one of the particularities of that learned man," &c. Now I must observe that this representation confutes itself; for it says that Mr. Mede "carried this notion of a Sacrifice higher than any Protestant writer had done before;" and yet says, that "nothing," according to him, "was to be offered, but prayer and praise:" for sure no Protestant writer ever asserted that prayer and praise are not offered in the Eucharist; and if Mr. Mede affirmed that nothing more was offered there, how did he carry this notion higher than other Protestants? But let Mr. Mede speak for himself, who in discoursing on Malachi i. 10, 11, says, "Incense here notes the rational part of the Sacrifice, which is prayer, thanksgiving, and commemoration; *mincha* the material part thereof, which is *oblatio farrea*, or an oblation of bread and wine[1]." Again, "the oblation of bread and wine is implied in St. Paul's parallel of the Lord's Supper, and the Sacrifices of Gentiles; 'ye cannot be partakers of the Lord's Table, and the table of devils[m].'" And a little after, "the Passover was a Sacrifice, and therefore the viands here, as in all other [holy] feasts, were first offered to God: now the bread and wine which our Saviour took when He blessed and gave thanks, was the *mincha*, or meat-offering of the Passover; if then He did, as the Jews used to do, He agnized His Father, and blessed Him, by oblation of these His creatures to Him." And as I observed in Propitiatory Oblation[n], Mr. Mede affirms that whereas in the Clementine Liturgy, prayer is made to God "that He would receive the gift up to His heavenly Altar; by the gift must be understood the bread and wine[o]:" but I will only further observe, that he asserts

---

[1] See his Works, 3rd edition, 1672, p. 358.

[m] Ibid., p. 374.

[n] Page 90.

[o] Page 374.

"the Eucharist to be a Sacrifice, not in a metaphorical, but
proper sense[p];" and spends a whole chapter to prove "that the
primitive Church, after Christ's example, first offered bread
and wine to God ; then received them again in a banquet, as
the symbols of the Body and Blood of His Son[q]."   My Lord,
I humbly recommend the consideration of this flat contradiction to truth, in the most valuable writer against the Sacrifice, next to yourself and my Lord Bishop of Oxford, to your
impartial examination : and it is the more gross and palpa-
ble, because it may be discovered by looking into an English
book, open to every vulgar eye.

It is true, Mr. Mede might safely say, in some sense, that
we offer nothing but prayer and praise in the Eucharist ; and
the same might be said of all the animal sacrifices of thanksgiving under the law : for the very animal itself was called,
when so offered, תודה, αἴνεσις, that is, 'praise;' as an offering
for sin was also called 'sin' in the abstract ; but this does not
at all prove that the Sacrifice itself in either case was perfectly immaterial, as I have shewed in the following book,
Chap. II. Sect. 2.

This same writer at another place perstringes the assertors
of a sacrifice for "ascribing a strange mystical efficacy to the
act of consecration ; and for placing he knows not what
mysterious powers in the act of consecration, and invocation
of the Holy Ghost[r] ;" and speaks of those divines as "perfecting our reformation," who (in Queen Elizabeth's time) "did not
bring in again that form of consecration and invocation of
the Holy Ghost :" by all which I cannot understand this
writer to mean less than that it is a fault to ascribe any mysterious efficacy, or power, to the prayer of consecration used
in the primitive Church, and that our Liturgy is more perfect without it than it was with it.   In answer to which I
will only appeal to another book, entituled, The Reasonable
Communicant, where we are informed that "a Divine power
and efficacy does accompany the holy Sacrament ;" and for
the proof of this, the author uses this argument, namely, that
"the Church of Christ did heretofore pray that the Holy
Spirit of God coming down on the creatures of bread and
wine, might make them the Body and Blood of Christ," and,

"that after the consecration such a Divine power and efficacy doth accompany the holy Sacrament, as makes the bread and wine become the spiritual and mystical Body and Blood of Christ[s]." Now this is all that either the ancient Church or we ascribe to the prayer of consecration. These two books are equally admired by the adversaries of the Sacrifice; but I cannot but think The Reasonable Communicant to have been written with a genius and temper much beyond that which appears in the Defence: and therefore from the censures of the latter I appeal to the primitive doctrine contained in the former. And I must add that this prayer of invocation for the descent of the Holy Ghost is very far from any just suspicion of Popery: for there is no such prayer in the present Roman Missal, nor has been for eleven hundred years last past; but in the time of Pope Gelasius the First, at the latter end of the fifth century, there probably was, as will hereafter appear.

2. The next objection of this sort against the writers for the Sacrifice is, that they trump up this doctrine with some indirect design, which they are afraid to own; and that the doctrine itself has an ill aspect on the civil government: and this I only take to be a proof of the jealousy of our adversaries, or rather a sorry artifice to render us suspected to the court. If they who were the chief ministers of state when Dr. Hickes, and Mr. Nelson, and some others, published their notions on this subject, had believed their own divines, they might have been ready enough to take this opportunity of crushing some men, upon whom they had an ill eye; but I am apt to think that they rather laughed in their sleeves when they observed how forward and officious some clergymen (unworthy of that name) are, to traduce and delate their brethren and their best friends, in order to signalize their zeal for those that were in a capacity to reward it. If the assertors of the Sacrifice had had any intentions against the state, they would certainly have chosen some more popular theme, they would have started some notions that were new at least, and better contrived to captivate the multitude. This is Popery, if our adversaries may be judges; and can

---

[s] See Reasonable Com., p. 12, 13. 3rd ed. [This is allowed by all, I think, to be Bishop Fleetwood's. (2nd ed.)]

they think that preaching, or writing for Popery, is a proper method to engage people against the government? It is rather an infallible way to provoke both governors and people against ourselves. I am of opinion that it would puzzle the most learned of our adversaries to give one single instance of any doctrine, whether old or new, true or false, that could with less probability be made use of, to seduce people from their allegiance to the Queen, than this which is now in dispute. If you consider the genius of the people, they are, or were, either averse to it, or altogether unconcerned for or against it : if you consider the doctrine itself, it has no relation to the civil government. Dr. Taylor, that was afterwards Bishop of Down and Connor, did, in the time of our confusions, while rebellion and fanaticism reigned, directly assert the doctrine of the Sacrifice. He did the same thing which Dr. Hancock, in his preface to his book against Dr. Hickes[t], charges as a fault on Mr. Nelson; that is, he brought the notion of a Sacrifice into a book of devotion, I mean his Holy Living and Dying[u]. [Nay, he did more than all this, he drew a Communion Office[x] in the English tongue according to the scheme of the ancient Greek and Apostolical Liturgies : only in one particular he differs from them, that is in placing the Consecration, or the prayer for the descent of the Holy Ghost on the Communicants, and on the Symbols, before the rehearsal of the words of institution. In all the ancient Liturgies we have first the institution, then the oblation, and last of all the prayer for the descent of the Holy Ghost. But Bishop Taylor follows the series of the first Liturgy of Edward VI.] And even Mr. Patrick, who was afterwards D.D. and Bishop of Ely, did, before those confusions were ended, openly declare for an oblation of bread and wine, as I shall presently shew; yet I am not sensible that they were by the enthusiastic and fanatical divines of that age represented as malignants, or disaffected to the government on that account : nor had either of those two

---

[t] Page 4.
[u] Pages 281, 334.
[x] See this Communion Office in a Collection of Offices, or Forms of Prayer, in cases ordinary and extraordinary, taken out of the Scripture, and the ancient Liturgies, &c., by Jer. Taylor, D.D., Bishop of Down and Connor. 2nd ed., printed for Luke Meredith, at the Angel, in Amen Corner. 1690.

great men the vanity to think that by this means they promoted the restoration of King Charles II., though it happened within half a year after Mr. Patrick's book was printed. And I conceive, if either of them had claimed a reward, as instruments of that happy turn of affairs, and attempted to prove it by shewing their books for the Sacrifice or oblation, they could not more effectually have exposed themselves. And I leave this to the reflection of those who would represent the publication of this primitive doctrine as a treasonable practice, and a plot against the state, in the reign of our most pious and merciful Queen, which yet passed unpunished and uncensured on this account even by fanatical rebels and usurpers; who were the most apt of any men living to make use of fictitious and imaginary crimes, and were pushed on by visionary fears, and the ill-bodings of their own consciences, to oppress truth and right.

3. It may be said that this doctrine tends to create divisions amongst us; and this may be said of any doctrine which is not universally received, when books are published for and against it. But then the question is, whether we ought from hence to conclude that truth is never to be published for fear of this consequence; and whether they who assert truth, or they who oppose it, are justly chargeable with those divisions which follow thereupon. And both these particulars I leave to your Lordship's determination. There is another question, which I humbly lay before your Lordship, and that is, why the publishing a book in behalf of the Sacrifice by Dr. Hickes, should be looked upon as more culpable and tending to division than by Mr. Mede. For, my Lord, it is notorious that Mr. Mede's Christian Sacrifice was a book as much celebrated as any other written by him, or by any of our most famous divines; and to say that he did not write for a material proper Sacrifice, is mere fiction. And what reason could Dr. Hickes have to suppose that his writings on the same subject should meet with more opposition from our Bishops and clergy, than Mr. Mede's had done? And as I believe Dr. Hickes's book yet remains unanswered, so I am not sensible that any man has attempted a reply to Mr. Mede. And if our divines had for the five or six years last past been as universally well affected to the Sacrifice, as

they had been for seventy years before, Dr. Hickes's book had occasioned no more division than Mr. Mede's; for it is opposition that causes division. Dr. Hickes and others have said no more than what Mr. Mede had said before in other words; and if his saying it cause animosities among us, this must in justice be resolved into a prejudice which some have conceived against the writer, rather than the book. Why else must the Christian Priesthood be assaulted, while the Christian Sacrifice remains unattacked, and has so remained for near eighty years together? It is scarce to be expected that this age should be more free from disputes than any of those that have already passed: for there are in all ages such as love truth, and such as hate it, or however, cannot see it in any opinion or practice maintained by those to whom they have an aversion upon other accounts, but oppose the truth for the sake of those who are advocates for it, and consider not so much what is said, as who speaks it, and it is therefore no more to be wondered that disputes and oppositions happen now, than that they have done so in all preceding times. And I am fully persuaded that there is no neglected truth that more deserves to be contended for than the doctrine of the Sacrifice; for I suppose it will appear to all unprejudiced inquirers to be a truth of very great moment and consequence. And though when some assert truth, and others contradict it, divisions must of necessity be the effect; yet the assertors in this case cannot but believe that as their cause is right, so the Divine Providence will not permit such divisions to be lasting; for great is the TRUTH, and will prevail, even against the most powerful opponents. I doubt not, but in the primitive Church, whatever Bishop had opposed, or depraved the Sacrifice, he would immediately have been obliged to give place to an orthodox successor: for I have reason to believe that the ancient Bishops, clergy, and people, were not more uniform in any point of doctrine or worship, than in their notions and practice concerning the Eucharistical oblation. And if any single Bishop, with the generality of his clergy and laity, had agreed together to maim or deface the Christian Sacrifice, and stood in defiance of their neighbouring Bishops and Synods; yet any particular clergyman or layman, who was dissatisfied with these innovations, might, in such a case, have removed into another diocese, where the Sacrifice was retained in its perfect purity and splendour; but it is evident that nothing of this sort is now practicable in this national Church; and that therefore such priests and pious discerning laymen, as are convinced of the truth and necessity of the primitive Sacrifice, and do not think that the public provision for it is sufficient, have no proper remedy left, but to labour with prayers to God, and with persuasions and arguments to men, for the perfect restitution of the sacrificial oblatory part of the Christian Liturgy; and in the mean time, to supply such defects as well as they can, by their own private silent devotions. In a word, the writers for the Sacrifice may be impleaded as the ringleaders of division and faction; but then this accusation may with as good reason be laid against them, who write for the necessity of Episcopacy in Scotland, or who contend for the Liturgy in the vulgar tongue in Spain or Italy.

4. But this doctrine of the Sacrifice (say some) tends to alienate the minds of dissenters from the clergy and communion of the Church, and thereby to put a stop to the union so much expected. But I conceive your Lordship by this time may be convinced, that this union of dissenters with the Church, is a mere airy phantom, and that we are never to expect that the main body of dissenters, as they now stand affected, would unite with the Church upon any reasonable terms; nor have they ever shewed any signs of, or tendencies to, a peaceable disposition; and the clergy have no method left of winning them to the Church, but as they can gradually, and man by man, by argument and persuasion, reconcile them to our communion. And I am fully persuaded, that we may as easily demonstrate the truth and necessity of the doctrine of a Sacrifice in the Eucharist, as any other point now in dispute between us. But if we must publish no doctrine but what agrees with the palates of dissenters, I am sure our sermons and writings must be very defective; nor can we be true to our Blessed Master, and teach our people ' to do all things which He hath commanded us.' And dissenters themselves will justly loathe us, and our communion, if once they find that we stifle our own real sentiments, and conceal our true principles in order to catch them. And

JOHNSON. c

there is nothing more inconsistent with Christian simplicity, and with that παῤῥησία, that integrity and assurance of mind, in speaking the whole truth and nothing but the truth, as it is in Christ; than to handle the Word of God deceitfully, either by curtailing what we believe to be the doctrine of the Gospel, or by adulterating it with sophistical mixtures, to make it go down the better with men whose palates are vitiated. I most heartily desire peace with the dissenters; but I desire it on Christian terms, and upon the primitive plan; and I am very sure, that no other peace can be either honourable or lasting.

5. It may be said that the public maintaining of this doctrine, especially if it were espoused by the generality of the Bishops and clergy, might give a handle to the enemies of the Church to persecute and destroy them. And must then the Pastors of Christ's flock be afraid of discharging their consciences, and executing their Master's commission, lest they should suffer for it? And shall the fear of men so far prevail over us, as to make us forget our duty to our God and Saviour? Can the Church of this age hope to flourish and enlarge its bounds by any other means than those by which the Apostolical Church did first overcome the world; that is, by boldness in speaking the truth, and by patience in suffering for it? I trust in God, there are now, as well as of old, men that are ready to suffer all things for the sake even of the least of those Commandments, which they have received from their ever blessed Redeemer, much more for so very momentous an institution. I am persuaded, that if God, in His gracious Providence, do ever intend any farther exaltation of our Church, and to perfect the glory of it, He will do it in the old method, that is, by the fiery trial of some at least of its most eminent or zealous members. And to say that a doctrine must not be taught for fear of provoking men, is in effect to say, that Christians and Priests must study to please men, lest they should become Martyrs or Confessors. I take it for certain, that God will never truly magnify His Church by human policies, or by the temporizing palliative arts of the wise men of this world; but by the sincere disinterested zeal, and firm constancy of the clergy and people, or of a number of them, in opposition to the frowns and smiles

of all its professed enemies or mistaken friends. It is very certain, my Lord, that the greatest and most formidable enemies of the Church are they who believe our very Creeds to be Popery, and our Sacraments priestcraft; who would reduce our Christian faith to one single article, that Jesus is the Messias, and look upon that too as far from being necessary. And, my Lord, the friendship of these men is never to be expected but upon a total renunciation of primitive Christianity. They may caress those who oppose the Sacrifice, and such like doctrines, as more moderate enemies; but if once they can crush them whom they call high-flyers, their next work will be to silence and suppress those that are for retaining the twelve old articles of the Christian faith; for they have the very same objection against these that the author of the Defence has against the mysterious power of Consecration, viz. that "it amuses the understandings, and confounds the devotion of the common people[y]." And though these men of short creeds are now the chief patriots and fautors of the dissenting interest, in opposition to that of the Church, yet if God in His displeasure should permit the dissenters to be made use of by such men as tools to the destruction of the established religion, they would soon find, by dear-bought experience, that these pretended patriots are no more friends to their principles than ours, (except it be in relation to civil government,) and that very few, in comparison, of those who separate from the Church, will find any countenance from those whom they now look upon as their chief supporters. For it is very evident, that they measure their own and other men's religion by the brevity and plainness of their creeds, and are known enemies to every thing that is mysterious and above reason; and will as soon become converts to the Quakers, as to the Presbyterians or Independents; and as easily be reconciled to the principles of Dr. Hickes or Mr. Dodwell, as of Calvin or Baxter. They can fawn upon fanatics, enthusiasts, or even Bishops, if they can hope by this means to serve a present turn; but Machiavel, Algernon Sidney, and such like writers, are their oracles in relation to civil government; and Socinus, Toland, or Blunt, as to matters of religion. And I cannot but won-

[y] Page 12.

c 2

der to see men, who, I in charity believe, are Christians at
the heart, espouse the interest, and put themselves under the
protection of such leaders ; and I can look upon it as little less
than a judicial infatuation, that men, who have any manner
of regard to that faith which was once delivered to the saints,
can court, or permit themselves to be courted by, such demagogues.   These are the chief enemies, from whom at present
the Church has reason to apprehend any mischief ; and these
are as inveterate against our Catholic forms of faith, and
other essentials of Christianity, as against the Sacrifice. But
give me leave to add, that these men do bear a most especial
hatred to those of your Lordship's venerable order : they
may for some private reasons like the man, but they cannot
but abhor the Bishop.   And I have reason to believe, that of
the two they would choose a Sacrifice without a Bishop,
rather than a Bishop without a Sacrifice. For, my Lord, with
these men that is the best religion that is the cheapest ; and,
next to the shortness of the Creed, the second best property
in it is the smallness of the cost.   It is well known that this
is one reason alleged, why so many Protestant States are not
capable of receiving Episcopacy ; viz. because they are not
able to support the dignity of Bishops, which they therefore
represent as extremely burdensome and expensive ; and no
doubt but these men would at any time of the day exchange
Episcopacy for the Eucharistical Sacrifice, and think it a good
bargain too ; and therefore I cannot believe that the most
terrible enemies of our Church can be so much provoked to
destroy it, on account of this doctrine of the Sacrifice, if it
were as universally received and practised as I could wish it
were ; as they already are by the Episcopal form of government, and the Bishops' lands.

It may be suspected by some, that our own people may be
inflamed against us on this account; but I must profess, I have
no reason to apprehend any such consequence.   There can
be no just cause for them to be averse from the Sacrifice,
more than the Eucharist itself.   Formerly indeed our people
were too ready to hearken to the malicious suggestions of
fanatics against the clergy; but I cannot but say, that dissenters have of late years, in a great measure, forfeited their
credit with the people of our communion.   It is commonly

said, I know, that Archbishop Laud's zeal for the Sacrifice
was the principal objection against him, and cost him his life,
and was one great occasion of all the public calamities that
ensued upon it ; and of this the Defence takes notice[z]. I
question not, but it was a comfort to Archbishop Laud that
he died a martyr in so good a cause ; and yet the odium
against Archbishop Laud was raised by the faction of that
age, altogether as much upon the score of his zeal for those
doctrines which were then called Arminianism, as for that of
the Sacrifice ; for the Divines who then prevailed, condemned
all those primitive principles as rank Popery, which yet has
not deterred the clergy, and even the Bishops themselves,
since those days, from openly espousing those doctrines and
principles, notwithstanding the hideous declamations of the
fierce dissenters against them on this account. And I believe it may be justly said, that the tenets which are falsely
called Arminian, do now generally obtain. And this is a
plain proof, that a doctrine thrives the better, for having
been watered by the blood of the holy Martyr. *Et Deus
secundet Omen.* They who look no further than to the out-
side of things, may imagine that this great man was perse-
cuted even to death for his opinions and notions; but they
who impartially read the history of those times, and reflect
upon the temper of the chief actors in that bloody tragedy,
will find it evident, that it was the man, the royal counsellor,
and the Christian Primate, they aimed at ; and when he and
his order were destined to destruction by the party which
then prevailed, some colours must be used, some specious
pretext contrived, for so barbarous and inhuman a murder,
for so execrable and sacrilegious a devastation of the purest
Church in the world. Our people, left to themselves, could
never have so far been inflamed against the Archbishop or
the Church, as to proceed to such furious excesses. The
puritanical preachers, who at that time had gotten possession
of, or borrowed pulpits in the city, and in all the populous
places of the nation, exasperated the minds of the people
against that great man, and his pious endeavours to perfect
our constitution ; and these preachers were the men, who
being set on by the heads of the party in the two Houses,

[z] Page 9.

did, under pretence of zeal against Popery, run down
Prelacy, Arminianism, Altars, and Sacrifice, and indeed the
Church itself, with one and the same breath. We have no
more reason to apprehend any danger to the Altar and
Sacrifice from our own people, than my lords the Bishops
have to their dignities and authority, or the whole Church to
our Liturgy and worship; unless it can be supposed, that
some of our own body can act the part which was then left
to the puritanical preachers, and make false alarms of
Popery, and other ill things, that were never meant, and
which can scarce be believed by them who would persuade
others to do so. The clamours of dissenters are now, in a
great measure, confined within the walls of their conventi-
cles; and the infection, God be praised, is not so spreading
as it was in those days. Our enemies of that sort can never
hurt us, if we be but true to ourselves, and can but contain
our tongues and pens from misrepresenting each other.

And further, in answer to all objections of this kind, in
which the merits of the cause are not concerned, but only
the prudence of the writers and the seasonableness of their
enterprise, I desire it may be considered; first, That Divine
truth is always seasonable, except to cunning men and politicians; and no truth can at any time be seasonable to them
if it do not fall in with their own schemes and projections;
nay, nothing is easily admitted for truth with them which is
disobliging or unagreeable to those whose friendship they
court, or by whose means they hope to advance their own interest. I am apt to believe that the very Gospel itself had
been yet unknown to the greatest part of Europe, if the first
publishers of it had stayed till they were called for by the
masters of politics in the several nations where it now prevails.
Nay, secondly, I cannot but think that Dr. Hickes's attempt
to establish this doctrine was as well timed as any thing of
this nature could be. It was when he saw a violent assault
made on the very being of the Church and Priesthood; when
a design was publicly set on foot to dissolve the Catholic
Church into numberless clans and clubs, and to degrade
Priests into mere tenders, or under-spur-leathers to those
clans or clubs; and not to assert the Sacrifice on such a very
urgent occasion, would have been interpreted as a tacit re-

nunciation of it. There had now passed seventy years since
the publication of Mr. Mede's Christian Sacrifice, and though
several divines had in this interval followed him in this particular, so far as to let the world know that they did believe
the Eucharist to be a proper Sacrifice, yet scarce any had
professedly and at large treated upon it. It was, therefore,
now high time to rénew this claim, when there was the most
violent provocation given that ever was, as I verily believe,
from the first institution of the Sacrifice and the Priesthood,
to this very day. Further, there had at that time, when
Dr. Hickes published the Christian Priesthood, been public
agitations for altering some particulars in the Liturgy of our
Church; and it is well known, that this had been proposed
to the Convocation soon after the Revolution; and it was with
good reason supposed, that the governors of the Church
waited only for a seasonable opportunity of renewing this
proposal. And sure no man will wonder, if a divine of
Dr. Hickes's eminence, who was himself perfectly convinced
of the truth and importance of this doctrine, did earnestly
desire, that when the Convocation should again sit upon this
weighty affair, some alterations might be made in favour of
this most primitive doctrine. And whatever reasons of state
or human prudence there might then be to the contrary, yet
it must be acknowledged that the thing itself was very desirable, that when so many alterations were meditated in compliance with the present age, some regard might be had to
Apostolical antiquity. If the Doctor did apprehend that this
effort of his was like to meet with opposition from several
persons of great authority in the Church, I cannot think that
this was a sufficient consideration to check his honest and
pious zeal, upon supposition that he was in his own conscience satisfied of the justice of his cause, which ought in
common equity to be presumed. Your Lordship knows very
well that the corruptions of the Church of Rome were first
discovered by private persons, and that a very great part of
this nation was, by the writings of particular men, convinced
of the necessity of a reformation long before any countenance
had been given to this cause, either by our King or Prelates.
And it is notorious that Christianity was introduced into most
nations by the care and courage of some one, or of a

few men, in opposition to all human power. If this
method prove inconvenient, it is most of all so to such as
are the undertakers. And they indeed often have incurred
severe penalties, and even death itself, for speaking bold
truths when politicians did not think it seasonable. And
Dr. Hickes is a man that has given effectual demonstration to
the world that he can suffer in a cause which he believes to be
good and righteous. When this doctrine was countenanced
by the ecclesiastical and civil powers, it pleased God to permit
it, together with the Church itself, to be run down by a popular fury, and a most horrid unnatural rebellion. And it is probable, that Divine Providence will choose to restore the primitive Sacrifice by the same method that Divine truth has
gained reception in all ages, that is gradually, by the endeavours
and patient sufferings of those who engage in the defence of
it. You, my Lord, together with my Lord Bishop of Oxford,
have consulted your own safety and taken effectual care
not to die martyrs, as the most Reverend Archbishop Laud in
some measure did, for this holy truth. And I have not heard
of more than one of that present venerable bench that has ever
been pleased publicly to declare in favour of it. I am sometimes
inclined to think, that the avowed opposition of two of our
Bishops against this doctrine, is so far from being an ill symp-
tom of the disposition of the clergy and people to embrace the
doctrine and practice of the Sacrifice, that I do not know but
it may in the event be one means of making way for its general
reception. I am not so sanguine as to hope that this whole
Church can be convinced of this truth all at once; nor yet
am I without hope, that by God's blessing on the labours of
them who do now, or may hereafter contend for the perfect
establishment of it, the prejudices of men may by degrees be
conquered, and the Unbloody Sacrifice and Altar recover its
pristine lustre and esteem, not by the force and imposition of
human authority, but by its own intrinsic excellence and reasonableness, and by the irresistible evidence of Scripture and
antiquity; for this is the way by which Divine truth delights
to diffuse itself. And though I cannot in reason expect to
live to that blessed day, yet I am full of hopes that it will not
be long before the primitive Sacrifice gains an establishment in our public councils, with a *nemine contradicente,*

with the concurrent desires and suffrages of the clergy and people.

And now, my Lord, I must have liberty to say, that I have answered all the objections I know of, both against the Sacrifice itself, and the defenders of it; the former in the book itself, the latter in this Prefatory Epistle, without concealing the force or strength of any one of them. Dr. Hancock, I remember, tells Dr. Hickes[a], "that he could help him to better proofs of the Sacrifice than those which he had produced." If there were any truth in this, Dr. Hancock by saying it only proved the weakness of his own performance; for all writers, that would do justice to their own cause, ought to assail the strongest arguments that they know against it; and he that does it not, leaves a just suspicion in his reader's mind, that the reason why he conceals them is, that he has no sufficient answer to make; and therefore the most charitable construction that can be put upon this saying of Dr. Hancock's is, that it was a mere gasconade.

Your Lordship might perhaps expect, that I should undertake to answer all the allegations produced from our modern divines against the sacrifice of the Mass; but I think I should undervalue the judgments of those great men by supposing that they would have argued against the Sacrifice as represented by Mr. Mede and Dr. Hickes, in the same manner that they have done against the Sacrifice of Transubstantiation in the Church of Rome. And I do seriously profess to your Lordship, that the two Charges published by yourself and my Lord of Oxford, are as full of authority against the Sacrifice as any of those citations which have so plentifully been produced from modern Bishops and Doctors; nay, your own opinion, in relation to the Sacrifice, would weigh as much with me as that of Bishop Overall, or any of your predecessors in the See of Norwich, upon supposition that your Lordship's opinion were supported with as good authorities from true antiquity as theirs; and without such support, I am confident your Lordship will not expect that your judgment should be thought decisive. I would as soon resign myself to the determination of my Lord Bishop of Oxford that now is, as to that of his most learned and generous pre-

[a] Answer, p. 207.

decessor, Bishop Fell, if his Lordship's sentiment were as agreeable to that of the primitive Church, as I believe Bishop Fell's to have been. If my most reverend patron, diocesan, and primate, should think fit to declare against the Sacrifice, I must own his personal authority to be as great and weighty in itself considered, as that of Archbishop Laud, or any of his Grace's predecessors, since the time of Augustine to this very day; but since our divines of late ages have very much differed in their judgments on this head of religion, therefore I know no other more proper course to bring this dispute to a just issue, than by appealing to genuine uncorrupted antiquity. The Reverend Dr. Hickes has produced a great number of citations from our Protestant Bishops and divines, many of which are very full and express for the Sacrifice; and I desire that these may be laid in the scale against those allegations, which, though aimed against the Popish Mass, yet may seem to bear hard upon the primitive Sacrifice itself. Since there is not so perfect a harmony and agreement on this subject amongst our English divines, as there is in other matters, it remains, that either these disputes continue still undecided, or that they be brought to a conclusion by an impartial inquiry into the judgment of the primitive Apostolical Church.

As for that trite objection which neither your Lordship, nor any of those who have opposed the Christian Sacrifice have omitted, I mean Mr. Mede's acknowledgment that "what the ancient Church understood by the Sacrifice is beyond belief obscure and intricate;" I hope the whole treatise annexed to this epistle is an effectual answer to it, though after all it was an objection that would have been thought of no weight in any other case, because, as I have elsewhere observed, Mr. Mede does not attribute the obscurity to the thing itself, but to the disputes raised about it. And if the obscurity of any doctrine be a sufficient proof against the truth of it, I am afraid there are very few doctrines in the Christian creed, or even in natural religion, nay in philosophy or metaphysics, that are not as much affected by this objection as the doctrine of the Sacrifice. I believe few of our Church do now doubt of the freedom of human actions because it is very hard to explain this doctrine so as to render it clearly consistent with the Divine pre-

science; and what orthodox Christian renounces the doctrine
of the Trinity because it is confessedly difficult to reconcile
the unity of the Deity with the co-existence of three really
Divine persons? and to disbelieve the Sacrifice because one
cannot satisfy himself in the modalities of it, is just as
rational as for a philosopher to deny the magnetic power
because he is not convinced that any one has yet given a full
and satisfactory solution of all the phenomena relating to
that great secret of nature. And this is but one instance of
many, which might be produced to shew that those objections
are thought to be of force against the Sacrifice, which would
not be thought to deserve an answer, if they were made
against any other doctrine.

It was the chief design of those who have formerly set
themselves to defend the Eucharistical Sacrifice, to prove the
thing itself, viz. that our Saviour instituted, and the Apostles
and primitive Church believed and practised this Sacrifice;
and I crave leave to say, that there was no necessity for me,
or any man else, to take any further pains in this matter, for
that our Saviour intended the Eucharist to be a Sacrifice, and
that the most primitive Church did so esteem and use it, was
as clear as anything need be. But because some men urged
Mr. Mede's confession of its obscurity as an argument against
the very existence of the thing itself, I have endeavoured in
the following sheets to present my reader with a draught of
the Christian Sacrifice, both as to the material substances
there offered, and as to the ends for which, and the Altar on
which, and the officers by whom it is offered, and as to the
manner of its consumption; and I conceive it will appear to
any unprejudiced examiner, that the main difficulty in the
whole scheme is to explain what that material thing or substance is which is offered, or how or in what manner the
bread and cup in the Sacrament are the Body and Blood of
Christ, and by what means they became so; and I conceive
that this difficulty does affect the Eucharist considered as a
Sacrament rather than considered as a Sacrifice. That the
nature of the Sacrament is very mysterious and obscure, is
very evident from the multitude of those voluminous books
that have been written upon that subject, and it is believed
to be so to this day by all, except those who follow Œcolam-

padius, Arminius, or Socinus, who have generally been looked
upon by all others to be erroneous in this point. If divines
were once unanimously agreed what that material substance
is which is given and received in the Eucharist, and by what
means it becomes what it is, the main difficulty of the doctrine of the Sacrifice would presently vanish; and because
the several bodies of divines of the Romish, Lutheran, and
Calvinistical persuasion, do so widely differ in this matter;
and the Church of England is, I think, allowed by all to have
made no precise determination in this point, but to have
satisfied herself by saying in general terms, that "the Body
and Blood of Christ is verily and indeed taken and received
by the faithful in the Lord's Supper;" therefore I have been
obliged to consider the doctrine of the primitive Church as
to this point; for without this it had been impossible to say
what that was which was offered in the primitive Church.
But it is evident that this difficulty does immediately concern
the Sacrament rather than the Sacrifice; and that therefore
they who would prove there was no Sacrifice in the Church,
because the nature of it is very obscure, might with much
more reason have asserted that there was no Sacrament
among the ancients; for he that can solve the notions of the
ancients in relation to the reality of the sacramental Body
and Blood, has overcome the grand difficulty of the primitive
Sacrifice; and I humbly submit what is offered upon this
subject in the Appendix to Chap. II. Sect. 1. to the judgment of your Lordship and the learned world.

Further, my Lord, though I have shewed that Mr. Mede
did assert a material Sacrifice, yet it must be confessed, that
he not living to see any book written in answer to his learned
works on this subject, was not so fully aware of the necessity of proving at large that the primitive Sacrifice was material, by a particular induction of authorities to this purpose.
He thought it sufficient to prove a Sacrifice of bread and
wine, an Unbloody Sacrifice; not suspecting that any men
could be so very exceptious as either to deny that a Sacrifice of
bread and wine was the Sacrifice of the Body and Blood of
Christ, or that such a Sacrifice would be deemed by Protestants to be the Sacrifice of the Mass; or that an Unbloody
Sacrifice would be construed to be an oblation of mere

prayer and praise. Farther, I found that many who did believe the Eucharist to be a proper Sacrifice, yet were not sufficiently apprized of the great importance of this doctrine, and of the great stress that the ancients with good reason laid upon it; nay, I found that some who could see no reason to doubt but that the Sacrifice was believed and practised by the primitive Church, were not sufficiently satisfied how this doctrine was reconcileable to the perfect satisfaction made by the personal oblation of Christ Himself. These considerations convinced me of the necessity of having those points cleared, and these obstacles to the reception of the Eucharistical Sacrifice removed.

It had been happy for the learned world if any one had published these objections and scruples while Mr. Mede was living and capable of writing an answer to them; for no man ever was more happy in understanding the Scripture and ancients than himself; but he was gone to his blessed rest before any now engaged in this controversy were born, as I have reason to believe. Archbishop Laud, his patron, a few years after fell a sacrifice to this doctrine among others; the most primitively learned Bishop Bull was some years ago " gathered to his fathers," whose doctrine he had so nobly followed and defended. Dr. Grabe soon followed him. Dr. Hickes, though yet alive, is worn out in the service of primitive Christianity and the study of antiquities, incapable of turning over books, and of the fatigue of writing or dictating anything that requires long application, and every day expecting his dissolution. Mr. Nelson was engaged in writing the Life of Bishop Bull, and publishing his works, and wholly employed since in works whereby he will merit of the present, and of future generations. And since I could hear of no person that was willing to undertake an affair of this nature, I at last came to a resolution of doing it myself; for though I was sensible how inferior I am in all respects to the least of those eminent servants of God whom I have now mentioned, yet I could discern no objections against this doctrine which were not capable of being answered by one of my mediocrity; and I hoped that it would be an additional evidence to the insufficience and feebleness of the arguments against the Sacrifice, if they could be refelled

by one that was so indifferently versed in antiquity, and
engaged in the sole service of so very large a cure of souls, as
I am.

It was my resolution from the beginning, to take my
measures and information from antiquity only, and therefore
not to look into any of those books that had been written
either by those of the Church of Rome for their corrupted
Sacrifice, or by the Protestants against it; and I can truly
say, I have most firmly and religiously observed this rule,
which I at first proposed to myself. The Defence[b] censures
Dr. Heylin for using the very texts, and "the Expositions of
them, which the Papists had done in defence of the Mass, in
his Antidotum Lincolniense." Now I declare, I have not
touched a book written by the modern Papists on their Sacrifice, nor did I ever see Dr. Heylin's Antidotum, or make
any inquiry after it. But if it be a crime to cite the same
texts that Papists do, it is impossible to avoid it; for, beside
the history of institution, there is but one context which our
adversaries will allow to be meant of the Eucharist, I mean
1 Cor. x. The history of institution is in substance and
effect but one, though four times repeated; and I cannot
myself believe that beside the history of institution there
are above four or five texts that do directly speak of the Eucharist. Now Scripture-proof is what our opponents do
almost wholly insist upon; and when we produce proofs
from Scripture we are told, these are the very texts which
the Papists use; for what is here said of Dr. Heylin as to
this point, must undoubtedly be true of all that ever did or
shall write upon this subject. Now I appeal to all the
rational world, whether it be possible to imagine how such
adversaries as these can think their cavils worthy of our consideration. Let them inform us of any one text in Scripture
that they will allow to relate to the Eucharist, which the
Papists have not cited, (for a man that never read their books
may easily presume that if there are so very few contexts
in the New Testament touching this matter, they will use
them all,) and I am pretty confident that no men of middling
sense could bear to read any writer that should so egre-
giously trifle upon any other subject; and the very same

[b] Page 8.

argument, *mutatis mutandis*, might with as good a face be made use of by Socinians against the very best of our writers upon the doctrine of the Trinity, which we hold in common with the Papists, and prove from the same texts of Scripture, and with the same expositions, that they do.

In order to pursue my resolutions, I drew up a collection of such authorities for the Sacrifice as might not only prove the Sacrifice itself, but give the best light I could expect into the nature and *modus* of it, according to the sentiments of the earliest writers; and because I look upon the Fathers of the fourth century to be the best expositors of the doctrine of the three former ages, therefore I proceeded to take as much information from them, and from the councils held in the same age, as I thought necessary for my purpose. I am far from pretending to have drawn up the whole force of all antiquity; nay, I have omitted very many testimonies of the fourth century, which I did know, and probably more and as good as those I have produced, because I was ignorant of them. I have taken some citations from Theodoret, and Cyril of Alexandria, as two of the most eminent and early writers of the fifth century, and who had their education in the fourth. I have avoided all citations from writers whom I could discover to be spurious, excepting only the constitutions called Apostolical, because they are allowed to be of very considerable antiquity, and drawn, save only some gross later interpolations, by very learned hands. It is very observable, that there is not any doctrine concerning the Eucharist, and particularly the Sacrifice, generally taught by the writers of the fourth century, according to the best of my observation, but what had been taught in the third, and second at least, and which I think I have proved to be the doctrine of our Saviour Himself. The reader cannot expect such numerous and large proofs from the few remaining writers of the second and third century, and especially the first, as from those of the fourth; but I cannot call to mind any particular of moment commonly asserted in the fourth century, which was not likewise asserted in the former ages, though more briefly and concisely. And though I cannot so much depend on the writers of the fourth century when they were destitute of the authority of the former ages; yet, when they fall in with them, it

seems a great proof that the Church of the former ages
looked upon the doctrine or practice wherein there is so visible an agreement, to be a matter of the greatest moment, and
therefore did inculcate it upon their rising posterity with the
greater earnestness and assiduity ; and that therefore their
consent with their ancestors in such particulars proceeded
from the unanimous judgment and faithful care of foregoing
ages, to transmit such doctrines and practices clearly and
fully to future generations. And what I have said of the
fourth age, I might, I believe, apply to three or four succeeding centuries, so far as concerns the matter now in dispute ;
for though there were, during this time, some additions made
to the Eucharistic Liturgies, which might well have been
spared, yet I am not apprehensive of any very gross corruptions introduced ; and I have given my reader a specimen
of the judgment of the Church in the eighth century, from
the Council of Constantinople that met to condemn image-
worship ; from which it will appear, that even thus late the
doctrine of the Eucharist and Sacrifice was preserved free
from any gross adulteration, and especially from that which
was afterwards called Transubstantiation ; and that therefore, if Gregory Nyssen, so early as the fourth century, did
teach a substantial change, as the most excellent Dr. Grabe
suspects, this was peculiar to that Father, or, at the most, can
be charged upon him and Cyril of Jerusalem only, (which
last I must confess is in my opinion innocent as to this
point,) and ought not to be looked upon as the current doctrine of the Church, in that, or even the following ages.

I likewise made extracts from the most ancient Liturgies
now extant ; and though none of them, except the Clementine, be truly primitive, yet in such particulars as they agree
with the Clementine, they do very much illustrate it, and
shew the consent of Churches even in later ages, to many of
the doctrines asserted in the following sheets. And it is very
evident, that some notions could never have begun so early,
as to be extant in the Clementine Liturgy, and yet be so far
diffused as to appear in all the Liturgies here cited, if they
had not had one common original, and that in the first times
of Christianity ; for though none but the Clementine is truly
ancient, yet the same series of the consecratory and more

solemn oblatory part of the service, their agreement in invocating the Holy Ghost, and in the end for which it is in-
voked, and in their intercessions or propitiations for others,
is a demonstration, that as to these particulars, they were all
formed by one rule and with one and the same view, and by
hands directed as it were by the very same mind and soul;
for as to these matters, they scarce differ in thought, but in
words only. There are indeed many gross additions and interpolations in all the Liturgies except that of St. Clement,
and yet among such heaps of rubbish the reader may observe
the true remains of antiquity sparkling in his eyes here and
there in every one of them.

When I had made such collections from antiquity as I
thought sufficient, I set myself to draw a scheme of the Eucharistical Sacrifice, according to the doctrine and judgment
of the ancients, without regard to what others, or I myself,
had formerly said on this subject. And I soon discovered an
excellent harmony of the ancients among themselves as to
this matter. I had an especial eye and regard to the Clementine Liturgy, and found that some things which at first
seemed very odd, yet by consulting that were made plain
and very intelligible. This I look upon as the only certain
plan upon which we can form a judgment concerning every
part of the primitive Eucharist and Sacrifice, and of the
series and connection of every part with the whole.

I must confess too, that in some particulars I discovered
that the assertors of the Sacrifice did not exactly agree with
the ancients. The most observable particular is this, that in
the primitive Church there was but one direct, solemn, vocal,
sacerdotal oblation of the bread and wine, and that immediately after the words of institution; whereas we have generally affirmed an ante-oblation of them. But since I cannot
find any certain evidence of any other oblation of them,
otherwise than as the representatives of Christ's Body and
Blood; therefore I have thought fit to declare, that I see no
grounds or reason to insist any longer on more than one oblation strictly so called. It may be said, that the bread and
wine were offered by being placed on the Altar by the celebrator, and this I do not deny; but I suppose this could not
be called the oblation of bread and wine, or the oblation of the

Eucharist, because other things beside the bread and wine were sometimes so offered. This could not be that new oblation of the New Testament spoken of by Irenæus, for that holy Father tells us that Christ taught us that oblation when He said, "This is My Body," &c., whereas the accepting the bread and wine from the hand of the lay-offerer and placing them on the Altar, was an action performed before, and in order to this more solemn sacerdotal oblation. And since the ancients speak but of one oblation in the Eucharist, and the Clementine Liturgy contains but one form of making this oblation, therefore I conceive that when in former books we made mention of two several oblations, we followed the scent which we took from later Liturgies, rather than the doctrine and practice of the truly primitive Church.

And let no man think that this frank confession of mine is any real prejudice to the cause, in the defence of which I am engaged, till he can shew that in any other cause, whether philosophical, juridical, or theological, where any number of advocates have written or spoken on the same side, there has not been some small dissonance in their pleas or arguings, or in the modifying or circumstantiating of them. And if the Sacrifice must be exploded on this account, I know no doctrine in the whole Bible so sacred, no truth in other sciences so evident, but that it is liable to the same objection; and if therefore this doctrine shall be thought worthy to be discarded on this account, I know not what doctrine can be safe.

And if two several acts of oblation, properly so called, be allowed, I apprehend no manner of danger to the Sacrifice itself on this account. When the lay-votary presented any animal to be sacrificed at the Jewish altar, this presentation of it might be called an oblation, and is so very often in the Scripture; so was the sprinkling the blood, the laying the animal on the altar, and the burning it in part or whole; and yet all this process was but one sacrificial celebrity, though it consisted of several sacrificial actions. So it is very evident that the presenting the bread and wine, or placing them on the Altar, may well enough be called an oblation; and if this action be attended with oblatory words, as it is in the later Liturgies,

I see no reason to blame this practice, especially since it is of very considerable antiquity, though not perfectly primitive. And the chief end which I promise to myself by this observation, is to render the Sacrifice, as spoken of by the most ancient writers, more clear and intelligible, and my proofs upon this head the more unexceptionable; for though the primitive writers do often call the layman's part in bringing his material offerings by the name of an oblation, as the law of Moses likewise did; and though the celebrator's placing them on the Lord's Table, be now commonly and properly enough said to be an oblation of them; yet the most proper Eucharistical sacerdotal oblation was always spoken of as one only in the most primitive writers. And that there was but one such oblation in the Clementine Liturgy, and that therefore the making but one oblation, and that by way of commemoration, is the most ancient method, that Liturgy itself is an irrefragable demonstration; and it is not worth while to dispute whether the presentation of them on the Altar was looked upon as a part of this one solemn oblation, or only as an action necessary in order to the other. It is sufficient for my purpose to observe, that they are never mentioned as two several oblations in the most early monuments of antiquity.

And by this, my Lord, I am insensibly brought to say something in relation to the censure your Lordship was pleased to pass, in your Charge, upon the author of the Clergyman's Vade Mecum. I can sincerely declare, that my only intention in affirming, as I did in the note on the second Apostolical Canon, " that bread and wine are actually to be offered to God, by the direction of the Church of England by virtue of the Rubric, immediately before the prayer 'For the whole state of Christ's Church,' and in and by that prayer," was to do justice to our constitution, and to represent our Church and Liturgy as conformable to the ancient model as in truth I could, according to the best of my knowledge. Your Lordship is pleased to resent this as an affront and injury done to the Church of England; lest therefore I should again incur your Lordship's displeasure upon this account, I have wholly forborne, in the following treatise, any intimation of the Church of England's agreeing, or not agreeing, with the primitive Church, in the doctrine or practice of the

D 2

Sacrifice; and have entirely left it to my reader to reflect under every head, how far our Church symbolizes with the primitive, or comes short of her. Nay, I have in the second edition of the second part of the Vade Mecum, omitted that paragraph which your Lordship has censured; not that I am not fully persuaded that the Church does, by the clause inserted into the prayer for the Church Militant, intend an oblation of the bread and wine, but because, upon maturer thoughts, I am perfectly convinced that the oblation meant in that canon is the commemorative oblation of the bread and wine, following after the words of institution in the ancient Liturgies, and not any previous oblation of the bread and wine, apart from the other lay-offerings.

But, my Lord, I cannot but express the sense I have of your severity toward me, in passing by other authors who have said the same thing in effect that I there do, and singling out so indifferent a writer as myself to bear the marks of your displeasure. Your Lordship has acquitted me from being any of the "chief promoters of this opinion;" for of these you are pleased to say, " that they are of the late separation[c]," meaning, I suppose, the non-jurors, of which number I never was; and the most incomparably learned Bishop Bull was alive when your Charge was delivered to the clergy, though he died about the time of the publication of it. Now whether your Lordship acted a generous part in choosing to condemn my book, who was the least capable of making a defence, I submit to your own consideration. And, my Lord, that in giving sentence against me, you condemned one of those English Bishops for whose memory you have the greatest honour, I am very sure you must yourself confess; I do not mean Bishop Bull, but Bishop Patrick; for though I can truly say that I did not learn this notion of the bread and wine being to be offered according to our Liturgy from that very learned Prelate, yet he that reads what I am now going to cite from him, and compares it with my note on the second Apostolical Canon in the first edition, would be apt to suspect me of a plagium. · " The spiritual sacrifice of ourselves, and the corporal sacrifice of our goods to God, may teach the Papists that we are sacrificers as well as they, and are made kings and priests unto God; yea, they may know, that the bread and wine of the Eucharist is an offering out of the stock of the whole congregation to this service, according as it was in the times of the primitive Church." And, my Lord, this book was published by Mr. Patrick while he was "minister of God's Word," as he styles himself, at Battersea in Surrey; and the Epistle Dedicatory bears date January, 1659; so that it was no crime in that age, and in so moderate a divine as Mr. Patrick, to say that bread and wine were offered according as it was in the primitive Church[d]. Nor did he alter his opinion as to this particular, after he became an eminent divine in the Church of England; nay, I think, he justifies all that your Lordship is pleased to censure in my book, in the following words: "It is not common bread and wine which the ancients prayed might become the Body and Blood of Christ to them, but bread and wine first sanctified by being offered to Him with thanksgiving.—This is to be understood when you see bread and wine set on God's Table by him that ministers in this Divine Service; then it is offered to God, for whatsoever is solemnly placed there becomes by that means a thing dedicated and appropriated to Him.—And if you observe the time when this bread is ordered to be placed there, which is immediately after the alms of the people have been received for the poor, you will see it is intended by our Church to be a thankful oblation to God of the fruits of the earth.—Desiring God to accept of these gifts as a small token of their grateful sense that they hold all they have of Him, as the great Lord of the world. And so we are taught to do in that prayer which immediately follows in our Liturgy, wherein we humbly beseech Him to accept, not only our alms but also our oblations; these are things distinct. And the former, 'alms,' signifying that which is given for the relief of the poor; the latter, 'oblations,' can signify nothing else, according to the language of the ancient Church, but this bread and wine." And now, my Lord, I crave leave to say, that there was much greater reason for your Lordship to censure Bishop Patrick's Christian Sacrifice, in the 77th page of which book, (the ninth edition,) these words are to be found, than the poor

d See Mensa Mystica, first edition, p. 44.

Clergyman's Vade Mecum; not only on account of the learning, dignity, and authority of the person who wrote it, but because it is certain that the Christian Sacrifice had come into
more hands when your Lordship was pleased to pass this
censure, than it was credible that the Vade Mecum ever can;
for the only reason hinted by your Lordship for making this
reflection on the book last mentioned is, that "it was designed to come into every clergyman's hands." This learned
Bishop does not only agree with the Vade Mecum in the
main, that bread and wine are or ought to be offered, but
that by being placed on the table they become dedicated
and appropriated to God; and this he says to prove that the
bread and wine are offered to Him: so that this great man
supposes, as I did when I wrote that note, that the bread
and wine is offered, or presented to God, by being placed
there by the hands of the Priest; which is what your Lordship charges on me, " as a misrepresentation of the Rubric,
and an assertion contrary to the Rubric." I own that in the
Rubric itself the word 'place' only refers to the bread and
wine, 'present' to the alms. But though the bread and
wine are not directed to be presented in the Rubric, yet they
are actually presented in the following Prayer, except it can
be made appear that in any oblatory prayer the word oblations be so used as to exclude the bread and wine. I must
confess that if I had expected so severe a Censor as your
Lordship, I ought to have expressed myself with greater caution. And yet I will hereby oblige myself, whenever your
Lordship is pleased to call for it, to present you with several
citations from the most accomplished human writers, in
which there is the same, or greater, liberty of expression
used, as there is by me in this passage, not excepting your
Lordship's own works. I was once thinking to insert some
instances of this sort; but I shall at present spare your
Lordship's patience, for I delight not in such reprisals, nor is
it my business to justify my own writings or reputation, so
much as the cause and doctrine the defence whereof I have
undertaken. I shall say no more on this head, but that I
am perfectly astonished to observe that Mr. Patrick could, in
the times of confusion, so far emancipate himself from vulgar
prejudices as to see and publicly declare for a material obla-

tion of bread and wine; and that after the review of our
Liturgy, he should understand the words of the Rubric and
the oblations in the following Prayer, as they were undoubtedly meant, of the Eucharistical elements; nay, that
Richard Baxter himself could say, that " in the consecration
the Church doth offer the creatures of bread and wine to be
accepted by God to this sacred use;" and that "ministers are
the agents of the people to God in offering or dedicating the
creatures[e];" and yet that a Priest of the Church of England, at a time when the Church was voted out of danger,
should, in the most public manner, incur the censure of a
Bishop of that Church only for saying the same thing which
they had done. I readily acknowledge, my Lord, that this
oblation of the bread and wine does not constitute the Eucharist a proper Sacrifice in the sense of the primitive
Church, nor come up to that notion which I have asserted in
the following sheets; and therefore I do not claim either
Bishop Patrick or Mr. Baxter as witnesses to the Eucharistic
Sacrifice, properly so called; I only produce them as declaring for me in that particular for which I stand condemned
in your Lordship's Charge.

Bishop Patrick was a man well read in all parts of divinity,
and I cannot but observe to your Lordship, that in the
above-written citation from his Christian Sacrifice, he argues
for the signification of the word 'oblations,' from the "universal
language of the ancient Church." And I cannot but take an
occasion here to express my wishes that this were better understood; for it is certain that the greatest obstacle to the
doctrine of the Sacrifice is, that the men of this age cannot
easily, by a spiritual, rational, unbloody, intellectual sacrifice, understand an oblation of bread and wine, considered
as the representative Body and Blood of Christ. By a Sacrifice of thanksgiving, of praise, of commemoration, they can
conceive nothing to be meant but what is verbal and mental.
It is one main design of these papers to apply a remedy to
this disease, and if I am successful in this particular, I have
no reason to doubt of carrying my cause, and obtaining the
verdict of all equal judges. Our adversaries cannot but be
sensible that they have a great advantage of us in this parti-

[e] See Append. to Christian Priesthood, p. 320.

cular, for there is a strange unaccountable magic in the
sound of words, and they who have the vulgar signification
of them on their own side, may enchant and charm the generality of people into their own opinions, whatever they are.
Your Lordship's own Order was in the last age run down by
this sort of fascination. Prelacy was the fatal word which
drove my Lords the Bishops first out of the House of Peers,
and then out of their churches. It is certain that the im-
parity of orders, which Christ instituted in His Church, cannot be better expressed than by the word Prelacy, and the
Greek word ἡγούμενοι, which denotes Bishops, Heb. xiii. 17,
cannot be more aptly rendered by any English noun than by
Prelates; but they who then had the people at their disposal,
first clapped an ill signification upon the word, as importing the
Popish hierarchy, or something very like it, and then applied
it to the governors of the Church of England, and by virtue
of that wrong application subverted the government and the
Church at once. This may serve for one instance to prove
of what dangerous consequence it is to permit people to run
away with the mistaken sense of a word; and they that indulge themselves in such errors, which at first sight seem
very small, may by this means be led into very mischievous
conclusions.

I must further add, my Lord, that it is of great use to all
divines to understand the language not only of the truly
ancient Church, but even of that of the middle and darker
ages. If I had been better acquainted with the liturgies of
those times, I might when I wrote the postscript to 'The
Propitiatory Oblation,' have laid before your Lordship clear
evidence, that when you take the word offertory to signify
the act of oblation or the things offered, you give such a
sense to that word as those Liturgies from whence our Reformers took it, never do. I have indeed in that postscript
given sufficient proof even from our own reformed Liturgies,
that offertory denotes the sentences sung or said while the
alms and devotions of the people are collected. And now,
my Lord, give me leave to add, that I have further authority
for this signification of that word. In Pope Gregory's Sacramentary, printed at Paris, 1642, are these words; *Postmodum legitur Evangelium, deinde offertorium;* "afterwards the

Gospel is read, then the Offertory :" on which words Menardus, the editor, has this note ; *Offertorium antiphona est, quæ dum caneretur, populus sua dona in altari offerebat juxta antiquum morem[f]:* "The offertory is an antiphone, and while that was sung the people made their oblations at the Altar, according to the ancient custom." In the old Liturgy published by Father Mabillon, are these words ; *Tum antiphona post Evangelium.* Mabillon explains the word *antiphona* thus ; *Nos, scilicet in ordine Romano, offertorium vocamus,* "We, in the Roman order, call this the offertory[g]." And Du Fresne in his Glossary says, " *Offerenda* and *offertorium* are the same, and signify what is sung *inter offerendum*[h], while the people make their oblations." Cardinal Bona, in his 66th page of his first book Rerum Liturgicarum, in giving an account of St. Ambrose's Liturgy, calls that *Antiphona post Evangelium,* (for the Creed was not rehearsed after the Gospel in that age,) which Mabillon calls *offertorium.* Other examples might be produced (if these were not sufficient) from Amalarius and Micrologus.

If Dr. Hancock had consulted these Liturgies he would never have been so far transported as to say that by " then" in the Rubric, which orders the Priest to place the bread and wine on the Lord's Table, we are to understand, "when there is a Communion." For by a diligent perusal of them he would have found that the stated time for doing this was immediately after the offertory. The first book of Edward VI. directed the Priest to place the bread on the corporas, or paten, and to put the wine in the chalice, or other vessel, as soon as these sentences had been sung or said. The present Rubric enforces the ancient practice of the Priest's placing the Eucharistical elements on the Holy Table precisely at this same time. And those incumbents, or curates, who leave this office to be performed by some layman, are guilty of non-conformity not only to the Church of England, but to the whole Catholic Church of Christ in the purest ages. For even in Justin Martyr's time, the elements were offered to the president or celebrator, who taking

---

[f] Page 582.
[g] Vid. Mabillon de Liturgiâ Gallicanâ, at Paris, 1685, p. 8.

[h] Offertorium, idea quod offerenda. Cantus qui inter offerendum cantatur.

them from the hands of the deacon or other idoneous person, presented them on the Altar, and then proceeded in the Eucharistical Service[i]. I might enlarge here, but the learned Dr. Nicols hath saved me that trouble, to whose note on this Rubric I refer my reader; but I the rather took notice of this because your Lordship's Clergy being assured by your Charge that Dr. Hancock's book is written "with good learning and judgment," may from thence conclude that it is left to their discretion how or when to place the bread and wine on the Lord's Table.

In another particular I cannot but think Dr. Nicols much mistaken; that is, in saying in his notes on the Prayer of Consecration, that the Church has not determined whether the Priest shall say that prayer standing or kneeling. Nay, he is not content with this, but goes so far as to say that " since it is a prayer, the posture of kneeling is most proper." That kneeling is the most proper posture for the people in prayer may be allowed, but if it be so for the Priest too, our Church is much to blame. For even in the matrimonial office, when the bridegroom and bride are come to the Communion Table, the Priest is expressly ordered to "stand," they to "kneel," while the prayers there are rehearsed. And in the Rubric before the prayer which immediately follows after the contract, the bridegroom and bride are directed to "kneel," but not the Priest; and indeed it is very improper for him to kneel, because that prayer is a benediction. And as to the main of the Communion Service, there is no question but that standing is the most proper posture for the Priest. At the beginning of the Service the Rubric expressly commands him "to stand at the north side of the Table, and to say the Lord's Prayer and the Collect following, the people kneeling;" and he is likewise directed to say the two Collects between the Commandments and the Epistle, "standing as before." The absolution, the following sentences, the *sursum corda*, and *trisagium*, are, I suppose, without all question to be pronounced standing; and yet this absolution itself is precatory. The question is not what is the most proper posture for prayer in general, but what is the most proper

---

[i] See Appendix A.

posture for a Priest in offering or blessing the sacramental bread and wine. And here I conceive it ought to be considered:

I. That it is contrary to the practice of all Churches, both ancient and modern, East and West, Popish and Reformed, for the Priest to kneel in making the oblation, or performing the consecration. If there be one single precedent for it, it is more than I am aware of.

II. It is inconsistent with the solemn action which he is now performing. For I apprehend that the common notions of mankind do all agree in this, that a sacred officer in making an oblation or conferring a benediction, is to use this posture of standing. So that if he be not allowed to be offering a sacrifice, yet except it be denied that he is blessing the bread and wine, he ought not to kneel.

III. I cannot but believe that the Priest is by our Rubric required to stand while he performs this most solemn part of his office. For, 1st. That he is to stand while he is ordering the bread and wine, is self-evident; and when he has ordered the bread and wine, he is presently directed to say the Prayer of Consecration. Now since he was before in a standing posture, he is not to alter this posture till he is directed so to do; and since the Rubric gives no intimation of making any such change of posture, I humbly conceive that he is to continue standing. 2ndly. The Rubric, till the Restoration, was, " the Priest standing shall say;" and there is no appearance or probability that the Convocation intended any alteration in this particular; and it is irrational to suppose that the governors of the Church intended to leave it to the Priest's discretion, whether he would use that posture which had hitherto been used upon this occasion in our own Church as well as all others, or whether he would choose a new one. And, 3rdly, I apprehend that the very words of the Rubric are a direct order to the Priest to stand in performing the consecration. They are these; " When the Priest standing before the Table, hath so ordered the bread and wine, that he may with the more readiness and decency break the bread before the people, and take the cup into his hands, he shall say the prayer of consecration as follows." For that the incidental proposition, " standing before the Table," relates to the Priest only while he is ordering the bread and wine, and not while he says the prayer, I cannot conceive. The natural construction of the words seems to me to be this, that "the Priest standing be-before the Table shall order," &c., and he, the same Priest, "standing before the Table shall say." For I can see no doubt, but that the Priest is to stand before the Table, while he consecrates. What those words, "before the Table," may import, I dare not say; but shall submit that and every thing else to your Lordship's judgment. And though this be not clear, yet the word "standing" is; and I think Dr. Nicols to have used too much liberty in attempting to expound away the plain meaning of it.

I beg your Lordship's pardon for using this freeness to a person of your character, who by the laws of the Church Catholic and of the Church of England, are one of those who have the sole authority, under the Primate, to determine the sense of all doubtful Rubrics. But I must confess I do not apprehend that these Rubrics are at all doubtful in themselves; but there is nothing so plain but that disputatious men may endeavour to puzzle and obscure them. And I am so far from any design of entrenching upon the prerogative of my Lords the Bishops on this account, that if my Diocesan and Primate, upon an application regularly made to him, should think fit to determine, that every Priest may place the bread and wine on the Holy Table at any time of the Communion Service that pleases him best, or that he may either stand or kneel while he says the Consecration Prayer, then it must be owned that the Clergy within this province are under no obligation to place the bread and wine on the Table at the end of the offertory, and that the Priest is not tied to stand at the consecration; and yet I should, notwithstanding this, humbly be of opinion that the words imply no such latitude in either case. But if any lawful judge do explain a law contrary to the meaning and intendment of it, that explanation is, I sup-pose, authoritative until it be overruled or superseded by some superior power. But all that appear as advocates in any cause, have liberty to allege their reasons against such interpretations, especially before such interpretations have been publicly pronounced e Cathedrâ. At least, I conceive, I have as just a right to plead for the true meaning of these

Rubrics, as Dr. Hancock and Dr. Nicols for that which I am persuaded is a wrong one.

And now, my Lord, I shall detain you no longer, but only to beg your pardon if any thing said by me in this epistle or elsewhere, seem to be expressed with more warmth or resentment than becomes me. I am one that never studied the arts of address, nor was ever solicitous to please any man by any other method but that of saying what I believed to be the truth, whether in season or out of season. I question not but I may have been guilty of several oversights in lesser matters, and that in my style and choice of words I very much need a corrector; but if any man shall take me to task upon these accounts, I shall not think myself obliged to answer him.

The argumentative part of my discourse, on which the main cause depends, is that for which alone I am greatly concerned; and if any man attack that part of my book, and do it in such a manner as becomes a scholar and one that understands the subject on which he writes, an answer will not be wanting if God grant me life and health. And if I die, yet I trust in God this noble truth will always find a succession of defenders; and if I should mistake in this presage, yet I shall think it much more honourable in the sight of God and my ever-blessed Redeemer, and of all truly judicious Christians, to be considered as the last Priest of this Church that ever wrote in defence of the primitive Sacrifice, than to have been the first Bishop that ever wrote against it. However, I dare say of all those who have of late years declared for the Sacrifice, as Origen did of himself and the Christians of his age, in words borrowed in part from St. Paul, Heb. x. 23, " We hold fast the OBLATION as long as we live." With this resolution I take leave to subscribe myself,

Your Lordship's

as in duty bound,

J. J.

May 18, 1713.

POSTSCRIPT.

When your Lordship published the first edition of your
Charge, 'The Propitiatory Oblation' was in the press, and well
near finished; 'The Unbloody Sacrifice' was in the printer's
hands, and this epistle ready for the press a considerable time
before your second edition appeared, by which means I have
been obliged to consider both the editions of your Charge in
a postscript.

Your Lordship's only argument, which seemed to me of
any force to prove that the word 'oblation' in the Prayer for
the Church Militant, did not signify bread and wine, was this,
that "there might be an offertory without a Communion."
This I readily acknowledged, but shewed at the same time
that your Lordship's supposition that offertory signified the
materials to be offered, was without any good grounds; for
I alleged a Rubric of the first Common Prayer-Book of
Edward VI. which directs the offertory to be sung by the
clerks, and it is certain that money or any other material thing
cannot be sung. And further I observed, that in our present
Rubric after the Communion Service, there is mention of
money given at the offertory, from which I inferred that the
money or other material thing given by way of devotion could
not be the offertory itself. Your Lordship in your second
edition has added some paragraphs, in which you are pleased
to confess, that "the offertory is in strict speaking the name
or title of the service that relates to the offerings or things
given[k]." And yet even in this second edition you continue
to assert as in the first, that "the matter of the offertory is
money[l]." My Lord, I crave leave to say, and I have fully
proved, that the matter of the offertory is nothing but the
words or sentences to be said or sung. Your Lordship acknowledges, as above cited, that it is "the service relating to
the offerings," therefore not the offerings themselves. You
are pleased to say, that "where you use it for the things
themselves, you take care not to be misunderstood," by
which I suppose your Lordship means that you have explained it in the second edition, by saying that it signifies

k Page 22.   l Page 20.

the service. I hope your Lordship does not mean that it comprises both the money and the service, and yet nothing else can reconcile these two propositions: and if they cannot otherwise be reconciled, I must leave the difficulty to your Lordship; for it is beyond my ability to prove that money put into a basin can be sung or said.

However, your Lordship can by no means allow that this name belongs to the sentences only, as this author (meaning the writer of 'The Propitiatory Oblation') restrains it; now I crave leave to say, that I have not at all restrained the use of this word, but take it as I find it in the Liturgy of Edward VI., and that which is now used in our Church. Nor did the compilers of these Liturgies restrain it; for it is evident from the citations in the foregoing epistle, that the word *offertorium*, as there used, signified nothing more nor less than the sentences of Scripture sung or said on this occasion, many hundred years before the reign of Edward VI. It seems to me that your Lordship is pleased to enlarge the signification of it, because I have nowhere found it to import what you assert it to do.

But I will consider your Lordship's reason for extending the signification of this word, and that is as follows: " For the very act of offering is doubtless a part of the offertory service, as it gives the name to the whole; the presenting what is offered upon the Table is another; and I believe it will be thought that the beseeching God to accept it is not the least considerable in this matter." Now, my Lord, this takes that for granted which is the point in dispute, viz. that the offertory is not the sentences; for if the offertory and sentences are the same, then there is an offertory when these sentences are read or sung, though nothing be given, presented, or recommended to the Divine acceptance, and this is indeed the truth of the matter. And to give full demonstration of this over and above what has been already said, I will lay before your Lordship another Rubric of Edward the Sixth's Liturgy, which stands just before these sentences; viz. " Then shall follow for the Offertory one or moe of these sentences of H. Scripture, to be song whiles the people dooe offer, or else one of theim to be saied by the Minister immediately afore the offeryng." By this it appears that the offertory

might be either during the offering, viz. if the offertory were
sung, and so there were time for the people to make their
offerings while the clerks were singing it, or it might be before the offering, viz. if the minister only read one sentence,
which in this case was the offertory, or for the offertory. In
both cases the offertory and the act of offering were two distinct things; and by this Liturgy the alms were not to be
presented on the Table, nor was there any prayer for their
acceptance; so that offertory is here used exclusively of all
the three actions here specified by your Lordship. Let me
further observe, that "offertory service" is a word new coined
by your Lordship, and though I own your authority to be
sufficient to coin a word, and to stamp what signification you
please upon it, yet, my Lord, you need not be told that our
Liturgy has no such word, nor any other Liturgy that I have
seen, and so your reasonings upon it affect no Rubrics of the
Church. I take leave further to observe, that though the
offertory, according to this Liturgy of Edward VI. and all
other Liturgies, was nothing but the sentences, yet the value
of the bread and wine is said to be offered in these words,
viz. "The parishioners of every parishe shall offre every
Sunday the just valour and pryce of the holy lofe at the time
of the offertory;" where still the offertory and the offering
are made things clearly distinct from each other.

If by "offertory service" you mean no more than what the
Church does by the offertory, it is evident that nothing can
be meant but the sentences sung or said; for the Church
always supposes an offertory when the Communion Service is
read, but cannot in reason suppose that every Sunday or
Holiday something shall be offered in every church. And to
give further proof of this, it is observable, that as these
sentences are most commonly called the offertory, so sometimes the vessel in which the bread was put passed by the
same name, of which see Mabillon de Liturg. Gall. p. 185.[m]
And your Lordship might argue upon this vessel just as you
do upon the sentences, viz. the very act of offering is doubt-

---

[m] Ad oblatas excipiendas inserviebat
offertorium: colum verò seu colato-
rium ad Vinum expurgandum. Offer-
toria vasa erant à Patinis distincta, in
quæ populus Panem oblatum ad Altare
deponebat; quæ primò solida erant,
deinde linea, seu sericea, aut ex quali-
bet simili materiâ: Unum aureum,
alia argentea memorat vetus Chronicon
Frontanellense in cap. 16.

less a part of the offertory, the presenting what is offered another, and the beseeching God to accept it a third; and you might as truly say, that the act of offering gives name to the vessel, of old called *offertorium*, as that it now gives name to what you are pleased to call the "offertory-service." Yet I fancy few would by this be convinced that the vessel itself implied or contained the act of offering, or the presenting the oblations, or the prayer for the Divine acceptance. Nay, all would easily perceive that the vessel, as well as the sentences, were the offertory, though not one mite or crumb of bread were put into the one, or one farthing given at the rehearsal of the other. And this may be sufficient also to shew that to argue from names or etymologies, as your Lordship here does, can do very little service to any cause.

If your Lordship still persist that the offertory takes in the Prayer for the Church Militant, I take leave to add that it must take in also the placing the Bread and Wine on the Holy Table, except you will suppose that the offertory-service breaks off at the end of these sentences, and then begins *de novo* with the Prayer for the Church Militant, and so in effect make two offertories in order to avoid the oblation of bread and wine. And if the placing the Bread and Wine on the Lord's Table be part of the offertory, then, according to your Lordship's own argument, it is to be offered, and presented, and recommended to the Divine acceptance; and using the word "place" instead of "offer" or "present," is no sufficient objection against this sense; for I conceive there is no occasion for me to point out those particular places, where the very action of offering the blood, which was the most essential action of offering the Jewish sacrifice, is by the English rendered 'putting the blood,' by the Latin *ponere sanguinem*, by the Greek ἐπιτιθέναι αἷμα, the Hebrew Nathan admitting of this rendition, because it signifies either, 'to give, present, put, or place.'

And, my Lord, the truth is, I know not whether you do after all persist in making the inserted clause of God's "accepting our alms and oblations" a part of the offertory, or not; for in the first paragraph of your addition[h], you seem to promise that you will "give me satisfaction," that the clause inserted in the Prayer for the Church Militant "is the

[h] Page 22.

offertory," and what follows looks the same way, if I understand it; in the third paragraph of this page you say expressly, that "this prayer immediately attends upon the
offertory," and therefore I should think were a thing distinct
from it; for if the thing *attending* be the same with the
thing *attended*, and if your Lordship upon recollection will
justify it, then all arguing is at an end.

Your Lordship justly suspects that what you had before
laid down would "be thought too much to be granted," and
you yourself I believe are by this time of the same mind; for
it is evident you demand that to be granted that subverts
your own hypothesis, viz. that the Prayer for the Church
Militant "attends the offertory;" and, my Lord, that the
Prayer for the Church Militant, or the inserted clause, is
either the offertory or a part of the offertory, is too much to
grant except there were some appearance of proof.

You insist "that the most obvious and reasonable interpretation of these words, 'Accept our alms and oblations,' is to
be had from considering what offerings there is any mention
made of in the office immediately preceding, and those are
confessed to relate only to the Minister and poor, which in
the Scotch Liturgy are expressly called oblations." Here
your Lordship, by "the office immediately preceding," must
mean the offertory sentences, for of them only it is confessed
that they relate only to the Minister and poor. You cannot
mean the placing the bread and wine on the Holy Table,
though that indeed "immediately precedes" the prayer, for
these I am sure you would not have called offerings; and if
these sentences be an "office," what other name can you give
it but the "offertory office?" and if the sentences be the offertory office, then the Prayer for the Church Militant is no
part of it.

In the next paragraph your Lordship proceeds thus; "He
who considers that the Scotch Liturgy was made upon ours
by several alterations and additions under Archbishop Laud's
own hand, and that great regard was had to these in the
review of the Liturgy, 1661, will I believe agree with me, that
the prayer to God to accept our alms and oblations respects
those offerings only which the foregoing sentences exhort us
to make." We own, my Lord, that during the offertory

nothing is to be given but money, or other materials for
charitable or pious uses; after the offertory the Bread and
Wine are placed on the table, and, as we believe, in order to
be solemnly offered by the Priest. But I cannot but express
my surprise to observe that your Lordship would enforce
what you here say, by observing that "at the review of our
Liturgy, 1661," when the clause in dispute was inserted,
"great regard was had to the alterations and additions made
with Archbishop Laud's own hand," and which he had made
in order to insert them into the Scotch Liturgy; for, my
Lord, the greater regard was had to the alterations and additions made with Archbishop Laud's own hand, the more sure
we are that bread and wine were designed to be offered, for
this was one particular on which Archbishop Laud and his
friends did always insist. It is evident they did not shew
their regard to Archbishop Laud's alterations by ordering
the elements to be "offered up" before the Prayer for the
Church Militant, as the Scotch Liturgy did, nor by calling
the alms 'oblations' (for that remains yet to be proved, my
Lord); it remains, therefore, that they paid this regard by
ordering both alms and bread and wine to be offered together
in the inserted clause. It was a poor regard indeed, if it only
consisted in calling the alms 'oblations;' the most proper
regard was paid by causing the elements to be offered to
God, which was the principal thing the good Archbishop intended in the alterations to be made in this part of the Communion office. I cannot persuade myself that your Lordship
can look on these arguings in the second edition, especially
when compared with those in the first, as sufficient finally to
determine your judgment.

It must be owned, that the Rubric next after the blessing
in the Post-communion service, calls the following prayers
Collects to be said after the Offertory, when there is no
Communion; and from hence your Lordship would conclude, that the Prayer for the Whole Estate, &c. is part of
the offertory, because these collects are universally read after
that prayer; but

1. The reader will take notice, that this title was first
given to these collects by the first book of Edward VI., and
then it properly belonged to them; for,

2. By this first book of King Edward, the Prayer for the Whole Estate was not to be read when there was no communion; and therefore these collects were at such times immediately to follow the sentences or offertory.

3. If the Prayer for the Whole Estate had been to be read at such times by that book of King Edward, yet it could not have been part of the offertory; not only because this prayer then stood at a greater distance from the sentences, viz. between the Trisagium and the Prayer of Consecration, but because there were then no oblatory words in that prayer; " accept our alms" was added, when this prayer was removed from its former place to that where it now stands; "and oblations" was added at the Restoration.

4. We now read the Prayer for the Whole Estate, when there is no communion, not by virtue of the Rubric next after the blessing and before the collects, but by virtue of the Rubric next after the collects, which runs thus; " Upon the Sundays and other holidays, if there be no communion, shall be said all that is appointed at the Communion, until the end of the General Prayer for the good Estate of Christ's Church, together with one or more of these collects last before rehearsed;" and this Rubric was not in the first book of Edward the Sixth.

The consequence is very clear, viz. that the title given to these prayers was very proper according to the first book of Edward the Sixth; for by that these collects were to be said immediately after the offertory, when there was no Communion; the title now belongs to them but very improperly; they are still indeed to be said after the offertory, but not immediately next after it, as formerly, for the Prayer for the Whole Estate comes between. Your Lordship's argument is grounded upon a misnomer, and therefore I dare presume that you will no longer insist upon it.

Cranbrook,
Oct. 17, 1713.

A NECESSARY

ADVERTISEMENT TO THE READER.

THE authorities made use of in this treatise are rarely printed in the original Greek or Latin, either in the text, or in the margin of the book itself; excepting only such as relate to some collateral point, and not to the main controversy, or some citations *ex abundanti*, and which I met with after I had finished my first design, and which I have occasion to mention but once; but lest my reader should suspect my fidelity, he is to observe,

I. That he has all the authorities from the Fathers, Councils, and Liturgies, on which the stress of my argument lies, printed in the Appendix in the original Greek or Latin; and whenever I cite any of these, I do not only give my reader the translation of the words in English, but refer him to the page of my Appendix where the original Greek or Latin is to be found, and not only to the page, but the letter by which that citation is marked or distinguished in that page, to which the reference is made; and if the words to which I refer stand above three or four lines from the beginning of that citation, then I further refer my reader to the line of that citation where the words that I mean stand, or at least begin; thus, when I allege the first citation from St. Clement of Rome, after I have mentioned the name of that Father, I add, (A. p. 1. Ap.) that is, at the letter A, in the first page of my Appendix; but if I cite those words, " Let every one of you brethren celebrate the Eucharist in his own rank," I not only put the letter B. the page 1. Ap. but I likewise add, l. 13, and in the 13th line of that citation the reader will find the Greek words to which I here refer him. If I allege those words of Justin, "The Deacons distribute it to every one of those who are present," I direct him to the Greek by prefixing (A. p. 2, 3. Ap. l. 9.) that is at the letter A. in the second and third page of my Appendix, in the ninth line, and there my reader will accordingly meet with the Greek words, for I never refer to the line of the page but of the citation. The reader may think it would have been more for his ease and satisfaction to have had the original citation produced in the text, or margin of the page, where it is alleged, but I thought the course I have taken more eligible.

1. Because very many of my shortest as well as longest citations prove several of the doctrines which are here advanced, and by consequence are often repeated; and I thought it would too much swell the volume to transcribe the citation in the original, as often as I had occasion to make use of it, especially if it were somewhat large; the lesser original citations might indeed have been once for all set down in the margin, and a reference made to that margin, whenever the citation was repeated; but then my reader must have had the same pains of turning to that margin, which he must now take in turning to the Appendix; and this method would have required my attendance on the press, which my circumstances would not admit of.

2. Several of my citations are very long, and such as I could have no occasion to allege all at once, as that of St. Cyprian's Epistle to Cæcilius, the first from Gregory Nyssen, several from Irenæus, that from the Synod of Constantinople; but I thought it proper that such large authorities, which I produce by piecemeals, should be once for all entirely represented to my reader's view, that so by the coherence and connection, the learned reader might be more capable of making a judgment of the pertinence of my allegations: and indeed these and some other citations seemed somewhat too large to be crowded into a margin.

3. It was especially necessary, that my citations from the Liturgies should at once be proposed to my reader's view; because some of my arguings depend on the series and connection of the several parts of those Liturgies; and I knew no method so proper for the attaining those ends which I proposed as that which I have therefore taken.

II. Some citations are here given in English only, as

1. Those which are taken from modern Latin writers; for I thought it would be an unnecessary piece of punctiliousness to produce the original words of authors whose language

is very plain and easy, and their books not so rare to be found as those of the ancients.

2. Some counter-citations taken from the adversaries of the doctrines which I here defend, are represented in the translation of them, by whom they are alleged; for the reader will not suspect that our adversaries are partial against themselves.

3. In the proof that John vi. is meant of the Eucharist, there are several citations from Origen's Homilies produced in English only; this is done for no other reason, but because these citations are somewhat long, and in which the main cause (that of the Sacrifice) is not directly concerned; and therefore I thought it best in this case to spare my reader's cost, and not to swell the volume by inserting the Latin.

If there are any other citations in English only, they are so few, or so trite and obvious, that I need make no apology for them.

PREFACE

THE SECOND EDITION.

It is some comfort to me that I live to see a second edition of a book, of which it is hard to say, whether it cost me more pains in composing, or more patience in bearing the severe censures that have been passed against me for it.

It is now more than ten years since the first publication[a]. During all this time nothing that deserves the name of an answer hath appeared against it; but only two or three impotent pamphlets; a fardel or two of calumny and buffoonery: and now and then a gird in a printed sermon or other discourse.

The generality of my adversaries have contented themselves with saying some wild rude things against the doctrine, or myself, and charging me in general with absurdities or contradictions, which yet they have not been able to point out, however, not to prove.

The most modish and compendious way of confuting my books on this subject, is by saying that the practice of some Churches is no necessary rule for all. Yet no one hath been able to shew us one single Church of two hundred years' standing, which did not own the Eucharist to be a Sacrifice, and practise it as such. The Gothic Missals may at first sight seem defective as to this particular; but when fully examined and understood, they too give evidence that the most rude and ignorant, as well as the most knowing and best informed Churches of old, did celebrate the Eucharist as a Sacrifice.

The silence of our most able divines against the doctrine of the Sacrifice, or the little notice they have taken of it, may seem a tacit approbation of it. However, if any of them are really adversaries to it, I should be glad if they would give the world a specimen of the strongest, or most specious argu-

---

[a] [The first Edition came out in 1714; the second (of which the present is a reprint) in 1724.]

ments that can be found against this doctrine. And I am persuaded this had been done, if such as are the best judges had any thing to offer on this head, which they thought would bear the test.

I was in hopes I had my wish, when some months since I was told by my correspondent at London, that the Reverend Mr. Rymer, in a book of his just then published[b], had strongly opposed this doctrine. And it must be confessed that this brother of ours hath acquired a great reputation in this diocese for his learning and good sense. And on this account I honour him, though personally unknown to me. Therefore what he hath said on this head claims a right to be considered by me, with a just regard to his character. I meddle not with any part of his book, excepting that which is supposed to have been particularly aimed against the doctrine which I assert. He speaks[c] of Sacraments in general. But I shall consider his words as if they had been meant of the Eucharist only. For what he says of both Sacraments cannot hold, unless it may be applied to the Eucharist as well as to Baptism.

His fundamental assertion as to this point is in the following words, viz.

" A Sacrament is not supposed (in its most essential part) an application made by men to God, but one made to men by God. It is not, in its essential and primary design, a service whereby men propitiate God. It is a gracious condescension of God's by which He converses with men, and exhibits to them spiritual blessings." Soon after he adds, " God's part is indeed the whole that is strictly and properly sacramental[d]."

Now, in direct opposition to this, I affirm, that not God (abstractedly) but God-Man, or Jesus Christ, is principal in this Sacrament; that He, as Mediator and partaker of the human nature as well as of the Divine, is the Author of this Sacrament; that He therein exhibits His Body and Blood in mystery; He exhibits them (by the hands of His ministers) as Mediator of the new, everlasting Covenant, and therefore

---

[b] A General Representation of Revealed Religion. Printed for Walthoe, 1723.

[c] In the first citation.
[d] Page 286.

first to God and then to men, to the whole Christian Church.

Our Saviour hath so expressly declared the Eucharist to be a covenant, that I conceive no judicious Christian can doubt of it. And to enter into covenant, or to renew a covenant without a mutual application of the parties concerned, is inconsistent with the nature of the thing. In truth, this Sacrament is a communion between God and man, as abundantly appears from the following book, but especially from the second part.

What I have hitherto cited from this author contains only the premisses of his argument. Let us next consider his conclusion, which is comprised in these words of his:

"If a Sacrament[e] exhibits to us some spiritual favour given to us, and is an application made by God to man, then changing the elements in the Lord's Supper into a material sacrifice of our own, and making them an application of men to God, exhibiting to Him what He is to be understood to exhibit to us, urging this continual remembrance on God, not on our own hearts; this is offering up strange fire, it is excluding the Sacrament by the Sacrifice."

Now here it is to be observed, that the conclusion contains more than the premisses, when both are fairly stated. And I appeal to himself, whether the sum of his premisses as contained in his book be not this, that "a Sacrament is principally an application made by God to men," and whether he did not intend the sum of his conclusion to be this, viz. "therefore the Lord's Supper is not an application made by men to God." If he did not intend this to be his conclusion, he could not mean any thing at all against the Sacrifice of the Eucharist. And if he did intend this for his conclusion, he meant more than can be found in the premisses. For the premisses only assert that "a Sacrament is principally an application of God to men," now this does by no means imply that "a Sacrament may not also be an application of men to God:" and yet this is the only conclusion that can be of any use to this writer. And that the Eucharist is an application of God to man, and of man to God, is the doctrine at large asserted by me in the following work, and is indeed suffi-

[e] Pages 297, 298.

ciently proved from its being a covenant, as I just before observed.

When our writer asserts that a Sacrament is principally an application of God to man, sure he would not be thought to deny that it is also an application of men to God. Nay, he himself does by implication own that it is so. His words are, " Herein consists man's part (of a Sacrament), a most hearty reverence and gratitude, a most affectionate love and devotion[f]." For how can these be paid without an application of men to God? But I am sorry that among the good qualities on man's part, he should omit the principal, which is faith, and without which the Sacrament cannot be discerned, or perceived to be what it is.

And if application is to be made by men to God in the Eucharist, then what more proper and solemn manner of doing it can be assigned than that of sacrifice? This is the way by which the patriarchs and all holy men of old were by God instructed to make their most important addresses to Him. This is the manner by which the primitive Church offered their devotions to Him. And thus they were taught to do by our blessed Saviour Himself.

Christ, as our Mediator, must first have offered the Sacrifice of His mysterious Body and Blood to God, before He could exhibit them to His Apostles to be eat and drunk, as pledges, symbols, and seals of the Divine promises. The blessings must first have been procured from God by sacrifice, before they could be exhibited to men, as tokens of the Divine favour. As the natural Body and Blood of Christ are the foundation of the Gospel covenant, so the sacramental Body and Blood are substituted instead of the natural; and are therefore first to be presented to the most worthy party in this covenant, the Infinite Granter of all the mercies belonging to it; and then in the next place to the least worthy persons, or the grantees, the whole body of Christian people. Therefore no man need stick to say in opposition to this writer, that the principal or primary part in the Sacrament of the Eucharist is the application of men to God, through the Body and Blood of Christ Jesus.

Our author would have it thought that by asserting the

[f] Page 287.

oblation in the Eucharist, we change the elements into a Sacrifice of our own. And when he hath proved that we have not the authority of Christ for making the oblation, we are willing to lie under the imputation of counterfeiting Divine institutions.

He aggravates our pretended crime by saying, that "we exclude the Sacrament by the Sacrifice." These words only shew that he is very angry with us, and, as I humbly conceive, without a cause. No man, to my remembrance, hath ever charged us with this crime before this writer; nor will he be able to point out the particular, in which we do impair or mutilate the Eucharist, considered as a Sacrament.

His next article of impeachment against us is, that "we urge the continual remembrance on God, not on our own hearts." I suppose he means the remembrance of Christ's death. I cannot suppose that he argues against us as guilty of a fault in frequently urging on God the remembrance of Christ's death, because the Church does this three times every week in the Litany. And I suppose all good Christians often do this in their private prayers, when they enforce them through the death, merits, or satisfaction of Christ Jesus. Therefore the fault he means must consist in not urging the remembrance of Christ's death "on our own hearts." If he knew the man that is wanting in this point, let him declare his name, and set a mark upon him. I am as ready as he can be to condemn this defect in him. But still the fault is personal, and may as well be fixed on them that deny the doctrine of the Sacrifice, as on them that defend it. This in either case cannot be the fault of the doctrine, but of the man.

But as if he had not yet sufficiently expressed his indignation against us, he proceeds to enhance our crime, and that he may do it in the most sanctified manner, he clothes his causeless wrath in Scripture language; he tells us, we "offer up strange fire." He might even as justly have accused us of offering human flesh, as the heathen did the primitive Christians. We offer, or desire to offer, the Sacrifice which Christ hath taught us, a Sacrifice "strange" to none that are Christians, except such as confine their views to modern ages and notions. The "fire" we offer is that of sincere prayers and

praise, "strange" to none but infidels and atheists. We offer
the same "fire," that this author and his friends do. The
difference is this; they choose to offer their fire in the
Eucharist without any proper Sacrifice, and by this means
render it a fire, strange, unknown to all Christians of the
preceding ages. We desire and endeavour to preserve the
pristine union betwixt the fire and the Sacrifice.

His professed design was to abolish and nullify the Sacrifice ordained by Christ: therefore I leave it to my reader to
judge, who it is that is guilty of sacrilege under the appearance of devotion. When he can shew that we do exclude, or
in any point derogate from the Eucharist as a Sacrament, we
may justly be charged with sacrilege. But he attempts not
to prove this, though he hath affirmed it. His allegations
against us are of a very high and heinous nature. What his
evidence and arguments are, I submit to the judgment of
others; declaring at the same time, that I shall always be
among the foremost in extolling and even magnifying his
great abilities. There are several other particulars, in which
this worthy person seems to me mistaken in the account he
gives us of a Sacrament. But this shall suffice at present.

Before I conclude, I think it necessary to renew a former
request to my reader, viz. That he would take my sentiments
not from the representation of others, but from my own
books only. And I must add, that even the citations made
from those books are not always to be depended upon. I
have fresh occasion given for this in a stitched book[g], entitled
'The Doctrine of the Eucharist stated.' The anonymous
author cites me for saying[h], "It must be confessed, that it
does not appear, from any of these writers, that the officiating
priest did offer the Sacrifice by prayer." By these words, as
there posted, he would insinuate my opinion to be, that
Sacrifice is not to be offered by prayer: though in the beginning of that very paragraph[i], and in the following pages,
I make it my business to prove, that prayer was always the
medium, by which the Sacrifice was offered. Again, he observes that in the words of institution, instead of "He gave
thanks," I have translated the text, "He eucharistized" the

g Printed 1720, for Bickerton.   i See Unbloody Sacrifice, Part II.
h Page 41.   pp. 82, 83.

bread and wine: upon which he cries out[j], "Eucharisted them! that is, thanked them, this is wonderful." Thus he leaves it to the reader to suppose, that I do really by eucharistizing mean giving of thanks, without giving the least hint that I have upon several occasions proved at large that the Greek[k] εὐχαριστεῖν is there used transitively, and hath the same signification with εὐλογεῖν, and that the blessing terminated on the bread and wine.

When this second edition was almost out of the press, I was informed that the famous Dr. Clarke of St. James's, in the twelfth of his seventeen sermons lately published, had undertaken to confute that sense of the context in John vi. which I have asserted.

Upon a perusal of the Doctor's discourse, I cannot but think that the substance of what the Doctor hath there advanced is sufficiently answered in my PROOF annexed to this volume, and in the Letter to my very learned friend. But because there are some peculiarities in this Doctor's way of managing the argument, therefore I will not esteem what he hath said wholly unworthy of my notice.

He spends two thirds of his sermon in proving what is granted by all, viz. that "meat, bread, wine, and water," do often signify "good instruction," and that to "eat and drink" denote the receiving such instruction. And upon this observation he undertakes to explain all that is said in this context. Page 272, he proceeds to the pinch of the argument in these words, "There remains only one phrase more in this chapter, wherein the same figure of speech is carried yet further. Our Lord, in the 51st, 53rd, and following verses, setting forth the same thing under the still higher figure of 'eating His flesh, and drinking His blood,' which in the text (ver. 35.) and in several other verses of this chapter, He had before expressed by styling Himself 'the Bread of life.' But this, when that which hath already been said, be well considered, will have no great difficulty in it." In the foregoing page he thus expresseth his sense of Christ's being "the

---

[j] See pp. 62, 63, of that book.
[k] See Unbloody Sacrifice, Part I. pp. 189, 194, 242, 278, edit. first; and 198, 246, 282, of this second edit. ; and Part II. p. 244.

Bread of life," viz. "That the belief, and consequent practice of the doctrine of the Gospel, is the support and preserver of the soul unto eternal life." Now the Doctor in what he says above supposes he hath explained what is meant by eating Christ's flesh and drinking His blood, by explaining those words, "I am the Bread" (or rather the meat) "of life." On the contrary, Christ explains bread or meat by flesh. For thus He speaks, "And the meat which I will give is My flesh." His flesh therefore was what He had promised His disciples in the former part of the chapter under the name of meat. And that we may be the more sure that He meant His flesh, not His doctrine, He gives this further description of it, "My flesh, which I will give for the life of the world." I am confident that neither the Doctor nor any judicious divine will dispute, whether this character do best agree with His flesh or with His Gospel. I conclude therefore that by bread or meat, in the foregoing part of the chapter, we are to understand Christ's flesh, according to our Saviour's own exposition. And I must further add, that by flesh Christ meant His sacramental flesh; which flesh He gave to God for us; as He clearly declares in the institution of the Eucharist. And this is His flesh, not in gross substance, but by that quickening spirit and life with which it is animated, not by a mere dry metaphor or cold figure of speech, as Dr. Clarke would have it, but by real power and energy.

Some lines here follow, which I cannot think worthy of a repetition. Then he goes on, page 273, "After our Lord's styling Himself the Bread of life, in the same sense as Wisdom, in the Book of Ecclesiasticus (chap. xxiv. vers. 21.), saying of herself, 'they that eat me,' &c. there cannot without great perverseness be put a wrong sense upon what He adds, vers. 56, 'He that eateth My flesh, and drinketh My blood, dwelleth in Me, and I in him.'" Now in answer to this, I must profess I see no justness of comparison between a fictitious personated Wisdom introduced in Ecclesiasticus, and resembling herself to various trees or plants, and speaking magnificently of the fruits which she produced, and the honey and honey-comb inclosed in her stock, and calling on men to entertain themselves with these provisions (which she expresses by saying, 'They that eat me,' &c.), and on the other side a real human person, such as our Saviour was, declaring that He would give His flesh to be eat, and especially His blood to be drunk. It ought to have been proved that some great master of religion, or philosophy, had used these phrases, and meant nothing by them but receiving his doctrine, or imbibing his precepts, before a sentence of perverseness had been passed against those that are not convinced by such defective proof. I have said what was sufficient on this head in the first edition of this book, p. 395, which may be found p. 401 of this edition.

But though no other master of religion did ever use these phrases, yet our Lord Himself hath upon another occasion used them, and used them there in a certain, and universally agreed sense, I mean, when He instituted the Eucharist. Then He commanded His disciples to " eat His Body," and " drink His Blood." These are the same phrases with those used here by St. John (for body and flesh are certainly the same) ; I cannot therefore but think it most enormously unreasonable to take Christ Jesus as meaning one thing in one place, another in the other, by the same phrases, and especially when He never used these phrases but twice in the whole course of His ministry. Dr. Clarke here unhappily forgot his own rule " of finding the sense of Scripture in the Scripture itself," p. 262 of this Sermon. I have spoken largely concerning this point of taking these same phrases in different senses in p. 407 of the first edition of this book, p. 412 of this edition.

But the Doctor proceeds in his argument, p. 273, in these words, " Why should not what our Lord calls ' eating His Flesh,' and ' drinking His Blood,' be as easily understood of our imbibing, and digesting His doctrine, as St. Paul is by all men understood to speak in a figurative sense, when he says of all good Christians, ' that they are members of Christ's Flesh, of His Body, and of His Bones.'" Now the answer here is very obvious, that we are clearly determined to understand St. Paul as speaking of Christ's union with, and affection to His Church, by another text of Scripture, viz. Gen. ii. 23, where this phrase is used in a sense very like this, if not the very same. When the Doctor can produce a text, where flesh and blood signifies doctrine, then his ques-

JOHNSON. F

tion will be to the purpose.   In the mean time let me have leave to ask him, why flesh and blood must in John vi. signify doctrine, when in the history of the institution of the Sacrament they certainly signify the consecrated elements?

After all, I know not whether, p. 261, and 278, the Doctor have not said some things that imply that this context is to be understood of the Eucharist.   But I am not at leisure to make disquisitions concerning the sense and meaning of his expressions.   And there are several particulars omitted by me, which are very extraordinary, and full of bold novelties, which yet I shall dismiss at present, especially because they are most of them, if not all, obviated in the following volume.

In truth this Sermon seems the most hasty performance that ever came from Dr. Clarke's pen.   I would have no man take a measure of the Doctor's acumen, or of his clearness of thought, or diction, from this little piece, which seems scarce worthy of his great name.

A DISCOURSE

UNBLOODY SACRIFICE, AND ALTAR.

INTRODUCTION.

CONTAINING SEVERAL DEFINITIONS OF SACRIFICE, AND THE
AUTHOR'S OPINION OF THEM, AND HIS OWN DESCRIPTION
OF IT.

HAVING undertaken, with the Divine assistance, to prove
that the Christian Eucharist is a Sacrifice properly so called,
I suppose the first step I am to take is to shew, not only
what I myself mean by the word Sacrifice, but that I take it
in the same sense that the most learned men of all parties
have understood it, and in such a sense as is most agreeable
to the thing denoted by it. Now to satisfy my reader that
my definition of a sacrifice is no invention of my own, made
to serve a present turn, I shall first present him with those
definitions, or descriptions of a sacrifice, which have been
given by men of the greatest name, both among the Protestants and the Papists.

Melancthon's definition of it is, a ceremony, or work, which
we render "to God, in order to do honour to Him[a]."

Mr. Calvin says, "Sacrifice in its general acceptation signifies whatever we offer to God; but we divide it," as he goes
on, "into two parts, the one we call λατρευτικὸν, or σεβαστικὸν, which consists in honouring and worshipping God; or, if
you will, you may call it Εὐχαριστικὸν, as being offered by

---

[a] ["Sacrificium est opus a Deo
mandatum, faciendum, ut Deo tribua-
tur honos, id est, ut ea obedientia
ostendamus nos affirmare Hunc solum
esse Deum, quem sic colimus, et nos
velle Ei subjectos esse." Melanchthon.
Explicatio in Malachiam, ed. Witeberg.
1601. tom. ii. p. 545.]

none, but such as are laden with immense blessings, and make to God a return of themselves, their whole selves, and all that they can do : the other we call propitiatory, or expiatory, the design of which is to pacify the wrath of God, to satisfy His justice, and by this means to wash, or wipe away sin." It ought not to be omitted, that he expressly declares, that he "calls that Sacrifice, which the Greeks sometimes call θυσία, sometimes προσφορὰ, according to the perpetual use of Scripture[b] :" so that this great man saw no difference between a proper oblation and a sacrifice[c].

The famous Dr. Spencer, who is as exact a writer on this subject, as any that has yet appeared, gives us this account of sacrifices, viz., "Formally considered, they are gifts offered to God, and solemnly consumed in honour to Him[d]. Materially considered, they are animate things, as oxen, sheep, goats ; or inanimate things, bread, wine, salt, and other things fit for food. Finally considered, they were called expiatory, when men brought gifts to the altar in order to appease God: they are called whole burnt offerings, when intended for the rendering honour to God, and acknowledging His dominion ; peace offerings, when they expressed a mind well and devoutly affected toward God ; Eucharistic, or sacrifices of thanksgiving, or vows, when to signify gratitude toward God ; euctic, when for the obtaining of any blessing[e]."

[b] [" Quod generaliter acceptum, complectitur quicquid omnino Deo offertur. —Proinde et nos in duo genera distribuamus, ac alterum, docendi causa, vocemus λατρευτικὸν et σεβαστικὸν : quoniam veneratione cultuque Dei constat, quem Illi fideles et debent et reddunt : vel si mavis εὐχαριστικὸν : quandoquidem a nullis Deo exhibetur nisi qui immensis Ejus beneficiis onusti, se totos cum actionibus suis omnibus Illi rependunt. Alterum propitiatorium, sive expiationis. Est autem expiationis sacrificium, cui propositum est iram Dei placare, Ipsius judicio satisfacere, eoque peccata abluere et abstergere.— Nos perpetuo Scripturæ usu sacrificium appellari scimus, quod Græci nunc θυσίαν, nunc προσφορὰν, nunc τελετὴν dicunt." Calvin. Institutt., lib. iv. cap. xviii. sect. 13. ed. Lugdun. 1654.]

[c] See Institutions.

[d] De Legib. Hebr., p. 640.

[e] [" Formaliter, quatenus munera fuerunt oblata Deo, et in Illius honorem solenniter consumpta." p. 640. " Cum autem sacrificiorum materia duplex esset, nempe res animatæ (boves, oves, et capræ) ; res etiam inanimatæ (panis, vinum, sal, aliaque mensis adhiberi solita)." p. 656. " Cum enim Altari dona ferebant, ad placandum Deum, Expiatoria dicebantur ; cum ad honorem exhibendum, Deique dominium agnoscendum, Holocausta vel sacra honoraria : cum ad amicum et benevolum animum erga Deum significandum, Pacifica : cum ad indicandam gratitudinem, Votiva vel Eucharistica : cum ad obtinendum beneficium, Εὐκτικα." De Legibus Hebræorum, lib. iii. cap. 3. p. 664. ed. Cantab. 1685.]

Thomas Aquinas's definition of a sacrifice is in these words, viz., "Any thing done as an honour due to God alone, in order to procure His favour[f]."

Bellarmine says, " Sacrifice is an external oblation made to God Alone, by which some sensible and permanent thing is consecrated, and changed by a lawful Minister, and by mystic rites, for an acknowledgment of our weakness, and the Divine greatness[g]."

[Dr. Outram's definition of a sacrifice is, " an oblation duly consumed." But to explain this he adds, "A sacrifice among the Jews was a holy thing offered to God, and with proper rites completed and consumed. And holy things were duly consumed, when they were killed, burnt, poured out, or made use of, for a sacred feast in a manner ordained by God[h]." And in the very next section he says, " Of those things, which were both offered and consumed in a proper manner, some had life, some had not." Now though this learned man's notion of a sacrifice be commonly esteemed contrary to the doctrine which I am now defending, and he expressly undertakes the definition of a Jewish sacrifice only; yet I see no occasion to make any exception against his definition of a sacrifice, as here explained by himself. The grand defect of his book seems to me to be this, that he makes the due consumption of the sacrifice to be the most necessary point of all, and yet never once offers to shew that the grand sacrifice of Christ was consumed either in whole or in part[i].]

If I should produce as many more descriptions, or definitions of sacrifice from authors of equal reputation with these, if any such there be, who have treated on this subject, there would, I conceive, be nothing considerable contained in them but what is to be found in these, which I have already

---

[f] [" Sacrificium proprie dicitur aliquid factum in honorem proprie Deo debitum, ad Eum placandum." Thomæ Aquin. Summæ Theologicæ, Pars iii. Quæst. xlviii. Art. 3. Conclusio. p. 101. ed. Duac. 1614.]

[g] [" Sacrificium est oblatio externa facta soli Deo, qua ad agnitionem humanæ infirmitatis et professionem Divinæ Majestatis, a legitimo ministro res aliqua sensibilis et permanens ritu mystico consecratur et transmutatur." De Missa, lib. i. cap. 2. ed. 1601.]

[h] [" Sacrificium, ad eorum (Judæorum) sententiam, ita definiri potest, ut sit προσφορὰ rite consumpta. Seu, ut paulo explicatius dicam, sacrificium, apud populum Hebræum, ejusmodi sacrum erat, tum rite confectum et consumptum." De Sacrificiis, lib. i. cap. viii. p. 82. ed. 1677.]

[i] [This paragraph is added in 2nd ed.]

laid before the reader: and I have not much to object
against any thing said by these very learned men: but yet I
ought to mention the exceptions, how few or small soever
which I have against them; or however to let my reader
know in what sense I take some particular expressions, and
in what sense I cannot admit of them. And

First, when Mr. Calvin supposes that a sacrifice must be a
satisfaction to Divine justice, if it be intended for the expiation of sin, I must observe that the words, if strictly taken,
can be applied to no sacrifice but that which was offered by
Christ in person. I shall not therefore think myself obliged
to prove that the Sacrifice of the Eucharist, as distinguished
and abstracted from the grand Sacrifice, is a satisfaction for
sin; nor can I believe that Mr. Calvin himself thought that
any other sacrifice, in itself considered, could by its own
intrinsic value expiate sin; and whoever asserts this doctrine
does not only annul the sacrifice of the Eucharist, but all
those sacrifices which were enjoined in the Levitical law; for
none of them were in themselves a satisfaction to Divine
justice.

Secondly, When Dr. Spencer asserts that a sacrifice is to
be consumed, as well as offered, in honour to Almighty God,
this is confessed to be true, if meant of the Levitical sacrifices, of which the Doctor was treating; and it is true of all
sacrifices, that they are to be consumed in the manner appointed by God; but if the Doctor intended that it is essential to all sacrifice to be consumed in the very act of oblation
or by fire, then I must crave leave to dissent from him. The
Passover was a perfect and solemn sacrifice, and owned as
such by Dr. Spencer, as will hereafter appear: and yet we
are assured, that it was neither in whole, nor in part, to be
burnt upon an altar, nor consumed in being offered; and
Dr. Spencer's words do not imply this way of consumption
to be in itself necessary: no, nor yet Dr. Outram's, as he
hath himself explained them.

Thirdly, When Bellarmine says a sacrifice must be consecrated, it is acknowledged to be true: nay, the very act of
oblation is a consecration of it: but when he speaks of its
being changed, I must solemnly protest against the change
by him intended, I mean, transubstantiation. A change is

confessed, that is, that the bread and wine from being common become holy, and the spiritual Body and Blood of Christ; but that the substance of bread and wine is changed into the substance of Christ's personal Body and Blood, I absolutely deny, and believe it to be as monstrous a doctrine as ever was believed by any that call themselves Christians.

Therefore allowing all these definitions or descriptions of sacrifice, excepting as before excepted, I shall add one particular not mentioned by any of them, I mean a *proper altar*. I cannot indeed say, that this was ever esteemed so essential to a sacrifice, as that an oblation was esteemed null without it (excepting the case of most of the Levitical sacrifices); but rather than make many words about it, I readily give it for granted, that an altar is necessary, though not to the essence, yet to the more commodious and solemn oblation of a sacrifice: and therefore I am now prepared to lay before my reader, what I think a full description of sacrifice: viz.

Sacrifice is, 1. some material thing, either animate, or inanimate, offered to God, 2. for the acknowledging the dominion, and other attributes of God, or for procuring Divine blessings, especially remission of sin, 3. upon a proper altar, (which yet is rather necessary for the external decorum than the internal perfection of the Sacrifice,) 4. by a proper officer, and with agreeable rites, 5. and consumed or otherwise disposed of in such a manner, as the Author of the Sacrifice has appointed. I shall speak to all these five particulars, by shewing,

I. In the first chapter, in what sense and degree every one of these five properties are necessary to a Sacrifice.

II. In the second, I shall shew that all these properties concur in the Eucharist, and that it is therefore a proper Sacrifice.

CHAP. I.

SECT. I.

Sacrifice is some material thing, either animate or inanimate,
offered to God.

CHAP.
I.

1. THAT nothing can properly be called a sacrifice, but
some material thing offered to God, is given for granted,
though neither Melanchthon, nor Mr. Calvin, nor Aquinas, do
expressly mention this particular; nay, the first and last of
the three suppose it is sufficient that it be some ceremony,
work, or action; but I shall not enlarge in a case where I
think all parties are now agreed.

2. That the matter of the sacrifice must be some animate
thing, some creature that has or had life, is a condition not
mentioned by any of the great men above mentioned; nay,
Mr. Calvin allows, that a sacrifice and oblation are the same,
according to the perpetual use of Scripture. And Dr. Spencer
affirms, that a sacrifice materially considered is not only some
animal, but bread and wine, or any thing fit for food; and
therefore I cannot but think, that they who will allow nothing
to be a sacrifice but what has life and blood, and is capable
of mactation, have neither good authority nor reason for
what they say.

[One of the most notable and constant sacrifices of the
Jews, was a cake[a] made of wheat-flour and oil, and wholly
burnt on the altar by the high priest, the one half in the
morning, the other in the evening, every day in the year.
This was called by the old Greek interpreters "a continual,

---

[a] Lev. vi. 20—22. The most judicious moderns instead of, ' in the day
when he is anointed,' say, ' from the day
on which he is anointed.'

a perpetual sacrifice;" and by our English, "an offering per-   S E C T.
petual, a statute for ever unto the Lord :" by both it is said ——————
to be offered "for a sweet savour unto the Lord;" and by
that priest of Aaron's sons, "who was to be anointed in his
stead." From this it appears, that the most noble, daily,
pontifical sacrifice among the Jews was a cake of flour;
and this was a most lively type of our High Priest's offering
His Sacramental Body. Josephus mentions this as still practised in his time; and he calls this daily action of the high
priest by the name of sacrificing[b]. Of these unbloody sacrifices I speak more largely in the second part of this
work[c].]

They who have asserted that nothing is a sacrifice but
what is slain, have done it on supposition that $\theta\acute{v}\omega$ does   That $\theta\acute{v}\omega$
properly and originally signify to kill, and that therefore   does not
originally
$\theta v\sigma\acute{\iota}a$, which denotes a sacrifice, must necessarily imply   signify to
slay, proved
something that is slain. But I need not tell my learned   from Aris-
reader, that no arguments are more fallacious than those   tophanes,
&c.
which are built upon etymologies. At this rate of arguing, a
man may deny that what I now write on is true paper, because it is not made of an Egyptian shrub, or flag called
$\pi\acute{a}\pi v\rho o\varsigma$; nay, it may safely be denied upon this hypothesis,
that there is any such thing as a book to be sold in St. Paul's
church-yard; because what we now call books do not consist
of the rind of that tree which our ancestors called *beoce*, and
from whence the present word book is commonly derived; for
just thus do they argue that deny any thing to be a sacrifice
but what is slain, because $\theta v\sigma\acute{\iota}a$ has $\theta\acute{v}\omega$ for its theme. Of
what force this way of arguing may be thought in this dis-
pute I cannot say; but I am sure it would be thought mere
chicanery in any cause but this. Yet, so far as I am capable
of discerning, this is the only pretence that some men have
for denying any thing that is unbloody to be a proper sacrifice; and this pretence is so thin, that our adversaries have
scarce the face to express it in words at length, but commonly content themselves with saying, that bread and wine
cannot strictly be a sacrifice. And if we enquire into the
bottom of their argument, it is only this, that $\theta\acute{v}\omega$ does originally signify to slay, according to their lexicons, or rather

---

[b] See Joseph., lib. iii. cap. 10. § 7. Hudson's edition.   [c] [Not in the 1st ed.]

CHAP.
I.

their own surmises; for if we look into the ancientest Greek writers, we shall certainly find that θύω did not at first signify to slay, but to offer any thing to the gods, by burning it in the fire, or by any other prevailing rite. Now that this may be made very evident, I will first produce the words of Aristophanes in Plutus[d]:

ὅτι οὐδ' ἂν εἷς θύσειεν ἀνθρώπων ἔτι,
οὐ βοῦν ἂν, οὐχὶ ψαιστὸν, οὐκ ἀλλ' οὐδεεν,
μὴ βουλομένου σοῦ. ——————

Chremylus tells Plutus the blind god of riches, that "no man would sacrifice a bullock, nor any dry crumbled thing, nor any thing at all, without his consent," that is, unless he gave them money to purchase what was to be offered. Nobody, I suppose, ever suspected these ψαιστὰ were animals, or any part of animals; and yet Aristophanes supposes they may be sacrificed, as well as a bullock. We have clear proof of this signification of the word in Homer, who tells us, that Eumæus having killed his best swine in honour to the nymphs, Mercury, and the other gods, by burning the several portions of those gods in the fire, and reserved the chine for Ulysses, who was come to him in disguise; after he had invited Ulysses to fall on, the poet adds,

'Η ῥὰ, καὶ ἄργματα θῦσε θεοῖς αἰειγενέτησιν·
Σπείσας δ' αἴθοπα οἶνον, 'Οδυσσῆϊ πτολιπόρθῳ
'Εν χείρεσσιν ἔθηκεν, ——————[e]

All that was done in relation to the sacrifice, before they came to the feasting part, is expressed by ἱερεύειν, σφάττειν, and εὕειν; but when they are going to eat, "Eumæus," says Homer, "sacrificed the nice bits, or first cut, to the eternal gods;" where θύειν cannot signify to kill; for the swine was not only slain, but all, except the chine, burnt before; therefore by ἄργματα θῦσε he can mean nothing but his offering some principal part of the viands, either by casting them into the fire, or by some other religious rite. And Eustathius, from this and other passages in Homer, concludes[f], that in this most ancient writer θύειν has the same sense with θυμιᾶν,

[d] Act I. scen. ii. [l. 137. ed. Dindorf.]
[e] Ὀδυσσ. Ξ. l. 446.

[f] [σφάξαι μὲν, τὸ ἱερουργῆσαι ζῶον· θῦσαι δὲ, τὸ θυμιάσαι. Vid. Eust. in loco. ed. Rom. 1551.]

that to sacrifice is only to burn, or make a perfume to the
gods, and therefore not to slay. Athenæus says[g], that
θύειν is never used by Homer for offering the victim; (for
in this sense he made use of ῥέζειν, and δρᾶν) but only of the
ψαιστὰ, the broken fruits and such like, the only sacrifices of
the ancient Greeks[h]. This would incline one to believe, that
the ἄργματα now mentioned was none of the swine's flesh, but
either some choice fruits or cakes; and what follows favours
this, viz. "he made a libation of wine." We have another great
authority for this from Theophrastus, Aristotle's scholar, cited
by Porphyry, and from him by Eusebius[i], and produced lately
by Mr. Dodwell in his learned book "Concerning the use of
Incense[j]." The words which make most for the present purpose
are as follows. Speaking of the inhabitants of the Egyptian
Delta, Τό γε πάντων λογιώτατον γένος ἤρξατο πρῶτον ἀφ᾽ ἑστίας
τοῖς οὐρανίοις θεοῖς θύειν· οὐ σμύρνης, οὐδὲ κασίας, καὶ λιβανω-
τοῦ κρόκῳ μιχθέντων ἀπαρχὰς, — ἀλλὰ χλόης, οἱονεί τινα τῆς
γονίμου φύσεως χνοῦν ταῖς χερσὶν ἀράμενοι — ἐκ δε τῆς θυμι-
άσεως τῶν ἀπὸ γῆς θυμιατήριά τε ἐκάλουν, καὶ τὸ θύειν, καὶ
θυσίας, ἃ δὴ ἡμεῖς οὐκ ὀρθῶς ἐξακούομεν, τὴν διὰ τῶν ζώων
δοκοῦσαν θεραπείαν καλοῦντες θυσίαν . . . πολλοὶ καὶ νῦν ἔτι
θύουσι συγκεκομμένα τῶν εὐωδῶν ξύλων τινα[k]. "This most
rational people began first to sacrifice to the heavenly gods
from the household fires, to sacrifice not the first-fruits of
myrrh, cassia, and frankincense mixed with saffron; but of
grass which they cropped with their hands, being as it were
a certain down of teeming nature. . . . It was from this burning the products of the earth, by way of incense, that they
gave the name of *thumiateria* to the censers, and of *thuein*
to the action of burning them, and of *thusia* to the thing
sacrificed, which we now do not rightly understand, when we
give the name of sacrifice to the pretended worship by animals. Many do to this day sacrifice some chips of the sweet-
scented trees." In which words Theophrastus declares that
the word θύσια, sacrifice, is improperly applied to offering of

---

[g] ['Ομηρός τε τὸ ῥέζειν, ἐπι τοῦ θύειν
τάσσει, τὸ δὲ θύειν ἐπι τοῦ ψαιστὰ μετα-
δόρπια θυμιᾶν. καὶ οἱ παλαιοὶ τὸ θύειν
δρᾶν ὠνόμαζον. Lib. xiv.]
[h] See Dr. Potter's Antiq. Gr. [B. II.
c. iv.]

[i] De Præp. Evangel., lib. i. cap. 9.
[p. 28. ed. Par. 1628.]
[j] P. 20.
[k] [Mr. Dodwell's reading is followed
here.]

CHAP.
I.

animals, and that originally it did not signify an oblation slain in honour to God, and that inanimate things are most properly sacrifices, if we regard either the thing itself, or the words used to denote it. And Plato, who was certainly one that very well understood both the notions and the language of the old Greeks, gives this account of it, θύειν δωρεῖσθαί ἐστι τοῖς θεοῖς[1]. "To sacrifice is to give to the gods." It is clear indeed by what Theophrastus says, that even in his time, who lived many hundred years after Homer, and about the time that the LXX made a translation of the Jewish law from the Hebrew into the Greek tongue, the word sacrifice was most commonly applied to the offering of animals; but he complains of it as an innovation, and as an instance of degeneracy, both as to the practice itself, and the language by which it was expressed; and the LXX translators were so sensible of this, that they use the word sacrifice for all altar oblations, inanimate as well as animate; and this is a thing so well known, that my reader will excuse me if I do not spend time in the proof of it. He that doubts of it, I will be bold to say, may be convinced by one single chapter, viz. Numb. vii., where he will find the Hebrew מנחה, which in strictness signifies no more than an offering of bread or meal, turned by the LXX θυσία thirteen times, if I number right, viz., ver. 13, 19, 25, 31, 37, 43, 49, 55, 61, 67, 73, 79, 87; and it is known that the writers of the New Testament do for the most part use the idioms of the LXX. St. Paul follows them in this particular; for he calls the fruits of the earth offered by Cain,

Heb. xi. 4. θυσία, "a sacrifice," as well as the cattle offered by Abel, as the
Gen.iv. 3-5. LXX had done before. And it is very evident that, in this particular, the idiom of the LXX was agreeable to the notions of the ancient Greeks, and to the critique of Theophrastus, Athenæus, and Eustathius, who seem rather to appropriate the word sacrifice to inanimate, than animate sacrifice, and to the definition of Plato, who says, "to sacrifice is to give to the gods." It is true, as Theophrastus intimates, that the Greeks of his age, and I may add of all ages after him, did commonly take the word θυσία to be derived from the verb θύω, as signifying "to slay;" but it is evident too, that this was but a vulgar prejudice, and that

---

[1] See Dr. Spencer, de Legib. Hebr., p. 665.

θύω was never thought to bear any such signification, until bloody sacrifices came in vogue, and by usually applying this verb to the offering these bloody sacrifices, the men of after ages began to think that it denoted mactation. It were easy to give instances of words in all known languages, that have thus in several ages varied their significations upon occasions; but the thing is so well known, that I may well spare my pains. Our adversaries seem to value their own notions and opinions more than those of the ancients, chiefly on this account, that they live in an age, in which the original languages are better understood, than they were by the primitive fathers; but if these languages are now better understood, it is evident, that they who value themselves on this account, are none of those who know Greek better than the Fathers did. Even the Latin Fathers knew well enough that an inanimate thing may be a sacrifice: the vulgar Italic Bible would teach them this, where מנחה, and θυσία, is often rendered by *sacrificium;* and it will appear by several citations hereafter to be produced, that they did actually so understand it. And though some of the Greek Fathers seem to think that θύω did originally signify to slay, (for what man is so wise, as not to be carried down the stream of vulgar mistakes, as to some particulars?) yet they never argued as our adversaries do, that therefore nothing can be a proper sacrifice, but what can be slain: they did not build their faith upon so airy a foundation as an etymology. As to the manner of consuming the sacrifice, viz., by burning, which some of the ancient Greeks seem to think is implied in the verb θύω, I shall have another occasion to speak of it ere long. In the mean time let our adversaries consider, that they cannot deny an inanimate thing to be capable of being made a sacrifice, but that they must suppose themselves better acquainted with the Greek tongue than Homer, Aristophanes, or Plato; and that they are better critics than Athenæus, or Theophrastus, or Eustathius; not to mention the authority of the LXX, the Apostle, and the most primitive Church, which are certainly sacred with all good Christian divines. And lest our adversaries or others should think that we contend for words, let them assure themselves, that if it be once granted, that an inanimate oblation may

We dispute not for words, ours is an unbloody sacrifice.

serve all the ends of a real sacrifice, this is all that we demand. For though we cannot see any reason to drop the use of a word that has been applied to the Eucharist for above fifteen hundred years together, without any observable contradiction, yet we at the same time declare with all antiquity, that ours is an unbloody Sacrifice. And because the Church of Rome has misapplied this title to their missatic Sacrifice, we therefore further declare, that we believe not the very substantial or personal Blood of Christ to be there offered, as the Papists do, and therefore cannot, in any tolerable sense, call that an unbloody Sacrifice. But lest my reader should surmise that I labour only to prove an oblation of mere material bread and wine, and that such an oblation seems not worthy of our zeal and concern, I shall only remind him, that a sacrifice, or oblation of bread and wine, though in itself considered it be of no great worth, yet may be of inestimable value on other considerations. And I cannot but admire to see one of our adversaries cite Greek upon us to prove that an ox or sheep is in itself better than a loaf of bread, as if he knew no other standard of the value of a sacrifice than the market price of it, or the external qualities inherent in it. They who estimate sacrifices by this rule, are just such appraisers of the representative sacrifice as Judas and the high priests were of the original, when they set It at thirty pieces of silver.

SECT. II.

That Sacrifice, properly so called, is offered for the acknowledging the dominion and other attributes of God, and for procuring Divine blessings, especially remission of sin.

THIS is a truth implied, if not expressed, in all the descriptions of a sacrifice above produced. It were very easy to make a great show of reading on this occasion; but since there is an unanimous consent on all sides as to this head, I shall no longer dwell upon it.

SECT. III.

*That a proper Sacrifice is to be offered on a proper Altar
(though the altar be rather necessary to the external decorum than the internal perfection of the sacrifice).*

I SUPPOSE any convenient utensil, table, or eminence,
whether natural or artificial, of whatsoever materials it be
framed, on which a material sacrifice is offered, may be
called an altar. If it be solely, or chiefly set apart, or dedicated to this use, it is a proper altar; and if it be erected for
offering sacrifice by fire, it must be furnished with a fire-
hearth, or be capable of being used as such; such was the
altar of burnt-offering at Jerusalem : if it be only used once,
or rarely, it is an occasional or vicarious altar. In this sense
the rock on which Manoah made an oblation is called an Judges xiii.
altar; and yet if the fabric be built on purpose for the mak- 20.
ing one single oblation, I see no reason why in this case it
may not be deemed a proper altar; as that, for instance,
which Abraham built, on which he intended to offer his son Gen. xxii.9.
Isaac, which was an oblation never to be repeated. There is
this difference between a fixed, proper, appropriated altar,
and an occasional or vicarious one; that an altar of the first
sort sanctifies the gifts laid on it, as our Saviour says of the
altar of burnt-offering at Jerusalem; and the same may be Matt. xxiii.
said, I apprehend, of all altars that are raised by due autho- 19.
rity, and designed and publicly known to be for no other use
but for receptacles of such things as are to be devoted to the
service of God; for in this case, the solemn placing of any
thing on it is an effectual declaration that the thing so placed
on it is God's peculiar right and property; but this I think
cannot be said of any other occasional tumultuary elevation
made for the offering sacrifice once and away. I should in
this case rather say, that the gift sanctifies the altar, than
the altar the gift; for I cannot conceive how such an altar
can have any sort of sanctity but what it receives from the
oblation made upon it, except it have been by some previous
act and deed consecrated to the worship of God. But this is
only my conjecture, and the present dispute does no way
depend upon it.

What is more pertinent, and more clear, is, that a proper fixed altar is not absolutely necessary to the internal perfection of a sacrifice ; the reasons of which opinion are, that it does not appear, that Abel or Cain made use of any, in offering the first sacrifices that are recorded in Holy Writ; and it seems utterly improbable, that every family of the Israelites should, in their several houses, have had a proper fixed altar for the first Paschal sacrifice offered in the land of Egypt; and if they had had such altars, it is not credible that they should have been commanded to sprinkle the blood of the

Ex. xii. 22. lamb "on the lintel, and the two side-posts of their doors," but as was done after they had a tabernacle, and other conve-

See 2 Chr. niences of worship, on the altar itself, and yet that the pass-
xxxv. 11. over was a sacrifice properly so called, I shall presently have occasion to shew. By the words of Theophrastus, just now cited, it appears that the ancient Grecians sacrificed in their domestic fires, and therefore, if they had altars, did not think them essential to a sacrifice[m].

I have not advanced this opinion, that an altar is not essential to a sacrifice, as if I had any apprehension that the

---

[m] [Here follows in the first edition, "The old Persians had neither temples, nor altars, and yet offered animal sacrifice. [Herod. Clio, c. 132.] See Propitiatory Oblation, p. 121, 122. The cross, on which the mactation of the grand sacrifice was performed, may be justly said to be an occasional altar, not indeed in the intention of those who erected it, but by the Divine decree and purpose. Nay, though no other sacrifice was ever designed to be made on it, yet it has this peculiar to itself, that by the all-wise will and pleasure of God, 'The Lamb that was to be slain was decreed to bear our sins in His own body on the tree;' (1 Pet. ii. 24.): and so that tree may in some sense be said to be a proper altar, not-withstanding its shape and figure ; and its being to be used but once, does no more prove this to be an improper altar, than it proves that which was built for the offering Isaac to be such. And I apprehend, that it is upon these considerations that the cross is called an altar by Origen, and by St. Ambrose." "Ubi vero tempus advenit crucis suæ, et accessurus erat ad altare ubi immolaret hostiam carnis suæ, ac-

cipiens, inquit, calicem, benedixit, et dedit discipulis suis : Accipite, et bibite ex hoc. Vos, inquit, bibite, qui modo accessuri non estis ad altare. Ipse autem tanquam accessurus ad altare, dicit de se : Amen dico vobis, quia non bibam de generatione vitis hujus, usquequo bibam illud vobiscum novum in regno Patris Mei." Origenis in Leviticum, Homilia vii. tom. ii. p. 220. ed. Paris. 1733. "An non tibi videtur effudisse sanguinem suum, de cujus latere supra ipsum passionis altare aqua cucurrit et sanguis?" S. Ambrosii Epistolarum Classis ii. Ep. lxv. tom. ii. p. 1054. ed. Paris. 1686. "Mirabile illud altare, in quo Unius Agni sacrificium tulit peccata mundi." S. Amb. in Ps. cxviii. Expositio, tom. i. p. 1002. Cf. Vitringa, Observationes Sacræ, l. ii. c. 13. p. 228. ed. Franequer. 1689. "Ara in quantum portavit sacrificium, idque in altum tulit, signum fuit crucis, in quam Christus tolleretur, in quam elevaretur, et in qua Se Ipsum ut sacrificium Patri suo sisteret, quæque Christum portaret." See Gothof. Voigti Thysiasteriologia, sive De Altaribus Veterum Christianorum, cap. xix. pp. 31, 2. ed. Hamburg. 1709.]

Eucharist is destitute of a proper Altar, for I shall hereafter S E C T.
III. prove a proper Altar in the Christian Church. And though —— I am not convinced that a proper Altar is absolutely necessary for a proper Sacrifice, yet I am fully persuaded that whatever is offered by a Priest on a proper Altar, may strictly be called a Sacrifice.

SECT. IV.

That a proper Sacrifice is to be offered by proper officers, and with agreeable rites.

THIS indeed is mentioned by Bellarmine only, in the descriptions of Sacrifice above produced, but it seems to have been the sense of all mankind; and, therefore, when great numbers of clans and families, whose several heads had before been their kings and priests, were embodied together by conquest or voluntary submission, or were by other means exceedingly enlarged and multiplied, and occupied many extensive countries, and had many cities and districts, governed by subordinate magistrates in civil matters, they all unanimously provided distinct officers for the inspection and celebration of divine offices. Such were the several fraternities of priests instituted in the infancy of the Roman empire by Numa, as Plutarch informs us in the history of his life[n]. Such were the several ranks of priests among the Grecians, for which I refer my reader to Dr. Potter's Antiquities[o], and others who have written on this subject. Such were the Magi among the Persians, as Herodotus informs us[p]. Egypt, as it was one of those countries that were first of all well stocked with people, who were invited thither by the fertility of the soil, so we are assured that there was in this country a settled priesthood, with an unalienable maintenance in lands, before Jacob's descent into Egypt, and before the date of any history now in being, excepting that of Moses. And Herodotus, the most ancient of the Greek historians, takes notice of these priests in his Euterpe, and says, they received their office by succession or inheritance[q]. And when God by His especial providence had multiplied Abraham's posterity into

Priests necessary for offering of Sacrifice.

Gen. xlvii. 22.

---

[n] [p. 68. ed. Francofurt. 1599.]　　[p] [Clio, c. 132.]
[o] [B. ii. c. 3.]　　[q] [c. 37.]

JOHNSON.　　G

CHAP.
I.

a nation, and resolved to form them, not only into a body politic, but a religious society, He Himself separated one of the twelve tribes of which their nation consisted, for the more immediate attendance on His Divine Majesty in religious worship. And it was declared to be present death for any man to intrude into the sacred office, or with unsanctified hands to touch any thing which God had committed to their care and direction. And though Sacrifice was not the only employment of these religious officers, yet this was always thought the most honorary and valuable function of the priesthood; and therefore only the elder house of that tribe, whom God was pleased to make choice of for the sacred ministry, were intrusted with the privilege of offering sacrifice. And even in the heathen nations, none were permitted to perform this office in public, but only such as had been solemnly dedicated to this function.

Rites necessary are only those actions by which the oblation is made.

And as all momentous actions are to be performed with a due decorum, and with just solemnity, so it is especially necessary that this most weighty negotiation betwixt God and man be executed with agreeable rites, and with circumstances befitting such holy institutions. But if we enquire into those rites which were peculiar to Sacrifice, we shall find them to be no other but the very actions of offering them. I will not pretend to say that there never were any ceremonies esteemed necessary by some particular people, for some particular sacrifices, but what I affirm is, that no rite is essential to Sacrifice in general, but only the very act or acts of oblation. For if it were otherwise, the Levitical sacrifices were in reality null; for no rites were necessary in offering them but sprinkling the blood, and burning the whole, or part of the sacrifice. And I suppose it needs no proof, that these, with the prayers, were the very rites by which the sacerdotal oblation was performed; by the sprinkling the blood, the whole sacrifice was consecrated to God, and the atonement made; and by burning the part or the whole on the Altar, God had what He required actually yielded to Him[r]. This

[r] ["So that these ritual actions were indeed no other but what were used as vocal signs, with which the sacrifice was presented to God. The priest used no words; but the actions were significant, and spake the thoughts of him that performed the office. Nor can I, upon the best enquiry I am able to make, find any ceremony generally thought necessary for offering a sacrifice, but only the actions, whereby the sacrifice was presented." First Ed.]

argument is more largely and clearly pursued, part ii. ch. i.
sect. vi.

SECT. V.

*A sacrifice must be consumed in such a manner as the author
of it, or God to whom it is offered, hath appointed.*

DR. SPENCER [and Dr. Outram] affirm this in express
words, and Bellarmine means the same; for the change, I
suppose, in his sense, is the consumption of the sacrifice.
And though we can allow of no such change, yet we must
confess, that God has so peculiar a right in things so solemnly
offered and appropriated to Him, that it would be profane
and sacrilegious to dispose of them otherwise, than He Himself has directed. If God indeed had expressly declared,
that the material sacrifice was to be bestowed or destroyed,
according to the discretion of those who offered it; then, I
suppose, no human authority could restrain this liberty
granted by God; but it is not rational to suppose, that God
should make no distinction between sacred and profane, between what had been offered to Him, and what had not; and
yet it appears from Herodotus, that the old Persians were
persuaded, that they might make what use of their sacrifices
they themselves pleased[s]. Our adversaries would have it, Consump-
that it is essential to sacrifice to be consumed by fire; but tion by fire
not abso-
upon what grounds they assert this, they inform us not. lutely necessary.
On the other side we are assured, that none of the Levitical
sacrifices, but burnt-offerings, and offerings for the sins of the
priest and congregation, were wholly consumed in this manner.
The greatest, much the greatest part of the usual sin and
trespass-offering was consumed by manducation. Nothing but
the fat, and the caul, and the kidneys, were to be burnt on Lev. iv.
the Altar, and the rump, if it were a trespass-offering; and the 27—35.
Lev. viii. 3.
same may be said of the peace-offerings. So that the only way Lev. iii. 9,
10.
of consuming the Levitical sacrifices was not by fire; nay,
the greatest part of them were consumed in another way; the
main of the sacrifices were to be eaten either by priest, or

---

[s] [ἀποφέρεται ὁ θύσας τὰ κρέα, καὶ χρᾶται ὅ τι μιν λόγος αἱρέει.—Clio, c. 132.]

people, or both. [Dr. Outram, as cited in the Introduction, allows that what was made use of for a sacred feast was consumed as a sacrifice.][t] And I presume no one can doubt, but that the carcase was as rightly consumed by manducation, as the fat, caul, kidneys, and rump were by fire. And by consequence, if the whole had been directed to be eaten by the law, then the whole had been by this means rightly consumed; for there is no reason but the will of the legislator, why the whole, as well as the greatest part of these sacrifices, might

Passover a proper Sacrifice, yet not consumed by fire. Ex. xii. 9.
not be consumed by manducation. And to make this more evident, it is to be considered that the Passover was entirely to be consumed by being eaten, even " the head, and the legs, and the purtenance thereof," as well as the body of the lamb. So that this is an unexceptionable instance of a sacrifice, wholly consumed, without fire, and by manducation. That the Passover was a Sacrifice, properly so called, we are assured in the narrative of its institution, Exod. xii. 27. " It is the Sacrifice of the Lord's Passover," or rather, " it is the Sacrifice of Passover to the Lord," as the LXX do justly, and even literally render the words[u]. Bochart[x] has proved by arguments drawn from Scripture and the writings of the Rabbies, that the Paschal lamb only is meant in that text, Exod. xxiii. 18, that this was that Sacrifice, of which God there says, " Thou shalt not offer the blood of My sacrifice with leaven, neither shall the fat of My sacrifice remain until the morning." And indeed it is so explained Exod. xxxiv. 25. " Thou shalt not offer the blood of My sacrifice with leaven, neither shall the sacrifice of the feast of Passover be left unto the morning." " God," says Dr. Spencer[y] on these words, " calls it, by way of excellence, My Sacrifice;" and he tells us, God made this law that none of the Paschal lamb should be left until the morning, that men might have no excuse if they should put a slight upon this singular Sacrifice[z]. It is true, this was none of the Levitical sacrifices, strictly so

---

[t] [Not in first edition.]

[u] [Θυσία τὸ πάσχα τοῦτο Κυρίῳ, but the author is right according to the Hebrew וְזָבַח־פֶּסַח הוּא לַיהֹוָה]

[x] De Animalib. Sacris, Pars I. lib. ii. col. 573.

[y] De Leg. Hebr., p. 150.

[z] [" Deus hanc legem ferens, mentionem Paschatis facit honorificam.

Nam Pascha, non agnum, sed זֶבַח sacrificium meum;—Quid autem Deus, hoc in loco, tam honorifice de Paschate loqueretur, nisi ut tacite indicaret, Se legem hanc ideo tulisse, ut contemptus alicujus ansa et species omnis a sacrificis tam insigni tolleretur?"—De Legg. Hebr., p. 150.]

called; for it was instituted a considerable time before there was any the least hint given to Moses concerning the tabernacle, or the service there to be performed. But Christians cannot esteem it the less on this account, no more than the sacrifices of Abel, Noah, Abraham, and the other patriarchs, for neither were they Levitical. It is sufficient that it had all the essentials of a Sacrifice, and God was pleased peculiarly to call it His own. Nay, Christians in reality ought to have a special regard to the Passover, as being in a more peculiar manner the prefiguration of the grand Sacrifice.

I therefore readily acknowledge, nay, I earnestly insist on it, that all Sacrifice must be consumed according to the directions of its Divine Author: it would be a great profanation, to dispose of what belongs to God, contrary to His own will and pleasure made known to us. There was not more precise care taken of any one thing in the old law, than how every part of every sacrifice and oblation should be consumed; what portion should be burnt; what might be eaten by the priests, or their families and dependants; and what by the people; in what place, within what time, and with what circumstances it should be eaten; with several penalties laid upon all that transgressed these directions. And though these provisions were part of the ceremonial law, done away by Christ, yet the reason upon which they are grounded is of eternal force, viz. that nothing offered to God shall be otherwise consumed or disposed of, than God has Himself prescribed. But that nothing but fire has a right to consume sacrifice, is a mere precarious notion, and contrary even to the Levitical law itself. For by that law the greatest part of the sacrifices were consumed by manducation; which therefore is at least as proper a method of consuming the whole, as any other, nay the most proper, when God is pleased to direct men to this method of consumption. Thus His own sacrifice the Passover was consumed, and this He intended as a type of a more perfect Sacrifice of His own foundation.

Lev. vi. 14—30; vii. per totum. xix. 5—8.

Thus have I described the nature of a proper Sacrifice, according to the best light I could receive from other men, or my own reflection. I proceed to shew that the Eucharist has all these properties now rehearsed, and is therefore a Sacrifice properly so called.

CHAP. II.

SECT. I.

*That material Bread and Wine, as the Sacramental Body and
Blood of Christ, were by a solemn act of oblation in the
Eucharist, offered to Almighty God in the primitive Church,
and that they were so offered by Christ Himself in the
institution.*

CHAP.
II.

IN order to prove the Eucharist a proper Sacrifice, I am
(according to the method proposed in the former chapter),
first to shew, that material things were actually offered to
God in the Eucharist by the primitive Church, and by Christ
Jesus Himself. But before I undertake this, I shall first, by
way of prevention, dispute one pass with our adversaries;
and it is the main evasion they have, when they feel themselves closely pressed with our arguments; I mean, that the
Sacrifice of the Eucharist is frequently called by the ancients
an unbloody, rational, spiritual Sacrifice: and when they find
any of these epithets given to the Sacrifice of the Eucharist,
they from thence conclude that it was by the ancients meant
to be a mere mental figurative Sacrifice. Now once for all
to silence this pretence, and that I may not have occasion
to make digressions on this account, when I am in pursuit
of my main argument, I shall beforehand shew that the
ancients were so far from thinking it was inconsistent with
a true material sacrifice, to be unbloody, rational, or spiritual,
that they do often in the same sentence express, or imply,
the Sacrifice of the Eucharist to be material, and yet unbloody, rational, or spiritual. What they meant when they
called a material sacrifice rational, or spiritual, I shall hereafter have occasion to shew: it will be sufficient at present to

prove, that they did so understand these words, as that it was no contrariety in their language, to give these epithets to the material Sacrifices of Christians.

1. As to the word 'unbloody,' it generally denotes some material thing, according to the best of my judgment and information. However, that it does so, when applied to the Sacrifice of the Eucharist, take these following instances. St. Cyril of Alexandria says[a], "the table which had the shew-bread denotes the unbloody Sacrifice of the bread or loaves." And elsewhere[b], speaking of the prophecy, he by the *mincha* Mal.i.10,11. understands, "the pure unbloody Sacrifice offered in every place;" and presently after adds, "the heavenly life-giving Sacrifice being here ordained, by which death is annulled, and this corruptible, earthly flesh puts on incorruption," by this, meaning the material Eucharist. St. Chrysostom speaks of the same prophecy, when he says[c], "See how brightly and illustriously he has explained the mystical table, and the unbloody Sacrifice; he calls the holy prayer, which is offered with the Sacrifice, pure incense; therefore the mystical table is the pure Sacrifice, the principal heavenly victim, to be preferred before the world." By the table he clearly means what is placed on the table; and this, as distinguished from the prayer offered with it, he calls the 'unbloody' Sacrifice. St. Gregory Nazianzen says[d], "Julian expiated his hands from the" pretended defilements of the "unbloody Sacrifice, by which we communicate with Christ and His sufferings." And again[e], he describes the Arians as "leaping or treading on the Altars, and defiling the unbloody Sacrifices with the blood of men, and heathen sacrifices." For the Apostate could not suppose, that the prayers and praises of Christians defiled his hands. Nor could St. Gregory imagine, that the mental devotions of Christians could be polluted by the Arians. St. Athanasius tells us[f], "Melchisedec was the first type of offering the unbloody Sacrifice, the holy oblation." And I suppose the reader need not be told, that the Sacrifice offered by Melchisedec, in the judgment of the ancients, was Bread and Wine; which therefore he here calls "the unbloody

[a] c. p. 43. Ap.
[b] e. p. 43. l. 3. 9. Ap.
[c] f. p. 38. Ap.
[d] b. p. 21. Ap.
[e] d. p. 21. Ap.
[f] c. p. 17. Ap.

Sacrifice." There is a citation in the Rev. Dr. Wise's book, as
from St. Athanasius in *Quæstiones ad Antiochum*, where 'unbloody' is taken in the same sense; I will give it the reader in
Dr. Wise's translation: "As all who think themselves bound to
offer sacrifice to God by the blood of animals and irrational
things, do pervert the unbloody Sacrifice of Christ, and make
It abominable; so all who circumcise the flesh, do set at
nought and overturn the spiritual circumcision of Christians,
to wit, Holy Baptism." I suppose this writer, by 'Baptism,' or
'spiritual circumcision,' must mean water-Baptism, unless it
can be shewed, that there was any other Baptism that could
be perverted.   And indeed, Holy Baptism, especially when
opposed to 'the circumcision of the flesh,' cannot in reason be
taken in any other sense: so that it is very evident he here
speaks of the two Sacraments. And as 'spiritual circumcision'
denotes water-Baptism, so 'unbloody Sacrifice' denotes the
Sacramental Bread and Wine. But I only crave so much aid
from this citation, as can be expected from a writer of the
seventh century, under the name of St. Athanasius; and can
only say, that his authority is as good for the right meaning
of the word 'unbloody,' as it would be against it; see Dr. W.'s
book[g]. Eusebius has a passage very apposite to this purpose[h], "Who but Our Saviour did ever by tradition instruct
His votaries to celebrate unbloody and rational Sacrifices, by
prayers, and an ineffable theology? therefore He erected
Altars throughout the habitable world," &c.   He calls the
Sacrifices unbloody and rational; but asks who ever did instruct his votaries to offer such, except Our Saviour. Now if
by unbloody and rational he had meant prayer, the question
might have been retorted upon him; for who that ever gave
divine laws, did not instruct men to offer prayers?   That
which is peculiar in Our Saviour's Sacrifices, is, that they are
offered only by 'prayer,' not by fire and smoke, as those of the
Jews and Gentiles; and by an 'ineffable theology,' by which
he means the mystical consecration, and the rites and devotions with which it was attended. And to 'erect altars' for invisible Sacrifices, is a work which no one but Dr. Hancock, I presume, will assign to Christ Jesus[i]. In the Clementine Liturgy,

g p. 305.   i ['Invisible' is Johnson's own infe-
h b. p. 15. Ap.   rence of Dr. Hancock's meaning, when

the officiating Bishop prays for the ordained Bishop thus[k], SECT. "That he may atone Thee, O God, by offering to Thee the pure and unbloody Sacrifice, which Thou hast ordained by Christ, the mysteries of the New Testament." For I take it for granted, that the Eucharistical Body and Blood are the mysteries of the New Testament here mentioned; and that you may be sure that a material Sacrifice is here intended, after the prayer is concluded, the officiating Bishop is directed "to offer the Sacrifice in the hands of the ordained:" in what sense soever you take these last words, they must import a material Sacrifice; for no other Sacrifice can be put into the hands of another. As in these places it is evident, beyond all doubt, that 'unbloody' and 'material' are epithets that may be applied to the same Sacrifice; so I am not sensible, that any one passage is to be produced from the Fathers or Councils, in which prayers, praise, or the like mental Sacrifices, are called unbloody; and Plutarch[l] applies the word to the libations of meal and wine, used by the Pythagoreans and ancient Romans (*in vitâ Numæ*, cited by me in the Propitiatory Oblation, p. 125, and by Dr. W. p. 276[m].) So that I take it for granted, that by the unbloody Sacrifice is always meant the Sacrifice of the sacramental Bread and Wine, in all ancient monuments of Christianity; and consequently, that when 'rational' or 'spiritual' go along with 'unbloody,' the same materials are thereby meant; and indeed in some particular places there are other concomitant words, which shew that Bread and Wine are meant, as in the Apostolical Constitutions[n]. "Instead of bloody Sacrifices, Christ enjoined the rational unbloody Sacrifice of His Body and Blood;" for where is

Rational or spiritual, joined with unbloody, denotes a Sacrifice of Bread and Wine.

he contrasts 'intellectual' with 'material,' and thereupon founds an argument against the Eucharistic Sacrifice's being understood of the Bread and Wine, understanding 'intellectual' and 'rational' in the sense of *mental*, as opposed to 'material.' The passage runs thus, "'Who,' (saith Eusebius, Ec. Hist. *Col. Ed. Vol.* i. p. 650,) 'except our Saviour hath taught us to perform unbloody and rational 'Sacrifices:' and in the same place, 'The services of intellectual and rational Sacrifices are offered to God, the King of all nations.' Here we may see what are the *unbloody Sacrifices* the Fathers speak of,

not *unbloody, material Sacrifices,* such as Bread and Wine, but *intellectual, rational Sacrifices.*" See Patres Vindicati, p. 17. Pamph. 283. 1709. Bodl.]

[k] a. p. 52. Ap. l. 6.

[l] Κομιδῆ δὲ καὶ τὰ τῶν θυσιῶν ἔχεται τῆς Πυθαγορικῆς ἁγιστείας· ἀναίμακτοι γὰρ ἦσαν, αἵ τε πολλαὶ δι' ἀλφίτου καὶ σπονδῆς, καὶ τῶν εὐτελεστάτων πεποιημέναι. [p. 65.]

[m] ["And indeed he who should talk of *unbloody prayer and praise,* would by all judicious readers be looked upon as one that affected a language by himself." First Ed.]

[n] c. p. 47. Ap.

CHAP.
II.

Christ's Blood sacrificed in an unbloody way, but in the Eucharistical chalice? So Cyril of Jerusalem[o], "When the spiritual victim, the unbloody service is consecrated, we beseech God over that Sacrifice of propitiation[p]," &c. for I suppose no Sacrifice can be said to be consecrated, and to have prayers said 'over it' in the Christian Church and Eucharist, of which Cyril was speaking, but the Bread and Wine; and therefore, when Athenagoras says[q], Τί δε μοι ὁλοκαυτώσεων, ὧν μὴ δεῖται ὁ Θεὸς; καί τοι προσφέρειν δέον ἀναίμακτον θυσίαν, καὶ τὴν λογικὴν προσάγειν λατρείαν· "What need I care for whole burnt-offerings of which God has no need? it is rather proper to offer to Him the unbloody Sacrifice, the rational service;" I can see no occasion to doubt, but that he means the oblation of material Bread and Wine. I suppose this to be the first time that the Eucharistic Sacrifice is called 'unbloody' in any remaining monument of Christianity, unless it be allowed that the Clementine Liturgy was used in this age, which I am very much inclined to believe[r].

[It is not necessary for me to assert that 'unbloody' does always imply something that is material. It is sufficient, that it so signifies when applied to the Eucharist. Constantine in his letter to Sapores king of Persia says[s], "Christians are content with unbloody prayers only in supplicating God:" and

[o] f. p. 19. Ap. l. 5.
[p] Mr. Lewis would thus obscure this illustrious passage with a translation of his own, I suppose, viz. " after this spiritual Sacrifice, and the unbloody worship on this Sacrifice of propitiation is completed, we beseech God," &c. The principal enquiry is, what Cyril means by the " Sacrifice of propitiation." I suppose Mr. L. would by this understand the grand personal Sacrifice. But ἐκείνης clearly points at some Sacrifice just before mentioned, and there is no Sacrifice before mentioned but the Eucharist, or " spiritual Sacrifice, the unbloody service." (See the next paragraph but one.) The Eucharist therefore is " that Sacrifice of propitiation." Behold and admire the laboured obscurity of these words : " this spiritual Sacrifice and unbloody worship upon this Sacrifice of propitiation," &c. To produce this darkness he hath deleted a comma after λατρείαν, added one after ἐκείνης, and inserted a conjunctive particle between θυσίαν and λατρείαν.

After all, the translation is contrary to his own hypothesis. For it supposes the Sacrifice and worship to be completed before the intercessions, and consequently before the distribution of the sacred symbols. [This note was added in second Ed.]
[q] [Legatio pro Christianis, 12. p.49. ed. Oxon. 1706.]
[r] [" And though I cannot from any other circumstance certainly conclude, that he meant the Sacrifice of Bread and Wine, yet I shall believe that this was Athenagoras's meaning, from his using the epithet 'unbloody,' till it be proved by our adversaries that it is ever applied to mere mental sacrifices; and consequently, that by the 'rational service' we are to understand the same Bread and Wine." First Ed.]
[s] Sozomen., lib. ii. cap. 15. Ed. Valesii. Paris. 1668. Μόναις εὐχαῖς ἀναιμάκτοις πρὸς ἱκεσίαν Θεοῦ ἀρκοῦνται — ἀποχρῆσαι Αὐτῷ εἰς νίκην τὸ τοῦ σταυροῦ σύμβολον καὶ εὐχὴν καθαρὰν αἱμάτων καὶ ῥύπου.

a little after, that "the sign of the cross, and prayer free from S E C T.
blood and filth, were sufficient to gain him victory." If he ——
by 'unbloody prayers' meant prayer without any Sacrifice at
all that was material, it is not much to be wondered at in an
emperor that was himself but a catechumen, especially when
writing to a professed heathen prince. But it is evident he
means 'prayers undefiled with blood and filth,' the filth of
animal sacrifices : as 'bloody prayers' denote devotions offered
with the sacrifice of living creatures; so 'unbloody prayers'
may denote devotions offered with sacrifices of creatures
without life, and such is the Eucharist. The word turned
'prayer' may, and very often does, signify a vow, and then it
will imply a material Sacrifice; as I shall prove, ch. ii. sect.
2. No. 5.] [t]

I know the word 'service' does, in common discourse, signify Service
actions rather than things; but as Grotius, on Romans ch. ix. may im-
ver. 4, truly observes[u], 'service' denotes all Sacrifices, and in port some
the institution of the Passover signifies the sacrificed lamb, material
as it evidently doth Exod. xii. 26, 27, "When your children thing.
shall say what is this service to you?" (this is the literal rendition) "It is the Sacrifice of Passover to the Lord;" where
'service' in the question is explained by 'Sacrifice' in the
answer; and in our lawbooks[x], if I mistake not, 'service' does
not only signify some respect, labour, or work, but some real
thing, paid, or yielded by the tenant, to the lord of the manor.

2. As for the word 'rational,' when applied to the Eucha- Rational
ristic Sacrifice, that it does not only denote some act of our Sacrifice
reason, or understanding, sufficiently appears by this, that applied to
the Sacramentary of Gregory[y], and other Latin Liturgies, in- what is
struct the Priest to pray to God, that He would "render it a material.

[t] [Not in first Ed.]

[u] ["καὶ ἡ λατρεία, et obsequium] צבודה [ceremonia]; quo nomine veniunt Sacrificia omnia, sed præcipue Agnus Paschalis, ut videre est Exodi xii. 25. ubi in Græco, φυλάξασθε τὴν λατρείαν ταύτην [observate ceremoniam hancce."] Grotii Annotatt. in Ep. ad Romanos, tom. ii. vol. ii. p. 726. Ed. Amstelodam. 1679.]

[x] [" Service (servitium) though it have a general signification of duty toward them unto whom we owe the performance of any corporal labour, or function ; yet more especially in our common law, it is used for that service, which the tenant by reason of his fee oweth unto his lord. And so doth it signify among the Feudists also. For Hotoman thus defineth it, 'Servitium est munus obsequii clientelaris.' Verbo Servitium. De verbis feudal. It is sometime called 'servage,' as anno 1 R. II. cap. 6." Cowell's Law Interpreter, sub voce 'Service.' Ed. Camb. 1607.]

[y] c. p. 58. Ap.

rational acceptable Sacrifice, and make it the Body and Blood
of Christ;" which can be understood of nothing, but the material Bread and Wine; for of nothing else can it be said, or
expected, that it should become the Body and Blood. And
the reader will observe, that several of the citations under
the foregoing head, prove, that a material Sacrifice may be
'rational,' as well as 'unbloody.' And, says Theodoret[z], " He
takes away the first, that He may establish the second; by
the first He means the Sacrifice of irrational creatures, by the
second the rational Sacrifice offered by Himself." Whether
he means the oblation of Christ's sacramental or of His
natural Body, it is all one to my present purpose, that is to
prove, that a material Sacrifice may be called a rational
Sacrifice, in the judgment of the ancients.

3. It may seem very strange to some moderns to be told,
that the ancients looked upon the oblation of a material
thing, when performed according to the laws of Christ and
the Church, to be a spiritual oblation; yet certainly such
were their thoughts, such were their words. St. James's
Liturgy, in the Prothesis, teaches the Priest to say[a], " I am
not worthy to hold up my eyes toward this spiritual Table."
I am indifferent whether by Table my reader understand the
proper Altar, or the side Altar, or the Bread and Wine placed
upon one or the other: for in which signification soever you
are pleased to take it, yet the thing is 'material,' but the epithet 'spiritual.' The Priest, when he presents the elements on
the Altar, is by the Liturgy of St. Chrysostom[b] directed to
say, " Enable us to offer the gifts and spiritual Sacrifices for
our own sins, and for the errors of the people." The Apostles
are introduced in the Constitutions saying[c], " Christ becoming Man for us, and offering to His God and Father a spiritual Sacrifice before His Passion, commanded us only to do
the same;" clearly referring to those words in the Institution, " Do this in remembrance of Me," which were spoken
to the Apostles only; and what Christ there gave, or offered
to God, was His Sacramental Body and Blood, the Bread and
Wine, which are therefore here called the spiritual Sacrifice.
And of no other Sacrifice, but the Sacramental Body and

[z] g. p. 46. Ap.
[a] a. p. 54. Ap.
[b] c. p. 57. Ap.
[c] f. p. 47. Ap.

Blood, could it be said that the Apostles *only* were commanded to offer it. For prayers, and praises, and lay offerings, were to be offered by the people; but the Apostles, and they who were commissioned by them, were the only proper officers for making the oblation of Bread and Wine as the Body and Blood, as shall hereafter be made to appear. Cyril of Jerusalem has these words[d], "Solomon, in Ecclesiastes, representing this grace in a mystery, says, Eat thy bread with gladness, thy spiritual bread — and drink thy wine with gladness, thy spiritual wine;" he undoubtedly speaks of the Eucharist, for the treatise from whence they are taken is wholly on this subject; and further, he had just before recited the words of Institution[e]: and if the Bread and Wine are spiritual, no wonder that the Sacrifice of them is spiritual too. Eusebius says[f], "Our Saviour, and all Priests from Him, celebrate a spiritual Sacrifice in bread and wine." Tertullian, having premised a distinction between earthly and spiritual sacrifices[g], adds, that "even from the beginning, the earthly sacrifices of the elder son, that is, Israel, were before hand exemplified in Cain; and the sacrifices of the younger brother Abel, that is, our people the Christians, shewed to have been contrary to them," that is, to have been spiritual, according to his present distinction; so that in Tertullian's opinion, Abel's was a 'spiritual sacrifice.' And since not only Cyril of Jerusalem, but even Clement of Alexandria[h], and many other of the ancients (as will hereafter appear) do give the epithet 'spiritual' to the Eucharistical symbols, which yet are certainly material things; I can conceive no reason why any man should conclude that they are not a material Sacrifice, (except he will first believe with the Papists, that the bread and wine are annihilated,) and yet at the same time a spiritual Sacrifice, for reasons which will in due time be laid before the reader.

Nay, it is further observable, that the ancients did not only assert the Bread and Wine in the Eucharist to have been rational and spiritual Sacrifices; but Theodoret expressly

---

[d] e. p. 19. Ap.

[e] The words immediately preceding are, Ὁρᾷς ἐνταῦθα ποτήριον λεγόμενον. ὃ λαβὼν Ἰησοῦς μετὰ χεῖρας, καὶ εὐχαριστήσας, εἶπε, Τοῦτο Μου ἐστὶ τὸ αἷμα τὸ ὑπὲρ πολλῶν ἐκχυνόμενον εἰς ἄφεσιν ἁμαρτιῶν.

[f] h. p. 16. Ap. l. 6.

[g] l. p. 8. Ap.

[h] b. p. 7. Ap.

says[i], "We find Melchisedec offering to God not irrational sacrifices, but Bread and Wine;" and St. Jerome says[k], "Irrational sacrifices are no longer to be offered, but Bread and Wine, that is, the Body and Blood of Christ." Eusebius Cæsariensis[l], "Melchisedec never appears to have offered corporeal Sacrifices, but blessed Abraham with Bread and Wine." Eusebius, and St. Jerome, and Theodoret, certainly understood the language of the primitive Church equally at least to any now living, and they were so far from thinking that a Sacrifice of bread and wine might not be a spiritual Sacrifice, that they do very clearly and roundly deny that such Sacrifices are irrational or corporeal.

It is evident that St. Paul uses the same language, for he speaks of a "spiritual body;" and in the same chapter calls the entire Person of Christ Jesus a "quickening spirit." Now if the ancient heretics, who denied that Christ had a real body, were again to appear in the world, how would our adversaries be able to confute them upon their hypothesis? If they should tell these heretics that the words 'spirit' and 'spiritual' are not always so meant as wholly to exclude matter and body, as they must do if they would in earnest answer the allegations of these men from the words of St. Paul, it is very evident that in answering them they must at once answer their own cavils against us, when they conclude that the Eucharist js a Sacrifice in which no material thing is offered, because it is often called a 'spiritual' Sacrifice.

If we enquire into the reason why men of such eminent learning and knowledge, as some that seem to have espoused this notion must be allowed to have been, were led into this opinion, I must profess I know of no other reason but this, that according to our modern philosophy, 'spirit' and 'spiritual' are opposed to 'matter' and 'material;' but it is evident from what has been said, that in this the language of the present and of the primitive ages do very much differ: but if the prejudices of our present adversaries are not very deeply rooted, they will certainly be convinced, that to be material and spiritual are not inconsistent in the judgment of the ancient Church, and of St. Paul himself: and it is very observable, that the Apostle uses this way of expression even when he speaks in allusion

---

[i] d. p. 44. Ap. l. 5.   [k] l. p. 29. Ap.   [l] h. p. 16. Ap. l. 4.

to the Eucharist. He calls the manna "spiritual meat," and SECT.
I.
1 Cor. x. 3, 4. the water of the rock "spiritual drink." Now will any man from thence conclude, that it was immaterial manna and water? Suppose some of this manna and water had been offered in sacrifice to God, and therefore been called a spiritual sacrifice, would any man of common sense have from thence concluded, that they had lost all their physical or corporeal latitude, longitude, and profundity, and were turned into spirits or mere ideas?

I own that the words 'spiritual' and 'rational' do sometimes, in the writings of the ancients, signify the same with 'mental' or 'intellectual,' and that prayers and praises are frequently called 'spiritual and rational Sacrifices;' and therefore I shall not conclude that any passage in the ancients is to be taken of the oblation of Bread and Wine, because either of these two epithets are joined with the word 'Sacrifice,' except some other circumstances concurring do determine this to be the writer's meaning; as, on the other side, our adversaries ought not to conclude, that any thing is perfectly immaterial, merely because it is called spiritual or rational: and when I call the Eucharistic Sacrifice material, I must here declare, that I mean nothing by it, but that it has such a real corporeal extension as natural bread and wine, as all other bodies are allowed to have; and that I do not intend it as a word of the same adequate import with the Greek ὑλικὸς; for I apprehend, that some of the ancients may have asserted, that the Eucharistic Sacrifice is ἄϋλος[m], as well as ἀσώματος, but then they did not mean 'perfectly immaterial' or 'without bodily substance,' but not gross or dreggy[n].

Now I shall proceed to produce my authorities for the offering material bread and wine in the Eucharist, when I have first desired my reader to observe the following particulars, viz. Method for the proving a material Sacrifice.

---

[m] [The Ed. has been unable to find any passage, but the one appended, to which Johnson himself afterwards refers; and which does not immediately belong to the Eucharistic Sacrifice. "Προσκομίζομεν γὰρ εἰς ὀσμὴν εὐωδίας τῷ Θεῷ πάντα τρόπον ἐπιεικείας, πίστιν, ἐλπίδα, ἀγάπην, δικαιοσύνην, ἐγκράτειαν, τὸ εὐπειθὲς καὶ εὐήνιον, ἀκαταλήκτους δοξολογίας, καὶ τὰς ἑτέρας τῶν ἀρετῶν.

ἀϋλοτάτη γὰρ αὕτη θυσία τῷ κατὰ φύσιν, ἁπλῷ καὶ ἀΰλῳ πρέπουσα Θεῷ." S. Cyril. Alex. contra Jul., lib. x.

[n] ["But still I look on the word unbloody as appropriated to the sacrifice or oblation of material and inanimate things; and by Christian writers to the Sacrifice of the Eucharist." Omitted in 2nd Ed.]

First, That I cite no authorities, but what relate to the
Eucharist strictly so called, or to the Sacrament of the Body
and Blood of Christ.

Secondly, That I indifferently cite those passages, in which
the things offered are called Bread and Wine, the Body and
Blood of Christ, Christ Himself, or the antitypes of Christ,
or of His Body and Blood; because I shall hereafter shew,
that the ancients styled the matter of the Sacrament and
Sacrifice by any of these names.

Thirdly, If the words do evidently express or imply something material to be offered in the Eucharist properly so
called, I take it for granted, that thereby is meant the
Eucharistical Bread and Wine, or the Sacramental Body of
Christ Jesus: for there is no other material thing there to
be offered.

Fourthly, Many of my citations will prove, not only that
the Sacramental Bread and Wine are called a Sacrifice, but
that they are offered up by a solemn act of oblation in the
Eucharist; and that therefore the Bread and Wine do not only
represent a Sacrifice, but are themselves a Sacrifice, though
they derive all their propitiatory virtue from the principal,
personal Sacrifice of Christ Himself. But because my next
collection of authorities will not every one of them reach this
last point, therefore I will subjoin a particular account of the
testimonies of antiquity on this head.

Fifthly, And because in some of my citations, the matter
of the oblation is called Bread and Wine, in others, the antitypes of Christ's Body and Blood, in others, His very Body and
Blood, in others, Christ, or our Redeemer; lest some should
from hence infer that two or three several things are meant
by these several expressions, and from thence endeavour to
obscure or annul my proof of the Sacrifice; I shall shew that
by all these expressions the same things are meant; and to
this purpose I shall be obliged to present my reader with a
scheme of the doctrine of the Eucharist, according to the
sentiments of the primitive Church of the first four centuries.

Evidence
for a mate-
rial Sacri-
fice from
single
Fathers.
And now I begin my authorities for a material Sacrifice;
first from Theodoret, who says[o], "that the Church offers the
symbols of Christ's Body and Blood;" and in one of his

[o] d. p. 45. Ap.

Dialogues, he introduces an orthodox Christian asking Eranistes a heretic[p], " Of what are the mystic symbols offered by
the Priests of God a sign?" Eranistes answers, " Of the Body
and Blood of our Lord." Orthodoxus in the following part of
the Dialogue allows of this. Cyril of Alexandria, as before
cited[q], " The table that had the shew-bread signifies the unbloody Sacrifice of the loaves," and[r], " We celebrate the unbloody Sacrifice in Churches, and so approach the mystic
eulogies," that is, the Sacramental Body and Blood. Chrysostom[s], " The Sacrifice is in [our] hands and all things lie
decorously prepared." "It is a great honour for them, be they
martyrs or more than martyrs, to have their names mentioned
in the presence of our Lord, when His death is celebrated,
even the tremendous Sacrifice of His ineffable mysteries[t];"
and[u] " can we do otherwise than prevail with God, when the
tremendous Sacrifice lies in open view?" again[v], " the priest
calls upon us to pray,—and give thanks, while the tremendous
Sacrifice lies in open view;" lastly[x], he interprets Malachi's
Mincha to be the unbloody Sacrifice, and the incense to be
the prayer offered with the Sacrifice; this he calls the chief
or first Sacrifice, the Sacrifice better than the world, and
reckons nine other, the last of which is Preaching. St. Austin
is very clear in this point, as when he says[y], " What shall I
say of the Body and Blood of Christ, the only Sacrifice for the
salvation of men? although our Lord Himself say, 'Except ye
eat the flesh of the Son of Man,' &c., yet does not the Apostle
teach us, that it is pernicious to those who misuse it? for he
says, 'Whosoever eateth and drinketh unworthily,'" &c. And[z],
" Christians celebrate the memory of that same Sacrifice, that
was offered by the sacred oblation and participation of His
Body and Blood." At another place[a], "To sacrifice to God,
as we very often do, according to that rite only which [God]
hath enjoined by the revelation of the New Testament, is
part of that worship which is due to God alone;" as also[b],
" Instead of all those oblations and Sacrifices, Christ's Body

p l. p. 46. Ap.
q c. p. 43. Ap.
r l. p. 44. Ap.
s C. p. 41. Ap.
t Ibid. l. 9. p. 41. Ap.
u O. p. 43. Ap.

v q. p. 39. Ap.
x f. p. 38. Ap.
y N. p. 36. Ap.
z H. p. 36. Ap.
a I. p. 36. Ap.
b E. p. 36. Ap. l. 9.

CHAP.
II.

is offered and communicated to the receivers." Again[c], " Thou art a Priest for ever, (speaking to Christ,) for the Priesthood and Sacrifice of Aaron is vanished, and what Melchisedec brought forth, when he blessed Abraham, is every where offered under the Priesthood of Christ:" and[d], " when Melchisedec blessed Abraham, then first that Sacrifice appeared, which is now offered by Christians throughout the world;" more fully yet[e], in those words, " what he adds of eating bread (he speaks of 1 Sam. ii. 36.) elegantly describes the very sort of Sacrifice, concerning which the Priest Himself saith, the Bread which I will give is My flesh; this is that sort of Sacrifice which is according to the order of Melchisedec, not of Aaron : he that readeth, let him understand;" by which he intimates that none could understand him that was not a communicant. In another place[f], " Christ is the offerer and the oblation, of which thing He designed the Sacrifice of the Church to be a Sacrament, which as being the Body of Him that is the Head, learns to offer herself by Him, of which our Sacrifice, the many and various sacrifices of the ancient saints, were but signs;" and[g], " We being many are one body, this is the Sacrifice of Christians;—in that oblation which she offers she herself is offered," for the bread represents the body of Christian people as well as the natural Body of Christ. Again[h], " when the Sacrifice of our Redeemer is offered, or alms-deeds are performed in the Church;" and elsewhere[i], " The sacrifice of the Jews was according to the order of Aaron in the victims of cattle, and this in a mystery; the Sacrifice of the Body and Blood of the Lord was not yet — which Sacrifice is now diffused throughout the world:" and lastly he says[k], " his mother Monica knew that from the Altar that Holy Victim was distributed, by which the hand-writing against us is blotted out." Gaudentius Brixiensis declares for the material Sacrifice, in saying[l], " Christ being offered in every Church under the mystery of Bread and Wine, does refresh and enliven, being believed," &c. And[m] " when He says in the Gospel, ' I am the true vine,' He

[c] D. p. 35. Ap.
[d] B. p. 35. Ap.
[e] C. p. 35. Ap.
[f] A. p. 35. Ap.
[g] z. p. 35. Ap.

[h] x. p. 35. Ap.
[i] q. p. 33. Ap.
[k] a. p. 31. Ap.
[l] a. p. 30. Ap.
[m] Ibid. p. 30. l. 10.

sufficiently shews, that whatever Wine is offered in the figure
of His Passion, is His Blood." And again[n], "Christ appointed
the Sacraments of His Body and Blood to be offered under
the figure of Bread and Wine." St. Hierom says of Melchisedec[o], that "representing Christ, he offered Bread and
Wine, and dedicated the Christian mystery in the Body and
Blood of our Saviour." At another place he asserts[p], that
"Christ instructed His Apostles to say, Our Father Which
art in Heaven, daily in the Sacrifice of His Body." And
again[q], "Melchisedec dedicated the Sacrament of Christ in
a pure and simple Sacrifice, that is, Bread and Wine." As
also[r], "our mystery is denoted in the word 'order,' irrational Ps. cx. 4.
victims being no longer to be offered by Aaron, but Bread
and Wine, that is, the Body and Blood of Christ being made
an oblation." And[s], "Ye [priests] do offer loaves, the loaves
of shew-bread, in all the churches throughout the world,
growing from one loaf:" I suppose, he means that in which
Christ instituted the Eucharist. Macarius says the same
thing plain enough[t], "At that time the great men, and
righteous, and prophets, knew that a Redeemer was coming;
but they knew not that Bread and Wine was to be offered
in the Church, as the antitypes of His Body and Blood."
St. Ambrose supports this doctrine, for[u] "Formerly," says
he, "a lamb was offered, a calf was offered; now Christ is
offered: and He offers Himself, as a Priest, for the forgiveness of our sins: in an image here [on earth], in the verity
there, where He interposes as an Advocate for us, with the
Father." And[x], "If you offer the Body on the Altars," &c.
and especially[y], "Though Christ is not now seen to offer, yet
He Himself is offered on earth, when His Body is offered;
nay, He apparently offers in" or "by us." Ephræm Syrus
says[z], "The tremendous mysteries full of immortality are
offered to God," meaning the Eucharistical Bread and Wine,
which in the foregoing words he calls "the gifts laid in open

[n] d. p. 31. Ap.
[o] b. p. 28. Ap.
[p] g. p. 28. Ap.
[q] h. p. 28. Ap.
[r] l. p. 29. Ap.
[s] n. p. 29. Ap.
[t] b. p. 26. Ap. Monsieur Larroque,
by a strange sleight of hand, for 'great
men,' 'righteous,' and 'prophets,' substitutes 'primitive believers.' History
of Eucharist, part i. c. 8. [2nd ed.]
["les anciens fidéles," p. 165. ed.
Amsterdam· 1671.]
[u] m. p. 27. Ap.
[x] n. p. 27. Ap.
[y] c. p. 26. Ap.
[z] a. p. 25. Ap.

view." We have already heard St. Gregory Nazianzen[a],
speaking, not only of 'unbloody' Sacrifices in the Christian
Church, but of Sacrifices, from the supposed defilement
whereof Julian, when he apostatized, 'expiated his hands;'
'Sacrifices' and 'Altars,' which were defiled by the Arians and
others; and therefore material, beyond all dispute or doubt.
And in another place, speaking of himself[b], "How should I
dare," says he, "to offer the external Sacrifice, the antitype
of the great mysteries, if I had not first offered myself a
sacrifice to God?" &c. And once more[c], "Will they drive
me from the Altars? I know another Altar — which is
wholly the work of the mind, and the ascent is by theory,
[i. e. contemplation:] by this Altar I will stand, on this I will
offer sacrifice, oblations, and holocausts, as much exceeding
those that are now offered, as the verity is more excellent
than the shadow." These words at first sight may seem to
give some countenance to the cause of our adversaries, as
supposing some mental Sacrifice more excellent than that of
the Eucharist; but let me observe, that though the supposed
Altar and Sacrifice of St. Gregory were really as much to be
preferred before the Altar and Sacrifice of the Church, as he
fancied them to be; yet still it must be allowed, that the
Altar and Sacrifice from which he expected to be driven,
were material and real; for he could be driven from none
that was immaterial. And as for the Father's theoretical
Altar and Sacrifice, I shall contentedly leave it to our adversaries, and let them make the best of it: for I believe it
will puzzle the most metaphysical head to imagine what
Sacrifice, either of prayer or praise, or whatever else they
please, could excel the Sacrifice of the Christian Church,
when offered as it ought to be, with all holy dispositions and
affections. I will suppose that St. Gregory meant an imaginary oblation of the very natural Body of Christ Jesus; and
yet cannot at the same time persuade myself, either that this
imaginary oblation was more excellent than that in the
Eucharist; or that this imaginary oblation could not be performed at the material Altar as well as any where else: nay,
if St. Gregory thought this imaginary oblation to be of so
great worth, I apprehend it was his duty to offer it, as often

[a] b. c. d. p. 21. Ap.   [b] a. p. 21. Ap.   [c] e. p. 21. Ap.

as he performed the external oblation; especially if it be con- SECT.
sidered, that the imaginary sacrifice of St. Gregory was to —— I.
be offered while he was in the body; while he could ascend
to the supernal regions "by theory only." We readily accept
the unanswerable proof, that the Father gives us of an external sacrifice; and as to the other sacrifice, we will further
consider it, when our adversaries háve first been pleased to
inform us what it was. And as for St. Gregory himself, I
can only say, that the greatest men, when they indulge the
warmth of their own present thoughts, have said things which
it would be very hard for themselves to explain. But St.
Gregory makes ample amends for this excess of rhetoric by
what he has said at other places, and especially where he
calls[d] "the gifts," or oblations made in the Eucharist,
"cleansing or expiatory Sacrifices;" and the Altar, "the
divine Table, the holy receptacle of these gifts." St. Basil
the Great[e] represents the great danger " of sacrificing the
Body of our Lord while we are under any defilement," and
speaks[f] of the Priest's " consummating and distributing the
Sacrifice." Hilary the Deacon says[g], "that the Bishop offers
the Sacrifice instead of Christ." Cyril of Jerusalem[h] [speaks]
of a "prayer offered while the holy and most tremendous
Sacrifice lies in open view;" and[i], " we offer Christ slain for our
sins." He has before been cited[k] for his speaking of " consecrating the spiritual oblation," and of " beseeching God over
the Sacrifice of propitiation." St. Athanasius says over and
again[l], "Melchisedec was the first example of offering the
unbloody Sacrifice, viz. Bread and Wine, and that therefore
it was said to our Saviour, Thou art a Priest according to the
order of Melchisedec." Eusebius[m] speaks of "offering the oblation, and giving to every one his share :" and[n] that "Altars
were every where erected for unbloody rational Sacrifices,
according to the new mysteries of the New Testament."
Mental devotions require no Altar, nor are they the new
mysteries. And again, as cited before in part[o], "Melchisedec

[d] g. p. 21. Ap.
[e] b. p. 23. Ap.
[f] d. p. 23. Ap.
[g] b. p. 20. Ap.
[h] f. p. 19. Ap. l. 15.
[i] g. p. 19. Ap.
[k] f. p. 19. Ap. l. 5.
[l] c. p. 17. Ap.
[m] a. p. 15. Ap.
[n] d. p. 15. Ap.
[o] h. p. 16. Ap.

CHAP.
II.

being a Priest of the Gentiles, nowhere appears to have used corporeal sacrifices, but blessed Abraham by bread and wine. Just in the same manner, first our Saviour, and then all Priests from Him, consummating the spiritual hierurgy [ἱερουργίαν] according to the laws of the Church, do represent the mysteries of His Body and saving Blood, in Bread and Wine." And elsewhere[p], "We celebrate the memorial of this Sacrifice on the Table, by the symbols of His Body and Blood, — and are taught by David to say, 'Thou hast prepared a Table before me; Thou hast anointed my head with oil:' expressly signifying the mystical chrism, and the venerable Sacrifices of Christ's Table; in which, offering unbloody and reasonable Sacrifices, and pleasing to Him, we are taught to make an oblation to God," &c. That which in the first place he calls 'the memorial of a Sacrifice by symbols,' in the next sentence he calls 'the Sacrifices of Christ's Table.' Dr. Hancock[q] artfully left out the first words in citing this

---

[p] f. p. 16. Ap.

[q] ["Many of the Fathers called even Baptism itself a Sacrifice, probably for this reason, because in Baptism we die with Christ, and by that Sacrament is applied to us the virtue of that Sacrifice upon the cross, as it is also in the other Sacrament. Eus. Dem. Ev. lib. i. c. 10. tells us, that in those words of the Psalmist, Ps. xxiii., 'Thou hast prepared a Table before me, Thou hast anointed my head with oil, my cup shall be full,' are plainly signified the mystical unction, (by which, no doubt, he means Baptism,) and the venerable Sacrifice of Christ's, whereby we are taught, through Christ our supreme High-Priest, to offer unto God over all, unbloody and rational Sacrifices continually all our life long.

"Melchior Canus tells us, that many of the Fathers called Baptism a Sacrifice. St. Chrysostom refers to Baptism those words of the Epistle to the Heb., chap. x. 26, 'There remaineth no more sacrifice for sin.' For though he means by Sacrifice that of Christ on the cross, yet being this is applied by Baptism, and that can be administered but once, he thinks it may be said on this account, 'there remains no more sacrifice for sin.' And Theophylact follows him in this, as he does in most other things. And St. Augustine likewise somewhere says, that 'many expound those fore-cited words of the author to

the Hebrews, of that Sacrifice of the Passion of our Saviour, that every one offers for his sins, when he is baptized.' And he after says, that 'to him that has received the knowledge of the truth, there remains no more sacrifice for sin, that is to say, he cannot be baptized anew.'"—Patres Vindicati, pp. 28-9.

"Sed quæris, quid causæ plerisque antiquorum fuerit, ut baptismum hostiam appellaverint, ideoque dixerint non superesse hostiam pro peccato, quia baptismus repeti non potest. Sane quia in baptismo Christo commorimur, et per hoc sacramentum applicatur nobis hostia crucis, ad plenam peccati remissionem, hinc illi baptisma translatitia hostiam nuncuparunt, ac post baptisma semel acceptum nullam hostiam esse reliquam interpretati sunt: quia baptisma secundum non est."— Melchior Canus, Opera, p. 680. ed. Colon. Ag. 1605.

"Οὐκέτι περὶ ἁμαρτιῶν ἀπολείπεται θυσία, ὃ δὲ λέγει τοιουτόν ἐστιν· ἐκαθάρθης, ἀπηλλάγης ἐγκλημάτων, γέγονας υἱός. ἂν τοίνυν ἐπὶ τὸν πρότερον ἔμετον ἐπιστρέψῃς, πάλιν ἀποκηρύξις μένει καὶ πῦρ, καὶ ὅσα τοιαῦτα. οὐ γάρ ἐστι θυσία δευτέρα."—S. Chrysostom. In Ep. ad Hebræos, cap. x. Hom. xx. tom. xii. p. 186. Ed. Paris. 1735.

"Οὐ τὴν μετανοίαν ἀναίρων λέγει ταῦτα, ὥς τινες ὑπενόησαν, ἀλλὰ δείκνυσιν, ὅτι οὐκ ἔστι δεύτερον βάπτισμα· διὸ οὐδὲ δεύτερος θάνατος τοῦ Χριστοῦ.

passage, and then would persuade his reader, that the rest is to be understood of the Sacrifice of Baptism, of which Sacrifice the Doctor (or those moderns from whom he took it) is the author. And at another place[r], "We offer the shewbread, and the Blood of sprinkling, the Blood of the Lamb, Which takes away the sins of the world, the expiation of our souls." And if this be not enough, I will add another passage, where he says[s], "Christ Himself delivered to His disciples the symbols of the divine œconomy, commanding them to offer the image of His own Body; for since God no longer designed bloody sacrifices,—He has by tradition instructed us to use Bread as a symbol of His Body; as another prophet has reminded us, saying, 'Sacrifice and offering Thou wouldest not, but a Body hast Thou prepared me.'" St. Cyprian is a most illustrious witness of this truth. I shall only at present transcribe one small part of an epistle written by him, against those who put nothing but water into the Eucharistical chalice[t], "We are given to understand, that the Lord's tradition be observed in offering the cup,—that the cup which is offered in commemoration of Him, be offered mixed with wine." And then he cites those words, "'Thou art a Priest for ever, after the order of Melchisedec,' which order being derived and descending from that Sacrifice, is this, that Melchisedec was priest of the most high God, that he offered bread and wine, that he blessed Abraham,—and that the blessing of Abraham might be duly celebrated, an image of the Sacrifice of Christ, consisting of bread and wine, goes before it. And the Holy Ghost by Solomon describes beforehand the figure of our Lord's Sacrifice, the immolated Sacrifice of Bread and Wine." And, "That Priest acts in Christ's stead, who imitates what Christ did, and offers to the Father a true and full Sacrifice in the Church of God, if he so begin to offer as he sees Christ to have offered." Origen teaches the same

---

Θυσίαν γὰρ τοῦτον καλεῖ, ὡς καὶ ἐν τοῖς κατόπιν. Μιᾷ γὰρ θυσίᾳ τετελείωκεν εἰς τὸ διηνεκές· τὸ γὰρ βάπτισμα ἡμῶν τὸν θάνατον εἰκονίζει τοῦ Χριστοῦ." —Theophylact. in eodem loco. p. 982. Ed. Lindsell. Londini. 1636.

"Non adhuc pro peccatis relinquitur sacrificium: sed de sacrificio de quo tunc loquebatur Apostolus, id est, holocausto Dominicæ passionis, quod eo tempore offert quisque pro peccatis suis, quo ejusdem passionis fide dedicatur, et Christianorum fidelium nomine baptizatus imbuitur."—S. Augustin. Ep. ad Romanos Expositio, tom. iii. pars 2. p. 937. Ed. Paris. 1680.]

[r] k. p. 17. Ap.
[s] i. p. 16. Ap.
[t] m. p. 11—13. Ap.

doctrine in those remarkable words[u], " Let Celsus, as being ignorant of God, render his Eucharistic Sacrifices to demons; but we, appeasing the Creator of the universe, do also eat the Bread that is offered with thanksgiving, and prayer made over the gifts, after they have been made a certain holy Body." He does not say the Body of Christ, because his discourse was chiefly intended for the confutation of the heathen; and immediately after, " Celsus is pleased to offer to demons, but we to Him that said, 'Let the earth bring forth,' " &c. as Gen. i. 11, &c.   Tertullian bears witness to the same truth in these words[x], " Very many on the stationary," that is, fasting " days, think they ought not to be present at the prayers of the Sacrifices, lest their fasts be broken, by receiving the Body of our Lord; does, therefore, the Eucharist slacken our devotion to God, or rather tie us faster to God? Will not your station be the more solemn, if you perform it at God's Altar?   However by taking the body of our Lord, and reserving It [to be eaten afterwards], both will be safe; the participation of the Sacrifice, and the performance of your duty, that is, fasting." He distinguishes between the prayers, and the Sacrifice; and he tells you, what the Sacrifice was, viz. the Sacramental Body of Christ; for 'to receive the Body of Christ,' and ' partake of the Sacrifice,' signify the same thing in this citation.   And[y], " The devil imitates the Divine Sacraments; he baptizes some that believe in him—and if I remember right, Mithra" a Persian idol "signs in the forehead his own soldiers, and celebrates the oblation of bread."   And it is to be considered, that it was such ' an oblation of bread' as was ' in the Divine Sacraments.'   Irenæus is very full to this purpose[z], " Christ charging His disciples to offer firstfruits to God of His own creatures—took such bread as is a creature, and gave thanks, saying, ' This is My Body;' and He declared likewise the Cup to be His Blood; which [Cup], according to our doctrine, is a thing created [by God];" this was what Irenæus's adversaries denied, " and taught the new oblation of the New Testament, which the Church, receiving from the Apostles, offers throughout the world." To this Sa-
chap. i. 10, crifice he applies the words of Malachi, and adds, " Manifestly
11.

[u] a. p. 9. Ap.   [y] r. p. 9. Ap.
[x] i. p. 8. Ap.   [z] c. p. 4. Ap. l. 15.

signifying by these words, that the former people, the Jews, SECT.
I. shall cease to offer to God; but that in every place sacrifices shall be offered, and that pure." He cannot mean mental sacrifices; for the Jews do not cease to offer prayers and praises; but material sacrifices, which the Jews cannot offer, since they have no temple. St. Justin Martyr is as clear in this point, as any Father whose words I have yet produced; as for instance, where he says[a], "The oblation of the cake, which was ordered to be offered for those that were cleansed of the leprosy, was a type of the Bread of the Eucharist, which the Lord Jesus Christ has by tradition instructed us to offer, for a memorial of His Passion." And presently after[b], "concerning the Sacrifices offered in every place to God by us Gentiles, that is, the Bread of the Eucharist and Cup of the Eucharist, He then foretold, saying, we should glorify His name." Here he refers to Mal. i. 10, 11. In the following citation[c] he refers to Isa. xxxiii. 16. "In this prophecy he clearly speaks of the Bread, which our Christ has by tradition instructed us to offer for a memorial of His Incarnation, for the sake of them that believe in Him." In the first and third of these citations from Justin, I have turned ποιεῖν, 'to offer,' as the most learned Dr. Hickes has proved that it here signifies[d]. It is an indignity to the Martyr to suppose, that our Saviour is by him represented as commanding us to 'make bread.' In the second citation, Justin uses the word προσφέρειν, and not ποιεῖν; and the learned Voigtus, though he was no friend to the Sacrifice, is forced to acknowledge that Justin asserts an oblation of Bread and Wine in the Eucharist[e].

I proceed to allege the public testimonies, which synods Evidence of
a material
Sacrifice
from coun-
cils. and councils have given to this doctrine. Now the synod of Constantinople, held A.D. 754, was too late to be cited upon this occasion, if there were not a very singular honour due to this numerous congress of learned and pious Bishops, on account of that noble opposition they made against image worship. They declared against images of wood and

---

a b. p. 3. Ap.
b c. p. 3. Ap.
c d. p. 3. Ap.
d See Christian Priesthood, pp. 58—68.

e ["Justinus certe Dial. cum Tryphone, f. 260. panem Eucharisticum vocat Sacrificium."—De Altaribus, p. 53.]

CHAP. stone, and that upon this principle; that Jesus Christ had
II. given us one only image of His Body in the Eucharist, and
therefore for this reason, among others, condemned the blind
zeal of those who were then for bringing other images into the
Church; but the adverse party, in less than forty years after,
did so far prevail, that in the second synod of Nice, they
got the decrees of this synod of Constantinople to be re-
versed, established the worship of molten and graven images,
and laid it down for a principle[f], that the Eucharist was not
an image of Christ, but Christ Himself: and though the
word 'transubstantiation' was not coined till some ages
after; yet from this time forward the ancient doctrine of
the Church, in relation to this article of religion, was gradually altered and corrupted, and at last wholly subverted.
Now the doctrine of the ancient Church, to which this synod
gave their authoritative testimony, was this[g], that "Christ
commanded the substance of material bread, selected [from
the main mass of oblations] to be offered as His image, not
representing the figure of a man, lest idolatry should be
introduced." It was not my design to swell my citations,
by producing authorities of the fifth, sixth, or seventh ages,
much less of those that are later; but I thought it not amiss
for once, to go a great deal out of my road, on purpose to
pay my respects to the synod of Constantinople, for which
all sincere Protestants ought to have a very singular veneration. The next synod I cite, is the third, alias the sixth of
Carthage, which in the twenty-fourth canon[h] charges, that
"in the Sacraments of the Body and Blood of Christ, nothing
be offered, but what the Lord hath delivered, that is, Bread
and Wine mixed with water." They not only mention the
material oblation, as made in the Sacrament, properly so
called; but suppose the oblation enjoined by Christ. Further,
Honoratus and Urbanus, in the forty-eighth canon of the
same council (according to the common division) observe[i],
that "it had both now, and in time past, been resolved to
prohibit Sacrifices after dinner;" and if any one doubt what
these Sacrifices were, that were to be offered fasting, he will

---

[f] The learned reader may see how   [g] p. 52. Ap. l. 14.
Du Pin countenances these Constan-   [h] See Appendix, p. 50.
tinopolitan Fathers, Cent. viii. p. 138.   [i] p. 50. Ap.
[2nd Ed.]

be informed by the twenty-ninth canon, which provides, that
"the Sacraments of the Altar be celebrated by such as are
fasting only;" and lest you should imagine, that the Sacrifice
mentioned in the forty-eighth canon, was that of prayer only,
it is added, that "if commendation of a deceased Bishop be
to be performed, it shall be done by prayers only, if it happen
that they who are to perform it have broken their fast." So
that prayers might be offered after dinner, but the Sacrifice
might not. The synod of Gangra[k], in the fourth canon,
censures them who "refuse to partake of the oblation, when
it is made by a married Priest;" and therefore by the 'oblation' can mean nothing but the Sacramental Body and
Blood. We have before seen, that one usual name given to
the Eucharistic Bread and Wine, by single Fathers, is that
of 'oblation,' or 'Sacrifice;' that they were as commonly distinguished by this title, as by the other of mysteries or Sacraments, is what no true antiquarian will dispute; and it is
very evident that this was the language of the Church itself,
if we may judge by the Nicene canons, which were compiled
by the most full representative of the whole Church, that
ever was held before; for by the eleventh of these canons[l] it
is provided, that "they who have transgressed," that is, done
sacrifice to idols, "without compulsion, shall continue three
years among the hearers, be *substrators* seven years, and
for three years communicate with the people in prayer, without the oblation." Prayer was so far from being thought,
or called 'the oblation,' that a man might partake of the
prayers, even those wherein the Sacrifice was offered, and yet
be denied the privilege of receiving the material oblation,
that is, the Sacramental Bread and Wine. That the penitents here spoken of, were allowed to be present during the
whole time that the Eucharist was celebrated, and so might
join in with the prayers and praises of the communicants,
appears from this, that they were called συνιστάμενοι, or
penitents that stood together with the faithful, after the
catechumens and other penitents were dismissed; and are
therefore said in this canon "to communicate with the people
in prayer;" and lest any one should please himself with a
fancy, that the Eucharist is called the oblation, because it was

[k] p. 49. Ap. [l] p. 50. Ap.

'given' or 'offered' to the people; let it be observed, that by
the eighteenth canon[m] of this council, the Deacons are prohibited to give the Eucharist, or distribute the consecrated
symbols to the Priest, "because," as these holy Fathers express
it, " neither canon nor custom permits, that the Deacons who
have not power to offer, should give the Body of Christ to
[the Priests], who do" or can " offer." It is certain the Deacons could offer, that is, distribute the Communion to the
people; but they could not offer in the sense here intended,
that is, they could not perform the solemn oblation of the
Eucharist, as a Sacrifice to Almighty God; and that therefore the Eucharistical symbols are called 'the oblation,'
from their having been thus offered to God, before they
were distributed. This will appear yet more evident from
the canons of the synod of Ancyra. The fifth canon of
this synod[n] requires, that they who had eaten things
offered to idols, but with tears in their eyes, thereby signifying their inward aversion, should after having been penitents for three years, be received to communion, " but without the oblation." But if they did not eat, but only went to
the idol temple, that then they should be penitents for two
years only, and the third year " should communicate without the oblation." By the sixth canon of the same synod[o],
they who were prevailed upon to eat things offered to idols
by threats only, were after somewhat more than three years'
penitence, to " communicate without the oblation for two
years." By canon the seventh, others are, after two years'
penitence, to be received to Communion; but " whether with
or without the oblation," is left to the Bishop's discretion.
By the eighth canon, they who had through compulsion twice
or thrice sacrificed to idols, were, after four years' penitence,
to be admitted to communicate without the oblation for two
years. By the ninth canon, they who had forced their Christian brethren to do sacrifice to idols, are admitted, after nine
years' penitence, " to communicate for one year without the
oblation." And by the twenty-fourth canon, diviners or con-
jurers, after three years' penitence, are admitted to " prayer
without the oblation for two years." Now the question is
what that 'oblation' was, which was denied to these penitents.

[m] p. 50. Ap.   [n] p. 49. Ap.   [o] p. 49. Ap.

Our adversaries, if they will be true to their cause, must say, either that it was prayer and praise, or at the most, alms for the poor, or first-fruits for the Bishop and Clergy. Now that it was not prayer, is evident to a demonstration; for the twenty-fourth canon admits them to prayer, but not to the oblation; by which not only a difference is made between the prayer and oblation; but the latter is clearly made the greater privilege of the two: for they that were thought worthy to join in prayer, are yet forbid to partake of the oblation; and therefore what can any rational man understand by the oblation, but the Bread and Wine offered and consecrated into the Body and Blood of Christ? So Balsamon, Zonaras, and Aristenus[p] explain this word; nor do I see that it is capable of any other meaning. If you suppose, that "to communicate without the oblation," is to eat and drink of the Sacrament, but not to be permitted to bring bread and wine, or any other material offerings to the Altar; this is to suppose, that it was less honourable to join in prayer, and in receiving the Eucharistical symbols, than to provide the outward elements; and that a man must first be fit to offer prayers to God, before he is worthy to make his oblation to the Priest; for this is the necessary consequence of this opinion; and yet this opinion is the only evasion that our adversaries can have, from the argument drawn from these canons. But further, the sixteenth canon of this synod does more directly prove that this could not be the meaning of these Fathers. The criminals there mentioned are condemned to fifteen years' penitence, and then, says the canon, "having completed five years in communion of prayer, let them touch, taste, approach, or come to the oblation;" for the word ἐφάπτεσθαι cannot with any justice be so turned, as to comport with bringing an oblation to the Church or Altar. The same canon enjoins twenty-five years' penitence to those who were grosser criminals, and then adds, "having completed five

---

p [Balsamon, on this canon, remarks: "Ὥρισαν οἱ πατέρες ἐπὶ πενταετίαν τούτους ἐπιτιμᾶσθαι ἤγουν ἐπὶ μὲν τρισὶν ἔτεσιν ὑποπίπτειν, ἐν δὲ δυσὶν εὔχεσθαι μετὰ τῶν πιστῶν, καὶ μετὰ ταῦτα ἀξιοῦσθαι τῶν θείων ἁγιασμάτων." And Zonaras: "Ὁ κανὼν ποιεῖται, ὡς τρία ἔτη ὑποπίπτειν, καὶ δύο ἔτη συνεύχεσθαι τοῖς πιστοῖς· μετὰ δὲ τὴν πενταετίαν, ἀξιοῦσθαι καὶ τῆς τοῦ ἀγαθοῦ μεταλήψεως." And Aristenus: "ἐπὶ διετίαν συστήσεται τοῖς πιστοῖς, καὶ μόνων τῶν εὐχῶν κοινωνήσει· καὶ οὕτω μετὰ τὴν πενταετίαν μεθέξει τῆς προσφορᾶς." See Beveregii Συνοδικὸν, tom. i. p. 400.]

years in communion of prayer, let them obtain the oblation."
Now 'obtaining the oblation' cannot in any propriety of
speech denote any thing but being admitted to receive the
offered and consecrated Bread and Wine. And let it not be
said, that 'to offer' signifies to consecrate; for it is certain
it does not primarily and directly, but only as oblation was
necessary in order to consecration, and as the solemn words
of oblation always made a part of the prayer of consecration;
but the offering and consecrating were ever distinguished in
all the Liturgies that I have laid my eyes on, and they were
ever denoted by several words; the one by προσφέρειν, προσ-
κομίζειν, ἱερατεύειν, &c., the other by ἁγιάζειν, ἀπαρτίζειν,
μεταβάλλειν, &c. And further, in the fifth, sixth, eighth,
and ninth, after specifying the term of years, during which
the several penitents were to continue in communion of
prayer without the oblation, it is immediately added, "let
them come to," or "partake of perfection," or "be perfectly
received," as it is in the eighth canon. Now I will leave it to
any impartial judge, whether bringing an offering, or receiving the Sacrament, (as we usually speak,) be most probably
meant by 'coming to perfection;' and it deserves our particular reflection, that the fifth canon expresses it by λαβεῖν
τέλειον; so that it is as evident, that τέλειον and προσφορὰ
do signify the Sacramental Body and Blood, as λαβεῖν signifies 'to take;' and consequently, that what was taken in
the Communion had first been offered. But I suppose that
the most ancient canons which are come down to us, are those
commonly called Apostolical. Now the second, *alias* third,
of these canons[q] provides, that "no Bishop or Priest do offer
any thing in Sacrifice on the Altar, beside what our Lord
hath commanded;" and if any one doubt what those things
are, which the Lord commanded to be offered, Justin Martyr,
Irenæus, the other Fathers above cited, and the synod of
Carthage above mentioned, will inform him that they are
Bread and Wine. This canon therefore supposes that truth
for which we contend; namely, that Christ commanded
Bread and Wine to be offered. The sixth, otherwise the
ninth of these canons, suspends those Bishops, Priests, Deacons, and others of the clerical list, "who do not partake of

q p. 48. Ap.

the oblation, when it is made." Now I apprehend, the greatest enemies of Priests and Altars will not suppose, that there could be any occasion to censure clergymen for refusing to take their share in the offerings which the people brought for their substance; and that therefore by the oblation here could be meant nothing but the Sacramental Body and Blood: but if any man still make a question, what is meant by 'partaking of the oblation,' I suppose the next canon will inform him; which suspends those laymen who enter into the Church, and hear the " Scriptures, but do not stay for prayers and the Communion;" to "partake of the oblation" and "Communion" was the same thing in the primitive Church. The thirty-eighth, *alias* forty-sixth of these canons provides, that no Bishop, Priest, or Deacon, that "has received Baptism or the Sacrifice from heretics," shall be continued in his office, but be deposed; and that by Sacrifice they meant the symbols of the Eucharist, is too plain to admit of any doubt; and on what account can they be supposed to be distinguished by this title, but because they had been solemnly offered to God in the preceding prayers?

As to the Liturgies, I shall allege no citations from the Latin; not because they do not speak home to the purpose; for there is not one of them, according to the best of my observation, which does not abundantly express in very plain words the material oblation, for which I now contend; but because they are none of them of greater antiquity than the eighth or at most the seventh century, excepting that of Gregory the Great, which therefore, as to what concerns the oblation, the reader has in the Appendix; and in which the Priest prays[r] that "the oblation may be accepted by God, that so it may become to us the Body and Blood of Christ Jesus." Now I suppose I need not inform my reader, what that was which they desired might become the Body and Blood of Christ. And again, after the words of Institution[s], "We offer unto Thee, O Lord, out of what Thou hast given us, a pure and immaculate Sacrifice, the holy Bread of eternal life, and the Cup of everlasting salvation." The Liturgy of St. Peter, being in reality no other than a Latin Liturgy translated into Greek, uses almost the very same expressions[t],

[r] c. p. 59. Ap.   [s] c. p. 59. Ap. l. 8, &c.   [t] c. p. 58, 59. Ap.

CHAP.
II.

which therefore I shall not repeat. St. Chrysostom's Liturgy does as plainly express the materiality of the Sacrifice; for in that, the Priest, having presented the Bread and Wine on the Altar, and rehearsed the words of institution, says[u], "We offer to Thee Thine own of Thine own;" and again, "We offer to Thee this reasonable and unbloody service; and we beseech Thee, send down Thine Holy Spirit on us, and on the gifts laid in open view." Now I suppose, what the Priest calls God's 'own of His own,' and 'the gifts laid in open view,' are the very same with the 'unbloody service;' and upon these gifts, this unbloody service, the Priest prays that the Spirit may descend, "and make them the Body and Blood." Nothing can be more clear, than that of St. Basil's Liturgy, which, besides what is common to that and others, hath there these words[x], "Most holy Lord, we approach Thine Altar, laying before Thee the antitypes of the Body and Blood of Thy Son Jesus Christ; and we beseech Thee that Thy Holy Spirit may come on these gifts laid in open view." The more direct oblation goes just before[y], and is thus expressed, "offering to Thee Thine own of Thine own, we sing hymns to Thee."

The words to this purpose in the Liturgy of St. Mark are[z], "Fill this Sacrifice with a blessing from Thee, by the coming of Thy most Holy Spirit;" and after the words of institution[a], "Of Thine own gifts have we laid Thine own before Thee; and we beseech Thee, send Thy Holy Spirit, and make this Bread the Body, and this Cup the Blood of the new covenant of the Lord." The Bread and Wine are indisputably the materials which the Priest prays to be made the Body and Blood; the Bread and Wine were what was laid before God; the Bread and Wine were the Sacrifices, on which a blessing from Heaven was expected. In St. James's Liturgy, the Priest, after pronouncing the words of institution, says thus[b], "We offer unto Thee, O Lord, this unbloody and tremendous Sacrifice — send Thy Holy Spirit upon us, and upon Thy Holy gifts lying here in open view[c],—and make the Bread the holy Body," &c. As sure as the Bread and Wine are meant,

[u] d. p. 58. Ap. l. 7.
[x] g. p. 57. Ap.
[y] f. p. 57. Ap. l. 7.
[z] c. p. 56. Ap.

[a] c. p. 56. Ap. l. 8, 9.
[b] g. p. 55. Ap.
[c] h. p. 55. Ap.

when the Priest prays, that the Bread may become the Body, the Wine the Blood; so sure is it, that the Bread and Wine were the 'gifts,' or the unbloody and tremendous Sacrifice. As the Clementine Liturgy is allowed to be the most ancient and valuable; so if the present assertors of the Sacrifice were themselves to compose a Liturgy, they could not express their sentiments in clearer or stronger words, than those which they here find ready drawn to their hand; I mean those words presently following the recital of the institution[d]. " We offer unto Thee, our King and our God, according to Christ's commandment, this Bread, and this Cup." Now when the most ancient authority is most clear and full, all the rest ought in reason to be explained by it; and this is the present case. For what St. James's expresses by "the tremendous and unbloody Sacrifice," the others by τὰ Σὰ ἐκ τῶν Σῶν, de Tuis donis ac datis, or the like, St. Clement's Liturgy explains in right down words, and calls it ' the Bread and Cup:' and though the other Liturgies do give sufficient light to themselves, and to each other, in this matter; yet I think it may be justly said, that this of St. Clement gives an additional light to all the rest; and by being the most ancient, reflects the greater lustre upon the material oblation. The plea of our adversaries might have looked less unreasonable, if in the most ancient Liturgy now extant, there had not been an oblation of the Eucharistic Bread and Wine, in such direct words, as will admit of no evasion. And when it is considered, that Tertullian, Irenæus, and Justin Martyr, do so expressly concur with this Liturgy, in asserting that Bread and Wine were offered in the Eucharist in that age; and the two elder, I mean Irenæus and Justin, do further say that this was done by Christ's instruction; I think it as clear a demonstration as a thing of this nature is capable of, that if this Liturgy was not used in the second century, yet that they had one, which in this respect at least agreed with that of Clement. If they had one single Liturgy to oppose to those six, from whence I have produced citations, they might indeed be said to have something to keep them in countenance : some parts of the latter Liturgies, cited by me, are no doubt interpolated, but if any part of them be

[d] c. p. 53. Ap. l. 29.

CHAP.
II.
ancient, of which no good antiquarian will doubt, then the
words I have cited from them are so; not only because they
all agree with that of St. Clement, in having solemn words of
oblation, and those placed after the words of institution, and
before the prayer for the Divine benediction, or the descent
of the Spirit, but because the most genuine undoubted writers
of the second century downward do so evidently inform us
that there was in those ages an oblation of Bread and Wine
made in the Eucharist.

The prayer
mentioned
Apost.
Const. lib.
vii. c. 25,
considered.
It may perhaps here be said by some that there is another
consecration prayer extant in the Constitutions, in which there
are no oblatory words. Mr. Whiston, if my memory do not
deceive me, somewhere in his late books concerning the Constitutions, supposes that the form called Εὐχαριστία Μυστικὴ[e],
was a sort of communion service for the use of the Gentile
converts; but this I look upon to be a very wide conjecture.
As there is in that form no oblation, so neither is there any
consecration, nor the words of institution. The Latin title
indeed is Gratiarum actio Sacramentalis, which probably may
have given occasion to this conjecture, of its being a consecration prayer; but I apprehend that the Greek title implies
no more than a thanksgiving to be said secretly or with a low
voice, at the Communion; and he that looks into the Liturgies
of St. Basil and St. Chrysostom will find many of these mystic prayers, and cannot but see that Μυστικῶς, 'softly' or
'secretly,' is opposed to ἐκφώνως, 'with a loud voice,' throughout those Liturgies: and I apprehend that this prayer was
intended to be used before the very long prayer of oblation
and consecration[f]: for before the beginning of that prayer
the Bishop is directed to pray καθ᾽ ἑαυτὸν ἅμα τοῖς πρεσβυτέροις, 'by himself together with the Priests;' and the words
suit very well with this occasion; they are these, according
to Mr. Whiston's translation : "We thank Thee, our Father,
for that life which Thou hast made known to us by Jesus
Thy Son, by Whom Thou madest all things, and takest care
of the whole world; Whom Thou hast sent to become man
for our salvation; Whom Thou hast permitted to suffer, and
to die; Whom Thou hast raised up, and been pleased to
glorify; and hast set Him down at Thy right hand; by

e Lib. vii. cap. 25.   f Lib. vii. cap. 12.

Whom Thou hast promised us the resurrection of the dead; S E C T.
do Thou, O Lord Almighty, everlasting God, so gather toge- I.
ther Thy Church from the ends of the earth into Thy kingdom, as this [corn] was once scattered, and is now become
one loaf. We also, our Father, thank Thee for the precious
Blood of Jesus Christ, which was shed for us, and for His
precious Body, whereof we celebrate this representation," (I
should rather have translated it 'the antitypes whereof we
are now going to celebrate;' Greek, οὗ καὶ ἀντίτυπα ταῦτα
ἐπιτελοῦμεν,) "as Himself appointed us, *to shew forth His
death*[g]." This is so far from a prayer of consecration, that it
does not so much as come up to the character of a grace
before meat; for there is no blessing craved, either on the
Bread and Wine, or on the communicants, but was proper
enough to be used by the Bishops and Priests before the
holy action. And I apprehend further, that the prayer in
the 26th chapter was to be used by the same persons, ἐπὶ τῇ
θείᾳ μεταλήψει, 'at' or 'upon' the communion or distribution,
that is, when the consecration was ended, while the deacon
was bidding prayer to the people[h], just before the administration of the symbols; for it seems contrary to the mind of
the constitution that it should be said after the receiving;
because at the end of that chapter it is said, " If any be holy
let him approach; if any one be not, let him become so by
repentance;" which supposes the distribution not yet begun:
and whereas the chapter begins with these words, Μετὰ τὴν
μετάληψιν οὕτως εὐχαριστήσατε, it must be said, that this
prayer was to be used after the clergy had received, and while
the people were drawing toward the Altar.

But there are in this Liturgy, and in the Constitutions, of
which it is now a part, further evidences of a material oblation; for it calls[i] "the unbloody Sacrifice the mystery of the
New Testament;" and the mystery of the New Testament is
certainly the Body and Blood of Christ, represented in Bread
and Wine. It orders the Sacrifice to be put "into the hands
of the Bishop," that is now in being ordained: and orders
the Bishop[k] "to give the oblation," that is, the Bread, "to

---

g [Primitive Christianity Revived,   i a. p. 52. Ap.
vol. iii.]   k d. p. 54. Ap. l. 14.
h Lib. viii. c. 13, &c.

the people;" and in a word, all that was produced from the
Constitutions under the former head, when I was proving
that the unbloody, rational, and spiritual Sacrifice was Bread
and Wine, is as apposite to my present purpose, as it was to
the former.

Now I am competently well assured, that it will be very
difficult for our adversaries to prove that any one of the
authorities here produced can otherwise be understood than
of the Eucharist strictly so called; and that they do every
one of them express, or necessarily suppose, the Sacrifice to
be material. I have not always used any words of my own
to point out to my reader the force of the proof, because I
have that good opinion of the authorities alleged, that if they
be not obscured by the printer or myself, they will make
their way into my reader's understanding.

Evasions of
our adver-
saries.
And now one would think that the materiality of the
Sacrifice were pretty well cleared, so far as the practice and
judgment of the primitive Church is capable of giving light
to any dispute in divinity; but my reader is to remember
that we have adversaries whose skill chiefly consists in
securing their retreat; and though they always make their
first onset by affirming and endeavouring to prove, in their
way, that the primitive Sacrifice was only an oblation of
prayer and praise; yet when they find they cannot maintain
this ground, their next refuge is this, that though the Eucharistical symbols be often called a Sacrifice and oblation, yet
this was only on account of their being a Sacrament; for
that representatives are often called by the name of their
principals; and that therefore the Eucharist, being the representative of the Sacrifice of Christ's Body and Blood, does
often go under the name of the Sacrifice itself. Now I
suppose it is an effectual answer to this pretence to say, and
prove, that the Eucharistical Bread and Wine were actually
presented to Almighty God by a solemn act of oblation. For
from hence it will follow, that the Bread and Wine, or, which
is the same thing, the Sacramental Body and Blood, were by
the ancients esteemed, not only the representation of a
Sacrifice, but a real Sacrifice; and that the sacred symbols
were thus offered to God, the Liturgies are a demonstration;
in every one of which a solemn tender of the symbols is made

to God, after the words of institution have first been pro- SECT. I.
nounced over them, as has been already shewed, and as the
reader may satisfy himself, by perusing the transcripts from
these Liturgies in the Appendix. It may be pretended that
some of these Liturgies are not of such antiquity as is necessary to make them evidences in this case; but since the
most ancient is most plain and express in this particular, if
one of them can be said to be more express than the rest,
they might from thence learn that the doctrine of the Sacrifice is none of those later additional notions, which the lower
you go in consulting the monuments of the Church, the
clearer proof you have of them; for if this were the case,
the later the Liturgy, the more full would the evidence be.
And since the case is quite otherwise, and the oldest Liturgy
now extant is a most uncontestable demonstration, that in
the ages and Churches where that was used, the symbols
were in a most devout and decorous manner presented to
Almighty God; I think this of itself so very strong an argument of the doctrine for which I now plead, that I dare lay
this single authority in the scale against all the artificial
reasonings of our adversaries, which are really nothing else
but shifts and palliations, in contradiction to plain and in-
controllable matter of fact. But this evidence will appear
more weighty still, if it be considered that we have not only
a form of words, and a description of the matter, how this
Sacrifice was offered, but we have the main body of the most
ancient valuable writers, giving their suffrage for us; for I
shall shew my reader, that the Fathers did not only assert
that the Sacrament was a Sacrifice, but that it was actually
offered to God.

Now Theodoret declares[1] that the Church "offers to God Evidence
the symbols," and[m] that the Lamb of God is "sacrificed," and[n] for the proof, an
that the mystical symbols "are offered" to God by the Priests. actual obla-
Cyril of Alexandria says[o], that holy offices are celebrated tion of the Bread and
with "sanctified hands, and incense is offered, and a pure Wine.
Sacrifice;" and says of heretics, that[p] they "sacrifice the
Lamb without doors." St. Chrysostom[q] speaks of prayer

[1] d. p. 45. Ap.
[m] dd. p. 45. Ap.
[n] l. p. 45. Ap.

[o] a. p. 43. Ap. l. 7.
[p] b. p. 43. Ap.
[q] f. p. 38. Ap.

CHAP.
II.

being " offered with Sacrifice," and[r] that Christ commanded Himself to be " offered." St. Austin[s], that " instead of all those (Levitical) sacrifices, Christ's Body is offered, and communicated to the receivers ;" that[t] what Melchisedec brought forth, " is every where offered ;" that[u] " in the Eucharistical symbols, the Church offers herself :" and that[x] in our memorial there is " an oblation," as well as participation " of Christ's Body." Gaudentius[y] mentions " the wine offered for a figure of His passion ;" and says[z], that " Christ commanded the Sacrament to be offered." St. Jerome brings in Christ saying[a], " ye [Priests] offer My loaves ;" and says, that[b] the Christian priesthood consists in " offering Bread and Wine, that is, Christ's Body and Blood ;" and[c] that the Bishop of Rome " offered a Sacrifice" over the bones of Peter and Paul ; and approves Jovinian's saying[d], viz. " Christ offered wine for a type of His Blood." St. Ambrose says[e], " If you offer on the Altars the Body to be transfigured ;" and again[f], " Christ offers by us, whose word sanctifies the Sacrifice which is offered." And at another place[g] he speaks of his own " presenting a Sacrifice ;" and says, that " Christ is offered." Macarius mentions[h] " Bread and Wine offered in the Church as antitypes of Christ's Body and Blood." Ephræm Syrus, speaking of the Eucharist, says[i], " when the tremendous mysteries are offered." St. Basil declares[k] his abhorrence of " offering the Body of Christ, while under defilement." St. Gregory Nazianzen speaks[l] " of his own offering the external Sacrifice, the antitypes of the great mysteries." Hilary the Deacon supposes[m], " the Priest offers the Sacrifice, as acting instead of our Lord." Cyril of Jerusalem[n] says, " we offer Christ slain for our sins." St. Athanasius[o], that " Melchisedec was the first type of offering the unbloody Sacrifice." Eusebius mentions[p] " making the oblation, and

[r] G. p. 42. Ap.
[s] E. p. 36. Ap. l. 9.
[t] D. p. 35. Ap.
[u] z. A. p. 34. Ap.
[x] H. p. 36. Ap.
[y] a. p. 30. Ap. l. 10.
[z] d. p. 31. Ap.
[a] n. p. 29. Ap.
[b] l. p. 29. Ap.
[c] e. p. 28. Ap.
[d] c. p. 28. Ap.

[e] n. p. 27. Ap.
[f] c. p. 26. Ap.
[g] d. p. 26. Ap.
[h] b. p. 26. Ap. l. 5.
[i] a. p. 25. Ap. l. 6.
[k] a. p. 23. Ap.
[l] a. p. 21. Ap.
[m] b. p. 20. Ap.
[n] g. p. 19. Ap.
[o] c. p. 17. Ap.
[p] a. p. 15. Ap.

giving to every one his part;" and further says[q], "We offer S E C T.
the shew-bread, and the Blood of sprinkling." St. Cyprian[r] ——I.——
declares that "the cup offered should be offered mixed with
wine." He speaks[s] of "offering wine in the Sacrifice of
God and Christ." He says[t], "neither wine nor water can
be offered alone." He shews, how the Priest in the Eucharist[u] "may offer a full and true Sacrifice;" and[x] mentions
over and again the "offering the cup of our Lord." And he
tells us[y] how Novatus was censured for "attempting to offer
sacrilegious sacrifices in opposition to the true priest." Origen says[z], "we eat loaves that are offered;" and[a] speaks of
the care Christians took in receiving the Eucharist, "lest any
crumb of the consecrated oblation should fall to the ground."
Tertullian[b] reflects on the priests of Mithra, for imitating the
divine Sacraments in the "offering" of bread. Irenæus,
speaking[c] of the new oblation of the New Testament, adds,
"which the Church offers to God throughout the world;"
and further says[d], "we offer to Him . . . as sanctifying the
creatures." St. Justin Martyr affirms[e], that Christ hath by
tradition instructed us to "offer" bread, &c., and speaks of
bread and wine as "offered" by Gentiles converted to Christianity, according to the prediction of Malachi.

The Constitutions are as forward evidence as the Fathers:
for in telling us what is the business of the Lord's day, they
reckon[f] "the offering" of the Sacrifice, and distribution of
the holy gift; and[g] the Bishops and Priests are ordered "to
offer" the Sacrifice which the Lord commanded, saying, "Do
this," &c. There is a complaint[h], that Eucharists "have
been offered" by such as ought not to have done it. And
there is a charge given[i] to "offer" the antitype of the royal
Body, as an acceptable Eucharist.

As to synods, that of Constantinople before cited, speaks[k]
of them who "offered" the image of Christ; and a little after[l]

[q] k. p. 17. Ap.
[r] m. p. 12—14.
[s] m. 6.
[t] m. 6.
[u] m. 9.
[x] m. 11, 12.
[y] n. p. 15. Ap.
[z] a. p. 9. Ap.
[a] aa. p. 10. Ap.
[b] r. p. 9. Ap.

[c] c. p. 4. Ap. l. 22.
[d] f. p. 5, 6. Ap. l. 32.
[e] b. d. p. 3. Ap.
[f] b. p. 47. Ap.
[g] bb. p. 47. Ap.
[h] e. p. 47. Ap.
[i] d. p. 47. Ap.
[k] p. 51. Ap. l. 3, 4.
[l] l. 21, 22.

CHAP. it is said, Christ commanded His image to be "offered." And
II.
further it makes mention[m] of the Body that is consecrated by
the Priest "who makes the oblation." The third, alias sixth
council of Carthage[n] orders, in the twenty-fourth canon,
that nothing "be offered" in the Sacraments of Christ's Body
and Blood, but Bread and Wine. The council of Laodicea[o],
canon nineteen, directs how and when the holy Sacrifice
shall be celebrated, or consummated. The synod of Nice[p],
in the eighteenth canon, affirms that deacons have not power
to "offer," that is, to offer the Sacramental Body of Christ,
which they are for that reason forbid to administer to the
Priests, who "could offer it." And the second and third apostolical canons[q] forbid the Priest to "offer" any thing but
Bread and Wine, as the synod of Carthage before mentioned
also did.

And now I must have leave to say, that I have good reason
to question whether any particular doctrine of Christianity
have a better foundation in the records of primitive Christianity than the material Sacrifice of the Eucharist, and the
solemn actual oblation of it in the Christian Church. And
these authorities are the more considerable and weighty, because there are not any abating or qualifying words. They
all call the Eucharist a Sacrifice; and intimate, if they do not
expressly assert, it to be a material Sacrifice of Bread and
Wine, or of the Body and Blood of Christ, or of the Sacrament;
by which it will hereafter appear that their meaning was the
same; and they declare that this Sacrifice was truly offered,
according to the rites of our most holy religion. But what
have our adversaries to say in answer to all these authorities
from the Fathers and canons of the first four centuries?
Why truly, the sum and substance of what they have to offer
is this, that St. Chrysostom, at the latter end of these four
centuries, or the beginning of the fifth, in his comments on
the Epistle to the Hebrews, has these words[r]; "Do this, says
Christ, in remembrance of Me, or, Offer this as My memorial.
We do not offer another sacrifice, as the [Jewish] high-
priest did, but always the same, or rather we perform a

---

[m] l. 31, 32.   [p] p. 50. Ap.
[n] p. 51. Ap.   [q] p. 48. Ap.
[o] p. 50. Ap.   [r] P. p. 43. Ap.

memorial." Now suppose St. Chrysostom did by these
words intend to detract from the proper sacrificial nature of
the Eucharist, yet we are to consider that four hundred years'
possession will be a better argument for the right the Eucharist has to this name, than the saying of one single Father
can be against it. And indeed the authority of one Father
of the fourth century is of very little weight, when what he
says is against the general stream of antiquity; but in reality,
what this Father says is what, I suppose, all the present
assertors of the Sacrifice do willingly subscribe to, nay, it is
this very opinion of St. Chrysostom which we contend for.
We do not think we offer another Sacrifice, but only continue
and perpetuate that which Christ offered; yet neither are we
so stupid as to believe that the Sacrifice we offer is substantially the same with that offered by Him. We pretend not
that His own natural Body is, or can be, sacrificed again, but
only His Sacramental; and therefore we allow that it is
commemorative: but we cannot see the consequence which
our adversaries would draw from thence, viz. that it is not a
real and proper Sacrifice. Prefigurative and commemorative
Sacrifices do both agree in this, namely, that they are representations. Now we believe, with all sound divines, that all
the sacrifices of the ancients, before and under the law, were
prefigurative of that Sacrifice which Jesus Christ offered in
His own person, and that they were therefore representative,
as well as that of the Eucharist; nor can we discern why
commemoration should extinguish the nature of a Sacrifice
any more than prefiguration. I add, further, that St. Chrysostom here calls the Eucharist, as our Saviour also does,
'Ανάμνησις, "the memorial;" now we know the critical meaning of this word, when applied to sacrificing, as it is here by
St. Chrysostom, is that portion of the oblation which, being
in a particular manner offered to God, did bring the whole
oblation in remembrance before Him[s]; and that, therefore,
this Father's meaning might probably be, that by offering
the Eucharist we do the same thing in effect that Jewish
priests did in offering their memorials; we apply the grand
Sacrifice, and render it operative and effectual to the purposes
for which it was intended; and if these words, when spoken

[s] See Levit. ii. 2. 9. 16; and Propitiatory Oblation, p. 18. 35.

CHAP.
II.
by St. Chrysostom, do not at all impair the sacrificial nature
of the Eucharist; much less can those of Eulogius, who wrote
at the latter end of the sixth century, or of Theophylact in
the eleventh century, (whose comments are little more than
transcripts from St. Chrysostom's,) do any prejudice to our
cause.

That the
Fathers
suppose
that Christ
offered
Himself in
the Eucha-
rist, yet do
not mention
two obla-
tions made
by Him.
However, from this passage it is evident that St. Chrysostom thought the frequent repetition of the Eucharist in the
Christian Church, was at first sight a seeming objection
against the one only oblation of Christ; but it is further to
be considered, that the ancients believed that Jesus Christ
offered Himself in the Eucharist, and it may at first sight
seem strange, that neither St. Chrysostom, nor any other of
the ancients, according to the best of my information, did
ever make it an objection against Christ's offering Himself
in the Eucharist, that according to this hypothesis, Christ
was twice offered by Himself, first in the institution of the
Sacrament, and then upon the cross. All that believe the
Eucharist to be a Sacrifice must, of consequence, believe that
Christ did in the institution in some sense offer His Body and
Blood; and if He did this again upon the cross, then it seems
that He offered Himself twice, which looks like a mighty
objection in the eyes of some modern writers; but it is such
an objection as the ancients seem to have been wholly insensible of. I shall now make it my business to prove that
the Fathers were fully aware that the Eucharist must have
been offered by Christ, or else that it ought not to be offered
by us; and by the account which they give of Christ's
offering Himself in the institution of the Eucharist, it will
plainly appear that this seeming objection was to them none
at all, because they believed that in the Eucharist He
executed His Melchisedecian priesthood, that there He
began the one only oblation of His Body and Blood, which
He finished on the cross. For it is to be observed[t], that the
Fathers from St. Cyprian downward, are scarce more unanimous in expounding any one text of Scripture, than that of
Gen. xiv. 18. "Melchisedec's bringing forth bread and wine," by which

[t] A notable adversary of the Sacrifice
in the Eucharist reckons this discourse
concerning Melchisedec my first argument or proof that Christ made the oblation at the institution of the Eucharist,
whereas I really begin my proofs above
twenty pages below this. [Not in First
Ed.]

they understood that he offered up those creatures to God before he gave them to Abraham; and that by offering them up, or giving them to God the Father, he prefigured the evangelical oblation, and conferred the blessing on Abraham, which afterwards he explained in words. From this meaning of the text they naturally concluded that one great part of our Saviour's Melchisedecian priesthood consisted in offering Bread and Wine; and that in offering them He did mysteriously, spiritually, and intentionally beforehand offer His own Body and Blood, and gave commandment to His Apostles and their successors for ever after to do the same.

That Melchisedec offered bread and wine.

I suppose there is no occasion for me particularly to prove that the Fathers believed that Melchisedec offered bread and wine, and that in so doing he was a type of Christ, by producing the several passages wherein they express these sentiments. Many citations from them have already been brought under the foregoing heads, which plainly speak their thoughts in this matter, and many more will hereafter occur, and a greater number might have been added, if it had been my design industriously to prove it; but my reader will think it more necessary and seasonable to say something in this place whereby to shew the grounds which the Fathers had for this opinion, than to labour in the proof of that, which is, I suppose, confessed by all that have in any measure looked into their writings. Now to shew that the ancients did not without reason suppose that Melchisedec offered bread and wine, let it be considered,

1. That Melchisedec was a priest, and superior to the patriarch Abraham, who was a priest also; and I suppose it needs no proof that he was a sacrificer, for this is imported in his being a priest; and we are expressly told by the author of the Epistle to the Hebrews, when he is speaking of this matter, that "every high-priest is ordained of God to chap.viii. 3. offer gifts and sacrifices." And it could not have been said that our Saviour was a Priest according to the order of Melchisedec, if the one had been a sacrificing priest, but not the other. As sure, therefore, as our Saviour offered Sacrifice, so sure is it that Melchisedec did so too.

2. It is very unreasonable to suppose that when Melchisedec had the very greatest occasion to execute all the most

principal parts of his priestly office, I mean upon his meeting and solemnly blessing Abraham, he should omit sacrifice, which was always thought, as the most essential, so the most honorary and eximious of the sacerdotal powers. And I suppose it will appear to any one that examines the matter thoroughly, that the most solemn benedictions, such as this of Melchisedec to Abraham, were not passed without previous sacrifices. After this, Abraham received from heaven two most gracious intimations of God's favour to him, or Divine benedictions; the one, after offering the heifer, the he-goat, and the ram; and the other, after his offering the ram in the stead of Isaac. And we read that Aaron, upon making his first sacrifices in behalf of himself and the children of Israel, "when he came down from offering, blessed the people." He seems to have done this by the particular direction of Moses, who was now with him to instruct him in the whole series of his sacrificial office; and what he did now was undoubtedly to be a pattern to him for the future; and what is more agreeable in the nature of things, than that the most solemn services and homages to God, such as sacrifice was always esteemed, should be an introduction to those assurances which God is pleased to give to men of His especial favour toward them? And it is probable that the ancients had much greater evidence of this truth, namely, that sacrifice was a constant and necessary preparation for the receiving the Divine blessing, than we in these ages, so remote from the institution and the practice of the old method of offering sacrifice and imparting benedictions, can in justice pretend to.

Gen. xv. ... benedictions; the one, after offering the heifer, the he-goat, and
Gen. xxii. ... the ram; and the other, after his offering the ram in the stead
Lev. ix. 22. ... "when he came down from offering, blessed the people."

3. If Melchisedec did offer sacrifice upon this great occasion, when it can scarce be supposed that he should omit it, then we have no cause to look any further for the materials which he offered, than to the brief history of Melchisedec in the fourteenth chapter of Genesis, where "bread and wine" are expressly said to have "been brought forth" by him. And indeed there was no occasion for Melchisedec to bring forth bread and wine for any other purpose than to make an oblation of thanksgiving for the victory, and in order to pronounce, or rather to administer the benediction to Abraham, with the proper preceding celebrity. Abraham and his retinue were sufficiently furnished with victuals in the booty

which they had retaken from their enemies, as we are assured ver. 11, 16, and we are informed, ver. 24, that they had
actually "eaten" of these provisions.

4. If I am thought by some men to be mistaken in my
reasonings upon this subject, it is very much to my satisfaction that I have so many and so great men under the same
condemnation with me; and perhaps I may meet with some
readers, who might have liked my notions and arguments if
they had been perfectly new and unheard of, but will be out
of conceit with them, merely because the notions are stale
with age, and the arguments not altogether new. However
I am much more concerned to maintain the integrity of the
Fathers, than the closeness of their arguings, or the niceness
of their critique; and if they did err in this point, it is evident that this error of theirs did not proceed from partiality
to their own cause, or from an indulgence to their own fancies; for even Philo, the Alexandrian Jew, and who lived and
died in infidelity, does expressly say of Melchisedec, "he
sacrificed victims," or "offered triumphal sacrifices[u]." And
since this latter could serve no cause by this opinion of his,
I may infer thus much at least from his saying so, that an
impartial inquirer may, by considering circumstances, fairly
argue himself into this persuasion; and I can safely say that
this is my own case, and for that reason I am disposed to
judge favourably of the ancients, as having, I believe, rea-
soned themselves into this opinion by such arguments as are
just before represented. And that it was upon these grounds
that the ancients believed that Melchisedec sacrificed the
bread and wine, I will mention three as great witnesses as
the ancient Church since the apostolic age did ever produce.
The first is Cyril of Alexandria; "Melchisedec," says he[x],
"receives the symbol of that priesthood which is above the
law, in order to bless Abraham, when he exhibited to him
bread and wine; for we are blessed no otherwise by Christ."
With whom accords Eusebius in these words[y], "Melchisedec

---

[u] Josephus indeed takes no notice
of the offering up the bread; but he
was junior to Philo. ["ὃν θεασάμενος
ὁ μέγας ἀρχιερεὺς τοῦ μεγίστου Θεοῦ
ἐπανίοντα—τὰς χεῖρας ἀνατείνας εἰς
οὐρανὸν, εὐχαῖς αὐτὸν γεραίρει, καὶ τὰ
ἐπινίκια ἔθυε, καὶ πάντας τοὺς συναραμέ-

νους τῷ ἀγῶνι λαμπρῶς εἰστία, γεγηθὼς
καὶ συνηδόμενος ὡς ἐπ᾽ οἰκείῳ κατορθώ-
ματι."—Philo Judæus, De Abrahamo,
vol. ii. p. 34. ed. Mangey. 1742.]

[x] a. p. 43. Ap.
[y] h. p. 16. Ap. l. 4.

CHAP.
II.
never appears to have used corporeal sacrifices, but blessed Abraham in, or by bread and wine." Nor is St. Cyprian less express when he says[z], "that therefore the blessing of Abraham by Melchisedec the priest might be rightly celebrated, the sacrifice of bread and wine goes before it." They all suppose that Melchisedec acted as priest, in relation to his bringing forth or offering the bread and wine, and that this oblation was a preparative to the benediction. Nor is the reader to wonder, that there is no express mention of Melchisedec's offering the bread and wine in Gen. xiv.; for all that are in any measure versed in the style of the Old Testament cannot be ignorant, that it abounds with ellipses, and often omits not only single words, but whole sentences; and there was the less occasion for Moses here precisely to express the oblation made by Melchisedec, because it was the known universal practice of the ancients to introduce their solemn feasts with sacrifices, or first to offer to God what they afterwards intended to be eaten and drunk as a festival banquet; and this is especially true, as to such feasts, where a priest presided at the entertainment, as Melchisedec did here. The learned Cudworth hath at large proved "that it was the custom of the Jews and heathens to feast upon things sacrificed[a]." [And Philo, in the place just now cited, expressly says, Melchisedec feasted all that assisted in the fight.]

St. Paul's silence of Melchisedec's sacrifice considered.
But I must acknowledge that there is one objection which deserves to be considered, and it is this, viz. that the Apostle in drawing a minute parallel betwixt Christ and Melchisedec, in the fifth, sixth, seventh, and eighth chapters of the Epistle to the Hebrews, takes no notice of the latter's offering bread and wine. To this it may be answered, that,

1. This argument proves too much; for if the Apostle's omission of Melchisedec's offering bread and wine be an argument, that he did not therefore offer them; it may as well from thence be proved, that his bringing forth bread and wine was not a type of the Eucharist at all, even though it be considered barely as a religious feast. Now I suppose no man, who believes Melchisedec to have been the most perfect type of Christ Jesus, can doubt but that Melchisedec,

[z] m. 4. p. 13. Ap.
[a] See Cudworth's Notion of the Lord's Supper, p. 2, &c.

in bringing forth the bread and wine, did typify the Christian Eucharist, though he should allow that he had no other design in view, but the entertainment of Abraham and his attendants. It is observable, that Clemens Alexandrinus, and Epiphanius, though they do no where, so far as I have observed, assert that Melchisedec offered these materials, yet do expressly assert that his bread and wine were types of the Christian mysteries: nay, this seeming argument proves too much upon another account, I mean, because it would prove that our Saviour never performed any act of the Melchisedecian priesthood; for if the Apostle's silence concerning the oblation of bread and wine be of sufficient validity to prove that none was offered; then his omission of the particular priestly action or actions, wherein Christ was prefigured by Melchisedec, will as effectually prove that Christ did, in no action performed by Him, execute the function of a priest according to that order. The Apostle, in his parallel between Christ and Melchisedec, expressly mentions his not coming to his priesthood by descent, his taking tithes of Heb. vii. 3. Abraham, the perpetuity of their priesthood. He mentions ver. 5, 6. ver. 12—16. also his being king of righteousness, and king of peace, and 23, 24. his blessing Abraham, but even these last particulars he does ver. 2. ver. 6, 7. not, in express words, apply to our blessed Saviour; and I apprehend very few of our adversaries will be disposed to think that Melchisedec typified our Saviour in all those instances here alleged by the Apostle, particularly in receiving tithes; and it must be owned, we have a very hard task if we argue with men, who will neither allow that all that is mentioned by the Apostle could be a parallel, or that any thing that is not mentioned was so. They take to themselves the privilege of arguing from the Apostle's silence, but will not permit others to argue from his words. If Christ then performed any function of the Melchisedecian priesthood here mentioned by the Apostle, it was either blessing the people, or receiving tithes, or both. St. Paul does not here say, that Christ did either the one or the other, and yet no man will from hence infer that Christ did neither of these; and on the other side very few will allow that Christ did both; and therefore we ought not to depend upon so weak and negative a proof as the Apostle's silence, nor to infer that what the

Apostle mentions of Melchisedec, is to be the standard of the parallel; except we will receive the parallel in all the particulars expressed by St. Paul, and not in some only. The Apostle does indeed directly apply Melchisedec's coming to the priesthood without any descent, or entail, to Christ Jesus, and so he does the perpetuity of it; but these are not parts or actions of the priestly office, but only circumstantial qualities of the priesthood itself. The only action in which the generality among us will be willing to acknowledge that Melchisedec represented Christ, is that of his blessing Abraham; which yet, as has been observed, St. Paul does not by any direct words apply to Him; and, therefore, we ought not to lay any stress upon an argument drawn from St. Paul's omission in one case, any more than in the other; so that the question truly stated is this, viz. why did the Apostle in this parallel omit Melchisedec's bringing forth the prefiguration of the Christian Eucharist? And to this

2. St. Jerome answers[b], "There was much to be said, and hard to be uttered; not that the Apostle could not have explained it, but because it was not seasonable at that time, for he was discoursing with the Hebrews, who were not yet confirmed in the faith, to whom he must have discovered the Sacraments," meaning undoubtedly the Eucharist. The Father supposes, that St. Paul did not think it proper to discourse of the Sacrament familiarly to people who were not yet fully settled in Christianity, which he apprehended to be the case of many of those to whom this Epistle was to be communicated. How far we may rely on this single judgment of St. Jerome, I presume not to determine; but I cannot but observe, that St. Paul does never in any of his Epistles, make any plain mention of the Sacrament, except in the first to the Corinthians; and perhaps the reason why he did it not was, that his Epistles were to be read in the public assembly, where there might be many present that were not thought fit hearers of that mystery; and if it be asked, why then did he speak of it so freely in the first Epistle to the Corinthians? I can but guess at the occasion, and it might be this; that the innovators there had permitted all the loose retainers to the Christian Church to approach the Lord's

[b] i. p. 28. Ap.

Table, without being instructed in the nature of the Eucha- S E C T.
rist. If this had not been the case, it is scarce accountable I.
how some that received the Eucharist in that Church should
"not discern the Lord's Body," or know what it was that they
received; and when by this means these loose retainers to
the Church knew what that outward solemnity of the Eucharist was, St. Paul could no longer consider it as a secret;
and, therefore, instead of that silence, or those short hints
concerning that ordinance, which are so remarkable in all
his other writings, he here endeavours at large to rectify
their notions and practice in this matter; and if the weakness
of understanding and judgment in relation to Christianity
were any reason why St. Paul should forbear to speak of the
Eucharist in words at length, then certainly the Hebrews,
to whom he now wrote (at least a considerable part of them),
were as indifferently qualified as any men to have a discovery
of these mysteries communicated to them in public; for the
Apostle in this very Epistle gives a sad account of their igno- chap. v. 12,
rance and dulness. It is true the Apostle complains of the 13.
Corinthians too, for being " babes, and not yet able to bear 1 Cor. iii.
strong meat;" but, as has been intimated, it was not in the 1, 2.
Apostle's power to conceal the outward part of the mystery
from them, who by the countenance of their new teachers
had been emboldened to break in upon the celebration of the
Eucharist without being duly qualified; and therefore the
only way that he had left to him to prevent their contempt and abuse of it, was to let them into the fuller knowledge of it: but it does not appear that he had any such
motive to do this to the Hebrews, or to any of the other
people to whom he wrote his Epistles. It may seem a
wonder to some, that St. Paul, after he had so severely
animadverted upon the defect of spiritual understanding in
the Hebrews, should yet speak to them so largely and particularly of the Melchisedecian priesthood, and other things
of like nature in the sequel of this Epistle; but they who
know that the allegorical way of interpreting Scripture did
now exceedingly prevail among the Jews, (as will appear
from the writings of Philo, who was contemporary with the
Apostles,) will be satisfied that this method of discourse could
not be looked upon as strong meat by those, that had had

JOHNSON. K

their education in the synagogue. This was what they really sucked in with their mothers' milk, and therefore in this St. Paul accommodates himself to their apprehensions and way of thinking; but if they had been told, that the bread and wine mentioned in the history of Melchisedec were a prefiguration of a new Sacrifice, to which all the bloody and other oblations of the law were to give way, this had indeed been meat so strong, as that they were not able to bear or digest. Thus much I have said in vindication of this learned Father's opinion, which I entirely submit to the judgment of my readers, for the question is too nice for me positively to determine.

3. I desire it may be considered, that when the types of the Old Testament are alleged in the New, the most principal and obvious correspondence of the one with the other is oftentimes omitted. I will instance in three, which seem to be some of the most remarkable types. 1. The first is the temple of Jerusalem, to which our Saviour expressly alludes, Joh. ii. 19. when He says, "Destroy this temple, and I will raise it up in three days." No one can doubt but our Saviour in these words affirms the temple to be a type of His Body, yet He omits to mention the main thing in which they agreed, that is, the inhabitation of the Deity, which was that which made our Saviour's Body a temple. 2. The second most remarkable type in the history of the Old Testament, expressly Num. xxi. 9. alleged in the New, is the brazen serpent, "which Moses made and put upon a pole;" this is likewise by our Saviour Joh. iii. 14. expressly applied to Himself, in these words, "as Moses lifted up the serpent in the wilderness, even so must the Son of man be lifted up." But our Saviour takes no notice of that which I suppose all will allow to be the most apt point of correspondence, viz. that as the sight of the brazen serpent was a cure to them that had been poisoned by the bite of the fiery serpents, so faith in Christ is a certain antidote against sin, and all the works of the old crooked serpent, which He came to destroy. 3. Again, St. Paul runs a parallel betwixt Sarah and Isaac, and the Christian Church and people, on one part; and Agar and Ishmael, and the Jewish synagogue and people, on the other part; but he omits that which was as clear a coincidence as any that he mentions; I mean, that

Ishmael was circumcised, and yet was cast out, and not permitted to be co-heir with Isaac; and I think, with submission, that no particular mentioned by the Apostle in this
parallel was more to his present purpose, than this of
Ishmael's being circumcised; for this whole Epistle is one
continued argument against the Judaizers, who pressed circumcision upon the Gentile converts, as a thing without
which they could not be saved; and the main inference from
his whole discourse is contained in these words : " In Christ ch. vi. 15.
Jesus neither circumcision availeth any thing, nor uncircum-
cision, but the new creature ;" and the case of Ishmael, who
was circumcised and yet disinherited, was a very irresistible
demonstration of this truth, yet passed over in silence by St.
Paul. And why may not Melchisedec's bread and wine be
a type of the Christian oblation, as well as God's symbolical
residence in the temple of Jerusalem was a type of the Deity's
more perfect residence in the Body of Christ Jesus; or as
the cure of the sting of those venomous insects in the wilderness was of that infallible remedy (the death of Christ)
against the wounds of Satan; or as the discarding of Ishmael
was of the reprobation of the circumcised unbelieving Jews;
though neither the one nor the others are expressly mentioned by our Saviour or St. Paul, when they are professedly
treating on this subject? The truth is, there are some things
so very plain and obvious, in all pertinent similitudes and
parallels, that they who best know the art of speaking,
think it a fault too much to dwell on particularities; and
it is imputed as a vice to some writers, that they do too
much *squeeze* their similitudes; and it ought not to be censured as an omission in inspired orators or writers, any more
than in others, that they often leave room to the thoughts
and reflections of the hearers or readers, to improve what
is said, and make proper applications of it, so that it be
done with modesty, discretion, and a godly fear of "wresting
the Scriptures to our own damnation." This is very evident
in the three cases before mentioned; where the omitted
correspondences are as plain, and as certain, and pertinent,
as those that are expressed in the words of our Saviour and
the Apostle; and I humbly conceive the same may be said
of the bread and wine spoken of Gen. xiv. 18. There is

no Christian, who knows that our Saviour instituted a Sacrament in those material symbols, and reads the history of Melchisedec, and knows him to be the type of the Messias, but his own sense must presently suggest to him, that he was a type of Him in bringing forth the bread and wine, as well as in other particulars; nay, I believe I may say without offence, that the bread and wine of Melchisedec are a proof of his being a type of Christ, and perhaps for that reason omitted by St. Paul; just as for the same reason the inhabitation of the Deity in the temple, and the curing the bite of the fiery serpents by the sight of the brazen, is a proof that those two are types of our blessed Saviour; and as Ishmael's being circumcised and yet turned out of doors, is an argument to prove, that he likewise was a type of the infidel part of the Jews. And therefore to retort this objection, I think we have reason to believe, that St. Paul might omit this particular at present, that if any one should afterwards call in question the justness of this parallel, he might have this matter of fact, as an argument in reserve to prove that the whole narrative is a prefiguration of the Messias. However the least that can be said is, that he must think the case so plain, and the correspondence so very visible, that even the most stupid of those to whom he wrote, if they knew any thing of the Sacrament, must discern the agreeableness without the help of a mystagogue; and therefore he rather labours to unfold the more secret and obscure resemblances between the historical and archetypal Melchisedec, than to insist upon a coincidence so plain and obvious, that he who runs may read it.

I have said thus much in order to vindicate the ancients from that misapplication of Scripture, which too many of this age are too rash in imputing to them on this occasion; and I must further observe to my unprejudiced reader, that the notion of the Sacrifice was certainly received in the Church, before the Fathers did ever, so far as appears by their writings, apply the oblation of Melchisedec to that of Christ. Justin Martyr, Tertullian, Origen, do plainly mention the Christian oblation, but take no notice, so far as I could ever observe, that it was prefigured by that of

Melchisedec[c]. This is a demonstration, that the Fathers did not take the preposterous method, that innovators usually do; I mean first to lay down the conclusion, and then hunt for arguments to support it. St. Cyprian, who called Tertullian his master, is the first that I have observed, who from these premisses did expressly infer, that Melchisedec's oblation did prefigure that of Christ.

And here it may not be amiss to consider, on what account the ancients, particularly Eusebius and Theodoret, denied that Melchisedec's sacrifice of bread and wine were corporeal and irrational; and it is, I suppose, evident, that they thought them spiritual and rational; not only because they were significant, mysterious, and predictive of the Sacrifice of the Eucharist, but because both Melchisedec and Abraham, by the eye of faith, did see and know them to be so: in a word, this sacrifice of Melchisedec was a spiritual, rational sacrifice, in the same sense that the Eucharist is so; viz. as St. Chrysostom expresses it[d], because "Our Lord has delivered nothing to us [in the Eucharist] to be perceived by the senses; but every thing to be apprehended by the understanding, in things perceptible by the senses," viz. bread and wine. And no wonder that they denied those to be corporeal sacrifices, when they believed, that the worth and value of them did not consist in the excellence of the visible materials, but in their inward, invisible, mysterious nature, which was to be discerned by the reason and spirit. We have no grounds to believe, that the generality of the Jewish priests or people did apprehend any thing in their animal sacrifices but what they saw. It is owned, that all sacrifices, instituted by God, were prefigurations of the grand Sacrifice; but they were mere bodily things to them, who looked no further, than to what they saw on the altar; but we are assured that "Abraham rejoiced to see the day of Christ, and did see it," and that therefore the bread and wine was to him a rational, spiritual sacrifice; because he

---

[c] "Nay, Tertullian affirms both the premisses, not only that the Eucharist was a Sacrifice, but that Melchisedec did offer sacrifice*, without drawing the inference, viz. that in this he typified the Messias." First Ed.

[d] t. p. 40. Ap. l. 6.

* Advers. Judæos, lib. i. cap. 2. ["Unde Melchisedec sacerdos Dei Summi nuncupatus, si non ante Leviticæ legis sacerdotium Levitæ fuerunt, qui sacrificia Deo offerabant ?" p. 184. Ed. Paris, 1664.]

CHAP.
II.

Heb. vii. 7.

That our
Saviour
sacrificed
in the
Eucharist.

believed, and knew it to be presignificative of the great Sacrifice. And we have no reason to suppose, that Melchisedec was less apprehensive of the grand Mystery, than the patriarch Abraham; for we are assured, that of the two Melchisedec was the better, or greater. Therefore Eusebius, having said[e] that Melchisedec "offered no corporeal sacrifice, but bread and wine," explains himself by adding, "that he foresaw the Mysteries by the Divine Spirit."

But after all, we cite the Fathers only as witnesses; and do not depend so much upon the acuteness of their arguings, and the politeness or aptness of their phraseology or diction, as upon the unanimity of their testimony, and the certain fixed meaning or intendment of the words, which they used to denote a material sacrifice. Granting that they were mistaken, which yet does not appear, in believing that Melchisedec offered bread and wine; it does not therefore follow, that they were or could be mistaken, in saying that they themselves, or the Church in their time, did offer those elements. And when they say that Melchisedec, in offering bread and wine, was a type of Christ Jesus; though we do suppose, with many of the moderns, that they were too hasty in seeing a type where none was meant; yet thus much we may infallibly conclude, that they who said this must believe that our Saviour offered Bread and Wine. Nor will it follow, that because they were mistaken in their reasonings, or their forwardness in receiving the traditions of the Jews in relation to a fact that was done so many ages past, that they therefore were deceived in a matter so (comparatively) late, as that of our Saviour's institution of the Eucharist; or that they did not rightly understand those words which our Saviour used on that occasion, nor the practice of the Church, from the times of the Apostles down to the ages in which they lived and wrote. And what I am chiefly concerned to prove is, that they who believed that Melchisedec offered bread and wine, and that in so doing he was a type of Christ, must believe, that Christ also did offer those materials; nay, that they who believed that such an oblation was, and ought to be made in the Christian Church, must believe also, that Christ in the insti-

e h. p. 16. l. 4. and 9.

tution did make this oblation. For it cannot in common
sense and charity be believed, that they thought any thing
was, or ought to be, done in the Eucharist by the Church,
but what our Saviour did, when He founded it; and indeed
several of them do express their sentiments to this purpose;
and therefore all the citations already produced on the foregoing heads, do by necessary consequence prove, that our
Saviour did offer Bread and Wine, in the judgment of
the ancients; except we will suppose that they thought the
Eucharist of the Church different from that of our Lord.
But to put the point beyond dispute, I shall further lay
before my reader the express affirmations of the ancients
to this purpose; namely, that our Saviour did in the original
Eucharist, offer His Body and Blood in the symbols of Bread
and Wine.

Theodoret speaks this plainly enough, where he says[f] "He
(St. Paul) reminded them of that holy sacred night, in which
Christ put an end to the typical passover, and exhibited the
archetype thereof, and opened the doors of the salutary
mystery." For the archetype of the passover is, in the
Apostle's language, "Christ our passover sacrificed for us;"
and in saying, that He exhibited, or shewed the archetype
of the passover, he does in effect assert, that Christ the true
passover was then sacrificed by Himself; and when he affirms
this to have been done in the night, when He put an end
to the typical passover, he must mean the night before His
crucifixion, when He instituted the Eucharist; but he says
this more plainly yet in these words[g], "Christ in that night,
after which He suffered, commenced His Priesthood, when
taking Bread He blessed it, and said, Take, eat," &c.; and
presently speaks of Melchisedec's being a type of our Saviour
in offering bread and wine. "On the same table," says
St. Chrysostom[h], "there are both passovers, that of the
type, and that of the verity: as painters on the same table
first draw the lines, and then cast the shade, and after that
add to it the just colours: so did Christ; He first represented the typical passover, and then added the true one."
And I hope I need not again tell my reader, what the true
passover was. St. Austin speaks fully to my purpose in

Proofs that our Saviour offered the Sacrifice.

[f] e. p. 46. Ap.   [g] d. p. 45. Ap.   [h] k. p. 38. Ap.

CHAP.
II.
these words[i], "Those [Jewish] sacrifices, as promissive words,
are set aside; completive are given to us. What is the completive word that is given us? A Body, which you [com-
municants] know, which all of you [catechumens] do not
know: I wish all you who know It, may not know It to
your own destruction. For Christ is our Lord, Who speaks
sometimes by His members, sometimes in His own person:
'Sacrifice and oblation,' says He, 'Thou wouldest not:' what
then, are we left now without sacrifice? God forbid. 'A Body
hast Thou prepared Me.' Thou refusedst those [sacrifices]
that Thou mightest prepare this. The performing of the
promises cancelled the promissive words; for if they were
yet promissive, then what was promised is not performed;
this was promised by certain signs. Those promissive signs
are cancelled, because the promissive Verity is exhibited.
We are now in this Body, we are partakers of this Body;
may you know It, who are now ignorant of It; and when
you understand It, may you receive It, not to condemnation; for he that eateth and drinketh unworthily, eateth
and drinketh condemnation to himself. We have a Body
prepared for us, let us be perfected in that Body." It is
evident to a demonstration, that by 'Body' is meant the
Sacramental Body, in St. Austin's judgment; and that
therefore our Saviour fulfilled that prophecy, and offered
this Sacrifice in the Eucharist. St. Jerome has been already
cited for using those words of Jovinian with approbation[k],
"Christ offered wine, not water, for a type of His Blood;"
and again[l], "When our Saviour had fulfilled the typical
passover,—He takes bread, which strengthens man's heart,
and passes to the true Sacrament of the passover; that
as Melchisedec, the priest of the most high God, to prefigure Him, had offered bread and wine; so He also might
represent the verity of His own Body and Blood." But
the words of St. Gregory Nyssen are most peculiarly remarkable to this purpose[m], "Christ, Whose œconomy regu-
lates all things, according to His sovereign authority, stays
not until He was under a necessity by being betrayed, and
until the Jews had seized Him by violence, or until Pilate

i r. p. 33. Ap.   l q. p. 29. Ap.
k c. p. 28. Ap.   m b. p. 24. Ap.

had unjustly condemned Him, and so their malice had proved SECT.
I.
the principal occasion and cause of the salvation of mankind;
but by His œconomy He prevents their seizure of Him; and
by a method of Sacrifice, which was ineffable and invisible
to men, He offered Himself an oblation and victim for us;
being Himself at the same time both the Priest, and the
Lamb of God, Which takes away the sins of the world.
When was this? When He made His own Body eatable,
and His Blood potable, to those who were with Him. For
this is manifest to all, that the Lamb could not be eaten
by men, if the slaughter had not made way for the manducation of It. He therefore that gave His Body for food to
His disciples, manifestly demonstrates, that a Sacrifice was
absolutely made under the figure of the Lamb. For the
Body of the Sacrifice had not been fit for manducation, if
It had been alive; therefore when He gave His Body to His
disciples to be eaten, His Body was already sacrificed in-
effably and invisibly, according to the will and pleasure of
Him, Who had the œconomy of this mystery." Eusebius
speaks fully to our purpose in the following words[n], "Our
Saviour Jesus, the Christ of God, does even to this present
time celebrate Sacrifice among men, by His ministers, after
the manner of Melchisedec; for as he, being a Priest of the
Gentiles, nowhere appears to have used corporeal sacrifices,
but blessed Abraham in bread and wine; in the same
manner, first our Saviour and Lord, and afterwards all
Priests from Him, celebrating the spiritual Sacrifice in
Bread and Wine, do represent His Body and Blood in a
mystery." And again[o], "We with good reason daily celebrating the memorial of His Body and Blood, and being
dignified with a better Sacrifice and Hierurgy than the
ancients, judge it not safe to fall back to the weak elements,
which contain symbols and images, not the truth itself; for
saith He—'Sacrifice and offering Thou wouldest not, but a
Body hast Thou prepared Me'—and after all, He auspiciously
offered to God the miraculous Sacrifice, the eminent victim,
having delivered to us the memorial, instead of, or as a sacrifice." Dr. Hakewell[p], and others since him, have laboured

---

[n] h. p. 16. Ap.
[o] e. p. 16. Ap.
[p] [See his "Dissertation with Dr.

Heylyn, touching the Pretended Sacrifice in the Eucharist." Cap. iv. Pamph.
41. 1641. Bodl.]

CHAP. hard to wrest the last words of this citation from the
II.   assertors of the Eucharistic Sacrifice; and if they could
have done this, yet it seems to me, that the most full
evidence is left unanswered. For I apprehend, that by the
"better Hierurgy and Sacrifice," opposed to those sacrifices
of the Levitical law, he certainly means the Eucharist. For
we have, and shall see, that the Fathers often call the Sacrifice
of the sacramental Body and Blood 'the verity,' in comparison
to the types and shadows of the Levitical law; and it is very
evident, that by the 'Body prepared,' Eusebius means the
Eucharistical Body; as he does again in another place[q],
where he says, "For since He no longer desired bloody
sacrifices, nor such as were appointed by Moses, by the
slaughter of divers animals, He instructed us to use bread,
as a symbol of His Body; therefore He hath aptly represented the whiteness and purity of this food, saying, 'His
teeth are white as milk:' and of this also another prophet
hath reminded us, saying, 'Sacrifice and offering Thou
wouldest not, but a Body hast Thou prepared Me.'" In
which place, as the learned reader may see, he is expressly
speaking of the Eucharist. And it is plain enough, that
by 'the better victim,' and by 'the prepared Body,' he
means something distinct from the 'miraculous Sacrifice,
the eminent victim,' viz. Christ's natural Body. For when
he had mentioned the two former, he adds, 'after all He
offered,' &c. which implies, that the personal Flesh and
Blood of Christ were not yielded to God, until He had
first dignified us with a better Sacrifice than those of the
law, and fulfilled that prophecy, viz. 'a Body hast Thou
prepared Me;' which He must therefore be supposed to
have done in the Eucharist, according to what St. Austin
has said in the place just before recited; therefore it is
very evident, that Eusebius did not at all apprehend, that
he lessened the Sacrifice, when he called it a memory, or
memorial. For it is clear, that he supposed, that Christ
did the 'will of God,' and offered the 'prepared Body' in the
Eucharist, and that therefore by this memorial the whole
Sacrifice was to be brought in remembrance before God.
The excellent Dr. Hickes has shewed, that ἀντὶ θυσίας may

q i. p. 17. Ap.

signify either, 'instead of the great Sacrifice,' meaning that of the Cross, as we commonly speak, or that the Eucharist is 'for a Sacrifice,' as the "woman's hair is for a covering[r]." Athanasius teaches the same doctrine with little variation[s], "It is the Body [of Christ] to which [God the Father] says, 'Sit Thou on My right hand;' and to which the devil and his wicked powers, and the Jews and Gentiles, were enemies; by which Body He became the High-Priest and Apostle in the mystery which He delivered to us, saying, 'This is My Body,'" &c. He clearly asserts, that Christ was exercising the office of High-Priest, while He instituted the Eucharist; and that therefore therein He offered an oblation; and he tells us, what it was He offered, viz. His Body; he passes from Christ's natural Body to His sacramental Body, without making any express difference; which yet he does plainly enough in other places of His writings. What he would hereby teach us is, that Christ, in offering His sacramental Body, did virtually and intentionally consign His natural Body to the Altar of the Cross; which is what the other Fathers do likewise mean beyond all doubt. When he says, that "Christ by This Body became a High-Priest and Apostle in the mystery which He delivered," he alludes to the words of St. Paul, who calls Christ Jesus the High-Priest of our profession, Heb. iii. 1; but I cannot but observe, that the word turned by us 'profession,' I mean ὁμολογία, is used five times by the LXX for 'a free-will offering.' [First, Lev. xxii. 18, 19, in the Greek stands thus—Ἄνθρωπος, ἄνθρωπος, ἀπὸ τῶν υἱῶν Ἰσραὴλ, ἢ ἀπὸ τῶν προσηλύτων, τῶν προσκειμένων πρὸς αὐτοὺς ἐν Ἰσραὴλ, ὃς ἂν προσενέγκῃ τὰ δῶρα αὐτοῦ κατὰ πᾶσαν ὁμολογίαν αὐτῶν, ἢ κατὰ πᾶσαν αἵρεσιν αὐτῶν, ὅσα ἂν προσενέγκωσιν τῷ Κυρίῳ εἰς ὁλοκαυτώματα (19.) δεκτὰ

[r] ["We must observe of the preposition Ἀντι, that it signifies first pro, FOR, as pro denotes loco, vice, instead, of which I need give no examples; secondly, it signifies propter, and gratia, as gratia is used in the ablative case; of which, not to bring proofs out of lexicographers, we have one in Heb. xii. 16; Ὃς ἀντὶ βρώσεως μιᾶς ἀπέδοτο, &c. Qui propter unam escam vendidit suum jus primogeniti, Who for one morsel of meat sold his birthright. So also it signifies Matt. xx. 28, and Mark x. 45; Ἀντὶ πολλῶν, pro multis,

The Son of Man came not to be ministered unto, but to minister, and to give His Soul a Ransom for many. And thirdly, with little difference from this second signification, it denotes the end, and signifies pro, for, in that sense which the Latins also express by ut, or eo ut, as in 1 Cor. xi. 15; Ὅτι ἡ κόμη ἀντὶ περιβολαίου δίδοται αὐτῇ, quoniam capilli pro velamine ei dati sunt, for her hair is given her for a covering or veil." Christian Priesthood, vol. ii. Account of the Third Edition, p. xiv.]

[s] d. p. 17. Ap.

ὑμῖν, κ. τ. λ. " Whosoever he be of the sons of Israel, or of the proselytes who cleave to them, who offers his gifts after the manner of every vow, and after the manner of every free-will offering of theirs, whatever they offer for a burnt-offering, (19.) Let it be acceptable or well-pleasing to yourselves, &c." Here the material thing 'vowed' is by the LXX turned ὁμολογία.

[Secondly, you have this word in the same sense, Jer. xliv. 25.—ὑμεῖς, γυναῖκες, τῷ στόματι ὑμῶν ἐλαλήσατε, καὶ ταῖς χερσὶν ἐπληρώσατε λέγουσαι, ποιοῦσαι ποιήσομεν τὰς ὁμολογίας ἡμῶν ὡς ὡμολογήσαμεν, θυμιᾶν τῇ βασιλίσσῃ τοῦ οὐρανοῦ καὶ σπένδειν αὐτῇ σπονδάς· ἐμμείνασαι ἀνεμείνατε ταῖς ὁμολογίαις ὑμῶν, καὶ ποιοῦσαι ἐποιήσατε. " Ye, women, have spoken with your mouth, and fulfilled it with your hands, saying, We will surely do, or offer our vows which we have vowed, to burn incense to the queen of heaven, and to make libations to her: ye have obstinately persisted in your vows, and done or offered them." Here the 'vows,' which they made with their mouths and offered with 'their hands,' were incense and liquid libations; yet they are twice styled homologies by the LXX. The Hebrew 'neder' is used in the original of both these texts; and the verb 'nadar' is rendered by ὁμολογεῖν, which therefore imports the dedicating of some material thing to the queen of heaven; for the difference between the vow and the free-will offering was very small, and consisted in this[t], that if the animal, or other thing which was vowed, were lost, or died of itself, another must be offered in its stead, which was not necessary in case of a free-will offering; therefore by a 'vow,' they understood a thing actually dedicated to some deity; and the vowing of it was a dedication, as I have shewed, ch. ii. sect. 4.

[In the three following texts, the Hebrew 'nedaba' is turned by ὁμολογία.

[Thirdly, the third text which I shall produce, whereby to prove, that this Greek word has the signification which I have assigned to it, is Deut. xii. 17. Οὐ δυνήσῃ φαγεῖν ἐν ταῖς πόλεσίν σου τὸ ἐπιδέκατον τοῦ σίτου σου, καὶ τοῦ οἴνου σου, καὶ τοῦ ἐλαίου σου, τὰ πρωτότοκα τῶν βοῶν σου, καὶ τῶν προβάτων σου, καὶ πάσας τὰς εὐχὰς, ὅσας ἂν εὔξασθε, καὶ τὰς

t See Ainsw. on Levit. vii. 16.

ὁμολογίας ὑμῶν, καὶ τὰς ἀπαρχὰς τῶν χειρῶν ὑμων· that is,
"Thou mayest not eat within thy cities the tythe of thy
corn, or of thy wine, or of thine oil, the firstlings of thy
bullocks, or of thy sheep, nor any of thy vows, which thou
hast vowed, nor your free-will offerings, nor the first-fruits
of your hands." Here are clearly such 'homologies' as may
be eaten; and therefore, in this respect, of the same sort with
the Christian Eucharist.

[Fourthly, the next is, Ezek. xlvi. 12. Ἐὰν δὲ ποιήσῃ ὁ
ἀφηγούμενος ὁμολογίαν ὁλοκαύτωμα σωτηρίου τῷ Κυρίῳ, κ.τ.λ.
"If a prince make, or offer a free-will offering, [which is] a
whole burnt sacrifice of a peace offering to the Lord," &c.
N.B. The LXX did not read the conjunction וא, and therefore took 'nedaba' as put in apposition with 'gnola;' and
so by an 'homology,' they understood a whole burnt sacrifice.

[Fifthly, the last place where I find ὁμολογία used by the
LXX, is Amos iv. 5, καὶ ἀνέγνωσαν ἔξω νόμον, καὶ ἐπεκαλέ-
σαντο ὁμολογίας. "They read a foreign law, and called
[them] free-will offerings," by 'them' meaning the 'sacrifices'
and 'tythes' offered to idols in the former verse. The reader
may see in the larger critics, how the LXX read the Hebrew
of this place. In all five places, the Hebrew as well as Greek
intends a material oblation. Of the word 'homology,' see
more toward the end of this section[u].] And therefore I
think, in reason it ought to be so rendered in this text of
St. Paul; and I cannot but observe, that St. Clement of
Rome[x], who is observed by learned men to transcribe several
passages from the epistle to the Hebrews, has τῶν προσφορῶν
instead of ὁμολογίας. I shall hereafter have occasion to
make use of this reflection. In the mean time let us proceed to the most illustrious attestation, which St. Cyprian
gives to this doctrine of Christ's offering Himself in the
Eucharist, taken from his epistle against the Aquarians, who
offered only fair water in the chalice[y]; 1. "Some either
through ignorance or simplicity, in consecrating the Lord's
Blood, and administering It to the people, do not that which
our Lord Jesus Christ, the author and teacher of this Sacri-

---

[u] Not in First Ed.   [y] m. p. 12—14. Ap.
[x] In Epistol. ad Corinth. prima, c. 36.

fice did, and taught. 2. Now we are given to understand, that in offering the Cup, the tradition of the Lord should be observed; and that no other thing be done by us, than what our Lord first did for us; that the Cup, which is offered in commemoration of Him, be offered mixed with Wine. 4. Who is more a Priest of God, than our Lord Jesus Christ, Who offered a Sacrifice to God and offered the same that Melchisedec had offered, that is, Bread and Wine, His own Body and Blood? That therefore the blessing of Abraham in Genesis might be rightly celebrated, an image of the Sacrifice of Christ in Bread and Wine goes before it; which thing our Lord perfecting and completing, offered Bread, and the Cup mixed with Wine; and He that is fulness, perfected the verity of the image, which was formed long before. 5. But the Holy Ghost also by Solomon, making mention of the Lord's Sacrifice, the immolated Sacrifice of Bread and Wine, as also of the Altar, and of the Apostles, (he cites Prov. ix. 1—5,) speaks with a prophetic voice of mingled Wine, that is, the Cup of our Lord mixed of wine and water; that it might appear, that nothing was done in the passion of our Lord, but what had been before predicted." 6. He cites the words of institution, and adds, " From whence it appears, that the Blood of our Lord is not offered, if Wine be not in the Cup; and that our Lord's Sacrifice is not celebrated with a due consecration, unless our Sacrifice and oblation answer the Passion. 9. If in the Sacrifice that Christ offered, none but Christ is to be followed, then we are to obey, and to do what Christ did,—for if Jesus Christ, our Lord and God, be the High-Priest of God the Father, and first offered up Himself a Sacrifice to the Father, and commanded this to be done in commemoration of Him; then that priest truly acts as in his Master's stead, who imitates what Christ did; and then offers a true and full Sacrifice in the Church of God, if he begin so to offer, as he sees Christ to have offered before him. 11. But Christ offered not in the morning, but after supper: should we therefore offer the Lord's Sacrifice after supper, that so, in repeating the Lord's Sacrifice, we may offer a mixed Cup?" (the meaning is, as I apprehend, that they who fasted, thought that drinking wine in the Eucharist would break their fast, and so delayed the offering and receiving the Eucharist, until they had fasted the whole day,) "but we celebrate the resurrection of the Lord in the morning; and because in all our Sacrifices we make a commemoration of His Passion, (for the Passion of our Lord is the Sacrifice which we offer,) we ought to do nothing but what He did. As often therefore as we offer the Cup in commemoration of our Lord, let us do what we are sure He did. We are unpardonable, who have now been admonished and instructed by the Lord, to offer the Lord's Cup mixed with Wine, according as our Lord offered it, viz., unless we comply. It is therefore agreeable to conscience and [godly] fear, and the place and office of our Priesthood, in mingling and offering the Lord's Cup, to observe the tradition of our Lord." Thus does this holy Father ingeminate his opinion, or rather speak the familiar language of Christians in that age, concerning Christ's offering His Body and Blood under the symbols of Bread and Wine. And it is observable, that he lays so great a stress on the oblation there made, that he gives the name of 'the Passion' to the Eucharist; I mean, he principally intends the Eucharist by this title, though not so as to exclude the personal or bloody oblation on the cross; for having mentioned the prefiguration of the Eucharist by Melchisedec and Solomon, he presently adds, "That nothing was done in the Passion of our Lord, but what had been predicted." Now the predictions mentioned by him relate directly to the Eucharist only, and to our Saviour's Body being crucified, and the Blood and Water that flowed out of His side, more remotely, and without any express mention of them. He does in another place of this epistle expressly hint, that he takes our Saviour's sufferings on the cross, in conjunction with His mysterious oblation of Himself in the Eucharist, into the full import and meaning of this word; for speaking[z] of some confessors, who were afraid of taking the Eucharist in Bread and Wine, lest their gaolers should by the smell of their breath discover what they had drunk; he says[a], "Our brethren begin to hang back from the Passion of Christ in the persecutions, since they learn to be ashamed of His Cross and Blood in the Sacrifices." To 'hang back from the Passion,' is undoubtedly to be indis-

[z] m. 10.   [a] m. 10.

posed to the receiving the Eucharist; and this, in St. Cyprian's
sense, implied the being ashamed of Christ's Blood and
Cross. And when he says, 'that our Sacrifice and oblation
must answer the Passion,' what he first and chiefly means
is, that the Eucharist, celebrated in the Church, must be
done with the same materials which Christ used in the first
Eucharist, which first Eucharist he therefore denotes by the
word 'Passion.' And to demonstrate that this is his meaning, the reader will observe that he had just before rehearsed
the words of institution, and that he draws this conclusion
from those words. I question not, but the holy martyr had
also a tacit regard to the Water and Blood which flowed from
our Saviour's side, in this passage as well as the former;
but the words must primarily be meant of the holy Sacrament. And thus Gaudentius uses the word, when he calls
the Eucharist[b], 'The propriety of our Lord's Passion.' And
so I understand St. Austin, when he says[c], "We must communicate in the Passion of our Lord." By this the reader
may see how strongly our adversaries argue, when they cite
the words of St. Cyprian out of this very epistle just now
cited by me, viz., "the Passion of our Lord is the Sacrifice
which we offer;" and from thence conclude that it is our
inward remembrance or calling to mind our Lord's sufferings,
which is the Sacrifice intended by St. Cyprian; whereas it
is evident beyond all reasonable doubt, that by the Passion
here he means the material Eucharist, the Bread and Wine
mixed with Water, though with a special regard to the personal sufferings of Christ, as has been before hinted. And
therefore in St. Cyprian's judgment, 'the Passion of which
we make a commemoration,' is directly, and in the first place,
the original Eucharist, celebrated personally by our Saviour,
and ultimately the bloody Passion upon the Cross; as the
reader may satisfy himself, by comparing together the several
parts of the epistle relating to this purpose.

The sum of what these Fathers teach us is, that Christ
entered upon His priestly office in the Eucharist; that there
He began the one oblation; there He offered Himself in a
spiritual mystical manner, as He afterwards did corporally
upon the Cross. He had, from before the beginning of the

[b] a. p. 30. Ap.   [c] e. p. 31. Ap.

world, decreed and resolved to die for the salvation of mankind; in the Eucharist, He actually yielded and consigned
Himself up to these sufferings; whereupon the powers of
hell were presently let loose upon Him, and raised that per-
turbation and agony in His mind, with which He was exercised in the garden; and before that was well over, He permitted Himself to be seized by the soldiers, and carried to
His trial: all this was the consequence of His offering Himself up to do and suffer the will of God; as was also all that
followed upon it, until having breathed out His soul upon
the cross, He said, "It is finished." Upon the cross, beyond
all dispute, the ransom was paid, the satisfaction made; His
natural Body and Blood were the price, which He had
agreed to deposit for the salvation of men. But these
Fathers give their judgment, that in the institution of the
Eucharist this Sacrifice was first made, in our Saviour's will
and intention; that then He made the tender of His Body
and Blood, after which the actual payment presently followed. It would be too nice, and altogether a needless disquisition to dispute, whether the voluntary resignation of
Himself to His Father, by His own free act and deed, before
He was under any appearance of necessity and compulsion,
ere He was yet under custody and confinement, (as Gregory
Nyssen[d] admirably well observes,) or His actual crucifixion,
which was consequent upon this resignation, were in themselves most meritorious. These two parts of the oblation
were but one continued solemnity; nay, we may add, that
the ascension of Christ into heaven many days after, was
but the finishing of this one oblation. The distinguishing
the oblation in the Eucharist from that on the cross, and
that afterwards performed in heaven, is really a confounding
or obscuring the whole mystery, and rendering it perplexed
and intricate. We ought no more to reckon them two or
three several oblations, than we would say an animal was
three several sacrifices, because it was first immolated, then
slain, afterwards burnt, and the blood of it ritually sprinkled.
Any one of these actions may be called an oblation; and the
animal, by having any one of these actions passed upon it,

[d] ["ὁ γὰρ πάντα κατὰ τὴν δεσποτικὴν ἐκ τῆς προδοσίας ἀνάγκην."—Tom. iii.
αὐθεντίαν οἰκονομῶν, οὐκ ἀναμένει τὴν p. 359. Ed. Paris. 1638.]

was rightly called a sacrifice; and yet the whole process was really but one and the same sacrifice.

The synod of Constantinople, before cited, seems to magnify our Saviour's oblation in the Eucharist, on the same score, that Gregory Nyssen had done so before, in the following words[e], "The Sacrificer Himself, our God, having wholly assumed our doughy nature at the time of His voluntary Passion, delivered the Sacrifice for a type and effectual memorial to His disciples." By the 'effectual memorial' meaning most probably such an one as that in the Levitical law, which was the very life and essence of the Sacrifice itself. And I apprehend that we are taught the same doctrine in the Constitutions, in those excellent words[f], "Christ, the first and only-begotten High-Priest by nature, that did not assume this honour to Himself, but being constituted by His Father, becoming man for us, and offering a spiritual Sacrifice to His God and Father, before His Passion, commanded us [the Apostles] only to offer the same." I shall leave it to my reader to determine what that Sacrifice was, which the Apostles only were to offer; for I conceive that none but Dr. Hancock or Dr. Wise will believe, that none but the Apostles only were to offer prayer and praise; nor can they themselves believe it, though they should be forced to say it. And we have already heard the twenty-fourth canon of the third, alias the sixth council of Carthage, and the second and third of the Apostolical canons, enjoining Priests and Bishops to offer nothing but what the Lord commanded, viz., Bread and Wine; and it is certain, that Christ commanded nothing to be done in the Eucharist, but what Himself had done before. And this consideration last mentioned will, by necessary consequence, prove Justin Martyr and Irenæus to have been of the same judgment; for the one asserts, that Christ, when He said, "This is My Body," taught the new oblation of the New Testament; and the other, that Christ hath by tradition instructed us to offer Bread and Wine, for a memorial of His Passion; and it is certain, Christ taught us to do nothing but what He had done before in His own person[g].

---

e p. 51. Ap. l. 4.
f f. p. 47. Ap.

g " But there is another authority, not much inferior in time to these now

There are two Latin Fathers who give their verdict to the same effect, though not in such strong words, I mean, St. Hilary of Poictiers, and St. Ambrose of Milan; the first asks[h], " How our Saviour could pray that the cup might pass from Him? Was it," says he, "possible that Christ should not suffer? Nay, but even from the foundation of the world this mystery had been published; nay, He had but just before consecrated the Blood of His own Body, to be poured out for the remission of sins." The other says[i], "The passover is the Passion of our Lord, as the blessed Apostle says, 'Christ our Passover is sacrificed for us :' therefore Christ assuming a human body, consecrated Himself to the Passion in the mystery of the passover;" the least that either of them can justly be deemed to say is, that Christ in the last Paschal solemnity, offered, devoted, and freely resigned Himself to suffer death for our sins.

Now I must have leave to say, that I have reason to believe, few truths of Christianity can more plainly or more copiously be proved from the Fathers, than those heads relating to the Christian Eucharist, which I have hitherto been confirming from their writings. We have sufficient proof of a material Sacrifice, from the canons of the most ancient synods; which yet had rarely any occasion to mention the Eucharist, except it were to regulate some innovations in the administration of It, or to deprive men of It for a time by way of censure; for canons are made in relation to the discipline of the Church and the external œconomy of it, rather than in regard to the doctrine or dogmata of religion. If any men of new light had started up in the first ages of Christianity, and asserted that the Eucharist was not a Sacrifice, but a feast upon a Sacrifice; or broached any fantastical

---

mentioned, which, I conceive, my reader will look upon as saying too much, rather than too little; it is that of Clemens Alexandrinus*, ' Christ being about to shed His Blood, or to be sacrificed, and giving Himself a ransom, left us the Blood of the New Testament.' For I suppose ' His being about to be sacrificed,'and ' giving Himself a ransom,' must refer to the same point of time; and that they both refer to the Eucharist, where He left us the Blood of the New Testament; or in other words, He gave Himself a ransom, and left us the Blood of the New Testament, while He was yet about to be sacrificed, or to shed His Blood; and therefore at, or just after, His last supper." [First Ed.]

[h] b. p. 20. Ap.
[i] f. p. 26. Ap.

* g. p. 7. Ap.

C H A P.
II.

Heretics
owned a
Sacrifice
and Altar.
opinion, subversive of the Eucharistical oblation; I question
not, but we had had councils assembled to silence and suppress them: but it is evident, that the heretics, that retained
the use and practice of the Eucharist in those ages, retained
It as a Sacrifice; and therefore the current phrase, whereby
heresy and schism were denoted in the primitive times, were,
erecting altar against altar, or *new altars,* or *making sacrifices apart,* or *out of the Church;* for no clan of men in those
times thought that they could have the appearance or shadow
of a Church, without an altar and a sacrifice: and even the
heathen, who had pried into the Christian mysteries, aped
their oblation of the sacramental Bread. And as to the
earliest Liturgies now extant, I apprehend that they clearly
set this doctrine above dispute, in the opinion of all, that
are not immoderately prejudiced.

But I expect to be told, that the authority of Fathers and
councils, and of all the diffusive bodies of Christians, expressed
in their Liturgies, put together, is not sufficient to establish
a doctrine of so great consequence; except I can prove by
the words of institution, or some incontestable evidence from
the Scriptures, that the offering of the sacramental Body
and Blood is essential to the Eucharist. To which I answer,

1. It is certain, that the great men, whose names and
words I have used in the foregoing pages, did believe, that
this Sacrifice was enjoined by Christ Himself; and though I
do not owe an implicit faith to them, yet when so many
venerable sages, to whom next after the Apostles Christianity chiefly owes its growth and settlement, do so frequently and positively affirm a thing of this nature; I think
myself in common equity and prudence obliged seriously to
examine, and impartially to consider, whether these things
are so. Further I am persuaded, that some of these Fathers
were more capable of giving us true light in this particular,
than all the most learned professors of languages and other
sciences, now in Christendom: for they had not only the
Scriptures, which we, God be praised, enjoy in common with
them; but they had, some of them at least, the knowledge
of the use and practice, if not of the Apostles, yet of those
who had personally conversed with them, and been witnesses
of the words, actions, and rites, with which they celebrated

the holy Sacrament. I will mention no more of those before
cited, than Irenæus and Justin Martyr; and I cannot but
think their evidence most unanswerably clear and unexceptionable. The first of them was the disciple of Polycarp, who
was consecrated Bishop of Smyrna by St. John; and he
says positively, that Christ instituted a new oblation, in and
by the words of institution; and that the Church received
the new oblation of the New Testament from the Apostles.
The other calls himself a disciple of the Apostles, and assures us over and again, that Christ instructed us to offer
Bread and Wine in the Eucharist; and if these great men
were inferior to the *literati* of this age in critique and philosophy, yet they were much beyond them in those qualifications, which are proper to make men able interpreters of the
New Testament; I mean, in the knowledge of those instructions, which the Apostles delivered to the Bishops and Priests,
which they constituted in the Church, and the manner and
method of celebrating the Eucharist and other religious
offices; in which particulars it must be acknowledged, we
most of all want information from the writers of the New
Testament; and we shall make our wants the greater, if we
refuse to receive that additional light, which they, who come
so near to them in time, hold out to us. We have justly re-
pudiated the oral traditions of the Church of Rome; but, I
suppose, we live in an age, when men are able to distinguish
between such traditions as are written (though not by inspired writers), and such as are unwritten, and therefore more
liable to be mistaken, or misreported. I have said thus much,
not that I think the Christian Sacrifice wants sufficient proof
from Scripture to determine any impartial inquirer; but it
fares with us in this respect, as it does with the assertors
of the doctrine of the Trinity, of the baptism of infants,
of episcopacy, and liturgies. Our proofs from Scripture,
though we believe them to be just and full, and know,
that they are such as our adversaries cannot answer; yet
when we are told, that they are not satisfactory, and the
question is simply this, whether they, or we, understand the
Scripture right; we take the same course, that our adversaries of our own communion do in the cases before mentioned; we appeal to the ancient monuments of the Church,

to those very writers, whom our adversaries themselves, who are in communion of the Church of England, think the most fair arbitrators in those controversies before mentioned; and if they do not speak as directly and expressly for the doctrine of the Sacrifice, as for any other point, for the decision of which we commonly appeal to them; if their testimonies for the Eucharistic oblation be not as many and as strong, as for any other principle or practice, which is now disputed among us; we are ready to submit, to confess ourselves in the wrong, and to yield ourselves up to all that shame and contempt which our adversaries are able to pour upon us, and which is in justice due to any men, and especially to divines, when they turn barrators: but if our authorities from the primitive Church are very numerous and very cogent; then we apprehend, that unless they can wholly confute our arguments from the Scriptures, our abundant demonstration of this doctrine from the earliest records of the Christian Church, and from such of them as are in age and authority next to the Holy Scriptures, will cast the scale on our side, in the opinion of all competent judges.

Evidence from St. Ignatius and Clemens R.
And the mention of these very early monuments of antiquity will naturally remind my reader, of St. Ignatius and St. Clement of Rome; for as to St. Barnabas and Hermas, they do never, to the best of my observation, expressly mention the celebration of the Eucharist; and therefore their silence concerning the oblation is no more an objection against the Sacrifice, than against the Sacrament itself. It is true, the former does mention an oblation to be made by Christians; and what that oblation is, we shall hereafter have occasion to consider. And he mentions an Altar[k], to which Christians are to approach, and which our adversaries will never be able to prove to be any other than that on which the Eucharist was offered. Nor can I on the other side affirm, that what he says is any full evidence for the visible external Sacrifice; but I cannot but think, that Ignatius is entirely ours. He mentions the Altar four times, as we shall hereafter more particularly observe; and that he meant a material Altar is as evident, as that he speaks of a human Bishop; for he joins

[k] [" Sicut ergo locutus est, honestius et altius accedere ad aram Illius."— Cap. 1.]

both together in declaring[1] for " one Altar, and one Bishop ;" SECT.
and in admonishing the Magnesians[m] to run together "as I.
to one house or temple of God, and to one Altar :" and he
sufficiently intimates what use they then had for an Altar in
the Christian Church, when he charges the Philadelphians[n]
to " use but one Eucharist, because there is but one Flesh of
Jesus Christ, and one Cup in the unity of His Blood, and one
Altar," &c. And he does the same again at another place, where
he says[o], that " he who is not within the Altar is deprived of
the Bread of God," for no impartial man can doubt, but that
by 'the Bread of God' he meant the Bread of the Eucharist :
that the Bread of God does perpetually in Scripture denote
some material oblation made to God, is what I shall hereafter
have a more fit opportunity to prove ; and in the interim,
taking this for granted, I think Ignatius says what is sufficient to establish the Sacrifice of the Eucharist in the judgment of all that are not pertinacious. The only exception,
that our adversaries can have against these passages in Ignatius in behalf of the Sacrifice, is this, that there is no direct
intimation of any solemn act performed in the Church,
whereby the Eucharist was presented to God as a Sacrifice
or oblation ; and our adversaries' known evasion is in this
case to say, that the Bread and Wine are called an oblation,
or the Bread of God, as representing the Body and Blood
offered for mankind. Now we should not be destitute of a
very peremptory and decisive reply to this exception, if we
could content ourselves in arguing from the concessions of
our adversaries. Dr. Hancock once at least[p], and Dr. Wise
very often, cites the words following, as the words of this
blessed martyr ; viz., " It is not lawful without the Bishop
to baptize, or to offer, or to bring" (or rather to present) " the
Sacrifice." It is true, the first of these doctors would by the
Sacrifice here understand only the lay-oblations ; but this
might easily be confuted by this one observation (to say no
more at present), viz., that the words going next before do
expressly speak of the Eucharist ; and therefore these words
must in common sense and justice be meant of the oblation

[1] g. p. 2. Ap.
[m] d. p. 2. Ap.
[n] g. p. 2. Ap.

[o] a. p. 1. Ap.
[p] Veteres Vindicati, p. 21.

in the Eucharist, strictly and properly speaking, but the
misfortune is, that these words are only in the interpolated
epistles, and so are no just evidence with us : but when this
glorious saint calls[q] the material Eucharist "the gift of God,"
as he had before called it "the Bread of God," these words
bid very fair for an actual oblation.   For thus what was cast
Luke xxi.4. into the Korban was called "the gifts of God," as being
religiously presented to Him.   But if St. Ignatius do not
support our cause in this particularity, yet it is clear he does
it in the rest ; and I persuade myself, I shall meet with very
few readers so excessively hardened against the belief of the
Sacrifice, as not to think it sufficient that he points out to
us a visible Altar with proper officers attending it, and a
material Sacrifice, the Bread of God, wherewith this Altar
is furnished ; even though they should not be convinced, that
he uses any words necessarily importing an act of oblation.
But as to myself, I cannot believe that St. Ignatius would
call the Eucharist the Bread of God, and the gift of, or to,
God, if he had not known that it was then solemnly offered
in the Church of Christ.

But to advance one step nearer yet to the Apostles, and
even to Christ Jesus Himself : St. Clement of Rome I look
upon as an eminent witness of the Sacrifice in the Eucharist.
Now he was infallibly a companion and fellow-labourer of
the Apostles ; and during their lifetime, constituted Bishop
of the Christian Church in the imperial city of Rome.   Clement of Alexandria expressly calls him an Apostle ; and the
epistle of his, to which I am now going to appeal, was once
of so great authority, that lessons were read in many Christian Churches out of those venerable remains of this Apostolical prelate ; whose words to our present purpose, take
as follows[r] ; "We ought to do all things in order, whatsoever our Lord hath commanded us to observe ; to celebrate the oblations and liturgies at the appointed times :
and He has commanded them to be done, not in a vain dis-
orderly manner, but at appointed times and seasons.   He
Himself has determined, where and by whom He would
have them celebrated, by His sovereign authority ; that so
all things, being done in a holy and well-pleasing manner,

may be acceptable to His will: they therefore, that offer their
oblations at the stated times, are acceptable and blessed;
for, following the institutes of the Lord, they transgress not:
for there are proper Liturgies delivered to the High-Priest,
and a proper place assigned for the Priests; and there are
proper ministrations incumbent on the Levites; and the
layman is under the obligation of such injunctions, as are
incumbent on laymen. Let every one of you, my brethren,
celebrate the Eucharist to God in his proper station, with
a good conscience, with gravity, not transgressing the canon
of his Liturgy. Perpetual sacrifices, vows, sacrifices for sin,
and trespass offerings, are not offered every where, my
brethren, but at Jerusalem only; and the oblation is made,
not in every place there neither, but before[s] the sanctuary,
and at the Altar." And afterwards, in the same epistle, having
shewed what care the Apostles took to continue a succession
of pastors in the Church, he adds[t], "It will be no small
crime, if we eject those from the episcopal function, who
offer the gifts in an unblameable and holy manner." And
here,

(1.) I take it for certain, that when he speaks of sacrifices,
and of the time and place of offering them, and of the persons
who are the proper ministers of them; he is not so to be
understood, as if he was speaking to Jews, concerning the
Levitical priesthood, and of the sacrifices to be offered by
the law. For he was writing to Christians, who lived many
hundred miles from Jerusalem, and of whom a very great
part, I may say the majority, were Gentiles by birth and
education, and never were under any obligation to the ritual
laws of Moses. And it cannot be supposed, that St. Clement
was persuading the Gentile converts to judaize, in opposition
to the doctrine of St. Paul, to whose name in these epistles
he pays so singular a deference.

(2.) And yet it is evident to a demonstration, that he
speaks to these Christians of sacrifices, and of a Priesthood
still in force; of "oblations and Liturgies, which we (Christians) ought to celebrate," and which "the Lord had commanded," and which they who duly perform, "are acceptable,

[s] Or in the foremost, or upper part
of. So ἔμπροσθεν τοῦ πλοίου, on the
forecastle of the ship.
[t] c. p. l. Ap.

CHAP.
II.
and blessed." Many of our divines do, with good reason, from this place argue, that St. Clement here asserts the three orders of ecclesiastical officers, Bishops, Priests, and Deacons, under the title of High-Priest, Priests, and Levites. And certainly the proof is as clear and strong for the sacrifice, as for the priesthood. And I am persuaded, that they, who will not allow both in the Christian Church, will never be able to shew the pertinence of this holy prelate's discourse.

(3.) The truth is, he plainly enough points out to us both the priesthood and the Sacrifice of the Christian Church : for if you would know, who were the persons designed under the character of High-Priest, he tells you they were the Bishops, whom he describes under the periphrasis of "offering the gifts;" and represents it as a crime, to "eject them from the function of the episcopal office," so long as they do this "in an unblameable and holy manner." And what the 'gifts' were, which the Bishops offered, I believe no man of good judgment will dispute. I know our adversaries would have nothing understood by that word, but the material oblations of laymen, without any immediate or necessary relation to, or dependence upon, the Eucharist. But then they ought to shew us, that these lay oblations were ever otherwise offered in the Church by the Bishops, than at the Altar, and in the Eucharist.

But one oblation in the Eucharist. It is pretty evident from the citations I have produced from St. Cyprian, Origen, St. Irenæus, and Justin Martyr, that they knew but of one solemn act of oblation, and that in the Eucharist properly so called, which oblation St. Irenæus says was taught by our Lord in the words of institution. And it is "the Bread and Wine of the Eucharist," which Justin Martyr says Christ instructed us to offer; and which Origen and St. Cyprian assure us were offered; and Tertullian speaks of the Bread offered in the divine Sacraments. I am sensible, that, in the later Liturgies, the oblations of the people were, by a solemn prayer, presented to God on the prothesis, before the more solemn oblation of them, as a memorial of the grand Sacrifice; but in the Clementine Liturgy[u], there is but one direct form of oblation, wherein

u c. p. 53. Ap.

the elements, presently after the words of institution, are
offered to God in commemoration of our Saviour's Passion.
And I am not sensible of any distinct oblation of them
mentioned in any early record of Christianity. There is
indeed a form of thanksgiving to be used over the first-
fruits, in the fortieth chapter of the eighth book of Constitutions; but this is so far from containing any formal act of
oblation, that it does expressly speak of them, as "having
been already offered," (προσενεχθεῖσι,) and which was indeed
no other than a prayer to be used by the Bishop, or clergymen, upon their eating of them. But it will be asked, how
or when the first-fruits or other lay oblations were presented
to God by the Bishop, or officiating Priest; I answer, just
as the carcasses of those animals, that were offered to God
under the law, for sin-offerings or peace-offerings; for it
does not appear, that they were presented to God by the
priest whole or entire, otherwise than by the priest's sprinkling some of the blood, and burning some parts of these
animals in the fire; for by this means the whole animal
was offered to God. And in like manner, the whole mass
of oblations made by the people was called and esteemed
a Sacrifice, on the account of that portion of Bread and
Wine, which was separated from them, and with most
solemn prayers and praises tendered to Almighty God. I
am sensible, the Bishop or celebrating Priest did receive all
the oblations of the people from the hands of the Deacon,
and deposited them on the Altar; and this act of the celebrator may be called an oblation; but I apprehend, that the
sacerdotal oblation, which is by the most ancient writers
spoken of as one single action, is chiefly to be understood
of the commemorative oblation, after the words of institution, though not exclusively of the celebrator's first presenting them on the Altar. For they were first placed on
the Altar, in order to the more solemn oblation, which soon
after followed. But suppose it could be proved, that in the
most primitive times of Christianity, and even before St. Clement wrote this epistle, the main mass of oblations were
offered by the Priest, in a distinct prayer before the Eucharistical oblation strictly so called; yet I apprehend it
would be no great commendation to the Bishop, that he had

duly performed this part of his office. But now St. Clement
gives it as a character of good and sound Bishops, that "they
offer the gifts in an unblameable holy manner;" and therefore must in reason be thought to speak of that part of the
Bishop's office, which was of the greatest moment. But now
I presume, that neither the friends nor the adversaries of
the Eucharistic Sacrifice can suppose, that the presenting
the mere lay oblations was such a considerable part of the
Bishop's office, that the measure of his merits and qualifications should be taken, by his performing this part of his
ministration without blame. The most momentous and
sacred office of our religion is, beyond all doubt, the Eucharist; and to have performed this with a due regard to so
holy an institution, was what might in justice entitle a man
to the reputation of a good Bishop, and to a reverential treatment by the people; and therefore, when St. Clement expresses himself in such a manner, as that it is clear he
thought, that they who had rightly offered the gifts had
filled up the character of Bishops; he cannot in common
reason be thought to speak of any gifts but those offered
in the Eucharist. The worthy Mr. Bennet was fully sensible
of this; and therefore, speaking of this passage, he says,
"St. Clement of Rome, who wrote in the Apostles' time,
plainly speaks of the Bishop's presiding in the celebration
of the Lord's Supper; for nothing else can be meant by
their offering the gifts; especially if we consider, that the
Eucharistical elements are called a gift, by St. Ignatius,"
(he refers to the place in St. Ignatius last above cited;) "and
that this language is used by innumerable other writers,
particularly those that are the most ancient; and it is
notorious, that προσφέρειν signifies to offer a sacrifice, such
as all antiquity thought the holy Eucharist to be[x];" and I
take this opportunity to pay my public acknowledgments to
him for this frank and full declaration in behalf of the doctrine
for which I am now pleading; and I dare lay this verdict of
Mr. Bennet in the scale against the two or three books, which
Dr. Hancock and Dr. Wise have printed against it.

But indeed we need not go so far as his forty-fourth chapter

---

[x] [See Bennet's "Rights of the Clergy of the Christian Church," cap. iii.
p. 52. Ed. 1711.]

to prove, that what he had said in the fortieth, was meant of the Eucharist. For he explains himself in the words immediately following; which, though they begin a new chapter in the common division, yet have a close connexion with the words, which conclude the fortieth chapter; and therefore in my translation, I take no notice of breaking off of the fortieth chapter. And further, I turn εὐχαριστεῖν, by "celebrating the Eucharist;" for so it signifies again in St. Justin Martyr[y], and in several other passages of the ancients; and indeed this place will, by itself considered, justify this version: for if no more were meant by this word than singing a hymn, or joining in a prayer of thanksgiving pronounced by the Bishop, or the celebrating Priest; I think it would be somewhat harsh for St. Clement to speak of every one's doing of it in his proper "station, rank," or "order;" especially if it be remembered, that in the words next before, the High-Priest, Priest, Levite, and layman, are expressly said to have their distinct parts in the Liturgies; and in the words next following, caution is given to every one not to transgress or exceed the canon of his Liturgy, or the regularity to be observed in the divine administrations. Now in bare verbal and mental thanksgivings, the share of all is equal or the same, except of him that officiates only; and the layman does the same with the Priest or Deacon, when the Bishop is present to pronounce the words; and I suppose there is no public office of religion in the Christian Church, where all, viz. Priests, Deacons, and laymen had their several parts to perform, but the Eucharist only; in which the layman brought his material oblation to the Deacon, by whom it was presented to the Bishop or officiating Priest, and by him laid on the Altar; and afterwards the whole Sacrifice solemnly presented to God, all the Priests standing by him that officiated; the Deacons attending, and keeping a decorum among the people; and (after the oblation and consecration) the celebrator first receiving himself, then the Priests and Deacons; after which the celebrator and the Deacons administered or distributed the Eucharistical symbols to the people. And as these words cannot properly be applied to any other part of religious worship; so it appears,

[y] d. p. 3. Ap.

that they do most exactly fit the celebration of the Eucharist, when performed in the manner just now hinted.
In a word, it must either be in singing psalms or saying
prayers of thanksgiving, that every one is to observe his
own particular station; which I suppose borders upon
absurdity: or else it must be in the administration of the
Sacrament. If the former, then I own, that such thanksgiving must be the Sacrifice here hinted at (and let my reader
too believe it if he can, that Bishops Priests and Deacons
were originally ordained for the keeping the better concert
and harmony, in offering up the hymns and verbal thanksgivings of the Church; nay, he must believe too, that such
hymns and thanksgivings are sacrifices for sin, and trespass-
offerings:) but if these thanksgivings are not that Sacrifice,
then certainly the material Eucharist is; which was to be
proved.

And that I may give some further confirmation to this,
I shall consider the occasion St. Clement had to speak on
this subject. It is evident to any man who reads this epistle
with application, that a sedition had been raised among the
Christians at Corinth against their lawful pastors, whom the
malcontent party endeavoured, at least so far as in them lay,
to remove and depose. And because the lawful pastors were
still supported by a considerable number of the people, who
kept to them, and to their former place of worship; therefore these malcontents form a separate assembly, set up some
of themselves or of the Deacons of their own side, to perform
the part of pastors, without any authority from the Bishop
and Presbytery, from whom they had made a defection;
and (as schism is a contradictious thing) they seem to have
chosen another day, in which to perform their devotions;
and not that which the Apostles, by our Saviour's direction,
had appropriated to this purpose. But it is observable, that
whatever innovations they made in other matters, yet they
affected to have the Sacrifice offered in the same external
form and manner that was used by the Bishop and Presbytery
and the uncorrupted part of the people, who still adhered to
them; only that they had no Bishop, or Priests, regularly
ordained. It was St. Clement's design, by this epistle, to
reconcile this mutinous party to their lawful pastors. Thus

it is easy to account for St. Clement's reminding them of SECT.
the stated place and time for celebrating the Eucharist; and ——I.——
for his insisting so much on the distinction of orders in the
Church, and for the hinted parallel between the Jewish
Church, as to their priesthood and sacrifice; and if they had
laid aside the Sacrifice, as they had their lawful pastors, he
would, no question, have laboured to convince them of their
mistake; but he speaks to them, as to men that were sensible
of the necessity of the Sacrifice; and therefore discourses
upon this supposition; but argues only against the irre-
gularity they were guilty of in offering It, by telling them,
that "Sacrifice is not offered at every place, but Jerusalem
only; and not at every place there neither, but before the
sanctuary and at the Altar." And St. Cyril of Alexandria
explains these words admirably well, when he observes[z],
"That the country of the Jews abounded with numberless
cities and villas; but God, by way of type, enjoined the
celebration of sacred offices and the paschal solemnity, to
be performed in Jerusalem only—so that it is not lawful
to fulfil the mystery of Christ, in any manner and place
at discretion; for the only fit and peculiar place is, in truth,
the Holy City, that is, the Church: in which there is also
a lawful Priest; and the holy offices are celebrated by
sanctified hands; and incense is offered to God the Sovereign
of all, and a pure Sacrifice, according to the voice of the
Prophet." I shall dismiss this head, when I have first desired Malachi i.
my reader to understand what I say of times appointed for 10, 11.
the Sacrifice, not to be so meant, as if I thought that the
Lord's day was the only time for celebrating the Eucharist,
in St. Clement's judgment; but that this was the day on
which it was performed with a greater concourse of people,
with more large devotions and oblations, than on other days.
For (says Justin Martyr), "On the day called Sunday, all
that live either in city or country, meet together at the same
place, where the writings of the Apostles and Prophets are
read, &c.; the Bishop makes a sermon; and prayers being
over, there is bread and wine and water offered to the
president[a]." And again, "Upon the Sunday we all meet
together[b]." From what has been said on these words of

---

[z] d. p. 43. Ap.   [a] Apology i. c. 66.   [b] c. 89.

CHAP. St. Clement, it is very evident that he does assert the Sacri-
II.   fice for which we contend; and consequently, we have the
testimony of the most unexceptionable piece of antiquity
now extant, next to the Scriptures themselves; of a piece
of antiquity which some Churches looked upon as part of
the sacred code. And I must believe, that this holy man
knew the mind of the Apostles, and the practice of the
Churches settled by them, much better than any that lived
in after ages, and infinitely beyond any of our modern
divines, though they were able to understand all the tongues
of men, and even of angels; nay, I look upon the testimony
of St. Clement to be, in effect, the testimony of St. Peter
and St. Paul both in one; for he was disciple to them,
and the Church of Rome, of which he was Bishop, was by
them regulated; and from them St. Clement received instructions in all things relating to the Christian doctrine
and worship. But further, to them who demand the authority of Christ Jesus and the Apostles for the Eucharistical
Sacrifice, I answer, that

That Christ   2. We have the express words of Christ Jesus Himself,
sacrificed   recorded by St. Matthew, St. Mark, St. Luke, and St. Paul,
in the in-
stitution.   fully attesting this great truth; namely, that He did, in the
institution of this Sacrament, actually offer Bread and Wine
to God, as His mysterious Body and Blood; and that He
commanded His Apostles to do the same.

(1.) I will shew that these words, "This is My Body given
for you, This is My Blood shed for you," do prove, that
Christ gave, or offered the Bread and Wine to God, as
His mysterious Body and Blood: and (2.) that He commanded His Apostles to do the same. [See this more
illustrated in Introduction to Part the Second.]

From our   Now in order to prove the first point, I take it for granted,
Saviour's   that when our Saviour says, "This is My Body given," by
saying,
τοῦτό ἐστι 'given' He means offered, or sacrificed to God. This is a
σῶμα διδό-
μενον.   thing very plain in itself, and is, nay, must be acknowledged
by all. When He said, "Take, eat," He gave His sacra-
mental Body 'to' His Disciples; when He adds "given
for you," He must mean given or offered in sacrifice to
God 'for' them. The giving His Body 'to' His Apostles,
and giving it 'for' them, are two things perfectly distinct.

His putting It into their hands or mouths, was not giving
His Body for them; this was an action performed *to the*
Apostles : His giving, or offering It *for* them, was an action directed *to God ;* which as it is very plain in itself, so
it is expressly taught us by St. Paul; "for Christ," says he, Eph. v. 2.
"has given Himself for us, an offering and sacrifice to God[c]."
[Whatever is offered to God is said very often in Scripture
to be given to Him. And in a particular manner all sacrifices are frequently called *gifts;* and the most eminent and
valuable Sacrifice that ever was presented to God is most
justly expressed by this word ; which, though small in sound,
is very big in signification. It imports Christ's free voluntary
resigning His own most precious Body and Blood to God the
Father as a ransom and Sacrifice for the sins of men.]

I take it for certain and indisputable, that the Body here
spoken of was now actually given, yielded, offered to God by
our Saviour, as a Priest according to the order of Melchisedec.
The three Evangelists before mentioned, and St. Paul, do
every one of them speak in the present tense, διδόμενον, Luke
xxii. 19, κλώμενον, 1 Cor. xi. 24, ἐκχυνόμενον, Matt. xxvi. 28,
Mark xiv. 24, Luke xxii. 20; the Spirit, by Which they wrote,
directed them all with an unanimous harmony to represent
our Saviour as now performing the most solemn act of His
Melchisedecian priesthood ; and, therefore, as offering His
Body and Blood to God, under the symbols of Bread and
Wine. It is well known by all that are not perfect strangers
to the Hebrew and Hellenistic diction, that the strongest and
most strict way they have of expressing the time present, is
by a participle of that tense. This way of expressing Himself
our Saviour uses; and all the four holy writers, who give us
the history of the institution, do agree in using this present
participle ; and do therefore most gloriously conspire to teach
us this truth, that our Saviour did now actually offer Himself to God, under the representatives of Bread broken and
Wine poured out. The rankest Deist, I apprehend, will scarce
be able to persuade himself, that four writers should all by
mere chance, in describing the same action, use the same

[c] "And if we duly consider this particular, which can be denied by none,
that do not want common sense and
judgment, the rest inevitably follows."
[First Ed.]

tense, and yet use it in the stead of another tense; that they should all speak of the same thing as done in the present instant of time, and yet mean, that it was to be done some considerable time after.   What then can we think of those Christians, who can believe, that these holy penmen were all moved by the Holy Ghost to speak improperly, concerning an action of the greatest moment; and, particularly, to say, that it was done now, at this instant moment of time; when yet they believed, and knew, that it was yet to be done; that twenty hours were to pass before it was to be completed?   If indeed one or two of these inspired writers had represented our Saviour as speaking in the present tense, and the others had expressed it in the future, our adversaries might have had some umbrage for saying, that the two former were to be interpreted by the two latter; but that they had no regard to grammatical niceties, nor are we to build any thing upon such uncertain bottoms.   But when every one of those holy penmen, who give us the minutes of this action, which was one of the most considerable that ever He did, and which is related by four of them, do all say, that our Saviour said, " is given," or "broken," "is shed;" I cannot think it becomes wise or modest men to pretend to correct these holy writers, as if they knew the meaning of Christ's words better than they who were present, when they were spoken.   It is therefore pre-posterous to tell us, that by *is* we are to understand *shall be*.   Nor have our adversaries any pretence for giving so un-natural a sense to these words.   They tell you, it is the present tense for the future; and if you ask, upon what grounds this is said, they have nothing to reply but this, viz. That Christ's Body was not in any sense given, or offered to God, until It was crucified.   Which is to take that for granted, which my reader sees, was denied by the ancient Fathers. [What if some few MSS., and the old Italic translation, and St. Cyprian, and the translator of Irenæus, and the canon of the mass in the Church of Rome, say " shall be given, shall be shed?"   Those can be of no weight, when laid in the scale against the concurrent authority of most and the best of the Greek books.]   Nor does the Scripture give any countenance to our adversaries, while they would persuade us, that Christ's oblation was performed on the cross only.   The four histories

of the institution plainly declare, that Christ's Body was S E C T.
given, or sacrificed in the Eucharist; nor is there one word ———I.———
in all the New Testament, that can be urged in contradiction
to it. Christ is often said to have " given Himself for us ;" but
that by this phrase is meant nothing but His dying for us
upon the cross, we are nowhere told ; and since He Himself
has informed us, that in the Eucharist His Body was given,
His Blood shed for us, we have just reason to believe Him.
He is sometimes said to have "borne our sins ;" and that this
was done upon the cross, that the mactation was there performed, is not disputed. It is said, that "Christ was once Heb. ix. 28.
offered, to bear the sins of many." And that the oblation
was but one is a most certain apostolical truth ; and yet they,
who limit this one oblation to the six hours' time during
which He hung upon the cross, are destitute of any proof
from Scripture. That the Sacrifice was not finished until
our Saviour expired on the cross, nay, until He entered into
the Holy of Holies, even heaven itself, is evident enough; nor
is it less evident, that He began this sacrificial solemnity by
offering His own Body and Blood, when He instituted the
Eucharist. Christ indeed bore the punishment of " our sin 1Pet.xi.24.
in His own" natural " Body on the tree." But when St. Paul,
as above cited, says, "He was offered to bear the sins of many;"
it is manifest, that there was an oblation previous to the sufferings, or ' bearing' there mentioned ; as when the Apostle
says, in the 26th verse of that chapter, that Christ " appeared
once to put away sin," His appearing was before His putting
away ; so when he says here, that He was " once offered to
bear," He must in some sense 'offer' Himself, before He could
be capable of 'bearing;' and it is evident, that His crucifixion
was a consequence of His offering Himself; and this is the
full of what St. Paul says, viz. that " Christ was not often to Heb. ix. 25,
offer Himself; for then He must often have suffered;" He 26.
offered Himself but once, and therefore suffered but once.
He began this oblation in the Eucharist, and continued it on
the cross. Nothing but His death could be a satisfaction for
our sins; and this was actually accomplished on the cross :
and this death of His was never to be repeated; it was the
effect of His personal oblation of Himself, which He began
in the Eucharist ; and since He was but once to offer, He was

but once to die. [See much more of this in Introduction to Part Second.]

It seems clear to me, that the one personal oblation, performed by our Saviour Himself, is not to be confined to any one instant of time; but commenced with the Paschal solemnity, and was finished at His ascension into heaven, there to appear in the presence of God for us. And if our adversaries will restrain the oblation to the cross alone, then they must exclude Christ's sacerdotal entry into heaven as the holy of holies, and say, that the oblation was finished before the Blood of the Sacrifice was brought into the most holy

Heb. ix. 7. place, and there offered, contrary to what the Apostle teaches us, and therefore few, I suppose, will presume thus far. And if it was consistent with the one oblation, to be made in the Holy of Holies as well as on the Altar, in heaven, as well as on the cross; then I cannot conceive, why the oblation made in the Eucharist should make the oblation cease to be *one*, any more than the double offering it on the cross and in the Holy of Holies, already mentioned. If our adversaries will needs have it, that the sacerdotal act of oblation was instantaneous and transient, and performed on the cross only; I am pretty confident, they will find no proof of this singular opinion. That the mactation and satisfaction was made and done upon the cross; that the substantial Sacrifice of Christ's natural Body was there once for all yielded to God the Father, is owned on all hands. But my ingenious reader will distinguish between the mactation, and the sacerdotal act or act of oblation; and though the former belongs to the cross only, yet this cannot truly be affirmed of the other: if our adversaries will have it, that Christ never acted as a sacrificing Priest here on earth, but in His crucifixion; they must first prove, that He did not solemnly *give* His sacramental Body to God; and then they must produce some cogent argument, whereby to make it appear, that He did upon the cross, by an internal act of His mind, if not in express words, make a sacerdotal oblation of Himself, which I conceive will be a very hard task; that He did so in the Eucharist, is clear.

If it could be proved, that our Saviour offered Himself on the cross only; it would from thence follow, that in this one oblation He did not at all act as a Priest according to the order of Melchisedec. For Melchisedec, as the ancients observe, is never reported to have offered a bloody sacrifice; if he offered any, which will not admit of a dispute, it was a sacrifice of bread and wine, as a prefiguration of the grand Sacrifice. And if, therefore, our Saviour did ever make an oblation according to the order of Melchisedec; He must have done it in the same materials, and therefore in the Eucharist. And from this my reader will observe, how much more agreeable the notions of the Fathers were, who believed that Christ blessed the spiritual progeny of Abraham, as Melchisedec did the father of the faithful, by an oblation of Bread and Wine; than the notions of those, who must assert, if they will discourse consistently with their own hypothesis, that though our Saviour was a Priest according to the order of Melchisedec; yet in the main point of the priestly office, that is, sacrifice, there was no correspondence between them. In a word, it is agreed, that Melchisedec typified the Priesthood of Christ in blessing Abraham, and that the foundation of all the blessings conferred on Abraham and his spiritual posterity, was the mactation of Christ's natural Body. It is evident, that the way of deriving the merits of Christ to particular persons, or imparting benedictions to them, has always been by Sacrifice. It is clear, that Melchisedec's priesthood was a sacrificing priesthood; but there is no probability, that he offered bloody sacrifices, but bread and wine only; and that therefore in such a sacrifice he imparted a benediction to Abraham; and by consequence, that our Saviour, as a Priest of the same order, did intend to confer benedictions on the people, as Melchisedec did on Abraham; and therefore performed the sacerdotal oblation in Bread and Wine. And here, as has been proved, we have the judgment of the ancients with us; who do generally assert, that Christ did offer Bread and Wine in the Eucharist, and offered them as a Melchisedecian priest, and as symbols of His Body and Blood; and that in, and by these symbols, He did mysteriously devote His natural Body to suffer according to the will of God; and this is a certain proof, that the Fathers took 'given,' not only as expressing, but as meaning and intending the time then present. Let the Papists then go on with their *dabitur* and *effundetur*, "shall be given," "shall be shed;" and it fits their notion well enough, who believe that the same Body and Blood was substantially offered in the Eucharist and on the cross; but let Protestants stick close to the primitive Church, and to the Evangelists, and to Christ Jesus Himself; Who undoubtedly declared, that in that very instant of time, in which He celebrated the original Eucharist, He did at once offer, or give to God Bread and Wine, and gave them as a pledge and earnest of the natural Body and Blood, which was soon after yielded to God on the cross. But to make this matter more clear if possible, I will propose two questions.

(1.) What is That which Christ here calls His Body and Blood? And here all antiquity, as we shall soon see, and the greatest part of Protestants, but especially the Church of England, give in their unanimous answer, that It is consecrated Bread and Wine.

(2.) The other question is, What is That of which Christ here says, that It is given, or offered to God? And yet it seems strange to me, that this should be a question with those, who believe that Christ here calls Bread His Body, Wine His Blood; for certainly if this Bread, of which our Saviour speaks, is His Body, then this Bread is also given to God, if our Saviour speak according to the common rules of construction; for the Bread and the Body of Christ are here the same thing. For no other Body of Christ could be eaten, no other Body of Christ had yet been substantially offered to God. The argument used by Protestants to prove that what Christ gave to His Apostles, and what they received, was Bread, runs thus: What He took, That He blessed; what He blessed, That He brake; what He brake, That He gave; what He gave, That they received; therefore what they received was Bread: for that was what He took. But there are some words omitted in this induction, viz. "My Body given for you;" and therefore I must take leave to add, what He gave was His Body; what was His Body, was given for them; what was given for them, was given to them; what was given to them they received, therefore what they received was Bread, actually offered to God as His (sacramental) Body. And this is to be applied to the Wine, *mutatis mutandis.* And indeed St. Luke so expresses our Saviour's words at the delivery of the Cup, that 'poured out' cannot be understood to belong to the natural Blood of Christ, but to the representative Blood, or the Wine. This cannot be perceived by reading our translation; but the words grammatically rendered are these, "This cup poured out for you," or offered as a libation to God for you, "is the New Testament," or covenant "in My Blood:" for ἐκχυνόμενον, being a nominative, cannot agree with αἵματι, which is in the dative; but our adversaries will rather make St. Luke guilty of a solecism, than allow that he could speak so decisively against their notions: for this is their way of dealing with the holy writers upon this occasion. I desire my reader further to observe, that when I vary 'poured out,' by those words 'offered as a libation,' I had an eye not only to truth, but to Mr. Calvin, who in his " Harmony on the Gospels," says, that our Saviour made a libation with the cup, and that "it used so to be done in sacrifices[e]." *O si sic omnia!* It is certain to a demonstration, that all the other particulars are predicated of the Bread and Wine; it is certain, in particular, that when He says, "This [Bread] is My Body," Body is predicated of the Bread; and it must be a strange sleight that can grant the word "Body" to be so predicated; yet when we come to the next word " given," we must find another subject for it. For it is to be observed, that this proposition, " This [Bread] is My Body," is false, if meant of His natural Body, which could not be eaten; it must therefore be meant of His sacramental Body, and therefore of His sacramental Body it is also said, that It is " given for us."

But I may be told that our Saviour's meaning is, " This

---

[e] [" Quia Lucas bis porrectum a Christo calicem memorat, quærendum est primo loco sitne repetitio (ut interdum Evangelistæ bis rem unam dicere solent) an vero Christus, postquam ex calice libaverat, hoc idem secundo iteraverit. Quod posterius mihi verisimile est. Scimus enim solennem in sacrificiis libandi ritum observatum fuisse a sanctis Patribus. Unde illud Psalmi cxvi. ver. 13, 'Calicem salutis accipiam, et nomen Domini invocabo.' Itaque non dubito, Christum ex more vetusto libasse in sacro convivio, quod rite peragi aliter non poterat: idque diserte refert Lucas antequam ad novi mysterii narrationem descendat: cujus ratio distincta est ab Agno Paschali. Hoc quoque ex recepto solennique usu fuit, quod *gratias egisse* nominatim dicitur *Accepto calice.* Nam initio Cœnæ precatum fuisse non dubito, ut nunquam sine Dei invocatione ad mensam accedere solitus est. Sed nunc rursum eodem officio defungi voluit, ne cæremoniam omitteret quam sacræ libationi fuisse annexam nuper ostendi."—Calvin. Harmonia Evangel., p. 321. Ed. Genevæ. 1595.]

[Bread] is [a symbol of] My Body given for you;" to which I answer,

(1.) That though I do allow this to be true in some sense, which will hereafter be seen; yet I do not think it fair, first to suppose that our Saviour meant the words in our sense, and then to build arguments upon that supposition.

(2.) I answer, that this will not at all clear the point under debate; for supposing the words stood, as just now represented, in the English tongue, yet the question is, how our Saviour and the Evangelists would have expressed it in the Greek, that is, whether it would have been τοῦτό ἐστι σύμβολον τοῦ σώματός Μου διδομένου, or διδόμενον; or whether the meaning of those English words should be, "This is a symbol of My natural Body, which natural Body is given for you;" or whether it should be, "This is a symbol of My natural Body, which symbol is given for you." If it were to be expressed in the first manner, it might seem favourable to them that may make this allegation; and yet in reality it must be against them; for so long as the participle is in the present tense, the Body must be now given; and if the Bread was a symbol of the Body which was given, while our Saviour was alive, it is certain that That Body was not yet substantially given, but only symbolically; and if symbolically, then under the pledges or symbols of Bread and Wine; and if it was given or offered under the pledges of Bread and Wine, then the Bread and Wine must be offered; and if they were not then offered, it could not be said that our Saviour's Body was then in any sense given to God: if in the latter, it would be directly against them. But it is vain for any man to assume to himself the liberty of determining positively, which manner of exposition our Saviour would have thought most proper; and to say the least of it, it is begging the question, for any man to assert peremptorily that it ought to be varied according to his own sentiments.

(3.) I answer, the most safe and just way of proceeding is to reason upon the words as they stand in the text; and I apprehend that neither of these modes of expression would have come up to our Saviour's meaning and intention; for it appears, by His using the present tense, that His design was not to say, "This is a symbol of My natural Body now

given for you;" because this was not yet actually given ; nor
only to say, "This symbol of My Body is given for you :"
for it has been shewed that He intended somewhat more,
viz. under this symbol actually to resign His Body to the
cross, there to be slain. And further it will appear ere long,
that the Eucharistical Bread is somewhat more than a type,
or symbol; that it is Christ's Body in power and effect,
though not in substance; and therefore fitly presented to
God as a pledge and earnest. And this may indeed be sufficiently inferred from our Saviour's choosing to express Himself in these words rather than any other. For it savours of
impiety, to suppose that our blessed Lord, in speaking on so
extraordinary a subject, did not make choice of the most apt
and adequate words, whereby to let His disciples into His
meaning; and He did so express Himself, that in many
hundred years after His ascension the main body of Christians throughout the world, however they differed in other
particulars, yet had no disputes about this.

Thus the reader may see, that the main stress of the dispute lies in effect in this single question, Whether our
Saviour did offer His Body and Blood in the Eucharist ; to
which our Saviour's express answer is, "This Bread is My
Body now given for you : This Wine is My Blood now shed
for you." Our adversaries, to shift off this, tell us, our
Saviour used one tense, but meant another; He said, "is
given," He meant, "shall be given ;" and further, they will
not allow the word 'given' to be applied to His sacramental
Body, though every word in the sentence, excepting that, is
by them acknowledged to belong to that Body. Now this is
perfectly precarious and evasive; and because our adversaries
will not be convinced with the most plain, natural, obvious
construction of the words, we have no means left us but to
refer our cause to the arbitration of the most competent, disinterested, and uncorrupted judges, the primitive Fathers
and councils, and the earliest liturgies, that are now in being;
and they do unanimously, whenever they have occasion to
speak of this matter, pronounce in favour of us; and I am
bold to say, that none of them ever said the contrary. They
say indeed that they have no such sacrifices as the Jews and
heathen had, offered by blood and fire; but those very

Fathers do upon occasion assert the unbloody Sacrifice; and if this be not sufficient to establish this doctrine in the opinion of all equal judges, we know not what will. We know that nothing can be so plainly and decisively expressed by any writer, in relating a matter of fact, but that cunning men, by virtue of some fetch, or by pretending that the expression is figurative, may evade the sense and meaning of the author; and especially if they may be allowed to affirm at discretion, that one tense is used for another; that the writer for instance uses the present, but means the preterperfect, or future. For though it is owned that such enallages do sometimes occur, yet no man, that has not some turn to serve, will suppose any such figure used by his author, when a fair account can be given of the words, without any such supposition; and our adversaries in this case have no pretence for an enallage, but only this, that they must either assert such a figure to be here used, or else for ever abandon their cause. But neither are we destitute of other proof from the words of institution; for,

(2.) Whatever Christ did Himself, the same He commanded us to do. If therefore He offered His own sacramental Body and Blood in the Eucharist, He has positively commanded us to do the same; and we are without excuse, if we do wilfully and designedly omit it. Having therefore before shewed that Christ did here make an oblation, it inevitably follows, that we must do so too, taking those words, "Do this in remembrance of Me," in the sense, which our adversaries themselves put upon them; but we affirm further, that the word ποιεῖν, when joined with a noun that signifies any thing proper to be offered to God, does very often signify to offer, or present to the Divine Majesty, by way of sacrifice. Dr. Hickes, in his "Christian Priesthood," has produced a very great number of proofs to this purpose, from p. 58 to 68; and when our Saviour says of the Cup, τοῦτο ποιεῖτε ὁσάκις ἂν πίνητε, it cannot in strictness be otherwise rendered than, "Offer this as oft as ye drink it." For it is certain, that ποιεῖτε affects τοῦτο, in the same manner that πίνητε affects it; and that therefore we are to 'do,' or 'make' what we 'drink,' or else we are to offer it; and since we cannot be, in any propriety of speech, said to make or to do the Cup in the Eucharist, it remains,

that we are to *offer* it; for that τοῦτο has ποτήριον for its S E C T
antecedent, is evident from this, that we cannot be said to ———— <u>I.</u>
' drink' any thing there spoken of, but the Cup only. See
" Propitiatory Oblation," p. 33. And lest my reader should
not have the " Christian Priesthood" at hand, thereby to be
convinced that ποιεῖν has this signification, I will only just
mention the places which are there referred to, viz. Herodotus,
lib. i. c. cxxxi. cxxxii; the LXX Greek translators, Exod.
xxix. 36. 38, 39; x. 25; Levit. iv. 20; vi. 22; ix. 7. 16. 22;
xiv. 19. 30; xvii. 9; xxiii. 12; Deut. xvi. 1; 1 Kings viii. 64;
xviii. 23. 25, 26. 29, (the words are not in the Hebrew;)
2 Kings x. 21. 24, 25; 2 Chron. xxx. 1, 2; xxxv. 1; Ezra vi.
19; Numb. ix. 2; Josh. v. 10; 2 Kings xxiii. 21; 2 Chron.
xxxv. 17, 18, 19; Psalm lxv. 19; Baruch i. 10; Heb. xi. 28;
1 Tim. ii. 1. The same is proved from Justin Martyr, Chrysostom, the Constitutions, &c.

I must also remind my reader, that the word Ἀνάμνησις,
" memorial," which is rendered by the English translators
" remembrance," is a sacrificial word; and is by the LXX
translators applied to the offering the shew-bread, which was
a most plain type of the Christian Sacrifice, Levit. xxiv. 6, 7.
And it is from this text of the LXX that the ancient Fathers
and Liturgists take the word προκείμενα, which I commonly
have rendered " lying in open view;" and this shew-bread
is, in the text now cited, expressly called " an offering of
the Lord." And it is well known, that the memorial was
the most essential part of the oblation; indeed, no part of it
but this was directly presented to God by a solemn act of oblation; but the whole sacrifice was rendered operative and
beneficial, by virtue of this memorial; as you may see, Levit. ii.
And we do not pretend, that in the Eucharist the substantial
Body of Christ is offered, (that we leave to the Papists); but
only, that we offer the sacramental Body and Blood, as a memorial of the natural; not as a cold remembrance, but as a
powerful, efficacious, prevalent oblation.

There is in the Apostolical Constitutions an observable
passage, which I cannot but recommend to my reader's
perusal on this occasion[f]; "Do ye," say the Constitutions,
" on our Saviour's resurrection offer that Sacrifice, which

[f] bb. p. 47. Ap.

Christ gave you in charge, by us [the Apostles,] saying, ' Offer this for a memorial of Me.' " If we turn the last words, " Do this in remembrance of Me," it will not be easy to see, how they could suppose, that a Sacrifice was here enjoined, taking the words apart from those that are before; I therefore turn them in that sense, in which I suppose the Constitutions understood them, and by this means their way of expressing themselves is very intelligible. There is, I own, another supposition, upon which this conclusion may be drawn from the words, as usually translated, " Do this in remembrance of Me;" the supposition is, that our Saviour, in the foregoing words, had declared the Bread and Wine given to God, as His representative Body and Blood; for if our Saviour did declare, in the former sentence, that His Body was actually offered, (as I have proved He did); then it is confessed, that it was sufficient for Him to say, " Do this," that is, offer Bread and Wine, as I have done. And let our adversaries choose which of the two they please; for upon either of the suppositions the doctrine of the Sacrifice is effectually established. And I persuade myself, that with all impartial readers, both will be thought more than suppositions; and that our adversaries will find them so by their own experience, if they think fit to try their skill and strength upon them.

That this was not only the notion of him, or them, who drew these Constitutions, but of St. Paul himself, will seem very probable to him that reads with attention 1 Cor. x. 16—21: where the Apostle, having cautioned the people against idolatry, that is, eating meats offered to idols in the heathen temples, proceeds to prove, that by eating such meats, they honoured and communicated with those false gods, to whom they were offered: and to make this good, he runs a parallel between things offered to the true God, and things offered to idols. He begins with the Christian Eucharist, and asks, ver. 16, whether " the Cup there blessed were not the communion of the Blood of Christ, and the Bread there broken, the communion of the Body of Christ?" he must take it for granted, that this Eucharistical Cup and Bread had been offered to God: for otherwise the parallel is lost: for the Apostle's argument proceeds thus; viz. the Bread and Cup in the Sacrament is the eating and drinking of a Sacrifice, as the banquets in the heathen temples are; and by partaking of the Sacrifice, we communicate with one another, and with that God to Whom the Sacrifice is offered: "For we," says St. Paul, "being many are one Bread and one Body, for we are all partakers of that one Bread," or "loaf;" and so united to God, and Christ Jesus, and each other, by partaking of that one Sacrifice: and that St. Paul supposes what was eaten and drunk to have been first offered, appears further, by the following instance, ver. 18, "Behold Israel after the flesh," or the Jewish people; and "are not they who eat of the sacrifices" offered by them, reputed to be "partakers of," or "guests at," their "Altar;" and so to communicate with that God, to Whom the sacrifices are offered, as well as with those men, who eat together with them? St. Paul applies both these instances to the case of eating heathen sacrifices in the idol temple, ver. 20, in those words, viz. "I say that the things, which the Gentiles sacrifice, they sacrifice to devils, and not to God," as the Christians do in their Eucharist, and the Jews in their temple service; and I would not "that ye should have fellowship with devils," by eating things offered to them, as Christians and Jews communicate with the true God, by eating things offered to Him. And this the Apostle speaks yet more clearly in the 21st verse, "Ye cannot" consistently "drink the Cup of the Lord, and the cup of devils;" that is, the Wine offered to the true God in the Eucharist, and that libated to the false gods in the heathen temples; "Ye cannot" consistently "be partakers of," or guests at, "the Lord's Table," or Altar, "and the table" or altar "of devils." For I suppose it is as evident, that the Cup of the Lord, here mentioned, had been offered in honour to Him, as that the cup of devils had been offered in honour to them; and that the Table of the Lord denotes an Altar erected for His worship, as the table of devils denotes an altar raised for the worship of devils; for by the table of devils you cannot justly understand feasting tables distinct from the Altar; because to "be partakers of the table" in this verse, is parallel to that of being "partakers of the Altar," ver. 18: and from hence

CHAP. we might conclude, that the "Table of the Lord" is a phrase
II. signifying His Altar, if we had no other proof of it.

And that this is the true state of the Apostle's argument,
I allege the authority of Dr. Whitby himself, who introduces
St. Paul thus explaining himself (in the last paragraph of his
annotation upon ver. 21.) "This I say to complete this argument, and to render the sacrifice offered to idols parallel to
those of Christians, and of Jews; that as these are offered
to the honour of Christ and of the God of Israel, so the
things which the Gentiles sacrificed they sacrificed to devils
and not to God[g]." I would not have my reader from hence
conclude, that the doctor is a friend to the Christian Sacrifice; (he has sufficiently declared the contrary;) but only
desire him to observe the force of Divine truth, which will
sometimes make its way into the eyes of men though they
wink never so hard.

It may seem a just objection against what is here offered,
that the Cup and Bread, ver. 16, are simply called the communion of Christ's Blood and Body, and not of His Blood
shed, and of His Body given for us, as at other places: for if
those words had been added, the argument had been plain
and obvious to all.   But to this I answer,

I. That St. Paul frequently speaks elliptically; nay, he
does so in this very chapter; the word 'water' is clearly
omitted, ver. 4, for not the rock itself but "the water which
flowed out of the rock followed the Israelites in the wilderness;" as, I suppose, everybody will allow. Another remarkable ellipsis occurs, ver. 7, for to prove that some of the
people were idolaters, he cites those words, Exod. xxxii. 6,
"the people sat down to eat, and drink, and rose up to play:"
he takes no notice, that what they eat had first been offered
to the golden calf, to whom they had erected an altar, and
offered burnt-offerings, and brought peace-offerings, as appears by the words immediately foregoing: and this is an
ellipsis of the same sort with that, ver. 16, where he mentions
not the bread and wine as offered to God, ver. 7, he takes no
notice, that what the people eat had been sacrificed to the calf.

2. The reason of his using an ellipsis, ver. 7, and ver. 16,
seems to have been one and the same, viz. that the history of

[g] [Whitby's Paraphrase, vol. ii. p. 175.]

the golden calf, and [that] of the institution of the Eucharist, were so well known to the Corinthian communicants, that he thought it needless minutely and *verbatim* to rehearse them: and if either were known to them better than the other, it was certainly the institution of the Eucharist; for they had it rehearsed to them once a week at furthest. St. Paul's chief aim was to prove, that men cannot eat, or partake of things offered to a God, whether a true or false one, but he must be supposed to intend this eating or participation done in honour to that God, and with a design to communicate with Him: the eating or partaking being the main thing he had in his view, whereby he intended to convince those loose Corinthians of their sin, in eating of things sacrificed to idols; he did not think it necessary always to repeat the circumstance of its being offered before it was eaten. And since it is evident, that he does not mention, ver. 7, the oblation of the peace-offerings upon which the Israelites feasted, we are not to wonder, that he omits in the sixteenth verse the oblation of the Body and Blood of Christ: but in the twenty-first verse he does as strongly intimate, that the Cup in the Eucharist was offered in honour of Christ, as that the cup in the idol feasts had been offered to devils. I think more need not be said to shew, that he does as necessarily imply the offering of the latter, as of the former; and that without this supposition the pertinence and consequence of the Apostle's reasonings are not to be perceived.

Thus, I conceive, I have fully established the doctrine of the Sacrifice, not only from the monuments of the primitive Church, but from the words of Christ Jesus Himself, and of His Apostle St. Paul. And I must continue of this opinion, till I am convinced by some direct evidence from Scripture, that Christ did at any other time or place here on earth, perform any sacerdotal act of oblation; that Christ's Body was substantially sacrificed on the cross, must be acknowledged by all; but by "sacrificed on the cross," we must then mean, that He was slain as an expiatory victim, and not that He offered Himself as a Melchisedecian Priest: for He declares, that He did this in the Eucharist: for "This," says He, "is My Body given" to God "for you."

And though we ought in every Eucharist to do what Christ

We do not
offer the
Eucharist
for the same
ends that
Christ did.

did; yet we are not to do it in all respects, with the same ends and designs that He did. The chief end, or primary intention, which Christ seems to have had in the celebration of the first Eucharist, was to devote and resign Himself up to God, as a Sacrifice for the life of the world, and to institute a perpetual commemoration of It: but we do neither the one, nor the other. We do not offer the Body of Christ in order to It's being crucified; but as a memorial of It's having been thus devoted to crucifixion, or mactation, now long since past. We do not institute either a Sacrament, or a Sacrifice; but put in practice the institution made so many hundred years since by Christ Himself. We have a parallel to this in the Paschal type: for the original sacrifice of the lamb in the land of Egypt was chiefly designed for propitiating the Divine Majesty, in order to avert that judgment (viz. the death of the first-born) from the Israelites, which befell the Egyptians, and to be the pattern of the Paschal sacrifice to the Jews in all succeeding generations; but the annual passover, though it were as truly a sacrifice as the original, was rather a commemoration of the deliverance of the Israelites from that calamity, than an apotreptic sacrifice; and was not intended as an institution, but as a continuation of the passover; though it was propitiatory, as well as other sacrifices.

[And thus I have beyond all just contradiction proved, that Jesus performed the office of a sacrificing Priest, when He first instituted the Holy Communion; and that He at the same time ordained His Apostles and their successors to succeed Him in that sacred office; and whether Melchisedec's priesthood were a type of Christ's in offering bread or wine or not (of which, I believe, few impartial readers will doubt), yet that in thus offering a meal-sacrifice He fulfilled the prefiguration of the pontifical sacrifice[h] offered under the law, and that He intended the latter as well as the former to be a perpetual daily Sacrifice, will be granted me, by all that are not very hard to be convinced.]

Sacrifices
in general
never
abolished.

It is true, our adversaries have an effectual answer to all this, and whatever else can be said in defence of the Sacrifice of the Eucharist; and that is, that all Sacrifice is abolished by Jesus Christ. Our adversaries do never speak with more

[h] See Levit. vi. 20—22; and ch. i. sect. 1. of this book *mox ab initio.*

assurance, than under this head; and they think they may
very well spare themselves the pains of an argument to prove
this, when they have vulgar prejudice on their side; and in
truth this is the only proof they have. Christ is nowhere
said to have abolished Sacrifice. Nay, I am bold to say, that
there is not a text in Scripture, that can in the eyes of any
judicious man seem to countenance our adversaries in such
an assertion. The only passage in the New Testament, that may
seem to look this way, is that [wherein] St. Paul transcribes the
words of David from Psalm the fortieth, and represents Christ
as saying, "Sacrifice and offering Thou wouldest not; but a
Body hast Thou prepared Me: in burnt-offerings and sacrifices for sin Thou hast had no pleasure; then said I, Lo, I
come to offer the delightful thing, or Sacrifice, O God—
Above, when He said, Sacrifice and burnt-offering, and
offering for sin Thou wouldest not, neither hadst pleasure
therein, which are offered by the law; then, said He, Lo, I
come to offer the delightful thing, or Sacrifice, O God: He
taketh away the first, that He may establish the second,"
that is, He taketh away sacrifice and burnt-offering and
offering for sin, "which are offered by the law of Moses:"
for the Apostle expressly tells us, that He meant no other
sacrifices; and that the Mosaical sacrifices are abolished, we
all gratefully acknowledge; but that the delightful Sacrifice,
the prepared or consecrated Body is abolished, our adversaries themselves will not dare to say. And we have seen
several of the Fathers expressly interpreting these words, of
the Eucharistical Sacrifice, offered by Christ Jesus the night
before He suffered, and this Sacrifice He has commanded to
be perpetuated until His second coming. So that I cannot
apprehend, that they have the appearance of any word in the
Holy Scripture for so bold an assertion as this, that all Sacrifice is abolished by Christ: and we have heard the ancientest
of the Fathers, Irenæus, Justin Martyr, nay, Ignatius, and
St. Clement of Rome, affirming the contrary. And as for
my construction of the phrase τὸ θέλημα ποιεῖν, by "offering
the acceptable thing, or Sacrifice," I elsewhere account for
it. [But I shall speak more of this in the Second Part.]

The only specious objection against the doctrine of the
Sacrifice, which comes now to be considered, is that which is

CHAP.
II.
————
chap. x.
10. 14.

chap. x.
12. 18.
drawn from the ninth and tenth chapters of the Epistle to the Hebrews ; viz. that Christians are said to be "sanctified" and "perfected" by the one Sacrifice offered by Christ in person; and especially, that since "remission of sin" is obtained by Christ's once offering Himself, therefore "now there remaineth no more sacrifice, or offering for sin." Now to this I answer,

1. That the most that can be argued from these passages, taken in the sense of those who make these objections, is, that the Eucharist cannot be a piacular or expiatory victim ; that there is no occasion for any sacrifice but that of the cross, for the taking away the guilt and punishment of sin. And let us at present grant this ; yet it will not from thence follow, that it is not a Sacrifice of thanksgiving properly so called, in which Bread and Wine are offered as the representatives of the Body and Blood of Christ, and as testimonies of our gratitude to God, for the redemption of the world by Christ Jesus. For if the Apostle had in express terms declared, that the Eucharist is no sacrifice for sin; yet no rational man would from thence infer, that it is not a material Sacrifice of praise. The very same thing may be said of the Passover, that it was no sin-offering, not primarily, at least, intended for the expiation of guilt; and yet we cannot doubt, but that it was a Sacrifice properly so called, unless we will contradict the Scriptures. And indeed the very name Eucharist imports what is so called to be principally, and in the first place, a Sacrifice of praise. And if we consider it as such, we must be forced to own at the same time, that it is such a Sacrifice of praise, as was intended to be a means of conveying to us all the effects of that piacular victim, which Christ offered in His own person. For as it is allowed on all hands, I think, that sacrifices are federal solemnities between that God, to whom they are offered, and the votaries or worshippers ; so it is, I think, a truth acknowledged by all Christians, that are not of a very base allay, that the Christian Eucharist is a rite, whereby the covenant between God and man in Christ Jesus is ratified and renewed ; and if it be once granted, that the Eucharist is a material Sacrifice of thanksgiving, and such a Sacrifice of thanksgiving, as that in, and by it, pardon and grace are actually applied to the souls

of the communicants; I am apt to believe, that the more SECT.
ingenuous part of our adversaries would scarce think it I.
worth while to dispute, whether it were directly and properly an expiatory sacrifice for sin, or not. For if it were so
allowed to be in effect, why should they contend about names
and words? And therefore what follows is not added, as if I
thought it necessary for the support of the Altar and Sacrifice;
(for a sacrifice of thanksgiving is in all respects as much a
sacrifice, as a sin-offering;) but it is added, in defence of
several of the ancients, and even of the Apostle himself,
whom I apprehend to speak elsewhere of the Eucharist, as
of a sacrifice for sin. And therefore,

2. I shall answer more directly to the allegations from the
Epistle to the Hebrews.

(1.) By considering what the Apostle means by perfecting,
and sanctifying, and by sacrifice for sin.

(2.) By shewing, that the perfecting, sanctifying, and
sacrifice for sin here meant by the Apostle, are not exclusive
of further perfection, sanctification, and sacrifice.

(3.) And that the Apostle afterwards, in the tenth chapter,
speaks of the oblation in the Eucharist.

(1.) I shall consider, what is here meant by "perfecting,"
and "sanctifying," and by "sacrifice," or "offering for sin."
And we cannot but know, what sort of sin-offering is here
meant; if we do but first understand, what the Apostle intended by the words "perfecting," and "sanctifying." And
here we must lay it down, as a certain foundation to all that
follows, that it is something performed *once for all*, and *for
ever*: some privilege purchased and conferred by the personal
oblation of Christ, never to be forfeited, or revoked. For the
Apostle argues the imperfection of the Jewish sacrifices, from
this consideration, that they "could not for ever make the chap. x. 1.
comers thereunto perfect;" (for so Dr. Whitby[i] and others
do justly construe the words). The perfection therefore
here said to be procured by the Sacrifice of Christ, must
be a perpetual perfection, without any end, or intermission,
so long as the world endures. And to this purpose the Apo- chap. x. 20.
stle remarks, that we are "sanctified by the offering of the
Body of Jesus Christ once for all." And again, "by one ver. 14.

[i] [vol. ii. p. 638.]

offering He hath perfected for ever them that are sanctified." They are so perfected, as that God will "no more
remember their sins;" and by consequence, they shall have
ver. 17, 18. no more occasion "for an offering for sin;" nay, the perfec-
ver. 2. tion is so great, that "the worshippers, once purged, have no
more conscience of sin." Now before I proceed, I shall from
hence observe, that the Apostle cannot here intend a moral
sanctification; as Grotius, with the Socinians and Quakers,
would have it[k]. For that is a thing not wrought all at once,
but gradually. There is no man so sanctified in this life, but
he may lapse into sin; and if the greatest saint on earth
commits a known sin, no doubt but God imputes it to him,
and therefore remembers it, until it be repented of and expiated. No grace is indefectible, no human holiness without
some intermissions, on this side of heaven; and therefore
none in this life can, in this sense, be "sanctified for ever," or
exempted from having a "consciousness of sin;" except you
will suppose, that the death of Christ makes the elect im-
peccable; or with the Antinomians assert, that God does not
impute sinful actions to the elect. I should dwell longer on
these particulars, if I had any reason to apprehend, that I
were like to have any readers infected with such pestilential
notions; nor can those baptized Christians be said to be perfected for ever, who, upon their repentance and proper application to the Divine mercy, have the pardon of their former
actual known sins sealed to them. For they may relapse, and
too often do, into the very same sins. Nor can it, I suppose,
in reason be doubted, that the Jewish sacrifices did, by virtue
of the Divine promise, "take away sin" for the time past; but
they could not do it "for ever," for the time to come; and this
was that particular, wherein the Sacrifice of Christ does so
much excel those of the Law. But neither does the Sacrifice

---

[k] [Grotius thus annotates on ver. 2.
" Si semel purgati fuissent (quemadmodum sunt veri Christiani 1 Pet. i.
22.) non ultra conscii sibi essent novo-
rum quotannis peccatorum, quæ ex-
piatione egerent."—Grotii Opera, tom.
ii. vol. ii. p. 1046. ed. Amstel. 1679.
    Socinus says: "Sacrificia illa (sci-
licet Legis) a peccatis retrahendi nullam vim habebant: quapropter, cum,
peractis illis, homines in eosdem errores
denuo laberentur, eadem offerenda sæ-
pius erant, et quotannis per ipsa peccatorum expiatio procuranda; Christi
vero sacrificium a peccando cessare
facit, et perpetuo hanc vim obtinet.
Quo consecuto, jam necessario etiam
omnium peccatorum remissio conse-
quitur. Et ita nulla amplius pro peccatis oblatione est opus."—Fausti Socini Opera, tom. ii. p. 167. ed. 1656.]

of Christ take away the moral turpitude of sin, nor the ob- SECT.
I.noxiousness to punishment, in those that are guilty of it, but for the time past only. It remains therefore, that I directly and positively shew, in what sense Christ does once for all perfect, or take away sin, for the future, as well as for the time past. For it is evident, that to "perfect for ever," and to purge, or sanctify the worshipper, so that he may never again "have conscience of sin," are two phrases signifying the same thing, in the first and second verses of this tenth chapter. It is clear beyond all dispute, that no sacrifice does once for all take away the moral stain, or guilt of sins, hereafter to be committed; or exempt men from sin for the time to come; therefore the Apostle cannot be understood in this context of any such perfection. If I am now asked, what else can be the Apostle's meaning?

I answer: By perfecting and taking away sin once for all, St. Paul plainly describes that privilege purchased by Christ's death, and once for all conferred upon His Church, whereby the whole body of Christian Priests and people are qualified to make their public addresses to God with acceptance, notwithstanding their corruption of nature, and the known actual sins of particular members. It is the universal opinion of the main bulk of mankind, or at least was so of old, that men are not fit to approach the Divine nature, without some mediator, or some preparative lustrations; and therefore not only the heathen, but the Jews, by God's appointment, had variety of rites and sacrifices, whereby not only to propitiate the Deity, but whereby to initiate and fit themselves to perform those propitiatory services. It were very easy to enlarge on this head, both from the sacred and profane writers; but it is a thing so generally known and allowed, that I shall not insist upon it; but only observe to my reader, that St. Paul, who is now granted by all men of learning, I think, to be the penman of this Epistle, does frequently insist upon this particular, as a very eminent privilege of the Christian Church, which makes it the more credible, that he should speak of it so largely here. He tells us, that "through Christ we have access to the Father," that "in Christ Jesus we have boldness, and access with confidence," that "by Him we have access into this grace wherein we stand." But in this Epistle to the Eph. ii. 18.
Eph. iii. 12.
Rom. v. 2.

CHAP.
II.

chap. iv.
15, 16.

chap. x. 19.
22.

John x. 9;
xiv. 6.

Hebrews, he is more copious on this subject. " For," says he, " we have not an high-priest, who cannot be touched with a feeling of our infirmities—Let us therefore come boldly unto the throne of grace." Nay, which is much more to our present purpose, he winds up his discourse in the ninth and tenth chapters, concerning the perfecting and sanctifying power of the one Sacrifice of Christ, with this application, viz. " Having therefore, brethren, boldness to enter into the Holies, by the Blood of Jesus—Let us draw near with a true heart, in full assurance of faith ;" and in this sense I suppose it is, that our Saviour calls Himself " the door" and " the way ;" and says, " no man can come to the Father but by Him," that is, it is by virtue of the merits of His death, that we have admittance into the Divine presence in this life, notwithstanding the pollutions and infirmities of our nature, and even our known sins. It is a privilege granted to the whole Church ; and in this respect it is indefeasible. Some particular men may lose this privilege by apostasy ; but the very essence and being of a Church depends entirely on this privilege. The Church is a society of men, incorporated together for the sake of Divine worship ; but if the infirmities and sins of Priests, or people, do render their worship unacceptable to God, then they are incorporated to no purpose at all. Nay, we cannot be sure, that the Sacraments themselves are valid, if either the known or unknown pollutions of the Priests who officiate, or the members of the Church assembled together with us, could obstruct the communications of Divine grace. So that this franchise was one of the principal ends of Christ's death ; and without it the Church itself could not be, and particular men could never have their consciences purged from the terror of their own sins, or of other men's sin, who join with them in the worship of God, so as that they could, with due confidence and assurance, approach the throne of grace ; and this franchise was once for all, and for ever, purchased and conferred upon the Church of Christ. And further to confirm and establish this notion, I will first shew, that the words and phrases used by the Apostle, in treating on this subject, are such as were used in the old Law, in relation to the lustrative rites and sacrifices thereby enjoined. And I shall further observe, that the sacrifices mentioned by

the Apostle in these two chapters, as types of the Sacrifice of S E C T.
I.
Christ, were such initiative or lustrative sacrifices.

Now the words and phrases used by the Apostle here, and used by Moses, and the Greek translators of him, in relation to these initiative or lustrative rites and sacrifices, are these, viz. τελειοῦν, which we turn (with no great exactness) 'perfecting,' but which properly signifies to 'consecrate' to some office, or dignity; the words καθαρίζειν, and ἀγιάζειν, rendered in the English 'purge' and 'sanctify,' carry a signification much the same with τελειοῦν, though not so full and strong. 'Sin,' ἁμαρτία, denotes that incapacity which is in all creatures, in this corrupted state, for the worship of God; to 'take away sin,' signifies the removing this incapacity; and the 'offering,' or 'sacrifice for sin,' the material oblations that were to be used for this end. I will give some proofs of each particular.

Τελειοῦν does most commonly signify to 'consecrate' to the Priest's office: so Heb. ii. 10, Christ is said to have been 'perfected,' that is, consecrated to His Priesthood. And again, Christ "being made perfect," that is, 'consecrated,' (Gr. τελειωθεὶς,) " He became the author of eternal salvation," &c. And it is so rendered by our translators, in those words, "the law maketh men high-priests, who have infirmities; but the word of the oath, which is since the law, maketh the Son, Who is consecrated for evermore," εἰς αἰῶνα τετελειωμένον. The consecration of Aaron and his sons is usually expressed by this word. What is in Hebrew " thou shalt fill," or rather " perfect the hand of Aaron," and is by the English there rendered, "thou shalt consecrate them," is by the LXX rendered τελειώσεις Ἀαρὼν, &c. Exod. xxix. 9. 29. 33. And again, Num. iii. 3. So the consecrated priest is τετελειωμένος, Lev. xxi. 10; the day of his consecration ἡμέρα τελειώσεως, Lev. viii. 33; the burnt-offering on that occasion ὁλοκαύτωμα τῆς τελειώσεως.

Ἀγιάζειν has much the same signification. God directs Moses, what he shall do to Aaron and his sons, to 'hallow,' or 'consecrate' them (Gr. ἀγιάσαι αὐτοὺς) " to minimister in the Exod. xxix.
1. priest's office;" and again, "Aaron shall be hallowed (Gr. ἀγιασθήσεται) and his garments," ver. 9; and in the next chapter, " thou shalt anoint Aaron, and his sons to hallow

CHAP.
II.

John xvii.
19.

Lev. xvi.
6. 15.

John xiii. 1.

them," or 'consecrate' them (as the English very justly has it) "that they may minister unto Me in the Priest's office," ver. 30; and we have the same words repeated chap. xl. 13. "And in this sense" (saith Dr. Whitby, from whom I have borrowed most of the references) "our Saviour saith, 'for their sakes I consecrate [sanctify] Myself, that they may be sanctified in the truth,' that they may be consecrated to their office, and set apart for My service. For as Aaron and his sons were hallowed, and set apart for God's service by a Sacrifice; so Christ's Apostles were sanctified, and set apart to their office, not only by the unction of the Holy Ghost, but also by the piacular victim, which Christ offered for their sins; and accordingly in these words, 'he that sanctifies' is Christ, that offered Himself,—'and they that are sanctified,' are they that by His Blood are purified from their sins, and fitted to draw nigh to God, and make a royal priesthood[1]." And if the learned Doctor had remembered this his excellent annotation on Heb. ii. 11, when he was writing his notes on Heb. vii. 27, he would most probably have given us a clearer explication of it, than he has. The words in the English translation stand thus, "Such an High-Priest became us — Who needeth not daily, as those high-priests, to offer up Sacrifice, first for Himself, and then for the people; for this He did once, when He offered up Himself." There can be no doubt, but these words are meant of the sacrifices offered on the day of expiation; for then only the high-priest offered first for the sins of "his own house," or family, the priests; and then for "the sins of the people:" and therefore καθ' ἡμέραν must signify on 'every day' of expiation. But what I would especially remark is, that Christ can in no sense be said to offer for His own sins, whatever Grotius conceited[m]; nor does Dr. Whitby allow of Grotius's wild notion; but then he gives no account, how the Apostle could say that our Saviour did what the high-priest used to do, viz. offer first, ὑπὲρ τῶν ἰδίων ἁμαρτιῶν, " and then for the people;" whereas by making ἰδίων to relate to the Apostles, who are called Christ's ἴδιοι, as being those "who did peculiarly belong to

---

[1] [vol. ii. p. 599.]

m ["Grotius and the Socinians contend, that Christ is here said to have offered up Himself *for His own* sins; but then, by sins, they say, is improperly signified His natural infirmities and sufferings."—Whitby in loco, vol. ii. p. 624.]

Him;" and supposing the word ἀποστόλων understood to be
the latter substantive to ἁμαρτιῶν, the words may fairly be
rendered, " He offered first for the sins of them who belonged
to Him, and then for the people ;" and this Jesus undoubtedly
did, " when He offered up Himself." And as for the word
καθαρίζειν, it is applied to the purgation of the people by the
sacrifices offered on the day of expiation (which will hereafter
appear to have been lustrative sacrifices :) " The priests shall
make an atonement for you, to cleanse you (Gr. καθα-
ρίσαι ὑμᾶς) from all your sins, and ye shall be cleansed,"
(Gr. καὶ καθαρισθήσεσθε.) And though the word be not
often used in relation to Aaron's being consecrated, yet the
day on which this was performed is called ἡμέρα καθαρισμοῦ
by the LXX, in the Hebrew יום הכפרים, which is otherwise
rendered by our translators ; and in the same verse, these
two words of which I am now speaking are promiscuously
used, and applied to the same sense, " and thou shalt Exod. xxix.
cleanse" (Gr. καθαριεῖς) " the altar, when thou hast made ^36.
atonement" (Gr. ἐν τῷ ἁγιάζειν) " for it, and thou shalt
anoint it to sanctify it." And the leper that had been cured
of his disease, and comes to offer his oblation upon that occasion, is called καθαριζόμενος ; and it is added καθαρισθήσεται,
" he shall be clean :" not cleansed of the disease ; for the Lev. xiv.
offering was made on presumption that he was already cured ; ^19, 20.
but he shall be acquitted from the disability he was under,
of entering into the tabernacle for public worship. And the
reader cannot but observe, that the altar was cleansed or
purged, and sanctified, and had an atonement made for it, as
well as the priest ; and therefore the consecration, sanctification, or whatever else you please to call it, could not consist in having a discharge from moral guilt, or from obnoxiousness to punishment. For the altar was not capable of
that ; and the leprosy was no moral sin, but a bodily pollution ; and therefore they do but deceive themselves, who are
so far carried away with the vulgar sense of these words as to
imagine, that any internal moral holiness is implied in them,
in these places. It is true, I have not observed that τελειοῦν
is in the Levitical law applied to any inanimate thing, or to
any other persons, but to the priests only ; but it ought not
to be omitted, that in most of the places above cited, from

Exod. xxix. and Numb. iii. the Greek is τελειοῦν χεῖρας, " to
consecrate the hands," as the Hebrew also signifies " to
fill," or " perfect the hands ;" and therefore it cannot rationally import any intrinsical holiness or innocence, but such a
separation for holy offices, as might give the people and themselves assurance that what they did in the service of God was
valid and acceptable, notwithstanding any personal sins or
infirmities.   For the case of the Jewish people had been
miserable indeed, if the success of their sacrifices and devotions had depended upon the real internal graces of the
priest, or on his being free from the stain of moral guilt.
This was what it was impossible they could certainly know ;
it was sufficient for them that they might be eye-witnesses to
the high-priests and priests performing those lustrative rites
and sacrifices, whereby they were qualified to continue the
holy functions, for which they were separated ; and by the
repetition whereof, their other oblations and services for
themselves and the people were acceptable in the sight of
God.

ʼAφελεῖν, or ἀφαίρειν ἁμαρτίαν is a phrase, which undoubtedly sometimes signifies to take away the guilt of any
immorality, and to free the offender from all punishment;
2 Sam. xii.
13.
as in the case of David, to whom Nathan said, " the Lord
hath put," or taken " away thy sin ;" but in other places it
imports no more, than to remove from men the incapacity
they are under to appear before God, or to perform their
part in holy offices ; so when the angel, who touched Isaiah's
Isa. vi. 7.
lips with a coal, said, " thine iniquity is taken away, and thy
sin is purged," there is, I believe, no sufficient reason to
believe, that any more is meant by it, than that some impedi-
ment in the prophet's speech, or some legal uncleanness, that
he was then under, was thereby removed.   And when the
Zech. iii. 4.
Lord said unto Joshua the high-priest, " I have caused thy
sin to pass from thee, and will clothe thee with change of
raiment," or " with the long robe," as the LXX render it ; it
seems probable, that the meaning was, that God would restore
him to the function of the high-priesthood, and accept his
ministrations ; notwithstanding his long conversation with the
heathen under his captivity, by which he must have contracted many legal uncleannesses, by which he was under a

disability for the performance of his office. But there is more SECT.
decisive evidence for this signification of the phrase, where —— I.
God charges Aaron, that the golden plate shall be upon his Ex. xxviii.
forehead, that he may bear, (Gr. καὶ ἀφαρεῖ,) or, and "he
shall take away the iniquity of the holy things, which the
children of Israel shall hallow — that they may be accepted
before the Lord." And Numb. xviii. 1, "The Lord said
unto Aaron, Thou and thy sons shall bear the iniquity of the
sanctuary;" for by the words here rendered "bear the iniquity," by the LXX λήψονται ἁμαρτίαν, I suppose no man can
doubt, but that we are to understand, that they shall bear or
carry them away, viz. by lustrative sacrifices, particularly
those on the day of expiation. Now since no man can believe, that there is in any inanimate creatures sin, or iniquity,
according to the sense in which the word is now commonly
taken among us; it remains, that we must thereby understand that ineptitude, that is in all creatures, to be made use
of in the service of God, without a previous lustration. There
can be no other pollution in any creatures void of sense, and
dedicated to religious uses, but what proceeds either from
that universal corruption, which upon the fall of man spread
itself through the whole terrestrial system; or from the relation it bears to them that offer it, that is, sinful men; or from
the abuse of it, by the profaneness and sacrilege of others:
and any of these might for a time render it unfit for holy
uses; but nothing could render it liable to any real guilt or
punishment; and therefore "taking away sin," in some cases,
must indisputably signify no more, than relieving men or
other creatures from some disability which they are under,
of worshipping God in public, or of being made use of to this
purpose; and by consequence, 'sin' must in such cases signify
no more than an incapacity of worshipping God, or being
made use of in the worship of God; "and a sacrifice, or
offering for sin" must signify, what is offered to God in
order to remove this incapacity, and to reinstate men in the
enjoyment of this privilege. And there is abundant proof of
this in the law of Moses; from which the Apostle, especially
in this Epistle, generally takes both his ideas and diction.
Now it is very evident, to all that read the books of Moses
with any degree of attention, that the English 'sin,' the Greek

CHAP.
II.

Numb. xix.
9. 17.
Lev. v. 2. 6.

Lev. xiv.
12, 13. 19,
20. 22. 31.

Lev. xv.
15. 30.

ἁμαρτία, and the Hebrew חטאה signify, not only immorality, but 'uncleanness' and 'impurity;' and the same may be said of what is commonly turned 'iniquity' by the English, ἁμαρτία by the Greek, and is עון in the Hebrew. You have just now heard Moses speak of " the iniquity of the sanctuary, and of the things hallowed" to God. So the ashes of a red heifer are said to be " a purification for sin," and the sin was touching a dead body, grave, &c.; and "if a soul," that is, a person, "touch any unclean thing,—he shall bring his trespass-offering to the Lord for the sin that he hath sinned." Nay, we read of a sin-offering and a trespass-offering, to be made for a man that was to be purified after the leprosy, which was a disease which, to be sure, no one chose; nay, which it was impossible in some cases for a man to avoid: there was nothing voluntary, and therefore nothing morally culpable in it; and yet the man, who had laboured under it, before he could be admitted as a worshipper in the tabernacle, must have a sin-offering presented in his behalf. And the case was the same with the man or woman that had an issue, by what means soever they came by it, whether through their fault, or their misfortune; a sin-offering was required, before they could be restored to the privilege of making their appearance before God in the place of worship; and in all these cases an atonement was to be made for the person, that came to be cleansed, or purified. So that I judge it clear beyond any reasonable doubt, that these phrases may fairly be taken in this sense; and that in the ninth and tenth chapters to the Hebrews, they cannot safely be taken in any other, than what I now contend for. But that this may further appear, I will also consider all those sacrifices, of which the Apostle here makes mention, in the same order that the Apostle speaks of them. And I suppose, the consideration of these sacrifices, and the connexion of St. Paul's discourse, will give us some additional light into the subject, of which I am treating.

Now the Apostle, having given a brief description of the sanctuary, or court of the priest, which he calls " the Holies;" and of the innermost *adytum* of the tabernacle, which he calls " the holiest of all," or " the Holy of Holies;" and of the sacred furniture of both, in the five first verses of the ninth chapter: in the sixth verse he observes, that " the priests who

celebrated the Divine service went continually into the first;"
and so he drops his discourse of this particular for the present;
but he proceeds to speak of the second, or the Holy of Holies,
"into which," says he, " the high-priest went once every year,
not without blood, which he offered for himself, and the errors
of the people." In which words, without dispute, he alludes
to the solemn sacrifices performed on the day of expiation;
and those were lustrative sacrifices, whereby both priest and
people were, by a sort of reconsecration, prepared for the
worship of God for the ensuing year. Our translators very
aptly turn the twentieth verse of Levit. xvi. by saying, that
Aaron was " to reconcile the holy place, and the tabernacle,
and the altar, and the congregation." The Jews had no right
or tenure in God's house, but what was renewable from year
to year; and therefore, at the return of every day of expiation,
their term expired ; and if they expected to enjoy this privilege for the year now coming, they must renew their services
and devotions, by which they held this privilege of appearing
before God. The virtue of the sacrifices offered on the last
day of expiation was spent; and priest, people, tabernacle,
and altar must be reconciled, before they could have any
claim, or pretence to the honour of appearing, or being used,
before the Divine majesty in the ensuing year; and therefore the Apostle truly observes, that "these sacrifices could ver. 9.
not consecrate him that did the service," that is, the high-
priest himself, as "pertaining to conscience;" that is, they
could not consecrate him "for ever," or for a perpetuity, as
the Apostle explains himself. The high-priest knew in his chap. x. 1.
own conscience, that his reconsecration was but for the
term of one year, and that the whole system of their worship
and polity must at the end of that term be reconciled again,
as being not founded upon so durable a bottom as ours is, so
as to remain without any renewal or reconsecration " unto
the end of the world." The Apostle further depreciates
the Mosaical œconomy, as " standing only in meats, and ver. 10.
drinks, and divers washings," &c. and in the next words
exalts Christ Jesus, and His religious institutions, by calling
Him " a High-Priest of good things to come." Now as the
state of things under the Messias is called by the Apostle, according to the familiar language of the Jews, " the world to

come," which is said " not to be put in subjection to angels," and as the efficacy of Christian ordinances is called " the powers of the world to come," so " the good things to come," of which Christ is here styled the High-Priest, seem plainly to be the Sacrifice of His Body and Blood; [as St. Jerome hath observed, that the Apostle speaks to the Hebrews with great reserve concerning the Eucharist; so this is apparent in this place and in ch. x. 1. He clearly opposes the Christian ordinances to those of the Jews: as he calls the former ' carnal,' so he calls the latter ' good.' You may, if you please, render the words, " Christ being come an High-Priest of good ordinances;" for δικαιώματα is the substantive going next before. We shall soon have occasion to observe, that St. Paul in other places of this Epistle calls Christ " the High-Priest of our oblation." And I take this to be of much the same signification with the title here given Him, viz. " High-Priest of the good ordinances," or of His own Body and Blood,] and in this eleventh and the twelfth verse he tells us, that Christ entered into the holy place, viz. heaven, " by," or " through a more perfect tabernacle," than that erected by Moses, " a tabernacle not made with hands, that is to say, not of this [sort of] building," that the Jewish place of worship was. It is strange to me, that there should be any dispute, what is here meant by " the tabernacle not made with hands, through which Christ entered into heaven." It seems so plain a description of " the Church of the first-born," the Apostles, and other converts which Christ made while He was here on earth, and with whom alone He conversed for the forty days between His resurrection and ascension, and from the midst of whom He was afterwards assumed into heaven; that I see no room to doubt, but that the Church is this tabernacle; and if the reader please to consult commentators upon this place, he will be more inclined to believe so still, by observing the incongruity of those conjectures, which have been advanced by some others. As then the high-priest, on the day of expiation, went from the altar through the second court, or the apartment of the priests, into the Holy of Holies; so Christ Jesus from the altar of the cross proceeded with triumph into heaven through His new sanctuary the Church, not made with hands; and this, says the Apostle, He did, " having

obtained eternal redemption for us;" an eternal redemption SECT.
from the incapacity, we are under by nature, of rendering I.
acceptable worship to God; and from an endless repetition
of these burthensome rites and sacrifices, by which the Jews
annually purged themselves from this incapacity.

The Apostle proceeds, in the 13th verse, to mention another
method of lustration, prescribed by the law of Moses, where Numb. xix.
the ashes of a red heifer mingled with water, and sprinkling
the unclean person, that is, him who had touched a dead
corpse, grave, &c., are made a necessary preparative to the
being readmitted into the tabernacle, the place of public
worship. The Apostle says, these ashes "sanctified to the
purifying of the flesh;" that is, the man was thereby anew
dedicated or prepared for the service of God: the defilement
he had contracted by the touch of the corpse, or grave, was
taken off, so that he was no longer debarred from making
his public addresses to God; to this sense Dr. Whitby, after
Dr. Hammond, interprets the words very justly. And if
the unclean person presumed to appear in the tabernacle,
before he had submitted to this method of purgation, he
is said "to defile the sanctuary of the Lord." Therefore Numb. xix.
by the "blood of bulls and goats," in this verse, he must 13. 20.
mean the sacrifices offered on the day of expiation; because
he attributes the same effects to them, that he does to the
ashes of the red heifer, namely, that they "sanctify to the
purifying of the flesh," or procure admittance into the
presence of God. The difference between them seems only
this, viz. that the ashes of the heifer were to be used by
single persons, in case of one particular defilement; the
sacrifices on the day of expiation were intended for the
benefit of the whole body of priests and people, and for
all sorts of sin and uncleanness, that they might be no
hinderance to the acceptableness of the public worship;
and particularly, that by this means they might be qualified
to offer such sacrifices for sin, as had a promise of full pardon
annexed to them; of which see Levit. iv. 20. 26. 32. 35.
And since the Apostle in the *protasis* mentions only lustrative sacrifices and rites, whereby men were prepared for the
solemn worship of God; therefore it is very unreasonable and
incongruous, to suppose, that in the *apodosis* he considers

CHAP.
II.

"the Blood of Christ" any otherwise than as a lustrative sacrifice, whereby we are 'purged,' or 'dedicated,' to "serve the living God;" the word λατρεύειν signifies the serving or worshipping God in a solemn public manner; nay, in the sixth verse of this chapter it evidently signifies, to perform the priest's part in the public service; and in the ninth verse, λατρεία denotes the functions that were peculiar to the priests; but we will give it for granted, that in this verse it imports the worship both of priest and people; and St. Paul argues very strongly, that if the ashes of the red heifer could so far expiate the uncleanness of men, as to prepare them for the Levitical worship; much more may the Blood of Christ give us confidence to make our approaches to God. The Apostle expresses the purgation or preparation we receive for the service of the living God, by the phrase of "purging our consciences from dead works;" because by Baptism all past sin whatsoever is forgiven; and there particular men have the effects of Christ's death so communicated to them, that by it, as by a most perfect lustrative sacrifice, they are for ever after emboldened to join in the public devotions of the Church, so long as they continue members of it; but no man can from hence in reason argue, that sins to come are forgiven in Baptism, as well as sins past; or that Baptism does exempt us from sin, or the imputation of it; or that sins committed after Baptism are not pardoned in and by the public worship, especially the Eucharist; and that therefore the conscience of such, as have relapsed into sin after Baptism, is only so far purged from dead works by virtue of Baptism, or by any other means, as that it is permitted and encouraged to make application to God for pardon in the evangelical way, that is, especially in and by the Eucharist, as has and will appear. And the main, of those to whom the Apostle here speaks, were undoubtedly baptized Christians, who do not receive forgiveness of sins before worship; but by the means of that public worship and Sacrament of His Body and Blood, which was intended by Him for the remission of sins. And therefore the Apostle, ver. 15, seems to say, that Christ's death was designed chiefly "for the remission of transgressions, under the first covenant," meaning that of Moses. He was speaking to such as had been born and

bred in the Jewish religion, and such men had no sins to be
forgiven, upon their conversion to Christianity and Baptism,
but only such as they had committed under the first covenant
or testament, or while they had been Moses's disciples: as
for sins committed after Baptism, the Apostle, toward the end
of the Epistle, reminds them of an Altar and Sacrifice, where
remission was to be had. Some perhaps may from hence
infer, that I would confine the effects of Christ's death to
the pardon of sins, which we receive in Baptism only; and
therefore I add, for the avoiding of all such misconstruction,
that it is very evident from the words of institution and
from the suffrage of antiquity, that all the blessings of the
New Testament, and whatever graces we receive in the
Eucharist, are derived from the effusion of the natural
Blood of Christ upon the cross; that this was the original
Blood of the New Testament, and the other only the full
and perfect representative of that Blood; that by the oblation and effusion of Christ's personal Blood, the new covenant
was once for all enacted and established; that by virtue of
this covenant, all baptized Christians and ordained Priests
have a perpetual right of being admitted to perform their
parts in the Christian worship, the most solemn and essential
article of which worship is the holy Eucharist. And therefore
the death of Christ is the foundation of all that pardon of sin,
which we receive in the Sacrament; not only because by
the death of Christ we have a right to all Christian ordinances purchased for us; but because the Eucharist derives
all its efficacy and power from the first and grand Sacrifice,
personally offered by Christ. But I cannot apprehend, how
the pardon purchased by Christ can be applied to baptized
Christians, in and by the service and worship of God, as
it is beyond all dispute; and yet, that we receive this pardon
as previous to this worship, and in order to our due performance of it; as they must think, who make the Apostle
say, that there must be a full pardon of all sin, before we
can be in covenant with God; or, that " God can enter into
covenant with none, who lie under the guilt of sin," as
Dr. Whitby expresses his sentiment on this text[n]. This is

---

[n] [" God, being an holy God, can
enter into covenant with none, or admit

them into His service, whilst they lie
under the guilt of sin unpardoned, and

a very strange opinion, and supported with as strange proofs.
He says, "Noah found grace with God, and with him He
established His covenant." Whereas it is very obvious,
that God established His covenant not only with Noah, but
with his sons, and with his seed after him, and will the
Doctor answer for the innocence and integrity of them?
He says, "Abraham believed God, and this was imputed
to him for righteousness, and then the Lord makes a covenant with him by sacrifice." But, with submission, this
covenant was not perfectly confirmed, until circumcision
was instituted. And this covenant was made, not only with
Abraham, but with his seed and his family; and will the
Doctor give his word for it, that Ishmael, and all the 318
servants of Abraham, before they were circumcised, were
free from all guilt and sin? But the most unhappy instance
of all is, what he mentions in the last place, I mean, that
of the Jews: "They," says Dr. Whitby, "offered burnt-offerings, &c. and then God enters into covenant with them."
The Doctor takes the liberty to represent the covenant as
yet to be made, when the sacrifices had already been offered;
whereas, in reality, the covenant was plighted and confirmed
by offering the sacrifice, and sprinkling the blood, as the
words of Moses sufficiently testify, viz. "This is the blood
of the covenant, which God hath made with you;" but the
Doctor knew very well, that the Jews were a stiff-necked
people, and that God Himself complains "of them, that from
the day they departed out of Egypt, they had been rebellious
against the Lord." And that but a little while before this
covenant was made, they had made a head, and murmured
against God and Moses. And therefore he was very sensible,
that in order to prove, that they did not now lie under the guilt
of sin, there was no way left but to intimate that this guilt
was taken away by sacrifice, and this sacrifice offered as
previous and in order to the establishing of the covenant.
Whereas the truth is, that the blood of those sacrifices was

so have not found grace in His sight. *Noah found grace in the eyes of God*, and with him He established His covenant, Gen. vi. 8. 18. Abraham believes in God, and *this was counted to him for righteousness;* and then the Lord makes a covenant with him by sacrifice, Gen.

xv. 10. 18. So, Exod. xxiv. 6, the Jews offer burnt-offerings, and sacrifice peace-offerings to the Lord, and the blood is sprinkled upon all the people, and then He enters into covenant with them."—Vol. ii. p. 634.]

the very blood of the covenant; and by the sprinkling of S E C T. this blood, the covenant was struck; and by the very same ——I.—— act, they were so far acquitted from all conscience of sin, as to have liberty to appear before God in His worship. Until men have entered into covenant, they must lie under the guilt of sin; for guilt can be taken away by no other means than the Divine grace and mercy; and the Divine grace and mercy is no other way certainly to be obtained but by covenant; and until that covenant be sealed, our pardon must, to say the least, be very dubious. But, to apply this to the Christian covenant, will the Doctor say, that no man can be baptized, that lies under the guilt of unpardoned sin? I should rather say with the Scriptures, that we are " baptized for the remission of sins;" and that therefore we enter into covenant with God; because, without doing so, our sins cannot be pardoned. And again, that we are under a necessity of renewing this covenant by the Eucharist: because we have committed sin since Baptism; and there is no way to procure pardon but by covenant; and we have no way to renew the covenant but by the holy Eucharist: and, therefore, to say, that God enters into covenant with none " that lie under the guilt of sin unpardoned," seems to me a very unwarrantable paradox.

But I proceed to take notice of the next sacrifices, which the Apostle speaks of on this occasion; and they are those offered by Moses, upon the dedication of that covenant, of Exod.xxiv. which he was mediator. The Apostle had observed, ver. 15, that Christ is Mediator of the New Testament by that Blood of His, which he had mentioned in the foregoing verse; (for as Dr. Whitby well observes, διὰ τοῦτο may more consistently be so rendered than ' for this cause,' as our English translation has it;) and to shew the necessity of blood for the enacting a Divine covenant, he observes, ver. 18—22, that the " old covenant was not dedicated without blood." " For when Moses," says St. Paul, " had spoken every precept to all the people, he took the blood of calves and goats, and sprinkled both the book and all the people, saying, This is the blood of the covenant which the Lord hath enjoined you. Moreover he sprinkled with blood both the tabernacle and all the vessels of the ministry. And almost all things are by the

Law purged with blood, and without shedding of blood is no
remission." Now by these sacrifices, the whole body of the
Israelites, and the tabernacle, with its furniture, was dedicated to the worship of God; that is, both the people and the
whole apparatus were admitted, by virtue of these sacrifices,
notwithstanding the ineptitude they were under by nature,
to the most honourable employment that either inanimate or
animate creatures are capable of, that is, the service of God.
And the Apostle seems to speak upon a supposition, which I
have already hinted more than once; namely, that there is a
sort of remission of sin implied in every consecration of things
void of sense. For when the Apostle says in the same verse,
first " all things are consecrated by blood;" and then, " there
is no remission of sin without blood;" either they are two propositions containing the same sense, and so ' remission of sin'
in the latter is the same with 'consecration' in the former; or
else the Apostle gives it as a reason, why consecration cannot
be without blood, that remission of sin can be had only by
this means. And this cannot be said but upon supposition,
that whatever is consecrated does need a remission of sin;
and this remission can only be a taking off the natural
ineptitude before spoken of. For the reader will observe,
that the Apostle is here speaking of things, rather than
persons; and had, in the words next before, mentioned "the
tabernacle and all the vessels of the ministry," as " sprinkled
with blood," in order to their consecration or remission. It is
true, when the same tabernacle was to be " purged" or consecrated on every day of expiation, the reason given for this
rite of "making an atonement for the holy place" is, "because
of the uncleanness of the children of Israel, and because of
their transgressions." And the atonement was to be made
Lev. xvi.16. for the tabernacle, because " it remained among them in the
midst of their uncleanness;" but when the tabernacle was
new made and just now erected, and had never been made
use of for religious worship, and so could not have been
defiled by the people's approaching it under their sin and
uncleanness; this reason could not take place. It may be
said, that all the materials of the tabernacle, with its orna-
ments and utensils, were the oblations of the people; and so
needed a purgation, as coming from polluted hands; but this

cannot be said of the "book" which was written by Moses,
and contained the words of God Himself; which yet, the
Apostle assures us, was sprinkled with blood, as being intended to be lodged in the most holy place; and which
therefore, according to the sentiments of that age, was not
capable of that honour, as being written with and upon
materials sordid by nature, until it had first been consecrated in this solemn manner. And here, I think, we
have the certain precise signification of the word καθαρίζειν,
so often used in this discourse of the Apostle; and I suppose
it very evident, that it does not denote any internal purification from moral guilt; but only a relief or releasement from
that unfitness, which all terrestrial nature is under, from
being employed in the service of God; and therefore that
remission of sin, implied in this consecration, can strictly
import no more, than God's receiving men and things so far
to a Divine use, as to allow public addresses to be made to
Him by those men, in and with the things thus separated for
the exercise of religion. This may at first seem a thing of
too little consequence for the Apostle so much to insist upon,
but is really in itself very great: for by this men are put into
a capacity of drawing down from God all mercies necessary
for them, either in relation to this life, or that which is to
come; and this is especially true as to the new covenant;
which, as it was ratified by a Sacrifice infinitely more valuable
than those offered by Moses, so the consecration is not only
more lasting and durable, so as to need no repetition; but
qualifies the Church for a more perfect internal holiness, and
for much more weighty rewards. And the Apostle, in the
next words, does very much magnify the Christian institutions, and the consecration of them by the Blood of Christ,
beyond those of the Law. "It was necessary that the patterns of things in the heavens" (that is, the Jewish institutions) "should be purified" or consecrated "with these" sacrifices of beasts; "but the heavenly," that is, the evangelical
institutions themselves, "with better sacrifices than these,"
that is, with the Body and Blood of Christ. Here the Greek
commentators do, by the τὰ ἐπουράνια, which I render 'the
heavenly institutions,' understand the Sacraments and services of the Gospel, or the whole Christian œconomy and

CHAP.
II.

polity°. And it was evidently the Apostle's design to assert, that these were ratified and established by the personal Sacrifice of Christ; and that from thence all our ministrations and holy offices do receive their validity and efficacy. Nor is it any extraordinary flight in St. Paul to give the title of 'heavenly' to the Christian institutions. He evidently calls the Chris-

Gal. iv. 26. tian Church, "the Jerusalem above (or from above) which is

Eph. i. 3. the mother of us all;" and he says, God "hath blessed us with all spiritual blessings, in the heavenly institutions in Christ;"

Eph. ii. 6. and again, "He hath made us sit together in the heavenly institutions in Christ Jesus." I make 'institutions' the substantive to ἐπουράνια; because I cannot at present think of any English word, that seems more agreeable to the Apostle's meaning. For I cannot doubt but every impartial reader will own, that either that word, or some other of a like signification, is necessary to express the full meaning of St. Paul; and he who considers, that our Saviour did so familiarly style His Church the "kingdom of heaven," cannot think it strange, that one of His Apostles should call the Sacraments and services of this Church, and the whole system of its doctrine, worship, and government, the heavenly institutions. Dr. Whitby labours to prove, that the heavenly 'places' here (for he makes 'places' the substantive to ἐπουράνιαᴾ) denote those mansions, which Christ is gone to prepare for us; and there is no doubt but that heaven is the *sanctum sanctorum,* the most holy place in the Christian scheme; and the fundamental institution of the evangelical œconomy is, that the heavens must receive our High-Priest, until the time of restitution; and if the most sacred place, where our High-Priest stands officiating and appearing in the presence of God for us, is heaven itself, the heaven of the blessed; no wonder, that the Apostle calls that state of things, that building which is erected on the foundation of the Apostles and Prophets, and which is the only passage or entrance into heaven, by the sublime and honourable title of the τὰ ἐπουράνια, the celestial state, the supernal institutions. In a word, our Saviour is

---

° ["Καὶ ἡμῶν τὸ πολίτευμά ἐστι ἐν οὐρανοῖς, καίτοι ἐνταῦθα πολιτευόμεθα. αὐτὰ δὲ τὰ ἐπουράνια· τουτέστι, τὴν φιλοσοφίαν τὴν παρ' ἡμῖν."—S. Jo. Chrys. in Ep. ad Hebr., cap. ix. Hom.

xvi. tom. xii. p. 160. ed. Savile.]

ᴾ In his notes; but in his paraphrase our bodies are the τὰ ἐπουράνια.

"the minister of the whole tabernacle, which the Lord hath SECT.
pitched, and not men," and therefore hath consecrated or I.
reconciled, not the Holy of Holies only, but the entire sanc- Heb. viii.
tuary, with all its services and appendages.

Now the Apostle, to prove that the whole heavenly temple, ver. 24.
of which the Church is a part, was consecrated by the Sacrifice of Christ, returns to the sacrifices offered on the day of
expiation; and because the sanctuary and altar could not by
the law of Moses be purged or reconciled but by the high-
priest's carrying the blood of the sacrifices into the most
holy place; therefore he observes, that "Christ went into
heaven itself, now to appear in the presence of God for us."
But now, if Christ had perfected His people by what He did
and suffered on the cross, it will not be easy to say, to what
purpose He now appears in the presence of God for us. If
it be said, that the Sacrifice was not consummated until our
High-Priest appeared before God in the true Holy of Holies, I
allow that; but observe, that He had made that appearance
many years, before this Epistle was written: and it is certain,
that Christ is now appearing in our behalf, as well as in the
days of the Apostle; and therefore His Church is not yet
perfected in such a sense, as not still to want a High-Priest
and Sacrifice; and therefore, when the Apostle says, that
Christ appeared "to put away sin by the Sacrifice of Him- ver. 26.
self," it is certainly most proper, by 'sin' to understand that
disability we are under by nature, to appear in the presence
of God, or to make our addresses to Him. Ἀθέτησις does
properly signify an entire 'abolition' and 'disannulling,' (it is
rendered by the last English word, in our translation.) Now it Heb. vii. 18.
is evident, that Christ hath not disannulled sin, either as to
its guilt or dominion, any otherwise than as He has once for
all so effectually dedicated or consecrated His Church, that
the sins of particular men can never wholly unhallow or extinguish it. Sin will still be committed, even by honest and
sincere Christians; and whoever commits sin is not to think,
that he is exempted from the imputation of it by the evangelical covenant. It may indeed be truly said, that Christ appeared for the gradual annulling of the guilt and dominion of
sin; but then this end of His appearing will not be fully attained, so long as the world stands; and in order to His ac-

complishing of it, it was not only necessary that He should once offer Himself, but that He should perpetually intercede in heaven for His people; and He cannot therefore be said in this sense to have perfected them by offering Himself once for all; He cannot be said to have done that once for all, which He is still doing. I wish therefore Dr. Whitby had explained himself, when in his note on Heb. x. 18, he asserts, that Christ "hath perfectly and fully expiated, and that for ever, them that are sanctified;" and then argues against the Sacrifice of the Eucharist, by asking, "what necessity of, what virtue can there be in doing that again," (that is, expiating men,) "which is perfectly and fully done already, and that for ever?" He seems to me to suppose, that Christ, by His Sacrifice on the cross, did actually blot out the sins of all believers, even before they had been repented of, nay, before they were committed. "He was" indeed "once offered to bear the sins of many," even as many as should believe in His name; and He certainly did on the cross suffer, as the only perfect Sacrifice for sin; and it is only through the merits of His death, that Christians ever since have assurance of pardon, upon proper application made. But this is not that, which the Apostle had here in his eye; for he was speaking of the sacrifices offered on the day of expiation, which were not intended to take away the stain of moral guilt, as has been shewed; and ' sin' may here signify, what it evidently does in other parts of these chapters, our natural unfitness for the service or worship of God. And Christ did certainly as a Sacrifice suffer, in order to deliver believers once for all from this miserable state, or ' to take away,' or 'remove' this unfitness, as the word ἀνενεγκεῖν may be turned.

But I must not here omit the consideration of that vulgar argument against the Sacrifice of the Eucharist, viz. that Christ is said "to have been offered once," and that it is ver. 28, 25. expressly denied that " He was often to offer Himself." Now it is strange to me, that any man should pretend to argue upon any subject, and yet betray such an excess of ignorance or disingenuousness, as to suppose, that any who assert the Sacrifice of the Eucharist among us do believe or say, that Christ does personally offer Himself in the Eucharist. I am

apt to think, that even a Papist would scarce own this. We
are so far from believing, that Christ literally offers Himself
in the Eucharist, that we do not believe Him to be personally
there present in His human nature. It is true, several of
the ancients have said, that Christ offers Himself in the Eucharist; but they certainly meant no more, than that He did
so representatively, by His Priests, and under the substituted
symbols of Bread and Wine. He offers Himself in the Eucharist, as He performs the ablution in Baptism, as He instructs the people in public sermons, viz. by the hands and
mouths of His ministers; He there by substitution offers,
not His real self or His natural Body and Blood, but the mysteries or sacramental representations of them; and what inconsistence there is in doing this daily or hourly, I cannot perceive.
I have shewed, that the action, whereby Christ offered Himself as a Melchisedecian Priest, was performed in the Eucharist; and that what He did there was to be done again,
He has Himself informed us. But if they will still insist
upon it, notwithstanding this command of Christ, that what
was done once by Him is never again to be repeated by us; I
must further remind them, that if this arguing will hold, then
Priests must leave off to preach and catechise, or any way to
instruct the people in principles of Christianity. For we are
assured, that " the faith was once delivered to the saints;" [Jude, ver.
and it may as well be argued, that it is presumption for any 3.]
man to preach that again, which was once preached by
Christ, as that it is a presumption to offer that again, which
was once offered; and I am bold to say, that the commission
of Priests to offer the sacramental Body and Blood is as clear
to him that inspects it with impartial eyes, as that which He
gave them to preach the Gospel. But some think, that this
argument receives great addition of strength from the word
ἐφάπαξ; and tell us, that "we are perfected by the offering
of the Body of Christ once for all." And that Christians are
consecrated once for all, and that too by the offering made
personally by Christ, I have before shewed; but yet that
ἐφάπαξ does there, or elsewhere, signify " once for all," I am
yet to learn; nay, it is certain, it signifies ' all at once,' or ' at
one same time.' So Christ was seen of above five hundred
brethren, ἐφάπαξ, not ' once for all,' but ' all at once,' or

CHAP.
II.

1 Cor. xv. 6.
Heb. vii. 27.

Heb. ix.
11, 12.
Rom. vi. 10.

'at one and the same time;' and so Christ offered "for His own" [Apostles] "and for the people," ἐφάπαξ, 'all at once,' or 'at the same time.' So "Christ being made an High-Priest, and having obtained eternal redemption for us," did ἐφάπαξ, "at the same time, enter into heaven," (for that is the true series of those words.) Again, "in that Christ died, He died at the same time to sin." I am not sensible that the word is elsewhere used in the New Testament; and it does not appear, that there is any necessity of ever understanding it as if it signified 'once for all;' but that it must sometimes signify 'all at once,' is evident from the texts here cited, viz. 1 Cor. xv. 6. Though neither have we any reason to apprehend any hurt from the word as commonly understood; but this I have added, to shew upon how very loose a bottom they build, who would draw any conclusion in prejudice of the Eucharistical Sacrifice from this word ἐφάπαξ. And this is a full answer to the learned Dr. Whitby's first argument [q] against the Christian Sacrifice, in his note on Heb. x. 18, viz. "Christ cannot offer Himself, but He must suffer;" He could suffer but once, therefore He could offer but once; as if because Christ does not personally offer His Body and Blood in the Eucharist, therefore they cannot be offered there at all. And when the same Doctor argues, that the Eucharist is either a bloody Sacrifice, or else no remission of sin can be obtained by it; he is already answered; for we assert no such remission of sin in the Eucharist, as the Apostle there means; no release from our disability to offer our devotions to God. We must be discharged from this disability, before we are allowed to appear at the Lord's Table; and the whole Church was discharged from it at once, by the personal Sacrifice of Christ. It is true, these arguments were by the Doctor aimed against the Sacri-

---

[q] ["From these, and many other passages of this Epistle, the Sacrifice of the mass declared by the Trent council, Sess. 22. Can. 2, 3, to be a true and proper propitiatory sacrifice for sins, is utterly overthrown. For, first, from these words of the Apostle, 'It was not needful that He should offer Himself often, for then must He have often suffered,' chap. ix. 24—26, it is very evident that Christ cannot offer Himself, but He must suffer. Since then they dare not say that Christ suffers in the mass, neither can they say that Christ offers Himself there. Secondly, from those words, 'Without shedding of blood there is no remission,' chap. ix. 22, it follows, either that the Sacrifice of the mass must be a bloody sacrifice, and so Christ's Blood must be as often shed as He is offered in the mass, or else that it obtaineth no remission of sin."—Whitby in loco.]

fice of the mass; and how full of proof they may be against SECT.
the Popish sacrifice, I am not concerned to say; nor indeed ——— I.
do I pretend to know, how the modern doctors of the Church
of Rome have modified their notions upon this subject; but I
know very well the charity of our adversaries here at home,
and that they do upon all occasions declare us Papists in this
point; and I was apprehensive, that what Dr. Whitby has
written in confutation of the Sacrifice of the Church of Rome
in so famous a book, as his Paraphrase and Commentary on
the New Testament, might by unwary readers be applied to
the primitive Sacrifice, which I am now defending; and therefore I have said thus much by way of prevention.

The Apostle in the beginning of the tenth chapter, has
his eye still fixed upon the sacrifices offered on the day of
expiation. And that I may not too much trespass on my Lev. xvi.
reader's patience, I will, instead of a long disquisition,
which it were easy to make on this occasion, only present
him with a paraphrase on the four first verses, with some
brief reflections.

"The Law having" only "a" faint previous "shadow of the chap. x. 1.
good things to come," that is, of Christ's Body and Blood,
of which He was the High-Priest[r], in those sacrifices offered
on the day of expiation, which were not intended to be the
"very image" according to the life of the things by them
represented, as the Sacrifice of the Eucharist is; "can never
by those sacrifices, which they [the high-priests] offer year
by year, consecrate for ever those that come," or draw nigh
to God, by them, or with them.

In making the "very image" to be the Eucharist, I have
the authority of many of the ancients: that τελειοῦν properly signifies to consecrate, I have before proved. Dr.
Whitby agrees with me in construing εἰς τὸ διηνεκὲς with
τελειοῦν[s].

"For then," that is, if they had been able for ever to con- ver. 2.
secrate those who made use of them, "would they not have
ceased to be offered?" Yes, certainly, "because the cultors

---

[r] See my explication of chap. ix. 11.

[s] ["That which he (St. Paul) here
denies to the legal sacrifices, must be
also this, that they could τελειῶσαι εἰς

τὸ διηνεκὲς, 'expiate sins for ever;' or
so as that they, who were once purged
by them, 'should have no more conscience of sin.'"]

CHAP.
II.
once purged," or consecrated, would have no more [such] "conscience for sin," as to make them sensible of the necessity of being consecrated again the next year.

Lev. x. 3.

chap. ix. 9.

As the προσερχόμενοι may denote the priests themselves, because they are peculiarly said "to draw near to God," so it is very highly probable, that the λατρεύοντες can be no other than they, if it be considered, that τὸν λατρεύοντα does certainly characterize the high-priest. I suppose the Apostle first treats of the consecration of the priests, and afterwards of the people, in this chapter. And I suppose there is a very apparent reason, why the sacrifices on the day of expiation would have ceased, if they could have had a perpetual permanent effect; and that is, because they were only intended as lustrative or preparative sacrifices; and if they could once for all have taken off men's natural ineptitude and disability for Divine worship, there would have been no further occasion for the use of them; but this reason does not at all affect the Sacrifice of the Eucharist, for that is not intended as an initiative or lustrative sacrifice. Christ did once for all personally offer His Body and Blood, for the perpetual consecration, lustration, or initiation of His whole Church; and this is therefore never to be offered again; but then it does not follow, that the Eucharist may not be a Sacrifice for other intents and purposes, though not for this.

ver. 3.

"But in those sacrifices there is a remembrance again made of sins every year," by the high-priest.

And indeed it appears, that the high-priest was obliged to make atonement for his own sins on this day, whether he had committed any sin, or contracted any legal uncleanness in the foregoing year, or not; and the reason is very obvious, upon the supposition so often mentioned; viz. that these sacrifices were not intended to take away wholly the guilt of disobedience; but to remove that unfitness for the worship of God, which proceeded from natural corruption, as well as from the known transgressions of the Divine law, [but that this unfitness could be removed only for one year's time, that is, till the next day of expiation.]

ver. 4.

"For it is not possible, that the blood of bulls and of goats should for ever take away sin;" that is, the incapacity of men to appear in the presence of God to worship Him.

I add "for ever" from the first verse, where the Apostle SECT. I. is his own interpreter; and I suppose there can be no doubt, but that the sacrifices offered on the day of expiation being of Divine appointment were effectual to the ends for which they were designed; but that being designed only to relieve men from their ineptitude to Divine worship for one year, they could not therefore do it once for all, as the Sacrifice of Christ Jesus hath.

The Apostle proceeds, from verse the fifth to the end of ver. 5—9. the ninth, to prove from the words of David, that God did Ps. xl. 6—8. very little esteem the sacrifices and offerings of the Law, in comparison of the Body of Christ, Which was in due time to be offered to Him. It is not indeed certain from the words of the psalm, that David did particularly mean the sacrifices on the day of expiation. "Sacrifices and offerings" are general words, but yet they are restrained by the mentioning of "burnt-offerings, and sacrifices for sin." And it is observable, that all the solemn sacrifices appointed for the day of expiation, were either burnt-offerings or sacrifices for sin. Aaron is ordered on this day to "come into Lev. xvi. 3. the holy place, with a bullock for a sin-offering, and a ram for a burnt-offering," and with these he was to "make ver. 6. atonement for himself and his house;" and further he was to "take of the children of Israel two kids of the goats for a sin-offering, and a ram for a burnt-offering;" and these were the only sacrifices peculiar to that day. And though David gives us no other hint, whereby we can learn, that he meant these sacrifices; yet the Apostle, who wrote by the same Spirit, to prove that the blood of bulls and goats offered on this day (for of those he was speaking) could not for ever ver. 4. take away sin, in the sense so often before mentioned, alleges these words of the psalm; and I suppose therefore, that St. Paul is clear in this point; and that he looked upon it as a certain truth, that the Sacrifice offered by Christ Jesus in person was to do that for ever, which the Levitical sacrifices could only do from year to year. I have before observed, that several of the ancients did believe, that Christ did fulfil this prophecy of David in the original Eucharist, where He did spiritually, intentionally, and mystically, offer His own

Body to God, under the symbols and pledges of Bread and Wine, which He had consecrated for this purpose; but the reader is not from thence to infer, that we do in our Eucharists offer the Sacramental Body and Blood, for the reconsecrating the Church and its ministrations, or to make a new satisfaction for the sins of the world; these were the first ends our Saviour had in view in the first oblation, and these were then obtained by Him once for all. I have before observed, and do now seasonably remind my reader, that as the first Passover was not sacrificed precisely for the same ends, that the future Passovers were offered; so neither did our Saviour in the original Eucharist present His Body and Blood to the Father altogether for the same purposes that we are now to do it. We offer it as a memorial, or commemorative sacrifice: our Saviour did not so. For the first oblation was then *in fieri,* and in present; and what is present cannot properly be said to be commemorated. We offer it for the application of the merits of the first and grand oblation; whereas our Saviour offered His Body to be a perpetual stock of those merits, which we by our Eucharists are from time to time to draw from that inexhaustible treasure; and to say no more, our Saviour in and by the first Eucharist, and His crucifixion or mactation consequent upon that Eucharist, offered an initiatory Sacrifice, whereby He for ever enabled and qualified His Church, without any other lustrative rites or oblations, to make the nearest approaches to God, and especially to continue this Sacrifice; not for the reconsecrating either Priest or people, but for the acknowledging the consecration once for all-performed, and all other benefits of His death; and for the perpetual application of the merits thereof to ourselves. I must further observe, that the words "I come to do Thy will," are not a full rendition of the Greek or Hebrew. It has sufficiently been proved, as I have said, by Dr. Hickes, that the Greek ποιεῖν and the Hebrew עשה when applied to sacrifice, do signify to 'offer:' and it is also evident that the Greek θέλημα and the Hebrew רצון do signify something 'peculiarly acceptable and delightful.' It is a common observation that θέλειν signifies 'to take pleasure' in any thing, and by parity of reason θέλημα denotes 'the thing with which one is pleased,' or which is 'in a peculiar manner desired, or pleasing' to another. The Hebrew word is at other places rendered δεκτὸν, 'acceptable, or singularly pleasing;' see LXX. Levit. i. 4; xxii. 19; Deut. xxxiii. 23; Isa. lxi. 2; lx. 7: so that instead of "I come to do Thy will," I crave leave to say, "I come to offer the acceptable thing or Sacrifice, that is, My Body." I have made this digression, not so much from any advantage to the cause which I am pleading, as to make this text more clear than it is in our modern translations; and accordingly the tenth verse is thus to be rendered, "In, or by which acceptable [Sacrifice] we have been consecrated, we [I say, have been consecrated] through the offering of the Body of Christ, all at once." I apprehend that the Apostle speaks here of our Saviour's consecrating His Apostles by the oblation of Himself. It is expressed in the Greek in the præterperfect tense ἡγιασμένοι ἐσμὲν; and when he says 'we,' it is most proper to understand those of the apostolical order, and their successors for ever. It has before been observed, that ἐφάπαξ signifies 'all at once,' or 'at one and the same time;' and this seems best to fit the sense here; for ἐφάπαξ does most probably affect the verb. It is an adverb, and therefore, according to the common rules of construction, cannot be put with the substantive προσφορὰ; and the Apostles and whole Christian hierarchy were consecrated or enabled to be ministers of the New Testament all at once, by the personal oblation of Christ; though if it be said, they were consecrated 'once,' or 'once for all,' neither does that much alter the sense, but only somewhat obscures it. For it is to be considered, that the office of Priesthood itself was consecrated or founded in the persons of the Apostles; and as the office itself was here founded, so was that part or branch of it, whereby the Apostles and their successors were empowered to adopt others into a partnership of that office; and the ordination or consecration of particular men to the episcopal office is only an exercise of that power, which was for ever conferred upon the apostolical college, by the first oblation performed by Christ Himself. It is not the founding of a new dignity, or office; but admitting one into that which

CHAP. was erected, and confirmed once for all by our great High-
  II.   Priest[t].

ver. 11.   And having thus far spoke of the Christian Priesthood, he
       now proceeds to shew the same of all that belong to the
       Christian Church, whom he calls the ἁγιαζόμενοι, such as are,
       by becoming members of His Body, ' purged,' ' sanctified,' as
ver. 14. it is in our translation, that is, released from their natural
       incapacity of offering their devotions to God; for whereas he
       before spake in the præterperfect tense, as having an eye
       particularly to the Apostles, who were in the first place in-
       vested with this privilege in a very eminent manner, and to
John xvii. whom He had beforehand given a promise of it, as was before
19.   observed; he now descends to speak of all, who had hitherto
       joined themselves to that Church which He had purchased
       with His own Blood, and become, by this means, a people
       near to God.   The Apostle, to introduce what he was to say
ver. 11. on this head, takes notice, that " every high-priest [among
       the Jews] stood on every day [of expiation] ministering and
       offering oftentimes the same sacrifices, which can never take
       away sin" all at once.   I translate the Greek " every high-
       priest," because not only the Syriac and Ethiopic versions
       have it, but also Theodoret, and St. Cyril of Alexandria so
       read it, and seven MSS. and among these the Alexandrian.
       And indeed these were the only sacrifices for sin often of-
       fered, of which the Apostle could say, that they did not take
       away sin; for of those other sin-offerings occasionally to be
       made, it is expressly said of them that bring them to be
Lev. xiv. 20. offered, that their sins " shall be forgiven them."   So that it
26. 31. is, I suppose, clear, that the words were meant of the sacri-

---

[t] The reader will pardon me, if I offer a conjecture, which I shall build nothing upon, but barely propose to his consideration.   The words οἱ διὰ προσφορᾶς τοῦ σώματος τοῦ Ἰησοῦ Χριστοῦ seem to me capable of this rendition, "we, who are employed, or are conversant in the offering of the Body of Jesus Christ."   For ' we ' is implied in ἐσμὲν, and the particle οἱ with a preposition usually signifies office, employment, or the like; so οἱ κατ' ἀγορὰν, 'pleaders,' or ' whose employment is in courts of judicature ;' οἱ ἀπὸ βήματος, ' orators,' or ' they whose business is in the pulpit;' and by analogy οἱ διὰ προσφορᾶς should be ' offerers' or ' sacrificers.'   I cannot doubt but οἱ was written with the Apostle's own hand; for it is unaccountable how a word, which in the general opinion rather clouds the sense than otherwise, should ever be added by any other hand; and it is in all MSS. excepting six or seven.   Nor is it any wonder, that transcribers should leave out what they thought redundant, or did not understand.   If I had any evidence that the preposition διὰ was ever so used, as it is certain several others are, I should think this a very considerable evidence, that St. Paul spoke of all the Apostles as sacrificing Priests.

fices on the day of expiation, so often before mentioned; and
therefore I need give no other reason, why I turn καθ᾽ ἡμέραν
'on every day' of expiation, as before.   " But this Man
[Jesus] after He had offered one Sacrifice for sin for ever,"
stood no longer ministering, or offering Sacrifice; but "sat
down on the right hand of God, from henceforth expecting,
until His enemies be made His footstool; for He hath by
one offering consecrated for ever all that are sanctified" by
Baptism. The Apostle is so far from intending to say, that
all Christian people are so perfected by the one oblation, that
by that oblation the practice and guilt of moral sin was abolished in them; that he says in effect the direct contrary:
for he gives us to understand, that Christ is still expecting,
until His enemies be made His footstool.   And sin is none
of the most inconsiderable of these enemies.   And it is evident, that what is expected is not yet accomplished: and
it is certain in fact, that even good Christians are still obliged
often and with great difficulty to strive with the guilt and
power of sin; and therefore the victory over sin in this sense
was not achieved all at once, but by degrees; and it will
never be finished or completed by particular men, while
they are in this state, where the flesh lusteth against the
spirit; nor by the whole Church, until death and Satan are at
the same time entirely and finally subdued ; and Dr. Whitby,
as if he had here been conscious of the defect of his hypothesis, mentions in his paraphrase " Satan, Antichrist, and
death," as enemies yet to be conquered; but omits sin, as
being sensible, that the mention of it in the sense in [which]
he all along takes it would confute his whole comment on
this place: and yet it is certain to a demonstration, that sin
cannot be said to be totally vanquished until the devil be
wholly and finally disarmed; and that therefore Christ did
not so perfect His people by the one oblation, as once for all
to take away the guilt and power of sin; and that therefore
my interpretation stands good; viz. that He hath, by offering
Himself, qualified His sincere servants for the perpetual worship of God, by which means they are gradually to attain a
final and total conquest.   The Apostle proves this from the
words of the Prophet Jeremiah, where God promises to put
" His laws in the people's hearts, and to write them in their

CHAP.
II.
minds;" He does not mean, He would give them a sinless
perfection, or exempt them from the power of temptations;
but that He would dispose their minds to the worship and
service of Himself, and " that He would remember their sins
and iniquities no more." In which words, no rational man
can believe, that God debarred Himself from imputing sin
to them, if they were guilty of it; or from punishing them
either in this life, or the next, or both, if they continued im-
penitent in it; but what He promises is, that as the people
should have pious inclinations to the public worship of Him;
so He would not, for the future, remember their sins, as He
had now done, by causing them to be transported into a
remote country, where they wanted the convenience and opportunity of public worship. For Jeremiah prophesied under
the Babylonish captivity; and God promises that He would
never treat His redeemed people again in the same manner.
And He so speaks, as that the words may be better and more
properly applied to the Christian Church, to which God had
undoubtedly an eye in this prophecy, than to the Jewish:
and what He promises to the Christian Church is, that though
much sin and weakness was to remain in particular members,
yet this sin and weakness should not be so remembered by
God, as that He would therefore annul their Sacraments;
or reject, or refuse His gracious presence to their public assemblies. If any thing more be contained in this promise, it
is this, that the sins of the whole Christian Church shall never
so far provoke God, as to make Him proceed to an utter ex-
cision of it, or to cause the Church to be no more. And indeed these words seem so to be explained, by those which
Jer. xxxi.
35.
immediately follow. " Thus saith the Lord, that giveth the
sun for a light by day, and the ordinances of the moon and
stars for a light by night — If these ordinances pass from
before Me, saith the Lord, then the seed of Israel shall also
cease from being a nation from before Me, saith the Lord, for
ever." In which words the Christian Church has a promise
of perpetual duration unto the end of the world: and this is
indeed implied in her being consecrated once for ever. And
now we are come to those words, which seem to some to
contain an unanswerable objection against the Sacrifice of the
ver. 18.
Eucharist, viz. " where remission of these [sins and iniqui-

ties] is, there is no more sacrifice for sin." But I apprehend, my judicious reader can by this time see no manner of
objection or difficulty in them ; or if there be any, it may be
removed by answering these three questions, viz. 1. What
is meant by sins ? 2. What by remission ? 3. What by offering for sin ?

1. What is meant by sins ? And the answer is, that actual
known transgression of the moral or positive law, whereby
we are obnoxious to guilt in this world and punishment in
the next, cannot be meant by the word 'sin' in this context,
nor even in these very words : for the sins here mentioned
are such as are not remembered, or imputed to Christians;
whereas it is certain, that all immoral actions are imputed to
Christians, as well as others. Nay, the sins here spoken of
are such as were actually remitted at the offering of the
grand Sacrifice; whereas the known actual sins of Christians
are not forgiven, until they are repented of. Nor does the
addition of the word 'iniquities' alter the case; for it has
been shewed, that עון, commonly rendered by the LXX
ἀνομία, signifies no more than חטאה, which is generally rendered as here, ἁμαρτία. And that both these words do frequently signify no more than that impurity, which is either
inherent in the nature of all sublunary beings, or otherwise contracted; whereby they are unfit for the service or
worship of God.

2. What is meant by remission of sins? And it is evident
that remission of sins is either the same with being 'consecrated,' or purged, ver. 14, or the immediate and necessary
effect of it: for the Apostle produces these words of the
Prophet Jeremiah to prove, that "Christ, by one offering,
consecrated them that are purged, or cleansed." For he
presently adds, "whereof the Holy Ghost is witness;" and
then cites the words of the prophet: so that it is evident,
that the remission here spoken of was actually passed, by and
upon our Saviour's offering Himself. And therefore it cannot import absolution from the guilt and punishment of
known actual sin, because this cannot be passed, until the
sin has been committed and repented of; the remission, of
which the Apostle speaks, was obtained and granted once for
all, and never to be repeated; whereas the remission of guilt

and punishment for particular Christians is to be obtained and granted occasionally from time to time, by a proper application of the merits of the death of Christ.

3. What is meant by an offering for sin? And it is evident from what has been before discoursed, that it must be such an offering (I mean as to its ends and design) as was offered by Moses for the dedication or ratification of the covenant between God and the Israelites; or upon his erecting and consecrating the tabernacle and the Jewish œconomy. It must be a Sacrifice intended for the qualifying men to attend and assist in the worship of God, as the ashes of the red heifer did. It must be a Sacrifice, or offering designed for the enabling men to continue the public worship and service of God, notwithstanding such defilements and corruptions as are necessarily incident to human nature; as the sacrifices offered on the day of expiation were; only more perfect than all of them joined together; for it did that all at once, which all these lustrative rites could not do. It gave all Christian people a right for ever after to join together to worship God: it formed them into a perpetual body or society of Priests and people, for performing a Divine and spiritual service, so that they need no new sacrifice to reconsecrate them: so that, in a word, 'remitting sin' in the eighteenth verse, and 'purging' and 'consecrating' in the fourteenth verse, and 'taking away sin' in the fourth verse, and 'consecrating as pertaining to conscience,' ch. ix. 9, are all phrases signifying in effect the same thing. And since it is evident, that consecrating signifies here, and in the Levitical Law, dedicating to the service of God by initiative sacrifices and rites; and that 'taking away sin' has the same signification, and imports the purging men and things from these defilements, which render them unfit for the service of Almighty God: therefore 'remission of sin' here is to be taken in the same sense; and men that are sensible of this privilege are said to be purged 'as to their conscience;' because they are not under such inward checks as the Jews must be, when they presumed to approach the sanctuary under such defilements, as by the tenor of their Law made them, until they had reconsecrated themselves, incapable of appearing before the Divine Majesty in the tabernacle, or temple. As the effects of Christ's death

are various; so are the manner and seasons of dispersing or conferring those effects on those for whom they were intended. The pardon of actions and habits morally sinful in believers is, and ever shall be, administered to penitents as occasion requires; and the same may be said of that "grace to help in time of need," which Christ purchased for His people. There are other effects of His death, which were not only purchased by the one offering Himself; but were likewise all at once and for ever actually conferred upon His Church, as liberty from the yoke of the Jewish Law, and a free access to God to make our wants and our joys known unto Him. It is true, the charter of pardon upon repentance, and of all necessary grace, were sealed at and by His death; but these blessings could not be actually applied then to all that were hereafter to have occasion for them; because they were conditional, and could not be bestowed until these conditions were performed; nay, they cannot now be applied to every single Christian all at once; especially remission of actual known guilt cannot be thus applied, before that guilt is contracted, and proper means are used for the removing of it. But freedom from the yoke of the Jewish Law was absolute and without any restraint, because the very force and authority of it was taken away by Christ's death; and so was the liberty which Christ procured for His whole Church, and every member of it in their proper stations, to make their addresses to God; and these privileges are now, and have in all former ages, been applied to Christians once for all, viz. at their Baptism. And so by this time my reader will conclude with me, that the sense of this eighteenth verse is, that "where there is" such "remission of sins and iniquities," that is, of such defilements, as before Christ's coming made men incapable of presenting themselves in the place of public worship, there is no further occasion of such "offering for sin," as the Apostle had been speaking of; or "there is no longer" (that is the true import of οὐκ ἔτι) such "an offering for sin," as was prescribed on the day of expiation, for reconciling priests, people, and the tabernacle itself, for the service of the ensuing year: for it is evident, that the Apostle in this place considers the Sacrifice of Christ only, as such an offering for sin, as was initiative, lustrative, or consecrative; and

CHAP.
II.
not as such a Sacrifice for sin as wiped off all guilt and obnoxiousness to punishment, when applied in a proper manner.
St. Paul does frequently in other places speak of the Sacrifice
offered by Christ in person, as a price and ransom for the
guilt and punishment of all sins committed by believers; but
here he treats of it with another view. And we are to remember, that he was writing to the Hebrews, to whom these
words and phrases, in the several significations above mentioned, were known and familiar; and I persuade myself, that
the greatest difficulty I labour under in writing upon this
subject is, that my readers of all sorts are such as have not
been used to take these words and phrases in such a sense,
as the Apostle did first intend them. And yet I am persuaded, that if the most learned amongst our adversaries will
please to apply the word τελειοῦν to any other fixed and de-
terminate sense than that which I have above given to it;
they will themselves be soon convinced, that it is not reconcileable to, or consistent with, the Apostle's arguings in this
context; for this word imports the same thing with the
phrase of 'taking away sin,' as the reader will find, by comparing the first and fourth verses of the tenth chaper. And
that our Saviour did, by His Sacrifice on the cross, actually
take away sin in any other meaning than that which I have
offered, will be very hard for them to prove, and, I humbly
conceive, impossible.

But if our adversaries do persist in that sense of 'taking
away sin,' and 'remitting of sin,' which these phrases bear
in common discourse, then neither they nor we can say that
"there remains no more sacrifice or offering for sin;" or if
any of our adversaries will be so hardy as to affirm it, then
they must give me leave to say, that they make the condition
of the lapsing Christian to be the same with that of an apostate. For the Apostle, in the twenty-sixth and twenty-seventh
verses of the tenth chapter, to shew the miserable and desperate condition of them who 'sin wilfully' after Baptism, that
is, who renounce Christianity, says of them, that "there remains no sacrifice for sin, but a certain fearful looking for of
judgment." The Apostle here evidently speaks upon this supposition, viz. that there can be no forgiveness without a sacrifice; and it is this that makes the case of the apostates with-

out redress or remedy. He is unpardonable, because there remains no sacrifice for his sin. But now, if there be no longer a sacrifice for the sins of offending Christians, how does their condition differ from that of apostates? And therefore if our adversaries will, by remission of sin, understand taking off totally and finally the guilt and punishment, they as well as we must be obliged to read the eighteenth verse interrogatively, viz. " Now where remission of these is, is there not yet an offering for sin?" Yes, undoubtedly, for there is no remission without sacrifice; and what makes the state of apostates deplorable is this, that they have committed sin, and have no sacrifice with which to expiate it; and therefore according to the Apostle's own reasoning, where there is remission of sin, there must be yet an offering for sin; upon supposition, that by sin is meant known and actual transgression, according to our adversaries' notions. If it be said, that there remains indeed a Sacrifice for believers that "have been overtaken in a fault," but no other sacrifice except that offered by Christ Jesus: so say we too, for we believe that the Sacrifice offered by the Church is no other than that offered by Christ, (though for ends somewhat different;) if it be said that this Sacrifice was once offered by Christ, but must be offered no more, that is the very point in dispute between us. That it was once offered by Christ is confessed on all hands; that it is to be offered no more, is the inference drawn by our adversaries, which we cannot allow. The Apostle nowhere says, that the Body and Blood of Christ is no more to be offered. All that can be proved from his discourse is, that it cannot be offered as an initiatory or consecratory sacrifice; and there is this manifest difference in the grand Sacrifice considered as initiatory, and considered as having a power for making satisfaction for known sin; that the benefits of It, as initiatory, were conferred once for all upon the Church, and by consequence on every member of it; but the benefits thereof, as It has a power of absolving men from known actual sin, were not so bestowed actually all at once, but gradually and occasionally, as has before been observed; and this shews the Apostle's meaning, when he says that there remains no more sacrifice for the apostate, who had forsaken the Christian assemblies, and so deserted the Church;

CHAP. namely, that there is no reconsecrative Sacrifice under the
 II.   Gospel, whereby either the Church, or any member of it, can
be anew separated to the service of God; and he therefore
that has thus shut himself out of the Church, of which he
was once a member, can never be re-admitted. By renouncing Christ he has lost the benefit, and forfeited the privilege
purchased by the first and principal oblation; and so cannot
by virtue of that be restored to Christian communion; and
there remains no other such initiatory Sacrifice; and therefore the apostate remains without hope of any possible reconsecration to the service of God. He is so far from being in
a capacity to obtain forgiveness of sin, that he is driven and
ejected from the presence of God, and not permitted to join
that one body of men, the Church, among whom only this
privilege of having sins pardoned upon repentance does reside. And if the lapsing Christian, as well as the apostate,
is destitute of a reconsecratory Sacrifice, there remains no
such oblation, either for the one or the other: but the lapsing Christian wants no such reconsecratory Sacrifice, though
he for a time be suspended or excluded from the communion
of the Church; because when that suspension is taken off, he
remains fully instated in the privilege of being admitted to
the Christian worship, whereby his pardon may be perfected.
And it is to be observed, that the censure of excommunication
was never designed by our Saviour, or His Apostles, to be
an exclusion from the Church totally and finally; but only
a depriving men of the privileges and benefits of communion
for a time, in order to reduce them to their duty. If excommunication be perpetual, it is the obstinacy of the offender
that makes it so, and not the law of Christ or His Church.
On the other side, the apostate, as has been shewed, can be
never the better for the consecration, which was procured
and passed at the oblation of the principal Sacrifice; and
by renouncing this Sacrifice, he for ever disables himself
from receiving the benefit of It again; and so he remains
incurable. But if both the lapsing Christian and the apostate do want a sacrifice for the expiation of moral guilt,
and yet no sacrifice remains for either of them; then the
case of both must be equally desperate, and without remedy;
which God forbid. If therefore by 'offering for sin' in the

eighteenth verse, my reader understand the same thing, that
he does by 'sacrifice for sin' in the twenty-sixth verse;
and in both places take it for an initiatory consecratory
oblation, the sense runs clear; and it is owned, that neither
the baptized Christian persevering in his profession, has any
occasion for such a sacrifice; nor can he that is a renegade
or revolter from Christianity receive any advantage from
such sacrifice; and so it may be said in relation to both,
that "there is yet no longer such sacrifice or offering for
sins," and this is the sense which I prefer. But if my
reader will, by a sacrifice for sin, understand a sacrifice that
may be satisfactory for the removing guilt and punishment;
then he must give me leave to conclude, that the eighteenth
verse is to be read interrogatively, and that that interrogation
is to be resolved into an affirmation; q. d. where "remission
of sins is, there is yet an offering for sin;" or if he do not
allow this, he must consider, whether it be possible to discover any difference between the lapsing Christian and the
apostate. When both are equally destitute of a sacrifice, and
without a sacrifice there can be no expiation of guilt; and
if it were the Apostle's intention to say, "there is yet a sacrifice;" then the conclusion of St. Paul's discourse is directly
contrary to that, which our adversaries would have it[u]. I
leave them to choose which they please; and if they choose
the last, but add, that though there be a sacrifice, yet that
it is not to be re-offered; I answer, no such consequence can
be drawn from any thing, which the Apostle says in these
chapters; nay, I apprehend, he says, what will in effect be
a proof of the contrary, even in this Epistle, as we shall hereafter see. In the mean time, I submit it to the judgment
of my learned reader to determine, whether this context,
which is commonly thought to favour the cause of our
adversaries, more than any other in the whole Bible, be not

---

[u] The necessity of a sacrifice to be
offered for a lapsing Christian may
grate hard upon the ears of some Protestants. But the judgment of St.
Cyprian is of more weight with me
than a thousand modern commentators.
He[*] complains of some lapsing Christians, that they had presumed to speak
peace to themselves "before their sins
were expiated, before confession of
their crime had been made, before their
conscience had been cleansed by Sacrifice and the hand of the Priest, before
the wrath of an angry, threatening
God had been pacified." [2nd Ed.]

[*] e. p. 11. Ap.

rather for us, than against us; for here we are instructed in this great truth, that our Saviour by His first Sacrifice consecrated His Apostles, and His whole Church, for some special Divine services; if the oblation of Christ's Body be not also expressly mentioned as one of these services. However, that is in effect already proved, which I promised to shew

That the perfecting mentioned Heb. x. is not exclusive of farther perfecting. 2. In the second place, viz. that the perfecting, and sanctifying, and sacrifice for sin, meant by the Apostle, are not exclusive of other perfecting, and sanctifying, and sacrifice for sin; this, I say, is already proved; for the perfecting here meant is only consecrating the whole Church, especially the Priests, to the service of God. The sanctifying here intended imports no more, than freeing men and things from the disability they are under by nature, or otherwise, for the service of God; and by the sacrifice for sin is here meant such a sacrifice as effected this consecration or dedication. For if the consecratory, or initiatory sacrifices offered by Moses, or the reconsecratory oblations made on the day of expiation, had been never so perfect in their kind; though they had once for all effectually attained their end, and conferred a perpetual indelible consecration on priests, and people, and tabernacle; yet it does by no means follow, that they were therefore to offer no other sacrifices, either for pardon of sin, or for any other ends. The Hebrews, to whom St. Paul wrote this Epistle, could not be so ignorant, as to draw any such conclusion from this discourse; they well knew, and so may we too, that the sacrifices offered by Moses, and the red heifer, and the sacrifices on the day of expiation, were not intended by God to excuse or free men from the obligation of offering other sacrifices: nay, they were sensible, that the main end and intention of the sacrifices of Moses, and [those] on the day of expiation, was to put men into a condition and capacity to offer other sacrifices and devotions appointed by the Law of Moses. And by parity of reason, the consecrative or initiative power of the first Sacrifice offered by Christ in person is so far from proving, that no sacrifice is for the future to be offered, that it rather proves the direct contrary; for there had been no occasion for such initiatory, consecratory Sacrifice, if it had not been in order to prepare

and qualify the Church for some very solemn and eximious
service; and since it does appear from other evidence, if
not from these chapters, that our blessed Saviour did
before and by His death offer, and for ever institute the
most Divine and beneficial Sacrifice that was ever presented
to God by mere men; and did, by this first oblation and
institution, intend to consecrate His Priests and people (as
appears from this chapter) as to all other religious offices,
so especially to that which was most excellent; therefore
the most proper conclusion from these things put together
is, that this most solemn service and Sacrifice is for ever
to be offered and observed by us: is for ever to be celebrated by Priests, clergy, and people in their several stations,
with a full assurance, that the pollutions of men can never
defile or invalidate a Sacrifice, that receives its power and
sanction from the most precious Blood of the Son of
God. And thus it appears, that the consequence of this
consecration, which the Church of Christ acquires by the
first oblation of the grand Sacrifice, is this; that all the
members of this Church have a certain, infallible remedy
against the guilt of all actual sin; that is, they have a right
of access to God in the public assembly; and by virtue of
the holy offices there performed, and especially of the Sacrifice of the Eucharist there offered, they have an application
of the merits of Christ's death made to them, for the taking
away that obnoxiousness to punishment which they had incurred; and therefore the full effect and consequence of
our being consecrated, perfected, or admitted to the service
and worship of God once for all, is this; that we are by this
means made capable of pardon upon repentance, and of all
the blessings purchased by Christ, upon condition that we
apply ourselves to God in the method appointed by Him.
I proceed therefore,

Thirdly, to shew further what reason we have to believe, St. Paul
that the Apostle had an eye to the Eucharistical oblation, hints the
even in these very chapters. The reason I have to think so cal Sacri-
is taken from the inference, which he draws from the fore- fice, Heb. x.
going discourse: for having said, "there remains yet no sacri- 19—23.
fice or offering for sin," meaning such initiatory sacrifice or
offering as Moses made upon the ratification of the old cove-

CHAP.
II.

nant, and the dedication of the tabernacle, or reconsecratory sacrifices, as were enjoined on the day of expiation; and having shewed them just before, what a more perfect consecration to the service of God they had obtained through the personal Sacrifice, he first concludes, that they ought to make use of this privilege, in " drawing near to the Holies," by the way that Christ had ' dedicated' for them, that is, the chap. ix. 11. Church, (which was the tabernacle through which He entered into heaven;) and it is certain that we must follow the way which Christ did first tread out for us. This is the Apostle's meaning, when he says, " we have freedom of access to the Holy of Holies," that is, heaven ; " and having a new and living way," through His tabernacle the Church, which was " first consecrated by the Body of Christ," which is therefore as the ' vail' by which we must be let into this tabernacle ; " let us approach to the Holies," that is, to heaven ; and then we make our nearest approaches to heaven, when we join in the solemn devotions of the Church. Now this is the most natural and obvious application of the foregoing context ; taking it, as I have done, to contain a proof, that Christ did by His first Sacrifice once for all prepare us for Divine worship. For it is to say, since we have this privilege purchased by Christ, let us make use of it. But if, on the other hand, it had been the Apostle's design to tell us, that by the one Sacrifice of Christ we are perfectly pardoned, and have the perfection of Divine grace assured to us; wherefore should he send people to church, as if any addition could be made to these blessings by the ministry of men? They amongst us, who are best versed in such glosses as these, if they do come to church, or to any religious congregation, yet they take care to let the world know, that they disdain the very ministry and Divine ordinances, which they use. And the Quakers, who have indulged themselves in the full consequence of this doctrine, have laid aside all ministry and ordinances; and a contempt of Priests and Sacraments is with them a certain sign of perfection; but it is very evident, that the Apostle's inference is directly contrary to the vain conceits of these men. For he speaks to the Hebrews, as to a body of men associated for Divine worship; and in order to enter into heaven, he charges them to " draw near with a true heart, in fulness of faith;"

that is, with a full assurance, that Christ hath purchased for
them the perpetual privilege of public worship; and that we
may be sure he meant drawing near in public worship, he
charges them first to be baptized; for that is the undoubted
meaning of those words, "having your hearts sprinkled from
an evil conscience, and your bodies washed with pure water."
For it is by Baptism, that men are sprinkled from an evil
conscience; because thereby they have not only forgiveness
of all past sin, but admittance into the Church and liberty to
join in the public addresses and devotions of God's people;
as the Jews of old were qualified to enter into the tabernacle,
by having water mingled with the ashes of the red heifer
sprinkled upon them: see Dr. Whitby's excellent note on
this place[v]. Further, the Apostle bids them "hold fast," or
carefully retain the use of "the oblation of their hope," or
"faith" (choose which reading you please) "without wavering."
I have before observed, that ὁμολογία signifies an oblation, and
so I turn it here. For it is very certain, that the word has
this signification with the Hellenists, and that it has any other
signification is not certain. St. Paul twice uses this exhor-
tation of holding fast our *homology*; first, chap. iv. 14, and
the English word 'oblation' admirably well falls in with the
sense of the Apostle in that place; for "seeing we have a
great High-Priest," says the Apostle, "that is passed into
the heavens, Jesus the Son of God, let us hold fast," or retain
the use of "our oblation. For we have not an High-Priest,
that cannot be touched with a feeling of our infirmities — Let
us therefore come boldly unto the throne of grace, that we
may obtain mercy," &c. The whole cannot more aptly be
understood than by applying it to the Eucharist, which is our

---

[v] ["God appoints the water made of the ashes of the red heifer to cleanse them from those legal impurities, which rendered them unfit to come into His tabernacle, and made it dangerous for them to approach unto it; styling it on that account '*a purification from sin*:' and this water was to be sprinkled on the unclean, and he was to wash his clothes, and bathe himself in water, and being thus purified might come into the sanctuary, Numb. xvii. 19, 20; this sprinkling of the blood and water sanctifying to the purification of the flesh, Heb. ix. 13. Let us therefore, saith the Apostle, who have (*not our flesh only*, but) our consciences purified from the guilt of sin, by the sprinkling (*not of the blood of bulls and goats*, but) of the Blood of Christ, and have our *High-Priest* still presenting this Blood before the mercy-seat, and who have our bodies washed with the pure water of Baptism, the laver of regeneration (as the clothes and bodies of the unclean were with fountain-water), draw near to God with greater freedom than they could."]

homology or oblation; and of which Christ Jesus is the High-Priest. And since He is passed into the heavens, to make way for its acceptance; we have all the encouragement we can desire, to persevere in offering It up to God; and there-

fore when he bids the Hebrews "come boldly to the throne of grace," I apprehend we cannot more congruously interpret the Apostle, than by supposing that he invites them to approach the Altar with a becoming modest assurance; the same which St. Barnabas means, when he speaks of *altius ad altare accedere,* cap. 1, "coming up higher to the Altar." For it is certain, that in the primitive Church all the most momentous and important petitions were presented to God at the Lord's Table; and to such prayers a gracious answer was expected on account of the Sacrifice there exhibited to God; and therefore no title does more properly belong to it than this of "the throne of grace," as being the most eminent utensil in the Christian Church, "the seat of the Body of Christ," and "on which the Holy Ghost descends upon the invocation," as Optatus observes, and where the devotions of the Church were offered with the greatest assurance of success. I am sensible, that commentators usually say, that Christ Himself is this throne; but to make the same person both the High-Priest and the throne, in the very same text, seems not consistent with the common obvious rules of analogy and concinnity, especially when there is no manner of occasion for it; since this title does so exactly comport with the Holy Table. And when the Apostle here (chap. x. 23,) does again repeat this admonition of "holding fast our *homology,*" I cannot but take him in the same sense; because by this *homology* (whatever it be) we are to draw near to the Holy of Holies; we cannot come to it without Baptism, as appears by

the foregoing verse; and it was to be made in the Christian assemblies, and I suppose nothing does so well answer these characters, as the Eucharist. And as I have before in this section observed, that ὁμολογία has no other signification in the Greek version of the Old Testament; so neither have I any reason to believe, that it has any other in the New. I have in 'the Propitiatory Oblation,' p. 12, shewed, that this word in the ninth chapter of the second Epistle to the Corinthians, ver. 13, does most probably signify the oblation

made by the people of Corinth, at the Eucharist; and that he
there commends them for their " subjecting their oblation to
the Gospel of Christ" in His Church, rather than to the Law
of Moses in the temple. And I do not find that the word is
elsewhere used in the New Testament, except in the sixth
chapter of the first Epistle of St. Paul to Timothy; where
at the twelfth and thirteenth verses, first Timothy and then
Jesus Christ are mentioned, as witnesses to the Christian
oblation. He says of Timothy, ὡμολόγησας τὴν καλὴν ὁμολογίαν ἐνώπιον πολλῶν μαρτύρων, "thou madest the good
oblation before many witnesses." I suppose the Apostle
alludes to the specimen, which Timothy gave, of his suffi-
cience for the office of a Priest or Bishop, when upon his
ordination he did in the face of the public assembly make
the Eucharistical oblation to the great satisfaction and edifi-
cation of all that were present? And it is to be observed, that
as all nouns do sometimes give an unusual signification to
their conjugate verbs, so may ὁμολογία here determine the
sense of the verb ὁμολογεῖν, though there is no necessity to
recur to this expedient : for ὁμολογεῖν is a word by which the
LXX turn the Hebrew נדר, Jeremiah xliv. 25; and as 'to
vow' does perpetually imply some material thing, which is the
object of that action ; so we are sure it does so in that place.
For the thing vowed was 'incense,' and 'a drink offering.'
" We will surely perform the vows that we have vowed, to burn
incense, and to pour out drink offerings." And in the next
verse it is said of Jesus Christ, that "He attested" or confirmed
" the good oblation under Pontius Pilate ;" that is, during the
time of his præfecture. We say in our Creed, that Jesus
Christ suffered " under Pontius Pilate," ἐπὶ Ποντίου Πιλάτου,
as here ; and it was upon His death, under this Roman præ-
fect, that He made His Apostles the authentic witnesses of
His offering His Body and Blood in the Eucharist, and instituting the oblation of It in His Church for ever after. The
'good *homology*,' made first by Christ, afterwards by Timothy,
must, I apprehend, be the very same thing ; otherwise it is
not accountable, why the Apostle should express it in the
same words, in two verses together. It may indeed be supposed, that Timothy at his Baptism did make confession, that
" Jesus was King of the Jews ;" and that this was the same

CHAP.   confession, that Jesus made to Pontius Pilate.   But that this
II.
—————— was ever part of the Baptismal confession is wholly uncer-
Joh. xviii.
37.   tain; and if it were so, I leave it to the reader to determine,
whether it be more probable, that St. Paul would take an occasion to commend a Christian Bishop, from having made his
Baptismal confessions as he ought to do, and which every the
meanest Christian under his care had done, as well as himself; or from his being well versed in the most solemn and
sublime office of the Christian religion, I mean, the Eucharist;
it is the more credible that St. Paul should ascribe it as a
very reputable qualification to Timothy, that " he had offered
the good oblation before many witnesses ;" because his fellow-
labourer, St. Clement of Rome, does thus characterize good
Bishops, that " they offer the gifts in a holy unblameable
manner." I know Dr. Whitby by the *homology* understands
his professing Christ in time of persecution; but this is
merely *gratis dictum*, except it did appear, that Timothy
before the writing of this Epistle had been under sufferings
for Christ's sake, of which I see no signs.   And I would not
have my reader despise this, as a mean conjecture of mine;
nor ought he to look upon it as such; for I really learned it
from Origen, who, when he is arguing with Celsus, and speaking of sacrifices and particularly of the Eucharistical Bread as
offered to God, adds immediately, *καὶ κρατοῦμεν τὴν ὁμολογίαν
ἕως ἂν ζῶμεν*[x]; which I cannot otherwise render, without doing
violence to the coherence of Origen's discourse, than thus;
viz. " and we hold fast our oblation as long as we live ;" and
I am pretty sure that my judicious reader will take it in this
sense.   There is also a passage in Cyril of Alexandria's letter

Heb. iii. 1.   to Nestorius, where the title given by the Apostle is understood in that sense, which I now plead for; the Greek words
are these, *Εἰ δὲ δὴ καλοῖτο καὶ Ἀπόστολος καὶ Ἀρχιερεὺς
τῆς ὁμολογίας ἡμῶν, ὡς ἱερουργῶν τῷ Θεῷ καὶ Πατρὶ τὴν πρὸς
ἡμῶν Αὐτῷ τε καὶ δι᾽ Αὐτοῦ τῷ Θεῷ καὶ Πατρὶ προσκομιζομένην
τῆς πίστεως ὁμολογίαν — πάλιν Αὐτὸν εἶναι φάμεν τὴν ἐκ Θεοῦ
κατὰ φύσιν Υἱὸν μονογενῆ*[y]: that is, though (Christ) be called
"the Apostle and High-Priest of our oblation, as sacrificing
to God and the Father the oblation of our faith, offered to

---

x a. p. 10. Ap. l. 9.   1636 ; Vid. Routh, Opuscula, vol. ii.
y [Binius, tom. ii. pars i. p. 211. ed.   p. 27.]

Him, and by Him to God the Father in our behalf;—yet
we assert Him to be the natural and only-begotten Son of
God." And he uses it so again in the defence of the tenth
Anathema[z], " οὐχ᾽ ὡς μείζονι Θεῷ προσκομίζων τὴν ἱερουργίαν,
ἀλλ᾽ Ἑαυτῷ τε καὶ τῷ Πατρὶ τῆς πίστεως ἡμῶν τὴν ὁμολογίαν
πραγματευόμενος," " not as offering a Sacrifice to a greater
God [than Himself], but as contriving the *homology* or oblation of our faith to Himself and the Father :" where by
' the *homology* of faith' he seems plainly to mean the Eucharist.   And Dr. Grabe will inform us, that this oblation
is offered, not only to the Father, but to the Son, according
to a passage in Origen ; which you may see in Grabe's edition
of Irenæus, p. 324[a].

I may be told, that oblation here consists of *faith*, or *hope*,
(according to which lection the reader chooses,) for the words
of the Apostle are, " Let us hold fast the oblation of our
faith," or hope.   And it is a settled rule with our adversaries,
if the word ' oblation' have a genitive case after it, to suppose,
that the oblation or sacrifice consists of the thing signified by
that genitive case : thus a sacrifice of praise or thanksgiving
signifies nothing in their language but bare praise, or thanksgiving ; a sacrifice of commemoration, nothing but an act
of the memory or a calling to mind some past mercy.   I
shall hereafter have occasion to shew particularly, and at large,
the insufficiency of this answer.   In the mean time, I shall
only observe in general, that this is a very fallacious rule.
When St. James, in his Epistle speaks of the " prayer of chap. v. 15.
faith," will any man from hence conclude, that the prayer
he meant consisted of nothing but faith ?   Must not prayer
consist of words, desires, and inward application to God ?
And is not faith, or a well-grounded assurance of being
heard, a commendable and necessary qualification of prayers
rather than the substance of them ?   And the same may be
said of the oblation of faith and hope ; namely, these graces

[z] Tom. i. pars iii. p. 466.

[a] [" Quomodo preces atque oblationes tum Christo, tum Deo Patri per
Christum offerantur, egregie declarat
locus Origenis, lib. viii. contra Celsum,
ita sonans: Τὸν ἕνα Θεὸν, καὶ τὸν ἕνα
Υἱὸν, Αὐτοῦ καὶ λόγον, καὶ εἰκόνα, ταῖς
κατὰ τὸ δυνατὸν ἡμῖν ἱκεσίαις καὶ ἀξιώ-
σεσι σέβομεν· προσάγοντες τῷ Θεῷ τῶν
ὅλων τὰς εὐχὰς διὰ τοῦ Μονογενοῦς
Αὐτοῦ, ᵉΩι πρῶτον προσφέρομεν αὐτὰς,
ἀξιοῦντες Αὐτὸν, ἱλασμὸν ὄντα (περὶ)
τῶν ἁμαρτιῶν ἡμῶν, προσαγάγειν, ὡς
Ἀρχιερέα, καὶ εὐχὰς, καὶ τὰς θυσίας,
καὶ ἐντεύξεις ἡμῶν τῷ ἐπὶ πᾶσι Θεῷ."]

are the salt with which our oblation must be seasoned, rather than the substance of our oblation.   And it must be owned, that all sacrifices offered without these graces are only a vain profusion of God's creatures.   But it does by no means follow, that we are to offer nothing else.   Nay, since it does appear, that there was a very eminent oblation instituted by Christ, in which none have a right to join but such only as believe or hope in Christ; therefore by "the good *homology*, the *homology* of our faith" or hope, it is most rational to believe, that St. Paul designed the Christian Sacrifice; for just so the covenant made between God and men by Christ is called Rom.iii.27; "the law of faith," and circumcision, "the seal of faith." iv. 11. And whereas the word *homology*, in those places where it is used in the Old Testament, does denote a freewill offering; this does more properly express the nature of the Christian oblation, than any other word commonly used by the LXX in their translation; (for I think they never use εὐχαριστία for a sacrifice, though Aquila does).   And it is well known that St. Irenæus does very much magnify the oblation of the Eucharist, as "made by sons, not slaves," as being offered "freely and cheerfully[b]."

SUBSECTION TO CHAP. II. SECT. I.

An additional subsection to Chap. 2. Sect. 1. shewing, that the Body and Blood of Christ, offered and received in the Eucharist, is Bread and Wine: that the Bread and Wine was believed by the ancients to be, not only the typical, but the true Body and Blood of Christ in power and effect. By what means the Eucharistical Bread and Wine were believed to become the true Body and Blood of Christ.

THE adversaries of the Sacrifice in the Eucharist have no other way left, to evade the proofs I have produced for it, but by betaking themselves to their old refuge, which is this; if the ancients speak of the oblation of Bread and Wine; the answer is, that this is not the oblation of the Eucharist, but of the alms or first-fruits offered by the laity:

[b] Lib. iv. c. 34. [p. 325. ed. Grabe. Oxon. 1702.]

if the ancients speak of the offering the Body and Blood of
Christ, they tell us this is the Sacrifice of the Mass, and so
give over all the ancients who mention this for transubstan-
tiators, and condemn the Fathers for fools, and us for knaves;
for this is the plain English of all they say upon this head.
Now to vindicate at once the primitive Church and Fathers,
and ourselves, and to shew the insufficiency of the answer
which our adversaries would put us off with upon this
occasion; and at the same time to justify myself for bringing promiscuously what is said by the ancients, of offering
the Eucharistical Bread and Wine, the Body and Blood of
Christ, or the types and symbols of that Body and Blood^c,
I will shew,

I. That the primitive Church believed the Body and Blood
in the Sacrament to be Bread and Wine.

II. That they believed them not to be the Body and Blood
of Christ in substance; and therefore often called them types,
figures, symbols of the Body and Blood.

SECT.
I.

^c " For I apprehend it will appear upon a scrutiny, that there was no oblation of the Bread and Wine, distinct from the other oblations, but what was performed in the Eucharist strictly so called; and that this Bread and Wine were offered only as representations of the Body and Blood of Christ, or as His true spiritual Body and Blood, as memorials of the grand Sacrifice. I can see no evidence in the first four centuries, that the Bread and Wine were offered to God separate, and apart from the main mass of oblations, any otherwise, or by any other act of oblation, than that which in the Clementine Liturgy followed after the words of institution. And I take it for certain, that the offering other materials toge-ther with the Bread and Wine is not the new oblation of the New Testament, is not that oblation instituted by Christ after the Passover Supper, but only previous and in order to it. And therefore, that when the ancients speak of offering Bread and Wine, especially if they give us to understand that this oblation was performed in the Sacra-ment, they can thereby mean no other oblation than that which was made in commemoration of Christ's passion. And lest our adversaries should think that they do effectually answer this by replying, that the Eucharistical obla-tion spoken of by the ancients was esteemed by them to be a Sacrifice of the Body and Blood, and therefore not of Bread and Wine; I shall therefore

Prove, that the ancients did believe that the Body and Blood of Christ, in the Sacrament, were the consecrated Bread and Wine; and that they there-fore did, at discretion, call them either Bread and Wine, or the Body and Blood, or the types of the Body and Blood; and by this means, I suppose, I shall at the same time vindicate the Fathers from the imputation of believ-ing the real presence in the sense of the Church of Rome; and give a con-vincing proof, that the offering of Bread and Wine in the Eucharist, pro-perly so called, and the offering the Body and Blood, or of Christ, of our Redeemer, and the like, and the anti-types or symbols of the Body and Blood, are several phrases importing the same thing; and that therefore I may as justly argue for the Sacrifice in the Eucharist from those places where Bread and Wine are said to be offered, as from those places where the Body and Blood, or Christ, or our Redeemer, or the types and figures of them, are styled an oblation, or said to be pre-sented to God." [Omitted in 2nd ed.]

III. That they did not esteem them such cold and imperfect types, as those before and under the Law. Nay,

IV. They believed them to be the true spiritual Body and Blood of Christ, though not in substance, yet in power and effect.

V. That the ancients laid a great stress on the belief of this doctrine.

VI. I shall shew by what means the primitive Church did believe the Bread and Wine (their substance still remaining) to become the spiritual Body and Blood.

VII. I shall consider some seeming excesses of the ancients on this head.

That the Body and Blood offered in the Eucharist are Bread and Wine.

I. I am to prove, that the primitive Church believed the Body and Blood in the Sacrament to be Bread and Wine. And that the most primitive Church of the two or three first centuries did so believe, our adversaries are willing to grant. And it is certain, that few doctrines of Christianity have more plain evidence of their being received in those first ages, than this which I am now asserting, I mean, the Sacrifice of the Eucharist; and therefore there can be no doubt but the Body and Blood, by them offered, was believed to be Bread and Wine. Our adversaries are very jealous of the ancient Fathers of the next succeeding ages; as if they had formed new notions of the real presence, very favourable to the doctrine of transubstantiation. Now suppose this were true; yet it is certain, that the doctrine of the Sacrifice in the Eucharist was as fully established in the second century (as appears by the writings of Justin Martyr, Irenæus, and Tertullian, and I might say in the first by the writings of Ignatius, St. Clement, but especially by the words of institution) as it ever was, or could be, in ages to come. So that the oblation of Christ's Sacramental Body has no manner of dependence on the notions of the real presence, which were afterwards broached. What we contend for is, that the Eucharistical Body of Christ Jesus is, or ought to be, offered to God. Whether this Eucharistical Body be the very personal, substantial Body of Christ, is another question. And men may believe, and the Lutherans do actually believe, that the very substantial Body of Christ is in the Eucharist; and yet not think, that it is there to be offered to God. And on the

other side, the most primitive Fathers, and the present assertors of the Sacrifice here in England, do agree in maintaining that the Sacramental Body and Blood are, as to their
gross substance, Bread and Wine; and yet that they are in
every Eucharist to be presented to God by a solemn act of
oblation; but in truth I am fully persuaded, that the Fathers even down to the seventh or eighth century did still retain a belief, that the Sacramental Body and Blood was Bread
and Wine; and the chief reason why some among us think
otherwise is this, that the ancients did not look upon the
Bread and Wine to be mere empty figures; and therefore
expressed themselves in such a manner, as cannot indeed be
reconciled to the loose notions of too many in this age, who
call every thing ' transubstantiation' that does not fall in with
Socinus and Arminius; but are very far from countenancing
the opinions either of the Papists or Lutherans. However I
shall at present confine my inquiry to the Fathers of the first
four centuries, or to those at furthest who had their education in the fourth century, as St. Cyril of Alexandria and
Theodoret. And though I will not too positively affirm, that
no single writer within this compass of time was ever guilty of
any excess as to this particular; yet I do not at all despair
of convincing my reader, that it was the current prevailing
opinion, that the Bread and Wine did still remain, even after
the oblation and consecration. And no man is more clear
in this point than the latest single Father, whose authority
I shall cite, I mean Theodoret; for he affirms[d], that our
Saviour, "in delivering the mysteries, taking the symbol,
said, 'This is My Body.'" And again[e], " He that called His
own natural Body Corn and Bread, and at another time
called Himself a Vine, He honoured the visible symbols with
the title of His Body and Blood, not changing their nature,
but adding grace to nature." But he yet more fully declares
himself in his dialogue between Orthodoxus and Eranistes a
heretic[f]; where he introduces Eranistes asking Orthodoxus,
" What do you call that gift that is offered, before the Priest
has made the invocation?" Orthodoxus having excused himself from saying plainly, ' Bread,' because some catechumens
are supposed to be present, answers, " Food made of certain

<hr />

[d] h. p. 46. Ap.   [e] i. p. 46. Ap. l. 5.   [f] m. p. 46. Ap.

grains," meaning bread made of wheat. *Eranist.* " And
what do you call the other symbol?" *Orthod.* " That also is
a common name, denoting a certain sort of liquor." *Eranist.*
" But what name do you give them, after consecration ?"
Orthod. " The Body and Blood of Christ." *Eranist.* " And
do you believe, that you partake of the Body and Blood of
Christ?" *Orthod.* " I do." *Eranist.* " As therefore the
symbols of the Lord's Body and Blood are one thing before
the invocation made by the Priest, but are changed and
become quite other things after the invocation ; so our Lord's
Body was, after the assumption, changed into the Divine
substance," (this was Eranistes's heresy.) *Orthod.* " You are
caught in the net, which yourself have woven. For the
mystical symbols, after consecration, do not depart from
their own nature, but remain in their former substance,
figure, and shape." Cyril of Alexandria having said[g] that
Melchisedec blessed " Abraham, by exhibiting to him bread
and wine," adds, " We are blessed no otherwise by Christ."
And presently after, " He plainly declares the manner of
the Priesthood for a demonstration of the thing; for Melchisedec brought forth bread and wine." And as before
cited[h], " The table that had the shew-bread represents the
unbloody Sacrifice of the loaves, by which we are blessed,
eating the Bread from Heaven, that is, Christ." St. Chrysostom on Psalm cix.[i] asks this question, " And why does he
say, according to the order of Melchisedec? Even because of
the mysteries; for he offered bread and wine to Abraham."
And again[k], " What is the Bread? His Body." But his
epistle to Cæsarius against Apollinaris is a most illustrious
testimony to this truth, in the following words[l]. " As we
call the bread Bread, before it is blessed; but when the
Divine grace has sanctified it by the intervention of the
Priest, it quits the name of Bread, and is thought worthy
to be called the Lord's Body, although the nature of bread
remain in it.—So the Divine nature taking the government
of the Body of Christ, both these made but one Son, one
Person." St. Austin gives us his verdict to the same pur-

g a. p. 43. Ap.
h c. p. 43. Ap.
i d. p. 38. Ap.

k I. p. 42. Ap. l. 5.
l Q. p. 43. Ap.

pose, when he says[m], "What Melchisedec brought forth,
when he blessed Abraham, is every where offered under the
Priesthood of Christ." Therefore I conceive, what is offered
"under the Priesthood of Christ" must be Bread and Wine,
consecrated into the Body and Blood. Nor was the Bread and
Wine offered in the primitive Church apart from the other oblations[n], [until the words of institution had been pronounced
over them.] And[o], "To eat Bread is the Sacrifice of Christians in the New Testament." More fully yet in those words[p],
"We call neither the tongue, nor membranes, nor significant
words pronounced by the tongue, nor literal characters wrote
on parchment, the Body and Blood of Christ; but that only,
which being taken from the fruits of the earth," that is,
bread, "and being consecrated with a mystical prayer, we
receive to our spiritual health." He had observed just
before, that the Apostle might preach Christ either with the
tongue or pen, or by the Eucharist. Gaudentius is very
clear in this point; for, says he[q], "The same Christ is
sacrificed in every Church, in the mystery of Bread and
Wine.—And Christ declares, that whatever Wine is offered
for a figure of His passion is His Blood." And again[r],
"When Christ held forth consecrated Bread and Wine to
His disciples, He said thus, This is My Body, This is My
Blood." And to mention no more[s], "Christ appointed the
Sacraments of His Body and Blood to be offered in the figure
of Bread and Wine." St. Jerome teaches the same doctrine;
for he bids us[t] hear or understand, that "the Bread, which
our Lord brake and gave to His disciples, is the Body of our
Lord and Saviour; since He Himself says to them, Take, eat,
This is My Body," &c. And[u], "Wheat is also that of which the
heavenly Bread is made; concerning which our Lord says,
My flesh is meat indeed," &c. Again[x], "Ye [Priests] offer My
loaves, the loaves of shew-bread in every Church—springing
from one loaf." And[y], "We pollute the Bread that is the
Body of our Lord, when we go unworthily to the Altar."

[m] D. p. 35. Ap.
[n] "Until they had been made the Sacrament by the words of institution." [1st ed.]
[o] C. p. 35. Ap.
[p] R. p. 37. Ap.
[q] a. p. 30. Ap. l. 6.
[r] b. p. 30. Ap.
[s] d. p. 31. Ap.
[t] k. p. 28. Ap.
[u] m. p. 29. Ap.
[x] n. p. 29. Ap.
[y] o. p. 29. Ap.

St. Ambrose testifies this truth in these words[z], "This Bread Christ gave to His Apostles, to distribute to the multitude of believers; and gives it at this day, which the Priest daily consecrates with His words." Ephræm Syrus bids us[a] "earnestly consider, how Christ took bread in His hands, blessed it, and brake it into a figure of His Body; and blessed the cup into a figure of His Blood, and gave them to His disciples." St. Gregory Nyssen gives us his suffrage in these words[b], "It is at first common bread; but when the mystery has made it a Sacrifice, it is called the Body of our Lord, and is so." For it is the Bread that is at first common that is made a Sacrifice; it is the Bread that is called the Body; it is the Bread [that is] the Body of our Lord. Macarius says[c], "Bread and Wine is offered in the Church, as an antitype of Christ's Body and Blood; and they who partake of the visible Bread do spiritually eat the flesh of the Lord." Epiphanius gives testimony to this truth; though he speak with some reserve, lest he should be understood by them that were not yet communicants[d]. "We see our Saviour took into His hands, as it is mentioned in the Gospel; that He rose up at supper, and took certain things, and having given thanks He said, 'This is My'—somewhat: and yet we see it is not equal nor like to His image [body] of flesh, nor to His invisible Deity, nor to the shapes and features of His parts: for this is of a round shape, and as to its faculties wholly without sense; yet by grace He was pleased to say, 'This is My Body;' and nobody disbelieves the word." Cyril of Jerusalem, who speaks as magnificently of the Sacrament, as any of the ancients, yet clearly affirms, that the Bread is the Body[e], "As the Bread and Wine of the Eucharist, before the invocation of the adorable Trinity, was mere bread and wine; but when the invocation is once made, the Bread becomes the Body of Christ, the Wine His Blood; so such meals as are used in the pompous worship of Satan, being in their own nature mere meats, become abominable by the invocation of demons." And he affirms[f], that "Christ said of the Bread, 'it is My Body.'" Again[g], "In the figure" or

z a. p. 26. Ap.   d c. p. 22. Ap.
a b. p. 25. Ap.   e a. p. 18. Ap.
h c. p. 25. Ap.   f b. p. 18. Ap.
c b. p. 26. Ap. l. 5.   g c. p. 18. Ap.

type "of Bread, the Body is given thee; in the figure of
Wine, the Blood." Eusebius Cæsariensis says[h], "First Christ,
and then His Priests, do mysteriously represent His Body
and salutary Blood in Bread and Wine." St. Cyprian gives
clear evidence for us; for he asserts[i], that "Christ Jesus
offered the same Sacrifice that Melchisedec did, that is,
Bread and Wine, viz. His own Body and Blood." "Nor[k]
can His Blood appear to be in the Cup, if Wine be not
there." Origen is very positive in this point, in those words[l],
"We eat the loaves offered to God, they being made a certain holy Body." And[m], "He that partakes of the Bread partakes of the Body of the Lord; for we do not regard the
nature of the things that lie visible before us, but we conduct our souls by faith to the body of the *Logos*." And[n],
"Not the material Bread, but the Word spoken over it, is
profitable to those that eat it, in a manner not unbecoming
[the mysteries] of our Lord." Tertullian instructs us[o], that
"Christ's Body is authoritatively declared to be in the Bread,
censetur in pane;" and in another place[p], "Jesus Christ
taking Bread, and distributing it to His Disciples, made it
His Body." And[q], alluding to Gen. xlix. 11, "He shall
wash his robe in wine," he says, "so now He consecrates
His Blood in the Wine, who then represented Wine by
Blood." He has, in these last words, an eye to Isa. lxiii. 4,
which he had cited just before. Clemens Alexandrinus seems
of the same opinion; for he tells us[r], "the mixture of both
these, viz. the liquor," or Wine, "and the Word, makes the
Eucharist." But this truth cannot be taught more plainly
than it is by Irenæus. For "Christ," says he[s], "took that
which is the creature of Bread, and gave thanks, saying,
'This is My Body;' and also the Cup, which, according to
our doctrine, is part of the same creation, He pronounced
it to be His Blood." N.B. By the Cup He clearly means
the Wine; and He intimates, that orthodox Christians believed the Bread and Wine to have been created by God the
Father, which the heretics, against whom he wrote, denied;

[h] h. p. 16. Ap. l. 5.
[i] m. 4. p. 13. Ap.
[k] m. 3.
[l] a. p. 9. Ap.
[m] g. p. 10. Ap.
[n] f. p. 10. Ap. l. 6.
[o] g. p. 8. Ap. l. 6.
[p] o. p. 9. Ap.
[q] p. p. 9. Ap.
[r] b. p. 7. Ap. l. 7.
[s] c. p. 4. Ap. l. 19.

and he thus disputes against these heretics again[t], "How can they be sure, that the Bread of the Eucharist is the Body of the Lord, and the Wine His Blood, if they do not allow Him to be the Son of that God, Who made the world?" And to the same purpose[u], "How could our Lord in justice take Bread,—if He belong to another Father (who is not the creator of bread) and declare it to be His Body? How could He affirm the mingled Cup to be His Blood?" Again[x], "At this rate neither is the Cup of the Eucharist the communication of His Blood, nor the Bread which we break the communication of His Body;" and presently after, "Christ pronounced the Cup of the creature to be His Blood, and the Bread, which is likewise a creature, to be His own Body;" nay, he supposes, that the "bodies" of communicants "are irrigated, and increased or nourished by this Body and Blood of Christ;" as you may see, by reading the paragraph next after the foregoing citation[y]. Nor is St. Justin Martyr behind him, when he says[z], "We have been instructed, that the food which has been blessed, or made the Eucharist by prayer, is the Flesh and Blood of Jesus, Who was incarnate for us." When Ignatius speaks[a] of "breaking the one Bread," or loaf, he can mean no other than that of the Eucharist; and when, in the very next words, he calls this ἕνα ἄρτον κλῶντες, ὅς ἐστιν φάρμακον ἀθανασίας· ἀντίδοτον τοῦ μὴ ἀποθανεῖν, ἀλλὰ ζῆν ἐν Ἰησοῦ Χριστῷ διὰ παντός· *Epist. ad Ephes.*; "the medicine of immortality," and "the antidote against death, that we should not die but live for ever in Jesus Christ;" he must be supposed to speak of it, as consecrated into the Sacramental Body of Christ; for in no other capacity can the Bread broken be the medicine of immortality. So then we have here the main body of the most noted writers, from the beginning of the second to the end of the fourth century, declaring the Bread of the Eucharist to be His Body, the Wine His Blood; or, which is the same thing, that His Body and Blood offered and received in the Eucharist is Bread and Wine. I am sensible, that some of these Fathers do so express themselves at some

[t] f. p. 5. Ap. l. 17.
[u] ff. p. 6. Ap.
[x] g. p. 6. Ap.

[y] p. 6. Ap.
[z] a. p. 2. Ap.
[a] b. p. 1. Ap.

places, that their words may be capable of that sense, which SECT. the Lutherans would put upon them, viz. that the Body of ——— I. Christ is in the Bread, the Blood in the Wine; not that the very Bread is the Body, or the Wine the Blood. Thus for instance, Cyril of Jerusalem may be understood[b], "in the figure of Bread the Body is given thee;" and so may the words of Tertullian[c]; but it seems evident to me, that when the ancients say we receive the Body in Bread, they are to be understood just as that Englishman would be, who should say "he had received a hundred pound in silver;" and as the silver, and the hundred pounds, in this way of speaking, are the same; so likewise is the Body of Christ, and the Bread, the same in these passages of the Fathers: that Cyril of Jerusalem so meant is evident; for in the two other citations he directly calls the Bread Christ's Body. And Tertullian at another place says[d], "Christ made Bread His Body;" and lest you should suppose that he imagined the Bread to be transubstantiated, he says immediately after, "Christ said 'This is My Body,' that is, the figure of My Body."

The synods of the ancient Fathers do evidently speak this doctrine. I begin with that which I may call the Protestant synod of Constantinople, as being assembled on purpose to condemn images in the worship of God; which, speaking of the Eucharist, and having a little before rehearsed the words of institution, says, that[e] "Christ commanded the substance of material bread, taken out [of the mass of obla- tions], to be offered, as an image of His Body." And the 24th canon of the third, alias sixth council of Carthage, pro- vides[f], "that in Sacraments of our Lord's Body and Blood, nothing more be offered than what the Lord commanded, that is, Bread and Wine mixed with water;" and I suppose, that when they speak of "offering in the Sacraments," they can mean no other oblation than that of the symbols of Christ's Body and Blood. The Greek translation runs thus, "Ἵνα ἐν τοῖς ἁγίοις μηδὲν πλέον τοῦ Σώματος καὶ τοῦ Αἵματος Κυρίου προσενεχθείη, ὡς καὶ αὐτὸς ὁ Κύριος παρέδωκεν, του-

[b] c. p. 18. Ap.
[c] g. p. 8. Ap.
o. p. 9. Ap.

[e] p. 51. Ap. l. 21.
[f] p. 50. Ap.

τέστι, ἄρτου καὶ οἴνου ὕδατι μεμιγμένου· that "in the holy
[mysteries] nothing be offered beside the Body and Blood
of our Lord, that is, Bread, and Wine mixed with water, as
the Lord hath commanded." They evidently speak of the
Body and Blood, and the Bread and Wine mixed with water,
as numerically the same. The council of Laodicea, can. 49[g],
forbids "Bread to be offered in Lent, except on the Sabbath
and Lord's day." And by 'offering Bread' must be intended
offering the Sacramental Body of Christ; until it does appear,
that the ancient Church did any where offer Bread separated
from other materials, excepting at the Eucharist.

And as to the Liturgies, it is very evident, that after the
words of institution rehearsed they all agree in offering to
God τὰ Σὰ ἐκ τῶν Σῶν, "Thine own out of Thine own,"
which is certainly a periphrasis of the Bread and Wine;
for men cannot be said to offer the substantial Body and
Blood, as things or gifts "out of other things or gifts." For
if Christ's personal Body or Blood are on the Altar, they
cannot be supposed to have been brought from home by
the communicants, or to have been taken out of the mass
of oblations by the celebrator; therefore this expression fits
nothing but the Bread and Wine, just before by the words
of institution pronounced to be the Body and Blood, and
yet remaining what they were, as to their gross substance;
and, indeed, the Clementine Liturgy has these express words,
"We offer to Thee, our King and God, this Bread and this
Cup." And it will hereafter more plainly appear, that the
Body and Blood of Christ, as offered by the ancients in the
Sacrament, could be no other than Bread and Wine.

But it is now time for us to inquire, in what manner they
called and thought the Eucharistical Bread and Wine, Christ's
Body and Blood; and this brings me,

Ancients
believed
the Eucha-
ristical
Body and
Blood to
be types
and images.

Secondly, to shew, that as they deemed the Eucharistical
Body and Blood to be Bread and Wine, and so could not
believe that the substantial Body and Blood of Christ were
in the Eucharist; so they did often call the Sacramental
Bread and Wine, types, anti-types, figures, likenesses,
images, and symbols of Christ's natural Body and Blood.
We have already heard several of the ancients applying

these names to the consecrated Bread and Wine. Theodoret[h] calls them "symbols." Gaudentius[i] calls them "figures ;"
and so does Ephræm Syrus[j]: Cyril of Jerusalem[k], "types."
Eusebius[l] uses the phrase αἰνίττεσθαι τὰ μυστήρια, which I
have rendered with some latitude, "mysteriously represent."
Abundance of authorities might be produced to the same
purpose; but in so plain a case my reader will be content
with the following. Victor Antiochenus says[m], "that men
are made partakers of the Body of Christ by the symbol of
Bread; of the Blood of Christ, by the symbol of Wine."
St. Chrysostom calls[n] the Sacramental Blood "the symbol
of death," that is, of Christ's effused Blood, "but a cause
of life ;" and he calls the elements[o] "symbols" again, in a
place presently to be cited more at large. Macarius speaks,
as just before cited, of "Bread and Wine being offered in
the Church, as antitypes of Christ's Flesh and Blood."
Gregory Nazianzen calls the elements[p] "the antitypes of
the mysteries." Epiphanius tells us[q], "that the Bread and
Wine offered by Melchisedec did typify the antitypes of
our Lord's Body, Who said, 'I am the Bread of life ;' and
the antitypes of the Blood, which flowed out of His side."
Eusebius explains his notion of the Sacrifice, by saying[r],
"We celebrate the memorial of this Sacrifice upon the Table,
by the symbols of Christ's Body and Blood ;" and[s], "He gave
the symbols of His Divine œconomy to His Disciples, commanding them to offer the image of His Body." Tertullian,
as just now cited, interprets those words 'This is My Body,'
by adding, "that is, a figure of My Body." The Constitutions charge men[t] "to offer the antitypes of the royal Body
of Christ ;" and the Liturgy of St. Basil calls the elements,
after the words of institution have been pronounced upon
them[u], "the antitypes of Christ's Body and Blood." And
the reader, by reflecting on these citations, will find, that
in many of them the Sacramental Body and Blood are

[h] h. p. 46. Ap.; i. p. 46. Ap. l. 7;
m. p. 46. Ap.
[i] a. p. 30; d. p. 31. l. 8. Ap.
[j] b. p. 25. Ap.
[k] c. p. 18. Ap.
[l] h. p. 16. Ap. l. 10.
[m] p. 43. Ap.
[n] p. p. 39. Ap.

[o] e. p. 38. Ap.
[p] a. p. 20. Ap. l. 6.
[q] b. p. 21. Ap.
[r] f. p. 16. Ap.
[s] i. p. 16. Ap.
[t] d. p. 47. Ap.
[u] g. p. 57. Ap.

CHAP.
II.

called types and figures, even when they are distributed to be eaten and drunk; but I proceed to shew,

Yet not
such im-
perfect
types and
images as
those be-
fore and
under the
Law.

Thirdly, that they did not believe the Eucharistical Bread and Wine to be such cold imperfect types, as those under and before the Law; for it is evident, that the ancient Church believed the old types to be figures of the Sacrament, and therefore much more faint and less full of instruction and efficacy than the Sacrament is. Of this we have very great evidence in the writings of the Fathers. Thus Theodoret makes the Eucharist the accomplishment of the Passover, in these words[x], " It became them by the symbol to learn the providence of God," (that is, it was fit that the Jews, by the Paschal lamb, should be taught how God had miraculously preserved their forefathers in Egypt;) " and us that sacrifice the Lamb, to know the type before described." And[y], " In that night, before the crucifixion, Christ gave an accomplishment to the typical Passover, and made the archetype of that type." Chrysostom speaks very home to this purpose, not only as to the Passover, but the whole Jewish œconomy[z]; " How much greater holiness becomes thee, O Christian, who hast received greater symbols than the Holy of Holies contained; for you have not the Cherubim, but the Lord of the Cherubim dwelling in you. You have not the urn and the manna and the tables of stone and the rod of Aaron, but the Body and Blood of our Lord—the greater symbols you are honoured with, and the more tremendous the mysteries are, so much the greater holiness you are obliged to." He plainly makes the Sacramental Body and Blood to be but ' symbols,' and yet much to be preferred to any thing under the Law; nay, in the same paragraph he says, " we have received the Spirit instead of the letter, and grace exceeding human reasoning, and an unspeakable gift;" all which is meant of the Eucharist. And as before cited[a], " On the same Table Christ described the typical Passover, and superadded the true one." Again[b], speaking of the Law and Gospel, " There was sanctification, here is sanctification; there was baptism, here is Baptism; there was sacrifice, here

[x] b. p. 45. Ap.
[y] e. p. 45. Ap.
[z] e. p. 38. Ap.

[a] k. p. 38. Ap.
[b] x. p. 40. Ap.

is Sacrifice—But those as types, these as the verity." But especially he elevates the Sacrifice of the Eucharist above those of Moses, in the following words[c], "This Blood worthily received drives away devils—It invites the angels to us, and the Lord of angels—This Blood ordained the Priests; this Blood, even in the type, washed away sin. If It had so great power in the type, if death were so affrighted at the shadow; tell, how it would be affrighted at the verity Itself. Truly tremendous are the mysteries of the Church; truly tremendous are our Altars." St. Austin teaches us the same thing[d], where, speaking of the Sacrifice of the Eucharist, he says, "The ancient sacrifices of holy men were manifold and various signs of this true Sacrifice." And elsewhere[e], "Instead of all those sacrifices and oblations, Christ's Body is offered, and communicated to the receivers." And again[f], "The former sacrifices are abolished, and others instituted; greater, as to their virtue; better, as to their benefit; easier to be performed, fewer in number." Gaudentius[g] calls "the Passover a figure, and not the proper Passion of the Lord; but under the verity, which we are [under], Christ is offered in every Church." St. Jerome uses much the same way of expression; for he styles[h] "the lamb the typical Passover, and the Bread given by our Saviour the true Sacrament or mystery of the Passover." And[i], "There is as much difference between the shew-bread and the Body of Christ" (he means the Sacramental Body; for he is speaking of the preparative holiness necessary in the administering and receiving It) "as between the image and the verity, between the patterns of things to come and what was by those [patterns] prefigured." St. Ambrose speaking of the Sacrament says[k], "The Apostle says of the type thereof," viz. manna, "our Fathers did eat of the same spiritual meat." St. Gregory Nazianzen says[l], "We will partake of the Passover, which is yet a type, but much more plain than the old one. The legal Passover, I boldly pronounce, was an obscure type of a type," or a type more obscure than [our] type. "There were," says Cyril

[c] A. p. 41. Ap.
[d] A. p. 35. Ap.
[e] E. p. 35. Ap. l. 9.
[f] G. p. 36. Ap.
[g] a. p. 30. Ap.

[h] q. p. 29. Ap.
[i] r. p. 29. Ap.
[k] k. p. 27. Ap.
[l] f. p. 21. Ap.

of Jerusalem[m], "in the Old Testament the loaves of shew-
bread; but these loaves of the Old Testament have received
their accomplishment; the heavenly Bread and the Cup of
salvation sanctify both body and soul." Eusebius Cæsariensis teaches the same doctrine, when he says[n], "We with
good reason daily celebrating the memorial of Christ's Body
and Blood, and being dignified with a better victim and
hierurgy than the old people, do not think it safe to fall back
to the former weak elements, that contain symbols and
images, and not the verity." He as plainly speaks of the
Eucharist, as any of those before cited on this head; nor
does he say more than several of them, whom I have before
produced. We have already heard Justin Martyr affirming,
that[o] the cake offered for him that was purified from the
leprosy was a type of the Eucharist. Nay, Clemens Alexandrinus[p], and several others of the ancients, make Melchisedec's bread and wine (the most perfect mystery and oblation,
in their judgment, that ever was offered before that of Christ)
to have been but a figure or sign of the Eucharist; which is
a clear proof, that this latter was, in their opinion, much
more excellent and efficacious than the former. And St.
Clement of Rome does, as we have seen, discourse of the
Christian Priesthood and Sacrifice, under the emblem of the
Levitical; and then introduces the Christian Bishop as offering the Eucharistical gifts, which must be said upon this
supposition, that the Levitical types had given place to the
Evangelical, as being much inferior to them in true value.
And therefore we have no reason to dispute a citation, which
Bulenger produces from Origen's MS. works[q]; "Christ said
not, this is a symbol, but 'This is [My] Body,' clearly, lest
any one should think it a type." And for the same reason,
we may allow those words in the same sense to be genuine,
which are cited by Bulenger, as from Magnes[r] the Priest of
Jerusalem (concerning whom see Dr. Cave, Histor. Literar.,
vol. ii. A.D. 265), viz. "The Eucharist is not a type of the
Body and Blood, as some men defective in their understanding have prated, but rather the Body and Blood." He does

m d. p. 19. Ap. l. 4.   p e. p. 7. Ap.
n e. p. 16. Ap.   q [g. p. 10. Ap.]
o b. p. 3. Ap.   r [p. 14. Ap.]

not say, the very personal or substantial Body and Blood;
but rather the Body and Blood, than bare types. And so we
must understand the words of Origen; they are not types, as
the manna, the shew-bread, the Passover, the Jewish sacrifices were, as the other Fathers before cited explain it; but if
you call them types, you must at the same time acknowledge,
that as to real benefit and efficacy they are the things signified, as well as the significators; just as an exemplification,
made according to law, is as effectual to be shewed or pleaded,
as the original itself. It is a copy, and yet more than a copy;
for it is in effect the very record or letters patents, the words
and meaning whereof it contains. It is a copy, for it was
transcribed from the original; it is not a copy, for it cannot
be set aside in pleading, as a copy may. And here I judge
it very proper to observe the several degrees of types or
symbols, exceeding, or falling short of each other, as to
their power or clearness of signification, the intention of
God in instituting them, and their beneficialness in relation
to men.

1. There were types, which had only a bare aptitude to Degrees
resemble Christ to come; and of these, 1. Some were pro- of types.
bably not known, or discovered to be prefigurations of Christ,
by them to whom they were first exhibited. It does not
appear, that the Passover, or brazen serpent, were perceived
by the Israelites in the land of Egypt and the wilderness, to
contain any promise or representation of the death of Christ.
I am not obliged positively to determine, that the knowledge
of their signification was hid from the eyes of the Israelites:
but I may have the liberty of supposing at least, that the
meaning of these, or some other types of Christ in the Old
Testament, was not discovered to them, to whom they were
first exhibited. And I shall take it for certain, that, 2. God's
primary intention in instituting the Passover, and erecting
the brazen serpent, was not to prefigure the death of Christ;
but the first was ordained principally for the redemption of
the first-born from present death, and to entreat God's
favour on the people in order to their *Exodus* from Egypt,
and for a perpetual commemoration of it: 3. and the other,
the brazen serpent, was primarily designed by God, as a
remedy against the bites of the venomous insects in the

wilderness. That God did so contrive both the one and the
other, that they might be fit to resemble and prefigure the
death of Christ, I do not in the least question; but I suppose
it evident, that this was not His principal, or however not His
sole intention.

2. There were, or might be types of Christ, that were
known to be such by those, to whom they were first exhibited; and such as were principally, or solely, intended by
God for this purpose. 1. If there were any such types in
the Old Testament as were understood by those to whom
they were first exhibited, they were the manna, and water
that issued out of the rock, and Melchisedec's bread and
1 Cor. x. 1,2. wine. Of the manna and the water St. Paul speaks. "Our
Fathers did all eat the same spiritual meat, and drink the
same spiritual drink."   Some, both of the ancients and
the moderns, have believed, that the Apostle means, that the
old Israelites in the wilderness did apprehend the manna
which they ate, and the water which they drank, to have
been prefigurations of the Body and Blood of Christ.   And
it is very evident, that when the Apostle calls them ' spiritual
meat and drink,' his design was to instruct us, that the
manna and the water of the rock did beforehand describe
Christ, not to the outward senses, to the eyes and taste, but
to the mind or spirit; or that the Israelites ate and drank
the Body and Blood of Christ, not substantially, or in a
sensible manner, but under a vail and cover, discernible only
to the eye of the soul.   But I think, with others both of the
ancients and moderns, that it is not absolutely necessary,
that we suppose the old Israelites actually to have discovered
the meaning of this meat and drink; but that it was sufficient to the Apostle's purpose, that the manna and the
water were certain signs of God's favour to that people; and
that Christians, "who have the vail taken away from their
eyes," may in that manna and water spiritually discern the
Body and Blood of Christ thereby typified. 2. If there was
any such type under the Old Testament of Christ yet to come,
as was both understood by them who first used it, and was
primarily intended by God to be a prefiguration of Christ
Jesus, and particularly of the Eucharist; it was Melchisedec's
bread and wine.   For it has been before observed, that

Abraham did certainly see our Saviour's day; and therefore much more Melchisedec, whom St. Paul declares to have been greater or better than Abraham: and allowing what Philo says, that it was an ἐπινίκιον or a triumphal Sacrifice, yet both Melchisedec and Abraham, being prophets, and foreseeing the victory hereafter to be obtained over Satan, sin, and death; and knowing that this was represented by Abraham's victory over the kings, might, and probably did, by the intendment and direction of God Himself, design this Bread and Wine to be types of that unbloody Sacrifice, which was many ages afterwards to be instituted, for a standing commemoration of this grand conquest. And what can be more rational than to suppose, that God, Who overrules the actions of men to His own purposes and designs, and Who had certainly let these signal servants of His into the secret of His Son's incarnation and sufferings, should also give them to understand, that He had decreed this triumphal sacrifice to be a prefiguration of the perpetual Eucharistic Sacrifice under the Gospel? If there were any other sacrifice primarily intended by God, and notified to man to be a type of Christ, it was the intentional sacrifice, which Abraham by God's direction offered, of his only son Isaac; which therefore was one of the most perfect types of the future Sacrifice of Christ. And yet my reader will observe, that there is not in the whole New Testament any direct application of this type to the archetype, nor mention made, that it was designed as a figure of the grand Sacrifice. And therefore it is no more prejudice to Melchisedec's bread and wine than to Abraham's offering Isaac, that none of the writers of the New Testament do expressly take notice of it.

3. Such types as are commemorative of something past, and were chiefly designed by God, the Founder of them, to be commemorations, are not only more intelligible to them, for whose use they are designed; but carry along with them a more full and strong intimation of the Divine will and pleasure, that they are so to be used and understood. Thus the Jewish Passover, if considered as a prefigurative type of Christ, is but a very cold and imperfect type, because not primarily or solely intended by God for this purpose; nor (probably) apprehended by the generality of people before

Christ, to have any such signification. But if you consider
all the yearly passovers celebrated after the *Exodus,* as types
or memorials of the first Passover in the land of Egypt; it
will be found, that the sense and meaning of them must be
very clear and obvious to the main body of the nation; who
were not perfectly stupid and ignorant of so memorable a
fact, as the deliverance of their fathers from Egyptian bondage.   And the express will of God requiring them, when
they celebrated their yearly Passover, to call to mind the first
institution of it in the land of Egypt, and the history of what
went before it and followed after it; must be much more
than a bare hieroglyphical memento of that providence; and
must annually overflow their minds with a very high tide of
joy and thankfulness, not only for the benefits then remembered; but from that satisfaction that must fill the minds of
all rational men, while they are engaged in the performance
of any service or devotion, to which they are called by the
voice of God Himself; whereas commemorations instituted
by men, or such types and resemblances as are contrived by
their wit or are owing to their invention, can only for the
present soothe the fancy, or give a placid motion to the
spirits of those that use them.

4. And further, if there be any such type, as is significant
of the greatest mercies and blessings, and at the same time
intended by God the Founder to contain and to convey to
men all the chief mercies, for which the original archetype
was first designed; then it must be owned, that this infinitely
exceeds in true value and power all others that hitherto have,
or that ever can be mentioned; and that indeed it may be
fitly enough called by the name of the archetype itself, and
is so in power and effect.   The annual Passover, though it
was in other respects a full representative of the first Passover in the land of Egypt, yet did not convey to those who
partook of it, the deliverance from temporal death or from
the Egyptian bondage; and therefore, though it was in this
respect a commemorative type, yet not so perfect as the
Eucharist; because by this latter, the pardon and grace purchased by the archetypal Sacrifice are applied to every worthy
receiver.   The lambs every year slain as types of those that
were first sacrificed in the land of Egypt might indeed well

enough deserve the name of the Passover, because they were as to substance the same sort of animals, and were designed as representations of those that were offered in Egypt; much more then may the more powerful and efficacious representatives of Christ's Body and Blood claim the name of their archetypes, if only upon this account, that if you consider them as types yet they exceed all other types whatsoever; and that they do exceed all others, will appear, by reflecting on the particular degrees of types before rehearsed; for

1. Bread broken and Wine poured out have not only an aptitude to represent the crucified Body and the effused Blood of Christ; but they are, or may and ought to be, known and understood to have this signification, by all to whom they are exhibited; and this cannot be said of the generality of types under the Law; for as God did never clearly intimate His will, or command, that the Jewish priests or people should be informed that their rites and sacrifices were types of Christ to come, so neither does it appear, that the people had by any other means an apprehension, that these rites and sacrifices were, by the secret Divine intention, appointed to prefigure the Messias; whereas the Eucharistical types are such as are to be known and understood by all, for whose use they were intended; and "not to discern" the Eucharistical Bread to be "the Lord's Body is to eat and drink our own condemnation."

2. Further, it does not appear, that any type under or before the Law was wholly and solely designed by God to be a type of the Messias, or of His Body and Blood. Melchisedec's bread and wine were (probably) chiefly and primarily designed for types of Christ's Body and Blood, but directly and immediately, of His sacramental, and more remotely and ultimately, of His natural Body and Blood; and I conceive it can be said of the Eucharistical Bread and Wine only, that they were designed by Almighty God for no other use or purpose but to represent the Body and Blood of Christ, and to be that Body and Blood in power and effect. And whereas the sacrifice of Melchisedec may be supposed to have been offered, partly in regard to the late victory of Abraham; the Eucharist is offered in commemoration of no other conquest

The preeminence of the Eucharist as a type.

CHAP. but that of Christ. The Jewish sacrifices were first and
II. directly intended for services, by which that people were to
acknowledge the sovereignty of God, and to express their
wants and desires, and to procure a relief and supply of
them; and were so far from being primarily designed for
symbols of Christ's Body and Blood, that God never seems
to have published to them in the Old Testament His secret
contrivance, whereby those sacrifices were made types of
"the grand oblation of Christ Himself." However He did
it not in so clear and open a manner, as it is reasonable to
suppose He would have done, if this had been His first
and primary intention in enjoining them.

3. All the legal and patriarchal types were only adum-
brations of Christ as yet to come; and therefore, how well
soever they were adapted in their own nature to prefigure
the Sacrifice of Christ, yet men could not be so capable of
discerning and penetrating into the scope and meaning of
them before their completion, as we now are; who not only
see our types, but have a more perfect knowledge of the
archetype, Christ Jesus, than they who lived in the ages
before Him. And the Eucharistical Bread and Wine are,
I suppose, the only types instituted by God, to represent
the Sacrifice of Christ, since the first and personal oblation of It.

4. And lastly, this I apprehend is the only type of Christ's
Body, which conveys and applies to those for whose use
and benefit it was designed; and which, as to efficacy and
virtue, is what It represents; and therefore no wonder that
this type does so frequently and usually carry the name of
its archetype, and that the Bread and Wine in the Eucharist
do so currently pass under the title of Christ's Body and
Blood. Who would bear him that should say, Moses struck
Christ Jesus; or, the Israelites baked and ground the Body
of their Messias; or that King Hezekiah brake Christ Jesus
to pieces, or that the Jews every year roasted Christ Jesus?
And yet it is certain, that the rock which Moses struck was
a type of Christ; that the manna which the Israelites ground
and baked, and the brazen serpent which King Hezekiah
brake in pieces, and the Passover which the Jews were
annually obliged to roast, were all types of our Saviour;

but not such full, lively, and powerful types, as the Eucharist is of Christ's Body and Blood; and therefore of him
that profanes the Sacrament we may say with St. Paul,
that "he is guilty of the Body and Blood of the Lord," that
he "tramples under foot the Son of God." It may be
allowed, that the annual Passover was such a type of the
first Passover, as our Eucharist is of the Body and Blood
of Christ, (though it did not come up to It in power and
effect, as has been hinted;) and I conceive, that this is the
only type, beside that of the Eucharist, that has ordinarily
gone under the name of its original; though it is to be
observed, that the original, I mean that in the land of
Egypt, was itself a type, in respect of the Body and Blood
of Christ. And it is certain, that nothing but the Eucharistic Bread and Wine has ever had this title commonly given
to it. Christ is indeed once or twice in Scripture called the
Passover, the manna, the rock, the door, the vine, the way,
&c. But this does by no means prove, that the Eucharistical Bread and Wine are no otherwise His Body and
Blood, than as the Passover, manna, rock, as a door, a vine,
and a way are Christ Jesus; for none of these are any more
than bare types and metaphors; nor dare any one say, that
he who touched the manna or the Passover with unclean
hands was guilty of the Body and Blood of Christ Jesus,
or that he who trod upon the rock trampled under foot
the Son of God, or that he who kicks at a door insults
Christ Jesus, or the man who cuts a vine wounds His
Saviour, or that he who sweeps the way cleans his Redeemer; and therefore none of these types or metaphors
have ever been used, in the current language of the Church,
to denote our Saviour, or His Body and Blood, but that at
the same time some additional words have been used to
shew the meaning of them. Whereas on the other side, the
Eucharistical elements are usually denoted in Scripture by
the words Body and Blood, without any qualifying or abating
additions; and this way of speaking descended from the
Apostles to the Church of the succeeding ages; and 'to
offer,' 'to receive,' 'to eat and drink the Body and Blood of
Christ,' are as familiar phrases in the ancient monuments
of Christianity, when by the Body and Blood of Christ they

C H A P.
II.

The differ-
ence be-
tween Bap-
tism and
the Eucha-
rist in this
respect.

meant only the symbols, as 'to receive the Sacrament' or 'to administer the Communion' are now with us. It is true, the other Sacrament of Baptism is a most efficacious institution, and the water is commonly presumed to represent the Holy Ghost. But if by this is meant, that the water is a type of the blessed Spirit, the third Person of the Holy Trinity, I cannot subscribe to it; for there cannot properly be a type of a thing present; and I suppose all that believe Baptism to be somewhat more than " washing away the filth of the flesh" and a mere federal rite, must believe also, that the Holy Ghost is there present to perfect the Baptism. I dare not affirm therefore, that the dove at our Saviour's Baptism was a type of the Spirit, or that the mighty rushing wind and the fiery tongues were so; they were rather tokens and indications of the presence of the Divine Spirit; and such I take the baptismal water to be; not such a type or sign, as the brazen serpent was of Christ yet to come, but such a sign, as breathing is of life now present. Ammonius of Alexandria[s] supposes that "the water differs from the Spirit in our apprehension only ;" or that it is the water of the baptismal font, whereby the Holy Spirit is first conveyed to Christians ; or that Baptism by water is the Baptism of the Spirit, where there is not some incapacity on the side of the recipient. I apprehend that this will not easily be received in this age ; especially because it may seem to suppose, that the Holy Spirit, being given in Baptism, implies habits of grace to be thereby infused ; because the Holy Spirit must carry along with It all Its ordinary effects, where the recipient is capable of them. But I humbly conceive, that no human soul is, without some miraculous instantaneous operation, capable of taking habits of virtue all at once ; and though the operations of the Spirit are præternatural, yet not miraculous ; and I think the only immediate effect of the Spirit in Baptism is remission of all sin, and removing our natural disability to

the worship and service of God, and "the sentence of condemnation," under which we were all born ; and that other graces are wrought in us by that Holy Spirit, Which by Baptism receives us under Its protection, gradually, and according to the capacity of the recipient. And this doctrine I

[s] a. p. 9. Ap.

learned from those words of St. Barnabas, in his epistle, cap.
vi.; ἔπει οὖν ἀνακαινίσας ἡμᾶς ἐν τῇ ἀφέσει τῶν ἁμαρτιῶν,
ἐποίησεν ἡμᾶς ἄλλον τύπον, ὡς παιδίον[t] ἔχειν τὴν ψυχήν, ὡς
ἂν καὶ ἀναπλασσόμενος Αὐτὸς ἡμᾶς, which I thus render,
(taking the two participles as verbs, which is not unusual
with Hellenistic writers, and is here necessary to clear the
sense,) "After therefore that Christ had renewed us by the
remission of our sins, He made us [in] another shape, so as
to have an infant-like soul, even as He Himself reformed us:"
where he plainly makes renovation to consist in forgiving sins;
and makes the new moulding or reformation of our minds to
be not performed at the same time with the other, or all at
once, but to be consequent upon the former renovation; and
Christ is always thus reforming us, from our Baptism to our
death. And I look on these words of St. Barnabas to be a
better explication of the renovation or regeneration of Christians by Baptism, than whole volumes of modern writers upon
the same subject. And I may here very seasonably observe,
that as the Holy Spirit is present in our Baptism, to seal the
remission of sins, and to infuse the beginnings of Christian
life; so He is present in Confirmation, to shed further influences on them that receive it, for the further suscitation of the
gift of God bestowed in Baptism and in the Eucharist, as
will hereafter appear at large, for our farther progress and
increase in grace; and this is a sufficient reason, why the
water of Baptism is never called the Holy Spirit, as the Bread
and Wine are called the Body and Blood; viz. because it is
not peculiar to Baptism, that the Holy Spirit is thereby communicated to the receivers, if they be duly disposed for the
reception of it; for the two other evangelical ordinances are
attended with the same benefit; whereas on the other side, it
is peculiar to the Eucharist, that the Body and Blood of Christ
are there received. I know some grave men[u] have told us
that St. Augustine asserts, that the Body and Blood of Christ
are received in Baptism. Now if that Father has any where
dropped such words, I must declare I have not yet been able
to lay my eyes on them; but giving it at present for granted
that St. Augustine may have said so, we must look upon it
as a peculiarity of this Father. And I suppose my reader will

[t] [ὡς παιδίων, Hefele.]   [u] [Dr. Hancock, 'Patres Vindicati,' p. 29.]

CHAP.
II.
agree with me, that our judgments are not to be determined in a thing of this nature by the saying of one or two single Fathers of the fourth or fifth century, when it is not supported by any authority from Scripture, or from the more early writers of the Church.

Made types by a Divine power.
And that the Bread and Wine in the Eucharist were such types as exceeded all others, not only in clearness of signification, but in that power and energy, by which they became such images as are perfectly to the life, will appear from this; that they, who sometimes call them types and images, do at other times call them the very Body and Blood; and others suppose it is by virtue of the Divine benediction, that they become such types and figures. So for instance, Ephræm Syrus says[x], "Our Saviour blessed the Bread into a figure of His Body." And the synod of Constantinople, so often mentioned, calls it[y], "a most effectual type and memorial;" and "the unerring image of His natural flesh, sanctified by the coming of the Holy Ghost—Which the true Artist of nature delivered to us with His own voice." The Liturgy cited by Pseudo-Ambrosius de Sacramentis, lib. iv. c. 5, teaches the Priest to say, *Fac nobis hanc oblationem adscriptam, rationabilem, acceptabilem;* [*ut sit nobis in figuram*] *corporis et sanguinis Domini nostri Jesu Christi*[z]. Now to pray, "that the oblation may become the figure of Christ's Body and Blood," is to suppose, that the Divine will and power is necessary to this end; and that therefore there is something in the Eucharist beyond bare resemblance, or an aptitude to represent Christ's Body and Blood. For this resemblance is inherent in the nature and condition of types of the common sort; so that it is not consistent with common sense, to pray to God that He would make them to become so. Suppose that the Israelites, or any considerable body of them, had had a clear view of our Saviour's life and death; and did so far penetrate into the Divine secrets as to know, that the manna, and the rock, and the brazen serpent were types of

[x] b. p. 25. Ap.
[y] p. 51. Ap. l. 6. 24. 26.
[z] [The Editor is unable to find the words, which he has inclosed in brackets. 'Quod est figura' occurs in the edition, which Johnson used in his Appendix, i. e. that of Paris, 1686; the same is also in that of Basle, 1567. And in both editions the books 'De Sacramentis' are classed among the genuine works of S. Ambrose.]

Him; their very knowledge that they were types, would
teach them, that there was no occasion for them to pray
that they might be made types. Who ever in his wits prayed,
that the rainbow in the clouds might become a type or representative of that, which was first exhibited to Noah as a
sign of the covenant? Therefore it is evident, that the ancients, when they called the consecrated Bread and Wine
types, meant something more by this word than a bare
likeness or resemblance inherent in the nature or circumstances of the things themselves. They were types in such
a manner, as they could not have been without the concurrence of the Divine will and power. There is no occasion
for me to enlarge on this head any farther, considering that
I am next to prove,

Fourthly, that the ancients believed the Bread and Wine
to be the very spiritual Body and Blood of Christ.

1. I shall shew, that they believed them in some sense to
be the very Body and Blood.

2. Yet not in substance, but in power and effect.

I begin with the first proposition, that they believed them
in some sense to be the very Body and Blood.

We have heard Theodoret say this already; for when [a]
Eranistes asks Orthodoxus, whether he believed he did partake of the Body and Blood, he makes Orthodoxus answer,
"yes, I do;" and after having said, as before cited, that they
are still Bread and Wine in their own nature, he adds, "but
they are by the understanding apprehended to be what they
are made, and they are believed and venerated, as really being
what they are believed to be."

Cyril of Alexandria affirms [b], "that Christ is in us by His
own Body, Which quickens us by the Spirit. For we must
not say, that because the nature of the Deity is not eaten,
therefore the Holy Body of Christ is a common thing; but
it is necessary we should know, that it is the all-quickening
Word's own Body; nor do we consider this as the flesh of a
man that was one of us, but as truly made the own Flesh of
Him, Who for our sakes became, and was called, both Son
and Man." St. Chrysostom will rather be thought to say too
much than too little; as in the following words [c], "Thus let us

How the
ancients
believed
these types
to be the
very Body
and Blood.

---

[a] m. p. 45, 46. Ap. l. 14.   [b] i. p. 44. Ap.   [c] t. p. 40. Ap.

CHAP.
II.
do in the mysteries, not eyeing only what lies before us, but
faithfully retaining His words; for His word is without deceit,
our sense may be deceived. That has never failed us; but
this is in many things erroneous. Since then the Word says,
'This is My Body;' let us both be convinced, and believe,
and look on It with our intellectual eyes;" and[d], "Look
that you be not guilty of the Body and Blood of Christ.
They [the Jews] murdered the most Holy Body; thou receivest It with a polluted soul.—He prepares a Body, and
mingles Himself with us, not only as to our faith, but in
reality." Again[e], "If they who defile the royal purple are
punished, as if they had torn it; why is it not reasonable,
that they, who receive the Body of Christ with an unclean
mind, should expect the same punishment with those that
rent It with nails?" And[f], "The Cup which we bless, is it
not the Communion of the Blood of Christ? The Apostle
speaks so as to make us believe and tremble. What he
says is this, that That which is in the Cup flowed from
Christ's side." Lastly[g], "Why will ye receive the Body of
God above all, the spotless pure Body, that was so familiarly
conversant with the Divine Nature, by Which we are and
live, by Which the gates of hell were broken down and the
doors of heaven opened; why will ye receive this [Body]
with so much insolence?" St. Austin says the same thing[h],
"'A Body hast Thou prepared Me'—this was promised by
certain signs; the signs are taken away, because the promised verity is exhibited. We are in This Body; we are
partakers of This Body;—and I wish you may not receive
It to your own condemnation;" and[i] he calls the Eucharistical Body, "the one only Sacrifice for our sins;" and
again, in a place not mentioned in my Appendix, viz. De
Eucharistica, lib. i. c. 13, that "wicked men do sin, taking
the very Body of our Lord, the one only Sacrifice for our
salvation[k]." Gaudentius says the same very plainly[l], "He
that is the Creator and Lord of natural beings, Who produces

d u. p. 40. Ap.
e B. p. 41. Ap.
f F. p. 41. Ap.
g L. p. 42. Ap.
h r. p. 33. Ap. l. 11.
i N. p. 36. Ap.
k [" Quid, de ipso Corpore et San-

guine Domini, unico Sacrificio pro
salute nostra, quamvis Ipse Dominus
dicat, ' Nisi quis manducaverit,' &c.
Nonne idem Apostolus docet etiam hoc
perniciosum male utentibus fieri."—
Contra Cresconium, tom. ix. p. 403.]
l a. p. 30. Ap. l. 10.

bread out of the earth, does again out of bread make His own Body; and He that of water made wine, of wine makes His own Blood; for He is able, and hath promised to do it." And[m], "Believe what is declared, that what thou receivest is the Body of Him that is the heavenly Bread, and is the Blood of that heavenly Vine." St. Jerome says[n] of Christian Priests, that they make "the Body of Christ with their own mouths;" and again[o], he uses almost the same words. St. Ambrose says[p], that "the holy things are transfigured into the Body and Blood of Christ, by the mystery of the sacred prayer." Ephræm Syrus bids you[q] "partake of the spotless Body and Blood of Christ, being assured that by a perfect faith you eat the entire Lamb." St. Gregory Nyssen speaks more than enough to this purpose[r]; for he inquires, "how it is possible, that one Body of our Lord, perpetually distributed to so many myriads of believers throughout the world, is entirely in every portion; and yet remains entire in Itself?" and declares his belief[s] that "the Bread sanctified by the word of God is changed into the Body of God the Word,"—and[t], "these things or privileges He gives by virtue of the *eulogy*," that is, the Eucharist, "changing the nature of the visible things into That [Body]." St. Basil speaks of[u] "sacrificing and touching the Body of our Lord, Which is greater than the temple." Optatus asks[x], "What is the Altar, but the seat of the Body of Christ?" And St. Hilary speaks home to the purpose in those words[y], "by the declaration," or, rather, according to the declaration "of the Lord, and our faith, It is true Flesh and Blood; and these being received, do cause Christ to be in us, and us in Him;" nay, he there supposes, that we have in the Eucharist, in some sense[z], "the very nature of Christ's Flesh." Epiphanius observes[a], that Christ "was pleased to say, 'It is My Body,' and no [Christian] man disbelieves His words." Cyril of Jerusalem having observed[b] that "the Bread is His Body, the Wine His Blood," adds, "He once by His own

[m] b. p. 30. Ap.
[n] a. p. 28. Ap.
[o] s. p. 29. Ap.
[p] e. p. 26. Ap.
[q] c. p. 25. Ap.
[r] a. p. 23. Ap. l. 18.
[s] l. 28.

[t] l. 42.
[u] a. b. p. 23. Ap.
[x] c. p. 22. Ap.
[y] a. p. 20. l. 12.
[z] l. 19.
[a] c. p. 22. Ap. l. 7.
[b] b. p. 18. Ap.

CHAP. command changed water into wine in Cana of Galilee; and
II. does not He deserve to be believed, when He changed wine
into Blood?" And[c], "We do with full assurance partake of
It, as the Body and Blood of Christ." And[d], "Consider
them not as mere bread and wine; for they are the Body
and Blood of Christ, according to what our Saviour pronounced; though your taste suggests this to you, determine
not the matter by the taste; but be beyond all doubt assured
by faith, of your being vouchsafed the Body and Blood of
Christ." St. Athanasius gives us his sense in the following
words[e], "It is the Body, to Which [God] says, 'Sit Thou on
My right hand;' to Which the Devil, with his wicked powers,
was an enemy, as also the Jews and Gentiles; by Which
[Body] He is called the High-Priest and Apostle, by means
of the mystery which He delivered to us, when He said,
'This is My Body.'" He makes the Body in the Sacrament the same, in some sense, with That, Which sits at
God's right hand. St. Cyprian speaks in the same strain,
when he says of some that had sacrificed to idols, and presently after came to the Eucharist[f], "When they had scarce
done belching the fatal food of idols, and their jaws stunk of
their crime, and breathed forth mortal contagion, they invaded the Body of the Lord." Then he cites Lev. vii. 20;
xxii. 3; 1 Cor. x. 21; xi. 27; and presently adds, "but the
Body and Blood of our Lord is invaded with violence, in contempt of all these [Scriptures.] They sin more against the
Lord with their hands and mouths now, than when they
denied Him." Origen speaks thus of the two Sacraments[g],
"Baptism before was enigmatical in the cloud and the sea;
but now regeneration by water and the Spirit is in open
view. Then manna was the enigmatical food; now the Flesh
of the Word of God is the true food, in open view." I turn
in specie, 'in open view,' as being opposed to *in ænigmate*.
Tertullian says[h], "the flesh is fed with the Body and Blood
of Christ." Clemens Alexandrinus speaks thus of the Eucharistical Body[i], "The Word is every thing to an infant,
a parent, a preceptor, a foster-father. 'Eat My Flesh,' says

[c] c. p. 18. Ap.   [g] c. p. 10. Ap.
[d] d. p. 19. Ap.   [h] m. p. 8. Ap.
[e] d. p. 17. Ap.   [i] a. p. 7. Ap.
[f] e. p. 11. Ap.

He, 'and drink My Blood:'" (he evidently cites the words
of institution but *memoriter*, and therefore according to the
sense, not the letter;)—"He commands us, when we partake
of the new food of Christ, that receiving Him we may, if
possible, treasure Him up within us, and inclose our Saviour
in our breast." St. Irenæus's judgment may be known by
what was produced from him, to prove, that Bread and Wine
are the Body and Blood; and it is observable, that he so
calls them, without any qualifying or restraining words: he
supposes it to be a truth, of which men should be well
assured; and asks the heretics, against whom he disputes[k],
"How they can be certain, that the Eucharistized Bread is
the Body of Christ, if He be not the Son of the Creator of
the universe." He supposes It to be made the Body of Christ
by a Divine power, as we shall hereafter see; and asserts It
to be a preservative of our bodies for a happy resurrection;
all which particulars I shall have an occasion to prove from
him particularly; and in the mean time my reader may, if
he please, read these opinions of his, in my citations from
him in the Appendix. Now certainly he that believed this
must think the symbols more than bare types; and indeed
I cannot observe, that this Father does ever give them the
name of types; but perpetually, the Body and Blood, the
Eucharist; or the heavenly thing, that is, the Spirit, and the
earthly, that is, Bread and Wine. And when Justin Martyr[l]
affirms, that Christians were in his time instructed that the
Bread and Wine were the Flesh and Blood, and that they
were made so by prayer; he must intend something more
than naked types; for there is no occasion for prayer or for
the Divine concurrence *toties quoties,* to render any thing a
resemblance of another; and I dare say, that the Arminians
and Socinians will bear witness, that nothing but breaking
the Bread and pouring out the Wine is necessary to make
the elements the Body and Blood in their sense, who believe
them to be nothing more than mere memorandums. When
therefore Irenæus and Justin Martyr lay such a stress upon
the belief of this doctrine, and suppose a power from above
necessary to render the elements the Body and Blood; they
must suppose withal, that they are in some sense the very

[k] f. p. 5. Ap. l. 17.   [l] a. p. 2, 3. Ap. l. 18.

things which they represent. A Deist or an atheist may believe, that the Bread and Wine are types of Christ's Flesh and Blood, and were by Him appointed as such; but it is very evident, that these holy men did look upon this doctrine of the elements being the Body and Blood, as a truth of very considerable moment, and in which Christians ought to be fully informed and assured; and that they were made the Body and Blood at their solemn request. And St. Ignatius teaches us the same doctrine, when he charges it as a heresy on the *Docetæ*[m], "that they abstained from the Eucharist and prayer; because they did not acknowledge the Eucharist to be the Flesh of our Saviour Jesus Christ, Which suffered for our sins, and Which the Father by His goodness raised from the dead." For certainly these words sound something much beyond and above a type or metaphor; nay, his words imply, that whoever then received the Eucharist was thereby supposed to acknowledge, that the Eucharist was the Body of Christ, Which suffered and rose again. For why should they abstain from the Eucharist on this account, if they could communicate without some way or other professing their belief of this doctrine? If it be said, that these *Docetæ* believed our Saviour's Body to have been a mere phantom, and that He suffered and rose again in appearance only, not in reality; and that therefore they never used the Eucharist or any thing that was an imitation of the Eucharist, because by using the type or symbol they must have confessed the original to be a real substance; I may allow this argument to be true, and yet with good reason deny, that the *Docetæ* were sensible of this consequence. Nay, it is certain, the Marcionites in the next age, though they believed Christ's Body and Death and Resurrection to have been only appearances without any realities, yet did celebrate the Eucharist in their way; and though Irenæus and Tertullian argued against them, that by owning the Sacrament of the Body and Blood they confuted their own opinion; yet there is not any reason to believe, that they felt the force of this argument; therefore it is most probable, that they only abstained from the communion of the Catholic Church, because by joining in that they must have ac-

St. Ignatius's sense of the Body and Blood in the Eucharist. Epist. ad Smyrn.

[m] h. p. 2. Ap.

knowledged, that they received there, in some good sense,
that Body of Christ, which died and rose again; and it is
certain St. Ignatius allowed but one Eucharist, viz. that in
the Church; and might therefore justly say, according to
his principles, that they abstained from the Eucharist, though
they had something like it among themselves; for, however
that was celebrated, being out of the Church, he thought it,
ipso facto, null and invalid: but if these *Docetæ* differed from
the Marcionites, in supposing that the Eucharist, however
administered, implied confession that the Body and Blood
were there, then this shews, that heretics, as well as
Catholics, had this notion of the Bread and Wine in the
Eucharist; viz. that they were by common acceptation the
Body and Blood of Christ; though this was what they could
not consent to, and for this reason as well as others were
condemned by St. Ignatius. If it be said, that it is sufficient
to suppose that the Bread and Wine were typically the Body
and Blood, in the judgment of St. Ignatius and the Church
of his age; and that the *Docetæ* could not allow this, because
they believed the personal Body Itself to be but a phantom;
it has already been observed, that their descendants the
Marcionites did not believe, that a phantom could not be
typified; nor is there any ground for supposing, that these
Docetæ might not be of the same opinion: they might, as
the Marcionites did, own the Eucharist to be the Body, in
the same sense that the original was so, that is, in a mere
imaginary manner; but this did not come up to the sense of
the Church and the holy Martyr; for by them the Eucharist
was believed to be that Body of Christ, which suffered and
rose from the dead; and it seems highly probable, that communicants in St. Ignatius's days were obliged expressly to
acknowledge the Eucharist to be Christ's Body and Blood,
by answering Amen at the delivery of the Sacramental Body
and Blood, as well as by joining in prayer to God, that He
would make them so. And because the *Docetæ* could not do
this, therefore they absented themselves from the Christian
assemblies. They might perhaps have been brought to believe, that the Bread and Wine were types or shadows, and
have received them as such; but they could not subscribe to
the doctrine of the Church. If any man think that the

CHAP. words of St. Ignatius import, that they allowed of no Eucha-
II. rist or Sacrament in any sense; it must follow, that they
allowed of no prayer neither. For St. Ignatius says, that
they abstained from prayer as well as the Eucharist; but I
shall hereafter have occasion to shew, that by prayer he means
that of consecration used by the Church; and that therefore
it is most rational to believe, that he means, by the Eucharist,
only the true Eucharist as celebrated in the orthodox assemblies. It may indeed be granted, and is, I think, plain in itself,
that these *Docetæ* were a sort of heretics just now started
up, when St. Ignatius wrote, and so had not yet formed
themselves into separate assemblies; and till they had done
this, could not have any thing that was in any sense an
Eucharist. It is probable the holy Martyr might be apprehensive that they were now meditating a new scheme of worship and discipline; which makes him in the following words
caution the Smyrnæans to " shun divisions," and " follow
the Bishop." Nay, St. Ignatius seems apprized, that they
had taken some steps at least toward the drawing up a
liturgy of their own for celebrating a mock eucharist; which
was probably the occasion of his telling the Smyrnæans,
that° " that Eucharist was valid, which was [performed] by
the ,Bishop or one licensed by him; and that without the
Bishop it was not lawful to baptize, or make a love-feast."
However this is very evident beyond all dispute, that it is
heresy in the judgment of Ignatius not to believe that the
Eucharist is the Body of Christ, which suffered and was raised
from the dead. And though we have already heard this holy
Martyr asserting that Bread is the Eucharist, yet we see he
believed this Bread to be the Body of Christ. The words 'type,'
'figure,' 'sign,' or 'symbol' are never used by this most primitive writer in relation to the Eucharist, nor yet by the penmen of holy Scripture; and though Tertullian and they who
came after him do frequently use this way of speaking, and
in a very sound sense; for they do thereby mean that the
Eucharist is not the very natural or substantial Body of
Christ; yet because these words are commonly taken to
signify something that is only a faint umbratile resemblance
of another, and not so lively and powerful a representation

° i. p. 2. Ap.

as the holy Eucharist is; therefore the holy Scripture and
the most ancient writers forbear this way of expression. Our Saviour says, "This [Bread] is My Body; this [Wine] is My Blood." The Apostle says, "The Cup of blessing is the communion of Christ's Blood; the Bread which we break is the communion of Christ's Body." It is certain that the Bread and Wine remain; but when blessed, they are the Body and Blood: neither our Saviour nor the Apostle do add any qualifying or abating words; and therefore so far as those elements are capable of becoming Christ's Body and Blood, so far they are so. And I cannot but express my concern, to observe how these words of Christ and His Apostle are by too many melted down by new expositions into mere tropes and figures. The most that the learned Dr. Whitby can make of 1 Cor. x. 16, "The Cup which we bless, is it not the communion of the Blood of Christ? the Bread which we break, is it not the communion of the Body of Christ?" I say, the most he can make of this text is thus expressed by him: 'The Bread, thus broken and shared out, may be said to be the communion or communication of the Body of Christ, as being the communication of that Bread which represented His broken Body; and the Cup they severally drank of may be styled the communication of the Blood of Christ, as being the communication of that Wine, which represented His Blood shed.' "*It may be said*," "*it may be styled*," says the Doctor; by which is intimated, that if it be so said or styled, it is in a very remote and improper sense, only so as to bring our Saviour and the Apostle off from being guilty of an absurdity. And that he meant so, appears from what he says in his note on ver. 3 of this chapter, where he produces those texts of Scripture as parallel to each other, viz. "The three branches are three days." "The seven good kine, and the seven ears of corn, are seven years." "The four great beasts are four kings." "Thou art that head of gold;" and (after several other texts of the same sort with these) he ends with those words, "This Bread is My Body, this Cup is My Blood;" so that it should seem, the Bread of the Eucharist is in the Doctor's judgment no otherwise the Body of Christ, than the visionary head of gold was Nebuchadnezzar. I had not taken notice of this

Dr. Whitby's gloss on 1 Cor. x. 16, 17. considered.

Gen. xl. 12.
Gen. xli. 26.
Dan. vii. 17.
Dan. ii. 38.

s 2

CHAP. but to give my reader an instance, how modern interpreters
II. explain the Sacrament into as mere a type as any that is to
be found in the New or Old Testament, making It a mere
emblem, only not insignificant. The Fathers did not so; but
though they acknowledged It a type as being not the very
natural Body, yet they asserted It to be such a type as
was at the same time a verity, in comparison of all the types
of the old Law; and such a type as is, in some good sense,
the Body Which it represents. Our Saviour positively affirms,
" It is My Body ;" Dr. Whitby in good manners thinks himself obliged not to contradict Christ Jesus; and therefore
confesses, " *it may be so said*," " *it may be so styled*," just as
the three branches are said to be three days. Irenæus,
Justin Martyr, and Ignatius did not thus expound away
the life and efficacy of the Sacrament into mere cold and
empty types; and let my soul be with theirs. Another exposition of this text the Doctor gives us presently after, in
these words, " Do we not, by partaking of this Bread and
Wine consecrated in memorial of Christ giving His Body
broken and His Blood shed for us, hold communion or
declare our fellowship with Christ[p] ? " Whereas, to explain
the text is not to tell us what we do in the communion,
but in what sense the Bread is the communion of Christ's
Body, the Wine of His Blood. But another very learned
man, and for whose person and merits I have a very singular
esteem, tells his parishioners, in explaining the Lord's Supper
to them, that " the communion of the Body and Blood of
Christ is a name given to the Lord's Supper, as it is a
public declaration which every Christian makes of his being
a member of Christ's Body, and his living in communion and
charity with his fellow Christians, as members of the same
Body, under one common Head, the Lord Jesus." Now to
shew how far this is from a just explication of these words,
I only desire my reader to observe, that the words of St. Paul
are, " the Cup of blessing which we bless, is it not the communion of the Blood of Christ? the Bread which we break,
is it not the communion of the Body of Christ?" So that
beyond all possibility of doubt, it is the Cup and the Bread
which are here determined to be the communion of the Body

[p] p. 152.

and Blood. And if the Cup and Bread be the communion,
I cannot for my life conceive, how this communion is a
declaration which every Christian makes. A declaration is
something said or done by us; but the communion, here
spoken of, is the communion of the Body and Blood of
Christ. Sure our declaration cannot by this learned man
be thought the Body and Blood of Christ. If he had said,
that our receiving the Sacrament is a declaration of our
being members of Christ, I should have made no objection;
but not content with this, he asserts, that the communion
of the Body and Blood of Christ is a declaration, or as a
declaration; and so a thing is turned into an action, and a
blessing which we come to receive into a declaration made
by us. And the most reputable writer that he has with him
in this particular, is, I believe, Dr. Whitby; who, in his paraphrase of 1 Cor. x. 16, makes the Apostle call the Cup the
communion of the Blood of Christ, because it is the rite
whereby we profess to hold communion with Christ; and in
the same place he supposes the Apostle calls the Bread the
communion of Christ's Body, because by eating at Christ's
Table we declare our fellowship with Him. By which he
seems to me to make the Cup (by which I suppose he means
the contents of it, viz. the consecrated Wine) a ' rite,' and the
Bread a ' declaration,' as the other great man has done after
him. Now I must confess I should as soon believe transubstantiation, as that two substances are *declarations*. What
these learned men mean, by thus endeavouring in a catachrestical manner to resolve these words of the Apostle into
jejune dilute figures, I will not allow myself to guess; but
sure I am, that how well soever such glosses may be received
in this age, they would never have been relished in any other;
and I cannot at present think of a better account of the
reason why the Eucharist is called the communion of the
Body and Blood, than those words in the Church Catechism,
viz. that "the Body and Blood of Christ are verily and
indeed taken and received by the faithful in the Lord's
Supper." And he who observes the sense and judgment of
the ancients in this particular, as before delivered, cannot but
think it one instance of the degeneracy of this present age,
that men are so cautious of saying any thing that may not

please the palates of pretended philosophers and *virtuosi*,
that if we were not taught this doctrine in our Catechism
while we were children, we should scarce be informed by any
other means, unless laying aside all prejudice we read it in
our Bibles.   It is sad to consider, how men naturally run
from one extreme to another; and that nations and churches
do so too.   During the times of Popery, the real substantial
presence of Christ was a darling prevailing notion; and next
to the Pope's supremacy, it may be justly owned, that transubstantiation is the most ill-favoured and yet the most beloved
error of that Church.   But now we are run so far into the
opposite extreme, that we turn all that is said by Christ or
St. Paul on this subject, into type and allegory; and therefore it was not only to clear the notion of the Sacrifice, but to
enable myself to lay before my reader the doctrine of the
primitive Church on this important head of religion, that I
have, without prejudice or partiality, inquired into the notions
of the Fathers of the four first centuries and other monuments of antiquity in those ages; and it is their sense, which
I am reporting to you, without any regard to persons or
causes.   And when I reflect upon the new notions of this
age and the authors of them, I cannot but wonder, that men
of learning and judgment should prefer the novelties of
Zuinglius and Arminius to the good sense and correct exposition of St. Chrysostom; who in his homily on the tenth
chapter of the first Epistle to the Corinthians, ver. 16, 17,
says, that[q] " the Apostle speaks so as to make us believe and
tremble; for what he says is this, that what is in the Cup is
That Which flowed out of Christ's side, and of This we partake." And he adds, not far from the same place[r], "After he
had spoken of the communion of the Body, and because that
which partakes is different from the thing it partakes of, he
takes away the distinction, though it seem but a small one.
Having spoken of the communion of the Body, he endeavoured to say something that was yet more close still; wherefore he adds, we being many are one Bread and one Body;
for [says the Apostle] why do I speak of communion? We
are that very Body. For what is the Bread? says the Apostle:
The Body of Christ.   What are the partakers? The Body of

⁹ F. p. 41. Ap.   ʳ I. p. 42. Ap.

Christ; not many Bodies, but one Body." In which words,
as he speaks decisively against the Church of Rome, not only
in making Bread the Body of Christ, but likewise in making
the Sacramental Body to consist of the members, as well as
of the head; so he is very express, that in the Eucharistical
Bread and Wine we receive the Body of Christ Jesus, more
than in a type or figure. For what is there in a type, to make
a man tremble? And he makes the communion to be the
Eucharistical Body and Blood, not our 'declaration.' And I
am the more confirmed in this exposition of St. Chrysostom,
when I consider, that St. Irenæus understands the Body and
Blood in this text to be the Bread and Wine consecrated for
this purpose. For speaking to those heretics, who vilified
the creation, and would not allow it to be the workmanship
of the good God and Father; "Then," says he[s], "neither will
the Cup of the Eucharist be the communication of His Blood;
nor the Bread which we break, the communication of His
Body." And in another place[t], "How could our Lord, in
common justice, take that Bread, which is, according to our
doctrine, a part of this creation, and declare it to be His
Body, if He be [the Son] of another Father? And affirm the
mixed Cup to be His Blood?" Ignatius himself supposes the
Eucharist to be "the Body of Christ, which suffered for our
sins and was raised from the dead."

The truth is, it is not much to be wondered, that they who
deny the Sacrifice of the Body and Blood in the Eucharist
should shew no great zeal or concern for making them present there in any sense, except that which is very cold and
remote. The Lutherans do indeed earnestly contend for a
Real Presence, and such a presence as is, I firmly believe,
contrary to Scripture and antiquity. And when I reflect on
this, and some other notions, entertained by them upon very
slight and insufficient grounds, so far as I am capable of
judging; I am the less surprised that they have a very great
zeal for the belief of the real Body of Christ, and against the
offering of It in the Eucharist; for a real Altar, but against
the Sacrifice. But they who understand consistence and con-
gruity better than the Lutherans seem to do, are not insensible, that it will be very hard to give any good reason why

For what cause many of late are not concerned to assert, that the Eucharist is the Body and Blood.

[s] g. p. 6. Ap.   [t] f. p. 6. Ap.

the Body or Blood of Christ should be in the Eucharist, if
they are not there to be offered to Almighty God. They
whom I have discoursed with on this subject, when they have
been asked, what they understood by " the Body and Blood
of Christ's being verily and indeed taken and received by the
faithful in the Lord's Supper?" have never been able to give
any other answer than this, that we do in that institution
receive all the benefits purchased by Christ's death.   But if
this be all the account that can be given of this matter, without admitting the oblation, (and this is all the account that
I can find in the acquaintance and conversation that I have
had either with modern books or men,) then I must confess
I am very much at a loss, why our Saviour should make the
eating His Body and drinking His Blood so important a
duty.   It is true, the arbitrary will and pleasure of Christ
Jesus, made known to us, is a sufficient reason for our compliance and obedience; but since, in other commands of
Christ Jesus, we can with great delight see the grounds and
reasonableness of what He requires us to do, it would be
some satisfaction to us to see it in this, as well as in other
particulars.   Now it is certain that all the benefits of Christ's
death might be applied to us, without eating His Flesh and
drinking His Blood, if He had intended nothing else but this
by instituting the Eucharist. We know the benefits of Christ's
death are first applied to us by Baptism, and they might from
time to time have been again and again applied to us by that or
any other covenanting rite, if Christ had so pleased. Nor is it
to be presumed that Christ would have had the Eucharist the
Sacrament of His Body and Blood, except there had been a
very apparent reason why His Body and Blood should be
there.   The principle of immortality might have been conveyed to us, as it was intended to have been imparted to
Adam, by eating of the fruit of the tree of life, or by any
other means that God had approved of.   Nor do I believe
that our adversaries will easily find any solid and just reason
for Christ's Body and Blood being in the Sacrament, but in
order to their being presented to Almighty God for the procuring and applying the purchase of our Saviour's death.
God thought fit, that they should be procured and applied
by the same outward means, and would not burden us with

a multiplicity of outward performances; and since the authen- tic representatives of Christ's Body and Blood were the most proper materials of a Sacrifice for the pleading our cause with God, and moving Him to grant us such spiritual mercies as we stand in need of, therefore He resolved that these same materials first offered should be returned to those that offered them, filled with Divine blessings. They that are averse to the doctrine of the Sacrifice can shew no reason, why there is any more occasion for the Body of Christ in the Eucharist than in Baptism; they seem sensible of this, and therefore are not at all solicitous to assert this doctrine, and content themselves with putting such a sense on our Saviour's words as may signify the least that such words possibly can. But as all the ancients did fully believe the Sacrifice of the Eucharist; so they were careful at the same time to assert, that they had in the Eucharist something which was worthy to be offered to the Almighty, and not such poor and sorry types as the bullocks, sheep, and goats were under the Law. If it be asked, how it comes to pass that the benefits of Christ's death may be applied in Baptism without an actual Sacrifice at that time offered? I answer, no man is fit to offer Sacrifice, either as a Priest or layman, until he be first cleansed from his natural pollution. Men therefore must by Baptism be prepared for the Eucharist: before they join in offering Sacrifice, they must be sons of the Covenant. And it has before been shewed, that as the Sacrifice of Christ is a lustrative Sacrifice to prepare men for Divine worship, it is not to be repeated; and by virtue of the first and principal Sacrifice, the Church is empowered to prepare men for the Christian Sacrifice, by the laver of regeneration.

But I expect, that a reader not freed from vulgar prejudices should start two objections against what I have been advancing. The first is, that it is but a poor and seemingly inconsistent account I give from the ancients of the Body and Blood of Christ in the Sacrament, since it is evidently a Body and Blood of Bread and Wine; besides that Bread and Wine, of themselves considered, can be no more than types, and as sorry types as those under the Law. The second objection is, that I have already asserted the Sacrifice of the Eucharist to be a spiritual Sacrifice, and hinted the Body of

Christ in the Sacrament to be a spiritual Body; which seems
to be very irreconcileable to the common notions now prevailing; since I have withal represented the Bread and Wine,
which are corporeal things, to be this Sacramental Body and
Blood offered in the Eucharist. Now I hope effectually to
answer all this, by proving,

That the
ancients
believed
the Eucha-
rist to be
the Body
and Blood
in power
and effect.

2. That though the ancients believed the Bread and Wine
in the Eucharist to be the Body and Blood; yet they did not
believe, that they were the natural or substantial Body and
Blood, but that they were so in a spiritual manner, in power
and effect. So that the Bread and Wine are not the Body
and Blood, in themselves considered, nor merely by their resembling or representing the Body and Blood, but by the
inward invisible power of the Spirit; by Which the Sacramental Body and Blood are made as powerful and effectual
for the ends of religion, as the natural Body Itself could be
if It was present. And it is on this account that It is called
Christ's spiritual and mysterious Body, as being discerned to
be what It is by the inward, not the outward eye; by our
faith, our minds and spirits, not our senses. And this, when
proved, is a full answer to the objections above mentioned;
for though bread and wine, abstractedly considered, are indeed
weak elements; yet when enriched with the special presence,
and invisible operations of the Spirit, they are very efficacious and beneficial. Though bread and wine in themselves
can be no more than figures, yet when the Holy Ghost has
blessed and sanctified them, they are in power and effect to
us the same that the archetypes would be. And though we
cannot apprehend this by our taste or sight, yet we may by
our reason, informed by a right faith. I will therefore shew
under this head,

(1.) That the ancients did believe, that the Holy Spirit
was in an especial manner present with the holy symbols, to
render them the spiritual Body and Blood.

(2.) And that they did on this account look upon them as
mysteries, to be spiritually discerned and received.

(1.) The ancients did believe, that the Holy Spirit was in
an especial manner present with the holy symbols, to render
them the spiritual Body and Blood. This is a doctrine which,
as it was universally received in the primitive Church, so it

will not easily be admitted by those with whom seeing is believing. Our adversaries are willing to suppose, that when mention is made of the spiritual Body of Christ, the spiritual Sacrifice, and the like; nothing is thereby meant but something that is not real, but merely figurative, imaginary, or any thing else that is nearer to nothing. They suppose that the word 'spiritual' has a sort of annihilating power, and can turn any words that it comes near into mere airy empty sounds; or that when it has any real signification, it imports something divested of all matter, and that has no substance but in our thoughts. The ancients did not so; but believed the material Bread and Wine to be the spiritual Body and Blood of Christ, on account of the presence and invisible operation of the Holy Ghost, in and by those elements; and though they were fully sensible that the energy of the Sacrament could be perceived by the mind or understanding only, yet they firmly believed this energy to be there; though some men, for want of faith or other good dispositions, did not perceive it, and were therefore never the better for it.

I expect the contradiction of our adversaries on this head; because it is the very heart and life both of the Sacrament and Sacrifice, according to the judgment of the primitive Church. It is by this, that our Christian types and symbols are nobly distinguished from those under and before the Law. It is truly observed by our adversaries, that animal or bloody sacrifices, in themselves considered, are more apt representations of the Sacrifice of the Cross than Bread broken and Wine poured out; and yet they are not pleased to inform us, in what it is that our types exceed those; as if they could be content, that the old Levitical types should be esteemed superior to those of the Gospel, rather than they should lose an occasion to depress and, if possible, annul the Sacrifice of the Eucharist. But the holy Fathers had a just sense of the dignity of the Christian mysteries, and the very centre in which all their reasonings and arguments on this subject meet, is this; that the Holy Ghost, at the prayers of the Priests and people, is in a peculiar manner present, and imparts a secret power to the Sacramental Body and Blood, by which they are made to be in energy and effect, though not in substance, the very Body and Blood Which they represent. So that it greatly concerns them, who oppose the doctrine of the Sacrifice, to stifle and suppress this doctrine, and to en˚avour, what in them lies, to confute the Fathers and the primitive Church. And they have, by what they have already published, sufficiently expressed their good will, and given full demonstration, that they are not at all checked or damped by any reverence or regard to antiquity; and that they have a much greater value and esteem for modern, than for ancient Fathers. And they have no reason to despair; for though they are embarked on a leaky bottom, and their arms and tackle but indifferent, yet it must be owned that they have the wind and tide with them; for we live in an age, when nothing is more contemned than antiquity, especially by those who set themselves up for judges of all disputes and controversies relating to religion, in the coffee-houses and such like places of public resort. And therefore I have reason to suppose, that the doctrine, which I am now going to support by the authority of the ancients, will be one of the first which will be attacked; not only because it is a main pillar of the doctrine of the Sacrifice, but because all must know that it is not like to meet with approbation from the common stream even of learned men. A polite writer[u] has cautioned us against "placing" any "mysterious powers in the act of consecration, and invocation of the Holy Ghost;" and against "ascribing a strange mystical efficacy to the act of consecration." And we know well enough what Mr. Hales of Eton said upon this occasion, in more harsh terms bordering upon blasphemy; but then we know too, that the Founder of this holy institution was by His enemies laid under the imputation of the same crime, with which Mr. Hales charges (in language unfitting a Divine and Christian, and which the primitive Fathers would have branded with the mark of heresy and apostasy[x]) the use of the words of institution, in celebrating the holy Eucharist. Nor are we ignorant, that very

[u] Defence of the Doctrine and Practice of the Church of England, p. 11, 12. [ed. London, 1712. Pamph. 300. Bodl.]

[x] [Vid. 'A Tract on the Sacrament of the Lord's Supper. By Mr. Hales of Eaton.' Pamph. 403. Bodl. Where he says, "The main foundation that upholds the necessity of this form of action now in use, is Church-custom and Church-error."]

many of the sciolists of the age will be ready to hiss the SECT.
I. notion of the Holy Spirit's imparting a real sanctity to inanimate creatures such as bread and wine, out of doors. But it is our great satisfaction, that if the doctrine of the Sacrifice be exploded on this account, and the assertors of it suffer in their reputation or otherwise; they must suffer from such men, as would, if they had lived in the three first centuries of Christianity, have joined in persecuting and running down some of the greatest lights of the Christian Church, and, as we verily believe, the Christian Church itself: for we have no reason to doubt but that the main diffusive body of Christians throughout the world were then in this opinion. We are very sure that the Divine Spirit can act upon inanimate creatures, and that the natural Body of Christ Jesus was a " holy thing," because It was conceived Luke i. 35. by the operation of the Holy Ghost. Nor can we apprehend any reason, why He may not exert His power in consecrating and blessing the Sacramental Body of Christ Jesus, as well as in forming and perfecting the natural. We know that when Theophilus of Alexandria, at the latter end of the fourth century, to express his resentment against some monks who had displeased him, procured the works of Origen, which were assiduously read and immoderately admired by these monks, to be condemned in a synod held at Alexandria, and in another in the isle of Cyprus; one head, upon which Origen's works fell under this censure, was, that in the books περὶ ἀρχῶν he had affirmed that "the operation of the Holy Ghost does not affect inanimate or irrational things [y]." Whether Origen do say this or not in those books, I shall not pretend to determine; but it is certain, that in his thirteenth homily on Levit. [z] he says, " We must receive the sacred mysteries in a holy place by the grace of the Holy Spirit, by Which every thing that is holy is sanctified;" meaning, I conceive, that nothing can be consecrated in that manner, that the Sacrament is, but by the power of the Holy Ghost. And in his tenth book on the

That the
Holy Spirit
may ope-
rate on
inanimate
things.

---

[y] ["Dicit enim Spiritum Sanctum non operari ea quæ inanima sunt, nec ad irrationabilia pervenire."—Vid. Galland. Bibl. Vett. Patt., tom. vii. p. 627.]

[z] ["In loco sancto capiamus sancta mysteria per gratiam Spiritus Sancti, ex Quo sanctificatur omne quod sanctum est."—P. 258. tom. ii. ed. Paris. 1733.]

Epistle to the Romans, that "the Holy Ghost is the fountain of all sanctification or consecration[a]." And it is certain, that he over and again asserts[b], that the symbols of the Eucharist are sanctified or consecrated; and therefore, according to his former doctrine, must be consecrated by the Holy Ghost. Nay, he asserts in that very place, where he speaks less honourably of the Sacrament than perhaps any other of the ancients, or than he himself does elsewhere, that[c] the "consecrated food is a cause of illuminating the mind;" which is a property, that it must receive from the Holy Spirit. And when Theophilus charges Origen with this error, he does not wholly deny that Origen admitted the concurrence of the Holy Spirit in consecrating the symbols, but only, that "the Sacrament produced sanctification in us;" for he says, Origen affirmed that the Eucharist "did only dispose or excite our mind to apprehend the graces of the Holy Spirit." See Theophilus in his first Paschal Letter[d]. It is certain, that the holiness imparted to senseless creatures is of another sort from that which is conferred on rational and intelligent beings; nor is it possible for us to determine, wherein the sanctity of the Sacramental Body and Blood does precisely consist. But we take it for granted, that the Eucharistical Bread and Wine were intended to be consecrated in the most perfect manner that such creatures can be consecrated; and we believe, that it is the Holy Ghost alone can impart this greatest degree of consecration. Theophilus was so sensible that this was the universal opinion of learned Christians in and before his own age, that he thought he could not in any particular have a more plausible plea for condemning Origen and his adherents than this of his seeming in one of his works to deny what he elsewhere asserts, viz. that inanimate creatures are not capable of being consecrated by the Holy Ghost. He therefore takes this advantage, solicits, and procures a censure to be passed against Origen and his followers by the Bishops of the neighbouring Churches, and, among the rest, by the famous Epiphanius. But, it should seem, St. Chrysostom was not

---

[a] [" Sanctificationis fons Spiritus Sanctus est."—Tom. iv. p. 676.]
[b] a a a. p. 9, 10. Ap.
[c] e. p. 10. Ap.
[d] Biblioth Patr., vol. iv. [Such a passage does not occur there.]

satisfied with the justice of these proceedings; for he coun-tenanced and received those monks, whom Theophilus and Epiphanius had condemned, nor would he join with them in forbidding the works of Origen to be read. Now it is certain, that no man was more positive as to the consecration of the holy Eucharist by the illapse of the Holy Spirit than St. Chrysostom; and therefore the reason why he did not come into the measures of Theophilus must be, that he was not convinced that Origen was guilty of that error which Theo-philus and his friends imputed to him. The polite writer, lately named, says, that " the invocation of the Holy Ghost is no more than a solemn consecration of the Bread and Wine to holy uses[e]." Now this is, I think, a very degrading account of the most venerable mystery of the Christian Church. The Bread and Wine are consecrated for holy uses by being placed on the Altar. And we shall ere long hear Origen telling us, that whatever is by a private man dedicated or vowed for the service of the Altar is *Sanctum Domini*, "the holy of the Lord," even before it is brought to church, while it is yet in his own custody. If this be a just account of the consecration of the Eucharist, then it is evident there is no difference between what is sanctified by the advent of the Holy Ghost and what is barely separated for pious uses, between the consecration of a church, and the consecration of the Baptismal water, or the Eucharistical Bread and Wine; and so the walls of the church are as holy as the Sacramental Body and Blood. And this learned person cannot but know that the Eucharistical elements, in the primitive Church, had been dedicated to holy uses, not only by the lay-proprietors' offering them to the celebrator, but by the celebrator's offering them to God, before the solemn invocation was made for the descent of the Holy Ghost. And Dr. Hancock[f] says very well, that " sacrifice implies consecration;" that is, what-soever is solemnly offered to God is thereby supposed to be consecrated to His service. This Doctor adds, that " sacrifice implies the highest degree of consecration." And this is so

[e] Defence of the Doctrine of the Church of England, p. 14.

[f] Answer to Dr. Hickes, p. 157. [This was published anonymously, under the title of " A Presbyter of the Church of England," and is called " An Answer to some Things contained in Dr. Hickes's Christian Priesthood asserted, &c. &c. London: printed for James Round, at Seneca's Head, in Exchange Ally, 1709." It is numbered in the Bodleian Catalogue, 8°. Rawl. 404.]

far true, I believe, that nothing could acquire a greater sanctity under the Law than by being offered in sacrifice; but I
apprehend that the Eucharistical Sacrifice, that is, the representative Body and Blood of Christ, were, by the primitive
Fathers, supposed to be consecrated in a more perfect manner
than any sacrifice under the Law could be: for in all the
Liturgies, after the oblation of the Bread and Wine as the
memorials of the grand Sacrifice, there is a solemn prayer
that God would send His Spirit or His Divine benediction
for the further consecration of them, after they had first been
offered as a Sacrifice to God. And this is the most perfect
consecration that inanimate creatures are capable of; and
such a consecration does apparently best fit and comport with
the Eucharist, as being the most eminent mystery and hierurgy that ever was instituted by Almighty God. And it is
to be observed, that by this means the Eucharistical Bread
and Wine are made the most perfect and consummate representatives of the Body and Blood of Christ. They are not
only substituted by His appointment and command to this
purpose, but they are by the power of the Spirit, which is
communicated to them so often as the celebration of this
mystery is repeated, made the lively efficacious Sacrament of
His Body and Blood: for the Holy Spirit is Christ's invisible
Divine deputy in His Church. Our Saviour has promised
His presence with us to the end of the world, and we know
how He fulfilled this promise, viz. by the sending the *Paraclete*
to abide with us for ever. The visible material substitutes of
Christ's human nature are the Bread and Wine; and when
the Holy Spirit, Which is His invisible representative, communicates It's power and presence to the symbols, which are
His visible representatives, they do thereby become as full
and authentic substitutes as it is possible for them to be; and
the reader is to be advertised, that when the ancients speak
of the *Logos*, or the Divine nature of Christ, being present
in the Eucharist; or of the Sacramental Body's being united
to the natural Person or Body of our Saviour; they mean
the same thing as if they had expressly mentioned the Holy
Spirit; because it is the known opinion of the ancients, and
may be proved from Scripture, that whatever beneficial operations are performed in the Church are performed *immediately*

by the Holy Ghost, and *mediately* only by the Father and the Son; and that it is by means of the Spirit that the Church communicates with the other two Divine Persons; and the holy Sacraments are very justly, by many of our Divines, styled the channels by which all Divine graces are derived to us.

I now proceed to shew, that it was the judgment of the ancient Church, that the Holy Spirit was in an especial manner present with the Holy Symbols, to render them the spiritual Body and Blood. I will mention but one place from Theodoret[g], which is that where he asserts a " change made by grace" in the Sacramental symbols, and yet presently adds, " Not changing nature, but adding grace to nature." The words of Cyril of Alexandria[h] are very full, " Lest we should be ready to swoon at the sight of flesh and blood lying before us on the Holy Tables of the Church, Christ as God condescending to our infirmities sends an enlivening power into the gifts laid before us, and substitutes them to be, in effect or energy, His own Flesh, that we may enjoy them, so as to partake of their enlivening power." But St. Chrysostom is most copious on this head[i]: " When the Holy Spirit sheds His grace, when He descends, and gives the contact to the [gifts] lying in open view, then do you make a noise and a stir?" Again[k], " If we had not the earnest of the Spirit, we could not enjoy the holy mysteries: for the mystical Body and Blood of Christ cannot be without the grace of the Holy Spirit." And[l], " Thou seest Christ, not in a manger, but on the Altar; not held by a woman, but by the Priest, who stands at [the Altar;] and the Holy Ghost most elegantly spreading It's wings over the [gifts,] which lie in open view." And[m], " This Table fully supplies the place of the manger; for here the Body of our Lord will lie, not in swaddling-clothes as formerly, but surrounded on all sides by the Spirit. Thou[n] hast the Body and Blood of the Lord, and the Spirit instead of the letter, and grace exceeding human reasoning, and the unspeakable gift." At another place[o], " The Priest stands at [the Altar], not bringing fire

Marginal notes:

SECT. I.

Proofs that the ancients believed the symbols to be consecrated by the Holy Spirit.

---

[g] i. p. 46. Ap. l. 7.
[h] m. p. 45. Ap.
[i] m. p. 39. Ap. l. 4.
[k] n. p. 39. Ap.

[l] M. p. 42. Ap.
[m] c. p. 37. Ap.
[n] e. p. 38. Ap. l. 5.
[o] h. p. 38. Ap.

CHAP.
II.

but the Holy Spirit; and offers a long supplication, not that a torch let down from heaven may consume the [gifts] lying in open view, but that grace lighting upon the Sacrifice may, by that [Sacrifice], kindle a flame in our souls." St. Augustine calls the invisible power of the Spirit, exerting itself in the Eucharist, "the virtue of the Sacrament;" for, says he[p], "the Sacrament is one thing," viz. Bread and Wine, "the virtue of the Sacrament another," viz. the efficacious presence of the Divine Spirit; and again[q], "This is the Bread Which comes down from heaven.—But as to what concerns the virtue of the Sacrament, not as to what concerns the visible Sacrament," or sign; and what this virtue is he clearly tells us in these words, where speaking of the Eucharistical Bread he says that[r] "when by the hands of men it is wrought into that visible shape, it is not sanctified into so great a Sacrament but by the invisible operation of the Holy Ghost." Gaudentius, speaking of the Eucharist both as representing Christ's natural Body, and His collective Body the Church, has these words[s], "As we know that bread is made out of many grains of wheat reduced to meal, and must of necessity be brought to perfection by fire, in this a figure of Christ's Body is rationally conceived; for we know, that It is a Body kneaded together out of the multitude of mankind, perfected by the Holy Spirit; for He was conceived of the Holy Spirit." Ephræm Syrus expresses his opinion thus, in his lofty way[t], "It exceeds all wonder, all apprehension, what the only-begotten Christ our Saviour has done for us. For He hath given fire and the Spirit, that is, His own Body and Blood, to be eaten and drunk by us, who are clothed with flesh." He is evidently speaking of the Sacrament, as the reader may satisfy himself, by reading the foregoing words in the Appendix. St. Ambrose teaches the same doctrine in these words[u], "Christ is in this Sacrament, for it is the Body of Christ; therefore it is not corporeal but spiritual meat. Wherefore the Apostle says concerning the type of it, 'Our fathers eat the spiritual food, and drank the spiritual drink:' for the Divine Body is a spirit-

p k. p. 32. Ap.   s d. p. 31. Ap. l. 6.
q k. p. 32. Ap.   t c. p. 25. Ap. l. 7.
r R. p. 37. Ap.   u k. p. 27. Ap.

ual Body. The Body of Christ is the Body of the Divine SECT.
Spirit: for Christ is a Spirit." His argument proceeds thus: ——— I.
the Sacramental Body of Christ must be a spiritual Body, because His natural Body is so; His natural Body was formed
and sanctified, and had in It a quickening power, by virtue
of the Holy Spirit; therefore His Sacramental Body must
receive all It's excellencies from the same Spirit. He supposes that when St. Paul calls the Eucharistical Body "the 1 Cor. x. 2.
spiritual meat," he means it of the spiritual powers and effects
which belong to It; and that therefore the Israelites did not
eat the Body of Christ in the same manner that we do in the
Sacrament; they did it only in an umbratile and faint type,
but Christians do it in a more effectual and lively manner;
they did eat "the same spiritual meat," but they did it by
a bare cold type, which perhaps they themselves might not
understand; the Church of Christ does it in such a representation, as is only not the original. Gregory Nyssen, speaking of the Eucharist, says[x], "It is necessary to receive the
enlivening power of the Spirit in a way naturally possible;
but it is the Divine Body [of Christ] only that has received
this grace. We ought to consider how it is possible, that this
one Body, being shared among so many myriads of believers
—should remain entire," &c. This explains the words of
Optatus, who speaking of the Donatists' breaking the Altars
in the Catholic Churches, says[y], "What sacrilege is equal
to that of breaking the Altars, on which the Holy Ghost
descended?" This is evidently Epiphanius's meaning in that
place[z], "The power of the Bread is enforced; so that Bread
is not our strength, but the power of the Bread; what is eaten
is indeed Bread, but the power or the force of that Bread is
to vivification." He says the same of Baptismal water; and by
the power of the Bread he means the same that St. Augustine
does by the "virtue of the Sacrament." This shews what St.
Gregory Nazianzen means, when he said[a], that "by the unbloody Sacrifice we communicate of the Passion of Christ, and
the Divinity;" and when he calls the Altar[b] "the Table that
receives God." For by the Divinity we are not to understand

---

[x] a. p. 24. Ap. l. 14.
[y] a. p. 22. Ap. l. 1. 5.
[z] d. p. 22. Ap.

[a] b. p. 21. Ap.
[b] g. p. 21. Ap.

the Divine nature of Christ.   For it does not appear that the
ancient Church thought that believers received that in any
sense, but only as the union betwixt Christ and His Church
is by means of the Holy Spirit's presence in the Sacraments.
Cyril of Jerusalem gives us the sense of himself and of his
Church, expressed in the Liturgy which he used[c], "We
beseech God, Who is a lover of souls, to send down His Holy
Spirit on the [gifts] laid in open view, that He may make
the Bread the Body of Christ, the Wine the Blood of Christ.
For to whatsoever the Holy Ghost gives a contact, that thing
is consecrated and changed."   This lets us into the meaning
of St. Ambrose[d], when he calls the Sacramental Bread "a
spiritual Body," and "the Body of the Divine Spirit;" and
also of Julius Firmicus[e], when he says, "Christ delivered to
His Disciples the substance of majesty;" which he presently
after calls the "grace of the salutary food," that is, the holy
symbols ennobled by the peculiar presence of the Spirit, and
thereby made the Body and Blood in power and effect.   And
this is what Gelasius Bishop of Rome calls "the Divine thing,"
in that celebrated place cited by all that write against transubstantiation; and which, though I have not in my Appendix, as
being written in the latter end [A.D. 488.] of the fifth century,
I will here subjoin.   *Certe Sacramenta quæ sumimus Corporis
et Sanguinis Christi Divina res est, propter quod et per eadem
Divinæ efficimur consortes naturæ, et tamen esse non desinit substantia vel natura Panis et Vini.   Et certe imago, et similitudo
Corporis et Sanguinis Christi in actione mysteriorum celebran-
tur.—In hanc scilicet in Divinam transeunt, Spiritu Sancto perfi-
ciente, substantiam, permanente tamen suæ proprietate naturæ.*
(In Tractatu contra Nestorium et Eutychem[f].)   In English
thus; "The Sacraments of the Body and Blood of Christ are
certainly a Divine thing; for which reason also, by means of
them, we are made partakers of the Divine nature, and yet
the substance or nature of the Bread and Wine continue; and
certainly an image or similitude of the Body and Blood of
Christ is celebrated in the mysterious action.—They [the
Bread and Wine] pass into a Divine substance, their proper
nature remaining by the efficacy of the Holy Ghost."   He

[c] f. p. 19. Ap.
[d] k. p. 27. Ap.
[e] p. 18. Ap. l. 15.

[f] [Vid. Heroldi Hæresiologia, p. 689.
Basil. 1556.]

cannot be in common equity understood to mean that the elements are changed into the Deity; but that the Bread and Wine, which he affirms to remain, do by the operation of the Spirit become the Body and Blood in power as well as name. St. Athanasius witnesses the same doctrine in these cele-brated words[g], "Christ predicates of Himself both Flesh and Spirit, and distinguishes one from the other, that believers may learn what of Him is visible and what invisible; for what He says is not carnal but spiritual. For how many (rather how few) would His Body have satisfied, if It had been to be eaten, that this should be an entertainment for the whole world? Therefore He reminds them of the Son of Man's ascent into heaven, that He might draw them off from corporeal notions, and that they might learn, that the Flesh spoken of was heavenly spiritual food, given by Him. 'For what I have spoken of,' says He, 'is Spirit and Life;' as if He had said, the [Body] Which is shewed and given for the world shall be given for food, so as to be spiritually distributed to or in every one, as a preservative to the resurrection of eter-nal life." This is an unanswerable evidence against trans-substantiation : for it proves, that Christ never intended to give His visible Body to be eaten. He calls the Sacramental Body "heavenly spiritual food," as several others do, and as he himself has done at another place, as we shall hereafter see. He asserts, that It is to be distributed to or in every Christian, which can be understood of His Eucharistical Body only; that It is a preservative to a happy resurrection, which was what the ancients generally believed of the Sacramental Body and Blood. This Sacramental Body is said to be That Which was given for the world, not only because It is a per-fect representation of It; but because our Saviour, in offering the symbolical Body, did intend to consign His natural Body to the cross; and from the whole we may conclude, that when he calls It "spiritual food," he means food that has a vital power communicated to it by the Spirit; which he afterwards explains, by calling It "a preservative to the resurrection," &c. St. Cyprian says, "what is taken [in the Sacrament] profits not the unworthy; and that even the salutary grace is turned into dust or ashes, the sanctity departing from it."

[g] a. p. 17. Ap. [h] f. p. 11. Ap.

CHAP.
II.

He calls the material Eucharist "salutary grace," on account of the presence of the Holy Spirit; and by the "sanctity" he can mean nothing but the Divine benediction thereby conferred. Origen[i] speaks "of loaves being made a certain Holy Body by prayer, and sanctifying them that use them with a sound intention:" and we have before heard him declare, that nothing is sanctified or made holy but by the Spirit. Clemens Alexandrinus does not often speak plainer than in the following words[j], "The Blood of the Lord is twofold, the one carnal, Whereby we are redeemed from destruction; the other spiritual, by Which we are anointed. To drink of the Cup of the Lord is to partake of the Lord's immortality; and the power of the Word is the Spirit, as the Blood is of the Flesh: therefore the wine is agreeably mixed with water, and the Spirit with the man; the mixed liquor invites us to a draught, and the Spirit leads us to immortality; and lastly, the mixture of the liquor and the Word together is called the Eucharist," that is, "laudable and eximious grace." He does expressly distinguish between the natural or carnal and the Eucharistical Blood; he says, that by the latter Christians are anointed or receive the unction of the Spirit, and to this he attributes a principle of immortality; and I shall in the Second Part shew at large, that the ancients did believe the Eucharist to have this power. He supposes the Word, that is, the consecration, to give this power to the symbols, and that It gives it by the efficacy of the Spirit; for "the power of the Word is the Spirit." He plainly speaks all this of the Eucharist, and interprets this name, so as to make it denote the spiritual grace with which it is attended; and though none of the other very ancient Fathers do give this etymology of the word *Eucharist*, yet Isidorus Hispalensis does, in his book *Originum et Etymologiarum*, vi. c. 19[k]; and all the ancients own the thing, viz. that the Eucharist is made what it is by the operation of the Spirit, though they do not give us

---

i a. p. 9. Ap.
j b. p. 7. Ap.
k ["*Sacrificium* dictum, quasi sacrum factum: quia prece mystica consecratur, in memoriam pro nobis Dominicæ passionis: unde hoc, Eo jubente, Corpus Christi et Sanguinem dicimus, quod dum sit ex fructibus terræ sanctificatur et fit Sacramentum, operante invisibiliter Spiritu Dei, cujus panis et calicis sacramentum Græci *Eucharistiam* dicunt, quod Latine *bona gratia* interpretatur. Et quid melius Corpore et Sanguine Christi?"—Isid. Hispal. Opera, p. 52. ed. Col. Agripp. 1617.]

this derivation of the word; but none does more plainly speak this truth of the Holy Spirit's power and presence with the symbols, than St. Irenæus in those words[1], "Earthly bread receiving [the benefit of] the invocation of God is no longer mere bread but the Eucharist, consisting of two things, an earthly" [viz. the Bread], "and a heavenly" [viz. the power of the Spirit]. So Irenæus explains himself[m], in these words, viz. "What is earthly? The body. (Plasma.) What is heavenly? The Spirit[n]." And again[o], "When the mixed cup and the natural bread receives the Word of God, it becomes the Eucharist of the Body and Blood of Christ." He repeats this again in the same chapter, in almost the same words. The admirable Dr. Grabe by the Word of God here understands the same with "the benefit of the invocation" in the former citation; just as if he had said, the Divine power or Spirit [p], and I have no objection against this opinion; but if you suppose he meant the Divine nature of Jesus Christ, yet his meaning is the same; for by having the Holy Spirit in the Eucharist, we have in effect the *Logos*, Whose authentic representative the Spirit is, and by the means Whereof we alone can have union with the *Logos*. Or if by the Word of God we mean the words of institution or consecration, the sense is much the same; considering as has been said in the citation from Clemens Alexandrinus, that "the power of the Word is the Spirit;" and that the Spirit is the "heavenly thing" mentioned in the first citation from St. Irenæus. This I take to be the meaning of St. Justin Martyr, when he speaks[q] "of the food which is eucharistized by prayer—being made the Body and Blood of Christ." (I designedly omit λόγου τοῦ παρ' αὐτοῦ, because they are either mis-written or exceedingly obscure); for by "the Bread eucharistized by prayer" he plainly means the Bread over which prayer had been made, that the Holy Ghost might descend upon it, according to the forms of the ancient Liturgies; and when Irenæus, according to the Latin translation (which is far from being nice), mentions the Bread[r], *in quo gratiæ actæ sunt;* there is

[1] f. p. 5, 6. Ap. l. 27.
[m] l. 5. c. 9.
[n] ["Quid est ergo terrenum? Plasma. Quid autem cœleste? Spiritus." —P. 412.]
[o] g. p. 6. Ap.
[p] [Note 1. p. 400.]
[q] a. p. 2. Ap.
[r] f. p. 5. Ap.

CHAP.
II.
no reason to doubt, but that in the original Greek it was ἄρτος εὐχαριστηθεὶς, ' the eucharistized Bread,' or the Bread blessed by the invocation of the Spirit, or however made the Eucharist by reciting the words of institution. And I believe this truth is imported in the words of St. Irenæus's translator, which are omitted in my citation from him[s], from book iv. c. 34[t], *offerimus enim Ei quæ sunt Ejus, congruenter communicationem et unitatem prædicantes Carnis et Spiritus,* that is, "we offer to God what is His own, agreeably hereunto declaring the unity and communion of the Flesh and Spirit." This holy man is arguing against the heretics, who denied bread and wine to be the creatures of God, and yet acknowledged that they were to be offered to Him, and that they became the Body and Blood of Christ; and yet they denied a resurrection. Now St. Irenæus's argument runs thus; how can they believe that Bread and Wine are made the Body and Blood of Christ, when they are none of God's creatures? Or that our bodies shall not rise again, when they are nourished by the Body and Blood of Christ? "Therefore," says he, "let them cease from making their oblations, or let them alter their judgment; but our judgment is agreeable to the Eucharist, and again the Eucharist confirms our judgment; for we offer to God what is His own, agreeably hereunto declaring the unity and communion of the" Eucharistical "Flesh and Spirit." Whereas it was incredible, that God should communicate the Spirit to the Eucharistical Bread and Wine, if they were not His creatures, but made by another God than He Who was the Father of our Lord Jesus Christ; and then he proceeds to shew, how the Eucharistical Body of Christ, receiving the illapse of the Spirit, was a means of immortality. Dr. Grabe supposes that the Greek transcribed from John Damascene is to be corrected by this old translation; but the Greek words are capable of a very good sense, taking the word ἔγερσιν to denote, not the resurrection itself, but "the power" or "faculty of raising," which it will very well bear. The Greek words are, ἐμμελῶς κοινωνίαν καὶ ἑνωσιν ἀπαγγέλλοντες καὶ ὁμολογοῦντες σαρκὸς[u] καὶ πνεύματος ἔγερσιν· "agreeably de-

s f. p. 6. Ap.
t [p. 327.]

[u] The learned Pfaffius will have πνεύματος ἔγερσιν to signify the con-

claring the communion and union, and confessing the raising or reviving power of the Flesh and Spirit" of Christ in
the Eucharist, of which he was speaking.   I am pretty sure
this sense is very clear and coherent, and fits both the Greek
and Latin; and it is very probable that those three words
καὶ ὁμολογοῦντες ἔγερσιν were either omitted by the translator, because he did not apprehend the meaning of ἔγερσις
πνεύματος; or else were turned by him *resurrectionem Spiritus,* which some Latin transcriber (not knowing or advert-
ing, that *resurrectio* was the imperfect rendition of ἔγερσις,
and that ἔγερσις had the signification above assigned to it)
did omit to render the sense more obvious.   And it seems
probable at least, that when St. Ignatius wishes the Magnesians[x] " a union of the Flesh and Spirit of Jesus Christ,"
his meaning is, that their Eucharist may be always rendered
effectual and beneficial, by the union of the Holy Ghost
with the Sacramental Flesh of Christ; and this best explains
the meaning of this holy Martyr, when he says[y], " the Eucharist is one, the Flesh of Jesus Christ; the Cup one," viz.
as being animated by one and the same Spirit; and I apprehend that this sense is preferable to that which is commonly assigned; and by this means SS. Ignatius and Irenæus speak the same thing; and we may learn from the
words of the former, that the presence of the Spirit with the
Eucharistical Body of Christ was by him esteemed the grand
privilege of the Christian Church, the continuation whereof
he therefore prays for at the beginning of this epistle, as a
most Divine blessing to the Magnesian people.

And though the early councils had no occasion to give
their judgments in a point so unanimously received by the
primitive Church; yet when, at the latter end of the fourth
century, some took occasion it seems from some words of
Origen to say what was thought to have an ill aspect on
this doctrine; there was a synod convened at Alexandria,
and another in Cyprus, to nip those novel opinions in the
bud; and Epiphanius and other good and learned men

junction of the soul, in his S. Irenæi
Fragmenta, &c. p. 71, and argues
against my explanation of these words
in this place in his Dissertat. de Con-
secratione, p. 463, 464, margin. Yet
in his addenda to p. 71 of his own
book he says, " Egregie hæc verba ex-
plicat Johnsonius—etsi paulisper ab eo
dissentiamus."

[x] c. p. 1. Ap.
[y] g. p. 2. Ap.

would not so easily have been prevailed upon to condemn
Origen's writings, if they had not a great zeal for this and
other truths, which Theophilus persuaded them were very
much shaken and endangered by some hasty expressions of
Origen, or by the wrong construction that others had put
upon them. And when, in the eighth century, the Icono-
latræ seemed to entertain some new notions of the Sacramental Body and Blood, it is very observable, how the
orthodox Fathers in the synod of Constantinople express
their sense of this matter, viz.[z], "As the natural Body of
Christ was holy, as having been divinely sanctified; so also
His adoptive Body [in the Eucharist] is holy, as having
been divinely sanctified by the grace of consecration. For
this was what our Lord Christ aimed at, that as He had
divinely sanctified the Flesh which He assumed by a proper
natural sanctification proceeding from its union; so it was
His will and pleasure, that the Bread of the Eucharist, as
being the unerring image of His natural Flesh, should become a Divine Body, being sanctified[a] by the descent of the
Holy Ghost.—Further, the natural animate Flesh of Christ
was anointed with the Holy Ghost[b]. In like manner the
image of His Flesh, delivered to us by God, was replenished
with the Holy Spirit, together with the life-giving Cup of the
Blood, which [flowed] out of His side."

All the Greek Liturgies, except that of St. Peter, which is
but a Latin Missal translated, as the Rev. Dr. Hickes has
observed, do contain a prayer for the descent of the Holy

---

[z] p. 51. Ap. 1. 20.

[a] Here I have omitted to translate
τὴν Θεότητα, as not seeing how it can
be rendered consistently with the sense.
What I suspect is, that it should be
written οὐ κατὰ τὴν Θεότητα, and rendered, 'not as to His Divinity,' which
may intimate, that Christ was anointed
with the Holy Ghost, not as to His
Divine nature but His human only.
Learned men complain, that the reports of the judgment of the Constantinopolitan Fathers are very much obscured in the acts of the second council
of Nice, from whence only we can take
them. The learned reader, in comparing my translation with the original
in the Appendix, may at first sight
suppose that I have defectively turned

θεόομαι by 'divinely sanctified;' but I
have this to offer in vindication of this
version, that St. Gregory Nazianzen
does so understand this word in his
Paschal Oration, a good way before the
middle of it, where he says, Ἄνθρωπος
—ζῶον τῇ πρὸς τὸν Θεὸν νεύσει θεού-
μενον. And Stephanus, in his The-
saurus, cites him for these words, Ἐμὲ
θεοῖ διὰ τοῦ Βαπτίσματος.

[b] The Fathers of the second Nicene
council cavil thus against this expression, viz. ' If it be an image of the
Body, it cannot be a Divine Body.'
But I suppose this is sufficiently answered above, where I speak of Firmicus's 'Substance of Majesty,' and
Gelasius's ' Divine Substance.'

Ghost on the Sacramental Body and Blood, as the learned
reader may inform himself by viewing my short transcripts
from them in the Appendix; as for instance, St. Chrysostom's[c],
St. Basil's[d], St. Mark's[e], St. James's[f]. I will only translate
the words of the most ancient, viz. St. Clement's[g], "Look
graciously upon these [gifts,] O self-sufficient God, for the
honour of Thy Christ; and send down Thy Holy Spirit, the
witness of the sufferings of our Lord Jesus, upon this Sacrifice, that He may make this Bread the Body of Thy Christ,
this Cup the Blood of Thy Christ." There is nothing of this
sort now in the Church of Rome, nor has been for many ages
past; but we have no reason to doubt but that the most ancient Liturgies of that Church had words to this effect, especially because we have above heard Pope Gelasius, at the end
of the fifth century, expressly attributing the consecration to
the Holy Spirit. And the old Gallican Liturgy is mentioned
in a book called Micrologus[h], written in the eleventh century, as directing the Priest to say this prayer, " Come, Holy
Ghost the Sanctifier, eternal God, and bless this Sacrifice[i]."
And the old Gallican Missal on St. Germanus's day has these
words[j], "We beseech Thee, Almighty God, let Thy Holy Word
descend on what we now offer to Thee. Let the Spirit of
Thine infinite Majesty descend, the gift which Thou hast of
old indulged, that our oblation may be made a spiritual oblation[k]," &c. And there is no room to doubt but that such
like words were used in the Eucharistic Liturgies in the Gallican Church from the time of Irenæus, Bishop of Lyons, in
the second century, whose writings breathe this Divine truth;
and that Irenæus learned it from St. Polycarp, who was the
disciple of St. John the Apostle. The reason why for so many

[c] d. p. 57. Ap. l. 10.
[d] g. p. 57. Ap.
[e] c. p. 56. Ap.
[f] h. p. 54. Ap.
[g] c. p. 53. Ap.
[h] ["Prædictas orationes, quæ omnibus Missis communis erat, de qua
Micrologus in cap. ii. ' composita oblatione in Altari, dicit Sacerdos hanc
orationem juxta Gallicanum Ordinem:
Veni Sanctificator, Omnipotens Æterne
Deus, et benedic hoc Sacrificium Tuo
Nomini præparatum per Christum
Dominum Nostrum.' "]

[i] See Mabillon, de Liturgia Galli-
cana, Paris. 1685. p. 43.
[j] ["'Descendat precamur, Omnipotens Deus, super hæc quæ Tibi offerimus, Verbum Tuum Sanctum; descendat inæstimabilis gloriæ Tuæ Spiritus; descendat antiquæ indulgentiæ
Tuæ donum: ut fiat oblatio nostra
hostia Spiritalis in odorem suavitatis
accepta: etiam nos famulos Tuos per
sanguinem Christi Tua manus dextera
invicta custodiat.   Per Dominum.' "]
[k] Mabillon, ibid. p. 331.

CHAP.
II.

This incon-
sistent with
the doc-
trine of the
Church of
Rome.

ages the Holy Spirit has not been mentioned in the Canon of the Church of Rome seems to be this, viz. that it is utterly inconsistent with their notions, since they have thought that the consecration is finished by the words of institution, whereas the ancient Liturgies pray for the descent of the Holy Ghost, after the words of institution had been first pronounced. And further, they all pray that the Holy Spirit may make the Bread the Body, the Cup the Blood of Christ, or in words to this effect; whereas the Romanists believe no Bread or Wine to remain after these words are once spoken, "This is My Body, This is My Blood." And further, it is evident that the ancients, in praying that the Bread might be made the Body, the Wine the Blood, did intend no more than that the Bread remaining Bread might be spiritually and in effect the Body and Blood. The Romanists believe the Bread and Wine to be annihilated, and the Body and Blood by a strange, I know not what, *adduction*, as they express it, to be brought to the patin and chalice in their stead. So that this judgment of the primitive Church is wholly inconsistent with the doctrine which has of late ages prevailed in that Church; and they therefore, who will call it Popery, not only calumniate the primitive Fathers and the main body of the best Christians that ever were in the world, but betray their own ignorance and want of charity, and do a real honour to the Church of Rome, which she little deserves. I shall only further observe, that as it evidently appears that the ancient Churches of the east, where Justin Martyr lived and Irenæus had his education, where Athanasius was Bishop and Cyril of Jerusalem presided, and the Church of Rome to the time of Gelasius, and of Gaul in the west for several ages after, did consecrate the Eucharist by the invocation of the Holy Ghost; so it is very highly probable that the Church of Africa did the same. For to omit at present what has been cited from St. Cyprian and St. Augustine on this head, the words of Optatus of Milevis do sufficiently prove this; for he tells us that the "Holy Ghost descended on the Altars at the prayer or request made for this purpose;" *Quo postulatus descendit Spiritus*. See the words at large in the Appendix[1]. And I apprehend that very few

[1] a. p. 22. Ap.

articles of our holy religion are capable of a more convictive SECT.
evidence from antiquity than this, that the Holy Spirit, by I.
It's powerful presence, renders the elements in the Eucharist
the Body and Blood of Christ, not substantially indeed, but
effectually, and to all spiritual intents and purposes.

It may not be amiss to observe, that the ancient heretics The old
believed this, as well as the Catholic Christians; thus in the embraced
dialogue written by Origen or Maximus (for learned men are the same
not agreed which of them two is the author of it) against the
Marcionites, the heretic owns that the Holy Spirit ἐπὶ τῆς
εὐχαριστίας ἔρχεται, "descends on the Eucharist[m]." Nay,
Theodotus somewhat exceeds the orthodox in this point, in
those words, Ὁ ἄρτος ἁγιάζεται τῇ δυνάμει τοῦ Πνεύματος[n],
οὐ τὰ αὐτὰ ὄντα κατὰ τὸ φαινόμενον οἷα ἐλήφθη, ἀλλὰ δυνάμει
εἰς δύναμιν πνευματικὴν μεταβέβληται[o], that is, "the Bread
is consecrated by the power of the Spirit; the things are not
what they appear to be, or what they are apprehended to be,
but by the power [of the Spirit] are changed into a spiritual
power." And Irenæus informs us of a legerdemain which
the heretic Marcus made use of, whereby to make his followers believe the Eucharist celebrated by him was more divinely
consecrated than that of the Catholics[p]: Marcus "pretending
to eucharistize the cups mingled with wine, and drawing out
to a great length the words of invocation, causes them to
appear of a purple and red colour, that so the grace [*charis*]
may seem to instil its own [virtue] from the supreme powers
by means of his invocation, in this cup; and that those who
are present may have a longing to taste of this liquor, to the
end that this grace [*charis*], as this magician calls it, may
distil upon them too." This was no doubt an apish resemblance of the Eucharist in the primitive Church; and probably these heretics being told by the Catholics that their
sacraments wanted the concurrent power of the Holy Spirit,
which extends Itself to the one body, the Church, only, they
endeavoured to make a very extraordinary appearance in what
they in reality wanted, by this gross imposture. And it may
be observed, that they use the very word χάρις, which is by

[m] Sect. ii. p. 53. [ed. Wetsten.
1673.]
[n] [In this and in Potter's edition,
the reading is τοῦ 'Ονόματος.]

[o] Inter opera Clementis Alexandrini,
p. 800. [ed. Heins. Paris. 1629. Ed.
Potter, tom. ii. p. 988.]
[p] a. p. 3. Ap.

CHAP.
II.

Clemens Alexandrinus and Gregory Nyssen (as *gratia* by St. Cyprian, Julius Firmicus, and others) applied to the power of the Spirit in the Eucharist.

On what Scripture this doctrine was grounded.

Now I expect our adversaries should demand upon what authority of Scripture this doctrine of the ancients was grounded; to which I answer, that it seems evident that they thought, when our Saviour blessed or eucharistized the Bread and Wine, the meaning of those words is, that He caused a Divine benediction to rest upon them. It is allowed, I think, by learned men, that εὐχαριστεῖν has the same signification in the history of the institution with εὐλογεῖν; and it is very evident, that εὐχαριστεῖν as well as εὐλογεῖν is used transitively; and that therefore, as we render the Greek words, Matt. xxvi. 26, "Jesus took bread and blessed it;" so in strictness the following words, ver. 27, should be rendered, 'He took the cup, and blessed' or eucharistized 'it;' and the same may be said in relation to Mark xiv. 22, 23. St. Luke, chap. xxii. 19, 20; and St. Paul, 1 Cor. xi. 24, 25, use the word εὐχαριστεῖν only in relation both to the Bread and Cup; and therefore, to render these texts so as that they may fully come up to the sense of the Greek, there ought to be the accusative case expressed after the particle εὐχαριστήσας, viz. "He took bread; having blessed" or eucharistized "it, He brake it, and said:" for it is certain, the blessing or eucharistizing terminates on the Bread. It indeed imports, that Jesus addressed Himself in prayer to God for a Divine benediction; but it is clear beyond dispute, that this benediction was to rest on the elements. It was rational to suppose, that the most Divine institution was to be attended with the most eminent benediction; and it was justly believed that this consisted in the immediate presence of the Holy Spirit. In St. James's Liturgy, the words of institution, in relation to the Cup, run thus[q], "Taking the Cup—eucharistizing it, consecrating it, filling it with the Holy Ghost," &c. For they, or he, who drew [up] this Liturgy, did take for granted what I now argue for, viz. that εὐχαριστεῖν does import a consecration wrought by the grace of the Holy Spirit; and not only the ancient Fathers, but even the heretics of the first ages, as we have seen, allowed this; and the eucharistized

[q] g. p. 55. Ap.

Bread, in the language of Irenæus and Justin Martyr, is the
Bread that has by this means been sanctified; and indeed,
the Apostle St. Paul does give great countenance to this doctrine, in saying, "by one Spirit we have all been baptized 1Cor.xii.13.
into one Body—and we have been all made to drink into
one Spirit." For as in the first clause he speaks expressly
of Baptism, so in the other he does, not obscurely, speak of
our drinking the Cup blessed with the Holy Ghost in the
Eucharist. The Rev. Dr. Pelling has well observed, "that
even the Socinians, who were the most perverse interpreters
of Scripture that ever yet appeared, cannot but acknowledge,
that the Apostle's meaning is, that we have drunk of the
Spirit; and that in this particular they agree with St. Chrysostom; and that St. Jerome expresses it by '*potionati Spiritu*[r].'"
But I conceive the ancients chiefly built their judgment in
this particular on the sixty-third verse of John vi., viz. "It
is the Spirit that quickeneth, the flesh profiteth nothing. The
words which I speak unto you, they are Spirit, and they are
Life." I think it is universally agreed, that these words are
an explication of that mystery which He had spoken so much
of in the foregoing part of the chapter, viz. "eating His Flesh
and drinking His Blood." I hope to give my reader satisfactory proof, before I conclude this book, that this eating
and drinking the Flesh and Blood of Christ was by Him
meant of the Eucharist only; and that this was the sentiment of the generality of the ancients; and so taking this
at present for granted, I will only consider how they interpreted this verse in conformity to that opinion, and applied
it to the Eucharistical Body and Blood; and particularly, that
by 'Spirit' in this text they understood the Sacramental Body
consecrated by the Spirit. Mr. Calvin[s], upon this verse, takes
notice, that St. Augustine so takes these words, as that when
our Saviour says "the flesh profiteth nothing" the sense is, the
flesh alone profiteth nothing, without the quickening Spirit;
and that by the 'flesh' he understood the Sacramental Flesh,
will in due time be sufficiently proved. St. Augustine's words
are, *Quid est ergo, non prodest quicquam Caro? Non prodest*

---

[r] See Dr. Pelling's Discourse of the
Sacraments, p. 278.

[s] ["Augustinus subaudiendum pu-
tat *solam* et *per se*, quia debeat cum

Spiritu conjungi: quod cum re ipsa
consentaneum est."—Calvinus *in loco.*
Opera, tom. v. p. 75.]

quicquam; sed quomodo illi intellexerunt : Carnem quippe in-
tellexerunt, quomodo in cadavere dilaniatur, aut in macello ven-
ditur, non quomodo spiritu vegetatur.   Proinde sic dictum est,
Caro non prodest quicquam, quomodo dictum est scientia instat.
Jam ergo debemus scientiam odisse? Absit.   Et quid est scientia
instat? Sola, sine caritate.   Ideo adjunxit, Caritas vero ædi-
ficat.   Adde ergo scientiæ caritatem, et utilis erit scientia : sic
etiam nunc caro non prodest quicquam.   Accedat Spiritus ad
carnem, quomodo accedit caritas ad scientiam, et prodest plu-
rimum[t].   Cyril of Alexandria expressly says[u], " Christ calls
His Flesh Spirit ;" and he had given the reason for it in the
words foregoing, viz. " He fills His Body with the energy of the
Spirit ;" and that He means this of His Body in the Eucharist will hereafter be proved.   And again[x], " Common flesh
cannot give life ; of this our Saviour is a witness, saying, My
Flesh profiteth nothing, it is the Spirit that quickeneth ; for
since It is the Word's own Body, on this account It is considered, as giving life, and is so ;" and that he means it of
the Eucharist, the learned reader may convince himself, by
turning his eye to the original.   St. Ambrose, as already cited,
has sufficiently shewed that he was of this mind : for[y] he
proves the Eucharist to be " the Body of Christ, because It
is the Body of the Divine Spirit."   St. Athanasius has been
already cited, applying this text to the Eucharist, and telling
us[z] that " by Spirit and life" is meant " the Body given for
the world, and distributed to, or in every one," &c.   And yet
he speaks more expressly, if possible, to the same purpose[a],
when discoursing of the Eucharist, he says, " the Flesh of the
Lord is a quickening Spirit."   And Ammonius took it so
above a hundred years before him, in those words[b], " What
He here calls the Spirit, is the Flesh, replenished with the
energy of the life-giving Spirit."   Now considering that these
passages in the ancients are so directly for our present purpose, to prove that by 'the Spirit' here is meant the Sacramental Flesh of Christ ; and that all that goes before, concerning eating the Flesh and drinking the Blood of Christ,
relates to the Eucharist, as I am hereafter to shew ; we are

---

[t] *In loc.* p. 503. ed. Benedict. tom.
iii.
    [u] h. p. 44. Ap.
    [x] l. p. 45. Ap.

[y] k. p. 27. Ap.
[z] a. p. 17. Ap.
[a] b. p. 17. Ap. l. 6.
[b] b. p. 9. Ap.

not to wonder, that the Priest and people of these ages did expect, that at their prayers the Holy Ghost should communicate It's influences to the Holy Symbols. It must be owned, that the meaning of this text is far from being easy or obvious, even though it be acknowledged to be an explication of what goes before. It is indeed no difficult matter for any new interpreter to clap an arbitrary sense upon this place, and make it chime in with his own inventions; but I must declare, that if I had so good light from antiquity, for the explaining other obscure texts of the New Testament, as I have for this; and if the writers and the whole Church of the four first centuries did so clearly determine the meaning of any other context, as they do this of the sixth chapter of St. John, I should desire no other help for the understanding the Scriptures of the New Testament, but what I receive from them; and indeed we must once for all discard the authority of antiquity in determining any controversy, which either now does, or shall ever hereafter depend, in relation to any point of Christianity, if such evidence may not cast the scale when there is nothing to weigh against it but the airy conjectures of modern doctors.

And that the glosses of late interpreters on this verse are but mere conjectures, will, I suppose, be easy to be demonstrated, from the great variety and inconsistence of them. I will take no notice of the Popish or Lutheran commentators, but will confine my observations of this sort to those interpreters, who may be supposed to be most in vogue with those of our own country. Mr. Calvin[c] understands the word ' Spirit,' in the first place, to denote the Holy Ghost communicating It's influences to our Saviour's natural Flesh; and in the second place, by ' the Spirit' he understands spiritual construction of Christ's words. Mr. Beza[d], in the

[c] ["Tenemus nunc quomodo caro vere sit cibus, et tamen nihil prosit: nempe cibus est, quia per ipsam parta nobis est vita, quia in ipsa placatus nobis est Deus, quia in ipsa completas habemus omnes salutis partes: nihil prodest, si ex sua origine et natura æstimetur (neque enim vitam confert Abrahæ semen, quod per se morti est obnoxium) *sed a Spiritu accipit* unde nos pascat."—"Spiritus nomen hic diverso sensu accipit. Sed quia de arcana Spiritus virtute loquutus erat, eleganter hoc ad doctrinam suam transfert, quod Spiritualis sit. Nam vox *Spiritus* in adjectivum resolvi debet. Porro spiritualis vocatur sermo qui nos sursum invitat, ut Christum, duce Spiritu, fide, non carnis sensu, in cœlesti sua gloria quæramus: scimus enim eorum quæ dicta sunt nihil nisi fide comprehendi."—Calv. in loco, tom. v. p. 75. ed. Genev. 1614.]

[d] [" Et quod hic a plerisque tradi-

first place, for the Divine *Logos;* in the second place, for a spiritual construction. Grotius[e] by ' Spirit,' in the first place, understands the human soul; in the next place, the actions of it. Dr. Hammond[f] follows Grotius. Dr. Whitby[g] takes ' Spirit' for the Holy Ghost, as given to believers, in both places, without any regard to the Eucharist: for he supposes that Christ intended to inform them, that by eating and drinking His Flesh and Blood, that is, according to him, believing His doctrine, they should attain the Holy Ghost and eternal life. Dr. Clagett[h], by the ' Spirit,' in both places, supposes our Saviour meant spiritual actions, practising the precepts of a heavenly life, and embracing the promises of happiness. Dr. Samuel Clarke[i], though he varies his phrase, yet seems to agree in the main with Dr. Clagett, and par-

tur, carnis videlicet Christi appellatione Humanitatis Ipsius distincte et in sese consideratam hic intelligi, per Spiritum vero Λόγου Θεότητα significari, a qua una (quamvis carnis per fidem nobis spiritualiter communicatæ interventu) vis illa vivifica proficiscatur, vere quidem, sed fortasse parum apposite dicitur,"—" Illud vicissim verissimum est, quod ad rem ipsam attinet eandem esse statuendam Ejusdem et Unius Christi perceptionem, spiritualiter videlicet per fidem, sive in simplici verbo, sive adhibitis Sacramentalibus signis nostræ menti sumenda præbeatur."—Beza in Nov. Test., p. 254. ed. Cant. 1642.]

[e] [" Res sunt animi, quibus vita æterna comparatur. Diximus ad Matth. xxvi. 41. voce רוּחַ [*spiritus*] modo τὸ ἡγεμονικὸν [*vim illam quæ imperat*] significari, modo *animum* totum, ut infra xi. 33, xiii. 21. Actor. xix. 21. Atque hoc posteriore sensu hic sumere simplicius est."—Grotii Opera, tom. ii. vol. i. p. 508. ed. 1679.]

[f] [" And for the other particular of eating His Flesh, He tells them they cannot but know that it is the soul that enliveneth, and not the body; and agreeably, that it is not the gross carnal eating of His Flesh that He could speak of, when He talked of their eating, and His feeding them to life eternal; but certainly a more spiritual divine eating, or feeding on Him, which should bring them a durable eternal life; His words, that is, His doctrine being spiritually fed on by them, that is, being received into their hearts, not

only their ears, will quicken them to a spiritual life here, and that shall prove to them an eternal life hereafter; (so S. Chrysostom expounds, [the flesh] that is, the fleshly hearing profits nothing.")—Hammond on the New Test., p. 285. ed. 1659.]

[g] [" 63. (*But know that*) it is the Spirit (*imparted to believers,*) that quickeneth (*their mortal bodies,* Rom. viii. 11.) the Flesh (*even of My Body, could you eat It,*) profiteth nothing (*to that end; now*) the words that I speak to you, they are Spirit, and they are Life ; (i. e. *they are the means of obtaining this Spirit and Life by Him.*")— Whitby in loco.]

[h] [" 63. No; when I speak to you of the conditions of obtaining everlasting life, though I have now expressed them, by *eating My Flesh, and drinking My Blood*; yet you had reason to understand Me of spiritual actions, which do indeed tend to the bettering of the inward man.—If, I say, you would know what things are proper for the improvement of the mind, they are the *words that I speak unto you*; they are those precepts of a heavenly life, and those promises of eternal life, which I have laid before you."—Paraphrase on the Sixth Chapter of St. John, p. 37. ed. 1686.]

[i] [" 63. No; Know that it is of no use to take what I say, in the gross and literal sense ; but ye ought always to understand Me of spiritual actions, such as improve the soul, and tend to make men better."—Clarke's Works, vol. iii. p. 443. ed. 1738.]

ticularly in taking 'the Spirit' to signify 'spiritual actions;'
and they are the only two, whom I can at present consult,
that seem to agree in their notions on this text, except
Grotius and Dr. Hammond; and so from eight writers we
have six several senses. Dr. Pelling by 'Spirit' conceives
that our Saviour intended to let them know that He spake
mystically, and that they were to interpret His words after a
spiritual manner, and of a spiritual and Divine way of feeding
on Him. Now the only use I make of these glosses is to
convince my reader, that when men of the greatest learning
and judgment have no compass by which to steer their interpretations of the Holy Scripture, they must of consequence run wide of the truth, and of each other; and if
they do hit on the true sense, it is by mere chance; and I
crave leave to say that in this particular they have all missed
of their aim, and given us their own fanciful guesses instead
of the truth. What makes me bold to say so is, that the
primitive Church, as has and shall be seen, was unanimous
in supposing that our Saviour here speaks of the Eucharist;
and none of the great men above produced do in this particular agree with them; and they, who give us a particular
explication of the text, do agree that it is to be interpreted
of the Holy Ghost accompanying the holy symbols of Christ's
Flesh and Blood. And I hope it will be thought pardonable
in me to adhere to the ancients, where they are unanimous,
in opposition to all expositors whatsoever, especially in a
point, where scarce two of them keep harmony with each
other.

But as to the text now before us, though it must be owned
to be one of those that cannot be fully understood without
close attention and application; yet I apprehend that if we
impartially aim at truth, and diligently keep our eye to the
analogy and connection of our Saviour's discourse, we shall
with some degree of assurance be able to say what the meaning
of these words is. Our Saviour, having staggered His hearers
by inculcating upon them the important doctrine of eating
His Flesh and drinking His Blood, here in the close of His
discourse gives them such hints as might for the present
serve to quiet their minds, by letting them know that they
were to blame, to take what He had said as if it were meant

CHAP.
II.
ver. 62.

of eating His natural Flesh and Blood; and to this purpose He first says, "What and if ye shall see the Son of Man ascend up [into heaven,] where He was before," will ye not then be convinced, that what I now say of eating My Flesh and drinking My Blood cannot be understood literally of the Body you now see, and the Blood which now runs in My veins? And having intimated to them what He did not mean, He proceeds to explain the phrases of eating His Flesh and drinking His Blood, so far as He thought proper or seasonable for the present; and dismisses His hearers as persons that were yet in the state of Catechumens (if I may so say), without informing them what the materials were which He intended to make His mysterious Flesh and Blood; and does not let His Apostles themselves into this secret, until the time came when He did institute the Sacrament and Sacrifice; and in the mean time thought it sufficient to let them know what was to be the very life and soul of this mysterious Flesh and Blood, viz. the presence of the

ver. 63.

Holy Spirit; for says He, "It is the Spirit that quickeneth," or giveth life, which was the main privilege and benefit that men were to receive by eating His Flesh and drinking His

ver. 48. 50,
51. 53, 54.
57, 58.

Blood, as He had before told them, "The Flesh [even of the Son of Man Himself,]" whether natural or Sacramental, nakedly or in itself considered, or alone without the Spirit, as St. Augustine justly understood it, "profiteth not" toward the obtaining of eternal life: "the words which I have" just now "spoken" unto you, though they seem to import no more than material things to be externally eat and drunk, yet are so to be understood by you as intended to denote somewhat that, though it be of itself very common and of an earthly original, yet shall be replenished with inward force and power from the Holy Ghost, and therefore deserves rather to be called "Spirit and Life" than dead body and effused blood. It challenges the name of Spirit upon the same account that the entire Person of the Lord is called

2 Cor. iii. 17.

"Spirit," and that the human nature of Christ is said to be a "quickening Spirit," viz. because the spiritual principle was

1 Cor. xv. 45.

that which was the most prevailing, and derived a dignity to His human nature, and made Him capable of giving life to others. Just so we may say, it is God that is Heaven, or

perfect happiness; it is the soul that is the man: it is pride
or malice that is the devil.   For the denomination is often
taken from the greater or more prevailing part or principle.   Therefore Ammonius, the old Christian philosopher;
Athanasius, the most acute Divine of his age; Cyril of
Alexandria, one that was inferior to none of the ancients
in good sense and penetration, tell us, that Christ called
His Body [in the Sacrament] 'Spirit' in this place, and my
reader just now saw them speaking for themselves.   It
may perhaps seem strange to such readers as are not versed
in the language of the New Testament, that our Saviour
should so often, in the foregoing part of the chapter, promise eternal life to them that eat His Flesh and drink His
Blood, and yet here expressly say, that "the Flesh profiteth
nothing;" meaning undoubtedly the same thing by His Flesh
in the sixty-third verse, that His hearers had done in the
other places, viz. mere material flesh, destitute of life, and
blood extravasated, and therefore importing death.   He acknowledges, that such flesh and blood, whether received in
substance or in figure, could carry no benefit along with it;
and therefore here by flesh means, as His auditors did, flesh
alone, without any thing to invigorate or give it life and
efficacy.   But the Flesh and Blood, so often before mentioned
by Himself, are the true Sacramental Flesh and Blood, that
were to carry power and virtue along with them, by means
of the presence of the Holy Ghost vouchsafed to them.   If
our Saviour had said, "the Flesh *alone* profiteth not," I suppose this would have removed all scruple from the minds of
my readers.   St. Augustine says, 'alone' is to be supplied; and
as the authority of the Father is not to be despised, so the
reason of the thing and the whole connexion of the discourse speak St. Augustine's judgment to be right.   And it
may be observed, that no word is so often to be supplied in
the discourses of our Saviour, as represented by the Evangelists, in order to make the sense clear and full, as this
word 'alone' or 'only,' with its redditive or correlative 'also'
or 'chiefly.'   I will give the following instances: "Lay not up Matt. vi. 19, 20.
for yourselves treasures upon earth" only, "but lay up for
yourselves treasures in heaven" also, or chiefly.   "It is not ye Matt. x 20.
that speak" alone, "but it is the Spirit of God that" also,

CHAP.
II.
Matt. xxiii.
9.
ver. 10.
Luke xii.
4, 5.
Luke xiv.
12, 13.
John iv. 21.
John vii.16.
John v. 31,
32.
ver. 34. 36.

or chiefly, "speaketh in you." "Call no man upon earth your" only "Father; for one is" chiefly or principally "your Father, even God." "Neither be ye called" the only or sole "masters; for one is" chiefly "your master, even Christ." "Fear not them" only "who kill the body; but fear Him" also, or chiefly, "Who hath power to cast into hell." "When thou makest a dinner, call not" only "thy friends and thy brethren; but call the poor" also. "Ye shall neither in this mountain, nor in Jerusalem" only, "worship the Father." "My doctrine is not Mine" only, "but" also "His that sent Me." "If I" alone "bear witness of Myself, My witness is not true; but there is another" also "that beareth witness of Me." "I receive not testimony from man," that is, St. John Baptist, only; "for the works that the Father hath given Me, they bear witness of Me" also. As many more examples of this sort might be produced; but these are sufficient to shew, that this was an ellipsis very familiar to our Saviour, or rather to the sacred historiographers, and particularly to St. John. And upon this supposition, what our Saviour says is this, "It is the Spirit that quickeneth, the flesh" alone "profiteth nothing to this purpose; the words which I speak," or the promises which I make, "are" not only of My Sacramental Flesh, but of the "Spirit and Life" to be received in conjunction with them. And that this was His true meaning will be more than probable, if it be considered that these words were designed as an exposition of what He had said of eating His Flesh and drinking His Blood, so far as He thought proper at present to explain Himself. He expounds what He had said, by hinting to them what it chiefly was which He had promised them under the name of His Body and Blood. For it was that was the difficulty, which most of all gravelled His hearers; therefore He lets them know, that they were not to understand it of His natural Flesh; for that He, as Son of Man, and therefore clothed with His human Body, was to ascend up where He was before, as He was the Son of God; and that they therefore could not come at this natural Body of His; and that by consequence He meant some other thing by His Flesh, which what It was and why to be dignified with that name He did not

think fit to acquaint them until after His last Passover.
But He in the interim imparts thus much of His mind to
them, that the very essence of that Flesh they were to receive was the Divine Spirit; He supposes they might rationally infer thus much from what He had before said;
for He had often told them, that the effect of eating His
Flesh should be life; and, says He, "it is the Spirit that
quickens" or "gives life." He could not deny that the
thing to be eaten was His Flesh, for this He had over and
again affirmed before; nor could He deny, that the eating
of His Flesh, as they ought to do, conduced to this end;
for He had as expressly declared that by eating this Flesh
they should live for ever, as that He would give them this
Flesh. It remains, that we cannot in equity conceive our
Saviour to intend any thing else by these words, than that
the Flesh alone, without the Spirit, profiteth not to eternal
life; and that therefore, when He promised His Flesh, He
did implicitly and by consequence promise the Spirit too,
even that Spirit, Which first quickened His own natural Body
in the womb of the Blessed Virgin. I can see no pretence
for supposing that it was our Saviour's direct and primary
intention to explain, what He meant by the actions of eating
and drinking; nor do I apprehend that His words in the
sixty-third verse can rationally be understood of any action
performed by us. The "quickening Spirit" must denote
either the Divinity of Christ, or the Holy Spirit, the third
Person of the Trinity; for no other Spirit can give or cause
life: it therefore cannot import any action performed by
man, not even in the most remote or improper way of speaking. The Spirit and Life is what is promised, whereas eating
and drinking is the action by which that promise, whatever
it be, is received, and is not itself therefore that promise.
The Flesh which profiteth nothing must be something that
is either to be eaten or not to be eaten; but cannot import
the action of eating or the forbearance of that action. And
if our Saviour does not here directly and primarily explain
the sense of eating and drinking, then there is nothing left
for Him to explain, but the words Flesh and Blood. And
these had been the main subject of our Saviour's discourse
in this chapter; these were the things, to the participation

whereof He invited His disciples; these were the sum and
substance of the promise He had made them in the former
part of the chapter; and therefore this is what He does in
part unvail to them in this sixty-third verse. Indeed there
could be no occasion to spend any words upon them, in order
to inform them what sort of eating or drinking He meant;
for if once they did in any tolerable measure know, what
the feast or entertainment consisted of, their own common
sense would presently direct them to the proper manner and
method of receiving it; so that, as to myself, I am not only
inclined to this interpretation, because it is recommended
to us by the judgment of the ancient Church; but because
when I consider what our blessed Lord's intention was, in
pronouncing these words, I can apprehend nothing that He
could have in His view but only to give His hearers a fair
intimation, that the great work and benefit of the Flesh and
Blood He had promised them was to be derived from the
secret life-giving power and operation of the Holy Spirit.
And I think myself bound in common justice to pay the
tribute of a grateful acknowledgment to those venerable primitive writers, who have confirmed me in this sense of a very
difficult text of Scripture. And without their authority, I
should never have dared to speak so freely of the conjectural
glosses of modern commentators; which yet rather serve to
confute each other than to establish a man in a settled judgment concerning this or any such like text of Scripture.
And having thus shewed, that the ancients did believe the
Holy Spirit to be in an especial manner present in the Eucharist, and on what grounds they believed this; I now proceed to prove,

That the
ancients
believed
the Eucha-
rist to be a
mystery.
(2.) That the ancients did conceive the Eucharistical Bread
and Wine to be mysteries, and therefore spiritually to be discerned on the account of this especial presence of the Holy
Ghost, which rendered the Bread and Wine the Body and
Blood of Christ, in the sense so often mentioned. And
having but just now laid before my reader at large the
grounds on which the ancients entertained the belief of the
Spirit's presence in the Eucharist; and particularly proved

John vi. 63. that those words of our blessed Saviour were directly and
primarily intended to give an explication (in part) of what

is received in the Eucharist; I think fit not to reserve what
I have to offer from Scripture in defence of the judgment of
the ancients, until after I have produced their suffrages (as
I have hitherto done); but to shew that their believing the
Eucharist to be a mystery, and therefore to be spiritually
discerned, might safely be built upon that text, as interpreted
by them. For though I think it very clear that our Saviour's
first intention was, in some measure, to open to His hearers
the nature of that Flesh which He had promised to give
them; yet He could not explain this to them so far as He
did, but He must at the same time, by very evident consequence, let them see that what He had been speaking of was
a mystery. For He had told them that they were to receive
Flesh and Blood; and this, according to the common sense
of mankind, must import something that is capable of being
received with the mouth; and yet He had affirmed, that the
Holy Spirit was the principal thing which He designed, for
that "His words," or promises then made, "were Spirit and
Life." And the grossest of His auditors could not surely suppose that the Holy Ghost was capable of an oral manducation, or that the "grace of God could be devoured by mouth-
fuls," as St. Augustine expresses it[k]; for though they might
externally eat and drink what was made the Flesh and Blood,
yet their teeth could make no impression upon what was in
its own nature not subject to corporeal taste or touch. And
this was the mystery, which shocked the loose part of His
auditory, who hereupon "went back, and walked no more ver. 66.
with Him." They could not conceive themselves capable
of eating His natural Flesh and Blood, nor yet comprehend
what He meant by giving them Flesh and Blood, which was
Spirit and Life. And the ancients believed this to be the
mystery couched in the Sacramental Bread and Wine, viz.
that they were in substance what they were before, but by
the especial presence of the Spirit rendered the Body and
Blood of Christ, as carrying with them all the beneficial effects
that His natural Body and Blood, influenced and anointed by
the Holy Ghost, could have done, if it had been capable of
oral manducation. Thus St. Chrysostom explains the sense
of the word 'mystery,' when he is speaking of the two Sacra-

[k] n. p. 32. Ap.

CHAP. II. ments[1]; "It is called a mystery, when we look not at what we see, but when we see one thing, but believe it to be another thing." And the case is very clear, that since the Sacramental Body and Blood are what they are, by virtue of the presence of the Spirit; and that the secret operations of the Spirit are not to be perceived by our senses; and that therefore the Body and Blood of the Eucharist are such only in an invisible mysterious manner : therefore they are to be considered and received by us, not only outwardly as consecrated Bread and Wine, but inwardly with the eye and relish of our understanding and judgment; not only as bare types and figures, but as being in effect, though not in substance, what they represent. And thus St. Chrysostom elsewhere explains himself, speaking of John vi. 63 [m], "We should understand all this mystically and spiritually.—'They are Spirit, and they are Life,' that is, they are Divine and spiritual things. What then, is not His Flesh, Flesh? Yes, assuredly. How then does He say, 'the flesh profiteth nothing?' He does not speak this of His own Flesh, far be that from Him ; but of those that took what He said in a carnal sense. But what is it to take Him in a carnal sense? To look merely to the [gifts] which lie in open view. We ought not to judge by what is seen, but to look on all mysteries with the inward eye; for this it is [to do it] spiritually." The holy Father does not so directly give us our Saviour's primary sense, as St. Augustine does, when he says, that by the flesh which profiteth not, we are to understand "the Flesh only;" but he rather considers what is the necessary consequence of what Christ here says, namely, that since it is the Spirit which is the principal thing in the Eucharist and That Which makes the Bread the Flesh of our Saviour, therefore we are to apprehend and use it as a spiritual mystery; which by consequence makes these words very apposite to the purpose for which I cited him. And when this Father says, that "Christ could not mean that His Flesh profiteth nothing; but that He speaks of those who took Him in a carnal sense, that is, who regard nothing but the [gifts] lying in open view;" he means the same thing with St. Augustine, when he says, that our Saviour meant, that His Flesh

1 D. p. 41. Ap.   m y. p. 40. Ap.

"alone" profiteth nothing; for they who took it in a carnal
sense understood our Saviour of His Flesh alone, without
the Spirit. They minded only what they saw before them.
Perhaps, indeed, St. Chrysostom does not express himself
with his usual exactness, when he says, "Christ speaks of
those who took what was said in a carnal sense." If, instead of these words, he had said, "Christ speaks of His
Flesh carnally taken, or taken in a carnal sense," I conceive
he had said the very same thing that St. Augustine does in
other words. For if we take the Flesh of Christ in the sense
which our Saviour meant It in, ver. 51. 53. 55, no doubt It
is profitable; but if indeed in the sense that His loose hearers
took It in, of which He speaks, ver. 63, then It was not profitable. Thus much I have said on this matter, on account
of the great difference which Mr. Calvin, on this place, would
persuade us there is between St. Chrysostom and St. Augustine, which is indeed next to none; but St. Chrysostom speaks
of this spiritual mysterious Body and Blood in the Eucharist,
in several other places; and tells us how It is to be received[n],
"The Word says, 'This is My Body;' let us be convinced,
and believe, and see Him with our intellectual eyes; for
Christ hath delivered to us nothing to be perceived by the
senses, but all to be apprehended by the mind, in things
perceived by the sense," viz. Bread and Wine; and again[o],
"Thou hast the spiritual Table; would you know how? 'He
that eateth My Flesh, abideth in Me.'" For I am not sensible, that St. Chrysostom is suspected of ever speaking of
John vi. to be understood of any other thing but the Eucharist; and therefore the Eucharistical Flesh is here called
"Spiritual," as being discerned by the Spirit only. St. Augustine is as clear as St. Chrysostom, when speaking of this
Sacrament he says[p], "Fix not your thoughts upon the Flesh,
lest you be not enlivened by the Spirit;" and presently after
he thus explains John vi. 63, speaking in the person of our
Saviour, "Understand what I have said to you in a spiritual
manner; you are not to eat that Body Which you see: I
have commended to you a Sacrament; if spiritually understood, it will enliven you;" and again[q], "Then will the Body

[n] t. p. 40. Ap. [p] s. p. 33. Ap. l. 19.
[o] a. p. 37. Ap. [q] w. p. 34. Ap. l. 6.

CHAP.
II.

and Blood of Christ be life to every man, if what is visibly taken be spiritually eaten and spiritually drunk. For we have heard our Lord saying, ' It is the Spirit that quickens ;' " and by this we may clearly understand him, when he bids us[r] " eat even to the participation of the Spirit ;" and here I apprehend St. Augustine falls in with St. Chrysostom, as above cited. But I shall here also subjoin his words found in Fulgentius, *De Baptismo Æthiopis, c. ult.*[s], where he speaks to them that had been lately baptized, and were now admitted to the Eucharist. *Quod ergo videtis, panis est, et calix ; quod autem fides vestra postulat instruenda, panis est Corpus Christi, calix Sanguis Christi.—Quomodo est panis Corpus Ejus, et calix, vel quod habet calix, quomodo est Sanguis Ejus ? Ista, Fratres, ideo dicuntur Sacramenta, quia in eis aliud videtur, aliud intelligitur. Quod videtur, speciem habet corporalem ; quod intelligitur, fructum habet spiritalem.* " What you see is the Bread and the Cup ; but that in which your faith requires to be instructed is, that the Bread is the Body of Christ, the Cup His Blood.—How is the Bread His Body, the Cup or what the Cup contains, His Blood ? these things, brethren, are therefore called Sacraments, because it is seen [to be] one thing, it is believed [to be] another. What it is seen [to be] has a bodily figure, what it is believed [to be] has a spiritual fruit or effect." Where St. Augustine does not only agree with St. Chrysostom in other particulars ; but in his notion of a mystery, which he calls a Sacrament. And this is a clear proof that the Latin *Sacramentum* is taken in the same sense with the Greek μυστήριον, though not perpetually. St. Jerome means the same mysterious eating and drinking the Body and Blood in the Sacrament, in those words of his[t], " Let us hear, or understand, that the Bread, which Christ brake, and gave to His Disciples, is the Body of the Lord our Saviour.—He is both the convivator and the feast ; He eats with us, and Himself is eaten. We drink His Blood, and without Him we cannot drink—we drink new Wine of the Father's kingdom ; not in the oldness of the letter, but in the newness of the Spirit." Macarius says[u], "they who partake of the visible

[r] o. p. 33. Ap.
[s] [p. 210. ed. Lugd. 1633.]
[t] k. p. 28. Ap.
[u] b. p. 26. Ap. l. 7.

Bread do spiritually eat the Flesh of the Lord." Cyril of Jerusalem says[x], "When Christ discoursing with the Jews said, 'Except ye eat the Flesh of the Son of Man,' &c., they not understanding what He said in a spiritual manner were scandalized, and went back, supposing that He exhorted them to be cannibals;" and he presently tells us how we must understand our Saviour, spiritually, viz. "regard them not as mere bread and wine, but as the Body and Blood of Christ, according to the declaration of our Lord;" therefore he calls them[y], "spiritual Bread and Wine;" and these again[z] he calls a "spiritual Sacrifice." And we have heard St. Athanasius not only declaring that the Sacraments of the Body and Blood are "spiritual things," but to be "spiritually distributed;" not as what they appear to be outwardly, but as what they are in internal power and efficacy: and we have seen Eusebius speaking of[a] "a spiritual hierurgy in Bread and Wine." Tertullian clearly supposes the necessity of a spiritual communion in the Sacrament, in saying[b], "the flesh is fed with the Body and Blood of Christ, that the soul may be replenished with God;" that is, either with God the Holy Ghost, or with the Father and Son by means of the Holy Ghost. And St. Cyprian cannot rationally be otherwise understood, when he says, the Eucharist was "spiritually injoined," that is, as a mystery; not to be celebrated or received with the outward senses only, but with the inward apprehension and application of the mind: and this is what Clemens Alexandrinus teaches us, in those words[c], "Christ, taking bread, first spake and eucharistized it, then breaking it held it forth, that we might eat it in a rational manner." These citations are sufficient to prove, that as the ancients believed the consecrated Bread and Wine to be the Body and Blood of Christ, by the invisible presence of the Holy Spirit; so in consequence of this belief, they looked on them as mysteries, to be discerned and beneficially received with the soul as well as with the mouth; that as the benefit of them was intended for the soul as well as body, so they should be received internally by one as well as externally by the other.

[x] d. p. 19. Ap.
[y] e. p. 19. Ap.
[z] f. p. 19. Ap. l. 5.

[a] h. p. 16. Ap. l. 8.
[b] m. p. 8. Ap.
[c] d. p. 7. Ap.

CHAP.
II.

How the
Eucha-
rist was
thought a
spiritual
Body, and
to be spi-
ritually
received.

Now before I proceed to another head of discourse, I shall make some reflections on what I have said and proved, concerning Christ's real Body and Blood in the Sacrament; and it's being His real Body and Blood, not in substance, but in spirit and power; and as therefore requiring the exercise of our best faculties, our understanding, judgment, and devotion, regulated and instructed by a true faith, in order to a proper use of it.   And,

1. We may from hence learn, for what reason the ancients called the Eucharistical Bread the spiritual Body of Christ, viz. because it was what it was by the peculiar energy of the Holy Ghost?   And what they meant by spiritual eating and drinking, viz. doing those outward actions in the Eucharist with a sincere faith in the Passion of Christ, and receiving the symbols, not as bare Bread and Wine, but as Divine powerful representations of the original Body and Blood. And until I am better informed, I shall look upon all other spiritual receiving Christ's Body and Blood to be a mere human invention of the middle and dark ages of the Church, built upon no other bottom than some passages in the ancient Fathers, misunderstood or wrested by new glosses and unnatural constructions.   This notion of spiritual eating and drinking Christ in any other religious exercise or action as well as the Holy Eucharist, I look upon as a doctrine, especially as it has of late years been managed, subversive of, or extremely endangering, not only the Eucharist, but the very foundation of all discipline in the Church and even of the Church itself; for it is very certain, that the offering and receiving the Holy Eucharist was intended by Christ Jesus to be the main pillar of the external Christian œconomy, and the strongest ligament of the mutual communion of Christians with their Head and with each other; but now this notion of spiritual eating and drinking the Body and Blood of Christ cuts the nerves of this and all other means of external communion, by assuring men, that they may eat and drink the Body and Blood of Christ at home in their closets and kitchens, as well as at the Lord's Table.   And I apprehend, I cannot do a greater service to religion, than by shewing that this conceit of spiritual communion *extra Cœnam* is a mere imaginary thing, without any foundation in Scripture,

reason, or antiquity. And to this purpose I have shewed my reader, what the ancients understood by the spiritual Bread and the spiritual Body, and the spiritual eating and drinking; and it does not appear, that they intended any thing else but the material Sacrament, enlivened by the Holy Spirit, and received spiritually by faith as well as bodily with the mouth.

2. If what is eaten be a spiritual Body, and what is drunk be spiritual Blood, then why may not that which is offered be a spiritual Sacrifice, since what we offer is the very same with what we eat and drink? If the very material Sacrifice, which is offered, be accepted by Almighty God, and if He send His Holy Spirit on it, as the ancient Church on good grounds believed He did; why then must it be denied the name of a spiritual Sacrifice; if it be discerned to be offered as a memorial of Christ's death only by our minds or spirits, I cannot conceive, why it may not be called a spiritual Sacrifice, since on the same account it is also styled the spiritual Body of our Saviour. The ancients called the sacrifices of the Jews and heathen, corporeal and gross fœculent sacrifices, because they who offered them were supposed to have no further meaning than to offer a dead carcase or some such like worthless thing, without any other view or speculation; but they believed the sacrifice of bread and wine, offered by Melchisedec, not to be a corporeal sacrifice; because they apprehended, that Melchisedec and Abraham, in the oblation of bread and wine, saw and designedly prefigured the Sacrifice of the Christian Church: and with much greater reason then may this Sacrifice itself be called spiritual; since, as Chrysostom says, "our Saviour hath delivered to us nothing to be perceived by sense, but every thing to be apprehended by our understanding, though in things perceptible by sense." It is true, what He delivered was Bread and Wine; but they are to be considered by us as Christ's Body and Blood, as made so by His Holy Spirit and discerned to be so by ours. And if our adversaries, for the future, cannot contrive some better shelter against our arguments for a real Sacrifice than that pretence of it's being so often called a spiritual Sacrifice, and that therefore it cannot be a real one; I persuade myself, they will convince but few; and these few must be such as suppose that all words

How it is a spiritual Sacrifice.

must in all ages have had the same signification; and that
because 'spiritual' in our present philosophy signifies something perfectly immaterial, and in common discourse, something or nothing, according to the fancy of him that uses it;
therefore sixteen or seventeen hundred years ago it could not
have any other meaning; whereas in reality the standard of
words is as liable to change as that of money, and they that
will not be persuaded of this by the authorities I have alleged
from the ancients may be convinced by their own English
Bibles, where we have express mention of "a spiritual Body;"
and where the whole Church, consisting of Christian men, is
1 Pet. ii. 5. called a "spiritual house," or temple; and it is observable,
that in the very same verse the Apostle mentions "spiritual
sacrifices;" and why the sacrifices must be perfectly immaterial any more than the men who offer them, will, I conceive, be impossible to be shewed. The Church is a spiritual
temple, not only as it consists of men united together by one
common faith, and by the ties of love and charity; but also,
as this union is perfected by the common influences of the
ch. ii. last same Spirit; for St. Paul tells the Ephesians, that "they were
ver. builded together for an habitation of God through the Spirit."
And why the material Sacrifice of the Eucharist may not be
thought one of the sacrifices spoken of by St. Peter, and the
principal one too, I cannot for my life conceive; for bread
and wine are not more material than human bodies are;
and if men clothed with flesh can be framed into a "spiritual
building," then I can see no reason why bread and wine,
consecrated by the Spirit, may not be "spiritual sacrifices,"
[and yet material.]

A distinct 3. By what has been said upon this head we are able to
answer to give a distinct answer to our adversaries, if they demand
those who
ask what is what is offered in the blessed Eucharist. We offer the Bread
offered. and Wine, separated from all other oblations of the people;
we offer them, as having been solemnly pronounced by the
words of institution to be the full representatives of Christ's
Body and Blood. And we make propitiation with them, after
God has first, by the illapse of the Holy Spirit, perfected the
consecration of them. When we say, we offer Bread and
Wine, and that we offer the Body and Blood of Christ, we
mean the same material things; and I have proved that the

ancients used the very same language, and by that language
meant the very same things that we do. When we say we
offer Bread and Wine, we do not only mean the products
and first-fruits of the earth, but the memorials of Christ's
Passion, the authoritative representations of Christ's Body
and Blood; or, if you will speak with the primitive Church,
the true Body and Blood of Christ: and on the other side,
when we say we offer the Body and Blood, we do not mean
what is commonly called the Sacrifice of the Mass, not the
substantial Body and Blood of Christ, much less His Divinity; but the Bread and Wine substituted by the Divine
Word for His own Body and Blood, and upon which God,
at the prayers of the Priests and people, sends down His
peculiar spiritual benediction, by which it becomes a Sacrifice of a sweet-smelling savour, as being therefore fully consecrated into the spiritual Body and Blood of Christ, and
therefore fit wherewith to propitiate the Divine mercy.

4. From hence we may infallibly conclude, that the ancient Church of the four first centuries did not believe trans-
substantiation, though they expressed their thoughts of the
reality of Christ's Body in the Sacrament, oftentimes in very
strong and lofty expressions. But that they did not believe
a change of substance, appears from this, that they called
even that which was distributed to the communicants after
the consecration was finished, sometimes Bread and Wine,
and at other times figures and types; and though they believed them to be types, so full and big with the life as to be
justly dignified with the names of the archetypes, yet they
inform us, on what account they were called and in some
sense believed to be the archetypes; viz. as by the secret invisible operation of the Holy Spirit, they were made in effect,
and to all religious intents and purposes, the very Body and
Blood. And I apprehend that Protestants cannot so effectually answer the allegations produced by the Papists in behalf of transubstantiation, upon any other scheme as this of
the primitive Church. They who believe the Bread and Wine
to be mere symbols and figures, can never, so far as I am
able to judge, give a fair and satisfactory reply to the objections, which may be urged against them from Holy Scripture; however they will be utterly at a loss to answer those

SECT.
I.

That the
ancients
believed
not trans-
substan-
tiation.
Lutherans
and Cal-
vinists
come too
near to it.

JOHNSON.   X

texts, if taken in the sense which the Fathers of the second century, viz. Ignatius, Justin Martyr, Irenæus, and Tertullian took them in. And I conceive that man ought to suspect his own judgment and orthodoxy, whose opinions sink below the standard of the second age after Christ; and I see no reason to doubt, but that the notions of the second, third, and fourth centuries, were the same in the main, as to this important head of Christian doctrine and worship; and I might say the same of several of the following ages. It is easy enough indeed for Protestants to prove, that the Church, in these ages, did not believe transubstantiation; but it can never be maintained that they looked on the Sacramental Body and Blood, as mere figures or symbols; and therefore I look on this hypothesis as utterly indefensible, as an opinion reprobated by the generality of the first Reformers, embraced only by Zuinglius and Œcolampadius and their adherents, who were upon that account called Sacramentarians; and of late advanced by the Arminians and Socinians with too great success; but utterly inconsistent with the principles of the truly primitive Church, and even with Scripture itself, as has been shewed. The Lutheran doctrine, though it come nearest to that of transubstantiation (for it supposes the grand absurdity of transubstantiation to be true; which is, that the Body of Christ descends from heaven to many thousands of Altars, at one and the same time; but it denies the other great absurdity of transubstantiation, the annihilation of the Bread and Wine) yet in one respect is, I think, altogether worse and less tenable; viz. because it supposes two Bodies and Bloods in the Sacrament, the typical and the substantial. For the Bread and Wine are figures of the Body and Blood; and figures may bear the names of their principals; and further, together with this typical Body and Blood, they believe they have the very Body and Blood of Christ, which was born of the Blessed Virgin, and shed upon the cross. And indeed the opinion of Calvin, Beza, and their followers, did not come much short of the Lutherans in this respect. For their doctrine too was chargeable with this consequence, though they modified their notions in a way somewhat different from that of Luther. What is given in the Eucharist and received from the hands of the Minister, they

affirmed to be mere typical, symbolical Bread and Wine; and
that the unbelieving or unworthy communicant received no
more than mere types and shadows; but then they added, that
the faithful and worthy communicant received the very natural
Body and Blood of Christ by an act of faith. And they further
asserted, that this natural Body and Blood might be received,
not only at the Holy Communion, but in any other act of religion; and though they allowed that the natural Body and
Blood were received at the Sacrament, yet they denied that
it was received in the Sacrament, that is, in the Bread and
Wine, but that it was communicated in a Divine and unintelligible manner to the faithful only. Now that my reader
may be made sensible of the inconvenience of this notion, I
will only give him the brief history of the treaty of Poissy,
the substance of which I take from the moderate impartial
Thuanus[d]. The managers on the Papists' side were the Cardinals of Lorraine and Tournon, Mr. Espencée, and others.
On the Protestant side, Mr. Beza, Peter Martyr, &c. Lorraine had charged Beza with saying that Christ's Body is no
more *in Cœná*, ' in the Lord's Supper,' *quam in cœno*, ' than
in the dirt we tread on;' but Thuanus seems to clear Beza
of this, by saying that it was only a consequence, which Melancthon had formerly in a heat imputed to Œcolampadius,
by way of objection against his doctrine; which was, that
the things received in the Sacrament are mere signs. Beza
purged himself from this imputation, and declared his abhorrence of it, as blasphemous; but Beza himself, though he
confessed that believers do as surely partake of the Body and
Blood of Christ, as they see and touch and put into their
mouths the Sacrament, yet affirmed that the Body of Christ
was as distant from the Bread, as heaven was from the earth.
This was received with great indignation by Tournon, and so
the assembly broke up for that time. Beza excused himself
in a letter to the queen regent (who called this congress, and
was present at the conferences) by saying, he had not time
given him to explain himself; for he owns it would be blasphemy to assert, that Christ was absent from His Supper,
which yet some had charged him for affirming, and which
Thuanus seems to say he had affirmed. He owns[e], that

[d] Lib. 28. [tom. ii. p. 117. ed. Lond. 1733.] Anno Dom. 1561.   [e] [p. 121.]

" this tremendous mystery was instituted by the Son of
God, that we may more and more be partakers of the substance of His very Body and Blood; that God was every
where present, but that His Body was in heaven, circum-
scribed by space and place;" for which he cited St. Augustine, and Vigilius Bishop of Trent five hundred years before.
Hereupon the colloquy was renewed, in which Lorraine made
a very bright speech, says Thuanus, in which he used the
following words[f]; "If the Protestants continue in this opinion, that Christ is no otherwise upon earth since the time
of His ascension than He was before He put on our Flesh;
or that He now has any other Body but what is visible;—or
in a word, that to put on Christ in Baptism, and to receive
His Body in the Supper, is all one thing; he must retort
their own words upon them, and say, that his opinion was
as far distant from theirs as heaven is from earth."   Two
days after they meet again: Lorraine and his party insist
upon a subscription to the chapter concerning the Eucharist
in the Augustan, that is, the Lutheran Confession, which
had formerly been demanded of the Protestants; and urge
an expression of Mr. Calvin's, intimating the "substance of
Christ's Body" to be in the Sacrament.   Peter Martyr endeavours to mollify this expression by a gloss of his own, but
to no purpose.   Then they agreed upon a new method of
conference, that this controversy should be amicably adjusted
by delegates deputed from each side.   After long debates,
the Protestant Ministers draw up their judgment in these
words[g]; viz. " We confess, that Jesus Christ, in the Supper,
does truly give and exhibit to us the substance of His Body
and Blood, by the efficacy of His Holy Spirit; and that we
do receive and eat, spiritually and by faith, that very Body
Which was offered and immolated for us, so as to be bone of
His Bone, and flesh of His Flesh, to the end that we may
be enlivened thereby, and receive whatever is conducive to
our salvation: and because faith, supported by the Word of
God, makes those things present which it apprehends, and
by that faith we do in deed and reality receive the true
natural Body and Blood of Christ, by the power of the Holy
Spirit; by this means we confess and acknowledge the pre-

[f] [p. 122.]   [g] [p. 125.]

sence of His Body and Blood in the Supper."—Espencée, though he did not much dislike the rest, yet could not allow of the last clause, which he said would never be allowed by the Latins, by the West or East, by the Ethiopian or African Church, nor by the Protestants in Germany, that is, the Lutherans; and therefore he proposed, that the last clause should be thus expressed[h]; "And because the Divine Word and promise, by which our faith is supported, makes those things which are promised present to us, and by the power and efficacy of the Word, we do in deed and reality receive the true and natural Body and Blood of Christ; therefore we do by this means confess and acknowledge the presence of His Body and Blood in the Supper." After a debate on this occasion between the Ministers and the delegates on the other side, the Ministers are forbid to appear there any more; which when the Ministers understood, they endeavoured (says Thuanus) to help out their former declaration, by adding what follows; viz. "No distance of place can hinder us from communicating of the Body and Blood of Christ, for the Lord's Supper is a heavenly thing; and though on earth we receive Bread and Wine" (I think 'only' ought to be added) "which are the true signs of His Body and Blood, with our mouths, yet by faith and the efficacy of the Holy Ghost, our minds which are fed with this food are rapt up into heaven, and enjoy the presence of the Body and Blood; and that by this means it may be said, that the Body is truly joined to the Bread, and the Blood to the Wine; but after the manner of a Sacrament, and not at all according to place or natural position; but as they (the signs) do imply, that God does efficaciously exhibit them to faithful receivers, and they do by faith receive them." Thus the assembly was dissolved.

Now this story is very instructive on several accounts. And first and especially it should teach Protestants not to make such concessions to Papists, as Beza and Calvin before him had done; (and indeed Calvin had subscribed the Augustan Confession;) I mean, to acknowledge that Christ's Body is substantially present in or at the Sacrament. It is plain that Beza, according to his hypothesis, might either

[h] [p. 126.]

CHAP.
II.

deny or assert this.   For he believed It not to be present in the Bread or Wine, or by virtue of any thing done in the Eucharist only; but he believed It present to believers, by means of their faith, in all religious actions, and therefore in the Eucharist as well as in Baptism, prayer, &c.   To wipe off the aspersions cast upon him, he declares the substance of the Body and Blood to be received by the faithful in the Supper; and so was caught in his own net, from which he found it impossible to extricate himself.   For by his explanations he only further involved himself; if the reader can penetrate into his meaning, I must confess it is more than I can pretend to do.   The case is very plain; if Christ's natural Body and Blood be received either in the Sacrament, or any where else on earth, it must be done either by having that Body and Blood brought down from heaven to us, or by our being assumed into heaven and being brought into the presence of that Body and Blood, or by our meeting them in some third place; but all these three suppositions are equally absurd, and there is no fourth to be imagined. Beza and his friends, to avoid the known difficulties 'of the first supposition, ran themselves aground on the second. Secondly, from this we may learn that the primitive Church asserted nothing so harsh and incredible, in relation to the reality of Christ's Flesh and Blood in the Eucharist, as either the Lutherans or Calvinists, who are the two main bodies of Protestants.   I am not sensible that any single Father ever asserted, for the first four hundred years, that Christ's personal Body and Blood can be substantially present to us here on earth.   Even Gregory Nyssen, who goes farther, I think, than any had done before him, never supposes Christ's natural Body to be brought down from heaven to the communicants; but rather, that the Bread of the Eucharist was, by addition, converted into His true Body, if I understand him right.   They call the consecrated Bread, a Divine heavenly thing or substance, but they do not call it the substance of the Body of Christ; and they call it a Divine substance, because they believe it sanctified by the Holy Ghost. They call the Sacramental Bread and Wine the true very Body and Blood, meaning, that it was so in power and efficacy, as has been shewed.   They believed it to be the very Body

and Blood, not by a bare figure or metaphor, just as Christ is SECT.
I.
called the Passover, the Vine, the Way, and the Door; but
by way of a lively mystery, which though it do not come
up to the original, is yet far above and beyond all other
types and representations, and specially all tropes and lifeless
figures and emblems. But it does not appear to me, that
ever they thought of receiving the natural Body of Christ,
as both Papists and Protestants asserted they did, at this
treaty; but I shall further vindicate the ancients, when I
come to speak of their seeming excesses on this head.
Thirdly, from hence we may see where the stress or knot
of the controversy between the Papists and Calvinists then
lay. The question truly stated was not, whether the substance of Christ's Body were capable of being received; this
was allowed on both hands; but, whether that thing, which
was given by the Priest, and received by the communicants,
was the very substantial Body of Christ; and if the question
had been thus proposed, as I humbly conceive it ought to
have been, there could have been no room for a treaty; but
the Calvinists must once for ever have denied it, and the
Papists affirmed it. But the present project at court was to
reconcile contradictions, and to accommodate matters so far,
if possible, as to bring the two contending parties to subscribe one certain form of words in two different senses, and
to make them in appearance say the same thing, when their
thoughts and meanings were directly contrary to each other;
and therefore palliative expressions, and ambiguous circum-
locutions were made use of: and upon this occasion, I think
fit to present to my reader, in one short view, the true state
of the questions now depending between the Protestants and
Papists, in relation to the *matter* of the Sacrament, or the
thing or substance there received.

1. Whether there are two Bodies of Christ to be received Dispute be-
in the Sacrament, or only one? The Lutherans[i] and Calvin- tween Pro-
testants and

---

[i] The Lutheran notion of the Real
Presence being very subtle, and the
Lutheran books not much read among
us, I thought fit here to set it down.

First in the words of Luther himself,
as they stand in his Cogitationes MS.
CCCC.

" Nostra autem sententia est, Corpus
ita vel in pane esse, ut revera cum
pane manducetur; et quemcunque mo-
tum vel actionem panis habet, eun-
dem et Corpus Christi; ut Corpus
Christi vere dicatur ferri, dari, accipi,
manducari, quando panis fertur, datur,
accipitur, manducatur. Id est, *Hoc
est Corpus Meum.*"

ists, if they will speak the truth, without reserve or palliation, must say there are two Bodies there to be received, the typical Body of Bread, and the substantial Body of Christ Himself. The Papists assert, there is but one Body of Christ in the Sacrament; and so far they are right. But then they add, that this is the very substantial Body; and in this their gross error consists. The Arminians and Socinians agree with the Papists, in asserting but one Body of Christ in the Sacrament; but then they err in the contrary extreme; for they believe it to be a bare typical figurative Body only.

2. Whether the substance of Christ's Body and Blood be received from the hands of the celebrator? Both the Papists and Lutherans affirm that they are; the Calvinists and Arminians and Socinians deny it; the former add, that the believer receives This by faith. The Arminians and Socinians deny that they can be received at all.

3. Whether the only matter or substance given by the celebrator be the substantial Body and Blood? The Papists affirm this; for they say, that the accidents of bread and wine only remain, but the substance of them gives way to

Next from Gerhard, in loc. Theolog. de Sacr. Cœna, cap. x. § 69. [tom. v. p. 55. ed. 1657.] " Credimus in Eucharistiæ Sacramento veram realem et substantialem Corporis et Sanguinis Christi præsentiam, exhibitionem, manducationem, et bibitionem. Quæ præsentia non est essentialis conversio panis in Corpus, et vini in Sanguinem Christi, quam transubstantiationem vocant: neque est Corporis ad panem, ac Sanguinis ad vinum extra usum Cœnæ, localis aut durabilis affixio; neque est panis et Corporis Christi personalis unio, qualis est Divinæ et humanæ naturæ in Christo unio; neque est localis inclusio Corporis in panem; neque est impanatio; neque incorporatio in panem, qua panis cum Corpore Christi et vinum cum Ipsius Sanguine in unam massam physicam coalescat; neque est naturalis inexistentia; neque delitescentia Corpusculi sub pane; neque quicquam hujusmodi carnale, aut physicum: sed est præsentia et unio Sacramentalis, quæ ita comparata est, ut juxta Ipsius Salvatoris nostri veracis sapientis et omnipotentis institutionem, pani benedicto tanquam medio itidem divinitus ordinato Corpus, et vino bene-

dicto tanquam medio divinitus ordinato Sanguis Christi, modo nobis incomprehensibili, uniatur; ut cum illo pane Corpus Christi una manducatione Sacramentali, et cum illo vino Sanguinem Christi una bibitione Sacramentali in sublimi mysterio sumamus, manducemus, et bibamus.   Breviter non ἀπουσίαν absentiam, non ἐνουσίαν inexistentiam, non συνουσίαν consubstantiationem, non μετουσίαν transubstantiationem, sed παρουσίαν Corporis et Sanguinis Christi in Cœna statuimus."

In Form. Concil. Art. vii. dicitur " Corpus et Sanguinem Christi non tantum spiritualiter per fidem, sed etiam ore, non tamen Capernaitice, sed supernaturali et cœlesti modo, ratione Sacramentalis unionis cum pane et vino sumi."

In this form, Concil. p. 753, the Corporal Presence is denied; which yet is thus explained; that the Body of Christ is received with the mouth, yet in a spiritual manner.   By which they run into the Popish absurdity of a Body's being present in a spiritual manner. See Pfaffius, p. 461, 462. [This note was added in 2nd ed.]

the adduced substance of the Body and Blood. The Lutherans assert that the Sacrament consists of the substance of Christ's Body and Blood, together with the substance of Bread and Wine. The Calvinists, Arminians, and Socinians deny that any substance is given by the celebrator, except that of Bread and Wine.

And I will here subjoin the judgment of the ancient Church, in relation to the questions above proposed, according to the best of my information.

1. As to the first question, the primitive Church believed, as the Papists, Arminians, and Socinians do, that there is but one Body, one Blood of Christ in the Sacrament. This Body and Blood the primitive Church sometimes called the true and very Body and Blood, as the Papists also do; and sometimes the typical or symbolical Body and Blood, as the Arminians and Socinians now do. But they did not mean these words in the same sense, either with the Papists on one hand, or with the Arminians and Socinians on the other.

2, 3. As to the other two questions, the ancient Church did not believe that the true substance of Christ's Body and Blood was given by the celebrator, or by any other means, either with or without the Bread.

But then there is another question, which was never to my knowledge proposed or disputed, either between the Papists and Protestants, or among the Protestants themselves; and that is,

Whether the Body and Blood given by the celebrator in the Eucharist be the true Body and Blood of Christ in real substance, or only in spirit and power. And every body knows, how the Church of Rome must answer this question, or rather how she has answered it; though it was never formally and in express words proposed to her. For the substantial Presence of the Body and Blood in the Sacrament is one of the new articles of the Tridentine Creed; and in this particular the Church of Rome has decided the cause, not only contrary to reason and common sense, but also contrary to the primitive Church; which, as has been shewed, believed the Bread and Wine to remain, and that they were the true Body and Blood of Christ, by virtue of their true spiritual consecration; and therefore, though they called them types,

CHAP.
II.
as believing them to be bread and wine, and not the very Life
itself, yet they called them too the true Body and Blood, for
they believed them to be so in power and efficacy.

The advantage of the primitive doctrine beyond those both of the Calvinists and Lutherans.
What opinion Protestants may now have of this judgment
of the ancient Church, I cannot so much as divine; but I am
very sure it had been very happy, if the great leaders of the
Reformation had been pleased to take such light, as antiquity
would plentifully have given them in this particular; and
would have leaned less to their own judgments, and more to
the sentiments of the primitive Church, in interpreting the
texts of Scripture relating to this subject; and by this means
there would not only have been a better harmony between
Protestants themselves, the great want of which is the scandal
of the Reformation; but they would have been enabled to
give more full and satisfactory answers to such objections, as
Papists or other adversaries alleged against them; and at
the same time have promoted the two most valuable things
on earth, truth and peace. The Reformers were very far
from being strangers to the writings of the primitive Church
and the ancient Fathers; nay, they were very diligent in
searching for authorities from antiquity, whereby to confute
the errors of the Church of Rome; but the leaders of the
Reformation abroad seem rather to have made use of the
weapons which the ancients put into their hands, for the
destruction of the Popish cause, than of the materials and
models which antiquity would have afforded them, for building
up their own Churches and systems of divinity. However I will not despair of some success among the Clergy
and people of our own Church, when I am recommending
that scheme of the doctrine of the Eucharist which prevailed
for so many hundred years next after the Apostles. It is
commonly said, and I think truly, that the Church of England has not declared for any particular *modus* of the Presence
of Christ's Body in the Sacrament. We are indeed instructed
by the Church, that " Christ's Body and Blood are verily and
indeed taken and received by the faithful in the Lord's Supper;" but whether substantially, or in power or efficacy only,
is not determined: and I am not without hopes, that those
of our Church, who have senses exercised, and who have any
regard to antiquity, will embrace this doctrine; not only as

more consistent with reason than either that of the Luther- SECT.
ans or the Calvinists, but because it comes recommended to   I.
us by the venerable stamp of the primitive Church. As for
those who have no notion of any thing in the Sacrament beyond that of a mere significant ceremony, a shadow, or symbol, they ought to consider that they stand condemned, not
only by the voice of our own Church, but of all duly constituted Churches that are or ever were; as may be seen in the
Right Reverend Bishop Cosin's History of Transubstantiation: and I persuade myself, that they have none with
them, even in this most degenerate age, excepting the Arminians and Socinians, and such writers as they will be ashamed
to own in the presence of competent judges. I am apt to
think, that one great occasion of the growth of these loose
opinions concerning the Eucharist has been the great absurdity and apparent inconsistence of those hypotheses, which
have of late ages prevailed in the Christian Church, in relation to this article of Christianity. Transubstantiation is pro-
verbially irrational; consubstantiation comes not much behind it; and the spiritual Presence, as explained by Beza and
his associates, is as unintelligible as either of the former. And
it is very hard for men, if they be in any measure inquisitive,
to believe any thing that is mysterious, without having some
fixed and certain idea concerning the manner of it; because
without this they know not how to distinguish between mystery and nonsense, and because without knowing the *modus*
they really know not how to argue or reason concerning it in
their own minds, or to discourse of it to others. And when
all the commonly prevailing *modus*es of Christ's Body being
really and truly received in the Sacrament are so very harsh
and incongruous, it is not much to be wondered, if in a free-
thinking age men rather choose to believe that Christ's Body
is not at all in the Sacrament, than that It is there in the
manner, which the Papists or Lutherans or Calvinists conceit it; or than to suppose that It is there, they know not
how. But I have reason to think, that the reality of Christ's
Body in the Sacrament, as to Its spiritual power and effect,
will meet with a tolerable reception, at least from all candid
and impartial sons of the Church, that rejoice to see primitive
Truth unclouding itself and shewing its reverend face.

CHAP.
II.

The opinion
concerning
two per-
sonal Bodies
of Christ.

Fifthly and lastly, by reflecting on this doctrine of the primitive Church concerning the reality of Christ's Body in the Sacrament, and the spiritual mysterious manner of It, we may see upon what slight grounds some particular learned men amongst us have advanced a notion of Christ's having two personal Bodies, a carnal and a spiritual one; that the carnal Body cannot be received, but the spiritual may. This opinion is maintained by the worthy and learned Dr. Pelling, in his Discourse of the Sacrament. He calls these "two naturesᴶ," and cites Irenæus for saying the Eucharist "consists of two things, a heavenly and earthly." The 'heavenly' he supposes to be the "spiritual Body;" but I have shewed, that by the heavenly thing he means the power of the Holy Spirit. He cites Origen at the same place, for distinguishing "the symbolical body" from "the Word Which was made Flesh." This last he calls His human nature; whereas "the Word made Flesh" includes His whole entire Person; and by the "symbolical Body," he rightly understands the Bread in the Eucharist. Then he cites Tertullian for saying "Christ represents His Body by Bread." How the Doctor would prove his point from these passages, I cannot so much as guess. Then he quotes St. Augustine from Gratian, who very often corrupts and misrecites that Father's writings. And yet St. Augustine, as there cited, says nothing, but that there is in the Eucharist "the visible species and the invisible Flesh and Blood;" which rather countenances the Papists' than the Doctor's notion. He cites St. Chrysostom directly against his own opinion, viz. *Et non duo Corpora, sed unum Filii Corpus prædicatur.* He also observes, that the Fathers of the second Nicene council determined, that after consecration "the Bread and Wine are rightly called the Body and Blood; but why," says he, "must this be meant of Christ's natural Body, and not of His spiritual?" Yes, if he had proved, that Christ had such a personal spiritual Body, distinct from His natural; but that is the point in questionᵏ. "The Body of Christ," says he, "may be considered either in respect of It's own natural substance, consisting of flesh, bones, and blood; or else with respect to His Divinity, as That is united with It, as It is replenished with the presence

ᴶ p. 198.

ᵏ p. 211.

and energy of the Godhead, and fills all things with spiritual rays[l]." This supposes but one Body of our Saviour, but only diversely considered; and yet he expressly calls this "a distinction between His natural and spiritual Body[m]." The Doctor says "the primitive Christians insisted much" on this distinction; cites Clemens Alexandrinus[n]; but I have elsewhere shewed, that Clemens, by the "spiritual Blood," meant the Eucharistical Blood; and that he himself in effect tells us so. He cites St. Jerome for saying, "The Blood and Flesh of Christ is capable of a double meaning, either that which He speaks of (John vi.) or that Flesh and Blood which was crucified and let out by the soldier's spear." I doubt not but St. Jerome means the Eucharistical, and the natural Blood; and I had myself alleged this authority, but that something follows which might have given our adversaries a handle for cavil, though they can do our cause no hurt, nor their own any good by it. The Doctor again quotes St. Augustine to prove, that "the virtue of Christ's Body is in the Sacrament;" but I cannot conceive, how this proves His spiritual personal Body distinct from His natural. Then he produces St. Ambrose[o], which I have before sufficiently considered. St. Ambrose expressly mentions the spiritual Body, as in the Sacrament. The Doctor never does so much as pretend, that this personal spiritual Body of Christ is the Sacrament, or in the Sacrament, but only the virtue of It[p], and so he himself explains it[q]. He goes on to cite Pseudo-Cyprian *De Cœna*, a writer of the eleventh or twelfth century, who yet says not a word to the purpose, so far as I can see[r]. Cyril of Alexandria, cited in the same place, unquestionably speaks of Christ's one natural Body, and therefore rather against than for the Doctor[s]. He would have our Saviour John vi. speak of this spiritual Body. Of this I have said something already, and intend to enlarge myself hereafter. He produces Athanasius[t], who speaks evidently of the Eucharistical Body, (as I have shewed)[u]. He proceeds to cite Cyril of Alexandria[v],

[l] p. 230.
[m] p. 231.
[n] b. p. 7. Ap.
[o] k. p. 27. Ap.
[p] p. 233.
[q] p. 234.

[r] p. 237.
[s] p. 237.
[t] a. p. 17. Ap.
[u] p. 24.
[v] h. p. 44. Ap.

CHAP.
II.
in words which he expressly applies to the Sacrament[w]. He
applies what the Apostle says, 1 Cor. x. 2, 3, to this notion of
His " spiritual Body ;" but he does not mention it in terms,
because he knew our Saviour then had no Body[x]. He mentions
St. Augustine again, as speaking of the virtue of the Sacrament[y]. He cites the heretic Theodotus, in the words above
produced by me; the reader may judge how much they help
the Doctor's cause[z]. He says Origen, as before cited, by the
Word made Flesh "means the vital and Divine power, which
goes along with the symbols." If this be true, then the Doctor's
"vital and Divine power" is the whole Person of Christ Jesus[a].
For the establishing this bold doctrine, (I am sure I do not
exceed the bounds of moderation in giving it that epithet,) he
does not cite any one writer who mentions any spiritual Body
of Christ, distinguished from His natural and Eucharistical
Body. Dr. Henry More takes this scent, which he had from
Dr. Pelling, and pursues it in a way peculiar to himself, in
his book of "The Real Presence[b]." I have said thus much of
this singular opinion of these learned men ; not that I apprehend any danger of such notions prevailing or spreading
themselves, in such an age as this of ours. I would have been
more large and particular in my reflections, if I had had any
suspicions that the doctrine were adapted to the relish of the
men of this generation ; and yet, I think, I have said as much
as is sufficient to weigh down all the arguings of Dr. Pelling,
which are what Dr. More builds upon. And what use I further intended in the particular notice I have taken of this
opinion is, to observe to my reader, that studious and thinking men, who are very much under the power of religion, such
as, I believe, both these Doctors were, can never satisfy themselves with that cold and jejune account, which the generality
of men amongst us have of late taken up of the Holy Sacrament, as mere emblems and remembrancers, no more than
with the modern fanciful inventions of Luther and Calvin ;
and therefore rather indulge their imaginations in contriving
some new hypothesis, which may better satisfy them, both
because it is new, and because it is their own, than rest con-

w p. 243.   z p. 265.
x p. 244.   a p. 266.
y p. 247.   b [cap. vi.]

tent with the empty figures and types of Arminians or Socinians, or with the odd and incongruous notions of Luther
and Calvin.

And further, it particularly deserves our reflection, that all The occa-
the wrong notions which have been framed concerning the sion of modern
eating and drinking of the Body and Blood of our Lord, pro- mistakes about the
ceed from one single cause; and that is, from an opinion, that Eucharist.
Bread and Wine are too worthless and sorry things to be the
Body and Blood of Christ, any otherwise than as mere figures
or resemblances; therefore the main body of Christians in
the East and West, in the North and South, and throughout
the world, in the middle and dark ages of the Church, were
easily persuaded to believe that there is no bread or wine
remaining in the Eucharist, but that the entire substance
there consecrated is the Body and Blood of Christ: but this
was too gross and contrary to sense, to stand the scrutiny of
Martin Luther and Philip Melancthon and their adherents,
who had less deference to the authority of the Church than
to their own senses; they were sure there was bread and
wine remaining after consecration, and they were fully persuaded that the Body and Blood were there too; therefore
they conclude, that the Eucharist was a mixture of both, that
the Body and Blood of Christ were in the Eucharist in an invisible manner, [accompanying[c]] the visible substance of Bread
and Wine. Calvin and Beza go a step further; they will not
allow the Bread and Wine to be so much as the vehicle of the
Body and Blood, but make them things not only distinct, but
very far distant from one another. They allowed nothing but
bare elements to be taken from the celebrator; and if men did
over and above receive the Body and Blood of Christ, that was
to be attributed to their own faith, by which they imagined
they could communicate of the Body and Blood at any other
place and in any other religious action as well as at the Lord's
Table or at the Sacrament. Dr. Pelling and Dr. More were
men of too great sense to believe, that faith could make any
thing present that was really absent; or bring Christ's Body
down from Heaven, or waft us up thither to receive It; therefore they project a scheme, whereby they suppose, that we
may communicate, not indeed of the natural or carnal, but

[c] [In the 1st ed. the Author had written 'contained in.']

CHAP.
II.

of another Body of Christ, that is in virtue and effect diffused throughout the universe; and though Dr. Pelling calls
them two Bodies, yet in reality he makes the spiritual Body
to be only the virtue or energy of the natural.   It is evident
that this was only a grafting or refinement upon the Calvinistical plan; and they agree with the Calvinists in the main
point, viz. that " though the great feast on this heavenly food
is more especially and copiously enjoyed in the celebration of
the Holy Eucharist; yet we may, in some good measure, draw
it in, day by day, by faith and devotion," as Dr. More has it[d]:
and " we are not to imagine, that the Body of Christ quickens
none but at the Communion[e]."   I cannot but farther observe,
that this fictitious spiritual Body of Christ is not a Body of
these Doctors' own making; for Robert Barclay had published
his Apology many years before they wrote the pieces I am
now speaking of.   And he, in his thirteenth proposition, expressly asserts this spiritual Body of Christ; and makes It the
same with " the heavenly seed, that Divine, spiritual, heavenly
substance," which he and his friends commonly call " the light
within."   In one particular, Barclay has the advantage of
Dr. Pelling; for he asserts, that Christ had this spiritual Body,
even when He was "the Word of God;" and that by It He
revealed and communicated Himself to the Patriarchs, and
was Christ before His incarnation[f]; and therefore he might

1 Cor. x.2,3. properly apply the words of St. Paul to this spiritual Body of
Christ; which Dr. Pelling could not do, without contradict-
ing his own hypothesis: and yet he has ventured to do it[g].
When Calvin had separated the Body from the Bread, it was
easy for the Quakers to despise the latter, (which they could
not have without a Priesthood or ministry,) and to conceit

---

d [p. 56. ed. 1686.]

e Dr. Pelling, p. 251.

f ["So then, as there was the outward
visible Body and Temple of Jesus
Christ, which took its origin from the
Virgin Mary; so there is also the spiritual Body of Christ, by and through
which, He, that was the Word in the
beginning with God, and was and is
God, did reveal Himself to the sons of
men in all ages, and whereby men in
all ages come to be made partakers of
eternal life, and to have communion
and fellowship with God and Christ.
Of which Body of Christ, and Flesh
and Blood, if both Adam and Seth
and Enoch and Noah and Abraham
and Moses and David and all the
Prophets and holy men of God had
not eaten, they had not had life in
them: nor could their inward man
have been nourished."—Vid. Proposition xiii. of the Apology, p. 449. ed.
1736.]

g p. 244.

that they still enjoyed the former. And it must be owned, that the Arminians and Socinians, and their predecessors (in this point) Zuinglius and Œcolampadius, who wholly divided the Bread from the Body, chose for themselves the most contemptible part, the poor, typical, figurative bread and wine; and the Quakers, in taking their leavings (if they really had what they conceited themselves to have) got much the better of them. But what all ages and Christians before thought too mean and base to be the whole entertainment for pious souls at the Table of the Lord, that is, mere bread and wine, without either natural or spiritual Body and Blood joined to them or accompanying them, without any Divine grace or benediction shed on them by the Holy Ghost; these weak elements barely set apart for a pious use, our Arminians and Socinians have substituted, instead of the "medicine of immortality," "the sanctifying food," "the heavenly as well as earthly thing," "the spiritual nourishment," "the Divine substance," "the tremendous mystery" of the ancients. They do not indeed deny the elements set apart for this use to be in some sense the Body and Blood; but the more you depress the mystery and degrade the dignity of the Eucharist, the less you make our Saviour's words to signify, and the more flat and dead you affirm the types and symbols to be, the more orthodox you are in the opinion of these men. They do indeed agree with the ancient Church in many particulars, as in asserting, that Christ's natural personal Body cannot be received; that there is but one Body of Christ in the Eucharist; that the gross substance of the Eucharistical Body is Bread: but they still make it ψιλὸς ἄρτος, without any spiritual power, or real enlivening energy. They believe it to be made the Body of Christ by the will and action of the Minister and people rather than by the Divine agency of the Holy Spirit.

I shall only, before I pass to another head of discourse, observe, that all the propositions hitherto laid down concerning the nature of the Eucharist, are fairly consistent with each other; and to this end, I will again place them all together in the reader's view. *The consistence of the doctrines concerning the Eucharist.*

1. The Body and Blood in the Sacrament are the Bread and Wine.

2. The Body and Blood in the Sacrament, or the conse-

crated Bread and Wine, are types of the natural Body and Blood of Christ.

3. But they are not such cold and imperfect types as those before and under the Law.

4. Nay, they are the very Body and Blood, though not in substance, yet in spirit, power, and effect.

If there be any appearing inconsistence in these propositions, it is between the second and the fourth; the second affirms the Bread and Wine to be types; the fourth affirms them to be the very Body and Blood. And if by the very Body and Blood were meant the natural or substantial, it must be acknowledged that the inconsistence were too great to be reconciled by me. But since it is the Body and Blood in power and effect only, this seems to me to remove every thing that can look like contradiction. In this sense, an exemplification, made according to the statute, is itself the record; and every impressed broad seal is itself the original. For though it consist of a material very different from that of the impressor, yet the impressed wax carries as much authority with it, as the original seal itself could do. I will not say, that this or any other imaginable similitude does in all respects come up to the nature of the great thing I am speaking of. Nay, I am sure it falls a great way below It in several respects. An exemplification receives it's validity from a statute, or statutes, made by the legislative authority once for all; the broad seal is passed, and made effectual by a minister of the law, that has little or perhaps no share in the legislative power; but the Eucharistical Bread and Wine are made the Body and Blood of Christ, not only by virtue of the institution and command of Christ, Who did once for all order It; not only by the ministry of a man, who is invested with authority to this purpose; but by a Divine act of the Holy Spirit, repeated as often as the Eucharist is duly celebrated. And it ought freely to be owned, that so Divine an Agent may render the Bread and Wine the Body and Blood, in such a manner, and in so superlative a sense, as cannot be expressed by the tongue or pen of man. Nay, I believe, it must in truth and justice be said, that the Bread and Wine are so the Body and Blood of Christ, as no one thing in nature, beside these, can be

said to be another. This was the belief of the ancient Church;
and this they thought to be such a mystery, as could never be
fathomed by human understanding. And though I am not
sensible that they asserted any thing that contradicted the
reason and sense of mankind; yet they always spake of It as
a thing above our conceptions and capacities. I conclude
therefore, that though the Eucharistical elements are not the
substantial Body and Blood; nay, they are the figurative and
representative symbols of them; yet they are somewhat more
too; they are the mysterious Body and Blood of our ever-
blessed Redeemer. By the mysterious Body and Blood, the
reader will easily perceive, I mean neither substantial nor
yet merely figurative, but the middle between these extremes,
viz. the Bread and Wine made the Body and Blood of Christ,
by the secret power of the Spirit; and apprehended to be so,
not by our senses, but by our faith, directed and influenced
by the same Holy Spirit; and made the Body and Blood in
such a manner as human reason cannot perfectly comprehend. I proceed to shew,

V. That the ancients laid great stress on the belief of this
doctrine; and to this purpose I shall observe,

1. That they speak of this doctrine as a necessary point of Of the
faith. Thus Theodoret[h], after he had in his dialogue made stress the
ancients
Orthodoxus declare, what were the symbols of the Body and laid on the
belief of
Blood; and after Orthodoxus had declared, that they were Christ's
spiritual
"called the Body and Blood;" introduces Eranistes urging Body in the
Orthodoxus with this question, "And do you believe, that Sacrament.
you partake of the Body and Blood of Christ?" and Orthodoxus answers, "so I believe." In this age he is commonly
thought orthodox enough, that confesses the Bread and
Wine to be symbols; and he, who goes a little farther and
familiarly styles them the Body and Blood, shall be rather
thought to overdo; but even this was not then sufficient; but
the sound Christian must believe them to be the Body and
Blood more than in name and bare resemblance. For Orthodoxus adds, "They are apprehended to be what they were
made; and they are believed and venerated, as being what
they are believed." Epiphanius's words are very remarkable[i];
"Christ was pleased by grace to say, 'This is My' some-

[h] m. p. 46. Ap.   [i] c. p. 22. Ap. l. 7.

CHAP.
II.

what, meaning 'My Body,' and no [Christian] man disbelieves the Word, and he that believes not" (He may perhaps
mean, that he who believes not 'misses of the grace and
virtue' of the Sacrament; the Greek will well bear this sense)
" is fallen from grace and salvation. We believe what we
have heard, that It is His [Body]." "We do," says Cyril of
Jerusalem[k], "with full assurance partake of them, as of the
Body and Blood of Christ:" and[l], "Regard them not, as mere
Bread and Wine. For though your sense suggest this to
you, yet let faith confirm you; determine not the matter by
the taste, but be fully assured by faith, that you are undoubtedly honoured with the Body and Blood of Christ."
I shall not accumulate authorities in a case so notorious;
but only further observe upon these I have produced, that
they speak of it as of a doctrine not easy and obvious, but
such an article as is a trial of our faith; they speak of it, as
a thing not only necessary to be believed, but which will not
be believed but by a faith that is not governed by sense, by
a faith that is peculiar to good Christians; whereas a Deist
or an Atheist may believe, that Bread broken and Wine
poured out were appointed by Jesus Christ to be symbols of
His Body and Blood; even they that crucified Christ and
charged Him with imposture might be satisfied by the
testimony of Judas, that Christ did command His disciples
to remember His death by these typical ceremonies; but
none of these could or would believe, that the Bread and
Wine was His Body and Blood, in the sense above mentioned, as the primitive Christians did. And lest my reader
should suspect, that this is a doctrine broached in the fourth
century; let him consider the words of Irenæus, when,
speaking of the heretics against whom he wrote, he asks[m],
" How they will be sure that the eucharistized Bread is His
Body, the Wine His Blood, if they deny Him to be the Son
of Him Who made the universe." He supposes it to be
an article of very considerable moment, of which Christians
ought to be perfectly well convinced; and that Bread and
Wine, created by a God that was not the Father of Jesus
Christ, could never be made His Body and Blood. For it
was incredible, that God should send His Spirit to sanctify

k c. p. 18. Ap.   l d. p. 19. Ap. l. 8.   m f. p. 5. Ap. l. 17.

creatures that were not His own. In this the force of his SECT.
I. argument consists, as he explains it afterward, by saying of the Catholics, that they "agreeably declared a unity of the [Eucharistical] Flesh and the Spirit;" and it has been before proved, that he judged the elements to be made the Body and Blood by a spiritual and Divine power; and this therefore was the doctrine, of which he would have Christians fully persuaded. This is the doctrine in which Christians were "instructed" in the time of Justin Martyr[n]; and they who disbelieved it are by St. Ignatius[o] branded with a particular mark of infamy.

2. The primitive Church required an explicit belief of this, both from Clergy and people, as often as they administered or received the Communion. The known form of administering the Eucharist, in the Christian Church of the first ages, was thus. The Bishop or Priest, who distributed the Bread, holding the symbol out to the receiver, said, "the Body of Christ." The Deacon or Priest, holding out the Cup, said, "the Blood of Christ;" to both of which the receiver answered "Amen." Of this we have abundant evidence. Tertullian, speaking of those who went to the theatre to see prizes fought, cries out[p], "What a thing is this, that you should give applause to a gladiator from that very mouth, with which you have pronounced 'Amen' over the Holy of the Lord!" that is, over the offered Body and Blood. Cornelius Bishop of Rome, in the History of Eusebius, informs us, that Novatus swore them that communicated with him never to return to their Bishop[q], "and when he had made the oblation, and distributed his share to every one, instead of saying 'Amen,' he that received answered, 'I will not return to Cornelius.'" Cyril of Jerusalem, giving directions for the reverent receiving the Communion, charges every one[r] "to pronounce 'Amen' both over the Body—and the Cup." "With what conscience," says St. Jerome[s], "shall I come to the Eucharist of the Lord, and answer 'Amen,' when I doubt of the charity of him that holds it out to me?" I might produce citations from St. Augustine and other Fathers to the same purpose, but because I suppose this to be a truth

(margin note: The primitive Church required an explicit belief of it.*)*

[n] a. p. 2, 3. Ap. 1. 18.   [o] h. p. 2. Ap.   [p] b. p. 7. Ap.
[q] a. p. 15. Ap.   [r] i. p. 19. Ap.   [s] f. p. 28. Ap.

CHAP.
II.

that none will dispute with me, I will only mention that of St. Ambrose[t]; "Christ Himself calls It His Blood. Before consecration It goes by another name; after consecration it is styled His Blood : thou answerest 'Amen;' this is true. Let your mind consent to what your mouth pronounces." By this last authority it is evident, that this "Amen" was not supposed to be optative or precatory, but affirmative; and it has, and will appear, that the ancients believed that the Bread and Wine became the Body and Blood by and upon the consecration; and that therefore it is not reconcileable to their opinion to suppose, that there was any occasion after that to pray that it might be made the Body and Blood; and the words used by them who administered were, as has been said, "the Body of Christ, the Blood of Christ,"—(to which the Constitution Liturgy adds, "the Cup of Life")— and these words imply no wish or prayer, but express the belief of the Church and of the administrator, that what was now distributed was the Body or Blood. There was no article inserted into any creed relating to the Eucharist; and the reason is very obvious, namely, that creeds were forms of Faith to be taught the catechumens in order to their Baptism; but the doctrine of the Eucharist was never delivered to any in the primitive Church, until after Baptism and confirmation. Therefore this article was peculiar to the initiated or communicants, and they professed it as often as they approached to the Lord's Table. And this leads me to observe,

The doctrine of the Eucharist a secret to all but communicants.

Thirdly, that the primitive Church did industriously conceal the matter and the manner of celebrating the Eucharist from all that had not a right actually to partake of it. This is by all acknowledged to have been the general practice of the ancient Church, and therefore I shall not spend time in proving it. The use which I at present make of it is, to observe to my reader, that they looked upon this doctrine as one of those pearls which were not to be thrown to swine, and indeed as the principal of them; for this was the last secret which was communicated to converts. The whole creed was taught the catechumens for some time before they were baptized; but this was the "hidden manna, the

[t] i. p. 27. Ap. l. 14.

wisdom of God in a mystery," which they never speak of
in words at length, but to the 'perfect' only.   The other
heads of Christian Faith the Fathers treated of freely and
apertly, in their homilies or sermons to the catechumens as
well as the faithful; but the doctrine of the Sacraments,
especially the Eucharist, they reserved for them only, whom
they thought fit to receive them.   The reasons they had for
the concealment of these mysteries were, in sum, to shew
the great esteem they had of them, and which they by this
means endeavoured to imprint upon all that were admitted
to the knowledge and enjoyment of them; and at the same
time to guard, and, if possible, to secure these holy institutions from the flouts and objections of Jews and Heathen
and of all whom they thought too light and frothy to be
entrusted with things so very weighty and serious and yet
of so peculiar a nature, that there was nothing in the world
that could in all respects be compared to them.   For they
justly believed, that the Sacraments were consecrated by the
Holy Ghost, and that therefore a Divine power went along
with them; which was reason enough why they should set
the highest value upon them, and desire that others should
do so too: and yet they knew the visible signs of these Sacraments to be 'beggarly elements,' things in their own
nature very cheap and common; and they might without
the gift of prophecy easily foresee, that the enemies of Christianity would always be ringing in the ears of all that were
well affected to Christianity, (as the Deists and Quakers are
perpetually labouring to persuade our people,) that there can
be no such effects of Water, Bread, and Wine, as Priests of
the Christian Church would have them believe.   And there
is one thing peculiar to the Eucharist, which made it more
liable to the scoffs of Anti-christian spirits, than any other
part of our religion; which is, that the Bread and Wine were
believed to be the very Body and Blood of Christ: no wonder,
if they were much upon the reserve in this point; since all
must be sensible, that nothing in the Christian theology
could have afforded more agreeable entertainment to the
drolls and buffoons of the age; for whatsoever is most extraordinary and elevated above the condition of other things,
which seem to be of the same sort, lies most exposed to

profane wit and mirth, when that which gives it it's worth and excellency can only be believed and not seen. And no doubt but Tertullian spoke the sense of all the learned Fathers of his own and of the succeeding times, in those observable words, "There is nothing does so much harden the minds of men as the simplicity of the Divine ministrations, which is seen in the [outward] action; and the magnificence, as to [their] efficacy, which is promised [to us[u].]" If the ancient Church had had no other notion of the Eucharist but that which now prevails among too many, that it is only a refreshing of our memory, and a symbol of love, or a federal rite; I can see no occasion why they should set such a guard about it, and use such a solicitous caution against exposing it to the eyes or ears of the profaners. The heathen philosophers and the Jewish Rabbies could scarce sink it lower than the Arminians and Socinians have done of late. And the candid Pliny gives as gentleman-like an account of it, in his letter to Trajan the Emperor, as some that go for Christian Divines in these latter ages. I am sensible that the ancient Fathers have been damned for Priest-craft upon the score of their drawing a vail before the Christian mysteries; for it is by our sciolists represented as Popery, to hide mysteries from the eyes of others. But now I am apt to think, that if the Papists affected only to conceal their Sacraments from the sight and knowledge of bigoted Jews, Turks, or Heathens, who were ready to profane, or however to loath or despise them; no man, that has a due regard for those holy institutions, would think them culpable on this account. The fault of the ruling part of the Church of Rome is not, that they keep their own people from the sight or knowledge of the Sacraments, for this they do not; but that they use a great deal of art and severity, in restraining their laity from looking into the Bible and other books, by which they might be informed of the errors of that Church, in things relating to the Sacrament and other heads of Christianity. The primitive Church not only permitted, but exhorted the laity to read the Scriptures; and took great care to instruct and train up all the people in the knowledge of the Eucharist and all other saving doctrines of Christianity; and withheld

[u] See the Latin in the title-page.

their mysteries from none, but such as they had good reason
to believe would scorn and deride rather than believe or make
a proper use of them. The catechumens were a sort of people
in a middle state, candidates or probationers only for Christianity; and as soon as the governors of the Church were
satisfied, that they were fixed and settled in the belief of the
general doctrines of the Gospel, such as were frequently read
to them out of Scripture and explained in the sermons or
homilies of the pastors; they were at their own request baptized, and so forthwith let into all the mysteries of religion;
and I wish with all my heart, that they, who make the Bread
and Wine to be mere symbols empty of all Divine grace,
may not pour contempt on this doctrine of the Eucharist, as
it was received in the primitive Church; and thereby give us
a fresh proof, that the ancients were obliged, in common prudence, to conceal the nature of this mystery from all that
were not initiated; and so at the same time justify the
ancient Fathers, and condemn themselves. For if they, who
would now be thought best to understand Christianity, and
[who] despise the ancients, as men that were not such critics
in languages as themselves, shall reject these notions of the
Eucharist as vain and groundless, which the Fathers with
good reason thought they had learned from our Saviour and
His Apostles; how much more may it be supposed, that they
would do the same, who had been born and bred Jews and
Heathens, and that were blinded with violent prejudices
against Christianity itself? However, that awe and reverence
with which the ancients treated the holy Eucharist, and the
care they took that their converts should do so too, is an unexceptionable proof, that they looked upon It as the most holy
and venerable institution of the Christian Church, as a spiritual mystery not to be divulged to any until they had given
sufficient proof of their integrity. I proceed to consider,

VI. By what means the Bread and Wine in the Eucharist By what
were by the ancients believed to be made the Body and Blood subordinate
means the
of Christ, the substance of Bread and Wine yet remaining. Bread was
Now I have already proved, that the Holy Ghost was, by the be made
the Body
vote of antiquity, the principal immediate cause of the Bread of Christ.
and Wine's becoming the Body and Blood. It now remains
only that I shew, that the subordinate or mediate cause of it

CHAP.
II.
is, 1. The reciting the words of institution. 2. The oblation of the symbols. 3. The prayer of invocation. All these three did, in the ancient Liturgies, immediately follow each other, in the order that I have mentioned them; and each of them was believed to contribute toward the consecration of the elements into the Body and Blood.

By the words of institution.
1. As to the words of institution, what St. Chrysostom says is very observable[x], " The Priest fulfilling his office stands pronouncing those words, but the power and grace is of God; that Word, 'This is My Body,' &c. changes the [gifts] laid in open view; and as the Word that says, 'Increase and multiply,' was but once pronounced, but is actually operative on our nature throughout all ages for the procreation of children; so that Voice once pronounced has it's effects on the prepared Sacrifice, on every Table of the Churches, from that time to this, and until His own Advent." St. Augustine attributes much to these words, when he says[y], " Before the words of Christ, what is offered is called Bread; after the words of Christ have been pronounced, It is no longer called Bread, but the Body." And I suppose what he says, at another place, is to be understood of the Eucharist as well as of Baptism[z], viz. " The Word is added to the element, and it becomes a Sacrament." St. Ambrose speaks to the same purpose[a], " This Bread Christ gave to His Apostles to divide among the multitude of believers, and gives it us this day, which the Priest himself consecrates with His words;" and[b] " Christ is manifestly declared to offer by us, and His word consecrates the Sacrifice which is offered." Some may suppose, that these words of St. Augustine and St. Ambrose are meant of the Lord's Prayer; especially because St. Augustine himself says[c], that " almost every Church used that Prayer, at the conclusion of the consecration;" and St. Jerome[d] gives us an intimation of the same practice; but since no truly ancient writer attributes any such power to that Prayer in express words, as they do to those of the institution, therefore I think it most rational to understand these Fathers in the sense before mentioned. I am

[x] l. p. 38. Ap.
[y] tt. p. 34. Ap.
[z] p. p. 33. Ap.
[a] a. p. 26. Ap.

[b] c. p. 26. Ap.
[c] c. p. 31. Ap. l. 6.
[d] g. p. 28.

sensible Gregory the Great is often cited for saying, *Apostolis* SECT.
in more fuisse, ut ad ipsam solummodo Orationem Dominicam I.
oblationis Hostiam consecrarent[e], that is, " It was the practice
of the Apostles to consecrate the oblation, by saying the Lord's
Prayer only ;" but I cannot think, that a writer of the latter
end of the sixth century is a competent witness to establish a
fact of this moment, when destitute of all testimony of the
earlier ages. Gregory Nyssen expressly attributes the consecration or change[f] to ' the Word of God ;' and presently intimates, that by the Word of God he means ' This is My Body.'
Origen seems to mean the same in saying[g], that "not the
Bread, but the Word spoken over it, is profitable ;" and I must
confess I cannot but take Irenæus in the same sense, in those
words of his[h], " when the Bread and Cup receive the Word of
God, they are made the Eucharist." I am sensible the excellent Dr. Grabe is willing by ' the Word of God ' to understand
the Divine Word or power : and that may be imported too in
St. Irenæus's expression, for he might justly suppose, that
those words of Christ carried Divine power with them ; but I
think it most natural to understand him as primarily meaning the Word spoken. And it is very evident to any one that
looks into the ancient Liturgies, that the consecration begins
by the Priest's pronouncing the words of institution, is continued by the solemn act of oblation, and finished by the invocation of the Holy Ghost. The Church of Rome attributes
the consecration wholly to the words of institution ; the Greek
Church wholly to the prayer of invocation ; but I conceive
the ancients did not attribute the consecration to any one of
these actions in such a manner as to exclude the other ; nay,
further,

2. They thought the oblation of the symbols necessary in Oblation
order to obtain a perfect consecration of them. To this pur- contributes
to the con-
pose St. Ambrose[i] speaks of " offering the Body to be changed secration of
or transfigured on the Altars." He calls It " the Body ;" and ments.
the ele-
yet supposes It to be offered, in order to receive a further

---

[e] [The passage in St. Gregory runs p. 276. ed. Par. 1619.]
thus : " Orationem vero Dominicam [f] a. p. 23, 24. Ap. l. 29.
idcirco mox post precem dicimus : quia [g] f. p. 10. Ap.
mos Apostolorum fuit, ut ad ipsam [h] g. p. 6. Ap. l. 5.
solummodo Orationem oblationis Hos- [i] n. p. 27. Ap.
tiam consecrarent."—Tom. iv. Ep. 64.

CHAP. change or consecration. To this purpose it is very observable,
II. that in the Liturgy of St. Basil, the Priest, after having pronounced the words of institution, offers the Bread and Wine
under the name of [k] "antitypes of the Body and Blood of
Christ;" and after this, prays for the Holy Spirit to "come
down and bless the gifts, and make[l] the Bread the Body, the
Wine the Blood of Christ." This for ever confounds the
doctrine of the Church of Rome, which asserts the elements
to be transubstantiated by the words of institution; and rather
inclines one to believe, that the ancients thought the elements
to be made the symbols or representatives of the mere material dead body and effused blood of Christ, by the authority
of the words of institution; but that in order to render them
the spiritual life-giving Body and Blood of our Saviour, it was
further necessary, that they should be offered to God and
accepted by Him; and that He thereupon should cause the
Holy Spirit, at the request of Priest and people, to give them
the finishing consecration. It is certain, that the judicious
and pious Fathers of the Constantinopolitan Council so often
mentioned did not think that the symbols were entirely consecrated at one instant, as appears by those words of theirs[m],
"The Eucharist becomes a Divine Body by means of the Priest,
who makes the oblation in it's passage from being common
to become holy." They clearly suppose a gradual process in
the consecration; and that during this process, viz. between
the words of institution and the prayer of invocation, the
Priest makes the oblation; whether their words imply, that
the oblation of itself does promote the consecration, I
leave to my reader's judgment. And if these Fathers did
not mean so much in these words, yet there can be no
doubt of the thing itself, if it be considered, that the
Fathers of the third century, St. Cyprian and Dionysius
of Alexandria, call the Eucharistical elements, "the holy
and most holy things of the Lord;" the former in several
places[n], the latter in his second canon; and so does Tertullian[o], who was their senior. For it is known that this
Lev. vii. 6; was the title given to the flesh of the peace-offering and
xix. 8.

[k] g. p. 57. Ap.
[l] Ἀναδεῖξαι does certainly in the
Liturgic language signify to 'make,'
'render,' &c.

[m] p. 51. Ap. l. 26.
[n] b. p. 11. Ap.; e. p. 11. Ap.; f. p.
11. Ap.
[o] b. p. 7. Ap.

sin-offering; and the reason of their being so styled was, SECT.
that they had been solemnly offered to God. And I have ──I.──
before shewed, that benedictions were of old passed upon men
by offering sacrifice in their behalf; and it is evident that
sacrifices were the chief medium, by which Aaron and his
sons were themselves consecrated to the priest's office; by
which I suppose it is evident, that the matter of sacrifices
was always looked upon, not only to be itself holy, but to be
a means of transferring holiness to others; to which purpose
also see Levit. vi. 27. Now whatever can communicate sanctity of any sort to others must be supposed to have sanctity
itself in a more perfect and plentiful manner. No wonder
therefore, if the ancient Church thought it necessary, that
the Bread and Wine, the symbols of Christ's Body and Blood,
should be offered to God, in order to make them capable of
the highest degree of sanctification that such creatures are
capable of; and therefore all the ancient Liturgies direct the
Priest first to make the oblation, then to pray for the descent
of the Holy Spirit, or the Divine benediction, which last is
the usual expression of the Latin Liturgies : and they all
agree in begging of God " to look graciously on the gifts,"
and to vouchsafe the Spirit, or heavenly blessing, as the
effect of His accepting the oblation. So that the Eucharist
was supposed to acquire some degree of sanctification by
being presented to God; not only by reason that the very
offering it to God was a consecration of it, but because by
being offered to God and accepted by Him it was thought
to be prepared and qualified for the most eximious degree of
sanctification, that can be communicated to bread and wine[p].
I shall on this head further mention the words of Irenæus[q];
" We offer to God, as sanctifying the creatures ;" which sufficiently shews his opinion, that the symbols received some
degree of sanctification by being made an oblation. And
when St. Ignatius[r] calls the Eucharist " the Bread of God,"
he not only intimates that it was offered to God, but that by
being offered it was consecrated; for whatever was of old
styled " the Bread of God" was thought to be holy, and to

[p] "And indeed, by the law of Moses, nothing could be made the most holy, or 'the holy of the Lord,' but what had been first in the most solemn man-ner presented to God." [1st ed.]
[q] f. p. 5, 6. Ap. l. 32.
[r] a. p. l. Ap.

become holy, by being offered to the Almighty. We meet with this phrase, Lev. xxi. 6, where the priests are charged not to profane themselves, because "they offer the bread of their God." And again, ver. 7, 8, "The priest is holy unto God; for he offereth the bread of Thy God." And it is said to Aaron, ver. 17, "Whosoever he be of thy seed, that hath a blemish, let him not approach to offer the bread of His God." And ver. 21, "He hath a blemish, he shall not come near to offer the bread of His God." From these places it is evident to a demonstration, that what is called "the bread of God" was somewhat solemnly offered by the priest; and what part of the sacrifice was particularly distinguished by this name, you may learn, Lev. iii. 11, for there it is said of the two kidneys, the fat, and caul, taken from the beast sacrificed for a peace-offering, that "the priest shall burn it on the altar; it is the bread of the offering made by fire unto the Lord." It is evident then, that that portion of the sacrifice which was burnt on the altar was particularly distinguished by this name of 'the bread of God.' (Our English translators turn לחם 'food,' in the place last mentioned, but 'bread' in the other places.) And the very same thing is meant by the bread of God, Lev. xxii. 25, where the priest is forbid "to offer the bread of God from the hands of a stranger;" but in the twenty-second verse of the twenty-first chapter, it is taken in so large a sense, as to include that part of the sacrifice for sin and the peace-offerings, which were reserved to be eaten by the priest. For it is there said of the priest that had a blemish, that "he shall eat of the bread of His God, both of the most holy, and the holy." By the "most holy" is meant, the priest's part of the sin-offering; by "the holy," the priest's part of the peace-offering. The conclusion therefore is unavoidable, that when St. Ignatius calls the Eucharist "the Bread of God," he means some material thing offered to God, and sanctified or consecrated by means of that oblation. I now proceed to prove,

The consecration of the elements finished by the prayer of invocation.
3. That the ancients believed the consecration of the elements was finished by means of the prayer of invocation. And since I have already made it appear, that it is the Holy Spirit, Which consecrates the gifts, and makes the true life-giving Body of Christ; and that in the primitive Church, the prayer

for the descent of the Spirit to render the Bread the Body of
Christ comes after the words of institution and the commemorative oblation, therefore the thing is in effect proved already;
for if the elements were by either or both the former means
fully consecrated, what occasion to invoke the Holy Spirit for
the further consecration of them? They are indeed by the
words of institution deputed to represent the crucified Body
and effused Blood of Christ, and as such are offered to God;
but this Body of Christ is not quickened by the supervening
power of the Spirit of God, before That Spirit is by prayer
invited to consummate the holy mysteries; but I will further
(because it seems to me a matter of considerable moment)
shew, that it was the current opinion of the ancients, that it
was by this prayer of consecration that the elements were
finally and completely consecrated. Now the words of Theodoret, in his second Dialogue, are very home to this purpose[s];
" What do you call the gift" (says Eranistes) " before the invocation of the Priest?" Orthodoxus answers, " Food made
of such and such grains." Eranistes, " How do we call the
other symbol?" Orthodoxus, "A certain liquor," &c. Eranist.,
" How do you call them after consecration?" Orthod., " The
Body and Blood of Christ." It is observable, that the Clementine Constitutions, in the commemorative oblation, calls
what is offered[t], "The Bread and Cup;" not that they did
not look upon them to be the representative Body and Blood,
but because they deemed them to be made the Body and
Blood in a more exalted sense after the prayer of invocation
had been made. Theodoret in this very Dialogue[u] says, " The
mystical symbols offered by the Priests are the mystical
symbols of the Body and Blood." And at another place[x],
" The Church offers the symbols of His Body and Blood."
Victor Antiochenus says[y], " After the benediction is added
to the Bread and Cup, by the symbols of Bread men partake of the Body, by the Cup, of the Blood of Christ." Chrysostom[z] attributes the " consummation of the mysteries to
the invocation of the Holy Spirit." And[a], " When the Priest
stands before the Table, stretching out his hands to heaven,

[s] m. p. 46. Ap.
[t] c. p. 53. Ap. l. 29.
[u] l. p. 46. Ap.
[x] d. p. 45. Ap. l. 9.
[y] p. 43. Ap.
[z] i. p. 38. Ap.
[a] m. p. 39. Ap.

CHAP.
II.

invocating the Holy Spirit that He would come and give the contact, then all is whist[b], &c. but when the Holy Spirit sheds His grace," &c. He supposes that the contact is not vouchsafed, until after the prayer of consecration is ended. Again[c], "The Priest stands, bringing down not fire but the Holy Ghost; and makes an ample supplication, not that a torch let down from above may consume the [gifts] laid in open view, but that grace, lighting on the Sacrifice, may by that [Sacrifice] inflame the hearts of all." St. Augustine supposes[d], "The prayers properly so called (προσευχαὶ, he is speaking of 1 Tim. ii. 1.) to be made at the consecration of the Bread, and in preparing it for the distribution;" and more directly[e], "We call That only the Body and Blood of Christ, Which is consecrated by a mystic prayer," &c. St. Ambrose says[f], that "the sacred things are changed into the Flesh and Blood of Christ by a mystic prayer." Nay[g], that "the nature of the elements is changed by the benediction." Ephræm Syrus[h] represents Priests bowing down before the lofty Throne,—"praying that the Holy Spirit may descend, and consecrate the gifts placed in open view." "Which of the saints," says Basil the Great[i], "hath left us in writing the form of invocation, at the consecrating[k] the Bread of the Eucharist and the Cup of *eulogy?*" Optatus's *quo postulatus descendit Spiritus* has been mentioned before, and so need only be hinted here. Cyril of Jerusalem has been already produced, as mentioning a prayer[l], in which God was beseeched to "send His Holy Spirit to make the Bread the Body," &c. Again, he tells us[m], "Before the invocation of the adored Trinity, it was mere bread and wine; but the invocation once made, the Bread becomes the Body of Christ, the Wine the Blood." And[n], "The Bread of the Eucharist, after the invocation of the Holy Spirit, is not mere bread, but the Body of Christ." Origen[o] gives us his opinion, that "the loaves

---

[b] [πολλὴ ἡσυχία, 'there is great stillness.']
[c] h. p. 38. Ap.
[d] c. p. 31. Ap. l. 8.
[e] R. p. 37. Ap.
[f] e. p. 26. Ap.
[g] i. p. 27. Ap.
[h] a. p. 25. Ap.
[i] e. p. 23. Ap.

[k] 'Αναδείξις is the word here and elsewhere used for consecrating or rendering the Bread and Wine, the Body and Blood.
[l] f. p. 19. Ap.
[m] a. p. 18. Ap.
[n] aa. p. 18. Ap.
[o] a. p. 9. Ap.

are made a certain Holy Body by prayer." He does not say
the Body of Christ; because he was speaking to heathen.
And again[p], "That the sanctified Bread is profitable, according to the prayer made over it." And Irenæus[q], "The earthly
bread receiving the invocation is no longer common bread,
but the Eucharist, consisting of two things, an earthly and
heavenly." These two last mentioned were before produced
to prove the words of the institution, and so were St. Chrysostom, St. Augustine, and others; and I will here add, that
Gregory Nyssen[r] and some others do apply to the Eucharist
those words of the Apostle, "It is sanctified by the Word of
God and prayer;" which makes it evident, that the ancients
did not think it any way inconsistent to say, that the Eucharist was consecrated, both by one means and the other; nay,
that they thought both of them necessary to this purpose.
St. Justin Martyr is very express[s], "that the food is eucharistized by prayer, and becomes the Body and Blood of the
incarnate Jesus." St. Ignatius makes mention of this prayer,
though he does not expressly take notice of it's being designed
for the consecration; for he says, the heretics he spake of[t]
"abstained from the Eucharist and prayer, because they did
not acknowledge the Eucharist to be the Body of Christ
Jesus." The reason given why they abstained from prayer
is the same with that, for which they abstained from the Eucharist, viz. because they did not believe it to be the Body
of Christ; now this is no reason at all, why they should
abstain from all prayer; for I suppose there is no manner
of dependence or connexion between the duty of prayer in
general, and the real Body of Christ. Nor can it be conceived, how they could argue against the use of all prayer
whatsoever, though it were granted them, that Christ had
no Body, but only in appearance; but this opinion of theirs
was a very good reason, why they should abstain from the
prayer of consecration used in the Church, because that
prayer was formed upon these two certain truths, that Christ
had a real Body, which was born of the blessed Virgin and
suffered under Pontius Pilate, and that the Bread in the

p f. p. 10. Ap.
q f. p. 5, 6. Ap. l. 26.
r a. p. 23, 24. Ap. l. 34, 35.

s a. p. 2. Ap. l. 18.
t h. p. 2. Ap.

Sacrament was That Body in power and effect; and in such
a prayer they could not indeed sincerely join; and therefore
of such a prayer must these words be understood.   The
learned Cotelerius, in his note on these words[u], observes,
that by prayer is meant that of consecration; and cites the
words of St. Jerome, *ad Evagrium*[x], 85, where speaking of
Priests, he says, " at their prayers the Body and Blood of
Christ are perfectly consecrated," (*conficitur* is the Latin
word); they were before symbols, by this means they become
the true spiritual Body and Blood; and as the whole is sometimes denominated from one part, so he shews that by ' the
prayer' is sometimes understood the whole Eucharistical office;
as at other places, the word 'Sacrifice' or 'oblation' carries the
same signification.   He supposes, that by " the prayers of the
Sacrifices," mentioned by Tertullian[y], we are chiefly to understand this of consecration; and I may add, that when the
seventh *alias* tenth[z] Apostolical Canon[a] censures those who
come to church but " do not stay for the Communion and
prayers," we are to take those words in the same sense that
we do St. Ignatius's Eucharist and prayer.   And it is observable, that even heretics, when they invented new schemes of
worship, and erected new Altars, did also form new prayers
of consecration; as appears from those words of St. Cyprian[b],
" The enemy of the Altar, the rebel against the Sacrifice of
Christ, dares to constitute another Altar, and offer another
prayer with an unlicensed mouth;" and so Irenæus[c] represents Marcus as " spinning out a prayer of invocation to a
great length," in order to procure the *charis* to descend on
his Eucharistical Cup.   And indeed Ignatius seems to explain
what he means by prayer in the place now cited, by what he
says elsewhere; for immediately after those words[d], " If any
one be not within the Altar-place, he is deprived of the Bread
of God;" he adds, " If the prayer of one or two have so great

[u] [" Multa et gravia peccat ad hunc
locum oppugnator Epistolarum nostra-
rum. 1. perperam accipit vocem προσευχῆς latissimo modo pro omni prorsus oratione: cum Ignatius aut loqua-
tur de prece mystica, oratione sollenni,
qua Corpus Christi conficitur. Hie-
ronym. Epist. 85.—Aut potius intelligat preces Liturgicas sive Missam,
juxta—'Sacrificiorum orationes' in Ter-

tulliano, lib. De Oratione extremo."—
Cotelerius in S. Ign. Ep. ad Smyrn.
cap. vii.]
[x] [i. e. Evangelum.]
[y] i. p. 8. Ap.
[z] p. 48. Ap.
[a] [Canon 9.]
[b] d. p. 11. Ap.
[c] a. p. 3. Ap.
[d] a. p. 1. Ap.

force, how much more the prayer of the Bishop and the whole Church?" for these words seem to import, that the efficacy of the Eucharist, which he calls "the Bread of God," is in a great measure to be attributed to the prayer of consecration: so that few truths are better supported from antiquity than this. And when our Saviour is said by the Evangelists to have blessed or eucharistized the Bread and Cup, it probably implies that He did address Himself to His Divine Father, that the Sacrifice now offered by Him might be replenished with such inward energy, as was necessary for the ends to which It was intended. At another place this word $εὐχαριστεῖν$ is used, to denote our Saviour's working a very great miracle in nature, I mean, His multiplying the loaves, see John vi. 11. 23; and though I do not see any reason to believe, that either Jesus Christ in the first Eucharist, or His Apostles, or other Ministers afterward, did exert any miraculous power in consecrating the Sacrament; yet it must be asserted, that all the actings of the Spirit are preternatural, whether these actings do affect immaterial or material things. And when St. Paul speaks of "the Cup of blessing which we bless," as it is evident beyond dispute, that he means the Cup in the Eucharist; so neither is it less plain in itself, that the Apostle supposes, that there was a Divine benediction imparted to it, and that this benediction was procured by what we now call a prayer of consecration; for to suppose, that the Cup was blessed by no other means than by giving thanks over it, or by making an acknowledgment to God for the benefit of His material creatures, is neither consistent with the grammatical construction of the words, nor with the sentiments of the ancients just now laid before the reader; so that in this, as well as in other particulars, there is an admirable harmony between the words of the Apostle and the primitive Church. And it is evident, that the ancients promiscuously use the word Eucharist and *Eulogy*. St. Irenæus[e] instead of saying the Cup of *Eulogy* or blessing, when he cites the words of the Apostle St. Paul in the tenth chapter of 1 Cor. ver. 18, says, "the Cup of Eucharist;" and St. Cyril of Alexandria and Gregory Nyssen do familiarly use *Eulogy* for the Sacramental Body. I am sensible some of the Church of Rome

[e] g. p. 6. Ap.

CHAP.
II.
would persuade us, that this prayer in the ancient Greek Liturgies for the descent of the Holy Ghost, and in most of the Latin Liturgies for the Divine benediction, imports no more than a request to God, that the Body of Christ and the Blood of Christ in the Eucharist may be truly so to the receivers, and that they may take Them to their salvation, and not their condemnation; and therefore they so paraphrase them, as if the construction were, "make them the Body and the Blood of Christ [to us];" but these last words are in none of the ancient Liturgies, and this is only a gloss of theirs, without any foundation in the Liturgies themselves. The Clementine Liturgy prays for the Holy Ghost[f] "to make the Bread the Body of Christ," and this after the words of institution and commemorative oblation; which can never be reconciled to the present doctrine of the Church of Rome, which supposes the change wrought by these words, "This is My Body, This is My Blood;" and is an undeniable proof, that the composer of this Liturgy did not believe, that the Eucharistical symbols were fully consecrated before this prayer was uttered; and the same may be said of St. James's Liturgy[g], St. Mark's[h], St. Basil's[i], and St. Chrysostom's[k], as the reader may see in the Appendix.

Oblation not finished until after consecration.
There is one thing, of which I cannot advertise my reader more seasonably than in this place; namely, that though the solemn oblation begins in all the Liturgies after the words of institution, and before the [invocation of the] Holy Spirit or the Divine benediction; yet the sacrificial service is not ended until after the consecration. For it is to be observed, that the Clementine Liturgy[l], St. James's[m], St. Chrysostom's[n], St. Peter's[o], St. Gregory's[p], contain a prayer for the acceptance of the Sacrifice; and particularly, that it "may be received up to the heavenly Altar," after the consecration is fully ended: and the most solemn propitiations, intercessions, reconciliations for the whole Church, for all orders and degrees of men, for all the most desirable graces and favours, follow after the consecration, in the Clementine

[f] c. p. 52, 53. Ap. 1. 37.
[g] f. h. p. 55. Ap.
[h] c. p. 56. Ap.
[i] f. g. p. 56, 57. Ap.
[k] d. p. 57. Ap.

[l] d. p. 54. Ap.
[m] i. p. 55. Ap.
[n] f. p. 58. Ap.
[o] c. p. 58. Ap.
[p] c. p. 59. Ap.

Liturgy[q]. And these no doubt were esteemed a considerable
part of the sacrificial service; and these were performed, after
the symbols had been made the spiritual Body and Blood, in
the most perfect and complete manner that it was possible
for one thing, it's substance remaining, to become another.
It was the Eucharistical Body and Blood, Which were the
gifts or Sacrifice, Which they desired might be assumed up
to the Altar in heaven, in the same sense that Cornelius's The Altar
in heaven.
alms, Acts x., "came up for a memorial before God;" and
that the sacrifice of Melchisedec and Abel (which were
certainly material) had the same honour vouchsafed to them:
these last are particularly mentioned in the Liturgy of St.
Peter[r], [and of] St. Gregory[s]. And these propitiations, or
whatever other name the reader is pleased to give them, are
found in all the Liturgies; as the reader, who has opportunity
of inspecting the Liturgies themselves, may satisfy himself;
but they were too long to be transcribed. Now we cannot in
reason say, that this latter part of the sacrificial service is to
be distinguished from the former, so as to make two several
oblations; no more than the sprinkling the blood, and burning the flesh of the same animal, under the Law, made the
one animal to be two. It may be justly said, that the whole
animal was in some measure consecrated to God, by having
it's blood sprinkled on the altar; but in a more perfect
manner still, by being in whole or in part laid on the fire;
for by this means it became "the bread" or meat "of God,"
in the Levitical language; and the reader will not want a
mystagogue to help him in applying this to the Sacrifice of
the Eucharist.

There are two considerable inferences, which follow from
what we have been proving. The first is, that the Eucharist
was by the ancients believed to be made the Body and Blood
of Christ, not by the faith of the receiver or communicant,
but the power of the Holy Ghost, or Divine benediction, imparted to it by means of the invocation: the other is, that
the primitive Christians expected to receive no other Body
and Blood, but the Bread and Wine thus sanctified.

1. It is evident that they believed the Eucharist to be The faith of
the com-
made the Body and Blood, not by the faith of the communi- municant

[q] c. p. 53. Ap. l. 39.   [r] c. p. 58. Ap.   [s] c. p. 59. Ap.

CHAP.
II.

does not
make the
Bread the
Body.

cant, but by the power of the Holy Ghost, or Divine benediction, imparted to it by means of the invocation: (I mean
perfectly and finally imparted by this means, not exclusively
of the words of institution and the oblation.) And this I suppose fully appears from those authorities above cited; and if
any doubt of it, I must desire him to give himself the leisure
of reviewing the passages produced, to shew that the ancients
esteemed the symbols to be made the Body and Blood by
the supervening energy of the Spirit; and those under the
last head, which prove that they thought the words of institution, the oblation, and invocation, to be effectual for rendering the elements the spiritual mysterious Body and Blood.
And this further appears from their way of distributing the
Communion, which has before been mentioned. The administrator affirms what he gives to be the Body or Blood, without
any certain knowledge whether the receiver had faith or not;
the receiver answers 'Amen,' and by this gives his assent and
consent to the affirmation of the administrator, before he
had actually received what was held forth to him. And indeed, if the Eucharist were not the Body and Blood before
distribution, it could not be made so by any post-fact of the
communicants; for faith can give existence to nothing, cannot alter the nature of things. But I apprehend that this
may be further proved from the practice of the primitive
Church, in reserving some part of the Eucharistical Bread
and Wine; for this proves not only that they thought it the
Body and Blood, without any respect to the faith of the
receiver, but that its consecration was permanent, and remained after the holy action was at an end. What was not
received by any at the Holy Table could not there be made
the Body and Blood by the faith of the communicant; and yet
if they did not believe it to be the Body and Blood, for what
purpose should they reserve it? That the holy Eucharist
was reserved in the Church or in the Bishop's house, is a
thing so well known, that I see no occasion to repeat what
others have said; but St. Basil affords us an ample testimony
that the Eucharist was reserved in some places, even by the
laity; and that it was as effectually the Eucharist, as if it had
been really received at the Altar. These are his words[t], "In

Reserva-
tion of the
Sacrament
proves that
the ancients
believed
the conse-
cration to
be perma-
nent.

[t] d. p. 23. Ap.

Alexandria and in Egypt, every one of the laity has the Communion in his own house; for when the Priest has consummated the Sacrifice, and distributed It, he that takes It ought in reason to believe, that he so partakes and receives It, as that he partakes of the whole together in every part from him who distributed It." We have heard Tertullian[u] already advising the laymen in one case to this practice. And he has another remarkable passage to this purpose in lib. ii. *ad uxorem*, where he tells a Christian woman, that if she had a heathen for her husband, he would not know "what It was that she tasted privately before any other victuals, and if he know that It is bread, yet he will not believe It to be what It is called[x]." Which words, though they are in other respects dark, for which reason I have not made use of them under any other head of my discourse; yet I think it very evident that even women in Africa were permitted to reserve the Eucharist in their houses, and to receive at home at discretion, in Tertullian's time. Nay, we are certain that this practice was much more ancient than Tertullian, at least as to the Bishop's reserving some portions of It. For St. Irenæus, in his letter to Victor, tells him, that his predecessors, the Bishops of Rome, though they did not keep Easter in the same manner that other Bishops did, yet " sent the Eucharist" to those Bishops[y]. The story of the sick Priest's sending the Eucharist, which he had ready consecrated by him, to Serapion, a lapsed communicant, but a penitent and now at the point of death, as reported by Dionysius Bishop of Alexandria, is very remarkable to this purpose[z]. And even Justin Martyr[a] testifies, that Deacons did not only give the Eucharist to them that were present, but " carried It to those who were absent." Now certainly the primitive Fathers never thought of sending mere bread and wine to their brethren or to the faithful who could not attend the public congregation; and consequently, they thought the benediction which they had received on the Lord's Table was not transient, so as to cease as soon as the celebration was con-

[u] i. p. 8. Ap.
[x] ["Non sciet maritus quid secreto ante omnem cibum gustes ? et si sciverit panem, non Illum credit esse Qui dicitur ?"—P. 169. ed. Paris. 1664.]
[y] Irenæus, p. 466 of Grabe's ed.
[z] See Euseb. Eccl. Hist., lib. vi.
c 44.
[a] a. p. 2. Ap.

CHAP.
II.

cluded; and therefore they did not imagine that their being the Body and Blood of Christ depended on the faith of those who did eat or drink It. The words of St. Hilary seem to sound to a contrary sense, viz.[b], "By the declaration of the Lord, and by our faith, it is truly His Flesh and Blood." But these words may import no more than that by the declaration of the Lord and our faith we are assured or have a full conviction, that they are the Body and Blood; not that the faith of the communicant makes them to be so. However the authority of a single Father, that was not very ancient, can by no means stand against the whole stream of antiquity.

Ancients expected to receive no Body of Christ, but the Eucharistical.

2. The other inference is, that the primitive Church expected to receive no other Body and Blood of Christ, but the Bread and Wine thus consecrated. They had no occasion to desire any other. For though they believed it to be Bread and Wine, yet they were at the same time of opinion that they were filled with all that Divine grace and efficacy that His natural Body was; and that if they had had His very natural Body, and had had stomachs and consciences to have eaten It, It could not have conveyed to them any benefit, which was not as effectually communicated to them by the Eucharistical Body and Blood. Was His natural Body anointed with the Spirit? so was His Sacramental; was His natural Body a spiritual, life-giving Body? so was His Sacramental; was His natural Body made a Sacrifice for the life of men? so was His Sacramental, as has been shewed at large; so that it will be very difficult for a man to imagine any reason why they should have any thoughts of receiving two Bodies of Christ. Nay, they could not but know that if they had the very natural Body, It would have been impossible to receive It; for neither their teeth nor their appetites would have served them; and this notion carries so much absurdity with it, that I shall add no more but the *scomma* which St. Augustine made use of against the Manicheans; "Do you expect that any one should thrust Christ into your jaws, as the most proper sepulchre[c]?" If others please them-

---

[b] a. p. 20. Ap. l. 12.

[c] ["Ore aperto expectatis quis inferat Christum, tanquam optimæ se-

pulturæ, faucibus vestris?"—Contra Faustum Manichæum, lib. xx. cap. 11. tom. vi. p. 153. ed. Par. 1635.]

selves with a fancy of devouring the natural Body of Christ in-
tellectually, or by faith, let me ask them whether they suppose
This natural Body present in the Eucharist or not. If It be
present, It is so in an invisible manner; and for the natural
Body of Christ to be present in ten thousand places at once,
is impossible in the nature of things; and I cannot but think,
that it is as impossible for It to be present in an invisible
manner, as to be in several places at the same time. It can
therefore be only present in the imaginations of men, and
consequently their eating of It must be only imaginary; and
if It were present at every Eucharist in a visible manner, this
would be so far from feeding our faith, that it would in reality
destroy it. For " Faith is the substance" or confidence " of
things not seen ;" and if we had the enjoyment of the substance, our faith and hope must presently vanish away. If
they believe that they eat the natural Body of Christ by that
faith by which they are persuaded that this Body of Christ
suffered for their sins, and that this Body of Christ is now at
God's right hand, I will only say that this is not that eating
of His Flesh or Body which we are now speaking of, and
which is peculiar to the Eucharist. For they who entertain
this notion do at the same time suppose that they may as
effectually eat His Flesh in any other act of religion, as in
the Sacrament; and all this I believe to be the invention of
men, and not so much as an *ens rationis*, but a mere creature
of fancy. And as for any personal spiritual Body of Christ,
Which communicates Itself to faithful people, Which Barclay
calls the *heavenly seed* or the *light within;* It is, I dare affirm,
as far from the truth and from the judgment of the primitive
Church, and of the Apostles and holy penmen, as this eight-
teenth century is from the first and purest age of Christianity.
But I apprehend some of my readers may, notwithstanding
what I have yet said, suspect that the ancients did believe
that they had and received the very natural Body and Blood
in the Holy Eucharist; and therefore I shall,

Seventhly, consider some seeming excesses of the ancients
on this head. Now,

[1. In the first place it may be objected, that the Fathers Seeming
seem to speak of a sort of worship due to the Sacrament; and excesses of
the ancients
this must, with good reason, sound very harsh in the ears of considered.

Protestants, who believe the idolatry of the Papists, in worshipping the host, to be one of the greatest abominations of
the Church of Rome. The passages of the ancients, which
give umbrage to this objection, are that of Theodoret[d], "they
are believed and venerated as really being What they are
believed to be;" and that of Cyril of Jerusalem[e], who directs
his young communicant to take the Body of Christ with his
hands framed into somewhat like a throne; and to approach
the Cup in a bowing posture, and with a sort of veneration
or profound reverence. The Clementine Liturgy exhorts
people[f] to receive It "with awe and reverence," and to come
to It "as to the Body of the King." And that of St. Augustine looks the same way[g], where by "the footstool" of God
he understands "the earth," by "the earth" Christ's Flesh
Which He has given us to eat, and no man eats It, says He,
nisi prius adoraverit, "till he has first made adoration or
obeisance; therefore," as he adds, "when you stoop, or bend
down your body to any earth, look not upon it as earth, but
as that Holy One in honour of Whom you adore the footstool," &c. I must confess I think the words *quamlibet terram* cannot without a very unnatural force be wrested to
mean any thing but the Eucharistical Body, especially because it is evident by what follows, that he had that Sacrament in his eye; and it is probable there may be other
passages in the ancients, like these already mentioned; and
I desire my reader, in order to take off the force of this
objection, to consider,

They did
not pay to
Divine
honour.
(1.) That Theodoret does, in this very Dialogue, and in the
words immediately foregoing, declare, that "the Bread departs
not from its own nature," &c. as he has been before cited;
and no one can believe, that a man of Theodoret's sense would
pay Divine honour to bread; nay, he himself expressly declares
his mind to the contrary; for, says he[h], "It is the last folly
to worship what is eaten;" and[i], "How can any man in his
wits either call that a god, which he abominates and abhors,
or even what is offered to the true God and eaten by himself?" He is indeed in these places speaking directly of the

---

[d] m. p. 46. Ap. l. 14.   [g] s. p. 33. Ap. l. 7.
[e] i. p. 19. Ap.   [h] a. p. 45. Ap.
[f] d. p. 54. Ap. l. 13.   [i] c. p. 45. Ap.

reason of God's forbidding to the Jews the eating of some such things, as were worshipped as gods by the heathen; and of the Jews being commanded by Moses's law to offer those creatures, which were worshipped by the heathen, in sacrifice to the true God; but it is not to be supposed, that such a writer as Theodoret would have expressed himself in this manner, if he had known of any Divine worship paid by Christians to what they offered and eat in the Sacrament. It is therefore evident, that when he speaks of a veneration paid to the Eucharist, he can only mean such a decent and reverential respect as is due to a creature sanctified to such excellent purposes, as the Eucharist is; and the same may be said of the other citations; and to convince you, that when they speak of venerating the Sacrament, they meant no other honour but what was due to bread appointed for these purposes; I will desire you to observe, that Ambrose supposes that Abraham paid this respect to Melchisedec's bread and wine. For[j] Melchisedec "brought forth," says he, "what Abraham venerated," as being the symbols of Christ's Body and Blood. For it must be owned, that they looked on the consecrated symbols as creatures not to be treated otherwise than as the representative Body and Blood of Christ, consecrated by the Spirit of God; and this must be St. Augustine's meaning, when he says, "Look not on It as earth, but as the Holy One." Not as the personal Christ Jesus Himself, but as Bread and Wine deputed to be His Body and Blood; Which Body and Blood, by a usual metonymy, are often called Christ; and that this is his meaning is very evident from the next words, viz. "It is His footstool which you adore, for you adore on His account; therefore he subjoined, 'adore His footstool, because it is holy.' Who is holy? He, in honour of Whom you adore His footstool." He clearly distinguishes between Christ Himself, and His 'footstool,' or 'earth.' He makes all the honour or reverence paid to the latter to be done, not so much for it's own sake, as for His Whose footstool it is; so that, instead of making the Eucharist to be, or to contain the whole Person of Christ Jesus, he clearly makes it His footstool; but at the same time supposes, that an honour is

[j] h. p. 27. Ap.

CHAP. to be paid to it; and what the honour was, it will not be hard
II.   to conceive, if we consider,

(2.) That προσκυνεῖν and *adorare* do not in the ecclesiastical language necessarily import worshipping any thing
with Divine honour.   It is certain that the Hebrew שחה does
ordinarily signify no more than to ‘bow down,’ not so much
as ‘to prostrate one’s-self,’ except ארצה be added.   The Greek
turns it by προσκυνεῖν, the Latin by *adorare*, (see Gen. xxiii. 7,
and the parallel places,) and these are the words used by Theodoret and St. Augustine; and these words are very far from
importing Divine worship, unless you will suppose that Abraham made gods of the children of Heth in the place now
cited; nor will St. Augustine’s *prosternis* imply Divine
honour, except you will give it for granted that Joseph’s
brethren deified him, when “they bowed themselves” *in ter-*
Gen. xlii. 6. *ram,* ἐπὶ τὴν γῆν, “to the ground” to him.   It must be owned
that St. Augustine’s way of expression is not very clear in
this place; but the most he can mean is, that some in his
age did prostrate themselves, when they approached the
Eucharistical Body: but it is very evident that by this they
intended no more, if they did it in St. Augustine’s sense,
than to shew their respects to the footstool of Jesus Christ;
or if they meant any higher degree of worship, it was directed
to Christ Himself.   Cyril of Jerusalem, besides the word
προσκύνησις, uses σέβασμα; but neither will this word necessarily import Divine worship; except you will suppose that
as often as the holy penmen called the emperor Σεβαστὸς,
they meant thereby that he was to be worshipped as God;
and indeed this word being in those ages so familiarly applied
to the emperors, it cannot be wondered that a Christian writer
should speak of the honour which he thought due to the
Sacrament, in this style; and the Clementine Liturgy is the
best comment upon it, when it admonishes men to approach
the Sacrament as the body of a king, that is, with an honour
or reverence very far from what is properly due to God.

(3.) It is very evident that the ancients did not, could not
worship the Eucharist with Divine honour; because they did
not believe that the Divinity of Christ was hypostatically
united to the Bread and Wine, as they did believe It to
be united to His natural Body.   Here Theodoret is very

express[k], "Our Lord did not promise to give His invisible
nature, but His Body, for the life of the world; 'for the
Bread' says He, 'I will give is My Flesh,' &c., and in delivering the Divine mysteries He said, 'This is My Body;'" and
again[l], "Our Saviour taking the symbol said not, 'This is
My Divinity;' but, 'This is My Body.'" Cyril of Alexandria
makes the same distinction, when speaking of the Eucharist
he says[m], "We must not think the Body of the Lord a common thing, because the Divinity cannot be eaten." And so
does St. Ambrose[n], "If thou offerest His Body to be transfigured on the Altar, but dost not distinguish the nature of
His Divinity and of His Body, it is said to thee also (as it
was to Cain, according to the LXX, Gen. iv. 7), If thou
offerest rightly, but dividedst not rightly, thou hast sinned[o];"
and the Church of Rome is grossly guilty of this sin, by pretending to make an oblation of the whole Christ, God and
Man. Epiphanius[p] says of the Eucharistical Body, that "as
to It's power It is without sense;" when therefore St. Hilary
says[q], that "we receive the Word" in the Eucharist, and
when other ancients speak of Jesus Christ Himself as offered
and received there, they must be understood as expressing
their judgment, that they were united to the Second Divine
Person by means of the especial presence of the Spirit in the
Eucharist. And when the ancients say that the Spirit "descended" and "gave a contact" to the holy symbols, or that
It filled the gifts with "energy, power," or the like, they do
not mean that the Holy Ghost was united to the Sacrament,
as the soul is to a human body, or as the Divine nature was
to Christ's natural Body; but that the Eucharistical Body
and Blood were so affected by the Spirit, in a way imperceptible by us, as to exert Itself in a peculiar manner in and by
them, in producing such effects in the receivers as are beneficial to their bodies and souls. The Spirit was never hypostatically united to the natural Body of Christ, but yet did
exert Itself in a miraculous manner in and by that Body of
His; and though now we believe It ceases to act miracu-

---

[k] h. p. 46. Ap.
[l] k. p. 46. Ap.
[m] h. p. 44. Ap.
[n] n. p. 27. Ap.

[o] [Οὐκ ἐὰν ὀρθῶς προσενέγκῃς, ὀρθῶς δὲ μὴ διέλῃς, ἥμαρτες;]
[p] c. p. 22. Ap. l. 6.
[q] a. p. 20. Ap.

lously, yet we doubt not but that It is, upon all occasions, ready to work in It's usual method, and to convey It's graces by It's wonted channels to the whole Church and every member; but it does not therefore follow, that the Eucharistical symbols do upon that account deserve Divine worship.

(4.) Nay, we have certain evidence and direct proof that the Eucharist was not worshipped with Divine honour, from St. Chrysostom's Liturgy; where[r] the Priest says to God the Father, "Look down on those who have bowed their heads to Thee; for they bowed not to flesh and blood, but to Thee the tremendous God." The prayer ends with these words, "by the grace—of Jesus Christ, with Whom blessed art Thou with the most Holy Ghost;" which I add as a demonstration, that the prayer was directed to the First Person of the blessed Trinity. And the council of Constantinople so often mentioned, though it speaks of "honouring the image of Christ," and says, "the image of His Body (the Eucharist) was wrought in a very honourable manner;" nay, though it declare, that "as Christ's natural Body was holy, as being divinely sanctified, so His adoptive Body is holy, as being divinely consecrated by the grace of sanctification;" yet they expressly add[s], "that He commanded His image, that is, material bread, taken from [the main mass of oblations] to be offered, not resembling the shape of man, lest idolatry should be introduced." Now as this does evidently suppose that it would be idolatry to pay Divine worship to the Host, though it did appear in the form of Christ's human Flesh, so it does as clearly suppose, that Christ instituted this Sacrament in Bread and Wine, in order to prevent any Divine honour which the superstitions of men might have been tempted to pay to it, if this image had been a human portraiture. And the later these authorities are, the more weighty they ought to be esteemed, as to our present purpose. For nobody, I presume, suspects the three first centuries of so criminal a practice as this of worshipping the Eucharist as the very Christ both God and Man; but now as the Liturgy of St. Chrysostom (so called) is of an uncertain age, and has, since it's first composure, received many additions, so we are sure this synod of Constantinople was held in the year 754, and

this is an irrefragable evidence given by 338 very judicious S E C T.
and pious Bishops, that the worshipping of the Eucharist was I.
even then thought idolatrous; much more may it be presumed,
that any synod of Bishops in the foregoing ages of the Church
would have made the same determination, if any occasion had
been offered them to declare their judgments in this matter.
It were no difficult thing to give my reader the opinion of
several single writers of the same age, and some even after
this; but I have said enough on this head to shew, that
though the Fathers looked on the Eucharist as the most
honourable institution of our religion, yet they did not think
that Divine honour was due to it, whatever some may rashly
conclude from the words of the ancients first above cited.
Nay, it is known that this practice was not settled in the
Church of Rome before the thirteenth century, in the pope-
dom of Honorius the Third.

2. It has been objected against the Fathers, that they
frequently call the Eucharist, not only Christ's Body and
Blood, but His "own proper" Body and Blood; for so *suus*
and ἴδιος may in strictness be rendered; though I must confess I have not myself been so punctilious as to give them
always this rendition. Now

In answer to this, I will transcribe the words of the most In what
excellent Dr. Grabe in his notes on Irenæus[t]. "First he sense they believed
owns that Irenæus did not call the Bread and Wine figures, the Bread Christ's
types, memorials, because this would not have sufficiently own Body.
expressed his judgment; for he believed the holy elements
to be His very Body and Blood, in some sense, though not
substantially." Then he cites Maxentius, who says, "Propriety is variously understood; for the Church is Christ's
own or proper Body—and every one of the faithful is His
own or proper member.—The Bread also, of which the whole
Church partakes in memory of our Lord's Passion, is His own
or proper Body[u]." And this is indeed a demonstration, that
in the judgment of Maxentius, who wrote in the sixth century, it is not the same thing to say it is Christ's "own

---

[t] P. 396.
[u] ["Proprietas multis intelligitur
modis. Nam et Ecclesia Corpus Ejus
dicitur — Et unusquisque Fidelium
membrum Ejus est.—Sed et Panis

ille, quem universa Ecclesia in memoriam Dominicæ Passionis participat,
Corpus Ejus est."—Dial., lib. ii. cap.
13.]

proper" Body, and to say it is His personal substantial Body: for he expressly calls it 'Bread,' and yet Christ's own Body, in the same breath. Then he cites Gregory Nyssen for saying, Christ's " own or proper Body, which is the Church." And Maxentius used the same expression in relation to the Church, in the words just before produced. And indeed this objection can be of no force, because it affects so very ancient a writer as Irenæus, who yet says no more than St. Justin Martyr and St. Ignatius, though in other words. His own or proper Body means no more than that it was not a false, alien, or counterfeit Body.

3. The Fathers frequently mention a change made in the elements, which the Greeks express by μεταποιεῖν, μεταβάλλειν, μεταρρυθμίζειν, μεταστοιχειοῦν, μετασκευάζειν; the Latins by *muto, transmuto, transfiguro*, &c.

That the Fathers did not believe a change of substance in the Eucharist. To this, Protestants, in answering the allegations of Papists, have truly replied, that there may be a change of quality, where the substance yet remains. And the elements are changed by the consecration from being common bread and wine, into the mysterious spiritual Body and Blood. And the ancients did indeed believe an imperceptible change made in the holy symbols. The most observable passages to this purpose in the Fathers cited by me are those words of Ambrose, who supposes the symbolical Body offered in the commemorative oblation[x] to be yet further " transfigured" on the Altar; but it is certain that the Latin *transfigurare* there used does sometimes signify no more than a change of quality. So Calepine, in his Dictionary, cites Pliny[y] for saying, *Transfigurantur amygdalæ ex dulcibus in amaras;* " Almonds[z] are transfigured from sweet to bitter." And again, St. Ambrose supposes that[a] " Christ in the Eucharist changes the species of the elements." And though this seems a hard saying, yet it will by no means do any service to the Papists; for they, by the species, understand the accidents of the Bread and Wine, and they assert, as is true, that these are not changed. Nor can it be supposed that this Father should affirm that the bread loses it's whiteness, the wine

---

[x] n. p. 27. Ap.

[y] [Nat. Hist., lib. xvii. cap. 24.]

[z] [Sub voce ' Transfiguro.'—Tom.

ii. p. 743. ed. Lugd. 1681.]

[a] i. p. 27. Ap. l. 8.

it's taste and inebriating quality. Therefore by the species he most probably means the logical species, the two sorts of elements, viz. the bread and wine, which are changed, as has been said, as to their insensible qualities, not in substance; so in this very paragraph, St. Ambrose must be taken, when he says, "before the benediction it is called another species, or sort of thing." And this I apprehend must be his meaning; because he elsewhere expressly calls[b] that 'Bread,' which Christ gave to His Apostles. And Theodoret shews, that it was not at all inconsistent to believe a change, yet at the same time to believe, that the substance of bread and wine remained. No Protestant can more strongly affirm that the elements do not lose their nature and essence than this Father, and yet no man can more plainly assert a change than he does; for, says he[c], "Christ would have us believe a change made by grace." And in the very paragraph, which is so directly against transubstantiation, he yet declares[d], "that by the invocation the elements are changed, and become other things." And therefore when the Liturgies pray, that the Bread and Wine, or the gifts, may be made or changed into the Body and Blood; it is most rational to understand them as the ancients did, and particularly Theodoret, not as if they expected that they should be miraculously converted into the personal Body and Blood of Christ, but that by an internal spiritual alteration, they might become the Body and Blood in real power and effect. It is true, Julius Firmicus[e] calls the Sacrament "the substance of Majesty;" and Gelasius, a "Divine substance;" but I have before shewed, that they only mean the elements sanctified by the Holy Ghost, which is so true, that the latter calls the Eucharistical Body 'Bread' in the very same paragraph.

4. But further, St. Ambrose asserts[f], "that the nature is changed;" and St. Hilary[g], that "Christ does naturally remain in us, who receive the Word in the meat or food of the Lord; and that He mingles the nature of His Flesh with the Eternal Nature, (that is, the Holy Spirit,) under the Sacra-

[b] a. p. 26. Ap.
[c] i. p. 46. Ap.
[d] m. p. 46. Ap. l. 8.

[e] [p. 17. Ap.]
[f] i. p. 27. Ap.
[g] a. p. 20. Ap.

ment of His Flesh, to be communicated to us; and that we have the nature of His Flesh."

In what
sense they
believed a
change of
nature.
Now that the reader may be convinced, that these expressions are not to be taken in the strictest sense, he is to observe, that this Father is here arguing against the Arians, who would allow of no unity betwixt the Divine Father and Son but that of will or consent: in opposition to this, he asserts a natural union; and because the Arians urged, that the Father and Son were one only, as Christians are or ought to be one, St. Hilary asserts that Christians are one by the "nature of one faith," and calls this "a natural union." He asserts further, that they are "one by Baptism;" and says, "they who are one by one thing or means are one by nature." Then he proceeds to shew we are one with Christ by eating His Eucharistical Body, and this he calls a "natural unity;" but it is evident he meant only something more than a unity of consent in all these cases, excepting that of the Divine Father and Son, for it is impossible he should think that all Christians are but one individual natural substance; and it was sufficient for him to say, that there is more than a unity of consent between Christians that are baptized and are communicants; for they are animated by the same Holy Spirit, and have heavenly life imparted and continued to them by the same internal and external means, and have the same seed of immortality communicated to them by the same spiritual meat and drink, and are united to Christ their common Head by these and other unknown or ineffable bonds and ligaments. I cannot in reason suppose that the Father intended to assert, that the union between Christians did in all respects equal the unity betwixt the Father and Son; but only, that it was somewhat more than the Arians allowed, viz. an agreement of affections. And indeed it is evident that he meant a mysterious union; and so he explains himself by saying, " He mingles the nature of His Flesh with the Eternal Nature, under a Sacrament or mystery; and we truly take His Flesh under a mystery:" for by these expressions the words ' nature' and ' natural' are made to abate in their significations when applied to the Eucharist, and not to have so much power or import as when applied to the Divine Father and

Son. He expresses both unions by the same words, but qualifies the meaning of them when he speaks of our union with Christ by partaking of the Eucharistical Body. And though the word 'nature,' with it's adjective and adverb, may seem of too full an import to be used in this place, yet it is to be considered that there are scarce any words in the Latin dictionary of a more extensive signification. And since it is so common for us to say of a man, that his nature is changed, when we only mean his dispositions and inward qualities, we ought not to judge too severely of St. Hilary or St. Ambrose on this account. And indeed we have little less than demonstration, that St. Ambrose, by "the change of nature," means nothing else but a change of quality; for before he comes to the end of the paragraph he says, "Before the benediction of heavenly words it is called another sort [of thing]," meaning bread; "after the benediction, the Body of Christ is meant" or represented; for though *significatur* imports more than a bare typical shady signification, yet it necessarily implies also a distinction between the figure and the thing signified, that is, the Eucharistical and natural Body. Nay, and a little before he has these words, "It is the true Flesh of Christ, Which was crucified and buried; it is therefore truly the Sacrament or mystery of His Flesh." So that "to be Christ's Flesh," and "to be the Sacrament of His Flesh," is with St. Ambrose the same thing.

5. There is another charge against the ancients on this head, which is, that they often speak of the change of the Bread and Wine into the Body and Blood as miraculous; and therefore must mean some other change than what I have before mentioned. Thus St. Cyril of Jerusalem[h] and Gaudentius[i], to render the conversion of bread and wine into the Body and Blood more credible, argue from Christ's miraculous turning the water into wine. St. Ambrose[k] argues the same from Aaron's rod being turned into a serpent, the waters of Egypt being turned into blood, and such like. To this it may be replied,

(1.) It does not follow that the Fathers thought the change wrought in the Eucharist to be miraculous, from their enforcing the belief of it by appealing to the miraculous works

SECT. I.

Whether they believed a miraculous change.

[h] b. p. 18. Ap. [i] a. p. 30. Ap. l. 10. [k] l. p. 27. Ap.

A a 2

wrought by Christ or the Apostles and the Prophets. They might intend to argue *a majori ad minus,* if God did the greater, much more can He do the less. Cyril's argument does evidently proceed in this manner; for[1] having mentioned the miracle of turning the water into wine, he adds, "Shall not Christ be much the rather acknowledged to give the enjoyment of His Body and Blood to the sons of the bride-chamber?" And it is probable the others meant the same. I suppose that the Apostle St. Paul, when he calls the manna and the water of the rock the same spiritual meat and drink with that in the Eucharist, means that it was the same in type and figure, as being a very signal token of God's good-will toward them; and that the prefiguration consisted not so much in the nutritive power of the manna and water, (for if this had been all that the Apostle had meant, then all the wholesome victuals and liquors that were ever eaten or drunk might be said to be the same spiritual meat and drink), as in the manner by which they were prepared, viz. by the special providence and power of God. And this indeed is the main ground on which the manna and water are made types of the Sacrament; for by this it appears, that both the type and archetype are singular specimens of God's bounty and power in making provision for His own people: but who therefore will pretend to argue that because the manna and the water of the rock were furnished by a miracle, that therefore the Eucharist is made so by the same means? And it is fit we should interpret the Fathers with the same equity which we use in interpreting Scripture.

(2.) It is certain that the ancients believed the Eucharistical Body and Blood to be made so by the concurrence of the Divine Spirit, and that it was therefore a preternatural work; for all the graces of the Spirit must be allowed to be beyond the power of nature. Now I believe it will be very hard for the most metaphysical head precisely to determine which of these works may in strictness be called miraculous, which not. And we are not to suppose, that the simplicity of the primitive Fathers disposed them to make such nice and subtle distinctions as later ages have done; and therefore I should not wonder if some of them had in express words

[1] b. p. 18. Ap.

affirmed it to be miraculous, as yet I am not sensible they have done. Theodoret expresses the sense of the Church in this respect excellently well, when he says, that in the Eucharist[m] "Christ did not change nature, but added grace to nature." I remember I have met somewhere with terrible reflections on St. Chrysostom for using some interjections of wonder, when he is speaking of the Holy Sacrament; whereas if we will accept of the same language and expressions from Fathers, that we do from the men of our own age, we must allow some "miracles of nature" and much more of "miracles of grace;" and if any one shall take the Fathers or me to task on this score, I shall expect that they do exactly fix the standard of the power of nature, and then proceed to shew what works are only preternatural, not miraculous, and to settle exact bounds and limits betwixt them. It is certain all miraculous works are preternatural; that all preternatural works are miraculous, I do not say; but I may have leave to say, that there is a great resemblance between them: and things that are alike in the main do often go under the same name with them that do not study niceties; and I believe there are many things done by a preternatural power which we should call miracles if we did not see them every day, for nothing seems miraculous that is usual.

I am sensible that the most learned Grabe has declared, in his notes on Irenæus[n], that Cyril of Jerusalem and Gregory Nyssen asserted that the "substance of Bread in the Eucharist is transformed into the Flesh of Christ, which He took of the Virgin;" he directs us to Catech. Mystag. 4. of Cyril; and therefore meant, I suppose, the same which I above considered, and in which I do not see that he positively determines this point; and I am the rather willing to believe he does not, because he says[o] that "the Body is given us in the type of Bread," which seems to express his meaning that the Bread still remains; and[p] he only says it is not mere Bread but the Body. Now I can never believe that 'type' signifies 'accidents,' as the Romish writers would persuade us; and when Irenæus and others say that it is not 'mere Bread,' we justly suppose that they give it for granted, by that expression, that they thought it yet Bread as to it's gross sub-

Cyril of Jerusalem and Gregory Nyssen charged by Dr. Grabe with the belief of a substantial change, but this not certain.

---

[m] i. p. 46. Ap.   [n] p. 399.   [o] c. p. 18. Ap.   [p] a. p. 18. Ap.

stance. And I think Cyril has an equal right with others to
this interpretation. As to Gregory Nyssen, whose words you
have in the Appendix[q], and which are the very same that Dr.
Grabe seems to point at, it must be confessed that they look
more this way than any other that I have yet met with of
equal antiquity with him; and yet I cannot but say there are
some passages in that long paragraph, which would incline
one to think more favourably of him; as for instance, " He
that sees bread does after a sort see human body; for when
that is in this, it becomes this;" that is, when the bread is
in the body, by nutrition it becomes part of the body. (So
he had said before, "when these [Bread and Wine] are in me,
they are Body and Blood:") and "the Divine Body of Christ,
receiving the nutriment of Bread, was the same with it in a
manner; and in one case" (he means that of our Saviour's
Person) "the grace of the Word sanctified the Body, which
was composed of Bread, and in some sort was Bread; in the
other case (the Eucharist) the Bread is sanctified by the
Word of God and prayer, passing into the Body of the Word,
not by being eaten and drunk, but forthwith changed;" that
is, not by digestion, as Bread and Wine became His natural
Body, but all of a sudden. By this it appears that it was the
Father's design to render the alteration in the Eucharist very
credible, and not so operose as it appears to be at first sight,
on supposition that bread is changed into human flesh; and
therefore undoubtedly supposes such a change as other of the
ancients do not; but still, whether he meant, as Dr. Grabe
supposes, that the substance of Bread was changed, I dare
not say. He rather seems to me to aim at proving that there
is no occasion for a change of substance; for he all along
argues that bread and human flesh are as it were the same
thing; and that all the odds between the Eucharistical Bread
being made the Body of Christ, and common bread becoming
His Body while He was alive here on earth, was this, that in
the former the alteration was made without mastication or
digestion, by the elements being added to Christ's natural
Body by a Divine power. However he declares his intention
to explain the change "in a manner possible to nature;" and
therefore could never have reconciled himself to transubstan-

[q] a. p. 23, 24. Ap.

tiation; and then too he supposes the Bread and Wine to become the Body and Blood, by being 'added' to His natural Body and Blood; and not by having the substantial Body and Blood *advanced* [r] into the Eucharist instead of the Bread and Wine, as the Romanists suppose. And we have already heard him say [s] that "Bread after invocation is called, and is, the Body of Christ;" and he does not directly contradict this here, but rather countenances it by saying that even Christ's natural Body was in some sort Bread, &c. The Father undertook to philosophize upon a mystery; and this is one way to render it still more a mystery; and it would be strange indeed, if the writers of the Christian Church for four hundred years together should never have dropped any words upon a subject so very nice and mysterious, that will not bear the scrutiny of a very critical and censorious age such as this of ours; and therefore I never thought it necessary to maintain that none of the ancients were ever guilty of any excess in this particular, but that the generality of the most valuable writers asserted no more than what I at first laid down. If therefore Gregory Nyssen have shewed himself to be mistaken, in pretending to explain a mystery by principles of philosophy or by asserting a change of substance, I apprehend that in this respect he goes alone; and if my reader, notwithstanding what has been said by me or others on this head, do still believe, that Cyril or St. Hilary St. Ambrose or St. Augustine do assert transubstantiation or the paying Divine honour to the Eucharistical Body and Blood, I do hereby solemnly declare that, when I am convinced that they are indeed guilty of so gross an error, I am ready to enter my protest against them as to these particulars. And I suppose it is very evident, that though it should be granted that these venerable names have, in the several passages above produced, departed from the sense of the Church in those ages; yet in other places they have said what is enough to shew, that this was not their settled judgment, but proceeded from haste or inadvertency or the sudden flash of a warm imagination; but that they generally owned an invisible mysterious change is what is very evident from several citations already inserted, and might be proved from many more,

---

[r] [In the first ed. Johnson employs the term 'adduced.']   [s] c. p. 25. Ap.

if it were to my present purpose.   I will only leave with my
reader the words of Gaudentius[t], "Let us not pretend to
break that most solid bone, 'This is My Body, This is My
Blood;' and if any thing remain which is not understood, let
it be burnt by the ardent fire of faith."

CHAP. II. SECT. II.

*That the Eucharistical Bread and Wine, or Body and Blood,
are to be offered for the acknowledgment of God's dominion
and other attributes, and for procuring Divine blessings,
especially remission of sin.*

HAVING fully shewed what is offered in the Eucharist, I
now proceed to consider the ends for which it is to be offered.   Dr. Spencer, when he considers sacrifices in respect
to their end, is very minute in mentioning particulars; but
it is observable, that they all centre in the two ends above
specified.   He reckons five sorts of sacrifices; but three of
them are easily to be reduced to the first head, viz. acknowledging God's dominion and other attributes; for such were,
in the first place, "whole burnt offerings or honorary sacrifices, intended for the rendering of honour to God and acknowledging His dominion;" such were "the peace-offerings
which expressed a mind well and devoutly affected toward
God," that is, sensible of His goodness, and disposed to make
all possible returns; such were "the sacrifices of thanksgiving, or vows, which signified gratitude toward God;" and
indeed these latter differed from the former more in name
than in reality; and his two other sorts of sacrifices are as
clearly reducible to the other head of procuring Divine blessing, especially remission of sin; for according to him, "the
euctic sacrifices were for the obtaining of any blessing; the
expiatory, for the appeasing of God;" see the Introduction.
Therefore Mr. Calvin takes no notice of any other ends but
these two, viz. "honouring" or rendering our thanks to "God
for His favours," and "pacifying His wrath;" and so omits

[t] b. p. 30. Ap.

any other benefits to be obtained by Sacrifice; in which SECT. respect his definition is imperfect. When Bellarmine makes the ends of Sacrifice to be "the acknowledgment of our own weakness and the Divine greatness," he may be understood to mean much the same thing. For in recognising His dominion, goodness, and providence, we acknowledge His greatness; and when we address ourselves to Him for pardon of sin and other blessings, this is a confession of our own disability to confer these favours on ourselves or others, and of God's power in these respects. I proceed therefore,

First, to shew, that one and the primary end of the Eu- First end of charistical Christian Sacrifice is the acknowledgment of the Eucha-ristical God's dominion and other attributes; and I must add, what Sacrifice, is most especially implied, of His goodness, in redeeming the ledgment world by Christ Jesus, which is the foundation of all other dominion, spiritual mercies. And I apprehend, our adversaries them- &c. selves do so far consent to this, as to own that the Eucharist is a Sacrifice of thanksgiving, and a recognition of all the blessings and favours we receive from God, and more particularly of His sending His Son to die for us, and of all the inestimable mercies accruing to ourselves and others by this means : they only deny that the Bread and Wine or Eucharistical Body and Blood are this Sacrifice; and would have it believed, that the verbal and mental praises are the only thing meant by this Sacrifice : and therefore the authorities produced under this head shall chiefly be such as do effectually prove, that the Sacrifice of thanksgiving in the Christian Church was, in the judgment of the ancients, an oblation not only of words and thoughts but of the material Bread and Wine. And first, St. Chrysostom says[u], "the tremendous mysteries, that are full of salvation, which are consecrated offered or celebrated in every Communion, are called the Eucharist, because it is a memorial of many benefits; wherefore the Priest also bids us give thanks for the whole world—while the Sacrifice lies in open view." The mysteries are the Sacramental Body and Blood; for this is the language of antiquity. And these mysteries are called the Eucharist, as being the memorials of the greatest bene-

[u] q. p. 39. Ap.

CHAP.
II.

fits; these are the Sacrifices lying in open view; and the verbal and mental praises are so far from being either the mysteries or the memorial or the Sacrifice, that these latter are the motives or incentives to the former. For, because "the mysteries are memorials of great benefits, therefore the Priest bids us give thanks." St. Augustine asserts[x], "that to sacrifice to God, as we very often do, according to that only rite, by which He has commanded Sacrifice to be offered by the revelation of the New Testament, is part of that worship which is called *Latria,* and is due to God Alone." I dare leave it to my adversaries to determine, what that only rite in the New Testament is, by which we offer Sacrifice. All our services are indeed a sacrifice, in an improper remote sense; but there is one rite, by which alone we do it properly, and by which we do a peculiar honour to God; and again[y], "*Theosebia* may be said to be the worship of God, which consists chiefly in this, that the mind be grateful; therefore in that most true and singular Sacrifice, we are admonished to give thanks;" where the thanks is evidently distinguished from the Sacrifice; and indeed bare mental praise is no singular thing, but is common to all religions; the Sacrifice of the Body and Blood of Christ in a mystery is peculiar to ours. And because the principal blessing, which we commemorate in the Eucharist, is the Death of Christ, and the inward remembrance of it is by our adversaries called the Sacrifice; see how much otherwise St. Augustine expresses himself in that observable place[z], where he explains the manner, how Christians celebrated "the memory of the Sacrifice, viz. by the holy oblation, and participation of the Body and Blood of Christ;" which is an unanswerable proof, that this Father looked on the commemoration to be a material one, and to consist not in thought and speech but in offering and receiving the Sacramental Bread and Wine. The learned Mr. Bingham[a] cites Paulinus saying the following words of the *Paratorium,* the right-hand apartment of the Church, viz. *Immolanti Hostias jubilationis Antistiti parat,* "It is for preparing the Sacrifice of jubilation," that is, un-

---

[x] I. p. 36. Ap.
[y] O. p. 36. Ap.
[z] H. p. 36. Ap.

[a] Book viii. chap. vi. [p. 459. ed. Straker. 1840.]

questionably, the material Bread and Wine. Eusebius speaks very elegantly to this purpose[b]; "We offer therefore to God the Sacrifice of praise; we offer the Divine and venerable Sacrifice, which hath a decorous sanctity. We sacrifice in a new manner, according to the New Testament; we offer a clean Sacrifice;" and he proves it clean, because offered with a contrite heart. "And we offer the prophetic incense, presenting to Him in every place the well-savoured oblation of a most virtuous *theology* by prayer to Him: therefore we offer both Sacrifice and incense; the one, when we celebrate the memorial of the great Sacrifice according to the mysteries delivered to us by Him, and when we present the Eucharist," that is, the Sacrifice of thanksgiving "to God for our salvation, by pious hymns and prayers; the other, when we offer ourselves, wholly consecrating ourselves to Him and His High-Priest the Word, cleaving to Him both in body and soul." The sacrificing in a new manner can be meant of the Eucharist only; for all the other sacrifices, even that of a contrite heart, were as old as David at least. This is the only Sacrifice peculiar to the New Testament; and he distinguishes the *Mincha* from the incense. The *Mincha* is the Sacramental Bread and Wine; the incense is, according to him, those inward holy dispositions, which he calls a most virtuous *theology*, offered to God by prayer. Nay, he repeats this distinction again, and says, "we offer both Sacrifice and incense;" and makes the memorial to be the Sacrifice, and the oblation of ourselves cleaving to Him both in body and soul, the incense; which is the very same with the virtuous *theology* before mentioned. And he tells us, this memorial was celebrated by the mysteries delivered by Christ, that is, His Sacramental Body and Blood; and that this memorial or Eucharist is offered by prayers and hymns, which therefore are to be distinguished from the memorial offered by them; and the reader will remember, that St. Augustine has just now given us an account what this memorial was, viz. the oblation and participation of the Sacramental Body and Blood, not a bare act of reminiscence. I have, in the first section of this second chapter, produced further proof that Eusebius's me-

[b] g. p. 16. Ap.

morial was a material Sacrifice, and therefore shall say no
more of that matter in this place; but only observe, that a
very great man[c], in a most celebrated book upon the Eucharist, produces several of these passages from Eusebius to prove,
that "the remembrance or commemoration is the Sacrifice;"
and yet presently cites Fulgentius[d] for saying[e], "the Holy
Catholic Church throughout all the world ceases not to offer
the Sacrifice of Bread and Wine." Origen's opinion may be
learned from those words of his[f], "Let Celsus, as one that
knows not God, offer his eucharistic sacrifices to demons;
but we, appeasing the Creator of all things, eat the loaves
offered with thanksgiving and prayer over the gifts, they
being made a certain Holy Body by means of prayer."
When he tells us the loaves were offered or presented with
prayer and thanksgiving, he gives us the reason why they
were the Eucharistic Sacrifice of Christians.   For it was
his present business, to distinguish between the eucharistic
sacrifices of the heathen and that which was offered by the
worshippers of the true God.   But none of the primitive
writers speak so directly and copiously to this purpose as
St. Irenæus, even when he was speaking contemptuously of
the Jewish sacrifices; what he says is as follows[g], "The
Prophets speak most fully, that God did in the Law enjoin
certain observances for the sake of [the people] themselves,
not as if He stood in need of their services; and again, God
has plainly taught us, that He wants not the oblations of
men, except it be for the sake of him who offers them; for
at a time when He saw them negligent of justice and averse
to the love of God and hoping to propitiate God by sacrifices and other typical observances, Samuel told them, that
God required not burnt-offerings;" then he makes citations
to this purpose from Psalm xl. and l., Isaiah l. 11. 16, 17, 18;
and then he thus proceeds, "From all which it is manifest,
that God demanded not of them sacrifices and burnt-offerings, but faith obedience and righteousness, in order to
their salvation; and our Lord also taught them the same,

c Bishop Patrick On Christian Sacrifice, p. 24. edit. 9th.
d De Fide ad Petrum Diac. cap. 19.
e ["Sacrificium Panis et Vini in fide
et charitate Sancta Ecclesia Catholica
per universum orbem terræ offerre non
cessat."—p. 92. ed. Lugd. 1633.]
f a. p. 9. Ap.
g c. p. 4. Ap.

saying, 'If ye had known what that meaneth, I will have
mercy and not sacrifice, ye would not have condemned the
innocent.'" "Christ, bearing witness to the Prophets that
they preached the truth, but charging them as culpably
ignorant, and giving in charge to His own Disciples to
offer to God the first-fruits of His creatures (not as if He
wanted them, but that they might not be unfruitful or un-
grateful,) takes that Bread, which is [part] of the creation,
and gave thanks, saying, 'This is My Body;' and the Cup
also, which is, according to our doctrine, part of the creation,
and confessed it to be His Blood; and taught the new oblation of the New Testament, which the Church receiving
from the Apostles offers throughout the world to that God
which gives us food, I mean the first-fruits of their gifts,
according to the New Testament." Then he cites Malach.
i. 10, 11; and then he adds, "[the Prophet] manifestly
signifying by these words, that the former people shall cease
to offer to God; but that a Sacrifice shall be offered to Him
in every place, and that a pure one too, and His Name is
great among the Gentiles." And at another place[h], "therefore the oblation of the Church, which the Lord hath taught
to be offered in the whole world, is esteemed by God a pure
Sacrifice, and is accepted by Him; not that He wants a
sacrifice from us; but because he who offers is himself
honoured in what he offers, if his gifts be accepted. For our
honour and affection toward a king is declared by our gifts:"
and again[i], "It behoves us to make an oblation to God, and
to be in all things found grateful to the Creator of the world,
offering the first-fruits of the things which are His creatures.
This oblation the only pure congregation, the Church, offers
to the Creator, when she offers to Him His own creature with
thanksgiving."—"We[j] offer to Him, not as if He were in-
digent, but as paying the homage of thanks to His supreme
Majesty—as therefore He, though He want not these things
from us, yet will have them to be done by us, that we be not
unfruitful; so the same Word gave a commandment to the
people to make oblations to God, though He wanted them
not—as He would have us also offer a gift at the Altar,
frequently and without intermission; there is therefore an

[h] e. p. 5. Ap.   [i] f. p. 5. Ap. l. 6.   [j] f. p. 5, 6. Ap. l. 30.

Altar in Heaven, (for thither our prayers and oblations are directed,) and a Temple, as John in the Revelation says." Now as this holy man does particularly guard against that vain conceit, which prevailed amongst the heathen and the grosser part of the Jews, that God had His wants supplied by the sacrifices made at the altar; and that He desired sacrifice for His own sake: so he again and again repeats the doctrine which I am now insisting on, that oblations are to be made to God for a recognition of His dominion over His creatures, and as a testimony of our gratitude; he expressly teaches, that Christ gave charge that Christians should make oblations, in His instituting the Sacrament of His Body and Blood; and informs us, that this oblation was in his time made by Christians throughout the world: and no man of his age better knew the practice of the universal Church; for as he had his education in the East, so he lived a great part of his time in the West, being Bishop of Lyons in Gaul. And what is most particularly remarkable, he was so far from asserting the doctrine which now prevails, that mere airy thanks and praise was the only sacrifice which was then called the Eucharist; that he directly declares, that the oblations made by Christians were the first-fruits of God's creatures, that very Bread and Wine, which the heretics denied and the Catholics affirmed to be the workmanship of God. This Sacrifice he affirms to be offered by the command of Christ, when He instituted the Eucharist; and he asserts the Sacrifice of Christians to be such a sacrifice as the Jews "then ceased to offer." Now the Jews neither then did, nor now do cease to offer naked thanks and praise; but they cease from offering a *Mincha* or material Sacrifice. This he declares to be the new oblation of the New Testament, which the Church had received from the Apostles, and which Christ had enjoined when He said "This is My Body;" and they who can believe, that after all this Irenæus meant no more than an oblation of words and thoughts, must suppose that this holy Father, when he speaks of Christ's saying, "This is My Body," "This is My Blood," bade His Disciples eat and drink mere sounds and ideas; and that the Eucharistical Bread is no more than an act of our memory. And whereas he tells us, that "there is an Altar in Heaven, to which our prayers and oblations are SECT. directed;" he not only clearly distinguishes prayers from II. oblations, but evidently alludes to the ancient practice, which is not only legible in all the latter Liturgies, but in that of Clement; I mean, in praying that the gifts which had been offered to God as the mysterious Body and Blood of Christ might be received up to the heavenly Altar: for my reader will find such a prayer at the latter end of the extracts from the several ancient Liturgies in my Appendix, and I think I may dare say in all others that are now extant, except those that are perfectly modern; only St. Mark's Liturgy puts up this prayer, by a prolepsis, before the words of institution[k]. I dare presume to say, that the latest of those Liturgies, which I have or shall mention, does not in more strong and irresistible words, express a material sacrifice of praise, than some of these lines of Irenæus above produced; and they that will understand him of mere verbal and mental oblations may as well take all that has been said by Dr. Hickes and others in the same sense, which is indeed an effectual method of putting an end to the controversy. St. Justin Martyr[l] speaks of "the Sacrifices offered, that is, the Bread of Eucharist" or thanksgiving, and "the Cup of Eucharist" or thanksgiving; and says[m], that "Jesus has by tradition instructed us to offer the Cup in remembrance of His Blood, giving thanks," or celebrating the Eucharist. There is indeed one passage in the writings A place of of this holy man, which may at first sight seem to say more Just. Mart. than is consistent with what I have hitherto asserted. I will from the give my reader the entire paragraph in English. He is con- of our futing Trypho the Jew; and in order to do this, he urges adversaries. the famous prophecy, in those words[n], "God beforehand Mal. i. 10, accepting all Sacrifices made to Him in every place through 11. His Name, which Jesus Christ has by tradition instructed them to make, that is, in the Eucharist" or thanksgiving-Sacrifice of Bread and the Cup, "testifies that they are acceptable to Him; but He rejects those made by you and those priests of yours, saying, 'I will accept none of your sacrifices at your hands, for from the rising of the sun to the going down thereof My Name is glorified among the Gentiles:' but

[k] b. p. 55. Ap.   [l] c. p. 3. Ap.   [m] d. p. 3. Ap.   [n] e. p. 4. Ap.

ye have profaned It; and still loving disputes, ye say, that God accepts not sacrifice of the Israelites so-called that then dwelt at Jerusalem, but that He said He desires the prayers of those that were then in dispersion, being of the same stock of men; and that He calls their prayers sacrifices. Now that prayers and praises made by worthy men are the only perfect sacrifices and acceptable to God, I myself also say; for Christians have been instructed to offer none other, even in the memorial of their food both dry and liquid, in which also the Passion of the Son of God is commemorated." (N.B. I concern not myself with the dubious lection in these last words, viz. Υἱὸς Θεοῦ, or Υἱὸς Θεοῦ Θεὸς, because the present dispute does in no measure depend upon it.) As to the words themselves, they are very favourable to the doctrine of the Sacrifice in the main: but when He says, "Prayers and praise are the only perfect sacrifices acceptable to God, and that Christians offer no other in the Eucharist," it may be thought that he countenances the notion of our adversaries, who assert, that there is nothing to be offered there but vocal and mental devotions; therefore I answer,

1. That it is certainly true, that all sacrifices are either prayer or praise; they are all offered either as petitions for what we want or as acknowledgments for what we have received, as has been already observed; and it is further to be considered, that all sacrifices take their name from their use or end; so a sacrifice for sin is called ἁμαρτία, the trespass-offering πλημμέλεια, the peace-offering σωτήριον, the vow εὐχὴ, the sacrifice of thanksgiving αἴνεσις by the LXX, Εὐχαριστία by Aquila, the freewill-offering ὁμολογία or αἴρεσις, which are words signifying literally 'sin,' 'trespass,' 'salvation,' 'prayer,' 'praise,' 'confession' or 'choice;' but did ever any man from thence conclude, that nothing was offered to God in these sacrifices but sin, trespass, salvation, prayer, praise, confession, and freedom of will or choice. The words indeed originally are such as do not necessarily and of themselves signify anything more than the abstracted acts of sin, trespass, &c., but when applied to the several sorts of sacrifices by the Hellenistic or Eucharistical writers, they do at the same time connote the animal or other material thing

offered upon these several occasions. It is said of our Saviour, that He "was made sin for us;" and they who have looked no further than to the common signification of the word 'sin' in this place, have from thence drawn some very harsh as well as false conclusions. The answer, to them who do thus abasively understand those words, is, that ἁμαρτία, 'sin,' in that text, signifies a 'sacrifice for sin;' and our Saviour might be made a sacrifice for sin, as He certainly was, without becoming actually guilty by the imputation of our sins: and the same answer will serve those, who, when they hear of a sacrifice of prayer and praise, presently run away with these words, taking them in their abstracted sense; and from thence conclude, that nothing is meant but a pure act of the mind, or at most of the mouth; not considering, that sin, prayer, and praise, when applied to sacrifice, import not only or chiefly the actions commonly denoted by those words, but that material thing, whatever it was, that was appointed for a sacrifice on this occasion. And I shall hereafter shew, that praise, or a sacrifice of praise, oftentimes in Scripture signifies the animal offered to express men's gratitude to God; and they who will allow no sacrifice that is material in the Christian Church, because it is by Justin called "prayer and praise," may with the same reason assert, that there was no such material sacrifice offered in the temple of Solomon.

2. The reader will observe, that this ancient writer does not say, that all prayers and praises are the most perfect sacrifices; but only such as are offered by "worthy men," that is, Christians, and at the Eucharist: thus much is imported in those words, "These only we Christians have been by tradition instructed to offer, in the memorial of our food." He does not give this reason for it, which would best fit our adversaries, viz. that it is an immaterial oblation; but rather the contrary, viz. that the prayers and praises were offered in and by a material memorial. For what can make these devotions more excellent and prevalent than others, except it be the visible memorial, "that memorial in which the Passion of our Lord is commemorated," as Justin speaks? for I will thank no man for granting, what I have fully proved

CHAP.
II.
in the margin°, that by the 'memorial' here must be meant the Eucharistical symbols.

3. From these two considerations it is very evident what Justin means, in granting that prayer and praise, offered by worthy men, are the most perfect sacrifice, and that Christians offered no other in the Communion. For as all sacrifices whatever are prayers or praises, in the sense abovementioned; so those offered by worthy men in the Eucharist are the only perfect and most acceptable. And if it be asked, what renders them so perfect and acceptable, it is evident, that this holy writer thought that the inward desires and acknowledgments of Christians were enforced and perfumed by that memorial, which Christ commanded to be offered.

° St. Justin Martyr here says, that in the *anamnesis* of food, both dry and liquid, a commemoration was made of the Death of the Son of God. Now an *anamnesis* of food must either signify an acknowledgment of God's goodness in providing meat and drink for mankind, which is what our adversaries would have, or it must denote the Eucharistical Bread and Wine.

1. It does not mean an acknowledgment of God's goodness in giving us common meat or drink: for in the *anamnesis* here mentioned, a commemoration was made of Christ's Death; but we cannot be said to commemorate Christ's Death by making a recital of God's blessing, in giving us common meat and drink. Men may in the same prayer thank God for meat and drink, and for Christ's Death; but such a prayer, especially if used in the Sacrament, would never go by the name of a commemoration or remembrance of our food, but would take it's name *a majori*, that is, from the Death of Christ there commemorated. Further, the καὶ is evidently emphatical, and therefore the words cannot otherwise be rendered than ' *even* in the memorial or remembrance.' Now the reader may judge whether it be most probable that this ancient writer would lay an emphasis on the least considerable part of the Eucharist-service, namely thanking God for common meat and drink, or on that which is the substance of the Eucharist, the Bread and Wine; and lastly, it is very observable that in the

most ancient Liturgy, the Clementine, there is no express mention of Bread and Wine in the long recital of God's mercies to us, only in the words of oblation and consecration. I am sensible that Justin, when he is describing the celebration of the Eucharist, says*, " the President taking [the Bread and Cup] makes a long thanksgiving to the Father of the universe, through the name of the Son and Holy Ghost, for that God has vouchsafed them to us;" but by ' them' I think it more proper, both in grammar and good sense, to understand the Son and the Holy Spirit, than the Bread and Wine.

2. It therefore signifies the Eucharistical Bread and Wine, called a ' memorial,' in allusion to that part of the *Mincha* or meat offering, which was offered by fire to God, and called by this name in the Levitical Law, Lev. ii. 2. 9. 16. and elsewhere. There indeed the word μνημόσυνον is used by the LXX, which is perfectly of the same signification; but the very word ἀνάμνησις is used in relation to the shewbread, a very remarkable type of the Eucharist, Lev. xxiv. 7, and certainly no name or title better befits the Eucharistical elements, which are taken out of the whole mass of oblations, to be in a particular manner offered and consecrated to God; as Justin elsewhere assures us, the Bread and Wine of the Eucharist were, and in which a commemoration was indeed made of the Death of the Son of God. The word *anamnesis* is also used Numb. x. 10.

* a. p. 2. Ap.

All sacrifices presented to God, according to His own directions, are vocal; they "speak good things" to God in our
behalf, as Abel's did. The ancient sacrifices were only dumb
significations of the thoughts and affections of them who
offered them; but the Christian Church presents her Sacrifice to God by words, as well as thoughts and actions; by
words expressing at large the wishes, hopes, fears, and intentions of the Priests and people; and therefore may more
properly be called prayers and praises, than any other material
sacrifices of old instituted by God.

4. This must of necessity be Justin's meaning in this place,
if we will suppose that he discourses consistently; for in other
places of this very Dialogue with Trypho, he expressly asserts,
that Bread and Wine were offered in the Eucharist; as I
have shewed just before, and as an honest adversary confesses, (I mean Voigtus *De Altarib.*[p]). Nay, it is observable,
that in that very place[q], where Voigtus owns he speaks of
offering Bread and Wine, he says that Malachi foretold this
in chap. i. 10, 11. Now Justin, in this very place, maintains
against Trypho, that this prophecy of Malachi is to be understood of the Eucharist, and therefore certainly of a material
oblation; unless you will make Justin contradict himself.
To advance one step further still; it seems very probable, to
say no more, that in the beginning of this very paragraph
he asserts *a thanksgiving-Sacrifice of Bread and Wine.* If
the translation which I have given of them just before be
allowed of, it will not bear a dispute; and that translation I
think to be fair and unexceptionable. The words are capable
of another rendition, which also is as favourable to the doctrine of the Sacrifice; thus, "God accepting all Sacrifices
(that is, in the Eucharist) of Bread and the Cup, made to
Him in every place, through This Name which Jesus Christ
has," &c. Nay, Dr. Wise's translation of these words is
fairly consistent with a material Sacrifice, viz. "God now
receives everywhere from Christians, through the Name of
Christ, those Sacrifices which He appointed to be made, that
is, in the Eucharist of Bread and Wine;" (I only omit the
Doctor's 'blessing,' which is not in the original,) for certainly
"the Eucharist of Bread and Wine" denotes the Bread and

[p] p. 53.   [q] c. p. 3. Ap.

Wine itself; for " we call this food Eucharist," says Justin[r].
The least that can be said is, that the words, however construed, do rather countenance the Eucharistical Sacrifice
than otherwise; and it is most rational to take them in a
sense, which Justin himself has expressly declared for in
other parts of this work.

5. It especially deserves our remark, that Justin in these
words is answering an evasive cavil of the Jew; for whereas
Justin had alleged the prophecy of Malachi in behalf of
the Christian Eucharist, the Jew replies upon him, that
Malachi's *Mincha* denoted the prayers put up by the Jews
in their dispersion throughout the world. And all that
Justin says of prayer and praise is only by way of answer to
a captious adversary; [therefore granting that Justin is to
be understood in our adversaries' sense, which I do not believe; yet still] he argues *ad hominem*, allows " prayer and
praise offered by worthy men in the Eucharist" to be the
best sacrifice; but lets him know what makes them so, viz.
the memorial in and by which it is offered. Justin, when
left to his own sentiments and expression, speaks in quite
another manner; but when he was confuting a corrupt gloss
of the Jews, he thought fit to talk in their way, and as it
were to beat them with their own weapon. And I cannot
but observe, that the present adversaries of the Christian
Sacrifice take up with the very same shifts that the unbelieving Jews did in Justin's days; they would make us believe, that Malachi's *Mincha* is only one of their spiritual
sacrifices, consisting of nothing that is material. But they
can never serve themselves or their cause by Justin's answer;
until they can shew us on their hypothesis, why prayer and
praise, made in the memorial of Christ's Death, are the only
perfect and acceptable sacrifice; for according to their principles, any prayer offered with faith must be as effectual as
that which is offered in the Eucharist.

And lest it should seem harsh to an English reader not
used to such ways of expression, by prayer and thanksgiving
to understand a material sacrifice; he is to remember, what
is before shewed, that all material sacrifices were of old
called by the name which denoted the end for which they

were offered; as the sacrifice for sin went by the name of 'sin,' the sacrifice of thanksgiving by the name of 'thanksgiving' or 'praise;' and the oblation or sacrifice promised to God, in case a prayer was heard, was called εὐχὴ or προσευχή, 'prayer;' it is perpetually so termed by the LXX. A vow is a prayer with a material sacrifice annexed to it. We shall hereafter see, that the ancients called the material oblation in the Eucharist a vow or prayer, in the Latin *votum;* and in the mean time I shall observe, that St. Clement of Rome speaks[s] of the sacrifice of 'vows' or 'prayers' (εὐχῶν) as offered in the true Jerusalem, the Christian Church, together with 'the sacrifice for sin and transgression;' by which it is very evident, that it could not be thought unnatural in Justin, by prayer or vow to mean or connote a material oblation by the word εὐχή.

There is another instance of this sort in the Apostolical A place in the Constitutions, lib. ii. cap. 53, considered. Matt. v. 23. Constitutions[t]; for there it is said, that[u] "prayer and praise is the gift" meant by our Saviour. Now it is evident to a demonstration, that our Saviour intended a material gift, such a one as a man might "leave" behind him "before the Altar, while he went to be reconciled to his brother;" and the Constitutor was fully apprised of this, for no writer speaks more copiously of a material gift and Altar than he does; and therefore he too by εὐχή must be most probably supposed to mean a 'vow,' or an oblation brought to enforce a prayer, and render it more prevalent: and then it will be easy to account for that expression, προσευχή σου οὐκ εἰσακουσθήσεται; for a vow may be said to be heard or not heard as well as a mere prayer, to which the votary does not annex a material oblation. And thus David expresses himself, Ps. lxi. 5. "Thou, O God, hast heard my vows." The word נדר, which perpetually signifies a material oblation joined with a wish or prayer, is here used in the original; and it is turned by the Greek, προσευχή, the very word used by the Constitutor.

Clemens Alexandrinus has indeed said what looks more A place in Clemens Alexandrinus considered. favourable to the cause of our adversaries than any thing that I have met with in antiquity; the words follow, καὶ γὰρ ἐστὶν ἡ θυσία τῆς Ἐκκλησίας λόγος ἀπὸ τῶν ἁγίων ψυ-

---

[s] b. p. 1. Ap. l. 14.
[t] Lib. ii. cap. 53.

[u] ["Δῶρον δὲ ἐστιν Θεῷ ἡ ἑκάστου προσευχὴ καὶ εὐχαριστία."]

χῶν ἀναθυμιώμενος, ἐκκαλυπτομένης ἅμα τῆς θυσίας, καὶ τῆς διανοίας ἁπάσης τῷ Θεῷ[x]. The first part of the sentence is capable of a double rendition, viz. "reason" or speech, "exhaled from holy souls, is the Sacrifice of the Church;" or, "the Word, incensed or perfumed by holy souls, is the Sacrifice of the Church." The first rendition speaks an immaterial Sacrifice; the second may signify, that "the Blood of Christ is the Sacrifice of the Church." For this ancient writer, speaking of the Eucharist, says[y], "the holy liquor of gladness allegorically represents the *Logos* or Word, shed for many for the remission of sins;" and this sounds expressly for the Sacrifice, especially if we consider what follows, viz. "the Sacrifice, and the whole mind together with it, being uncovered to God;" for this undoubtedly alludes to the custom of laying the symbols in open view during the holy action. And therefore, if the connection did favour the doctrine of the Sacrifice so much, as the words themselves considered apart, I should not doubt to say that Clement was with us.

There is one consideration which is of itself an effectual answer to this and all other such like passages in antiquity, if there be any of the same sort; I mean, that by this way of arguing we may prove from Scripture, that none of the cattle offered at Jerusalem were true sacrifices, but only improperly and abasively so called. For those words of Psalm li. "The sacrifices of God are a contrite spirit," do as strongly and fully say, that a contrite spirit was the only sacrifice under the old Law, as Clement's words do import, that prayer is the only sacrifice under the Gospel. David might as truly have said, that "prayer exhaled from holy souls was the sacrifice of God," as that a contrite heart was so; and as by saying that a contrite heart was such a sacrifice, he did not, could not mean, that God required no other sacrifice but that, while the Law of Moses was in full force; so neither would any rational man have drawn such a conclusion from his words, if he had said the same thing of prayer. And the reason is plain, viz. that material sacrifice was enjoined by the plain express words of the Law very often repeated; and that David was so far from thinking that Law

1 Chron.
xxi. 26.

[x] [f. p. 7. Ap.]　　　　　　　　　　　[y] c. p. 7. Ap.

repealed, that he himself did offer material sacrifice. And f the words used by David do not prove, that material sacrifices offered at Jerusalem were not true sacrifices, no more do the words of Clement prove, that he did not believe the Eucharistical Bread and Wine to be a Sacrifice strictly so called. I will suppose for once, that Clement had said a great deal more than ever our adversaries suppose him to have said; as for instance, that God loathes a *Mincha*, that His soul hateth the Eucharist-Sacrifice, and that he who offers any material oblation is as he who blesseth an idol. Our adversaries would indeed triumph, if any such words could be found in the ancients; yet such words as these would no more annul the Christian Sacrifice than those Isa.i.11.13; words did the Jewish. [This argument is further pursued lxvi. 3. Part II. ch. ii. sect. ii.]

[But I labour not so much to prove that Clem. Alexandr. was an asserter of the Sacrifice, as that the Church in his age, as well as the following, did hold and practise It. And to this, Clement himself is a direct witness, in his first book of Stromata. For he tells of heretics, " who used bread and water only in the oblation ;" and says, this was " not according to the Canon of the Church." And this I take to be a certain proof not only of a material Sacrifice of thanksgiving, both in the Church and among the heretics, but of the Church's having a fixed rule or canon, whereby It was to be offered. If therefore Clement in his own judgment had been for an immaterial Sacrifice only; yet he gives full evidence against himself, as one that opposed the Church in this particular[z].]

I cannot but once more mention the words of St. Gregory Nazianzen[a]; " Knowing that no man is worthy of the great God and Sacrifice and High-Priest, who has not first presented himself a living holy sacrifice to God, and exhibited the rational acceptable Sacrifice, and offered to God the sacrifice of praise, and the contrite spirit (which is the only sacrifice which God demands from us), how should I dare offer to Him the external Sacrifice, the antitype of the great mysteries, or be invested with the character or title of a Priest ?"

[z] See Preface to Part II. of the Unbloody Sacrifice, p. vii.
[a] a. p. 21. Ap.

No words can be more expressive of a visible, real Sacrifice offered by a Priest; and he plainly supposes, that all mental sacrifices are only preparative or qualifications for offering this external Sacrifice; which consideration does very much exalt the nature of the Eucharistical oblation. And yet after all he says expressly, that praise and a contrite heart are "the only sacrifice" which God demands. These things may at first sight seem very inconsistent, but in reality the holy Father speaks very agreeably to himself and to the truth: for he does not say, that they are in themselves absolutely the only sacrifice, but that they are the only sacrifice which God demands from us; that is, which we can furnish out of our own stock, or offer of our own abilities. God demands the oblation of Christ's Sacramental Body and Blood; but this is a Sacrifice, which He first *et toties quoties* gives us, before we can give it Him; even the material Bread and Wine are things, which God must give to us, before we can offer them to Him. His Word and Spirit must make the Eucharist the Body and Blood, before we can present them as such to Him; so long as we are rational, and creatures, and enjoy the faculty of speech, we have the sacrifice of praise and contrition, ἐφ᾽ ἡμῖν, to offer to Him of our own, when and where we please. And therefore this is the only sacrifice God demands, as from ourselves, from within our own persons. And if we consider the Church as a body of such men, it may be truly said, that the only oblation which they can advance as from themselves is that mental sacrifice now spoken of; the Body and Blood, and even the Bread and Wine, are things which may be said to be οὐκ ἐφ᾽ ἡμῖν, not from within us; and therefore this is in some measure applicable to the words of Clemens Alexandrinus, just before cited: and these words of Gregory are a very plain demonstration, that all the great things said by Cyril of Alexandria and others concerning the excellence of internal intellectual sacrifices are not at all inconsistent with the belief of a real and visible Sacrifice in the Eucharist; for the reader sees, that this Father in the very same paragraph does, in such words as will admit of no dispute, assert the material Sacrifice in the Eucharist, and makes all those internal sacrifices previously necessary to the better offering of this; and yet at the same time says, that praise and a contrite heart are the S E C T. only sacrifice which God demands *of us*[b]. II.

If from single Fathers we turn our eyes to the ancient Of the long Liturgies, we shall find them filled with long recitals of God's recitals of God's mer- power, dominion, providence, and attributes, with Psalms of cies in the old Litur- David, and other hymns from canonical and apocryphal gies. Scripture, or of a private and more late composure; and these were commonly introductory to the *Trisagium*, and in all Liturgies ended with those angelical words; soon after which the Priest proceeds to the institution, and then to the commemorative oblation, and then to the finishing consecration. Now these particular and very large enumerations of God's mercy and care over the whole race of mankind, and especially the Church, were intended to be express declarations of the meaning and intentions of Christ Jesus', and His Priest and people's, instituting and celebrating the Eucharist; that it was designed, in an especial manner, to be a sacrifice of praise and thanksgiving for the creation and preservation and wise government of the world, and especially for our redemption by Christ Jesus; and that these recitals were very ample and very ancient is to be seen in Justin Martyr's account of the Eucharist, which the reader has in the Appendix[c]. I know our adversaries are willing to have men believe, that these acknowledgments and declarations of God's power and goodness were the very Sacrifice offered in the Communion; and that by these thanksgivings the Bread was sanctified, the Wine was blessed; but this is all mistake, as has been sufficiently shewed; though it must be owned that by perpetually translating εὐχαριστεῖν in the history of institution by "giving of thanks," and Justin Martyr and Irenæus's ἄρτος εὐχαριστηθεὶς, "bread over which thanks has been given," the generality of readers have taken occasion to draw such conclusions in their own minds. But having already shewed how the Bread and

---

[b] I have produced sufficient proof from the Fathers for a material sacrifice of praise in the Eucharist; and I have considered such particular sayings of the ancients, which are but three or four, where they seem to assert that the sacrifice consists of nothing but words and thoughts: and now, allowing them these authorities for an immaterial sacrifice in the Eucharist, what are they, if they are laid in the scale against so many and clear proofs for a Sacrifice of Bread and Wine? But in truth none of these are directly against us; the first and last are for us.—[1st Ed.]

[c] a. p. 2. Ap.

CHAP.
II.
Wine were consecrated, and that there was in the ancient Church a solemn oblation of them made to God, in commemoration of Christ's personal Sacrifice, I think it needless now to labour for a proof of that which must, I suppose, be allowed to have been sufficiently proved already to all such as are impartial inquirers; and therefore I shall at present only further observe, that they, who would have the prefatory lauds and hymns to be the only Eucharistic Sacrifices of Christians, argue as irrationally as if they should undertake to prove, that confession of sin was the only sin-offering or trespass-offering used in the temple or tabernacle of the Jews; because he that came thither to offer such a sacrifice must lay his hand on the beast which he brought

Lev. v. 5.
to be sacrificed, and "so confess his sin:" but as this confession of sin was in truth no more than a declaring the occasion of his bringing the sacrifice; so I apprehend, that the ancient way of introducing the oblation in the Eucharist, with a very ample and special recital of God's more singular blessings and favours, was no more than an express and most solemn profession of the Church's intention, in the Sacrifice now to be offered, to do glory to God, to agnize His dominion and other attributes, and to acknowledge all His mercies and favours, especially that which was the principal and the foundation of the rest, His sending Christ Jesus into the world to die for our sins. And that this was the first and primary design of the Eucharist they knew, not only from the nature of all Sacrifice, but because Christ had instituted this to be offered for a memorial of Him; and therefore, though it is certain, that εὐχαριστεῖν and εὐλογεῖν, Εὐχαριστία and Εὐλογία have the same signification in the history of institution and in several of the most ancient writers, and it was the Bread and Wine which were blessed or eucharistized; yet these words were taken in so extensive a signification, as that they were also believed to import blessing and praise offered to God, in and by this most sacred institution: and indeed the very offering the holy symbols to God was at the same time a recognition of God's goodness and other attributes, and a means of procuring the Divine blessing to descend upon them; and therefore by the very same act and deed, they blessed God and blessed His creatures.

There is a passage in St. Clement of Rome's first Epistle to the Corinthians, which deserves our particular considera-tion; the words are[d], "'The Sacrifice of praise shall glorify Me, and there is the way in which I will shew him My salvation.' This is the way in which we shall find our salva-tion, that is, Jesus Christ, the High-Priest of our oblations[e]." This holy Bishop had made a long citation from the fiftieth Psalm, in the end whereof are those words, which are at the beginning of those now produced by me. Now I suppose it will be easily granted, that by "the Sacrifice of praise" St. Clement meant the Eucharist; and indeed this is the only Sacrifice of praise, in which we can in any tolerable sense be said to "find the salvation of God." In the former part of this Psalm, God had declared He would reject the bloody sacrifices of the Jews; but lest any one should from hence conclude, that no proper Sacrifice was to be offered by God's new people under the Gospel, it is added, ver. 14, "offer unto God thanksgiving, and pay thy vows unto the Most High;" and here in the last verse, "the Sacrifice of praise shall glorify Me," &c.; which St. Clement rightly judged to be a prediction of our unbloody oblation. The only question then is, whether by the sacrifice of praise we are here to understand a material sacrifice. Now as to this point, we have elsewhere seen, that this most primitive writer does plainly enough teach an oblation of Bread and Wine in the Eucharist; see Sect. I. of this chapter; and our adversaries themselves own an offering made of Bread and Wine, though they cannot allow it to have been any essential part of the Eucharist in St. Clement's time : there remains therefore nothing to be considered under this head, but only, whether it be more probable, that Clement here speaks of a material or an immaterial Sacrifice of praise; and the only way I know to determine this question is, to examine how the expression was taken in all religious writings before and in his time; for it is not reasonable to suppose that St. Clement would

SECT.
II.
St. Clemens
R. of a
Sacrifice
of praise.

---

[d] N.B. St. Clement cites these words according to the Greek trans-lation. Now the LXX read זָבַח for the present זֶבַח and we translating from the Hebrew, as it now stands, have 'he that offereth,' instead of 'the Sacrifice;' and further the LXX read שָׁם for the present שָׂם, and so we have 'he that ordereth it aright,' in-stead of 'there;' and the word which we render 'conversation,' they render literally 'way.'

[e] [a. p. 1. Ap.]

CHAP. pretend to stamp a new sense upon it; or if he had, he
II. would certainly have hinted so much to us.

The Scrip-   Now it is certain, the current sense of "a sacrifice of
tural notion praise," before and to St. Clement's time, was an animal or
of a Sacri-
fice of   some other visible thing offered to God, as a testimony of
praise.   gratitude. This it infallibly signifies wherever it is used
in the Law of Moses; for a sacrifice of praise or thank-
offering (which is the same thing; it is styled θυσία αἰνέσεως
by the LXX in Leviticus, as well as Psalm l.) was only one
sort of peace-offering, and this peace-offering was either a
Lev. iii.   bullock or sheep or goat. But if it was intended for a sacrifice
of praise or a thank-offering, the votary was directed to offer
Lev. vii.   with it "cakes unleavened, mingled with oil," &c. "And the
12, 13.
ver. 15.   flesh of the sacrifice of peace-offering for thanksgiving shall
be eaten the same day that it is offered;" and again to the
Lev. xxii.   same purpose, "When ye will offer a sacrifice of thanksgiving
29, 30.   unto the Lord, offer it at your own will. On the same day
it shall be eaten up." So it signifies again in the story of
2 Chron.   Hezekiah, who bade the people "bring sacrifices and thank-
xxix. 31.   offerings into the house of the Lord; and the congregation
brought sacrifices and thank-offerings, and as many as were
of a free heart, burnt-offerings:" again, in the account we
2 Chron.   have of Manasseh's conversion, it is said, "He repaired the
xxxiii. 16. altar of the Lord, and sacrificed thereon peace-offerings
[ch. xxxiii. and thank-offerings." [And the Prophet Jeremiah speaks
11.]   of them that should "bring a sacrifice of praise into the
house of the Lord."] The word translated here in the two
last places 'thank-offerings' is in the Hebrew תּוֹדוֹת, that
is, 'praises' in the abstract; and yet I apprehend, that no
rational man can doubt but that it signifies animal sacrifices. The "sacrifice of thanksgiving with leaven" mentioned
Amos iv. 5, must of necessity be material. We are told that
1 Mac.iv.56. at the feast. of dedication the people "offered burnt-offerings, and sacrificed the sacrifice of deliverance and praise or
peace-offerings, and thank-offerings;" there are but three
other places that occur to me in the Old Testament, where
this expression is used; in Psalm cvii. 22; cxvi. 17; and
Jonah ii. 9. In these three places, vocal praises are added to
the sacrifice of thanksgiving; but sure, when the Psalmist
wishes that men would "offer to God the sacrifice of thanks-

giving, and tell out His works with gladness;" and when he says of himself, "I will offer the sacrifice of thanksgiving, and call upon the Name of the Lord;" he could not intend, by exhorting others to express their gratitude in words as well as by dumb sacrifices, and by doing the same himself, that the verbal praise or devotion should annihilate the animals that were to be offered on such occasions. He only desires, that men would not content themselves with offering the carcase of a dead beast, but that they would with their tongues express their good dispositions toward God; and he resolves to do so himself; and the same must be said of Jonah, who, in the whale's belly, promises not only to 'sacrifice,' but to do it with a "voice of thanksgiving" and to "pay his vows." The Psalmist and Jonah were born and bred Jews; and therefore, when they speak of sacrifice or the sacrifice of praise, they must in equity be understood to use those words in the sense, which God by His Law had given to them; in that sense, which the common use of the Jewish people had impressed upon them; unless there be some very obvious and cogent reason to the contrary: but in these places there is no such reason; nay, Jonah expressly adds 'vows;' and these were ever some material things offered to God, either in order to obtain some blessing, or to thank God for the receipt of it: and therefore I may conclude, that in the Old Testament a sacrifice of praise or thanksgiving perpetually signifies something that is material; for it is evident, that David at the offering sacrifice did use vocal devotions. When he "offered burnt-offerings and peace-offerings," he "called upon the Name of the Lord;" nay, "he appointed certain of the Levites to record, and thank, and praise the Name of the Lord; and he left Zadok the Priest to offer burnt-offerings, and Heman and Jeduthun to give thanks unto the Name of the Lord," yet no man will in common sense conclude, that the material sacrifices were by this means annulled, or converted into hymns and psalms. "The Sacrifice of praise" is mentioned but once in the New Testament, viz. Heb. xiii. 15; and I can see no reason, why it may not there be taken in the same sense that did formerly belong to it; I do not mean for an animal sacrifice, but still for a material one; for such a Sacrifice as Christians offered

SECT. II.

1 Chron. xxi. 26. 1 Chron. xvi. 4. 37. 39, 40, 41.

CHAP. in the Eucharist.   Nor does the phrase here added, viz. the
II.   "fruit of our lips" (or " the offering of our lips," for καρπὸν
here is allowed to be put for κάρπωμα)—this I say does not
impugn the notion of a material sacrifice of praise, at least
not such a one as we offer in the Eucharist; for this is really
an oblation of the lips, rather than of the hands; it is presented to God principally by prayer and praise, and is therefore ' an offering of the lips, making confession to God's
name.'   It is supposed, that the Apostle took this phrase
from Hosea xiv. 2, where it is rendered by us, according to
the present Hebrew copies, "the calves of our lips."   But
neither does this phrase necessarily import an immaterial
sacrifice.   The Prophet directs the people to address themselves to God, and say, " Take away all iniquity, and receive
us graciously, so will we render the calves of our lips."   It
seems to me most probable, that as the words are a form of
prayer, which the Prophet drew up for the ten tribes to be
used under their captivity; so the import of them is, that if
God would restore them to their native country and to the
public worship in the temple, they would upon their restoration render to God those calves, or other sacrifices, which
their lips had promised or vowed under their captivity.   So
Ps. lxvi. 14. that by ' the calves of their lips' we can more probably
understand nothing than those material sacrifices, which
the captive Israelites had vowed on condition that God
would give them the free enjoyment of their country and
religion.   And I shall hereafter have occasion to shew,
that the oblations made by lay-Christians were sometimes
called vows, and that too very properly; so that, in a word,
I can see no shadow of reason, why a sacrifice of praise
must have quite another signification in the writings of St.
Paul and his fellow-labourer St. Clement, from what it
has through the Old Testament.   Nor can I see any other
cause, why men when they hear mention of a sacrifice of
praise should presently form an idea of some invisible and
immaterial oblation, than that which Quakers have, when
they hear of " the Spirit" and " the Body of Christ," presently to apply it to their " light within;" or than others
have, when they hear of " praying by the Spirit," to apply that
phrase to praying without premeditation; or when they hear

the word 'presbytery,' to have in their minds a notion of ten
or a dozen grave men, perfectly of the same order and authority, and that have the gift of speaking extempore both
to God and men : and the reason is only this, that they have
many years used to link together these words and these
ideas, and they are so much under the power of prejudice,
that they know not how to turn their thoughts into a new
track. If it be said, that Christ came to instruct us " to
worship God in spirit;" and that therefore the phrases of
the Old Testament, when used in the New, must be taken
in a spiritual sense; all this I readily own. But then by
'spirit' I do not think we are to understand worshipping
God without any thing that is material. I can see no reason
why our Sacrifices must be more immaterial than our Sacraments. We worship God in spirit, when our minds go along
with our outward actions and words, and when we see and
acknowledge those promises to be fulfilled by the Gospel,
which were veiled under types and enigmatical predictions
in the Law and the Prophets. Men may pretend, and may
by mistake believe, that, while they contend for an immaterial sacrifice in opposition to a material one, they do it out
of true judgment and a well-informed zeal, which teaches them
to prefer the inward affections and dispositions of the heart
before every thing that is external : and it is upon this very
pretence that a very great number of our people despise or
neglect Sacraments; and others cry out against them as the
very dust of the serpent. But sure, by asserting a material
Sacrifice, so tremendous a Sacrifice as that I have been describing, we do not at all·lessen the value of any internal
grace or the necessity of a pious life and conversation; nay,
we believe, that, by endeavouring to raise the dignity of Sacraments to the primitive Apostolical standard, we take the
most effectual course to promote solid piety and practical
Christianity. There is no argument like that of experience;
piety never thrived so mightily in the Church of Christ as
during those times, when that doctrine of the Eucharist,
which I now plead for, did universally prevail : and on the
contrary, we justly complain of the great degeneracy of the
present generation of men, who call themselves Christians;
and certainly one radical cause of this degeneracy is the very

low opinion, which men have entertained of the Sacraments, and particularly of the Eucharist; which was of old esteemed, and certainly was, while duly practised, the most prevalent and efficacious method of addressing our services to God, and of drawing down blessings from Him upon ourselves. A man of the present age may please himself with an opinion, that if he do but "praise the Name of God" and "magnify it with thanksgiving" proceeding from his tongue and heart, he offers a better sacrifice to God than if he sacrificed "a bullock which hath horns and hoofs;" and he may conceit that the Sacrifice of the Eucharist is no better than that of a dead animal; nay, our adversaries have endeavoured to represent the latter as more valuable than the former: but certainly the royal Psalmist would never have drawn any comparison between a sacrifice that men can compose and offer by their own inherent powers and faculties, and a Sacrifice that was contrived by the Son of God Himself, and which He invigorates with perpetual streams of Divine grace, and has made the standing ordinance, whereby His merits are to be solicited, conveyed, and applied to the souls of men.   This brings me to shew,

The second end of the Eucharistical Sacrifice is propitiation and expiation.   2. That the other end of this Sacrifice is, to procure Divine blessings and especially pardon of sin. In the first respect it is propitiatory, in the second expiatory, by virtue of its principal, the grand Sacrifice. I join both of them together to render the citation of the authorities less tedious to my reader and myself; for the proofs of both these particulars are intermixed with each other, as the reader will perceive by a perusal of them. I begin with the words of St. Chrysostom[f]; "When the whole people and the body of the Clergy stand with hands stretched out, and the tremendous mystery is placed in open view, how can we do otherwise than prevail with God?" and he takes it very ill of some in his days, who thought[g], that "when the Sacrifice was in [the Priests'] hands, and all things being ordered in a decorous manner lay in open view," yet that the commemoration of Martyrs was "mere matter of form; then," as he adds, "other things are matters of form, the oblations made for the Priests and the body of the people; but God forbid, all

[f] O. p. 42. Ap.   [g] C. p. 41. Ap.

these things are done with faith." St. Augustine wonders[h], "why in this one Sacrifice for sin the people should be invited to drink the blood;" whereas they were forbidden it in all the sacrifices under the Law. He calls it[i] "the only Sacrifice of our salvation :" for he supposes it the same, which Christ offered in the original Eucharist. Nay, he says in commendation of his mother Monica[k], "She desired daily to be remembered at the Altar, from whence she knew That Victim was dispensed, by Which the hand-writing against us is blotted out." "Now," says St. Ambrose[l], "Christ is offered, He offers Himself as a Priest to remit our sins, here in effigy, there in verity, where He intercedes as an advocate to His Father for us." Ephrem Syrus affirms, that[m] "when the tremendous mysteries are offered, and the Priest makes a prayer for all, (meaning between the consecration and distribution,) then those souls, which make their approaches, receive a purification from all their sins through those tremendous mysteries." Cyril of Jerusalem tells us[n], "when the spiritual victim, the unbloody Sacrifice is finished, then we supplicate God over this Sacrifice of propitiation or expiation, (ἱλασμοῦ,) for the common peace of the Churches, for the well-ordering of the world, for kings, for soldiers, &c.—and to say all at once, for all that want our assistance;" and again[o], "We offer Christ slain for our sins, propitiating God for them [the people,] and for ourselves." Eusebius, speaking of some Bishops, who were not sufficient masters of eloquence to harangue the emperor and his court at a public congress, says[p], that "they propitiated the Deity with the unbloody victims, the mystic Sacrifices, for the common peace, for the Church of God, for the emperor himself, offering supplicatory prayers for the royal issue;" and at another place[q], "We offer the loaves of shew-bread, and the blood of sprinkling, of the Lamb of God, Which taketh away the sins of the world, Which expiates our souls, when we renew the salutary memorial." St. Cyprian[r] expresses his indignation against some that had lapsed in time of per-

---

[h] f. p. 31. Ap.
[i] N. p. 36. Ap.
[k] a. p. 31. Ap.
[l] m. p. 27. Ap.
[m] a. p. 25. Ap.

[n] f. p. 19. Ap.
[o] g. p. 19. Ap.
[p] c. p. 15. Ap.
[q] k. p. 17. Ap.
[r] e. p. 11. Ap.

secution, for that they attempted surreptitiously to take the Sacrament, "before their sins were expiated, before they had made public confession of their crimes, before their conscience was cleansed by the Sacrifice and hands of the Priest;" i. e. before the Eucharist had been offered for them in particular, and before the Priest had absolved them by imposition of hands, as the practice was in that age. Origen is very clear in this point[s]. "If these things," says he, "are referred to the great mystery, we shall find that that memorial has the effect of the grand propitiation. If you turn your thoughts to that Bread which comes down from heaven and gives life to this world, to that Shew-bread which God hath set in open view, as being propitiatory by faith in His Blood, of which our Lord saith, ' offer this for a memorial of Me ;' you will find this is the only memorial which renders God propitious to men." And when St. Clement of Rome says[t], that "the continual Sacrifice, the vow, the offering for sin and transgression, are offered only in Jerusalem," that is, in the Christian Church, as St. Cyril of Alexandria very justly explains it, he gives a very illustrious testimony to this truth.

The Liturgies are very full of proof to this purpose; the Gregorian prays[u] for "an acceptance of the gifts, and of those who offer them, and for whom they are offered, and of all who belong to them; for the redemption of their souls," &c. That of St. Peter, that[x] "God would bless the Sacrifice, and for the sake of it accept them who offer it;" and[y], that "God would bless the gifts which we offer for the whole Catholic Church." In St. Chrysostom's Liturgy the Priest begs[z], "that he may be sufficient to offer gifts and Sacrifices for his own sins and the errors of the people;" there are words to the same effect in the Liturgy of St. Basil[a], and in the Liturgy of St. James[b], which I shall not repeat, but refer my reader to them. But the Clementine Liturgy best deserves our notice; and in that the Bishop beseeches God[c] "to look favourably on the gifts, and to send down His Holy

s b. p. 10. Ap.
t b. p. 1. Ap. l. 14.
u b. p. 59. Ap.
x a. p. 58. Ap.
y b. p. 58. Ap.

z b. p. 57. Ap.
a b. p. 56. Ap.
b c. d. p. 54, 55. Ap.
c c. p. 53. Ap. l. 31.

Spirit on them; that they who partake of them may be con-
firmed in godliness, obtain remission of sins," &c. and then
goes on "to pray or offer" (these words are indifferently
used) for all sorts and degrees of men, and for blessings of
all kinds. But there is one thing very observable on this
head, and that is; whereas the Liturgy of Clement has these
intercessions or propitiations for all estates of men, and for
all Divine blessings, immediately after the oblation and con-
secration only, the other Liturgies have them interspersed
throughout: which seems plainly to be a proof, that the
most primitive Church thought it the only proper time to
prevail with God for the greatest favours and graces, when
the Sacrifice was just now consummated and lay in open
view; and that therefore the higher you go in Church an-
tiquity, the more clear and agreeable were the notions which
prevailed concerning the propitiatory and expiatory nature
of the Eucharist. It seems plain, that the Liturgies used
by SS. Chrysostom and Cyril of Jerusalem observed the same
method, that is still extant in the Liturgy of St. Clement;
for we have, in the citations just before, seen them expressing
and justifying these propitiatory devotions, as made when the
Sacrifice was consecrated.

There is one proof of the propitiatory nature of the Eu-
charist, according to the sentiments of the ancient Church,
which will be thought but only too great; and that is the
devotions used in the Liturgies, and so often spoken of by the
Fathers, in behalf of deceased souls. There is, I suppose, no
Liturgy without them, and the Fathers frequently speak of
them. St. Chrysostom mentions it[d], as an institution of the
Apostles. St. Augustine asserts[e], that such prayers are bene-
ficial to those who have led lives so moderately good as to
deserve them. Cyril of Jerusalem mentions[f] a prayer for
those[g] who are gone to sleep before us. And St. Cyprian[h]
mentions the denial of these prayers, as a censure passed
upon some men by his predecessors. Tertullian speaks of
this practice as prevailing in his time[i]; and the Constitu-

[d] O. p. 42. Ap.
[e] x. p. 35. Ap.
[f] f. p. 19. Ap. l. 10.
[g] [Rather, a commemoration of the departed, "that by their prayers and

intercessions God may receive our supplication."]
[h] i. p. 12. Ap.
[i] c. d. p. 8. Ap.

c c 2

CHAP. tions[k] do require Priests and people to use these sorts of
II.   devotion for the souls of those that die in the faith. I shall
say nothing of this doctrine : but

That the ancients did not use these prayers, as if they
thought of a purgatory ; it is certain this last is a modern
invention, in comparison of the oblations and prayers offered by the primitive Church in behalf of their deceased
brethren.

They did not allow prayers to be made for such as they
thought ill men, either as to principles or practice. They
prayed for the Virgin Mary, Apostles, Patriarchs, &c. and
such as they believed to be like them.

They seem to have learned this practice from the Synagogue; for it is probable the Jews in and before our Saviour's time did use it.

Dr. Whitby has fully proved in his annotation on 2 Tim.
iv. 4, that the primitive Fathers, and even the Apostles, did
not believe, that the souls of the faithful are admitted into
heaven before the day of judgment. It was, I suppose,
from hence concluded, that they were in the interim in a
state of expectance, and were capable of an increase of light
and refreshment.

Since praying for them while in this state was no where
forbidden, they judged it therefore lawful ; and if it were lawful, no more need be said ; nature will do the rest.

The only use I make of it is to prove, that the ancients
believed the Eucharist a propitiatory Sacrifice ; and therefore
put up these prayers for their deceased friends, in the most
solemn part of the Eucharistic office, after the symbols had
received the finishing consecration : for as no desires are more
sincere or affectionate than those which we conceive in behalf of our deceased friends; so certainly the ancients addressed these desires to God in such a manner, as they
thought most prevalent, that is, by virtue of the Eucharistical Sacrifice then lying in open view.

Upon whatever grounds it was, that the primitive Church
received this custom of praying for the dead, which I am not
now at leisure to consider so much at large as it deserves ;
it is certain, they had this notion of the propitiatory nature

k d. p. 47. Ap.; c. p. 53. Ap. l. 47.

of the Eucharist from the Scripture, and even from Christ SECT.
Jesus Himself. For if the Eucharistical Bread and Wine be II.
Christ's Body and Blood, given and poured out for us; if
our Saviour did in the institution give the one, and shed the
other for us; and if He commanded His Apostles and their
successors for ever after, to do the same as a memorial of
Him; then I think it is already sufficiently proved, that the
Eucharist is a propitiatory Sacrifice. And further, I con- Heb. xiii.
ceive the Apostle speaks of the Eucharist, both as a sacrifice the Chris-
for sin and a sacrifice of praise, in the thirteenth chapter of tian Sacri-
the Epistle to the Hebrews. The Apostle observes, ver. 9, expiatory
that " it is good, the heart be established with grace, not with ristical.
[such] meats," [as peace-offerings, unleavened bread, and the
like] " which have not profited them who have been occupied
therein." Now I must confess by " grace," as opposed to those
meats which the Law prescribed, I think it most reasonable to
understand the Eucharistical Bread and Wine. I have formerly observed, that Clemens Alexandrinus and others suppose the Sacrament to be called the Eucharist[1] from the
Divine grace communicated to it and by it. And it is pretty
plain, that even the lay-oblations pass by this name[m]. Much 2 Cor. viii. 1,
more credible is it, that the offered and consecrated symbols &c.
should have this honourable title given to them. I apprehend,
therefore, that in these words the Apostle exhorts Christians
not to trouble themselves, if the infidel Jews drove them from
their temple and sacrifices; and advises them to keep close
to the Christian Church, where they might be sure to " eat
the Bread of God," and to receive such meats as would indeed " establish the heart." In the tenth verse the Apostle advises the Hebrew Christians to comfort themselves with
this, that they had in the Church ' an Altar,' of the Sacrifice
offered whereon the Jews remaining in their infidelity " had
no power to eat," no, though they " served the tabernacle or
temple" in the quality of Priests or Levites. The reason
given by the Apostle, why neither the Priests nor people of
the Jews had any right to eat any thing that came from the
Christian Altar, was, that the Sacrifice there offered was not
only a sacrifice for sin, such as was offered in behalf of any
subordinate magistrate or common person; the main of which

---

[1] q. ab. εὖ et χάρις.　　　　[m] See Propitiatory Oblation, p. 22.

CHAP.
II.
Lev. iv.
22—35.
ver. 5. 16.
ver. 13. 21. was to be eaten by the Priests : but such a sin-offering, as was
enjoined for the Priests and the whole congregation, when
they had been guilty of any actual transgression against the
Law of God; such an offering for sin, as that " the blood
was carried into the sanctuary" and " the body burnt without the camp," and that therefore it was such a Sacrifice, as
the Jewish Priests were not to taste of, much less the people,
according to the prescripts of their own Law.   They who by
the " Altar" would understand the Cross, and by " eating" the
receiving Christ by faith; as they give us a very frigid and
jejune explication of the Apostle's words, and suppose that
for which they have no grounds in Scripture, viz. that eating
of Christ Jesus denotes bare faith in Him ; so they can never
reconcile this notion to the Apostle's reasonings and asser-
tions : for if by eating of the Sacrifice the Apostle meant
only believing the virtue and power of it; then it cannot be
said, that the Priest and people did not in this sense eat of
the body of those sacrifices, whose blood was carried into the
sanctuary.   For if they believed their own Law, they must

believe that " the blood made atonement for the soul;" and
if by believing in Christ we eat Him, then they, in believing
the efficacy of their sacrifices, might, in the same manner
and by the same figure, be said to eat their sacrifices.   Therefore I take the words of the Apostle in their most obvious
and natural sense.   I doubt not but by the " Altar" he meant
what all Christian writers did for many hundred years next
after him; and by " eating of" or from " it," I understand
an oral participation of the Sacrifice offered upon it.   And I
conceive, I have given sufficient reason for taking the text in
this sense.   And they that will run off from the literal
meaning of any text, purely to indulge their fancies, or to
serve a present turn, cannot be said to consult the honour
of those holy records.

[Nay, they do in effect contradict a certain truth contained
in these sacred books.   For there we are assured that Jesus
Christ was sent first to the Jews.   But now if they who served
the tabernacle had no right to eat from the Christian Altar,
and if eating from the Christian Altar signify only believing,
then it must follow that they who served the tabernacle had
no right to believe in Christ; whereas in truth they had a

right in this respect prior to the Gentiles. If it be said, while
they served the tabernacle they had no right to believe, I
answer yes. All infidels have not only a right, but are under
a command to believe in Christ.]

I conceive, that by " the Sacrifice of praise," ver. 15, I have
already proved, that St. Clement, who was the Apostle's fellow-labourer, meant the Eucharist; and it is probable that
he learned this language from St. Paul, by whom he was
instructed in the Christian faith, and in the doctrine and
method of celebrating the holy Eucharist. Several Protestants by "the Sacrifice of praise" do understand the alms
offered at the Eucharist; and these are certainly material
sacrifices; unless you will suppose, the Apostle intended
such alms, as St. James speaks of, " be ye clothed, and be
filled :" for such alms best fit the notions of those, who will
allow Christians no Sacrifice but what is spiritual; and believe nothing to be spiritual but what is immaterial. " He
that giveth alms sacrificeth praise," saith Ecclesiasticus,
chap. xxxv. ver. 2, that is, he offereth a material sacrifice
of thanksgiving; he does a thing as acceptable to God, as
if he presented Him with some brute animal to express his
gratitude; and much more may they be said to do this, who
offer to God the most valuable oblation that was ever offered
by mere men, I mean, the Eucharistical Body and Blood of
Christ. But if our adversaries are for confining these words
of St. Paul merely to the lay-oblation; yet I hope, when he
speaks of " communicating" in the next verse, this may be extended to the whole office of the Eucharist; I am sure it is
so now among us; and I will add, that it was so in the
primitive Church. For in the canons of one council, and
that I think the very earliest, whose constitutions are come
down to us, (I mean that of Eliberis, held A.D. 305,) the holy
Sacrament is called ' the Communion' fifty times, or very near
it. And if the canons of this council be genuine, this shews
that ' Communion' and ' communicate' were words used in
the same sense in that age that they are in this; and that
this was then a very familiar way of speaking. And the
Apostle, in the next words, declares what he had been speaking of to be sacrifices, and " such sacrifices as God is well
pleased with." We are sure the alms were material; and

why the other particulars should be deemed to be immaterial, we see not.

And thus having finished my proof of the Eucharistical and propitiatory nature of the Christian Sacrifice; I think it seasonable, before I close this chapter, to consider such exceptions as have [been] or may be made against it, as here asserted to be propitiatory and expiatory. I have already in the first Section answered or prevented those objections, which may be raised against it, as if it were a repetition of the grand Sacrifice; and have shewed, that it is not the repetition of the satisfaction made on the cross, but only of that oblation made by Christ in instituting this memorial. Yet still it may be thought by some, that in pretending to offer an expiatory Sacrifice, after the all-sufficient and most satisfactory Sacrifice offered by Christ, we lessen and depress the value and merits of It.

The Sacrifice of the Eucharist no diminution of the satisfaction made on the cross.

But I must confess, I do not perceive any force in this argument against the expiatory nature of the Eucharist any more than against the expiatory nature of the sacrifices offered by God's direction before or under the Law. If God had seen it necessary, in order to preserve the honour and esteem due to the grand Sacrifice, that no other oblation offered to Him should be looked upon to be an expiation for sin; He would surely never have expressly told the Israelites, that "by the blood of their sacrifices an atonement was made." He would rather have told them, that instead of sacrificing they ought to believe in that grand Sacrifice, which was hereafter to come; which was the only method, upon the supposition of our adversaries, to have secured the value and esteem, which men ought to have for the personal Sacrifice of Christ Jesus. And then to suppose that the faint shady types and figures of the Law should be of greater force and efficacy than what the ancients thought to be a completive Sacrifice under the Gospel, than a Sacrifice instituted with the mouth and hands of the Son of God Himself, is a doctrine very hard to be digested by those that have a hearty esteem for the Gospel Sacraments and the Founder of them. And I cannot but say on this occasion, that some great men, who have asserted the Eucharist to be a real Sacrifice but not propitiatory, have in this respect been more cautious than argute. For if

Lev. xvii. 11.

there ever was a sacrifice, truly so called, that was not propitiatory, it is what I am yet to learn. And I cannot but think,
that I have sufficiently consulted the honour of the grand
Sacrifice, by asserting and proving that the Eucharist was
never intended for the making a new satisfaction for the sins
of men; that this cannot, in the nature of things, be done
again; "for Christ, being once dead, dieth no more; death
hath no more dominion over Him." We do no more in
the Eucharist than what we firmly believe Christ hath commanded to be done over and again until His second coming.
We shew forth His death, only as He Himself did, when He
previously gave His Body and Blood to God before His
crucifixion. And we believe Christ Jesus Himself to be a
more proper judge in what degree and by what means we
are to secure the honour of His personal Sacrifice, than the
whole rational world beside.

It may further be said, that since so perfect a satisfaction
has been made by the one oblation of Christ; all further
propitiations and expiations must, to say the least, be perfectly unnecessary. To which I humbly reply, that

If by calling the Eucharist a propitiatory or expiatory Sacrifice, I am understood to mean, that we add to the merits
of our Saviour's death and sufferings; I must disclaim and
protest against all such thoughts and notions. It is the
natural Blood of Christ, Which is the inexhaustible treasure
of all those blessings that can be derived to us by the Eucharist, or by any other means. Whatever power or efficacy is
ascribed to the Eucharist, flows wholly from the original
Sacrifice. And yet we cannot think the Eucharistical Sacrifice needless; because the personal Sacrifice of Christ did not
and could not absolutely and actually discharge all Christians from the guilt of their sins. For there were many, I
may say, infinitely many sins, that were not yet committed,
when Christ was crucified; and I suppose none but the
rankest Antinomians will say, that sins are forgiven before
they are committed. Nay, I conceive, I am like to have no
adversaries, but such as will readily own, that sin cannot be
forgiven, until they who are guilty of it have sincerely repented and used the proper methods of obtaining pardon;
and that therefore, if Christ Jesus have instituted any Sacri-

The Sacri-
fice of the
Eucharist
as expi-
atory, not
unneces-
sary.

CHAP.
II.
fice as necessary to be offered in order to obtain this pardon, we are never to presume that we have gained the end, until we have used the means. In a word, all Christians, with whom I am now arguing, will grant, that Christ purchased forgiveness and other blessings by His death, conditionally only; and that until we have complied with these conditions, we have no reason to expect these blessings;

Two things necessary for applying the merits of Christ for the expiation of our sins.
In order therefore to procure pardon of sin or any other mercy, which we hope to receive by the shedding of His Blood, these two things are necessary;

1. That we apply ourselves to God in a proper manner; and if He have directed us in what manner to do it, we are to seek for no other. God decreed from the beginning, that the death of Christ should be the means of all that pardon and other graces and favours, which He intended for His Church and people. Yet this did not hinder Him from instituting sacrifices, whereby men should apply themselves to Him, in order to have these graces and favours imparted to them; and though He hath now abolished all other sacrifices, yet I have shewed, that He has enjoined a new one in their stead. And since the sins of Christians are more exceeding sinful than those of other men, as being committed against a more clear and full light than was ever enjoyed by others; therefore it seems reasonable, that they should make this application to God for pardon, by more valuable and powerful sacrifices, than others did or could. And since the mercies we expect are more great and weighty than any men, before Christ's coming, had any reason with confidence to ask of God; therefore the Sacrifice offered by us ought in reason to be of greater price and more full of persuasion than theirs were; and Christ hath accordingly furnished us with such a Sacrifice, even that of His spiritual Body and Blood. The Apostle excellently well teaches us this truth, when he tells us, that "God hath set forth Christ to be a propitiation," or rather a "propitiatory;" that is, Christ is to us, what the mercy-seat was to the Jews. Now the Jews were never the better for the mercy-seat, if they did not apply themselves to it in the method, which God by His Law had prescribed. And the method of making approach to the mercy-seat was by offering sacrifice, and sprinkling the blood thereof upon

Rom. iii. 25.

the vail, which was drawn before this throne, where the Divine Majesty did in so peculiar a manner reside; and our Saviour has directed us where and how we are to make our addresses to Him, as our mercy-seat; and that is by offering the memorial, which He Himself hath appointed. And it is strange, that Christians can think of making application to their mercy-seat in a less solemn manner, than the Jews did to theirs. The Apostle further tells us, that Christ is our pro-pitiatory, "through faith in His blood;" because faith is not only necessary to qualify us for pardon, but even for the application that is to be made for this purpose. But faith of itself can no more pardon a Christian that is baptized, than a catechumen that is not. We are justified by faith; because we are by faith led to Baptism and to the Eucha-ristical Sacrifice. But when we live in an age, wherein men are made to believe, that faith pardons, justifies, and saves men; it cannot be wondered, that men slight and disparage all other means: but God be thanked, that neither the Scrip-tures, nor the Church, teach us this doctrine; but it is a false conclusion that men draw from the Scriptures, to save them-selves the pains of using any other means. It appears then very evidently, that, notwithstanding Christ's death, yet par-don and other evangelical mercies cannot be obtained with-out particular application made to God; that the application made by Christians ought to be rather in a more solemn and prevalent manner than was ever used by others; that never any people did make application for pardon and other great favours, after they were once in covenant with God, but by Sacrifice. It therefore seems just and reasonable, that we should do it in the same manner; and it is very evident, that the Christians of the first and purest ages did thus make their application. It ought further to be considered, that nothing within, no external action performed by any person in behalf of himself, can properly be said to be pro-pitiatory or expiatory; the assiduous sincere performance of any duty undoubtedly inclines God to be merciful and pro-pitious to us; but no man ought to depend on any action of his own, for the procuring an actual application of pardon to himself. It is agreed on all hands, that the merit and satisfaction, whereby our sins are forgiven, flow purely from the grand Sacrifice; but I am now speaking of the actual application of these merits and this satisfaction, which was the end for which all sacrifices under the Law and the Eucharistical Sacrifice under the Gospel were appointed by God. And it is I suppose very evident, that none was ever allowed to make expiation for himself, by any thing that he was capable of doing as a private person. The High-Priest, when he had sinned, was indeed to expiate his own fact; but it was by virtue of an external sacrifice, instituted by God for this purpose; not by any prayer, or faith, or internal act of religion. He was to apply himself to God " by the blood of other" creatures, to shew, that nothing which proceeds *ab intus*, from within ourselves, can either make satisfaction for our sins, or make application of the satisfaction made by another. Moses indeed seems to have made atonement for Aaron and the people by prayer, but not for himself, for he was innocent; but this too seems to have been done, before the tabernacle and altar were erected and the priesthood instituted, and consequently before there was any solemn sacrifice appointed for this purpose; and it was in a case too, where the intended High-Priest Aaron had polluted himself by idolatry, and so had been under an incapacity for executing his office, if he had received his inauguration; and this therefore can never prove, that any particular person, or any body of men, can effectually apply themselves to God for pardon by virtue of their own prayers, or other good deeds, or even by faith in Christ, without using that method of application which God hath ordained. Far be it from me to say or think, that God hath tied His own hands, so as that He will accept of no other manner of address, when He sees a just reason for it; but what I say is, that neither prayer nor any mere internal act of the mind was ever appointed by God, either to make satisfaction or expiation, or to apply it to our souls; though we ought in reason or charity to believe, that in defect of the outward means God accepts what we are capable of doing. David indeed had no occasion to make use of sacrifice; for he had his pardon notified to him by an express revelation. And though the son of Sirach says, that " to depart from evil is a propitiation;" yet in the next words he advises the reader "not to appear before the Lord empty," that is, without a sacrifice; by which he lets us know, that when he calls repentance "propitiation," he means, it is a most excellent qualification to prepare us to appear before God, in order to have our sins expiated. I conclude, that neither prayer, nor faith, nor any other act or deed of ours, can be expiatory in any sense; by them no satisfaction can be made; nor did God ever intend them to be the ordinary means of applying the merits of the grand Sacrifice; if He had, Sacraments would have been needless things, as well as sacrifices; and this brings me to speak of,

2. The other thing necessary for the receiving pardon of our sin, or any other benefit of Christ's Passion; and this must be some Divine act passed by God the Father, Son, or Holy Ghost towards us. For since it is evident to a demonstration, that the purchase of Christ's death was not, could not be actually applied by either of these three Divine Persons, at the time of offering the grand Sacrifice; therefore it follows, that it must be applied from time to time, as occasion requires. And it is extremely vain and groundless to suppose, that any particular man can perform this Divine act of applying the merits of Christ's death to himself. It is an act of God, Who has the sole power of pardoning or conferring any spiritual grace upon His creatures; and since God does it not by express revelations made from time to time to His creatures, it is very evident, He performs it to Jews and heathens upon their conversion, in and by Baptism; to those that are already members of His Church, in and by the Eucharist. These are holy solemn actions, in which the Christian Priest is ordained to act "for men in things pertaining to God;" and they who are duly admitted by him to be "partakers of the Altar" or to be guests at the Lord's Table, by the holy action which he there performs by a Divine authority, and according to the instructions given him by "the High-Priest of our oblations," have the pardon of their sins sealed to them, and are put or continued in the possession of all those graces and benefits, which Christ by dying merited for us. This shews, that prayer or faith cannot impart these blessings to us, for they are our own acts; whereas the forgiveness of sin and the communication

of all spiritual mercies must be performed by God; and the
usual method in which God performs these acts is in and by
the Sacraments. And though Sacraments are administered
by the hands of men; yet I have shewed, that according to
the judgment of the ancients grounded upon Holy Scripture,
the Spirit of God does, by His particular power there present,
render the elements effectual to the ends for which they are
intended. Great things are said of prayer in the Holy Scriptures, and all blessings promised to those who duly practise
it; but I apprehend, that all judicious men will acknowledge,
that they are the prayers of the Church, put up in public
assemblies, to which these promises are made, rather than
the private prayers of single Christians; which though they
are a necessary duty, yet have not assurance of being accepted in that degree, that public prayers have; and I must
add, that the public prayers of the Church, for all the most
valuable and desirable blessings, were addressed to God in
the primitive Church in the Eucharistical office or Liturgy,
and were offered in virtue of the Sacrifice lying in open view.
So that all those proofs for the prevalence of prayer were in
reality evidences of the propitiatory nature of the Eucharist,
in the judgment of the ancients; and that which gave wings
and vigour to these prayers was the Sacrifice offered with
them and by them.

We do no
more lessen
the merits
of Christ's
death than
our adver-
saries.
Our adversaries agree, that the Sacramental Body and
Blood of Christ do convey pardon and all the benefits of
Christ's death to the souls of the receivers; and if they allow
that these mercies are bestowed by the Sacrament, they must
allow that there we must apply ourselves to God for them;
or else they must say, that God bestows these mercies without any application made to Him: but none of our adversaries will say this; for they all use prayer for pardon and
grace, in celebrating the Lord's Supper; and I cannot for
my life conceive, how it can lessen the grand Sacrifice more,
to apply ourselves to God by exhibiting the Eucharistical
Bread and Wine, than by offering what our adversaries call
the spiritual Sacrifice of prayer. Why is it a diminution to
the personal Sacrifice of Christ, to offer a Sacrifice in the
Eucharist? why because, say our adversaries, it supposes
that Christ's personal Sacrifice was not sufficient for the

pardon and salvation of men. If they be asked, how this follows, or how the Sacrifice of the Eucharist supposes the personal Sacrifice to be insufficient; they must say, that if we thought the personal Sacrifice sufficient we would use no other. Now the answer is obvious, that our Sacrifice is not offered to render the original Sacrifice more meritorious or more satisfactory, but to apply the benefit of It to particular men; and in order to this application, we believe a material Sacrifice necessary to be used: our adversaries own, by their practice at least, that what they call a spiritual Sacrifice is necessary for this purpose; else why do they pray for pardon and grace in the Eucharist? and it is impossible to assign any reason, why the offering of prayer for the application of the merits of Christ's death should not as much impeach the sufficiency of It, as offering Bread and Wine. Certainly he, who in the Eucharist prays for pardon of sin and grace to amend his life, does as effectually declare that he does not think that the benefits of the grand Sacrifice were applied all at once, and that Christians were finally perfected by the personal oblation, as he who offers the Eucharistical Body and Blood. And neither do they offer the one, nor we the other, as if we thought the satisfaction defective; but only for the deriving and applying the all-sufficient merits of Christ to the souls of particular men. Our adversaries must own, that they offer a spiritual Sacrifice to this end; and we do with the primitive Church believe, that our prayers are to be supported by the material oblation of Christ's Sacramental Body and Blood; and we cannot conceive, how our Sacrifice does impair or lessen the virtue of Christ's death more than theirs. And since it is allowed by our adversaries, that the effects of Christ's death are communicated by the Eucharistical Body and Blood to all that duly receive them; this is another tacit acknowledgment, that the grand Sacrifice does not set aside the necessity of a particular application; and that faith and prayer being human actions are not sufficient to make this application, but that it must be done by some Divine action; and where God does perform this action toward baptized Christians otherwise than in the Eucharist, I apprehend they will scarce undertake to inform us. They may say, that this application may be made by God in the

CHAP.
II.
Eucharist, considered as a Sacrament only, not as a Sacrifice; but then they must suppose, that God makes this application to us, without any application made by us to Him. For we cannot apply ourselves to God otherwise than by Sacrifice. Our adversaries grant this; but they assert this to be only a mental Sacrifice of prayer, faith, and such like inward devotions; and granting this, yet it is evident, that the Sacrament without some sort of Sacrifice is not sufficient for the application of Christ's merits; and whether this Sacrifice consist only of such internal actions of the mind, or of the Body and Blood of Christ there represented, I leave to be determined by Scripture and antiquity, which I have proved to be with us in this particular. It is therefore sufficiently clear, that God does apply the effects of the great Sacrifice to us in the Eucharist; and that in order to obtain this application, we must first apply to Him by Sacrifice, even the Sacrifice of Christ's Body and Blood. It is evident, that before the death of Christ, pardon was imparted to the Jews by the oblation of the sacrifice for sin, no part of which was returned to the lay-offerer; but Christ hath provided, that our offering for sin should be shared out among all that attend this Sacrifice, as a token of God's acceptance of it.

Application of the merits of Christ's death made by oblation only, in some cases, without actual communion. But in some cases it seems pretty clear, that the ancients were of opinion, that the application of the merits of Christ's death might be made by virtue of the oblation only, without eating and drinking the Eucharistical Body and Blood; as for instance, to those who, by banishment, imprisonment for Christ's sake, or other violent means, were debarred from the privilege of actual communion. As the case of such was always particularly recommended to God in the Eucharistical service; so no doubt it was done upon an apprehension, that by virtue of this propitiation they had the benefits of Christ's sufferings imparted to them: and we may remember, St. Cyprian reprehends the lapsing Christian for attempting to communicate, before the Sacrifice had been offered in his behalf; that is, before his name had been particularly mentioned in the Eucharistic service, among those penitents who were thought fit to be restored to the communion of the Church, the time of their penance being well-nigh completed. Other cases might be mentioned, whereby it would appear that the ancient Church believed, that men might receive the application and effects of the grand Sacrifice without receiving the symbols, though not without the oblation made for them by name, or however in general terms: which is an undeniable proof that they did believe that oblation could supply the want of communion; or that the merits of the grand Sacrifice might be applied by the Sacrifice of the Eucharist to such persons as were incapable of orally receiving. And let not any man suspect, that, by saying this, I intend to say any thing in behalf of the private solitary Masses of the Church of Rome; for I own them to be a modern corruption. In the ninth century, when the primitive ardour and purity of the Church was very much eclipsed, the people grew more backward and cold in the duty of communicating; then some Priests presumed to make the oblation without any distribution or communion; and yet even then it was not allowed, or approved; nay, they who did it were censured in divers councils held in France and Germany. I only speak of the efficacy of the oblation in behalf of such as were detained from the Communion by some involuntary and invincible obstacle; and am so far from having any good opinion of the solitary Masses among the Papists, that I am fully satisfied, that in the primitive Church the oblation and communion were inseparable; and that they had but one Altar in every Church, where all both Clergy and people attended and received: and as a multitude of Altars in the same Church is a most unprimitive practice, so the administering or consecrating the Eucharist in private houses, except in times of persecution, was not then used. Perhaps the earliest instance of it is in Uranius's Life of Paulinus[n], who had the oblation made in his presence, when he was on his death-bed, the Bishops who were present communicating with him; this was A. D. 431. And in a Penitentiary of the middle ages the Bishop is obliged to confess it as a crime, "if he had caused the Missal-service to be sung by the bed-side in a house, where there were many nauseous things[o]."

Private Masses censured.

---

[n] [Vid. Surii Sanctorum Histt., tom. iii. p. 733.]

[o] See Joan. de Deo, p. 19. (*non numerat.*) after Theodore's Penitential, &c., published by Petit. [ed. Paris. 1677.]

["Quadragesimum nonum est, quod non curavit de Divinis officiis propter

CHAP. II. SECT. III.

That the Communion Table is a proper Altar.

I HAVE shewed, chap. I. sect. III., that a proper Altar is
not absolutely necessary for the offering a proper Sacrifice.
The ancient Christian Priests, when under a state of persecution, and in want of external conveniences, might undoubtedly offer the Eucharist on the stump of a tree or any rough
and unhewed stone, as acceptably as if they had used a fabric
of the most costly materials or the most exquisite workmanship. Dr. Cave, from Philostorgius, tells of Lucian the Priest
and Martyr; that when he was in prison for the sake of his
religion, and by reason of his chains and the ulcers made in
his flesh by the scourges of his persecutors he could put himself into no other posture, he offered the tremendous Sacrifice, lying flat on his back, making use of his own breast instead of an Altar; and from thence administered it to the
Christians who were with him. And I suppose, no rational
man will doubt but in such cases the Sacrifice is perfect,
though the outward decorum of a proper fixed Altar be
wanting[p].

The Holy
Table an
Altar, in the
judgment of
the ancient
Church.

But yet I suppose nothing more evident, than that when
the Church was in a prosperous and quiet state, and enjoyed
the freedom of worshipping God and celebrating the Eucharist in a way that they thought most agreeable to the Divine
will and the nature of the holy mysteries; they always had,
in the most eminent place of their public assemblies, some
table or structure, which they used as an Altar, and deemed
it to be a real one. The proof of this is to be drawn from
the language of the Church, in which it was commonly called
an Altar, without any abating or mollifying additions. Chrysostom tells us[q], " Truly tremendous are the mysteries of the
Church, truly tremendous are the Altars;" and[r], " You see
Him not in a manger, but on the Altar; not a woman hold-

---

convivia sua contra auctoritatem Gre-
gorii 44. Di. c. et quia faciunt cantare
Missam juxta lectum in domo, ubi
spurcitiæ multæ sunt, et ideo Divinam
patientiam ad iracundiam provocant :
nam nunquam Missa in domo celebrari

debet."—This Penitentiary is published
in the Appendix by Petit.]
  p Vid. Lucian, in Cave's Historia
Literaria, [p. 107. tom. i.]
  q A. p. 41. Ap. l. 7.
  r M. p. 42. Ap.

ing Him, but the Priest standing by." St. Chrysostom is particularly cited by Mr. Mede, for asserting, that even in the British Isles Churches and Altars were erected[s]. It would be endless to go to particulars; and the same may be said in relation to St. Augustine, from whom I will therefore only produce two places[t]; "We being many are one Body; this is the Sacrifice which the Church often repeats in the Sacrament of the Altar, which the Church knows full well." I have before observed from the ancients and from the Apostle, that the Eucharistical Bread and Wine were believed to be symbols of Christ's political Body, the Church, as well as of His natural Body; at another place, he speaks of the Eucharist considered as a feast rather than a Sacrifice; and indeed most sacrifices were of old attended with a feast, as ours is; his words are[u], "The feast of our Lord is the unity of His Body, not only in the Sacrament of the Altar, but in the bond of peace." In these two places, the reader will observe, that the Sacrament and Altar were by St. Augustine thought inseparable; as he who calls the Eucharist the Sacrifice of the Church, means the Sacrifice offered only by and in the Church; so he, who calls the same Eucharist the Sacrament of the Altar, means the Sacrament ordinarily celebrated on the Altar only; and St. Augustine was present at the third *alias* fifth Council of Carthage; by the ninth canon[x] whereof it is provided, "that the Sacrament of the Altar be celebrated only by such as are lasting." St. Jerome evidently calls the Communion Table an Altar, in places already cited[y]; and St. Ambrose[z], which my reader may see in the Appendix. Optatus[a] speaks of the impiety of the Donatists, in breaking the Altars of the Catholics, on which, says he, "the vows of the people and the members of Christ have been borne;" and at another place[b] "calls it the seat of the Body of Christ." St. Gregory Nazianzen speaks familiarly of a material Altar in the Church,

---

[s] [Καὶ γὰρ αἱ Βρεττανικαὶ νῆσοι, αἱ τῆς θαλάττης ἐκτὸς κείμεναι ταύτης, καὶ ἐν αὐτῷ οὖσαι τῷ Ὠκεανῷ, τῆς δυνάμεως τοῦ ῥήματος ᾔσθοντο. καὶ γὰρ κἀκεῖ ἐκκλησίαι, καὶ θυσιαστήρια πεπήγασιν.—Tom. vi. p. 635. ed. Savile.] See Mede, "Of the name of Altar." —[Mede's Works, vol. i. p. 491. ed.

1664.]
[t] z. p. 35. Ap.
[u] d. p. 31. Ap.
[x] p. 51. Ap.
[y] e. p. 28, and o. p. 29. Ap.
[z] d. p. 26, and n. p. 27. Ap.
[a] a. p. 22. Ap.
[b] c. p. 22. Ap.

in places also before produced[c]. We have heard Eusebius
asserting[d] "that Christ erected Altars, and caused dedica-
tions of Churches." Mr. Mede also cites his description
of the Altar in the Church of Tyre[e], but in another place
he speaks of the translation of the Altar, as a principal
alteration made in the Christian œconomy, and by which
the Church is chiefly distinguished from the tabernacle or
temple; for, says he[f], "The Altar being translated, contrary
to the placits of Moses, there is an absolute necessity that
there should be a change of Moses' Law, and that an Altar
of unbloody rational sacrifices, according to the new mysteries
of the new Covenant, be erected through the whole habitable
world to the one only Lord:" and St. Athanasius explains
the word 'Table,' by 'Altar;' this latter being in that age
the most known name of that holy fabric. The words deserve
to be transcribed, viz., τράπεζαν, τούτεστι, τὸ ἅγιον θυσιαστήριον, καὶ ἐπ' αὐτῷ ἄρτον οὐράνιον καὶ ἄφθαρτον· "the Table,
that is, the holy Altar, and the heavenly uncorrupted Bread
upon it[g]." Mr. Mede further observes, that St. Cyprian
uses the word Altar, of the Lord's Table, ten times in his
Epistles only; and I must add, as that learned man does,
"whether he useth the name Table, I know not[h]." For
it does not appear to me, that the adversaries of the Sacrifice and Altar have been able, ever since the time of Mr.
Mede's writing, to produce a single instance of this Father's
applying that name to the sacred Board. The reader, by
casting his eye to my citations, will see that St. Cyprian
does very often give this compellation of Altar to the Communion Table; and I am apt to think, that if ever he had
called it otherwise, we should have heard of it long ago. He
says indeed more than once, that it was pointed out by " Solomon's table," but so the Eucharistical Sacrifice was prefigured
by the Paschal Lamb; but no man from thence did ever conclude, that the Eucharist was a bloody or animal sacrifice.
The industrious Voigtus observes, that Origen reprehends
some Priests for carrying themselves in a lofty theatric manner,

---

[c] c. d. e. p. 21. Ap.
[d] b. p. 15. Ap.
[e] [p. 490.]
[f] d. p. 15. Ap.

[g] Disput. contra Arium, [tom. i. p.
122. ed. Par. 1627.] See Mede, [p.
489.]
[h] [p. 488.]

in the "circle of the Altar," in his third Homily on Judges[1];
Mr. Bingham[j] cites him for so using the word in his tenth
Homily on Numbers; but I apprehend he does it much more
clearly in the eleventh Homily, in a passage cited in my Appendix[k]. Tertullian gives it the name of Altar[l] and of Ara[m];
and Mr. Mede cites him[n] as using the word Altar for the
same thing, in *De exhortatione castitatis*. St. Irenæus says[o],
"The Apostles of our Lord inherit neither lands nor houses,
but always attend God and the Altar." And Mr. Bingham[p]
cites him for saying[q], that "we ought to offer a gift at the
Altar frequently, without intermission;" both these citations
escaped the diligence of Mr. Mede and Voigtus too. It does
not appear, that Justin Martyr and Athenagoras or Clemens
Alexandrinus had ever any occasion in their writings to
mention this holy utensil; and so they can afford no evidence
either for or against us. St. Ignatius four several times expressly calls it an Altar. He speaks[r] of "one Eucharist, one
Flesh of Christ, one Cup, one Altar, one Bishop;" and[s] bids
the Magnesians "run to one Temple, one Altar, one Jesus
Christ;" he adds[t], "He that is within the Altar is clean," by
"the Altar" meaning the Altar-room, the Chancel; and
again[u], "He that is not within the Altar," or Altar-room, "is
deprived of the Bread of God." St. Clement of Rome tells
the Corinthians[v], that "Sacrifice is not to be offered every
where, but at the Altar;" and St. Barnabas is most probably
to be understood of the Holy Table, when he bids men "come
up higher, and in a more honourable manner, unto the
Altar[w]." In a word, it does not appear to me, that the Called a
Holy Board is ever called a Table in the three first centuries once in the
but once, and that is by Dionysius of Alexandria in his three first
letter to Xystus of Rome. The most diligent Voigtus has centuries.
discovered but this single instance[x]. It is in the narrative, which Dionysius gives, of a clergyman, who discovered
that the Baptism he had received was heretical and as he

[1] See Voigt. de Altarib., cap. ii. sect. 32.
[j] [vol. ii. p. 434.]
[k] e. p. 10. Ap.
[l] h. k. p. 8. Ap.
[m] i. p. 8. Ap.
[n] [Vid. Mede's Works, vol. i. p. 487.]
[o] b. p. 4. Ap.
[p] vol. ii. p. 434.
[q] f. p. 5, 6. Ap. l. 38.
[r] g. p. 2. Ap.
[s] d. p. 2. Ap.
[t] e. p. 2. Ap.
[u] a. p. 1. Ap.
[v] b. p. 1. Ap. l. 13.
[w] chap. i.
[x] [p. 76.]

CHAP.
II.
thought invalid; after he had long lived in the communion of the Catholic Church, and "standing at the Table (Gr. τρα-πέζῃ παράσταντα) had stretched forth his hands to receive the holy Food." In the fourth century, it is owned that it was frequently so called; but to shew that this was an innovation, Athanasius thought himself obliged to explain his own word, and to let the reader know that by 'Table' he meant 'Altar,' because the latter was the most known and familiar name. And I suppose it is altogether incredible, that the Church should call the most known part of the sacred furniture by a name not at all agreeable to the use of it, and very rarely indeed by that name which best fitted it; and if it therefore be an error to call the Holy Board an Altar, it is an error of a very particular nature, and contrary to all other that ever prevailed in the Church. It was in full force in the ages next succeeding that of the Apostles, but in the following ages it did very much abate; for whereas there is but one clear instance of it's being called a Table in the first three centuries, it was not unusual in the following times to call it 'the Holy Table,' 'the mystical or spiritual Table,' or 'the Table,' without an epithet; as may be seen in the citations from Eusebius, St. Chrysostom, and St. Augustine, in the Appendix. The Fathers of the three first centuries certainly knew the import of 'an Altar,' as well at least as any that ever lived since; and they knew very well the connexion between an Altar and a Sacrifice; and if they had in the least suspected, that the name would have given men a wrong idea of the thing, they would certainly have wholly forborne to use that name, or have taken care to intimate to their readers that they were not to take it in a proper sense; or if some particular men had ventured to give it that title, they would by others have been called upon to explain themselves and to remove the scandal: but contrary to all this, the name Altar was familiarly and even generally given to the Holy Table, without any appearance of question or dispute upon this subject; and it may as well be doubted, whether what the primitive Church called Baptism, Eucharist, Bishop, or the Holy Scripture, were those things which now pass under those names, as whether what they called an

Josh. xxii. altar was a real altar. When the Reubenites and Gadites gave the title of an altar to that monument, which they had erected for a testimony of their right and obligation to attend the worship of God in the tabernacle, as well as the rest of the Israelites; the rest of the tribes took umbrage at it, and supposed it to be an overt declaration of their intentions to offer "burnt-offerings and sacrifice" on that altar, if not to another God, yet in another place than what was prescribed by the Law of Moses; and the other tribes express their resentment and suspicions in a most zealous and unanimous manner against this presumed innovation; nor could they be pacified, until the Reubenites and Gadites had fully satisfied them, that though they had given the name of an altar to this monument, yet the structure was not intended for the use which the name imported. As this shews the natural coherence and relation between an altar and a sacrifice, according to the common conceptions of mankind; so it is not consistent with that common prudence, which all that are not malicious enemies to primitive Christianity must allow to the Fathers of the first ages, to suppose that they should so generally agree in calling the Communion Table an Altar, and that no one single writer should ever hint any dislike of this name, especially if the notion of a material sacrifice be so dangerous and full of mischief, as some would represent it. If the primitive Fathers of the two or three first ages had indifferently called it Table or Altar, it had been no prejudice to the cause of the Sacrifice. Dr. Lightfoot[y] tells us, that the altar of burnt-offerings was indifferently called an altar or a table by the Talmudists, in his note on 1 Cor. x. 21; but no one will from thence conclude that they did not think it an altar in the most proper and strict sense; for every altar is a table, though every table be not an altar. And I do not suppose it necessary, that men should perpetually call every thing by it's most proper and distinguishing name. If the ancients sometimes call the Eucharist "the Lord's Supper," of which I am not very sure, yet it does not by any means follow that they did not think it a Sacrifice; because it is very consistent for the same thing to be offered as a sacrifice, and to be eaten as a feast; but when it is in the three first centuries called above

[y] [Vid. vol. ii. p. 769. ed. 1684.]

twenty times an Altar, and a Table but once; if we may
not from hence conclude, that 'Altar' was then thought the
most proper name; we must for the future cease to argue
from the words of others, and learn some more sure way of
guessing at their thoughts.

But since our adversaries have so great an aversion to the
name 'Altar,' let them tell us what other appellation they can
prove to belong to it. Let them tell us, how it was called
by the Apostles or Christ Jesus Himself. To this they can
only say, that Dionysius, two hundred and fifty or sixty years
after Christ, calls it simply a Table; and must we suppose
that Dionysius better understood names and things than
St. Cyprian, Origen, Tertullian, St. Irenæus, St. Ignatius,
and St. Clement? And shall we take a measure of the
notions and language of the Church from six of the greatest
and most eminent writers of these ages, or from one single
person, who as he was the last in time, so he was not the
greatest in any other quality that makes him capable of
being an evidence in this case?

Lord's
Table and
Altar the
same thing
in Scrip-
ture.
If it be said, St. Paul calls the Holy Board a 'Table;' I
answer, no, not simply 'a Table,' as Dionysius does, but the
Lord's Table, 1 Cor. x. 21; and I have elsewhere proved,
that by this expression we are to understand an Altar; for
wherever else it is used in Scripture, that is clearly the
meaning of it; as the reader may be satisfied, by perusing
the four places where we meet with this word in the Old
Testament, viz. Ezek. xli. 22; xliv. 16, and Mal. i. 7, 12.
And he, that after having read these texts can doubt, whether
by the Lord's Table in every one of them be meant the Altar,
may please further to consider, what I have offered to this
purpose in the Propitiatory Oblation, p. 51—56; and since
this phrase does everywhere else denote an Altar, we must
be extremely prejudiced, if we will against such evidence
take it in another sense, in the text of St. Paul; the only
place where this utensil is mentioned in Holy Scripture, except that Heb. xiii. 10, where it is expressly called an Altar
by the same Apostle. The truth is, 'the Table of the Lord'
was the most honourable title that the Prophets and Apostle
could give to a proper Altar. I have at another place shewed
that our Saviour does plainly express His intentions, that He

would have an Altar in His Church, in that text, Matt. v. 23, "If thou bring thy gift to the Altar, &c.," which Mr. Mede has clearly demonstrated to be an evangelical precept[z]. It is true, our Saviour in that place does not directly inform His hearers, what He intended to be the principal Sacrifice to be offered at that Table; but He evidently supposes a material gift there to be offered, such a gift as might be left before the Altar. And the primitive Church, instructed in this point by the Apostles, did upon the same Altar present the material Bread and Wine, and solemnly offer part of that Bread and Wine to God, as the representative Body and Blood of Christ. And I have good reason to believe, that if our adversaries had the one half of that evidence against an Altar, which I have here produced for it, we should be impleaded of obstinacy and stupidity, if we persisted in our pretensions. But let us consider what our adversaries have to offer, by way of reply to these authorities.

I. It is said that the Holy Table was called an Altar, on account of the first-fruits and other provisions for the Clergy and poor, which were there offered. To this I answer, *Whether the Altar were so called only on account of the lay offerings.*

(1.) Be it so; yet this clearly supposes a material Altar and a material oblation.

(2.) Let it be shewed, that such oblations were ever brought to this Altar, but at and in order to the Holy Communion; or that the oblation of Bread and Wine was ever looked upon otherwise in the primitive Church than as a necessary part of the Eucharistical solemnity; the Bread and Wine, for the Sacrifice strictly so called; the other oblations, for the support of those who offered and attended on the Sacrifice and Altar. For if the offering of Bread and Wine on the Altar, and the offering of the Body and Blood of Christ, were always in the first ages inseparable actions; then we have no more reason to say that the Christian Altar was only for receiving first-fruits and alms, than that the altar of burnt-offering was only intended for the depositing such beasts or other things, animate or inanimate, as were brought thither by the Israelites; for the laying them on the Altar and the solemn offering them to God are, in both cases, but only two several parts of the same oblation.

[z] See Propitiatory Oblation, p. 19.

(3.) I have proved, that by the practice of the primitive Church which was learned from the Apostles, and by the intendment of Christ Jesus Himself, the Eucharist was thought a real Sacrifice, and offered as such; and that they judged a proper Altar, though not absolutely necessary to the internal perfection of the Sacrifice, yet very requisite to the outward decorum of it.

Whether the Altar be so called, only as it is a centre of unity.

II. It has been said that the Holy Table is called an Altar by way of allusion, because what the altar at Jerusalem was to the Jews, that the Communion Table is to us, viz., a centre of unity[a]; and this is said by way of reply to St. Ignatius's calling it an Altar four times in his Epistles. To this I answer,

(1.) If indeed St. Ignatius had once or twice by chance so called it, or if this name were given to it very rarely, or only by some one or two writers, this might seem somewhat better than a mere cavil; but since it appears that 'Altar' or 'Lord's Table' was the ordinary, nay, perpetual name of this utensil for the first 250 years; and since in after-ages, though the name 'Table,' without any addition, was frequently given to it, yet no single person can be produced that ever denied it to be an Altar for very many centuries; therefore we must believe that this was thought it's distinguishing characteristic title. For we must believe the Christian writers to be the most singular that ever yet appeared, if for so long a tract of time as 250 years they never gave it any other but a nickname; and in all succeeding ages, until now of late, this name has still been allowed to the Holy Board without any control or opposition.

(2.) If they had spoken only by way of allusion to it's being a centre of unity, they might rather have chosen the word 'Table' than 'Altar;' for every body knows that there were in the temple two altars by God's appointment, that of burnt-offering and that of incense; but there was but one table placed in the temple by God's direction, viz., that of shew-bread, and the Fathers do very frequently speak of this shew-bread as a prefiguration of the Eucharist; but when they speak of the eminence on which the Eucharist is offered and consecrated, they do for the most part style it an Altar, especially in the earliest times.

[a] See Dr. Hancock's Answer, p. 25.

(3.) Ignatius does not speak of the Altar only as a centre of unity, but as a sacred Table for the Bread of God; and for this reason declares[b] that "He who is not within the Altar-room is deprived of the Bread of God." And I have shewed that as by 'the Table of the Lord' is always meant an Altar, so by 'the Bread of God' is always meant some material offering, in the most solemn manner consecrated to God.

(4.) If this way of interpreting Scripture and antiquity be allowed of, it will soon evaporate all religion into mere airy notion. Thus Baptism does, according to the Quakers, denote only an inward washing by the Spirit, and is called by that name only with an allusion to the external washings of the Levitical Law and John the Baptist; eating the Body and Blood of Christ is nothing but regaling the soul with the heavenly Divine Seed and Light within, and is spoken in allusion to the divers meats and drinks of the Jewish Law. St. Clement's High-Priest, Priest, and Levite, and St. Ignatius's Bishop, Priest, and Deacon are not three real orders of evangelical officers, but the Gospel-ministry represented under the titles and degrees of the Jewish Priesthood; or rather they are the sanctified people, such as are under the conduct of the Divine Light.

III. The learned Voigtus[c] would have it, that the Altar was so called on account of the Sacramental Body of Christ; wherein, according to his sentiments, the personal Body was contained (for he was a Lutheran) and laid on this Table, and from thence distributed to the communicants; but

Whether the Altar be so called on account of the sacrificed Body of Christ lying on it.

(1.) It is without example for any thing to be called an Altar on account of a Sacrifice being laid upon it, except the act of oblation be there performed; and until some precedent be produced, whereby it may appear that a Table made for the receiving Sacrifices and oblations, after they have been first offered on some other fabric or utensil, was styled an Altar, all that is said by Voigtus on this head is perfectly precarious.

(2.) I have produced abundant proof that the Sacramental Body and Blood were not only laid on the Altar, but that they were there actually and solemnly offered to God; and that therefore it was not only called an Altar, but was one;

---

[b] a. p. 1. Ap.   [c] [cap. ii. sect. xlii.]

CHAP.
II.
It was not only the bier, on which the dead Body of Christ was laid; but that Table of the Lord, on which It was offered.

IV. It may be pretended that the Holy Table was called an Altar, on account of the spiritual Sacrifices, viz., prayer and praise there offered. But,

(1.) It is irrational to suppose that a material Altar should be raised for the offering of immaterial Sacrifices, such as our adversaries mean by 'spiritual.' A table is but a very indifferent convenience for offering prayer; a desk or pulpit much more eligible.

(2.) I have nowhere met with any passage in antiquity intimating that Altars were erected only for this purpose. And without this all that men write or say on this head must be mere conjecture. That prayers were indeed used at the Altar is as evident as that they were Altars; for by these prayers the oblation was made: nor do I confine the word 'prayers' to the oblatory and consecratory part of the Liturgy, but I mean it of the whole Eucharistical office, which was unquestionably performed by the celebrator standing at the Altar, excepting such parts as belonged to the Deacon. I now speak of the early times only, while the Clementine Liturgy, or one very like it, was everywhere used[d].

(3.) It is true Origen says, "It is on the Altar that we offer our prayers to God," in his ninth Homily on Leviticus[e]; and the reason of this is evident from what has before been shewed, viz., that the ancients believed that their supplications and prayers were rendered effectual by virtue of the Body and Blood of Christ, Which were offered on the Altar, and Which lay there in open view, during the time of their most solemn devotions and intercessions: and so must Optatus be understood, when he says to the Donatists[f], "Why have ye subverted the vows and desires of men together with the Altars? From thence the people's prayers used to ascend to the ears of God; why have ye cut off the intercourse of prayer, and laboured as it were to take away the ladder with an impious hand, lest our supplications should ascend to God

d "Nor does it appear that there were originally any other prayers used, as the common stated devotions of the Church, but in the Eucharist only, however not before the fourth century." [1st ed.]

e [Tom. ii. p. 236. "Altare enim est super quod orationes nostras offerimus Deo."]

f aa. p. 22. Ap.

in the accustomed manner?" It is said that "Abraham builded an altar, and called upon the name of the Lord." If any writer of the first ages had said this of the Apostles or primitive Christians, we have little reason to doubt but our adversaries would from thence have concluded, that the Altar was built only for immaterial Sacrifice; and yet I believe no one will doubt but Abraham called on the name of the Lord, by offering animate or inanimate creatures on his altar; for his sacrifices were 'speaking sacrifices' as well as those of Abel, though they consisted of dumb and dead creatures; and if he by offering such sacrifices be said "to call on the name of the Lord;" much more may the Sacramental Body and Blood be called "the prayers, vows, and desires of men;" and the Altar on which That Body and Blood lie, "the ladder by which they ascend to heaven."

SECT.
III.

Gen. xii. 8;
xiii. 4.

V. Our adversaries do frequently tell us that Justin Martyr, Athenagoras, Tertullian, Minutius Felix, Arnobius, and Lactantius, deny that Christians had Sacrifices or Altars. To which I answer, that

(1.) The writings of these ancients, in which they suppose that they deny any Sacrifice in the Christian Church, are such as were chiefly intended for the use of the heathen. The three first in their Apologies, and the other three in the books they wrote against the heathen worship and in behalf of the Christian religion, do say that which gives occasion to our adversaries to speak of them as if they favoured their notions. If therefore all or some of these ancients should have never so expressly told the heathen that Christians had no sacrifices nor altars; all that could in equity be meant by it was this, that they had no bloody sacrifices, no altars with fire-hearths; for they were speaking to the heathen, who in that age made no account of any other sacrifices or altars. Thus any Protestant of the Church of England, in disputing with a Dissenter, may safely and truly deny that our Liturgy is a Mass-book: because Dissenters have no other notion of a Mass, nor indeed the generality of Protestants, than that it signifies the corrupt office for the Sacrament of Christ's Body and Blood now used in the Church of Rome. And it is certainly true, that, according to this prevailing signification of the word, we have no Mass-book; but if by a Mass-book be meant a collection of rules and prayers for celebrating the Eucharist (as the word 'Mass' signifies in the sixth canon of the African Code[g]), then no learned Church-of-England-man would deny that we have such a book.

(2.) As to the three first writers above mentioned, they are very far from denying that Christians have Altars or Sacrifices. Justin Martyr says, that "Christians conceive that God does not stand in need of gross material oblations (ὑλικῆς προσφορᾶς)," and so say we too; nay, we say, that God wants no oblations at all. Tertullian says, "We sacrifice for the safety of the emperor—but, as God hath commanded, with pure prayer: for God, the Creator of the universe, does not want the perfume or blood of any creature[h]." A certain Doctor, in urging this citation, thought fit to add of his own, "nor any material thing." For he was conscious that Tertullian did not say enough for his purpose; and we can easily grant, nay, we believe it a certain truth, that God does not want any material thing or sacrifice, no, nor yet immaterial; so that it is not easy to conceive what our adversaries mean by producing such proofs, except it be to expose themselves. Both St. Justin and Tertullian do in other places expressly own the Christian Sacrifice. The former never mentions the Altar under any name or title; the other does give it the appellation, not only of Altar, but 'Ara,' as has been shewed; and in this very place, he owns the Christians did sacrifice, but with 'pure prayer;' that is, not with fire and smoke, as Jews and heathen did; for prayer was the only medium by which Christians offered their Sacrifice. Athenagoras says[i], "the Maker and Father of the universe wants not blood and *nidor*, flowers and fragrant perfumes:—but it is a very great sacrifice to Him, if we know Him that extended the heavens—that made man.

---

[g] ["Ab universis episcopis dictum est, chrismæ confectio, et puellarum consecratio a presbyteris non fiat, vel reconciliare quemquam in publica missa presbytero non licere, hoc omnibus placet."—Can. VI. See Codex Canonum Eccles. Africanæ, Ed. Justelli.]

[h] [q. p. 9. Ap.]

[i] ['Ο τοῦδε τοῦ παντὸς Δημιουργὸς καὶ Πατὴρ οὐ δεῖται αἵματος, οὐδὲ κνίσ-

σης, οὐδὲ τῆς ἀπὸ τῶν ἀνθῶν καὶ θυμιαμάτων εὐωδίας, Αὐτὸς ὢν ἡ τελεία εὐωδία, ἀνενδεὴς καὶ ἀπροσδεής· ἀλλὰ θυσία Αὐτῷ μεγίστη, ἂν γινώσκωμεν τίς ἐξέτεινε καὶ συνέσφαιρωσε τοὺς οὐρανοὺς—καὶ ἄνθρωπον ἔπλασεν.—Τί δέ μοι ὁλοκαυτώσεων, ὧν μὴ δεῖται ὁ Θεός; καίτοι προσφέρειν δέον ἀναίμακτον θυσίαν, καὶ τὴν λογικήν προσάγειν λατρείαν.—pp. 48, 49. ed. Oxon. 1706.]

—But what do I care for sacrifices and holocausts, for which God has no occasion? It rather becomes us to offer the unbloody Sacrifice to God, and present to Him the rational service."

As to Minucius Felix, his words run thus, as often cited by others, viz. *Nullas aras habent, templa nulla, nulla nota simulacra;* "They have neither altars, nor temples, nor images of note[j]." But it ought to be observed, that these are the words of Cæcilius; who, in this Dialogue of Minucius Felix, is the advocate for heathenism, and takes the liberty of saying what he pleases, by way of reproach against the Christians. He had just before charged them with the killing a child, and eating the flesh of it, and with incestuous mixtures. And is it not an extraordinary proof that Christians had no altars, to allege the words of one that was saying every thing of Christianity, true or false, that he thought would make it look odious in the eyes of others? It is certain, our atheists may as well cite the words of Cæcilius as a proof of the savageness and the incestuous mixtures of the primitive Christians, as the adversaries of the Sacrifice for what he says of altars and temples.

As for what is said by Arnobius and Lactantius, I do not think it of any moment in this controversy. Not that I think them to be so opposite to the doctrine of the Sacrifice, as our adversaries represent them; but because I look on their authority as none. No ancient writers (for they flourished in the beginning of the fourth century) are liable to more just exception. And I think St. Jerome's censure[k] of them allowed by the most judicious moderns; that " they destroy the Ethnic religion rather than establish the Christian." Arnobius wrote against the Gentiles, while he was yet but a catechumen, and therefore unacquainted with the Christian Sacrifice. Lactantius was his scholar, and though he outdid his master in rhetoric, and is called the Cicero of the Christians; yet they seem to have been both equally novices in the Christian theology. I can without any great difficulty or concern consider them as patrons, not only of

---

[j] [Chap. x. p. 9. ed. Oxon. 1662.]
[k] [" Lactantius quasi quidam fluvius eloquentiæ Tullianæ, utinam tam nostra confirmare potuisset, quam facile aliena destruxit."—Ad Paulinum, De institutione monachi, *circa finem.*]

them who are adversaries to the Christian Sacrifice, but even
of the Arians and other heterodox opiniators.   It is sufficient, that the Sacrifice and Altar are supported by those,
who best knew the Christian religion, and whose authority
will be of greatest weight in this and all other disputes.

Our adver-
saries' in-
consistence.   Before I proceed to another head of discourse, I cannot
but reflect on the inconsistence of those pleas, which have
been advanced against the Sacrifice.   Sometimes our adversaries tell us, that the ancients declared against the Altar
and Sacrifice; and to prove what they say, they can only
produce some passages out of these writers last mentioned,
wherein they do indeed seem to disown these things to un-
cautious readers.   At other times our adversaries say, that
the Fathers used to speak of Sacrifice and Altar in the Christian Church in order to reconcile the Jews and Gentiles to
Christianity, by representing it as like to their religion as
possible; and to make a Christian Church look as like the
temples of the Jews and heathens as they well could, and
more like than in truth it was, if we may believe some modern
Divines; but in reality, the ancient Fathers did directly the
contrary.   If they ever dropped any words that seem to import no Sacrifice or Altar among Christians, they did it in
their discourses to the heathen; and when our adversaries
produce their allegations from antiquity against the Sacrifice,
they are almost or altogether drawn from books that were
addressed to the Gentiles; which is a plain demonstration
of the integrity of these holy men, who were so far from
temporizing, or accommodating themselves to the erroneous
opinions of those heathen whom they endeavoured to convince, that they rather disown Sacrifice and Altar than study
to catch them with such baits.   Nay, it is very evident, that
they were very cautious and reserved in speaking to their
catechumens upon this head.   On the other side, they never
speak more frankly and copiously of the Sacrifice and Altar,
than when they speak in confidence to those who were the
dispensers of, or communicants in, the holy mysteries.   Thus
for instance, St. Irenæus has more largely and directly asserted the Eucharistical oblation than any other writer of the
two first centuries; and he does it in a book, that never was
intended for the perusal of Jews or heathen, but was com-

posed to be put into the hands of the Christian Clergy and people as an antidote against the heresies of that age. In the third century, St. Cyprian delivered his sentiments so fully and openly, in his letter to Bishop Cæcilius, that he says more on the subject of the Sacrifice, and wholly in favour of it, in that one Epistle, than you will find said concerning the Eucharist in all the writings of Justin, Tertullian, Athenagoras, Arnobius, and Lactantius, put all together. And in the fourth century, Cyril of Jerusalem, in five very short catechetical lectures, written for the instruction of young communicants, says more to the purpose of the real Sacrifice of the Eucharist, than can be found in all the works of some voluminous writers, who intended the main of their labours for the reading of Jews and heathens as well as Christians. So that in this respect, our adversaries represent things topsy-turvy; they would persuade their readers, that the Fathers spoke of Sacrifices to deceive Jews and heathens into a good opinion of Christianity; whereas, if the Fathers do ever disown Sacrifice in the Church, it is in their discourses to these Jews and heathen. And if ever they speak more frankly and apertly of the Sacrifice and Altar, it is between themselves; and certainly if men do ever speak the whole truth, it is when they are writing and discoursing to their most intimate friends and associates, to them who are, in the main, of the same sentiments with themselves. And since the ancients do never discourse so peremptorily and decisively of the Christian Altar and Sacrifice, and use so many and such strong words, as when they are treating with those who were partakers of the same holy mysteries; I think this consideration to be of very great moment, in determining the present controversy; as likewise a great proof of the integrity of those holy men. It evidently therefore appears, that 'Altar' is the most proper name of the Communion-Table; and though Altar is not essential to Sacrifice, yet I suppose whatever is offered on a proper Altar is a Sacrifice properly so called.

CHAP. II. SECT. IV.

That Bishops and Priests are the only proper officers for the solemn offering and consecrating of the Christian Eucharist.

AND I am apt to think, that this doctrine is capable of as clear proof from antiquity as any in the whole Christian system. As the oblation and consecration were inseparable and interwoven with each other in fact, so that he who performed one, must perform the other; so I take it for granted, that those authorities from the ancients, which prove, that the consecration was appropriated to the Priest, do equally prove the same of the oblation, and *vice versa.* I must further observe, that I take it for an unquestionable truth, that whatever power belonged to the Priest belonged to the Bishop also in a most eminent manner; and that therefore those citations, which mention Priests as proper officers, do imply Bishops to be so too. And that therefore all the following authorities prove this privilege to belong to Bishops; whereas those only, where the Priest is expressly mentioned, do prove him to be a proper officer for the offering and consecrating this mystery. Now I suppose it will not be expected, that every authority to be produced on this occasion should amount to an exclusion of all others from this right or prerogative; but that it will be sufficient to shew,

1. That Bishops and Priests were invested with this power.

2. That the inferior Clergy and laity were denied it.

3. That this power was thought the greatest privilege, that belonged to Priests, that is, the second order of Evangelical Ministers.

1. As to the first point, the reader will observe, that Theodoret[1] speaks of the symbols as " offered to God by such as have been consecrated," which words include both Bishop and Priest: for the distinction of *ordaining* a Priest, and *consecrating* a Bishop, was not, I suppose, so early as Theodoret. He[m] attributes " the change" in the elements " to

---

[1] l. p. 46. Ap.   [m] m. p. 46. Ap. l. 8.

the invocation made by the Priest." The suffrage of Cyril of Alexandria is very decisive[n]; "It is not lawful to consecrate the mystery in Christ in every place; for the only place agreeable and peculiar to it is the Holy City, that is, a Church in which there is a lawful Priest, and the holy Sacrifices are celebrated by consecrated hands." I say nothing of St. Chrysostom in this place, because his books *De Sacerdotio* are so well known of late to Englishmen, by the late learned Mr. Hughes's translation of them; and whoever looks into that translation must be satisfied, that St. Chrysostom is entirely ours. Gaudentius asserts[o], that Christ "commanded His faithful Disciples, whom He constituted the first Priests of His Church, that they should without ceasing celebrate the mysteries of eternal life—until Christ come again from heaven." St. Jerome[p], speaking of the Bishops, says, "Far be it from me to speak a sinister word of them, who, succeeding the order of the Apostles, do consummate the Body of Christ with their sacred voice." And he would have a Bishop[q] "dwell in the holy places, and be ready to offer victims for the people, as an agent between God and man, that consummates the Body of Christ with his sacred voice." St. Ambrose has the following remarkable words[r], "We have seen, and we hear the Prince of Priests offering for us His own Blood; let us that are Priests follow Him to our ability, though weak as to merit, yet honourable on account of our Sacrifice, let us offer a Sacrifice for the people; for though Christ is not seen to offer, yet He Himself is offered on earth, when His Body is offered; nay, He Himself does manifestly offer by us." Ephrem Syrus[s] reckons this the dignity of the Priesthood, that "it is dedicated to mysteries and Sacrifices:" and, soon after, attributes the consecration to the prayer of the Priest. St. Basil declares, that[t] "when the Priest has consummated the Sacrifice, and distributed It, he that receives receives the whole in every part." Optatus bids the uncharitable communicant "leave his gift before the Altar[u]; that the Priest may not offer for him," while he is in this

[n] d. p. 43. Ap.
[o] c. p. 30. Ap. l. 9.
[p] a. p. 28. Ap.
[q] s. p. 29. Ap.

[r] c. p. 26. Ap.
[s] a. p. 25. Ap.
[t] d. p. 23. Ap.
[u] b. p. 22. Ap.

CHAP. II. condition. Epiphanius gives his opinion[x], that " the Priesthood is translated to the order of Melchisedec, which [order] was before that of Levi and Aaron, which now even to this time officiates in the Church under Christ; not any one family, by way of succession, being selected for this purpose, but a character required as to virtue or ability," (Gr. κατ' ἀρετήν). The reader, upon considering these words of Epiphanius, will be naturally led to reflect on the words of St. Paul, viz. "This Man, because He continueth for ever, hath an unchangeable Priesthood," or a Priesthood " that passeth not from one to another:" for so Heb. vii. 24. I think it is best rendered in the margin of our translation. And these words must be understood of the High-Priesthood, with which our Saviour is invested; which is indeed without succession of any sort, because our High-Priest is immortal. But then the very notion of a High-Priest carries along with it a supposition of other inferior Priests acting under Him. And in this sense Epiphanius and other of the ancients, esteemed Christian Bishops and Priests to be of the order of Melchisedec, as officiating by virtue of a commission received from the Divine Melchisedec. And though the High-Priest be immortal, the inferior Priests are not so. St. Gregory Nazianzen[y] addresses the Bishops and Priests of Constantinople by calling them " Priests, who offer unbloody Sacrifices." And speaking of himself, and of the qualifications necessary for the Priesthood[z], " How durst I without these," says he, " offer the antitype of the great mysteries, or be invested with the character and title of a Priest?" St. Hilary says[a], *Sacrificii opus sine Presbytero esse non potuit*, " Sacrifice cannot be offered without a Priest." Hilary the Deacon, speaking of the words used at imposition of hands in ordination, says[b], that " by them he that is elected is authorized for his function, so as that he may dare to offer the Sacrifice instead of our Lord." In his commentary on Ephesians iv. he supposes, and only supposes, that believers in the beginning were allowed to preach and baptize; but he does not dare to say, that they were allowed to offer or consecrate the Eucha-

---

[x] a. p. 21. Ap.
[y] h. p. 21. Ap.
[z] a. p. 21. Ap.

[a] See Mr. Bingham's Antiquities, vol. i. pp. 269, 290.
[b] b. p. 20. Ap.

rist. Cyril Bishop of Jerusalem[c], speaking of himself and those of his order, has these words, " We offer Christ, Who was slain for our sins, propitiating That God, That is a lover of men, for them [the people] and for ourselves." Eusebius speaks very fully in the following words[d], " Our Saviour Jesus, the Christ of God, does yet celebrate by His Ministers the functions of His *hierurgy*, after the manner of Melchisedec ; for as he being a Priest of the Gentiles never appears to have offered corporeal Sacrifices, but blessed Abraham in bread and wine, in like manner first our Saviour, and then all Priests from Him, celebrating the spiritual *hierurgy* over all nations, according to the laws of the Church, mysteriously represent His Body and salutary Blood in Bread and Wine." St. Cyprian asks[e], " What Sacrifices the rivals of the Priests can celebrate ? " And thus describes a leader in schism[f], " Contemning the Bishops, and leaving the Priests of God, he dares erect another Altar, and profane the verity of our Lord's Victim by mock-sacrifices." He supposes that they who had lapsed in time of persecution[g] " ought to have their consciences purged by the Sacrifice of the Priest." And "Every one," says he[h], "that is dignified with the Priesthood, and constituted in the Clerical Ministry, ought to serve the Altar only—nor does he deserve to be named in the Priest's prayer at the Altar of God, who would call Priests and Clergymen from the Altar." And[i] he allows none but a Priest, attended with a Deacon, to make the oblation among the confessors in prison; though it is clear the Priest, by going thither to officiate, exposed himself to great danger. And at another place[k], " It is the great honour and glory of our episcopal office, as being Priests, who daily prepare victims, and offer Sacrifice to God, to give peace to the Martyrs." And yet he expresses himself still with greater force, if possible[l], in these memorable words, " If Jesus Christ our Lord and God be Himself the High-Priest of God the Father, and first offered Himself a Sacrifice to the Father, and commanded this to be offered for a memorial of Him; then certainly that

[c] g. p. 19. Ap.
[d] h. p. 16. Ap.
[e] c. p. 11. Ap.
[f] d. p. 11. Ap.
[g] e. p. 11. Ap. l. 7.

[h] i. p. 12. Ap.
[i] k. p. 12. Ap.
[k] l. p. 12. Ap.
[l] m. p. 12. 14. Ap.

Priest acts as the substitute of Christ, who imitates that
which Christ did; and then he offers a full and true Sacrifice
in the Church of God, if he so make the oblation, as he sees
Christ to have done." Origen describes the Priest[m] as
" standing at the Altar, and serving the Altar." Tertullian
speaks of a layman as making his offering[n], and " commending his wife's soul to God by the Priest." And every one
knows that souls were commended to God in and by the
Eucharist. At another place[o], " It is not permitted to a
woman to speak in the Church, nor yet to teach, nor baptize,
nor to offer, nor to challenge to herself the function of any
civil authority, or of the sacerdotal office." Nobody can
doubt but a woman might present a lay-offering, as well as a
man; therefore the offering here mentioned must be understood of making the sacerdotal oblation in the Eucharist.
And he plainly intimates what were the sacerdotal functions,
viz., to preach, baptize, and offer the Eucharist. It is true, at
other places, he allows a layman to baptize, and even to make
the oblation in want of Priests; and though some others have
allowed that laymen may baptize in case of necessity, yet in
the other particular of making the oblation he stands by
himself; and therefore what he says is of no weight, nor
does it deserve my consideration. They who would be further informed in this point cannot consult a better book
than Mr. Bennet's Rights of the Clergy, chap. xxii. St.
Justin Martyr, in his description of the celebration of the
Eucharist, says[p], " Bread and a mixed Cup was brought or
offered to him that presided over the brethren; and he
taking it sends up glory and praise—and the people make a
cheerful Amen." St. Ignatius[q] allows of no Eucharist "but
by the Bishop, or one licensed by him." " And let it," says
he[r], " be your endeavour to partake all of the same holy Eucharist; for there is but one Flesh of our Lord Jesus Christ,
one Cup in the unity of His Blood, one Altar; as there is
also one Bishop with his Presbytery and Deacons:" and he
expresses himself to the same purpose at another place[s],

[m] e p. 11. Ap.   [q] i. p. 2. Ap.
[n] d. p. 8. Ap.   [r] g. p. 2. Ap.
[o] f. p. 8. Ap.   [s] b. p. 1. Ap.
[p] a. p. 2. Ap.

joining together the Altar and the Eucharist, the Bishop and
Priests acting under him, and the Deacons attending both in
this holy solemnity. When St. Clement of Rome mentions[t]
"peculiar *Liturgies* or offices assigned to the High-Priest,
and a proper station to the Priests, and ministry to the Levites;" he explains himself in the words immediately following, viz., "Let every one of you, brethren, celebrate the
Eucharist in his own rank or station—not going beyond the
stated rule of his office or *Liturgy*." He does not specify
what particular share every one had in this holy action, but
clearly intimates that the Bishop, whom he calls High-Priest,
was to preside in it, if present; and in another place describes
the Bishop's office[u] by "offering the gifts in an unblameable
and holy manner."

The right of Bishops and Priests only to offer and consecrate the Eucharist is also established by councils. That
of Constantinople, so often mentioned, gives this judgment[x];
"It seemed good to Christ, that the unerring image of His
own Flesh, being consecrated by the Advent of the Holy
Ghost, should become a Body Divinely sanctified by means
of the Priest, who makes the oblation." Therefore the
fourth *alias* the seventh council of Carthage, in the thirty-
third canon[y], requires, that Bishops or Priests, coming to a
strange Church, "be invited to consecrate the oblation;"
there had been equal reason for the Deacons to have been
mentioned on this occasion, if they had been thought proper
officers for this purpose. By the second *alias* fifth council
of Carthage, in the fourth canon[z], the Priest is ordered to
"reconcile the penitent to the Altars, with the advice of the
Bishop, if the Bishop himself be absent." By 'reconciling'
to the Altars, is meant, I suppose, admitting to Communion,
which was the Bishop's prerogative, if he had been present,
and even in his absence he must be consulted; but the
Deacon and all below him were not thought proper officers
in such a case; because none of them could preside in celebrating the Eucharist; and in the eighth canon of the same
council[a], the Priest only, who "erects a new Altar and

[t] b. p. 1. Ap. l. 9.
[u] c. p. 1. Ap.
[x] p. 51. Ap. l. 29.
[y] p. 51. Ap.
[z] p. 50. Ap.
[a] p. 51. Ap.

makes the oblation separately, is censured." For it seems,
that even those schismatics and heretics did not think any
persons below a Priest, competent ministers of the Eucharist.
The fourth canon of the synod of Gangra[b] censures those,
who refuse to "receive the oblation, when the Priest, who
performed the Liturgy, was married." If Deacons had then
presumed to perform the Eucharistic oblation, these heretics
would no more have received the Eucharist from a married
Deacon than a married Priest; for their quarrel was against
matrimony itself, as any one may see by the first canon; for
there they are described, as people that "abhorred marriage."
And the second *alias* third[c] Apostolical Canon forbids "the
Bishop and Priest" only "to offer any thing on the Altar,
but what Christ commanded." For they, who made that
canon, knew no other persons, it should seem, who assumed
to themselves the power of making the oblation.

It would be endless to transcribe all that is said in the old
Liturgies to this purpose; it is sufficient to say, that if the
reader please to peruse the Liturgies themselves, he will find
no persons mentioned in them as celebrators of the Eucharist, inferior to Priests. I shall therefore only observe, that
in the prayer for the consecration of a Bishop in the Clementine Liturgy, there are these words[d]; "Grant, O God, Who
art the Discerner of hearts,—that he may gather together
the number of the saved, by propitiating Thy face; and that
he may offer to Thee the gifts of Thy Holy Church; and that
he may appease Thee, by offering constantly without blame
or accusation the pure unbloody Sacrifice, the mystery of the
New Testament, which Thou hast commanded by Christ, in
meekness and a pure heart." From which it is evident, that
in the age when this Liturgy was compiled and used, and
that was undoubtedly very early, the oblation of the Eucharist was esteemed a very principal part of the Bishop's office;
but that Priests were ever allowed to celebrate, appears from
the prayer drawn from the ordination of a Priest in the same
Liturgy, wherein the Bishop that performs the office prays,
that the elected or ordained person may[e] "consummate the
spotless *hierurgy* in behalf of the people through Christ."

[b] p. 50. Ap.
[c] p. 48. Ap.

[d] a. p. 52. Ap.
[e] aa. p. 52. Ap.

This is what we are taught in the Constitutions, over and again. For the author having, in the name of the Apostles, called on Bishops and Priests to baptize the catechumens, and preach to the people; at the beginning of chap. 19, of the fifth book, he proceeds to exhort them to "offer the Sacrifice, concerning which Christ charged you by us, saying, 'Offer This for My memorial';" and elsewhere[f], "Instead of a daily Baptism, Christ hath given us one only Baptism into His Death. Instead of one tribe, He has ordered the best of every nation to be ordained into the Priesthood; and not their bodies, but their religion and life, to be strictly examined: and for bloody sacrifice, the rational, unbloody, mystic Sacrifice." Again[g], "We foreseeing the danger justly imminent on those who do such things, and the little care that is taken about the Sacrifices and Eucharists, upon the account they are offered by such as they ought not, who impiously look upon the episcopal authority, which contains a resemblance of our Great High-Priest and King Christ Jesus, as a matter of sport;" we, I say, "had a necessity to give this admonition." Further[h], "The only-begotten Christ, being the first High-Priest by nature, did not snatch this honour to Himself, but was ordained by God the Father; Who being made Man for us, and offering a spiritual Sacrifice before His Passion to His God and Father, commanded us the Apostles only to offer this." Lastly[i], "After [Christ's] Assumption, we [the Apostles] offering the pure unbloody Sacrifice, ordained Bishops, Priests, and Deacons." I proceed to shew,

2. That Deacons, and all inferior to them, were denied this privilege of offering and consecrating the Eucharist. Now the eighteenth canon of the first council of Nice[k] does not only mention the Bishop and Priest, as the officers that had power "to make the oblation;" but expressly declares, that "Deacons had not this power." The synod of Arles[l], held some time before that of Nice, does in the fifteenth canon expressly censure the presumption of some Deacons, who usurped this power, and declare that it ought not to be done. Dr. Wise indeed observes, as the accurate Mr.

---

[f] c. p. 47. Ap.
[g] e. p. 47. Ap.
[h] f. p. 47. Ap.

[i] g. p. 47. Ap.
[k] p. 50. Ap.
[l] [p. 48. Ap.]

Bingham[m] had done before, that St. Cyprian has these
words, "The solemnity" [of the oblation and consecration]
"being finished, the Deacon began to offer the Cup to them
that were present[n]." 'Offering' here can import no more
than giving them to drink of it. For the solemnity is supposed to have been over, before the Deacon did thus offer
the Cup; and this, I apprehend, explains the second canon
of Ancyra[o], which forbids the Deacon "to offer the Bread
and Cup," in case he had committed idolatry, that is, to distribute them to the people. Justin Martyr[p] speaks of Deacons administering both the Body and Blood to the present,
and carrying them to the absent: but then the President,
that is, the Bishop, or celebrating Priest, is said first to have
eucharistized them. The Constitutions[q] not only expressly
say, that "it is not lawful for a Deacon to offer the Sacrifice;"
but in the Liturgy[r] direct "the Bishop to give the oblation,"
that is, the Bread, and "the Deacon, the Cup." But that
the Priest was permitted by the Constitutions to celebrate
the Eucharist, appears from the twenty-sixth chapter of the
seventh book; in the last words whereof the Bishops are
ordered "to give leave to the Priests to perform the Eucharist;" which is the undoubted meaning of St. Ignatius,
when he says[s], "That Eucharist is valid, which is performed
by the Bishop, or by one whom the Bishop shall license;"
for though he do not mention the Presbyter, yet he by the
common agreement of all is the only officer, to whom the
Bishop can grant this commission. St. Jerome gives his
opinion in those warm words of his, so well known that I
need not transcribe the Latin, "What is come to the minister
of tables and widows, that he should swell, and lift up himself against those, at whose prayers the Body and Blood of
Christ is consummated?" The reader will remember, that
the Bread and Wine were believed to become the Body and
Blood, by the recital of the words of institution over them;
but that by the oblation, and prayers[t] for the Holy Spirit, they

[m] [vol. i. p. 288.]
[n] [" Solemnibus adimpletis Calicem
Diaconis offerre præsentibus cœpit."—
De Lapsis, p. 132. ed. Oxon. 1682.]
[o] p. 49. Ap.
[p] a. p. 2. Ap. l. 9.

[q] c. p. 47. Ap. l. 6.
[r] d. p. 54. Ap. l. 15.
[s] i. p. 2. Ap.
[t] [i. e. for the descent of the Holy
Spirit on the consecrated elements.]

were believed to receive a more full and perfect consecration,
which explain the phrase of 'consummating the Body and
Blood.' The twenty-fifth canon of Laodicæa forbids the Sub-
deacon to "bless the Cup," which may at first sight seem to
intimate, that some of that rank had presumed to celebrate
the Eucharist; but it is pretty plain, that no more is meant,
than distributing it.   For the action forbidden to the Sub-
deacon, in relation to the Cup, is most probably the same,
that is forbidden him, in relation to the Bread.   Now what
was forbidden in relation to the Bread, in the foregoing
words of the canon, is "to give it."   However this was absolutely prohibited, and was beyond all dispute a gross usurpa-
tion.   For it was not allowed to the Sub-deacon, so much as
"to touch the holy vessels," by canon the twenty-first of the
same council.   But the words of St. Laurence the Deacon to
his Bishop Sixtus, when he was going to suffer martyrdom,
seem to imply, that St. Laurence had power to consecrate
the Eucharist; for St. Laurence, in the account given us of
this matter by St. Ambrose[u], says, "Where go you so fast,
O holy Priest, without your Deacon? You were never wont
to offer Sacrifice without your Minister.—Did you ever find
me degenerate—will you deny him a partnership of your
blood" [or sufferings], " to whom you have committed the
consecration of the Blood of Christ," [or the consecrated
Blood of Christ?] "and a partnership in consummating the
mysteries?" Mr. Bingham supposes, as others have done, that
"the consecration of the Blood" signifies no more than giving
the Cup, which is a sort of " ministerial consecration" as he
expresses it[v]: and this must certainly be the meaning of the
words; and I am apt to believe, that St. Ambrose's words are
to be rendered, "to whom you committed the consecrated
Blood of Christ," in order to administer it to the people.
All know that St. Ambrose's diction is very singular.   It is
particularly observable, that he frequently puts two substan-
tives, and the latter in the genitive case, instead of the substantive and adjective or participle.   Thus you have[x] *populo
credentium* for *populo fideli* or *credenti;* and[y] *orationis mysterium* for *oratio mystica,* and[z] *benedictionem verborum* for

u l. p. 27. Ap.   y e. p. 26. Ap.
v Antiquities, vol. i. p. 291.   z i. p. 27. Ap. l. 13.
x a. p. 26. Ap.

CHAP.
II.

verba benedictoria or *benedictio verbalis;* but perhaps it is
more to the present purpose, to take notice, that he says[a]
Panis hic est remissio peccatorum, "this Bread is the remission
of sins," which I suppose stands for *Panis hic est Panis remit-
tens peccata;* and by the same construction he might call the
Eucharistical Cup "the consecration of the Blood," or "the
consecrated Blood." St. Jerome seems[b] to call the consecrated elements *sanctificatio.* "There is one sanctification
for the master and servant," that is, one consecrated Bread
and Cup. And St. Cyprian seems to take the word in the
same sense[c], when he advises, that "we who abide and live in
Christ should not depart from His sanctification," that is, the
Eucharist, of which he was speaking; for the word *corpore,*
which follows, may denote the mystical Body or Church; or
'*a sanctificatione*' and '*corpore*' may be a hendiadys, q. *a corpore sanctificato.* St. Augustine[d] calls that material thing,
whatever it was, which was given to the Catechumens, and
which they called the Sacrament of the Catechumens, he
calls it, I say, the "sanctification of the Catechumens;" and
says, "It will not give them entrance into the kingdom of
heaven." And it is observable, that the Greek Fathers often
call the material Sacrament ἁγιασμὸς or ἁγίασμα, literally
'consecration;' [yet it is equivalent to the Latin *sacramentum.*] Enough has been said to shew, that Deacons were not
proper officers for the offering or consecrating the holy mysteries; and consequently, that this was not allowed to the
inferior Clergy or the laity. I add

That to
offer the
oblation
was the
highest
privilege
of Priests.

3. That the oblation and consecration of the Eucharist
was of old esteemed the most honourable part of the Priest's
office. The Bishop had the power of ordination, by which he
could impart this honourable office to others; and further,
Bishops had the direction of Priests in this point of offering
the Sacrifice, so that the latter were not to do it in any manner, time, or place, disallowed by the former; but to shew
how valuable a function this of offering the Body and Blood
of Christ was thought by the ancients, let me first recite the
words of St. Chrysostom[e]; "When [the Priest] invokes the

---

[a] a. p. 26. Ap. l. 9.
[b] d. p. 28. Ap.
[c] g. pp. 11, 12. Ap. l. 19.

[d] Q. [p. 37. Ap.]
[e] i. p. 38. Ap.

Holy Spirit, and is consummating the most tremendous Sacrifice, and makes his nearest approaches to the common Lord of all, what place of honour shall we assign to him?" He makes ten Sacrifices[f]; the first and principal of which is the Eucharist, the tenth and last is 'preaching.' When St. Jerome would dash the insolence of the Deacon, who had been guilty of some misbehaviour toward him who was a Priest, he calls the Deacon "a minister of tables;" and to speak, in one word, the dignity of those of his own order, he tells you, "they consummated the Body and Blood of Christ." When a Priest had committed a crime, which yet was not so gross as to deserve deposition, he is by the first canon of Ancyra[g] forbidden first to "offer," then to "preach," and lastly to "perform any priestly function," and yet "to retain the dignity of his seat in the presbytery;" and which is more observable, the synod of Neocæsarea in the first canon[h] forbids the delinquent Priest "to make the oblation," and yet allows him to continue in the exercise of his function, in other religious offices; for they, who were thought fit for less honourable ministrations, might yet, in the judgment of those Fathers, be unworthy of that eximious honour of offering and consecrating the Eucharist. Thus I apprehend, I have fully proved, what I at the beginning of this section laid down, viz., that Bishops and Priests were always esteemed the proper officers for celebrating the Eucharist; and I apprehend, there is not one single proof to the contrary in all antiquity. Tertullian allows the Bishop and Priest to be the proper officer, though he supposes a Deacon or layman may do it in case of necessity. And he is singular in this opinion; that, even in want of a Priest, another person may perform the oblation. However I know no other ancient writer of the same opinion with Tertullian; for the fable of Petronilla has been abundantly confuted by Mr. Dodwell[i], and by Mr. Bennet, in his Rights of the Clergy, ch. xxi. p. 288, &c.[k]; and I conceive, that I have no occasion to prove this from Scripture, as I

---

[f] g. p. 38. Ap.
[g] p. 49. Ap.
[h] p. 49. Ap.
[i] De Jure Laicorum Sacerdotali, p. 326.
[k] [St. Petronilla, the daughter of St. Peter, has been erroneously supposed to have offered the Eucharist, on the authority of Baronius; whereas he only says, "Mox ut Christi Sacramentum accepit, emisit spiritum."—Vid. Bar. in Maii 31.]

CHAP.
II.

have the other points; because the adversaries, with whom I am concerned, will readily grant, that if the Eucharist be a Sacrifice, and never allowed to be offered by any other but Bishops and Priests in the primitive Church, this is sufficient to shew that it ought to be offered by none others now. I shall only therefore desire my reader to reflect on the words of the Apostolical Constitutions, which I lately cited[1], viz., that Jesus Christ "ordered us [the Apostles] only to offer this." For though I am not persuaded, that the Apostles were really the authors of these Constitutions; yet the Scripture clearly asserts, that this commission was given to the Apostles only; and the Church has always so understood it, that none but their successors, or Priests authorized by them, should make this oblation.

No objection against this, that Bishops and Priests are not called Sacrificers in Scripture.

I cannot think it any just objection against the Priesthood of Christian pastors, or their right to Sacrifice, that they are nowhere in the New Testament distinguished by the title of Ἱερεῖς, or any equivalent name. For the Hebrew word כֹּהֵן does no more denote 'a Sacrifice' by its original import, than the Greek words, Ἀπόστολος, Ἐπίσκοπος, or Πρεσβύτερος; and the same may truly be said of the title of 'Magi,' which the Persians gave their sacrificers; and of Pontifex, Flamen, &c., which were the names that the Romans gave to their sacrificing officers. And though it be granted, that the Evangelical officers have no compellation given them in the New Testament, which does in strictness imply Sacrifice to be their proper function; yet St. Clement of Rome speaks of the three orders of the Church under the character of Sacrificing officers, as High-Priests, Priests, and Levites; and even hints the Sacrifice, which was offered by them, when he bids them in the next breath, "celebrate the Eucharist every one in his own order;" and supposes, that in the Eucharist we offer the 'perpetual Sacrifice,' 'vows,' and 'offerings for sin.' Nor can I see any shadow of reason, why St. Ignatius's καλοὶ ἱερεῖς should not be understood of Gospel-Priests[m]. The words stand thus, "Priests (ἱερεῖς, sacrificing Priests) "are honourable; but the High-Priest is somewhat more excellent; to whom alone the holy of holies is intrusted; who is alone intrusted with the secrets of God; he

---

[1] p. 47. Ap.   [m] See Ignatii ad Philadelph., cap. 9.

alone is a door to the Father;" the interpolator so under- SECT.
stood it, for he explains 'Priests' by 'Ministers of the Word,' IV.
the very title given to Evangelical officers; but since the thing Luke i. 2.
itself, I mean the Sacrifice, and the oblators, are so clearly
to be found in Scripture, I am sure the ingenuous part of
our adversaries will think it below men and Christians to
strive about words and names; though, as for myself, I look
upon the testimony of St. Clement to be in effect the testimony of the two Apostles, from whom he received his instructions in Christianity and in the *liturgy* of the Sacraments and all episcopal offices; and upon the language of
St. Ignatius, as the way of expression, which he had learned
from St. John the beloved Apostle, whose disciple he was;
and I am reasonably well assured, that they will bear us
out in giving the title of Sacrificers to Bishops and Priests.

I shall only make one short reflection upon the truth, This power
which I have now been proving, namely, that this sole power in Bishops
and Priests,
of offering the Eucharist and administering it, being an- the only
foundation
nexed to the episcopal dignity, and to the Presbyterate under of Christian
discipline.
the Bishops, is the foundation of all spiritual authority; for
they that have the sole power of consecrating and giving the
Eucharist, have the sole power of withholding it. This is
originally in the Bishops, and in Priests subordinately only;
for it must be allowed, that by the commission of Christ
Jesus and by the practice of the primitive Church the
Priests have only a secondary and dependent authority in
administering Sacraments, and are therefore under the check
and control of the Bishops, as the Prophets were under that
of the Apostles; as appears by the regulations made by
St. Paul in relation to the Prophets at Corinth, in his first
Epistle (ch. xiv.) to the Christians in that city. And as
Bishops are, under Christ, the sole source and origin of all
ecclesiastical authority strictly so called; so certainly it
would well become them, even at the peril of their lives,
to be the most zealous and resolute patrons of it; and to
screen their Priests from the fury of such Erastian or Athe-
istical demagogues, as would by virtue of civil sanctions
violate and break through the fences of primitive Apostolical
provisions: and to this purpose I cannot but wish, that the
following words of St. Chrysostom were written in letters of

CHAP.
II.
gold over the throne of every Bishop in Christendom. He is speaking to his Priests, and thus he expresses himself[n]; " If any one come unworthily, though he be a general, or lieutenant, nay, though he wears the imperial diadem, stop him; you have more power than he in this respect. If you dare not do it yourself, bring him to me; I will not permit such things to be done. I will spend my own blood, rather than profuse such tremendous Blood against right and reason."

The only
essential
rites, prayer
and praise.
I have shewed, ch. I. sect. IV. that no rites are necessary to Sacrifice, but only the action or actions, by which the oblation is made. And I have there and elsewhere observed, that the oblatory actions under the old Law were, sprinkling the blood, and burning the whole or some part of the material oblation. Now I shall shew, that the only necessary rites to be observed in offering the Christian Sacrifice, after the Priest has accepted and presented the oblation at the Altar (which is absolutely necessary in all proper Sacrifices), are the prayers and praises of the Eucharistic Liturgy. And I must further observe to my reader, that the Eucharist was especially prefigured by the Mincha and the shew-bread; and both these last were offered by burning frankincense on Lev. ii. 1—
4; xxiv. 7. the Altar. And this was the very rite, by which the meal- or bread-offering was presented to God by the priest. As therefore blood, fire, and incense were the mediums, by which the ancient sacrifices were offered; so are prayer and praise the mediums, by which the Christian Sacrifice is made to ascend to heaven, and rendered a עלָה, a culminating sacrifice, for so the Israelites called their burnt-offering. And I apprehend, that the action of prayer and praise are the only rites whereby the Eucharist is offered to God. I do not deny but that other rites may be used, but I affirm these are the only essential ones; and that this was the opinion of the ancients, I shall shew from what now follows. St. Chrysostom speaking of the prophecy of Malachi, ch. i. 10, 11, says[o], " How brightly and illustriously he interprets the mystical Table, the unbloody Sacrifice;" this he supposes to be Malachi's Mincha, "and he calls prayer the incense offered with the Sacrifice." St. Jerome alludes to the rite of making

[n] w. p. 40. Ap.   [o] f. p. 38. Ap.

the oblation by sprinkling the blood and burning incense
both at once, when he says[p], " Let them know, that spiritual
Sacrifices are to succeed the carnal victims, and not the
blood of goats, but incense, that is, prayers of the saints are
to be offered to God—and that in every place an oblation is
to be offered, not an impure one, as among the people of
Israel, but a clean one, as in the ceremonies of the Christians." And " Who beside our Saviour," says Eusebius[q],
" has by tradition instructed his votaries to offer unbloody
rational Sacrifices by prayer?" The last words shew, that
Prayer was by Eusebius thought the medium, by which the
material (and which he therefore calls unbloody) Sacrifice
was offered. And again[r], " We offer the Sacrifice of praise,
the Divine and venerable Sacrifice, with a decorous sanctity
to God over all. We sacrifice in a new manner, according
to the New Testament. And we offer the prophetic incense,
presenting to Him in every place the well-savoured incense
of a most virtuous *theology,* by prayers made to Him." He
supposes, that both the Mincha and the incense are to be
presented by prayer; the Mincha is clearly the matter of
the Eucharist, for I have already shewed that a Sacrifice of
praise is properly a material oblation; the incense he supposes to be pious and holy affections, which are to be offered
to God both with the Mincha and the prayer, which is still
the medium with which the whole Sacrifice is offered. Tertullian says[s], " We sacrifice to God with pure prayer." By
' sacrificing' is to be understood, as at other places, offering
a material oblation; and when he says, this was done "by
pure prayer," he means without blood or incense; so he explains himself in the next words, " for God does not want
a perfume or the blood of any creature;" for neither the
blood nor the incense were the sacrifice strictly speaking;
but the whole animal or Mincha. St. Irenæus has been produced already, asserting that the Mincha was the prefiguration of the material Eucharist. And at another place he
says[t], that "incense is the prayer of holy men." And from
hence we may certainly know what Tertullian means, when[u]

---

[p] p. p. 29. Ap.
[q] b. p. 15. Ap.
[r] g. p. 16. Ap.

[s] q. p. 9. Ap.
[t] d. p. 4. Ap.
[u] i. p. 8. Ap.

　　　　F f

he mentions "the prayers of the Sacrifices," that is, the prayers by which the Eucharistical Bread and Wine were presented to God as the memorials of Christ's Body and Blood. If he had thought prayer the sacrifice, he would rather have said "the sacrifices of prayers."

Before I close this section, I shall only observe, what share the people of old had in the oblatory service.

1. They furnished the Bread and Wine as the material Sacrifice; and they added whatever else was necessary for the subsistence of all that attended the Altar.

2. They joined in the devotions offered by the Priest.

3. They did likewise eat and drink a portion of the Sacrifice.

People furnished the material oblations, which were sometimes called vows.

1. I need not labour in the first point, it being a thing so commonly known and confessed on all sides. I will therefore only further observe, that what they thus offered was called a vow or prayer; that is, in truth, a material thing either actually offered on the Altar, or intended for that use by the proprietor, in order to render his prayers the more successful; which is, I think, the common signification of *votum*, and εὐχή, as used by the LXX in the translation of the Pentateuch. Now St. Augustine says[x], "Whatever is offered to God is vowed, especially the oblation of the Altar." Origen, in his eleventh Homily on Leviticus, speaks of these vows[y], and supposes a man, in imbarning his corn or barrelling his wine, resolves to offer such a portion of it to the Church; "If," says he, "afterwards he apply part of what he has vowed to his own use, he does not take of his own goods, but prophanes the holy things of God." And this gives light to the words of Optatus, who says[z], "that the vows of the people and members of Christ are borne by the Altar." Voigtus[a] would by the *vota populi* have us understand the verbal devotions of the people only; but I cannot conceive how bare words can be laid upon an Altar: but every one knows how vows or oblations joined with prayer, and therefore called Prayer, may be thus deposited. And I believe Origen and St. Augustine are much better commentators on Optatus, than the learned Voigtus. When Optatus imme-

x b. p. 31. Ap.
y fol. 83.

z a. p. 22. Ap.
a De Altarib., cap. viii. sect. 5.

diately adds "the members of Christ," he must mean the material oblation; though whether he speak of this oblation, as representing His natural members or His political members, is not worth disputing. And this explains St. Clement of Rome, when he speaks of εὐχαὶ, vows, immediately after "the continual Sacrifices."

I further observe, that Origen calls these vows "the holy things of the Lord," even while they remained in the possession of the proprietor; which confirms the observation I made in my subsection to sect. I. of this chapter, that every thing becomes holy by being dedicated to God, according to the degree by which it has been so dedicated: thus a beast, by being vowed to the Lord, became holy; yet no one can doubt but it acquired a greater degree of consecration, by being solemnly offered on the altar. St. Cyprian speaking to a wealthy lady, who was very close-handed, says[b], "You are rich, and can you think you celebrate the [Sacrifice] of the Lord, who have no regard to the Corban, who come into the Church without a Sacrifice, who take part of the Sacrifice which a poor person offered?" Here, what the private Christian brought to Church for the provision of the Altar is called a 'Sacrifice,' before any act of the Priest had been passed upon it; so the animal brought to the temple is frequently called a 'sacrifice,' while under the hands of the lay-votary. But no judicious person will from thence conclude, that both the one and the other did not acquire a much greater degree of holiness, or was not more perfectly consecrated, by the more solemn oblation performed by the Priest. The truth is, the people offered immediately to the Priest, and by the Priest to God. So Origen teaches us[c], "Whatever is given to the Priest is offered to God;" and adds, "the first-fruits of every thing must be offered to God; that is, to the Priests." And it is clearly in this sense, that the rich lady might have offered a Sacrifice, and eaten of it; and is reprehended by St. Cyprian for not doing so. In any other sense a woman could not offer a material Sacrifice; as we have heard before from Tertullian.

It is farther to be observed, that these offerings were free; the people were under no constraint, but what proceeded

Marginal notes:
Which by this means became holy and a Sacrifice.

Lev. xxvii. 9; Deut. xii. 6.

Those offerings were free.

---

[b] h. p. 12. Ap.   [c] d. p. 10. Ap.

CHAP. from conscience and a sense of duty. There are canons in
II. the ancient Church for prohibiting Priests and Bishops from
accepting oblations from vicious and unpeaceable persons[d]
and from[e] such as did not actually communicate[e], but none to
oblige the people to any quota in their altar-oblations. The
words of Tertullian are remarkable on this occasion[f], " Every
one deposits a moderate allowance once a month, if he be
willing, if he be able; for no man is compelled, but gives of
his free will; and this is a stock for pious uses." St. Irenæus
is very large on this head; he supposes our Saviour in instituting the Eucharist[g] " did give a charge to men to offer the
first-fruits of His creatures." He says[h], " Men ought to offer
Phil. iv. 18. frequently and without ceasing." He cites[i] where St. Paul
says, " I am full with those things, which were received by
Epaphroditus, which were sent by you for an odour of a
sweet savour, a sacrifice acceptable, well pleasing to God."
For Irenæus seems to suppose, that what St. Paul received
was some considerable part of what the people had offered
at the Altar. And the truth is, when St. Paul speaks of
bringing " alms and oblations " from other Churches to his
Acts xxiv. countrymen at Jerusalem, we cannot in reason understand
17. him otherwise than speaking of the oblations made at the
Eucharist for this purpose; for there is no proof, that sending the Eucharistical symbols themselves did yet prevail. The
words of Irenæus immediately going before those last cited
are, " Because the Church offers with simplicity," that is,
liberally, " her gift is esteemed pure in the sight of God; as
Paul also says to the Philippians, 'I am full,' " &c. He was
certainly speaking of offering at the Eucharist, and produces
these words as a proof, that these oblations were and ought
to be large. The following words are, " It becomes us to
make an oblation to God—offering the first-fruits of His
creatures; this oblation the Church, which alone is pure,
offers to the Creator." And he does more fully express the
largeness of their offerings, by observing, " the Jews gave
the tenth, Christians offered all they had to the Lord's use."

d See Can. 93, 94, of the fourth
alias seventh Council of Carthage, p.
51. Ap.
 e See 28th Canon of the Council of
Eliberis, in Appendix, p. 48.

f a p. 7. Ap.
g c. p. 4. Ap. l. 17.
h f. p. 5. Ap.
i f. p. 5. Ap.

And it is just before this he says[k], that "not sacrifice in
general is rejected, but the species of it is altered; for offerings are now made, not by servants, but by sons;" that is, not
by Jews, who were tied down to a beast of some particular
sort and sex and age, but by Christians, whom God treats
more like children than servants; and so leaves them more
at discretion; and who therefore make the most ample returns they can to This bountiful indulgent Father. Dr.
Hancock asks Dr. Hickes, how the "species or kind of sacrifices are changed, when bread and wine were offered under
the Law, and Bread and Wine are offered under the Gospel[l]."
But the Doctor takes it for granted, that "species" here is
taken in the logical sense for one particular sort of sacrifice
coming under a genus. But it is more probable, that 'species'
is the rendition of the Greek ἰδέα, as we are sure it is[m]. And
certainly *idea* or species there signifies number and bulk;
for he complains of the heretics for making the Gospels
more or less than four, and thereby "ἀθετοῦντες τὴν ἰδέαν
τοῦ εὐαγγελίου," quite destroying the certain bulk, *com-
pages*, or 'volume' of the Gospel. Thus the idea of the old
sacrifices is changed; for every Mincha was to be of a just
measure, the tenth part of an ephah, that is, a little more
than half a gallon; and the particular conditions of every
animal sacrifice were precisely determined: whereas, under
the Gospel, men were not stinted, as they had been under
the Law; and used their freedom like ingenuous children.
For Irenæus tells us, that instead of a tenth they were ready
to offer all. And whether the original word were ἰδέα or
εἶδος, St. Irenæus might mean that the "outward appearance" of the Sacrifice was much changed; for it was offered
without blood, fire, or smoke, the most essential ingredients
of a Levitical sacrifice; but I am the more inclined to think
that ἰδέα was the word used by Irenæus, because it is most
probable, he used εἶδος in the former part of the sentence;
and that the translator turned that word by 'genus.' And
St. Irenæus would never say, the εἶδος of sacrifice is not
rejected, but, the εἶδος is changed. Therefore I adhere to
the first sense; and it is to be observed, that of these lay-

SECT.
IV.

Lev. v. 11;
Numb.
xxviii. 5.

---

[k] e. p. 5. Ap. l. 9.
[l] [p. 134.]

[m] Lib. iii. cap. 11. *versus finem* [p.
134.]

CHAP.
II.
———

oblations those words of the same writer are to be understood, viz. "the Sacrifices do not sanctify the man, but the
conscience of him that offers being pure sanctifies the gift;"
not that he denies that the Eucharist has a sanctifying power
to such as duly receive it, for he says, it "consists of two
things, an earthly, and heavenly;" but that the mere Bread
and Wine, or rather materials offered at the Altar, have no
sanctifying power; nor can the sanctifying power in the Eucharist produce good effects on him that does not come with
a good conscience. And I cannot but understand St. Barnabas of these voluntary oblations in those words[n], where
having spoken of the Jewish institutions he says, *Hæc ergo
vacua fecit, ut nova Lex Jesu Christi, quæ sine jugo necessi-
tatis est, humanam habeat oblationem.* By the "human oblation" I understand one offered with freedom, and without any
law determining the properties and value of it; for the holy
man speaks of an oblation quite contrary to those of the
Jewish Law. The character he gives of the Jewish sacrifices
is, that they carry "a yoke of necessity" along with them;
and therefore the oblation contrary to these must be such a
one as proceeds from choice and free will; and such is a
truly human oblation; for what is voluntary is most agreeable to the nature of men.

People
joined in
with the
prayers and
praises pro-
nounced by
the priest.

Lev. iv.
13, 14.

Lev.xxiii.1.
8. 16.

Deut.xii.27.

2. A second part which the people bore in the sacrifices
was in joining in those prayers and praises that were on this
occasion offered; and as the whole people of the Jews are on
some occasions said to offer bloody sacrifices, as "when the
whole congregation had sinned they were to offer a young
bullock for their sin." And as God says to the whole Body
of the children of Israel, "Ye shall offer an offering by fire,
and a new meat-offering." Nay, it is said to the people of
Israel, "Thou shalt offer thy burnt-offerings, the flesh and
the blood upon Mine altar." So we are not at all to wonder
that the whole Christian Church are said to offer the Eucharist; for as in the former case the concurrence of the people
in their wishes and hearty desires did not in the least super-
sede the necessity of the Priest's performing his office, so
neither in the latter is it to be supposed, that the devotions of the people do at all impair or intrench upon the

[n] cap. ii.

prerogative of the Christian Bishop or Priest, in performing the sacerdotal oblation. The priest in the Jewish sacrifice sprinkled the blood, and laid that part of the sacrifice which was to be burnt on the fire that was upon the altar, with his own hands. The Christian celebrator presents all the oblations of the people on the Altar, and separates a proper portion of the Bread and Wine, and solemnly offers it to God as a memorial of Christ's Death, and presides in the prayers and praises, and in the whole sacred action; and I cannot see in what respect the Levitical priest was a more proper oblator than the Christian, if this latter perform his part in that manner that the primitive Priests and Bishops did. And the concurrence of the people in their earnest prayers for the validity and good success of the Sacrifice does no more affect us, than it did the sons of Aaron, as to the character of being sacrificing officers. The burning incense was an office as peculiar to the Jewish priests as offering bloody sacrifices; and while the priest burned the incense, we are told that the people prayed. And the priest could not preside in this prayer; for the people were "without" in their own apartment, the priest in the sanctuary where the altar of incense stood; which is a demonstration that the prayers sent up by the people, during the time that any material oblation is made, are no infringement on the oblatory power of the Priest, especially when the Priest presides in those prayers, as the Christian Priests ever did. In a word, the Priest in both cases was ever esteemed the principal in making the oblation; but the people were likewise allowed to be accessories in the primitive Church. The Priests were the proper oblators; the people were said to offer by them; and therefore the Eucharist is often styled "the oblation of the Church." Theodoret expresses this admirably well[o], "Jesus Christ, Who sprang from Judah, still sacrifices; not by offering any thing Himself, but by being styled the Head of them that do. For He calls the Church His Body—and the Church offers the symbols of His Body and Blood." St. Augustine[p] calls the Eucharist "the Sacrifice of the Church;" and further says "She herself is offered in the Sacrifice which she offers;" for the Bread and Wine are symbols of the political Body of

Luke i. 10.

---

[o] d. p. 45. Ap. l. 10.　　　　　[p] A. p. 35. Ap.

Christ (the Church) as well as of the natural. The Apostolical Constitutions[q] direct laymen "to offer the antitypes of
Christ's Body and Blood." And it were easy to add more
authorities, if I thought I were like to meet with any readers
hard of belief in this point. I shall therefore only add the
testimony of Irenæus[r]; who, speaking of the Sacrifice enjoined
by Christ in the institution, adds, that "this is the oblation
of the New Testament, which the Church, receiving from the
Apostles, offers throughout the world."

It is further to be observed on this head, that the ancient
Liturgies were composed in such a tongue as the people,
among whom they were to be used, best understood; and
therefore in the East, mostly in Greek, in the West and
Africa, in Latin; and Justin Martyr assures us[s] that the
people joined in the Eucharistical prayers and praises in his
time, by sounding out a cheerful Amen at the conclusion of
them. And St. Paul reprehends the innovating guides at
Corinth for blessing and giving thanks or celebrating the
Eucharist in an "unknown tongue," or rather in "the
tongue," as it is in the original, that is, the Hebrew, which
he so calls by way of eminence; for it seems that these in-
truders, who valued themselves much on the account of their
being born and bred in the country of Judæa, and therefore
called themselves Hebrews, had turned the Liturgy, which
St. Paul left with his Prophets at Corinth, into the holy
tongue, to shew their skill in that language. The Apostle
therefore owns that these innovators did Eucharistize or perform the holy action well; but the unlearned communicant
was not "edified," that is, he could not join in and concur
with that part of the congregation, and the celebrator, who
understood the Hebrew; the whole Body could not be ce-
mented together in putting up their devotions with one heart
and consent, and in token thereof answer Amen. The Apostle's argument, however you modify it, turns entirely upon
this supposition, that it is necessary that the people be edified,
or united with the celebrator and with one another, in putting up the very same wishes and desires, prayers and praises;
and that in order to this the oblation and consecration be
made in a tongue understood by the congregation. And I

1 Cor. xiv.
16.

2Cor. xi. 22.

1 Cor. xiv.
17.

q bb. p. 47. Ap.   r c. p. 4. Ap. l. 22.   s a. p. 2. Ap.

tremble to think what account the governing part of the Church of Rome have to give to God for depriving the people under them of that privilege, which is a part of their birthright; and for so engrossing the oblation and consecration to the Priest, that the most sensible of their people, who do not understand Latin, cannot without an implicit faith say Amen at the Eucharistical solemnity: and yet I think they are equally to blame, if not more, in denying their people

3. The last share that they have in the material Sacrifice, and which seems the greatest of all, that is, their eating and drinking of the Sacramental Body and Blood of Christ; for it is too well known, that the Church of Rome does not permit the people to taste of the Eucharistical Cup; though in many places, I am assured, they give the people unconsecrated wine to drink, and if I am not misinformed, do it in such a manner that the people are persuaded that they receive the very Blood of their Redeemer; which, if true, I must call not a pious but a most impious fraud. But the right of the people to partake of the Sacrifice falls in with

CHAP. II. SECT. V.

That the Sacrifice of the Eucharist is rightly consumed, by being solemnly eaten and drunk by the Priest, Clergy, and people.

THERE is no occasion for me now to prove either that the Eucharist is a Sacrifice, or that it is to be consumed by manducation; the first I have sufficiently proved already, the last is what all will grant, except the Divines of the Church of Rome, who make the consumption of the Sacrifice consist in the miraculous change, as I suppose, according to Bellarmine's notion of it expressed in his definition in the introduction to this discourse; and will not allow the people or noncelebrating Clergy to partake of the Cup. I have already shewed[t] that much the greatest part of the Jewish sacrifices was consumed in this manner; indeed all, except the whole

[t] chap. i. sect. 5.

burnt-offerings and sacrifices for sin, the bodies of which were burnt without the camp, were consumed by eating; for the fat, kidneys, and rump of the common sacrifice for sin and trespass-offering and the peace-offerings are scarce worth mentioning; and the whole carcases of these sacrifices were to be eaten by the priests or people; as likewise all the first-born, and the vows, and passovers. Now these sacrifices, which were ordered to be consumed by manducation, were, beyond all question, the very great majority of the Jewish sacrifices, both in bulk and number; and therefore under the Law it must be owned, that either manducation was a proper way of consumption, or that the greatest part of their sacrifices were not rightly consumed.

It is true that what was burnt in the fire on the altar was more directly offered to God, because this action of burning was then a rite of oblation; but from hence the grosser part of the Jews were apt to conclude, that God stood in need of sacrifice, and was refreshed with the *nidor* or steam of the altar, as we may learn from the fiftieth Psalm. Therefore God, to take off this objection against sacrifice, has commanded it to be consumed, as His own sacrifice the Passover was, wholly by manducation; and thereby gives us a demonstration of that, which I will express in the words of St. Irenæus[u], viz., "God wants not the oblations of men, but for the sake of those who make them."

Eucharistic
Sacrifice
most hon-
ourably
consumed.
And certainly this *modus* of consuming the Sacrifice was not only intended for the removing of that grand objection against consumption by fire, namely, that it gave occasion to men to think that the indigence of the Deity was by that means supplied; but likewise for the honour of the Sacrifice itself. For it is not easy to imagine how any creature can be disposed of in a more honourable manner than by being consumed in an act of the most solemn devotion, as the Eucharistical symbols are by the institution of Christ Jesus. The Jewish sacrifices were in part to be reduced to ashes, and the remainder to be eaten in such a place, and by such persons, and with such circumstances, as God had appointed; but it does not appear that they who eat them were obliged, during that action, to employ their minds in the service of

[u] c. p. 4. Ap.

God; only in the Passover they were to call to mind their deliverance from the Egyptian bondage. But on the other side, the manducation of the Christian Sacrifice is to be performed, as the most solemn and religious action that private Christians can do in their own persons. For the oblation and consecration have been shewed to be the acts of the Priest, in which the people are only accessories. It is true indeed, the consequence of this consumption by manducation is not for the honour of the Sacrifice, according to the notion of Origen; for he says, εἰς ἀφεδρῶνα ἐκβάλλεται. But Justin Martyr[x] asserts that the Sacramental Body and Blood "are by a change turned into the nutriment of our flesh and blood;" and Irenæus, that "our bodies are thereby increased and nourished, and have a principle of a happy resurrection conveyed to them[y]." And it is evident that St. Augustine[z] and St. Chrysostom[a] were of the same opinion, and so was Cyril of Jerusalem[b].

That the receiving of the Bread and Wine in the Communion is the consumption of a Sacrifice, or that the Eucharist is a feast upon a Sacrifice, has been asserted by several learned men in the last, and by some in this age. The most learned

Eucharist truly a feast on a Sacrifice.

[x] a. p. 2, 3. Ap. l. 19.

[y] It is true, that St. Irenæus and Justin Martyr do not directly deny that the symbols are cast into the draught; but they do it by consequence, when they say that they are converted into the nutriment of our bodies. And Cyril of Jerusalem and St. Chrysostom do in words at length deny it, in the places here referred to. St. Chrysostom is not content to say, that it is not cast into the draught; but explains his opinion by the similitude of wax cast into the fire, and wholly becoming the fuel of that fire, so that nothing of it remains. St. Augustine, in the place above cited, makes this difference between common food (though sanctified by the word of God and prayer) and the Eucharist, that the former is cast into the draught; which is more than an intimation that the latter is not.

[z] What St. Augustine here says concerning the Sacrament of catechumens has given occasion of dispute to learned men. Some will have it, that it was nothing but salt; others, that it was the bread offered by the laity on the Altar, and which had perhaps some prayers said over it, but was not consecrated or offered as the Body of Christ; and I must confess I incline to this latter opinion. It is true, the fifth canon of the third alias the sixth Council of Carthage, A.D. 397, prohibits any Sacrament to be given to the catechumens, but that of salt; but this supposes that some other had been given; otherwise what occasion had there been for such a canon? And we are not to conclude, that because this canon forbids any other Sacrament to be given, that therefore it was not given. All laws do not meet with the approbation or compliance of those for whom they are made. It appears that the African Bishops did not make such an account of this canon as to put it into their Code; and therefore it is not improbable, that this custom of giving bread to the catechumens, under the name of a Sacrament in a more loose sense, did still prevail when St. Augustine wrote this.

[zz] Q. p. 37. Ap.

[a] o. p. 39. Ap.

[b] h. p. 19. Ap.

CHAP.
II.

Dr. Cudworth, about forty or fifty years ago, published this notion as a discovery of his own; and yet in that very book which he wrote on this subject, he denies the Eucharist to be a Sacrifice. And so, it seems, Christians feast upon something that is a Sacrifice, but not offered. For this and other reasons I think his book, which he calls a Discourse concerning the True Notion of the Lord's Supper, very much misnamed. This notion of Dr. Cudworth's seems much of a piece with that conceit of the Calvinists, that we receive the natural Body of Christ in the Eucharist; though it be as far distant from us at the same time, as heaven is from the earth. Dr. Hancock seems very sensible of this absurdity; he is aware, that if the Communion be a feast on a Sacrifice, then what is there eaten and drunk must of consequence be a Sacrifice. Dr. Wise could not see this consequence, though the other had shewed it him, in his answer to Dr. Hickes[c]. Dr. Hancock justly supposes that the Eucharist cannot be a true Sacrifice, nor by consequence the Communion a true feast upon a Sacrifice, except "what is eaten and drunk be offered up just before;" and therefore he is only mistaken in denying that it is so offered: but his second, Dr. Wise, will not allow that it is so offered; and yet approves Dr. Cudworth's notion, that the Eucharist is a feast on a Sacrifice. Now I shall further observe, that the ancients did sometimes speak of receiving the Sacrament, as of a banquet upon what had been first offered to God. Thus St. Augustine speaks of "the Altar[d] from whence that Sacrifice is dispensed, whereby the hand-writing against us is blotted out," clearly hinting the distribution of the holy symbols; and when Gregory Nyssen tells us[e] that "the sacrificed sheep cannot be eaten unless the slaughter precede the manducation," and "that the body of the sacrifice could not be eaten while it was alive," and accommodates this to the Eucharist, he must mean the same thing. St. Basil spake with the same view, when reflecting upon that prohibition in the Law against eating of the sacrifice, while men were under any legal uncleanness. He said[f], "as much as our Saviour was greater than the temple, so much more heinous is it and more horrid, to dare touch the

[c] pp. 176, 177.
[d] a. p. 31. Ap.

[e] b. p. 24. Ap. l. 11.
[f] b. p. 23. Ap.

Body of Christ while we are under any pollution, than to SECT.
touch rams and bulls" offered in sacrifice. St. Cyprian ___V.___
speaks of the feast upon the Paschal sacrifice, when he
applies to the Eucharist those words[g], "'In one house shall it Exod. xii.
be eaten; ye shall not carry any of the flesh out of doors:' [46.]
the Flesh of Christ, and the Holy [thing or Sacrifice] of the
Lord cannot be carried out of doors; nor is there any other
house to believers than that one house, the Church." He
does not mean the material fabric, but the Body of Catholic
Christians, who alone enjoy the true Eucharist, according to
the doctrinè of St. Cyprian and the Divines of that age.
And when Tertullian[h] calls the Body of Christ in the Sacrament "the Holy of the Lord," as St. Cyprian does in the
words now cited; and when Dionysius of Alexandria, in his
second canon[i], and others call it "the most Holy," they do
beyond all doubt allude to those places in the Levitical Law,
where that part of the sacrifice of peace-offerings and sin-
offerings, which was to be eaten by the priests or the people,
are called "the holy," or "most holy of the Lord." Tertul- Lev. xix. 8;
lian speaks more plainly still, when he calls[k] receiving the vi. 17.
Sacrament *participatio Sacrificii*, "the participation of the very evi-
Sacrifice:" by which he can mean nothing but taking into ration for
the hands the holy symbols, and carrying them home; for he oblation,
advises the lay-Christian, that was resolved to keep his station- and the
fast, to take the Sacrifice, and reserve it to be eaten some tion of it.
other time, rather than not to assist at the Altar while the
oblation was made. He cannot mean receiving the natural
Body of Christ by faith, for That Body cannot be reserved;
nor does a man break his fast by eating the Body of Christ
spiritually, in the sense of our adversaries. And as I look
upon this to be as undeniable a proof of the material Sacrifice
as any in antiquity, as being a Sacrifice distinguished from
the prayers that were used on that occasion, a Sacrifice made
on an Altar, a Sacrifice that a man could not take without
breaking his fast, a Sacrifice that a man might take and not
eat presently but keep by him to be eaten hereafter, a Sacrifice which is in the same sentence called "the Body of our
Lord;" so the receiving of it in order to be eaten, is ex-

_____

[g] b. p. 11. Ap.
[h] b. p. 7. Ap.
[i] p. 48. Ap.
[k] i. p. 8. Ap.

CHAP.   pressly called "the participation of the Sacrifice." Dr. Han-
II.   cock did not "think it worth while to look for this citation[1]."
He had enough of it, as it stood in the margin of Dr.
Hickes's book; and whereas Dr. Hancock says that Tertullian calls it a Sacrifice only "in a general sense;" I am
bold to say, that he speaks of it as a Sacrifice in that very
sense for which Dr. Hickes contends. Origen[m] makes this
a characteristic difference between the Eucharistics offered
to dæmons by Celsus and his party, and the Eucharistic by
which Christians appeased God, viz. that the first were given
or wholly burnt in the fire to those dæmons; but the Christians "eat those loaves that were offered to God."

Therefore   And when St. Ignatius reckons it a dangerous thing[n] to be
called the   deprived of "the Bread of God," as it is certain that by that
Bread of
God.   phrase he means the Eucharist; so it is as plain, that he calls
Lev.xxi.22. it "the Bread of God," as typified by that part of the Levitical sacrifices, which was reserved to be eaten by the priests
and their families : for nothing is distinguished by that title in
Scripture but either the portion burnt in the fire in the act
of oblation, or what was reserved for the priest's use. When
therefore St. Ignatius calls the Eucharist the "Bread of
God," as he must mean some material oblation; for nothing
else was ever called "the Bread of God :" so, since he cannot
mean it of the Eucharist as a sacrifice or oblation by fire,
it must of consequence be understood of the Eucharist as a
sacrifice, which is not consumed either in whole or part by
oblation, but as wholly reserved to be consumed by manducation. And this brings me

This a   To reflect on the singular and honourable mark of distinc-
peculiar   tion, by which God has dignified the Christian people above
honour to
the Chris-   and beyond His old *peculium*, the Jews; and that is, that
tian laity. whereas the Christian Church has but One Sacrifice, instead
of that multitude and variety of sacrifices under the Law,
and whereas the Jewish laity were not permitted to eat of
any other sacrifices but the peace-offerings; the rest being
either wholly burnt in the fire, or reserved to be eaten by the
priests and their families : on the other side, now under the
Gospel our One Sacrifice is wholly to be consumed by Priest,

[1] See his Answer to Dr. Hickes, p.   [m] a. p. 9. Ap.
209.   [n] a. p. 1. Ap.

Clergy, and people jointly; and this I take to be a most
signal mark of favour to the Christian laity, that they are
admitted to a participation of the Sacrifice equally with the
Priests themselves. St. Chrysostom magnifies this privilege
of Christians in this respect, when he says°, "There is a time,
when the Priest differs not from his votary, as when we are
to enjoy the holy mysteries; for we are all equally dignified with them; there is one Body, one Cup for all, placed in
open view." No Romish Bishop can speak in this manner,
he cannot say that "the Cup is for all;" it is only for the
celebrator, according to the present corrupt decrees and
practice of that Church. St. Jerome describes the same
privilege, when he hints[p] that "all are equally partakers of
the Lord's Body; there is one consecration" or consecrated
[Eucharist] "in the mysteries, for the master and servant,
the noble and ignoble." And I apprehend, that this is the
meaning of St. Barnabas in inviting the people "to come
higher up towards the Altar," as well as "in a more holy
manner;" or it may be rendered, 'in a more honourable
manner;' whether St. Barnabas used εὐσχημονεστέρως or
ἀξιωτέρως or σεμνοτέρως or σεβασμιωτέρως, it is certain, that
any of those words may justly be rendered 'more honourably.'
And it was with reason esteemed an honour to the Christian
laity, that they were allowed and invited to come into the
Altar-room, which was the uppermost part of the Church, and
to eat and drink the Eucharist in the very same apartment
with the Bishops and Priests; and it is to be observed, that
the Altar itself in the primitive Church stood in a more honourable place than the altar of burnt-offering did in the
tabernacle or temple. It not only stood *within* the chancel,
if I may so speak, but toward the upper end of it. There was
nothing above it but the Bishop's throne. Whereas the
altar of burnt-offerings stood *without* the door of the sanctuary or the priests' apartment. Now as the Altar of Christians is promoted to a more high and honourable place than
the Jewish altar of burnt-offering was allowed; so the Christian people are dignified beyond the old *peculium*, by being
called up into the Altar-room, and there eating the Sacrifice,
the most Holy of the Lord, together with the Priests. I am

° E. p. 41. Ap.   p d. p. 28. Ap.

CHAP.
II.

sensible, that in after-ages none but the emperor was permitted to come within the *bema ;* and even by the nine-
teenth canon of Laodicæa[q], the people are prohibited from
entering into the Altar-room ; but in St. Ignatius's time[r]
" he that was not within the Altar-room was deprived of the
Bread of God[s]." And therefore all communicants did unquestionably in that age go within the *septum* in order to receive
the Eucharist ; and this Eucharist was by them esteemed
and believed to be the Bread of God, of which none under
the Law might eat but the priests and their families. For the
flesh of the peace-offering, which the people were allowed to
eat of, was never called the Bread of God ; so that Christian
people upon this account may claim the title of Priests in somewhat a more emphatical sense, than the Jews could. Philo,
in his book *De Vita Mosis*[t], is much mistaken, when he
asserts that the Jews did act as priests in the Passover, because every private person might kill the lamb as a sacrifice ;
for it is certain, the mactation was no sacerdotal act. The
layman was to kill the beast, which he offered either for a

Lev. i.5.11;
iii. 2. 8; iv.
4.

burnt-offering or sin-offering or peace-offering ; and Dr.
Lightfoot reports it as a saying of the Rabbins, that the
priest's work begins with the sprinkling of the blood, but
the mactation of the sacrifice may regularly be done by any
one, even by strangers or women[u]. Philo might with much
greater truth have said, that in the Paschal solemnity the
people acted as priests, in eating their share of it promiscuously and in common with the priests themselves ; and
what the Jews did once a year, that the primitive Christians
did daily.

This proved
from Scrip-
ture.

And it is very evident that our Saviour did intend the Eucharist to be not only a Sacrifice, but a feast upon a Sacrifice ; and therefore, when He was beforehand shewing to His

John vi. 33.

disciples the nature of his Sacramental Flesh, He calls It "the
Bread of God :" for, as Dr. Whitby justly observes, " The ob-

---

[q] p. 50. Ap.
[r] a. p. 1. Ap.
[s] See also Euseb. Hist., lib. vii. cap.
9. with Valesius' Annotatt. and Balsamon on the Second Can. of Dionys.
Alex. and Bingham. [2nd. Ed.]
[t] ['Εν ᾗ ᾗ (i. e. τῇ ἑορτῇ τοῦ Πάσχα) οὐχ
οἱ ἰδιῶται προσάγουσι τῷ βωμῷ τὰ ἱερεῖα,

θύουσι δ' οἱ ἱερεῖς, ἀλλὰ νόμου προστάξει
σύμπαν τὸ ἔθνος ἱερᾶται, τοῦ κατὰ μέρος
ἑκάστου τὰς ὑπὲρ αὑτοῦ θυσίας ἀνάγον-
τος τότε καὶ χειρουργοῦντος.—Lib. iii.
p. 169. ed. Mangey. 1742.]
[u] See Synopsis Critic. in Luc. xiii.
1. [p. 148. ed. Cant. 1674.]

lations made to God are styled in the Old Testament 'the Bread of God;' and accordingly Christ styles His piacular Victim by the same name[x]." And I must add, that nothing but what had been sacrificed is ever in Scripture called the Bread of God; and therefore, when our Saviour gives this character of what we receive in the Sacrament, that it is the Bread of God, we may safely from thence infer, that it was by Him designed as a feast on a Sacrifice. And when in the narrative of the institution He says, "Take, eat, This is My Body given," i. e. sacrificed " for you;" He does not more plainly say, that the Body which He reached out to them was now made an oblation for them, than He says that they were to eat of It as such. In the tenth chapter of the first Epistle to the Corinthians, St. Paul draws a parallel between the heathen feasts upon the sacrifices and the Christian Eucharist, or between " drinking the Cup of the Lord and the cup of devils," " being partakers of the Lord's Table" or Altar, " and the table" or altar " of devils." So that in all the-most observable contexts which treat of this Sacrament, it is represented to us as a Sacrifice consumed by manducation.

And thus, I apprehend, I have sufficiently established the doctrine of a real and proper Sacrifice in the Eucharist. I have shewed that a material oblation is there made, not indeed of the natural or personal Body and Blood of Christ, yet of the Bread and Wine, which are by a Divine authority substituted in their stead; and which, by the invisible operation of the Holy Ghost, are made the Body and Blood, so far as one thing (viz. Bread) can be another, (that is, the Body of Christ); and it is by this means the most valuable material Sacrifice that was ever offered, excepting the personal Sacrifice of Christ Himself. I have shewed that it is offered for those two great ends, for which all sacrifice was ever intended; that is, for an acknowledgment of God's sovereign dominion, and especially of His goodness in redeeming us by Christ Jesus; and as a propitiatory and expiatory Sacrifice, not by any new accession of satisfaction or merit, but by the application of the infinite and inexhaustible virtue of the grand oblation. I have shewed that this Sacrifice has a pro-

[x] [p. 485.]

per Altar, proper Priests, Ministers, and attendants; and that
it is to be rightly consumed by being eaten and drunk in
the most solemn and devout manner, that any thing can be
performed by men.

An objection proposed concerning wicked men's not eating the Body of Christ.
But our adversaries have given sufficient proof to the
world, that calumny is their best argument. I expect that
they will continue to oppress our cause and us with loads of
reproach and contumely; that they will scarce satisfy themselves with representing our real sentiments in the worst and
blackest colours, but impute to us such consequences of our
doctrine, as we can by no means own or allow. And since I
at large proved, that what is eaten and drunk in the Communion is the Body and Blood of Christ, before It is administered and received; and that the faith of the communicants cannot make It to be the Body and Blood any otherwise than It was made so by rehearsing the words of institution, by the oblation and prayer for the Holy Ghost; it may,
with some appearance of truth, be from hence inferred, that
I believe the Body and Blood to be received by the wicked
hypocritical communicant as well as by them who receive It
with true faith and devotion; and therefore to silence this
objection, I shall shew from the writings of the ancients,

1. That the wicked communicant does externally eat and
drink the Body and Blood.

2. But that he does not do it internally, nor, by consequence, beneficially.

That wicked men do externally eat the Body of Christ.
1. And that the wicked do externally eat and drink the
Body and Blood, the ancients are very clear; thus St. Chrysostom speaks this truth,[y] "Look that you be not guilty of
the Body and Blood of Christ; they (the crucifiers) murdered
His most sacred Body, and thou receivest It with a defiled
soul:" and[z], "If they who defile the royal purple are
punished, as if they had torn it; why is it unreasonable,
that they who receive the Body with an unclean mind should
undergo the same punishment with those who tore It with
nails?" St. Augustine speaks to the same purpose[a], "'A
Body hast Thou prepared Me;' in This Body are we, of This
Body are we partakers; and you [catechumens] that do not
know It, may you know It; and when you have learned It,

oh! may you not receive It to your own destruction!"
Again[b], "How shall we understand this, viz. 'if any man eat
of this Bread, he shall live for ever?' Can we here admit of
those, of whom the Apostle says, 'they eat and drink judgment,' when they eat the Flesh and drink the Blood Itself?"
He further there speaks of hypocrites and apostates, "who
eat That Flesh, and drink That Blood;" and in another place[c],
"Though our Lord says, 'except ye eat the Flesh of the Son
of Man,' &c., does not the Apostle teach us, that even this is
pernicious to those who misuse it?" St. Jerome is altogether
express[d], "We pollute the Bread, that is, the Body of Christ,
when we approach the Altar unworthily, and drink the Blood
of the Lord while we are polluted;" and again[e], "As we did
not equally receive the Body of Christ: there is one consecration" (or consecrated Bread) "in the mysteries." "The
mysteries of Christ," says Ephrem Syrus[f], "are an immortal
fire; take heed how you profanely pry into them, lest you be
consumed to ashes in the participation of them;" which
mysteries he had just before called "the immaculate Body
and Blood." St. Cyprian is altogether as clear and full in
this point, when he thus expresses himself against those, who
had sacrificed to idols, and then came to the Communion,
viz.[g], "Returning from the devil's altars, they approach the
Holy of the Lord with polluted hands, with hands infected
with the *nidor* of the heathen sacrifices. While they are yet
belching their deadly meats, and their jaws stink of their
wickedness and breathe out mortal contagion, they invade
the Body of our Lord—violence is offered to His Body and
Blood; and they sin more now against their Lord with
their hands and mouths, than when they denied Him." The
Liturgies were formed upon this supposition; St. Basil's
particularly, in which there is a prayer[h], that God "would
grant that none might receive the Body and Blood of Christ
to condemnation." And in the Clementine Liturgy, after the
distribution of the Bread and Cup, the Deacon bids prayer
in these words, "Let us, who have received the precious Body
and the precious Blood of Christ, give thanks to Him that

[b] t. p. 34. Ap.
[c] N. p. 36. Ap.
[d] o. p. 29. Ap.
[e] d. p. 28. Ap.

[f] c. p. 25. Ap.
[g] e. p. 11. Ap.
[h] h. p. 57. Ap.

CHAP.   hath dignified us with the participation of His holy mysteries;
II.   and let us request [of Him] that it may not be to our condemnation but salvation[i]." This is omitted in my Appendix;
but the reader will find it, Constitutt., lib. viii. cap. 14. I shall
in so plain a case add no more than that many of the ancients did believe, that Judas received the Sacrament from our
Lord's hands; and that Origen is cited by several of them
for saying, that what Judas received was of the "very same
kind (ὁμογενὲς) with what was given to the rest; but that it
was to him for judgment, to the others for salvation." And
I need not shew upon what authority of Scripture they
grounded this opinion. Several of them tell us, that it was
on those words of St. Paul, "He that eateth and drinketh
unworthily eateth and drinketh damnation to himself, not
discerning the Lord's Body;" for it could be no fault not
to discern It, if It were not there. What the wicked receive
is, therefore, the Body of Christ; and their fault is, that they
do not apprehend this mysterious Body to be what It is.

2. But the ancients did not believe that the wicked did
eat the Body and Blood of Christ internally, spiritually, or
beneficially. This I take to be St. Chrysostom's meaning in
those words[k], "How shall" or can "we receive the Body of
God over all, Which is spotless, pure, and joined to the Divine
Nature, by Which we are, and live; by Which the gates of
hell were broken and the doors of heaven opened,—with
such insolence?" We have before heard him affirming that
this Body might in some sense be received, even by those
who come with an unclean mind; therefore in this place,
he can intend no more than this, that they cannot receive It to their own spiritual good and advantage. This
is what St. Augustine means in that most famous passage[l],
"He who remains not in Christ, and in whom Christ does
not remain, he does not spiritually eat the Flesh of Christ
nor drink His Blood." I find some cite these words without the adverb 'spiritually;' and I shall not trouble myself
with the disputes of critics; but think it sufficient to observe, that since this Father does so expressly declare, as we

---

[i] [Μεταλαβόντες τοῦ τιμίου σώματος
καὶ τοῦ τιμίου αἵματος τοῦ Χριστοῦ,
εὐχαριστήσωμεν τῷ καταξιώσαντι ἡμᾶς
μεταλαβεῖν τῶν ἁγίων Αὐτοῦ μυστηρίων·

καὶ παρακαλέσωμεν, μὴ εἰς κρίμα ἀλλ'
εἰς σωτηρίαν ἡμῖν γενέσθαι.]
[k] L. p. 42. Ap.
[l] m. p. 32. Ap.

have seen, that in some sense, that is, externally, wicked
men do eat the Flesh of Christ; therefore, when on the other
side he declares they do not eat It, he must in common
equity be so understood to mean, that they do not receive It
as good Christians, with faith and other good affections:
and if he be not sufficiently clear in this place, yet he certainly is so elsewhere; as when he says[m], "Then will the
Body and Blood of Christ be Life to every one, if what is in
the Sacrament visibly taken be spiritually eaten and drunk."
He supposes, that what is given in the Sacrament visibly by
the Minister giveth Life; but then it is to those who receive It
spiritually, that is, as a mystery, and therefore with the mind
as well as with the mouth. St. Augustine does not distinguish
between what we receive outwardly from the Minister, and
what we receive inwardly from heaven; (but what is received
is "visibly taken," and is therefore the Sacrament Itself, enriched with the power of the Spirit;) but he distinguishes
between receiving It outwardly with the hands and mouth
only, and "spiritually," that is, with the concurrence of heart
and affections: he speaks not of two Bodies of Christ to be
received in the Sacrament, the typical and the real, the first
of which is conveyed to the worthy receiver by the hand of
the Priest, the other by the hand of his own faith; but of
one Body only, and that "visibly taken." But he makes a
clear distinction between the Sacrament and 'the virtue of
the Sacrament'; and he distinguishes too between receiving
It 'outwardly,' and receiving It 'inwardly:' yet he never
supposes that men receive It inwardly, except they receive
or desire to receive It outwardly; but he supposes many
receive It outwardly, who do not receive It inwardly. All
this he teaches plainly in the following citations, viz.[n], "The
Sacrament is one thing, the virtue of the Sacrament another:
—This is the Bread which comes down from heaven; but as
to what concerns the virtue of the Sacrament, not the visible
Sacrament," or sign; "him who eats internally, not him who
eats externally, with his heart, not with his teeth." For all
the spiritual advantage proceeds from the "virtue" of the
Sacrament; and which therefore is not ordinarily to be expected apart from the Sacrament itself; on which account

[m] w. p. 34. Ap.   [n] k. p. 32. Ap.

CHAP. he advises men[o] "so to eat the Flesh and drink the Blood
II.   of Christ, as not to receive It in the Sacrament or sign
[only], which many wicked men do; but so as to participate
of the Spirit: let us eat and drink so, as we may remain
members of His Body and be vegetated with His Spirit."
And therefore having proposed the difficulty and seeming
inconsistence between our Saviour's saying, that except we
eat His Flesh and drink His Blood, there is no Life in us;
and the words of St. Paul, that some eat and drink these
to their own condemnation, he solves it by adding these
words[p], "There is a certain manner of eating that Flesh and
drinking that Blood; and he that eats and drinks in that
manner, Christ remains in him, and he in Christ:" and he
describes the manner of doing it excellently well in those
words[q], "We betake ourselves to the Mediator of God and
man, Who gives His Flesh to be eaten, His Blood to be
drunk, by a faithful heart and mouth." St. Jerome means,
I suppose, the same thing in those words[r], "There is but
one sanctification," or sanctified Eucharist—"yet it is various
in it's effects, according to the merits or qualifications of the
receivers;" and it is probable St. Chrysostom means this,
when he charges them to absent themselves from the Altar[s],
"that could not discern the calf slain, that could not see the
Heavenly Blood poured out for remission of sin;" meaning,
I suppose, such as wanted a true faith. St. Cyprian[t] seems
to speak, as if he thought that the Sacramental Body, upon
the touch of an unworthy receiver, ceased to be what It was
before; as if our Lord withdrew Himself from such a man,
and as if the sanctity of the symbols vanished; but we
cannot conclude, that St. Cyprian believed that it was always
so, for he was now relating a miracle; and I have met
with nothing like this in any other ancient writer. And it
is evident by what was cited from St. Cyprian under the
former head, that he believed the Body of Christ to be externally received by wicked men; whereas if the sanctity
vanish, it is no longer the Body of Christ. Origen expresses
the whole truth excellently well in a few words[u], "The sanc-

[o] o. p. 33. Ap.
[p] t. p. 34. Ap.
[q] M. p. 36. Ap.
[r] d. p. 28. Ap

[s] oo. p. 39. Ap.
[t] f. p. 11. Ap.
[u] f. p. 10. Ap. l. 4.

tified food becomes profitable, according to the proportion of faith." He ascribes the effects to the food itself, not the natural bread, but the bread sanctified by prayer, and " over which the Word [of institution] hath been pronounced ;" but yet this bread is profitable only in proportion to the faith of the receiver; which is a demonstration that he thought it could not be profitably eaten without faith.

There are three reasons why a thing cannot be eaten, viz., first, that it is in it's own nature incapable of it, as wood or stone. This cannot be said of the Sacramental Body of Christ; for it is in it's gross substance bread, than which nothing is more proper for manducation and nutrition; and therefore it may be externally eaten not only by infidels but by brutes, and this latter is a much less profanation of it than the former. But then it is also mysterious Bread, where one thing is seen, another meant; and therefore cannot be truly eaten but by rational creatures, who can perceive the signification and virtue of it. 2. Another reason why a thing cannot be eaten is, that it is what we cannot come at, that it is at least for the present out of our reach. And it may so happen that the actual receiving the Eucharist, even in a Christian Church, may be impracticable for want of a Priest, or the elements, or of a competent number of communicants, (I say this last in relation to our Church ;) and I must confess, I cannot conceive, that he who does not externally receive the Sacrament can in act and reality receive It inwardly. But thus much is certain, that God in all such cases accepts the will for the deed, when the reason why the deed is not performed proceeds not from any wilful defect in ourselves. He that would relieve the wants of others if he had wherewithal, he that would attend the public worship if it were in his power, and has in the mean time a sincere desire, a holy hunger and thirst after these duties, but is incapable and disabled through some invincible obstacle, is undoubtedly an almsgiver and a public worshipper in the sight of God, though he cannot in fact either give alms or come to Church. So he who has earnest and longing desires after the receiving the Sacrament but has no possible opportunity of doing it, when the want of opportunity does not proceed from any voluntary cause, shall infallibly be deemed

Three particulars which make a thing incapable of manducation.

CHAP. and dealt with by a just God, as if he were an actual com-
II.   municant; and God can by extraordinary means supply the
want of Sacraments, when He sees just occasion; and therefore no man need stick to affirm of all honest Christians,
who wish for the Sacrament but cannot have It, that they
eat the Body and drink the Blood of Christ profitably to
their souls' health, although they do not receive the Sacrament with their mouths; not that the Body and Blood of
Christ is to be had anywhere in this life, save in the Eucharist; but because, as has been said, God takes the will for
the deed, when the will is sincere, and the deed is impossible to be done, through some intervening act of God, or when
it cannot be properly performed through some fault of other
men. A devout Christian receives the Sacramental Body and
Blood of Christ, by having a readiness and zeal for that duty,
Heb. xi. 17. though he cannot in fact do it; just as "Abraham offered
Isaac," that is, intentionally and beneficially to his soul's
health. A third reason why a thing cannot be eaten is,
because the person to whom it is offered, by reason of some
defect in himself, cannot eat, masticate, or swallow it. And
though there are very few indeed that cannot thus externally
eat the Sacramental Body as to It's gross substance, which
is Bread; yet there are very great numbers of men, that cannot receive It internally, as It is the mysterious Body of
Christ, and ennobled with the especial Presence of the
Spirit, for want of faith and other holy dispositions. They
can take It with their mouths and press It with their teeth,
but they cannot ruminate and digest It by "discerning the
Lord's Body," and converting It to the nourishment of their
souls; for It is a Spiritual Body, not so much intended for
the repast of our palates and stomachs as of our minds. It
conveys indeed to the body, as I intend to shew in the second
part of this work, a principle of happy immortality; but it is
on condition that our bodies be preserved pure and undefiled,
for there is no communion with Christ and Belial. Both the
bodies and souls of wicked men labour of a fatal lientery as
to this sacred Food, and for want of digestion receive no benefit from It. In a word, though the holy Sacrament abounds
with Divine blessings, yet wicked men are incapable of receiving or applying them; their faith is defective, their under-

standings and wills are vitiated; "the right eye" of such men
is "utterly darkened," as the prophet Zechariah expresses it,
that is, all their superior faculties are impaired, so as to be
wholly unfit to perceive these Divine mysteries, and render
them beneficial to themselves. Just so the blind man cannot receive light, even when he is surrounded with it. And
he only that internally and spiritually receives the Sacrament,
does "eat the Flesh of the Son of Man and drink His Blood,"
according to the design and intendment of our blessed Saviour; as will further appear by what I have to say in the next
place, concerning that most notable context in the sixth chapter of St. John's Gospel.

*A proof that the context in the sixth chapter of the Gospel of
St. John, from verse 26 to verse 36, and from verse 47 to
verse 64, is to be understood of Sacramental eating and
drinking.*

WHEN I affirm that this context is to be understood of
Sacramental eating and drinking; my reader will easily perceive, that I do not mean receiving with our mouths only, or
pressing with our teeth the outward signs, or taking the consecrated Bread and Wine, *sacramento tenus,* in the sense of
St. Augustine just before mentioned; but the receiving it as
a mystery, that is, as the Body and Blood of Christ, not only
in signification but in virtue and power, and therefore with
such holy affections and dispositions, as befit such a Divine
institution.

And when I affirm that it is so to be understood, my
meaning is, that I take it to have been our Saviour's primary
and direct intendment in this context to treat of the Sacramental eating His Flesh and drinking His Blood in the Eucharist. It was the common opinion of the Fathers and the
School-men, that all or most texts of Scripture had more than
one sense or meaning; and I shall not concern myself with
this notion any further than to own, that this is certainly true
of very many texts. Whether it can in strictness be said of
the context now in dispute, I shall not pretend positively to

CHAP.
II.

determine; but shall content myself, and, I hope, my reader too, if I can make it appear that our Saviour's principal and main design was, in these words, to instruct His hearers in the excellence and beneficialness of the Eucharist, which He resolved afterwards to institute. This I shall endeavour to prove,

First, From the general consent of the ancient Fathers, and primitive Church.

Secondly, From intrinsic arguments drawn from the words themselves.

I. In order to shew, that I have the general consent of the Fathers and primitive Church on my side, I shall,

1. Consider such allegations, as have been produced from antiquity against that sense of John vi. which I am now asserting.

2. I shall produce positive authorities from the ancients, in behalf of this sense.

It is con-
fessed that
the Fathers
sometimes
explain
John vi. of
doctrine;
but how?

(1.) I am to consider such allegations to the contrary, as others have produced from antiquity. I deny not but that some of the Fathers do interpret John vi. of hearing, receiving, or believing the doctrine of Christ; nor will I at present dispute, whether they meant receiving Christ's doctrine together with His Sacramental Body and Blood, which is certainly the most perfect way of receiving it; or whether they intended a bare receiving it by faith, and *extra cœnam*, as the moderns commonly express themselves. But it is certain that they who receive the Sacrament according to the will and design of Christ Jesus, do receive the Word and precepts of Christ together with the Bread and Wine. Nay, it is further certain, that we receive not the Word of God so effectually in any other way, or by any other means, as in and by the holy Eucharist: for therein only God seals all His evangelical promises to baptized Christians; and therein only baptized Christians do set their seal of fealty and obedience to His laws.

Various
senses of
the same
text in the
opinion
of the
ancients.

But my reader cannot have forgotten, what I so lately hinted, that it was the common opinion of the Fathers, that Scripture was capable of a double interpretation, viz., literal, and spiritual; and further, they often vary in the spiritual interpretation of a text, by sometimes affixing to it a mys-

tical signification, as supposing that even the historical nar-
rations in Scripture are intended to represent to us the hidden
wisdom of God in the redemption of mankind; sometimes by
giving a moral or tropological meaning to matters of fact
recorded in the Old or New Testament, as supposing that
over and above the historical sense the Holy Spirit designed
to give us instructions for the regulation of our lives; sometimes by giving such a construction to any doctrine or precept either of the New Testament or Old, as is not necessarily
implied in the words themselves, but only more remotely
hinted, as they conceived; and this last they commonly called
the *anagogical* sense. It is needless to give instances of all
these several sorts of interpretations; especially because there
are but two of them that do at all affect the present dispute;
that is, the mystical, and the anagogical. For it is given for
granted by the ancients and by all the Protestants of the
Church of England, that these words of our Saviour were
never meant by Him in a literal sense; or that He never intended to give His Body to be eaten, His Blood to be drunk,
in the sense that His unthinking hearers wotted; and that
therefore they must be understood in a spiritual sense only;
and to this I readily subscribe.

And this I suppose is to be applied to the words of institu- The spiri-
tion, viz., "This is My Body, This is My Blood;" as well as tual sense
to the "eating" His "Flesh," "drinking" His "Blood" here of John vi.
in John vi. And I conceive, that the Fathers never doubted
but that this mystical or spiritual sense was that which our
Saviour primarily intended in both places. But my reader,
if he have perused the foregoing sections, will easily perceive,
that when I speak of the "spiritual sense," I am not so to be
understood, as if I thought our Saviour spoke of feeding the
mind only and not the mouth; or as if He meant, as the
Papists do, that His Body is present in the Eucharist, after
the manner of a spirit; or that It is given to all the faithful
or worthy receivers, in an invisible or imaginary manner, as
the Calvinists fancy; but I take the spiritual sense, as opposed
to the literal, to imply, that we are not to take the phrase
of "eating His Flesh" in the most natural or obvious meaning, as if it imported feeding with our teeth only, or on His
substantial Body; but as importing the reception of Christ's

CHAP.
II.

The anago-
gical sense
of John vi.

None of the
Fathers do
say that
John vi. is
not meant
of the
Eucharist.

Sacramental Body or His mysterious Flesh both with our minds and mouths; for I have sufficiently shewed, that Christ's Eucharistical Body is a spiritual Body.

But then beside the primary and direct sense of the text, the ancients commonly supposed that there was a reductive or anagogical meaning, in which it might be taken. Thus we have already seen several of the Fathers interpreting that petition, "Give us this day our daily bread," as meant not only in relation to the necessary supplies of bodily food and raiment but of the Eucharistical Body and Blood. I suppose they did not doubt but that the words were primarily meant by our Saviour in the former sense; but that they might, by a reductive construction, be applied to the latter. And by parity of reason they might be fully persuaded, that John vi. was first and most properly to be understood of the Eucharist; and yet at the same time be of opinion, that it might likewise, in a more remote way, be applied to receiving of Christ's doctrine or precepts. And so far as I am able to penetrate into the judgment of the ancients in this particular, I can see no reason to believe that they did ever understand John vi. of believing Christ's doctrine, or receiving His Word by faith, *extra cœnam*, to be meant by our Saviour otherwise than in this anagogical way of interpretation.

It ought particularly to be observed, that none of the Fathers did ever say that John vi. was not meant of oral or Sacramental manducation; which yet is what Dr. Whitby has thought fit to assert, in his annotations on ver. 53, 54[v]. And he attempts to prove it chiefly by the authority of the ancients; with how good success he has done this we shall presently see: but in the mean time let the reader consider, that there is this grand objection lies against the Doctor's hypothesis, that not one of the ancients do say, in the words produced by him, that John vi. is not meant of the Sacrament; nay, they speak nothing that could give any just grounds for the Doctor's notion.

The most learned and ingenious Dr. Clagett had many years before published a tract on John vi., in which he asserts that this context is to be understood of "spiritual actions," by which he meant faith, obedience, &c., though he is pleased to

[v] p. 490.

own that the words may be accommodated to the Eucharist.
Both these Doctors use the same citations; the difference however is not very great in this point. And I will in charity believe that these two learned men have produced the strongest
proofs that antiquity affords, in maintenance of their own
opinion. And yet I suppose it will appear very clearly, that
the citations alleged by them prove at most no more than this,
that the context now in dispute may anagogically be applied
to believing in Christ or His doctrine; and so do not at all
affect the truth which I assert, viz., that John vi. is primarily
to be understood of the Eucharist. I will consider the citations produced by these learned men, in the same order that
Dr. Whitby ranges them.

He begins[x] with those words of Clemens Alexandrinus[y], Clemens
"The Word is all things to a babe, a father, a mother, a pre- Alexandrinus not
ceptor, a foster: [" eat," says He, " My Flesh" and "drink My for Dr.
Whitby's
Blood," allegorically signifying the clear liquor of faith and the sense.
promise:] He bids us put off the old carnal corruption and
food, and partake the other new Food of Christ, and receiving
Him to store Him up if possible in ourselves, and to inclose
our Saviour in our breasts." The Doctor only produces so
much of this paragraph as stands between the hooks. Now
I must declare, that I am not able to form any supposition,
upon which an argument can be fetched to serve his turn;
but I look upon the words rather as an argument against
that sense, which he has espoused: for these words, " Eat
My Flesh," &c. are meant either,

1. Of eating Christ's Flesh, and drinking His Blood, according to the intention of our Saviour in the sixth of
John;

2. Or of eating His Sacramental Flesh and Blood, according to the command in the words of institution; (for I now
argue upon the hypothesis of Dr. Whitby, which is, that the
eating Christ's Flesh in John vi. is a distinct thing from
eating His Sacramental Body.) But,

1. If Clement must be understood of eating Christ's Flesh,
according to the meaning of our Saviour in John vi., then we
are further to inquire what he means by ἀλληγορῶν, which
I render ' allegorically signifying.' Now ' allegorically signi-

fying' must import one of these two things, viz., either signifying in a remote and very figurative improper manner, which
is the common denotation of this word in ecclesiastical as
well as foreign writers; and from thence it follows, that
Clement was now designedly interpreting this context, not
in that sense which he thought to be first and principally
meant by our Saviour, but in a secondary and more improper one. And if therefore the Doctor be willing to understand this word in the most common acceptation, he must be
forced to grant that this is the allegorical meaning of John vi.,
and therefore not the proper or primary one. Or else by the
word ἀλληγορῶν, Clement intended to denote a Sacramental
representation; and then the words ought to have been rendered, " ' Eat,' says Christ, ' My Flesh,' and 'drink My Blood,'
Sacramentally representing the clear liquor of faith," &c.
And if he does therefore here speak of John vi., he by consequence interprets this context of the Eucharist; for no
other Blood of Christ but the Eucharistical can be said Sacramentally to signify or represent. And that St. Clement
does use the word in this sense, is evident from that passage[z],
" The liquor of gladness," that is, the Cup in the Eucharist,
ἀλληγορεῖ, "Sacramentally represents the Word poured out for
the remission of sins." And indeed Dr. Whitby gives another
instance of this signification of the word, not far from the
passage first cited, viz., " τὸ δὲ αἷμα οἶνος ἀλληγορεῖται[a],"
" Wine Sacramentally represents the Blood." The Doctor
left the words untranslated; but from this it appears, that
Clement took the Eucharistical Blood to represent the doctrine of Christ; and that therefore Clement here spoke of
John vi. if he had this context in his eye, as meant of the
holy Eucharist; for there only the Blood can Sacramentally
represent the doctrine of Christ.

2. If we understand the Father as speaking here of the
words of institution, then the Doctor did to no purpose allege this passage of St. Clement; for certainly it was not the
Doctor's intention to prove, that by eating Christ's Body or
Flesh, (which will soon appear to be the very same thing) and
drinking His Blood, according to the command of Christ
Jesus, in Matt. xxvi. 26, we are to understand nothing but

[z] c. p. 7. Ap.   [a] [Pæd., lib. i. cap. 6. ed. Potter, p. 126.]

believing.   And in truth I can see no shadow of reason, why
we should suppose that Clement had any other text directly
in his view, beside the history of institution.   For he introduces our Saviour as speaking imperatively, " Eat ye, drink
ye ;" and our Saviour never uses this style but in the Eucharist only; and it has been already shewed, that the word
ἀλληγορῶν does in this writer denote ' the Sacramental representation.'   And that all the promises of the Gospel, pardon, grace, and eternal happiness, are less directly or implicitly represented and exhibited to communicants in the
Eucharist, is what will be denied by none.   And it is evident
that Clement restrains his words to the promissive doctrine
only, when he calls the Eucharistical Cup " the clear liquor
of faith, and the promise ;" though I see no reason to question but by receiving the Eucharist we do implicitly receive
all the doctrines of the Gospel, for as much as the Eucharistical symbols are most perfect representatives of Christ crucified, and Christ crucified is the sum of the Gospel.   So that I
am perfectly at a loss to know, what Dr. Whitby intended by
producing these words of Clement, which, however you take
them, destroys his hypothesis.

Dr. Clagett, as well as Dr. Whitby, does also produce those
words of Clement[b], " The Word is diversely allegorized or Sacramentally represented as food, as flesh, as nourishment, as
bread, as blood, as milk."   'Αλληγορεῖται may here be turned
" Sacramentally represented ;" for that milk was in Clement's
age used in Baptism, there is no room to doubt. · But if you
choose by ἀλληγορεῖται, to understand the remote and improper signification of the " Blood" mentioned John vi., then
the most to be gained by it is this, that in the more loose
and remote sense, John vi. may be understood of the Word
spoken.   These citations therefore do not at all serve the
cause, which these two Doctors had espoused.

Nay, if what has been already observed does not shew that
Clement took John vi. to be meant of the Sacrament ; yet when
the reader reflects on that gloss he gives upon those words,
" Eat My Flesh" and " Drink My Blood," which are plainly
the words of institution, rehearsed *memoriter*, and therefore not
according to the original text; when, I say, he puts this gloss

[b] Pædag., lib. ii. cap. i.

upon them, viz. Christ "bids us put off the old corruption,"
he will see reason to believe that this ancient writer applies
those words in John vi. 58, "He that eateth of this Bread
shall live for ever," to the receiving the holy Sacrament.
And the same may be said of those words of Clement[c], where
distinguishing "the spiritual Blood of Christ" from "the
carnal," he says, that "by the spiritual Blood we partake of
incorruption ;" for that by the "spiritual Blood" he means
the Sacramental, has been already proved; and that the
Father does so explain himself, the citation, which is to be
seen at large in the Appendix, does sufficiently declare. And
indeed the very words, which I now hint at, seem to be another
proof of his understanding John vi. primarily of the Eucharist ; for, says he, "The mixture of the liquor and the Word
is called the Eucharist, of which they who partake with faith
are sanctified both as to body and soul." For I conceive that
the sanctifying power of the Eucharistical Flesh and Blood
can be directly proved from John vi. only, where Christ's
Flesh is called "the Bread of God," that is, "the most Holy
Meat," which sanctified men's bodies by it's touch under the
old Law; see Lev. vi. 27.   And indeed he could ground his
notion of the "spiritual Blood" in the Eucharist upon no
other text than John vi. 63; for though St. Paul calls it
1 Cor. x. 4. "spiritual drink," and says "We are all made to drink into
1 Cor.xii.13. the One Spirit," yet he does not so explain the spiritual
efficacy of the Sacrament as to make it a principle of incorruption or immortality, as Clement here does. So that I can
see no reason why I may not reckon upon Clement as an
evidence for that sense of John vi. which I believe to have
been first intended by our blessed Saviour.

Tertullian
shewed to
be not
against the
sense for
which I
plead, but
rather for it.
The next writer cited by Dr. Whitby and Dr. Clagett is
Tertullian, whose words he is pleased thus to represent;
"Our Lord all along urged His intent by allegory, calling
His Word 'Flesh,' as being to be hungered after, that we
might have Life ; to be devoured by the ear, ruminated upon
by the mind, and by faith digested." The reader, by turning his eye to the words of Tertullian in the margin[d], will see

---

[c] b. p. 7. Ap.
[d] "Exsequitur etiam quid velit intelligi Spiritum : 'Verba quæ locutus sum
vobis, Spiritus sunt, vita sunt,' sicut et
supra (he cites John v. 24.) Itaque
Sermonem constituens vivificatorem,
quia Spiritus et vita Sermo, eumdem
etiam carnem suam dixit; quia et

how faithful the Doctor is in his citations. But for brevity's
sake I will grant the Doctor his own translation. Let it be
allowed, that Tertullian supposes that these words may allegorically be understood, and that he by an allegory means a
remote and improper interpretation; doth it therefore follow
that the text has not a more strict and proper meaning? I
am sure Dr. Whitby and all learned men will allow, that
Tertullian himself does nowhere use a greater latitude and
liberty in glossing Scripture than in this passage. For
he supposes or rather asserts the Word spoken, and incarnate, the Spirit, the Flesh, even that Flesh which the sub-
stituting Word assumed, to be the same; and if he sup-
poseth that our Saviour intended these words in an allegorical as well as in a more direct sense, this only shews that
Dr. Whitby by the allegorical or secondary sense would set
aside the other sense, which is more proper and therefore
more eligible: but if by 'allegory' he means the Sacrament,
as it is evident that Clemens Alexandrinus by 'allegorizing'
means 'Sacramentally representing,' then the Doctor's argument is wholly lost. And it will be hard to prove that Tertullian by "the allegory of necessary food"[e] does not mean the
Eucharist. And when he adds that "our Saviour urged upon
them the memory of their fathers, who preferred the bread
and flesh of Egypt before the Divine will;" his meaning
seems to be, that Christ's present hearers were like their
ancestors, who desired the dainties of Egypt rather than
manna; for just thus His present hearers had a greater appetite to such food as He had the day before prepared for
them by a miracle, than to that Food from heaven which He
had been speaking of. And I see not any incongruity in his
supposition, that our Saviour, in reminding them of the
'quickening Spirit' and of His own powerful 'Word,' did design to admonish them of avoiding that carnal and sordid

Sermo caro erat factus; proinde in causam vitæ appetendus, et devorandus auditu, et ruminandus intellectu, et fide digerendus. Nam et paulo ante, car- nem suam panem quoque cælestem pronunciarat, urgens usquequaque per allegoriam necessariorum populorum, memoriam patrum, qui panes et carnes Ægyptiorum præverterant Divinæ vo- cationi. Igitur conversus ad recogi-

tatus illorum, quia senserat dispergen- dos, ' Caro,' ait, ' nihil prodest.' Quid hoc ad destruendam carnis resurrec- tionem."—De Resurrect., c. 37. [p. 347. Ed. Paris. 1664.]

[e] [Johnson read 'pabulorum,' ac- cording to Rigaltius's Edition. In the preceding note, the Benedictine read- ing ' populorum' has been followed.]

CHAP.
II.

disposition of mind, which had so provoked God against their ancestors; though this must be allowed to be but a conjectural gloss: but when Dr. W. represents these words of Tertullian, as if the Father had said that "Christ urged" His own intent "by allegories," he seems to me to take a greater liberty in rendering this saying of Tertullian, than Tertullian does in glossing the sacred text. We have seen that all true communicants do "hunger after, devour with their ears, ruminate by the mind, and by faith digest" the words of Christ, as well as the external symbols; and therefore as Tertullian asks the Marcionites, (who used to produce these words of Christ, "The flesh profiteth not," as a proof against the doctrine of our bodies being to be raised from the dead,) "How does this tend to destroy the doctrine of the resurrection?" so I may have leave humbly to ask the Doctor, how does this of Tertullian tend to destroy that sense of this context in John vi. for which I am now arguing? It is true in this place he makes no express mention of the Eucharist; but in p. 379[f] of this very book he does, and that in such terms as seem to imply that he understood John vi. of the Sacrament. I mean those remarkable words of his[g], "The flesh is fed with the Body and Blood of Christ, that the soul may be replenished with God;" for whether by "God" you understand the Second or Third Person of the Trinity, I suppose the truth itself must be learned from John vi. as understood of the Eucharist. For from thence only it can be proved that "he who eats Christ's Flesh and drinks His Blood has Christ abiding in him," or is "the habitation of
Eph. ii. 22.
God through the Spirit;" for Christ dwells in us by means of the Spirit, Which He hath given us. If by "God" you understand 'the Spirit,' I suppose I have shewed that the best proof of the Spirit's being conveyed to us by means of the Eucharist, is from John vi. 63, understood according to the sense of the ancient Church[h]. And that Tertullian understood John vi. of the Eucharist, appears pretty evidently from those words of his, in which he explains "our daily bread" in the Lord's Prayer[i], viz., "This may spiritually be understood;

---

[f] [It must be borne in mind, that the Author refers to the paging of the Edition, which he here employed, viz. Rigaltius's.]

[g] m. p. 8. Ap.
[h] See sub-section to chap. ii. sect. 1.
[i] g. p. 8. Ap.

for Christ is Bread, and Bread is life—as also because His
Body is authoritatively declared to be in Bread, 'This is My
Body;' therefore by asking daily bread we ask perpetuity in
Christ, and that we may remain undivided from His Body."
For by these last words he clearly alludes to that text, " He John vi. 56.
who eateth My Flesh abideth in Me," and as clearly applies
it to the Eucharist. Tertullian then is rather for me than
against me.

The next writer cited by Dr. W. in favour of his opinion, The same is
that John vi. is not to be understood of the Eucharist, is Ori- shewed
concerning
gen. Now it may be proper previously to observe, that Origen Origen.
is the most remarkable of any other ancient expositors for
the variety of senses, which he frequently applies to the same
text. And though Clement of Alexandria, who was his master, did probably teach him this way of expounding Scripture; yet it is certain, that Origen was one of those scholars,
who mightily outwent his master. He commonly calls his more
remote and anagogical constructions 'allegories;' not in the
sense that his master Clement says that " Wine allegorizes,"
that is, "Sacramentally represents the Blood," but as 'allegory'
denotes a very figurative and remote sense. And therefore,
when he owns himself to be in pursuit of an allegory, we
may safely conclude that it was not his intention to give
us the direct sense or proper meaning of the text which he
is handling.

Having premised thus much, I proceed to the first allegation from this writer, produced by Dr. W., which is this;
" We are said to drink the Blood of Christ, when we receive
His sayings, in which Life consists[j];" so the words are quoted
by the Doctor. But the words of Origen's translator are,
*Bibere autem dicimur Sanguinem Christi, non solum Sacra-
mentorum ritu, sed et cum sermones Ejus recipimus, in quibus
vita consistit, sicut et Ipse dicit,* John vi. 63. [k]In English, "We
are said to drink the Blood of Christ, not only in the rite of
the Sacraments, but when we receive His sayings," &c. The
Doctor had good reason to maim this evidence, because it is
directly against him. For he undertakes to prove from Origen,
that John vi. "is not to be understood of Sacramental oral manducation;" whereas Origen says, " We are said to drink the

[j] Homil. xvi. in Num. fol. 123.   [k] [tom. ii. p. 334.]

H h 2

CHAP.
II.

Blood of Christ, not only in the rite of the Sacraments," (and it has been more than once observed, that the ancients often call the Bread and Wine in the Eucharist 'Sacraments' in the plural number). And in these words he does as expressly contradict Dr. W.'s doctrine, as if he had said, "We do in the rite of the Sacraments drink the Blood of Christ, according to John vi." For it was of these words he was now discoursing, and he had just before rehearsed ver. 53, viz., "Except ye eat the Flesh of the Son of Man, and drink His Blood," &c., "and My Flesh is meat indeed," &c., and "He that says this was wounded for all; for He was wounded for our sins," as saith Esaias[1]. And then follow the words first cited; so that Origen's testimony recoils on them that use it. For it is certain that in those words he applies these verses in John vi. to the Eucharist. And though he does also say that "we drink the Blood of Christ by receiving His sayings;" yet his way of expression sufficiently shews, that the Sacramental drinking was the primary and acknowledged sense, and the other the allegorical. And indeed he was professedly upon the allegorical flight; for the occasion of all he says in this place was, that he thought the literal sense of those words, "He shall not sleep until he drink the blood of the slain," to be too harsh; for he supposes it to be a prophecy of the Christian Church, and that therefore "abhorring the sound of the letter we must recur to a sweetening allegory;" and so expounds these words by John vi. 53. And because 'slain' is in the plural number, and therefore to drink the Blood of Christ, Who was but one Person, did not come up to his purpose, therefore he adds that "the Apostles were also slain, and that when we read their writings we drink the blood of slain men." Therefore one may certainly pronounce this to be in Origen's own judgment the allegorical sense of John vi., and by unavoidable consequence, not to be that primary proper sense intended by our Saviour in these words.

Numb.
xxiii. 24.

And here my reader may observe, that neither Origen nor

---

[1] The reader will excuse me that I allege Origen here, and in the other citations on this head, in English only. The citations are numerous, and some of them long; and the Latin, from which they are translated, very plain, so that I think my reader may depend upon the rendition which I have given. I can assure him that I have not designedly misrepresented one word.

any other of the ancients does ever professedly labour to prove
that John vi. was to be understood of the Eucharist; not because they did not think that this was our Saviour's meaning in this place, for it will soon abundantly appear that
they did generally so take it; but because this sense of the
words was so obvious and so commonly received, that there
was no occasion to insist upon a particular demonstration of
it.   Origen's zeal for the allegorical sense makes him here
and elsewhere enlarge himself in justification of the gloss,
which Dr. Clagett and Dr. Whitby assert to be the true one.
But he saw no cause to use any persuasion or argument to
convince himself or his intelligent hearers, that Christ was
to be understood of the Sacrament; for which no reason can
so probably be alleged as this, that all were sufficiently apprised that this was the common prevailing sense in which
the words were generally taken; and therefore Origen thinks
it sufficient to mention it *en passant,* as a thing of which
nobody doubted: while on the other side he knew that his
allegorical construction of the words would not so easily
be admitted; and therefore he found it necessary to press
and enforce it; and this will appear more evident from that
citation from him, which Dr. Whitby next mentions.

This citation is as follows; "Christ's Flesh is meat indeed,
and His Blood drink indeed; because He feedeth all mankind with the Flesh and Blood of His Word, as with pure
meat and drink [m]."   I should rather have turned the words,
"He irrigates and refreshes every sort of men with," &c.,
for the Latin words are, *Potat ac reficit omne hominum
genus,* &c.   Now that Origen in this Homily is upon the
allegorical flight, is evident to all that ever looked into it.
He had indulged himself so far this way in the former part
of his discourse, that he apprehended his readers to be
offended with him; and therefore apologizes for himself in
fol. 72, by alleging the example of St. Paul.   And he goes
on to tell us that St. Peter went into an upper room to pray,
"to shew that he sought after the things which are above."
And because it was said to that Apostle, "'Kill and eat,' three
several times," he will thereby have this doctrine insinuated,
that "except we are cleansed by Father, Son, and Holy
Ghost, we cannot be clean."   No man certainly can believe,

SECT.
V.

Ancients
take it for
granted
that Joh. vi.
is meant
of the
Eucharist.

1 Cor. x.
1, 2, &c.
Acts x.

---

[m] Homil. vii. in Levitic., fol. 72, 73.

that Origen designed to persuade his hearers that this was the primary and direct intention of the holy writer, in giving us this narrative; nay, he himself supposes the contrary, for he says this in justification of his former allegorical expositions. He does indeed introduce his gloss on this passage of John vi. by saying, "That what we are speaking of may more evidently be made to appear, we will take an instance in things of greater moment;" and then cites John vi. 53. 55, and adds, "Because Jesus is wholly clean, His Flesh is wholly meat, His Blood is wholly drink, therefore He says, ' My Flesh is meat indeed;' " and so proceeds as first cited. And he presently subjoins, "Peter and Paul and all the Apostles are clean in the next place after Christ; and thirdly, all the disciples in proportion to their merits are clean food." He supposes that this allegory of his was better grounded than the rest, and therefore hopes to support the others by this; but if this had been the primary and direct intention of our Saviour in this text, it had been nothing to his present purpose, which was to justify a secondary and more remote exposition. And to give farther evidence of this, he says, "There is a killing letter in the Gospel as well as Law;" and gives John vi. as an instance of this killing letter; which is indeed a good proof against transubstantiation. And he alleges another instance of this in those words of our Saviour, "He that hath no sword, let him sell his garment, and buy one." He tells us that "there is in these words the quickening Spirit," meaning, I suppose, 'the sword of the Spirit.' No man can in equity suppose, that Origen intended to deny that there was a more proper and just interpretation of those words; or that the history recorded Luke xxii. 35—38 was meant of nothing but of a spiritual sword, which is the Word of God; and I am very confident that no impartial reader will see cause to suppose that Origen believed this construction of John vi. to be more proper and genuine than any of the rest. There is indeed this difference between John vi. and other texts here produced by Origen, that others of them have a literal meaning intended by the holy writers; but this of John vi. has no literal meaning intended either by Christ Jesus or St. John. But that Origen himself acknowledged that "we eat Christ's Flesh in the rite of the Sacraments," has been already observed; and that this is a more proper sense than that of 'receiving His doctrine,' needs no proof. For that the Eucharistical Bread and Wine are verily and indeed Christ's Body and Blood, though not literally, has been shewed at large; but this can never be said of His precepts, except in a very remote and loose way of speaking. If Origen, in all this disquisition about eating clean animals, which begins p. 72. col. 1. do give the proper sense of any one text that he cites, it is [that of] the parable of "the net which gathered of every kind." And it is certain, that by the good and bad fishes he justly understands men[n]; but when in the same place he supposes that these good or bad men are like clean or unclean fishes, to be tasted or eaten by discourse or conversation, he manifestly runs into an allegory: and he does this more manifestly still[o], where he says, "Those fishes, which are assisted by their fins and covered with scales, do rise upward, as seeking the liberty of the Spirit. And such," says he, "is every saint, who being inclosed in the net of faith is called a good fish by Christ Jesus." So that all which can be learnt from this citation is, that Origen is here allegorizing the words of our Saviour; and consequently, that believing Christ's doctrine is not eating His Flesh and drinking His Blood, in the most direct and primary manner intended by our Blessed Saviour. Dr. Whitby lays some stress on the words used by Origen on this occasion, viz., "If ye are the sons of the Church, acknowledge that what we say are the things of the Lord;" and if Origen had been performing the part of an interpreter, it must be owned that these words had been of considerable weight; but he himself, in the very beginning of the Homily, declares that this was not his design. *Non enim nunc exponendi Scripturas, sed ædificandi Ecclesias ministerium gerimus.* And it is very evident, he kept close to his purpose, and acts the allegorist through the whole discourse. And when he charges them as "sons of the Church" to allow of his glosses, the utmost he can mean is, that it was then a prevailing opinion, that secondary remote allegorical senses of Scripture were to be admitted over and above the direct genuine meaning; and yet this opinion did not so much prevail but that Origen found occasion to complain of some men, for

SECT. V.

Matt. xiii. 47, 48.

[n] fol. 72. col. 4. [o] fol. 73. col. 4.

charging him with 'offering violence to Scripture' by his
allegorical strains[p]; and he might have spared all his pains,
which he takes to defend himself on this occasion, if the
sense which he gives to this and other texts had been the
received sense of the Church in those days. I am pretty
confident, that neither Dr. Whitby nor any of his followers
will allow of any one of the allegorical glosses of Origen
above mentioned, excepting this only on John vi., but I conceive in this case he ought not to pick and choose, but to
take all or none; for it is the judgment or authority of
Origen, for which we are now arguing; and he does as
clearly declare that " thrice," Acts x. 16, denotes the trine im-
mersion; that Peter's going up into the upper room denotes
his seeking the things above; that the Apostles and disciples
of our Lord are " clean meat," and the other particulars before
mentioned; as that John vi. is to be understood of doctrine.
Nor ought any man in justice to impute this opinion to Origen; since it is evident beyond all dispute, that he does not
offer this as an interpretation, but only as an allegory; and
declares in the very front of his discourse that he was " not
interpreting Scripture, but edifying the Church," that is,
making such anagogical glosses as might elevate the affections or reform the morals of his hearers.

That Origen understood John vi., in the first place, of the
Eucharist, and in the second place or anagogical sense only,
of doctrine, we have a very direct proof from Homil. xiii. in
Levitic., fol. 87. col. 3, where having spoken of the Eucharist
as an effectual propitiation, as " the Bread Which comes
down from heaven and gives life to the world," as the reader
may see in the Appendix[q], he soon after adds, " We may otherwise understand it; for every word of God is bread;" for
here again, as in the citation first produced by Dr. Whitby,
he clearly speaks on a supposition, that the Eucharist was
primarily meant in John vi., doctrine or precepts secondarily
and remotely only.

And to give my reader a decisive proof, that no conclusion
ought to be drawn against that sense of John vi. for which I
now plead, from Origen's allegorical flights; I desire it may
be observed, that he uses the same liberty in relation to the

[p] fol. 72. col. 1, 2. [q] b. p. 10. Ap.

history of institution, that he does in relation to John vi. And I do with good reason presume, that it was not the intention of Origen nor of those against whom I argue, to prove that the words of institution are meant of instruction only. And though Dr. W. is willing to have John vi. to be understood primarily of doctrine and precepts; yet I cannot in charity believe, that he would serve the history of institution in the same manner. And I suppose it will appear from the following passages, that Origen's judgment was, that the words of institution and of John vi. carry the same sense; and that whosoever fulfils our Saviour's precept in receiving the Eucharist does also receive the promise of Christ's Flesh and Blood and [of] eternal Life mentioned in John vi., and that they who do not eat Christ's Flesh and drink His Blood according to John vi. do not comply with the institution of this holy Sacrament. The words of Origen, to which I now appeal, are in his thirty-fifth Homily on St. Matthew's Gospel; where he treats of our Saviour's celebrating the first Eucharist, according to the narrative which St. Matthew gives us of this memorable fact, in the twenty-sixth chapter of his Gospel. Now in the 75th fol. col. 1. of this Homily, speaking of our Saviour's preparing to eat the Passover with His disciples, he says, "We being under the virtue and spirit (not the letter) of the Law do fulfil all things, which are there commanded to be celebrated in a bodily manner, by celebrating them spiritually; for we put away the old leaven of malice and wickedness, and we keep the new Passover with the unleavened bread of sincerity and truth; Christ Himself feasting with us according to the will of the Lamb, Who says, 'Except ye eat the Flesh of the Son of Man and drink His Blood, ye have no Life in you.' He Who takes away the sins of the world does also forbid the destroyer of all mankind and not of Egypt only, to touch us; while we celebrate the Passover with Him, and ascend, the Lord being with us, from the places below to the upper region in which is a guest-chamber, which is shewed to the disciples of Christ by the master of the family, that is, the intellect which is in every man: but let this upper room be large enough to receive Jesus, the Word and Wisdom and Truth of God, and in all respects the Son of God, Who cannot

CHAP. be received but by those whose minds are enlarged." He
II. adds, that it must not only be "large" but "clean," that it
must be "in the City of God," that is, the Church. And
at the end of this page, " We ought to know, that they who
are taken up with feasting and secular cares do not go into
the upper room, nor behold it's greatness, nor consider it's
furniture ; nor do they celebrate the Passover with Jesus, nor
do they receive the Bread of blessing nor the Cup of the New
Testament from Him." Here in the first words he supposes,
that they who keep the Christian Passover do eat the Flesh
of the Son of Man, according to the meaning of John vi.;
and that it was Christ's will, in celebrating and instituting
this new Passover, that we should eat this Flesh ; and by
eating this Flesh, have Life abiding in us. And in the last
words he denies that worldly unprepared communicants do
receive " the Cup of the New Testament or the Bread of blessing." So that ' to eat the Flesh of the Son of Man' and ' to
receive the Cup of the New Testament or the Bread of blessing' are reciprocal things ; and he that does one does the
other. Modern Divines think it the peculiar privilege of
well-prepared communicants, that they eat the Flesh of Christ
and drink His Blood, according to John vi. Origen declares
that this is likewise their privilege, that they only eat the
Bread of blessing and [drink] the Cup of the New Testament ;
that is, they alone do truly receive the Eucharist. Modern
Divines say, that this Flesh and Blood may be eaten and drunk
extra cœnam, in any act of religion ; but Origen supposes
that eating the Flesh and drinking the Blood, and eating
the Bread and drinking the Cup, are the same action ; and
that none do it indeed, but they who come with suitable dispositions. He speaks of both in the same cryptical manner ;
and he does this last more clearly in the following words
of the same Homily[r] ; where after having recited the words
of institution, he immediately subjoins, " The Bread, which
God the Word confesses to be His Body, is the Word Which
nourishes souls. The Word proceeding from God the Word,
and the Bread from the heavenly Bread, Which is placed
on that Table, of which it is written, 'Thou hast prepared
a Table before Me in spite of them that trouble Me ;' and

[r] fol. 76. col. 2, 3.

the Drink, which God the Word confesses to be His Blood, is that Word Which irrigates and exhilarates most notably the hearts of them who drink It; Which is in that Cup, of which it is written, 'and Thy exhilarating Cup is very strong,' (according to the LXX[s]); and that Drink is the Cup of the true Vine," he cites John xv. 1. I suppose neither Origen nor any other writer could ever more expressly say that eating the Flesh of Christ according to John vi. denotes receiving His doctrine, than Origen here says the same of eating Christ's Body and drinking His Blood in the Eucharist; and this passage is the more observable, because Origen here is professedly speaking of the history of institution, and therefore one would think should give us what he thought to be the most proper meaning of that context. But he proceeds in the same strain, and at the foot of col. 3. he adds, " And what Jesus said, when He took Bread, and likewise when He took the Cup, he that is a babe in Christ and carnal may understand in a common sense : but let him that is wiser inquire, from whom Jesus receives it; for He receives it from God the Giver, and He gives it to them that are worthy to receive the Bread and Cup.—' Moses gave you not bread, but My Father giveth you the true Bread from heaven.' " In which words he plainly asserts that what our Saviour promised, John vi., was actually given in the institution; and he supposes that they only who are worthy do receive the Eucharistical Bread and Cup, and supposes them to be babes who think otherwise. And therefore in his judgment, to receive the Eucharistical Body, and to eat the Flesh according to John vi., are the same thing. He presently adds, as follows; " And Jesus always receives Bread from the Father, and gives thanks, and breaks it for them who keep the feast with Him. And He gives it to His disciples according to every one's capacity, and says, 'Take ye, eat ye;' and He shews, when He nourishes them with this Bread, that it is His own Body; since He is the Word Which we stand in need of, both now and when it is fulfilled in the Kingdom of God.—If therefore we will receive the Bread of blessing from Christ Who uses to give it, let us go into the city, into the house of a

[s] [Καὶ τὸ ποτήριόν Σου μεθύσκον ὡς κράτιστον.]

CHAP.
II.

certain man, where Jesus keeps the Passover with His Disciples, when His friends have prepared it : and let us go to
the upper part of the house, which is large, furnished, and
prepared; where [Jesus] receiving the Cup from the Father,
and giving thanks, gives It to those who go up with Him,
saying, 'Drink ye, for It is the Blood of the New Testament,'
Which is drunk by His Disciples and poured out for the
remission of sins committed by those who drink It.   If you
ask how It is poured out, earnestly consider, when you say
this, that which is written, that the love of God is poured out
in your hearts."   And in the Greek works of Origen[t], after
having said, that what our Saviour gave to Judas at the Eucharist was ὁμογενὲς, of the same sort that He gave to the
other Apostles, to them for salvation, to him for condemnation ; he adds, " Let the Bread and Wine be apprehended by
the simple, according to the common receiving in the Eucharist (Gr. κατὰ τὴν κοινοτέραν περὶ Εὐχαριστίας ἐκδοχὴν) ;
but by those who are more profoundly instructed, according to a more Divine explication or promise (Gr. ἐπαγγελίαν)
and concerning the nutritive Word of Truth."   It is evident
to a demonstration, that he gives the same turn to the
history of institution that he does to John vi.   It is certain, that he could not intend by these glosses to set aside
the necessity of the outward Eucharist; he himself owns
that "the eleven Apostles received it to salvation," and
that therefore it is a saving ordinance of religion ; nor
was he ever understood by the ancients to be guilty of
any heterodoxy upon this head of theology.   They, who
have so critically examined and so severely censured Origen upon other accounts, would never have spared him
for so unsound an opinion, if they had thought that there
had been any grounds for suspicion ; for as the ancients
universally believed the necessity of this Sacrament, so they
would never have borne with him, if he had so notoriously
opposed the known sense of the Christian Church.   And
therefore when he thus explains the institution of the Eucharist, he must be supposed either to mean, that what we
receive there is not the Body of Christ, in itself considered, but
by virtue of the words pronounced over it ; and that there-

[t] vol. ii. p. 411.

fore we must receive the words as well as the bread; nay, we must have a much greater concern to digest the words by faith than to masticate the bread with our mouths. And this agrees well enough with what he says in the last citation but one from him, which my reader will find in the Appendix[u], where he says, "The Bread is profitable by means of the Word spoken over it;" and I have before shewed, that we never do so effectually receive the whole Word of God as in the Eucharist. And this indeed must be his meaning in the citation just now mentioned, where he supposes that they who are "more profoundly instructed" do, by the Bread and Wine, understand "the nutritive Word of Truth;" which is the doctrine likewise of his master Clement. Or else it must be said, that, these discourses being delivered to a promiscuous auditory consisting of catechumens and chance-comers as well as communicants, it was not thought proper to speak of the mysteries of the Eucharist in such a manner, as that they who were not yet admitted to the Communion might fully know the nature of it. And I suppose that this account will appear very probable to him that considers the following words of this writer in his ninth Homily on Leviticus, fol. 81. " Thou that art come to the High-Priest, dwell not upon the blood of the flesh but learn rather the Blood of the Word, and hearken to Him Who says to thee, 'This is My Blood Which is shed for the remission of sins'. He that is initiated in the mysteries knows both the Flesh and the Blood of the Word of God. Let us not therefore dwell on these things, which are well known to them that are instructed," that is, to the communicants, "and which cannot be explained to the ignorant," that is, to the catechumens and infidels. By "the Blood of the Word," I apprehend, he clearly meant doctrine and instruction; and yet he certainly speaks of the Eucharist, for he bids us "hearken to Him Who says, 'This is My Blood.'" He does not directly and in words at length speak of the Eucharistical Blood, but only of the natural or carnal, and of the allegorical blood, that is, doctrine; which may be said too of some of the other citations to this purpose. And he hints his reason for it, viz. that his hearers were partly such as were " instructed," and so had no occasion for further infor-

[u] f. p. 10. Ap.

mation in this point; and partly the " ignorant" or unbaptized, who according to the discipline of those ages were not permitted to hear any discourse, whereby they might come to the clear knowledge of the Eucharist before their time. And therefore when Origen, in the course of his Homilies, was obliged to say something of the words in John vi., or in the institution, he thought it sufficient to say so much of them, that the catechumens might not think that they stood for nothing, and yet to say no more than what might be heard by the unbaptized; and the communicants were, by the public Liturgy and by private and personal application, not only taught the nature of this mystery, but the reason why it was not to be expected that they should hear it publicly divulged in sermons or homilies, pronounced in common to all that were pleased to be present at the Christian assemblies. Perhaps he nowhere in his Homilies speaks more plainly of the Eucharist than in the words I have more than once cited from him, and which must now be repeated[v], viz. " If these things are referred to the great Mystery, you will find that that commemoration has the effect of the great Propitiation. If you reflect on that Bread Which comes down from heaven and gives Life to the world, on that Shew-Bread Which God hath set forth as propitiatory through faith in His Blood; and if you look to that commemoration, of which our Lord says, ' Do this as a memorial of Me ;' you will find that is the only memorial which renders God propitious to men." Now though no words can more plainly speak Origen's opinion of the Eucharistical Sacrifice to them who are well acquainted with the phrases and texts of Scripture here used ; yet I am persuaded, my impartial reader will agree with me, that one who knew nothing of Christianity but what he had heard in such Homilies as these of Origen could never, from hearing these words once and away or by having them ten times repeated to him, penetrate into the nature of the Christian Eucharist. They could not from these words in themselves considered, without being acquainted with the process of the Eucharistical solemnity, know whether Origen meant natural or figurative bread, or in what sense it came down from heaven, or how it was a memorial, or of what it was a

[v] b. p. 10. Ap.

commemoration. And it is observable, that he turns short upon his hearers and excuses himself from any further explanation by presently adding, " But it is not convenient to enlarge on these things; because it is sufficient that they may be understood by remembrance," that is, by recollecting what they had formerly been taught upon this head, presently after Baptism, and upon their first admission to the Eucharist. Communicants might sufficiently understand what he meant; and he intended to instruct no other persons in this mystery. And so he proceeds to tell the catechumens, that " every word of God is bread," as is before mentioned. And indeed it seems probable that this was the usual rule by which preachers governed themselves, while their auditories were known to consist of infidels or almost-Christians as well as of those who had received Baptism. And this is the account which he himself seems to me to give of this matter.

I have been the more large in examining the citations of Origen, because they seem to give more countenance to the cause of Dr. Whitby and Dr. Clagett than any thing else to be met with in antiquity. And now let us briefly reflect on what we find Origen to have said in this matter.

It is freely owned that Origen does several times explain eating and drinking Christ's Flesh and Blood in John vi. by receiving His doctrine. But,

1. He does in the same manner explain eating the Bread and drinking the Cup in the history of the institution; now it is very certain, that the words of institution are meant of the Eucharist, and that Origen himself did so understand them. When therefore he takes no more liberty with John vi. than he does with the words of institution, it does by no means follow, that by eating Christ's Flesh and drinking His Blood in John vi. he believed that receiving Christ's doctrine was primarily meant, any more than that the words of institution, by bidding us ' eat this Bread,' ' drink this Cup,' require us only to believe His Gospel.

2. It is certain, that when Origen gives this meaning either to John vi., or to the words of institution, he gives it as an allegorical remote sense only. All will easily believe this as to the words of institution. And the whole process of his

Marginal notes:
SECT.
V.

Origen's evidence summed up.

discourse in those Homilies, from which Dr. Clagett and Dr. Whitby have taken their citations, is a clear demonstration that he was wholly on the allegorical strain, when he explained John vi. by faith and doctrine. Nay, I have shewed that Origen himself does declare as much. Since then this is by Origen himself confessed to be the allegorical sense only, therefore it cannot be the first and direct sense, after which only I am now searching. So that the very citations produced by Dr. Clagett and Dr. Whitby are, if we observe their connection with what goes before and follows, a proof that Origen did not look upon this gloss to be the proper sense of John vi.

3. It is very clear that he does over and again apply John vi. to the Eucharist, without giving us any grounds to suspect that he does it in an anagogical or improper sense; nay, he does it sometimes in such a manner, that we have good reason to conclude he took this to be the primary meaning of our Saviour. I will here add one instance not yet mentioned [x]. "Baptism was formerly enigmatical in the cloud and the sea; but now regeneration by water and the Spirit is in open view. Then manna was the enigmatical food; but now the Flesh of the Son of God is true meat in open view, as He Himself hath said, 'My Flesh is meat indeed, and My Blood is drink indeed.'" I suppose no man can rationally doubt, but that as he speaks of Baptism in the first clause, so he speaks of the Eucharist in the other; and he calls this latter Sacrament the Flesh of Christ, as he could not have done, if Christians in that age had used by 'the Flesh of Christ' to understand doctrine and mere precepts. And he supports this name of the Sacrament by John vi. 55, which had been impertinent if it had not then been generally allowed that this text was meant of the Eucharist. And it will soon appear from St. Augustine, that 'to receive the Flesh of the Son of Man' was a phrase commonly used among the African Christians for 'receiving the Sacrament,' as we now speak.

4. And it deserves our particular reflection, that neither Origen nor any other writer does ever industriously and designedly make it their business to prove, that John vi. was to be understood of the Eucharist, as some of them at least

[x] c. p. 10. Ap.

would have done, if it had been a disputable point; but when
they apply John vi. to this Sacrament, they speak of it as a
thing which all then allowed; but it appears by the two first
citations from Origen, that when he would have this text to
be understood of doctrine and precepts, he thought it necessary to spend many words upon it, as being a notion not
so generally received. And I need not tell my intelligent
reader, that it is not so much my concern to prove that I
have Origen on my side, as that the Church or generality
of Christians did in those ages take John vi. to be meant
of the Holy Sacrament. And I cannot but be of opinion,
that both Origen, and especially the Christians, to whom he
preached, were in my sentiment as to this matter.

If indeed Origen, when he says, that "The Bread and
Wine may be apprehended by the more simple, according to
the common receiving in the Sacrament, but by them who
are more profoundly instructed, concerning the nutritive
Word:" if, I say, by these words he intended to express his
opinion that men may fulfil the institution of the Eucharist
by believing the Gospel without receiving the symbols; I
conceive this opinion of his ought to be abhorred by all men
that are judicious and of a true Catholic spirit; but it is
evident, that these words were spoken in relation to the
Bread and Wine administered by our Saviour, when He
celebrated the first Eucharist, and so cannot serve the turn
of Dr. Whitby or his followers.

There is indeed a passage of Origen, on Matt. xv. p. 253.
vol. i. of Monsieur Huet's edition, which I cannot pretend to
understand. If any learned person, who dislikes the doctrine
for which I am now an advocate, shall please to form an
argument against me from those words, I shall not despair
of returning a proper answer; but that place does not at all
favour the opinion of Dr. Whitby. And I apprehend it will
be no hard matter to prove, that whoever undertakes to
maintain any modern notion from those words will find
himself disappointed.

The next writer cited by Dr. Whitby, is Eusebius Cæsari- Allegation
ensis[z], who introduces our Saviour saying, "Do not think I from Eusebius con-

---

[z] [Contra Marcellum, De Ecclesias-
tica Theologia, lib. iii. cap. 12. p. 180,
appended to the Demonstratio Evangelica, ed. Paris. 1628. Μὴ γὰρ τὴν
σάρκα, ἣν περίκειμαι, νομίσητέ Με λέγειν, ὡς δέον αὐτὴν ἐσθίειν· μηδὲ τὸ

speak of the Flesh with which I am clothed, as if you must eat
that, nor that I command you to drink My corporeal sensible
Blood; but know well, that the words, which I have spoken
to you, are Spirit and Life.   So that the very words and
speeches of Christ are the Flesh and Blood."   Now I conceive, that by this last sentence his meaning is, either that the
Word of Christ makes the Sacrament the Body and Blood;
just so our Saviour says, "I am the Resurrection and the Life;"
He is the efficient cause of the resurrection, as His words are
of the Sacramental Body and Blood: or else his design was
to say, that the main or principal thing required on our part
in receiving the Sacrament is to receive all the holy instructions which He has given us.   However, that Eusebius did
not believe that bare words and precepts were intended by
our Saviour in John vi. is sufficiently clear from what he
speaks in this very discourse[a], that when our Saviour says,
'the flesh profiteth nothing,' "He did not speak of the
Flesh which He had assumed, but of His mystical Body and
Blood[b]."   And this indeed is his most probable meaning in
these words, and those cited next before, viz., that, as Origen
expresses it, "Not the consecrated food" or the material
Bread, which is His mystical Body, "but the Word spoken
over it is profitable."   I conceive 'the mystical Body' can
be understood of nothing but the material Eucharist, in this
place: the Church is indeed Christ's mystical Body; but as
I am not aware that any man ever asserted that Christ by
His Flesh and Blood in John vi. did intend His Church, so
it is utterly inconsistent with common sense so to understand it; for the Flesh which Christ speaks of John vi.
"was given for the Life of the world," which cannot be
applied to the Church.   Nor am I sensible, that Christ's doctrine is ever called His 'mystical Body;' and if it were,
yet to suppose that Eusebius should say in one place, that
Christ's mystical Body (that is, His doctrine,) profiteth not,
and then within a page or two from that place to assert, that
this doctrine of His, this mystical Body, is Spirit and Life,
is to make this great man directly contradict himself.   I

αἰσθητὸν καὶ σωματικὸν αἷμα πίνειν
ὑπολαμβάνετέ Με προστάττειν. 'Αλλ'
εὖ ἴστε, ὅτι τὰ ῥήματά Μου ἃ λελάληκα
ὑμῖν, πνεῦμά ἐστι καὶ ζωή ἐστι· ὥστε,
αὐτὰ εἶναι τὰ ῥήματα καὶ τοὺς λόγους

Αὐτου, τὴν σάρκα καὶ τὸ αἷμα.]
     [a] p. 179.
     [b] οὐ περὶ ἧς ἀνείληφε σαρκὸς διελέ-
γετο, περὶ δὲ τοῦ μυστικοῦ σώματός τε
καὶ αἵματος.

conclude therefore, that if Eusebius be not a witness to the doctrine which I now assert, yet neither is he against it.

St. Athanasius is next cited by Dr. Whitby, for saying, "The words which Christ spake are not carnal, but spiritual; for how could His Body have sufficed for meat, that It should be made the food of the whole world?" Thus he maims a paragraph, which the reader may peruse more at large in my Appendix[c]; and yet in the words, as cited by the Doctor, there is nothing that does at all affect the doctrine of oral or Sacramental manducation. Nor can I conceive to what purpose Dr. Whitby and Dr. Clagett produced these words; they are indeed directly against transubstantiation, but are an illustrious proof of the doctrine of the Sacrament which prevailed in the primitive Church; and particularly, they are an evidence that he understood John vi. of the Eucharist. For this great man declares that "Christ predicates of Himself," (that is, of His Sacramental Body; for the Fathers use the word ' Christ' or 'Christ's Flesh and Blood' promiscuously, as our Saviour Himself uses 'I' and 'Me' in this chapter as words equivalent to 'My Flesh and Blood,') "both Flesh and Spirit;" and therefore was very far from the opinion of these Doctors, that Christ meant nothing but precepts and instruction by Flesh and Blood: though he says, "Christ speaks not of carnal things but spiritual;" yet he affirms too, that there is something 'seen,' something 'invisible.' By Spirit and Life he understands "spiritual and supernal food, heavenly nutriment, distributed among all as a preservative to the resurrection to eternal life." And he has formerly been cited as from Mr. Mede, calling the Eucharist "heavenly incorruptible Bread," clearly alluding to the words of our Saviour, "This is the Bread which cometh John vi. 50. down from heaven, that a man may eat thereof and not die." To this let me add those decisive words[d], "We have the first-fruits of the future repast in this present life, in the Communion of the Body of our Lord, as He hath said, 'The Bread which I will give is My Flesh,' &c., for the Flesh of the Lord is a reviving Spirit." No writer can speak more directly and positively than St. Athanasius does, for oral manducation being meant in John vi. And I must profess myself amazed

[c] a. p. 17. Ap. [d] b. p. 17. Ap.

to see two such learned men as Dr. Whitby and Dr. Clagett suppose that he favours the contrary opinion.

Allegations
from St.
Jerome
considered
and re-
felled.
The next writer cited by both these Doctors is St. Jerome; the treatise cited by them is spurious, I mean their Commen- taries on the Psalms; for Erasmus and all editors since his time, and Dr. Cave our learned countryman, give them over as the work of some later hand. I will only add that this pretended St. Jerome says, that John vi. " may be under- stood of the mysteries." This is contrary to what Dr. Whitby asserts, which is, that our Saviour is " not to be understood of Sacramental manducation." The true St. Jerome does say[e], that " Christ's Flesh and Blood may be eaten and drunk, not only in the mysteries, but in reading the Scripture." But he first fairly tells his reader that he is speaking *juxta ἀνα- γωγὴν*; which makes me believe that other Fathers, when they speak as St. Jerome here does, are to be understood anagogically; and I shall not enlarge on these words, be- cause they are in effect what Origen had said before. Let us observe then, how he mixes the anagogical and the proper sense of John vi. and of the institution, in those words[f], " Let us understand, that the Bread, which Christ brake and gave to His disciples, was the Body of our Lord and Saviour— if therefore the Bread which came down from heaven is the Body of our Lord, and the Wine He gave to His dis- ciples, the Blood Which was shed for the remission of sins— let us go with our Lord into the upper room furnished and clean, and let us receive from Him the Cup of the New Tes- tament from above; and celebrating the Passover with Him, let us be exhilarated with the wine of sobriety; for the king- dom of God is not meat and drink, &c. Moses gave us not the true Bread, but our Lord Jesus, Who is Himself both the Convivator and the Feast, that eats with us and is eaten by us." He very evidently speaks of the Sacrament, and applies to it the title of the " Bread which came down from heaven," and of "the true Bread," which he took from John vi.; and yet he gives such an anagogical dash to his discourse, that if it were not plain to a demonstration, that he speaks of the in- stitution as well as of the context in dispute, this would·be thought an unanswerable evidence against me. But from

e On Ecclesiast. cap. 3.   f k. p. 28. Ap.

this instance it appears, that the ancients used the same latitude in relation to the words of institution, that they do in
speaking of John vi.   And it is observable that St. Jerome,
when these words came from him, had Origen's Homily on
the twenty-sixth chapter of St. Matthew, ver. 26, 27, which
I just now quoted from him, lying before him, or fresh in his
memory.   And by the turn which he gives them, it seems
pretty plain that he took the words of Origen as I do.   But
St. Jerome fully delivers his testimony of the proper sense
of John vi. when he says of 'wheat[g],' that "out of it the
heavenly Bread is made, of which our Lord declares, 'My
Flesh is meat indeed, and My Blood is drink indeed.'"   And
from all this put together, I conclude that he certainly understood John vi. to be most properly understood of the Eucharist; and it is for the primary and proper sense that I am
now arguing.

Dr. Whitby proceeds to St. Augustine; and Dr. Clagett Allegations
from St.
Augustine
considered
and re-
felled.
too, many years before, had cited to the same purpose those
words of his, "Why providest[h]" (I should rather say, 'why
preparest') "thou [thy] teeth and stomach? believe, and
thou hast eaten[i]; for to believe in Him is to eat the Living
Bread."   He was evidently speaking to some ignorant care-
less Africans, who were more concerned to come to the Sacrament with clean mouths and empty stomachs than with
hearts filled with faith and holy affections; and all that the
Father can mean is, that faith is more necessary than any
external preparation for eating and drinking the Sacrament
to our soul's health.   It is very evident, that the Father
speaks to them, who came to Church in order to communicate and had to that purpose kept themselves fasting.   Now
I have that opinion of Dr. Whitby, that he will not suppose
that it was St. Augustine's intention to send these men home
again without receiving the Sacrament, or that he designed
to convince them that oral manducation was unnecessary, that
it was sufficient for them to eat the Body of Christ by an

---

[g] in. p. 29. Ap.
[h] The Latin is, 'Ut quid paras' &c.
[i] Just so he says of the woman that
had the issue of blood, "Tetigit, id est,
credidit," she touched, that is, she believed, Conc. 1. on Psalm lxxviii. He
does not mean, she did not touch the
hem of Christ's garment, but that she
believed as well as touched. So St.
Augustine intended not to say, that we
need not eat if we believe, but that we
must believe as well as eat.

CHAP.
II.

internal act of faith only. He therefore speaks to them upon supposition that they were to eat and drink the symbols; and to such a person any Bishop or Priest may say, ' Believe, and thou hast eaten; and if thou believest not, thou hast not eaten.' The question is, whether this holy Father would have used these words to any that were not actual communicants, and told them that they might eat Christ's Flesh and drink His Blood, without the assistance of Church or Priest, in their own closets or at their own tables, by the exercise of their faith or by any other act of religion. Nothing else will serve the purpose of Dr. Whitby; and I am much mistaken, if St. Augustine ever dropped any words that look this way. Dr. Whitby refers us to St. Augustine's twenty-sixth Tract on St. John, where we have the following words [k], " To believe in Him is to eat the Living Bread. He that believes eats, because he is inwardly replenished; any one may come in, and go to the Altar, and receive the Sacrament with an unwilling mind; he cannot believe but with his own consent." And in these words again he strongly affirms the necessity of faith in order to a proper eating and drinking the Sacrament, but still he speaks of and to actual communicants; and the question still is, whether the Father would have said so to one that wilfully abstained. And it will soon appear that he could not so speak according to his own principles. Dr. Clagett further cites St. Augustine for saying [l], " The Sacrament of this is taken by some to life, by some to destruction; but the thing itself, whereof this is a Sacrament, is to all for life, to none for death." The reader is to observe that ' the thing itself' here spoken of is *unity*, for that was what the holy Father had just before been treating of; and I cannot at present conceive, how they that believe these words to be a proof that John vi. is not meant of the Sacrament would form their argument or draw their conclusion from these words. And I have no reason to apprehend that it is possible for them to make these words serve their purpose.

Dr. Clagett cites St. Augustine for saying [m], " To receive the Body of Christ truly and not by the Sacrament, this is to remain in Christ." But the Doctor takes the liberty of

<hr />

[k] i. p. 32. Ap.   [l] l. p. 32. Ap.   [m] F. p. 36. Ap.

turning, *non Sacramento tenus*, ' not by the Sacrament,' which
really signifies, ' not in the Sacrament' or sign ' only ;' so,
ore tenus, ' in words only ;' *titulo tenus*, ' in name,' or title
' only ;' *aurium tenus*, ' with the ears only.' "To eat the Body
of Christ truly," in the sense of St. Augustine and the
ancients, is to eat It internally and with faith, as has been
shewed; and to do it ' by the Sacrament only' is a phrase intimating the reception of the ' external sign' (so St. Augustine
sometimes explains Sacrament) without faith and other internal preparations.

But the most learned and ingenious Dr. Clagett, whose
labours against Dr. Owen and the Papists will immortalize
his name, does confess that " St. Augustine in writing against
the Pelagians owns this context in St. John's Gospel to be a
direct and proper command to receive the Eucharist." Therefore I wish this excellent man had never studied to make this
Father contradict himself. But I think it is very evident
that he has laboured in vain, for I am not sensible that he
has produced any passage from St. Augustine or any other
Father but what has been considered and answered; for as
to what concerns St. Augustine's denying that the wicked eat
the Body of Christ, that has formerly been accounted for under
another head[n]; and as to the passage from St. Augustine,
De Doctrina Christiana[o], the Doctor uses it against transubstantiation only, and indeed it could serve him to no other
purpose. It is true, St. Augustine (and the same may be
said of several others) does understand what goes before
those words in the fifty-first verse of John vi., viz., " And the
Bread which I give is My Flesh," &c., they understand, I
say, our Saviour sometimes, in what goes before, to speak of
His giving the Holy Ghost: so in Tom. iii. p. 703. Tract 26.
on St. John's Gospel, *Daturus Dominus Spiritum Sanctum
dixit se panem, qui de cœlo descendit*. And of this I suppose
he is to be understood in his second book *De Sermone Domini
in Monte;* where interpreting those words in the Lord's
Prayer, " Give us this day our daily bread," by ' daily
bread' he understands the things necessary for this life, or
the Sacrament of Christ's Body, or "that spiritual Bread of
which our Lord says, ' I am the Bread of Life ;'" for He is

[n] chap. ii. sect. v. *versus finem.*   [o] e. p. 31. Ap.

CHAP.
II.

St. Augus-
tine gives
testimony
very
largely,
that John
vi. was
meant of
the Eucha-
rist.

with us by the Spirit. And it was not incongruous by what
went before those words, where He declares "His Flesh to
be Bread," to understand the promise of that Holy Spirit,
whereby His Sacramental Body became what It was. But
this does not in the least serve the purpose of any modern
glossators; for St. Augustine does not understand either
doctrine or any spiritual action of ours, or the natural Body
of Christ, to be understood by our Saviour in this passage;
and the words from verse 51. forward, he perpetually took
to be meant of Sacramentally communicating, though not
orally or externally only.

And this I look upon to be the common judgment of the
ancient Fathers; however, this was beyond all doubt the
sentiment of St. Augustine, as appears from the following
citations: first[p], "Does the flesh give Life? The Lord Himself said, when He was commending to us this earth, (that is,
the Sacramental Body,) 'It is the Spirit that giveth Life but
the flesh profiteth not.' Therefore when you reverentially
approach any earth, look not on it as earth," &c. And in
the next page[q] he introduces Christ, as saying, "Understand
what I say in a spiritual manner, you are not to eat that
Body which you see; I have commended to you a Sacrament;
it will give you Life, if spiritually understood; though it is
necessary to be celebrated in a visible manner, yet it must
invisibly be apprehended:" in which words he professedly
expounds John vi. 53, 63. Again[r], "How are we to understand that which is said, 'If any man eat of this Bread he
shall live for ever?' Can we admit of those [to live for ever]
of whom the Apostle says, that they 'eat and drink their
own damnation?'" This is the main, I may say, the only
difficulty that I am aware of, in maintaining that John vi. is
to be understood of the Eucharist; and I am not sensible of
any reason that others have to oppose this sense, but that they
imagine, that if the words are so taken, then he who externally
receives the Eucharist cannot miss of Life eternal: and for this
reason it is thought safest by most now-a-days, to deny that this
context is to be understood of the Eucharist. You see St. Augustine was pressed with this difficulty; he was fully sensible
of the force of this objection; and therefore, if he had not been

P s. p. 33. Ap. l. 12.   q s. p. 33. Ap. l. 21.   r t. p. 34. Ap.

fully convinced that this context was to be understood of the
Eucharist, he would infallibly have let us known it on this occasion. If his judgment had not been perfectly determined in
the point, he would have been glad to make use of the evasion
which is now with too many thought to be a certain truth;
viz., that Christ Jesus does not here speak of oral or Sacramental manducation; which had been an effectual way to
cut the knot, and to escape the objection with which he was
pinched. And we are not therefore to doubt but he would
have made this answer, if he had not been under an absolute
persuasion that he should thereby have done injury to the
truth. And therefore instead of saying that this context was
not meant of Sacramental eating and drinking, he answers
it upon a direct presumption of the contrary: for, says he,
"There is a certain manner of eating that Flesh and drinking
that Blood; and he who eats and drinks in that manner, he
dwells in Christ and Christ in him." And I have before
shewed what the 'manner' was, here meant by St. Augustine,
namely, eating and drinking the Sacrament inwardly as well
as outwardly, with faith as well as with the mouth. In other
places he is altogether as express for understanding John vi.
of the Holy Sacrament; as for instance, where he asks[s],
"What is the Bread of the kingdom of God but He Who
says, 'I am the Living Bread which came down from heaven?'
prepare not your mouth but your heart. This is the commendation of this Supper. See, we believe in Christ, we receive with faith, in receiving we know what is the subject of
our meditation. We take a little, yet we are replenished in
heart." And again[t], "We have heard the veracious Master,
the Divine Redeemer, commending to us our own ransom, His
Blood; for He spake to us of His own Body and Blood; the
one He called 'Meat,' the other 'Drink,' which is the Sacrament
of the faithful; for we have heard our Lord saying, 'It is the
Spirit that quickeneth.'" I will produce no more proofs of
St. Augustine's opinion at large, but refer my reader to those
passages[u], which do as clearly speak St. Augustine's judgment
as any other which I have produced in words at length translated into English. I will only add two paragraphs, which do
not so much declare what this Father's opinion was, as the

[s] u. p. 34. Ap.   [t] w. p. 34. Ap.   [u] f. p. 31. Ap.; C. p. 35. Ap.

general sense of Christians in that age, in the Church of Africa at least.   The first is that, where he says[x], " Christ does not commit Himself to catechumens.   Ask a catechumen, 'Dost thou believe?' He answers, 'I do,' and signs himself with the cross of Christ.   He is not ashamed of the cross of Christ; but bears it in his forehead.   Let us ask him, ' Dost thou eat the Flesh and drink the Blood of the Son of Man ?' He does not know what we mean, for Christ hath not committed Himself to him; catechumens do not know what Christians receive." Every one knows that what the ancients did most industriously hide from the catechumens was the nature of the Eucharist.   And to keep them in the dark as to this particular, they did not permit them to be informed in the proper sense or primary meaning of John vi.; and here we may learn the reason why they did this, namely, because they believed that John vi. was to be understood of the Eucharist.   Our modern Divines, who by Flesh and Blood mean doctrine, when they come to explain those words, " the Bread which I will give is My Flesh," do own that these words are especially meant of the " belief or our Saviour's Death and the benefits of it ;" and therefore do suppose that this is the condition on which eternal Life depends.   Now the ancients were clearly of another mind ; for they taught men before they were baptized to believe in the Cross of Christ, and yet did not on this account think them in a state of salvation.   And we of this age have been endeavouring to persuade men that what the primitive Church taught the catechumens is the very perfection of our religion, the principal or, in effect, the only condition for the obtaining eternal Life.   The other passage I had in my eye is that in which he informs us[y], that " the Punic Christians do rightly call Baptism nothing but Salvation, and the Sacrament of the Body of Christ nothing but Life.   And whence have they this but from an ancient and, I think, Apostolical tradition, by which they hold it to be a principle innate in the Church of Christ, that the Kingdom [of Heaven] or Salvation cannot be had without Baptism.   And what do they hold, who call the Sacrament of the Lord's Table, Life, but that which was said, 'I am the Bread of Life ;' and 'Except ye eat the Flesh of the Son of Man and drink His Blood ye have no Life in you ?' "

[x] h. p. 32. Ap.   [y] P. p. 36. Ap.

This is a most ample testimony that the African Christians did believe John vi. to be meant of the Sacrament; and it seems this way of speaking was of so long standing, that St. Augustine thought it an "Apostolical tradition, an innate principle" of Christianity. Nothing greater could be said in behalf of this doctrine.

Thus I have examined the citations alleged by these two very learned men; and as they reckon upon seven Fathers on their side, so I am pretty well assured they have not one. St. Augustine is a flaming and copious evidence against them. St. Jerome, St. Athanasius, Tertullian, and Clement of Alexandria, are clearly enough for the truth which I assert. Origen, rightly understood, gives no real support to their cause, but rather countenances what I believe to be the true sense of John vi. And even Eusebius says, that John vi. is to be understood of the "mystical Body;" by which he cannot mean the Church, but the Eucharistical Body of Christ. I will proceed to shew,

These seven Fathers not against this sense, rather directly for it.

(2.) That the primitive Church and Fathers did generally take John vi. to be meant of the Sacrament. Theodoret is very clear in those words [z]: "Our Lord did not promise to give His invisible Nature, but His Body; 'for the Bread [which] I will give is My Flesh;' and in the delivery of the Divine mysteries, taking the symbol, He said, 'This is My Body.'" [a] He understood John vi. and the institution to be meant of the same Body. Cyril of Alexandria is a very willing and copious evidence: who [a], mentioning "the unbloody Sacrifice of the loaves," adds, "by it we are blest, eating the Bread which came down from heaven." In which words he applies John vi. 32 and 50 to the Holy Eucharist. Again [b], he styles it "the heavenly Life-giving Sacrifice by which this mortal flesh puts on incorruption;" which he could not say of the Eucharist on any other grounds but those words of our Saviour, "He that eateth of this Bread shall live for ever." He expresses himself more fully still to this purpose [c], where designedly treating on John vi. he says, "Christ did not there shew the manner of eating His Flesh but the advantage of it, and required [His hearers] to believe rather

That John vi. was generally understood of the Eucharist. Theodoret.

Cyril Alex. and third general Council.

John vi. 58.

---

[z] h. p. 46. Ap.
[a] c. p. 43. Ap.

[b] e. p. 44. Ap.
[c] f. p. 44. Ap.

than to be inquisitive;" and then applies the words of institution to John vi. "He brake the Bread, and gave it to
them who believed, saying, 'This is My Body:' you see He
declares not the manner of the mystery to them who were
ignorant and refused to believe without demur; but He is
found of them who already believed;" and citing those

John vi. 53. words, "Except ye eat the Flesh of the Son of Man ye have
no Life in you," he immediately subjoins, "They remain
wholly destitute of a holy and happy life, who receive not
the Son by the mystical *eulogy*;" that is, the Eucharist.
And at another place [d], speaking of John vi. 63, our Saviour
"calls the [Sacramental] Flesh 'the Spirit,' not denying it
to be Flesh; but because it is united to It [the Spirit] and
receives all its efficacy, and therefore ought to be called by
that Name;" and elsewhere [e], "Christ is with us by His
Flesh, which quickens us by the Spirit." But those words
of his, and of the whole Synod of Alexandria, and which are
repeated by Cyril in his explanation of the eleventh Anathematism [f], are of the greatest force and authority, as being
read and approved by the third General Council, held at
Ephesus; they are as follows [g]: "We celebrate the unbloody
Life-giving Sacrifice in the Churches, believing that which
lies in open view to be the Body, not of common man, such
as ourselves, (as also the precious Blood), but receiving it
rather as Christ's own Body, and as the Blood of the Word,
Which quickeneth all things; for common flesh cannot give
Life; and of this our Saviour is a witness, saying, 'The Flesh
profiteth not, but it is the Spirit Which quickeneth;' for because it is made the Word's own Flesh, therefore it is conceived to be quickening, and is so; as our Saviour Himself

John vi. 57. says, 'As the living Father hath sent Me, and I live by the
Father, so he that eateth Me, even he shall live by Me.'"
Cyril himself in his letter to the monks [h], having recited
some part of these words, adds, "The chorus of the Fathers
is of our mind," (he means the Fathers of the General Council of Ephesus,) "and Proclus, who adorns the throne of Constantinople [i]." And it is observable that the Orientalists did

---

d h. p. 44. Ap.   g l. p. 44. Ap.
e i. p. 44. Ap.   h Binius, vol. ii. p. 651.
f Binius, vol. ii. p. 440.   i [ταῦτα φρονεῖ μεθ' ἡμῶν ὁ φιλόχρισ·

not deny these words to be understood of the Eucharist, as SECT.
Cyril himself sufficiently hints in his defence of the eleventh V.
Anathematism; for he takes notice, that the main of what
Nestorius and his party objected as to this point was, that
"the Deity was not eaten[k];" which indeed gives it for
granted, that Christ speaks of Sacramental manducation.
For the Deity may be eaten by faith, as well as the Body
and Blood; so that it is evident both parties took it for
granted, that John vi. was meant of Sacramental manducation; and in fine, both Church and heretics then agreed that
our Saviour treats of the Eucharist in this chapter. St. Chry- Chrysos-
sostom expresses his opinion, when he calls the Sacramental tom.
Cup[l] "the Life-giving Blood and the cause of Life;" when
he says[m], that the Sacramental Body "is full of Life;" and in
those very many places where we have seen him affirming,
that the Divine grace and Holy Spirit descends on the sacred symbols: but further he directly declares his sense of
this context, when he says[n], "Christ drank of the Cup, that
they who heard Him say these things might not say, 'what
then, do we drink Blood and eat Flesh,' and so be disturbed
on this occasion; for when He discoursed of these things,
many were offended at His sayings;" where he refers evidently to John vi. 61, and therefore takes it for certain, that
Christ is there speaking of the Eucharist. Again[o], speaking
of John vi. 63, he says (as before cited), "We must take all
these things in a spiritual manner; they are Spirit and Life,
that is, they are divine and spiritual; what then, is it not
His Flesh? yes, certainly.—We ought not to judge by what
we see, but to look into the mystery with our internal eyes."
And Gaudentius, speaking of the Eucharist, says[p], "This Gaudentius
is our provision for our journey, by which we are subsisted
and nourished in this life, until departing this world we go
to Him; on which account our Saviour said, 'Except ye eat
the Flesh of the Son of Man and drink His Blood, ye have
no Life in you.'" Ambrose gives very full evidence in this Ambrose.

τος τῶν ἁγίων πατέρων χορὸς, καὶ αὐτὸς δὲ ὁ νυνὶ τὸν τῆς ἁγίας Κωνσταν-
τινουπολιτῶν ἐκκλησίας κατακοσμήσας
θρόνον—Πρόκλος.]

k [" Ὁ τρώγων Με, κἀκεῖνος ζήσε-
ται· τίνα ἐσθίομεν, τὴν θεότητα· ἢ τὴν

σάρκα;"—Binius, vol. ii. p. 469.]
l p. p. 39. Ap.
m K. p. 41. Ap.
n s. p. 40. Ap.
o y. p. 40. Ap.
p c. p. 30. Ap.

CHAP.
II.

cause in those words[q], "Christ gave this Bread to His Apostles to distribute it to the faithful people. This Bread is the food of Saints. We may receive even the Lord Himself, Who gave us His Flesh, as He Himself says, ' I am the Bread of Life,'—for he receives Him, who examines himself, and he who receives Him dies not the death of a sinner." And in his discourse to them who were just now admitted to the Eucharist[r], "The food which ye receive is the Living Bread, Which comes down from heaven and affords the substance of eternal Life; and whoso eats of this Bread shall live for ever." And in the same discourse[s], "Christ is in this Sacrament; for it is the Body of Christ; it is not therefore bodily but spiritual food.—The Body of Christ is the Body of the Divine Spirit," referring to John vi. 63. Macarius says[t], "Christ transforms Himself into meat and drink, as it is written in the Gospel, 'He that eateth of this Bread shall live for ever.'" Ephrem Syrus[u] calls the symbols, "Mysteries full of immortality:" and therefore interprets those words, "He that eateth of this Bread shall live for ever," of the Holy Sacrament. Gregory Nyssen[x] labours to shew the manner, how the Eucharist conveys a principle of happy resurrection to the bodies of Christians, and therefore supposes that this principle is in the Eucharist; which he could believe on no other grounds but the words in John vi. now mentioned. St. Basil declares[y] that "it is good and profitable to communicate daily of the Body and Blood of Christ; since He Himself says, 'He that feeds on My Flesh, and makes My Blood his drink, hath eternal Life.'" Optatus calls the Eucharist[z] "the pledge of eternal salvation, and the hope of our resurrection," with a view to John vi. 54. St. Hilary having cited those words from John vi., "My Flesh is meat indeed," &c., from thence concludes[a] that the Eucharist is "the true Flesh and Blood of Christ by the declaration of Christ." Cyril of Jerusalem observes[b], that "Christ once discoursing with the Jews said, 'Except ye eat the Flesh,' &c., they not understanding the

Side notes: Macarius. / Gregory Nyssen. / St. Basil. / Optatus. / St. Hilary. / Cyril of Jerusalem.

[q] a. p. 26. Ap.
[r] g. p. 26. Ap.
[s] k. p. 27. Ap.
[t] a. p. 25. Ap.
[u] a. p. 25. Ap.

[x] a. p. 23. Ap.
[y] c. p. 23. Ap.
[z] a. p. 22. Ap.
[a] a. p. 20. Ap.
[b] d. p. 19. Ap.

things that were spoken in a spiritual manner, but supposing that He exhorted them to eat flesh [like cannibals]
were scandalized, and went back from Him;—but the heavenly Bread, and the Cup of salvation in the New Testament,
sanctify both body and soul." Julius Firmicus[c] calls the Sacrament, "the nutriment and ensign of immortality." He
cites Prov. ix. 1—5. and the history of Melchisedec, which
the ancients did generally believe to be prefigurations of the
Eucharist; and adds, " Our Lord, that He might more plainly
declare what that Bread is by which the mischief of death
is overcome, says in the Gospel, ' I am the Bread of Life.'"
St. Cyprian is very full in this point; for he interprets[d]
' daily bread,' in the Lord's Prayer, of the Eucharist; and
adds, " We desire this Bread to be given us daily, lest we
that are in Christ and daily receive the Eucharist as the
food of salvation, while we are repelled and forbid the heavenly Bread by reason of some grievous sin, are thus also,
by not communicating, separated from the Body of Christ;
since He Himself hath advertised us, ' I am the Bread of
Life,'&c., since then He has said, ' He who eateth of this Bread
shall live for ever;' as it is manifest, that they are alive who
take hold of this Body by right of Communion, so on the
other side we ought to pray and fear, lest any one being repelled be separated from the Body of Christ, and remain far
from salvation; since He threatens, and says, ' Except ye eat
the Flesh of the Son of Man,' &c. Therefore we desire our
Bread, that is, Christ, to be given us daily, that we who dwell
and live in Christ may not depart from His sanctification (f. consecrated Eucharist) and Body." Dr. Clagett[e] is willing to believe, that *Corpus Ejus attingere*, which I have rendered, ' take
hold of His Body,' is a phrase that "may be understood of all
the means of grace." Now let this be granted, yet I cannot
conceive, what inference the Doctor would have drawn from
thence for the service of his cause. For if it do import all the
means of grace, it is evidently for this reason, that they who
do " take hold of Christ's Body" in the Eucharist " by right
of Communion," (and not by stealth, as this Father observes

[c] p. 18. Ap.
[d] g. p. 11. Ap.

[e] [Preface to Paraphrase on John vi.,
p. xi.]

some lapsing Christians had done,) could not be deprived of any other means of grace; for he, who has a right to receive the Communion, has a right to all other essential privileges of a Christian. It is certain, as to the main cause now in dispute, St. Cyprian wants no comment; nor is it possible for the most perverse interpreter to stifle so plain an evidence.

St. Irenæus. St. Irenæus's Discourses[f] turn entirely on this supposition, that those promises made by our Saviour, that "He who eateth this Bread shall live for ever," are to be applied to the due receiving of the holy Eucharist. For he asserts, that it is by the Eucharistical symbols that we have the principle of a blessed immortality conveyed into our bodies, for which there is not the least appearance of proof from any other text of Scripture, but John vi. He never indeed does expressly cite any of the words of this context, either in the places to which I have referred my reader, or in any other part of his works, to the best of my observation; but his repeated assertion that bodies nourished by the Eucharist cannot be liable to a final mortality, is as clear a proof that he so understood this context, as if he had cited and transcribed it in words at length.

St. Igna-
tius. But St. Ignatius, after all, is instead of a thousand witnesses. He, who was the disciple of St. John the Evangelist 'who wrote these things,' and who had lain in the bosom of that Apostle as the Apostle had in the bosom of Christ, who was by him constituted Bishop of Antioch, and received the sense and meaning of St. John's Gospel from the holy penman himself, does expressly apply such virtues and privileges to the Eucharist, as cannot belong to it upon any other consideration but this, that John vi. is to be understood of this holy Sacrament. This he does principally in those excellent words, where he exhorts the Ephesians[g] "to make haste together to one place, in one common faith in one Jesus Christ, breaking one loaf, which is the medicine of immortality; our antidote against death [and] for eternal Life, through Jesus Christ." And in another place, speaking of those heretics who abstained from the Eucharist, he pronounces sentence upon them in those words[h], "It were better

f f. g. p. 5, 6. Ap.   g h. p. 2. Ap.   h h. p. 2. Ap.

for them to[i] receive it [the Eucharist], that through it they
might one day rise again." Now that the Eucharist is a means
of a happy resurrection, cannot be allowed to the doctrine of
Scripture, except John vi. be meant of the Eucharist; and
therefore this holy Martyr, when he does once and again assert
that this is a privilege conferred on us by the Eucharist, must
of consequence be in this sentiment, that our Saviour there
spake of His Sacramental Body and Blood. This most primitive Father does not cite the Evangelists or other holy
penmen by name, as was usual in after-ages; and very
seldom (if at all) does expressly produce their words; but he
does directly and in plain terms apply the greatest privilege
or benefit of eating Christ's Flesh to the receiving the Eucharist; and therefore leaves no reasonable occasion for us
to doubt but that he understood John vi. of that Sacrament.
I conceive one principal motive that modern Divines have to
deny that John vi. is to be taken of the Eucharist, is this,
viz., that the effects and consequences there attributed to
the eating and drinking Christ's Flesh and Blood (especially
that of eternal Life) are too great and valuable to be applied
to the Communion. But it is evident St. Ignatius was of
another judgment; he believed immortality itself to be the
effect of duly receiving the Sacrament. It is certain, he
learned his principles from the Apostle St. John; and if St.
John had not believed this doctrine, he would never have
taught it his scholar. And if St. John himself believed it,
from whence should he receive this Divine truth but from
that discourse of our Saviour, which the Apostle himself has
recorded in the sixth chapter of his Gospel? There is another
passage of St. Ignatius, which I cannot but take as meant of
the Eucharist; but I will submit it to the judgment of the
reader. In his Epistle to the Romans, which he sent to them
before his own arrival, when he was going to suffer martyrdom
in the imperial city, where they dwelt, he thus expresses
himself[k]; " I delight not in corruptible food, nor in the plea-
sures of this life; I desire the Bread of God, which is the
Flesh of Christ Jesus; the drink I long for is His Blood,
which is incorruptible love," or 'an incorruptible love-feast.'
I own he was just before speaking of " going to the Father;"

'Αγαπᾶν.   [k] f. p. 2. Ap.

CHAP. and in the following words he declares, that he "desires not
II.   human life." And if this be thought a decisive argument
against understanding those words of the Eucharist, they
must be taken of eating the Flesh of Christ in another world;
and perhaps some parallel expressions may be found in some
writers of the fourth century, yet scarce in the more primitive
Fathers. But I cannot think it any incoherence, when he
was speaking of going to the Father and not desiring to live
here, to express his holy hunger and thirst after that, which
has always been thought the most proper *viaticum*, the holy
Eucharist. It is probable he had not been permitted, while
under the custody of his inhuman keepers in his voyage, to
celebrate the Eucharist; or that he durst not do it, for fear
of having the mysteries profaned by them; but he hoped,
when he came to Rome, to have an opportunity of refreshing
himself with that Divine repast; and, I suppose, he expresses
these hopes and desires in the words now cited. And I am
pretty sure, that there is no incongruity in this supposition;
whereas eating of Christ's Flesh in another world is a way of
expression somewhat unaccountable. 'To receive the Flesh
of Christ in the Eucharist' is the familiar language of the
primitive Church, and of the holy Martyr; 'to receive the very
Christ by faith' is a way of speaking common among modern
Divines; but this cannot be applied to eating Him in another
world, for there faith vanishes in enjoyment. 'To eat Christ's
natural Body by love and devotion toward Him' is a phrase
not so agreeable to primitive simplicity, as 'to eat and drink
His Eucharistical Flesh and Blood:' and therefore I think it
most probable that he is so to be interpreted in this place;
and by calling the Eucharist "the Bread of God," he clearly
refers to John vi. 33. The Right Reverend Bishops Pearson[1]
and Wake[m] by ἀγαπᾶν understand "receiving the Communion" in the citation just before produced[n]; and though I
am persuaded that the Eucharist and the common love-feast
were not usually, in well-regulated Churches, celebrated at
the same time and place; yet it is not improbable that the
Eucharist might in a wide sense pass under that name, and

[1] ["'Αγαπᾶν videtur significare ἀγάπην ποιεῖν, Agapen celebrare, et Eucharistiam percipere."—Vid. Pearsoni Annotatt. in D. Ignatium, p. 18. Ed. Oxon.

1709.]
[m] [See Transl. of S. Ign. Ep. ad
Smyrn. cap. 7.]
[n] h. [p. 2. Ap.]

that it does so in this place. So $E\dot{v}\chi\alpha\rho\iota\sigma\tau\acute{\iota}\alpha$ is used in the Apostolical age both for thanksgiving at large, and for the Eucharist strictly so called; $\Delta\iota\acute{\alpha}\kappa o\nu o\varsigma$ for any Minister, and yet for the Deacon; $M\alpha\theta\eta\tau\grave{\eta}\varsigma$ for any disciple of Christ, and yet for an Apostle. But if instead of translating the words 'an incorruptible love-feast,' we turn them 'incorruptible love,' the citation from St. Ignatius may be applied to the Sacramental Blood as well as to the natural, though not in so exalted a sense. They are both, in their several degrees, motives to us to love God, and assurances of His love toward us; so that I can see no reason to understand Ignatius of any other Blood but the Eucharistical.

Dr. Whitby, in his Examen Var. Lection. on John vi. 56, reflects on Dr. Mill, for supposing that some words found in the Cambridge MS. might be genuine text, though not extant in our present copies; and would prove the contrary by observing, that $\Sigma\hat{\omega}\mu\alpha$ is used in those words of the MS. instead of $\Sigma\acute{\alpha}\rho\xi$; for, says Dr. W., "Christ never in this discourse uses the word Body; nor does He in this discourse speak of His Sacramental Body[o]." By saying this, he supposes that Christ makes a distinction between His Flesh and His Body; or at least, that the Evangelist does so. It is evident this criticism will not bear the test, except the Doctor will lay his own judgment in the scale against that of St. Ignatius; for this holy Martyr[p] supposes it to be heretical to deny the Eucharist to be the Flesh of Christ. Justin Martyr testifies, that the Christians of his age[q] "were taught that the Eucharistized Bread was the Flesh of Christ;" and Clemens Alexandrinus thus expresses the words of institution[r], "Eat My Flesh," &c. These are three of the earliest writers next after the Apostles, that mention the Eucharist; and they unanimously call it 'the Flesh of Christ.' As this is a

Eucharist the Flesh of Christ.

[o] ["Ad finem v. 56. Stephanus et Cant. addunt $\kappa\alpha\theta\grave{\omega}\varsigma$ $\grave{\epsilon}\nu$ '$E\mu o\grave{\iota}$ $\acute{o}$ $\Pi\alpha\tau\grave{\eta}\rho$, $\kappa\grave{\alpha}\gamma\grave{\omega}$ $\grave{\epsilon}\nu$ $\tau\hat{\wp}$ $\Pi\alpha\tau\rho\acute{\iota}$· '$A\mu\grave{\eta}\nu$, '$A\mu\grave{\eta}\nu$, $\lambda\acute{\epsilon}\gamma\omega$ $\grave{v}\mu\hat{\iota}\nu$, $\grave{\epsilon}\grave{\alpha}\nu$ $\mu\grave{\eta}$ $\lambda\acute{\alpha}\beta\epsilon\tau\epsilon$ $\tau\grave{o}$ $\sigma\hat{\omega}\mu\alpha$ $\tau o\hat{v}$ '$Y\iota o\hat{v}$ $\tau o\hat{v}$ $\grave{\alpha}\nu\theta\rho\acute{\omega}\pi o v$, $\grave{\omega}\varsigma$ $\tau\grave{o}\nu$ $\acute{\alpha}\rho\tau o\nu$ $\tau\hat{\eta}\varsigma$ $\zeta\omega\hat{\eta}\varsigma$, $o\grave{v}\kappa$ $\acute{\epsilon}\chi\epsilon\tau\epsilon$ $\zeta\omega\grave{\eta}\nu$ $\grave{\epsilon}\nu$ $A\grave{v}\tau\hat{\wp}$. *Hæc ipsius Johannis verba esse asserit Millius* in Appendice, ex fide sc. Cant. (de quo tamen codice mirum in modum interpolato vide judicium Millii, Proleg. p. 132. col. 2.) Agnoscit illa nullus Pater, nulla versio, nullus commentator; at-

que iis omissis citat hoc caput a v. 53. ad v. 58. Origenes, $\pi\epsilon\rho\grave{\iota}$ $\epsilon\grave{v}\chi\hat{\eta}\varsigma$, p. 88, 89. Nec Christus per totum hoc caput vocabulum $\sigma\hat{\omega}\mu\alpha$ usurpat, nec loquitur de Corpore Suo Sacramentaliter capiendo, ut alibi fusius ostensum est. Nihilominus *restituta* vult Millius, Proleg. p. 74."—p. 49.]

[p] h. p. 2. Ap.

[q] a. p. 2, 3. Ap. l. 20.

[r] a. p. 7. Ap.

CHAP. II.

clear confutation of Dr. W.'s note, if these Fathers may be the judges; so it is a very probable argument, that they understood John vi. of the Eucharist; since they use that word in speaking of the Sacrament, which is there used by St. John. And since we are sure, that St. Ignatius by 'the Flesh of Christ' means the Eucharist in his Epistle to the Smyrnæans; it is most likely, that by the same words he means the same thing in the Epistle to the Romans.

The judgment of the primitive Church on my side.

If any one do still think that some one particular Father, or even two or three of them, did understand John vi. otherwise than I do; yet all must acknowledge, that I have the generality of the ancients, and, above all, St. Ignatius, with me in this particular. Nay, I have a very great human authority, beside that of Ignatius, for taking John vi. as I do, viz., the judgment of the third General Council. These two, especially in conjunction, are as weighty a proof as can be produced from antiquity for taking any text of Scripture in any particular sense. And over and above all this I insist, that there were several doctrines which prevailed in the first ages of Christianity, that could not be grounded upon any other authority of Scripture than this of John vi. as understood of the Eucharist. The doctrines I mean are such as these, viz.

That by abstaining from the holy Eucharist, Christians do incur the penalty of eternal damnation. This is a doctrine which can hardly be preached without censure in a congregation, where there are any hearers well versed in our modern systems. It is true, that the duty of communicating has been much inculcated of late years; but I am not sensible that the neglect of it is usually taxed as a sin, whereby eternal happiness is forfeited;

That the Holy Spirit is particularly present in the Eucharist;

That the Eucharistical symbols convey to all worthy receivers a principle of happy immortality.

If any of these doctrines can be proved from other places of Scripture, yet not with so great force, as from the fifth of St. John. And this is very evident from this consideration, viz., that none of these doctrines are now commonly believed by Christians in the purest Church now in the world; and of

this no other account can be given, but that it passes for a SECT.
certain principle, that John vi. is meant of doctrine or I know ⎯⎯V.⎯⎯
not what mere notional manducation.   One of the doctrines
above specified has already been shewed to have been the
sentiment of all antiquity.   The others will appear to have
been so, in the second Part. [See Part II. chap. ii. sect. 1.]

Having said what I judge sufficient to prove, that John vi. John vi.
was by the primitive Church primarily understood of the is to be
understood
Eucharist; I proceed to shew the same, of the
Eucharist,
II.[s] By a particular consideration of the context itself; proved
and here I shall from a con-
sideration
1. Prove, that it cannot rationally be understood to have of the context itself.
been primarily meant in either of those senses, in which it is
now commonly taken.

2. And that it is most properly to be understood of eating
and drinking Christ's Sacramental Body and Blood.

1. In order to prove that John vi. cannot rationally be
understood in either of the two senses now prevailing; I am
first to inform my reader what these two senses are:

(1.) The first is, that our Saviour, by eating and drinking
His Flesh and Blood, primarily means spiritual actions in
general, or a belief of the doctrine of the Gospel and particularly of His Death, and the benefits of it.

(2.) The second is, that our Saviour here speaks of eating
and drinking His natural Flesh and Blood by faith.

(1.) Our Saviour cannot rationally be understood, by John vi.
eating and drinking His Flesh and Blood, in St. John, pri- cannot
rationally
marily to mean spiritual actions in general; or a belief of the be understood of
doctrine of the Gospel, and particularly of His Death, and the what Dr.
benefits of it. Clagett
calls 'spiri-
It is to be observed, that by 'spiritual actions' Dr. Clagett tual actions,' and
understands moral virtues as taught by our Saviour, the Dr. Whitby
'faith.'
practising of the precepts of a heavenly life, whatever tends
to the improvement of the mind, the following Christ's example, believing in His Death; so that I take 'spiritual
actions' in the sense of those who are adversaries of that
truth, which I am now advancing.   For I deny not the receiving of the Sacrament with due preparation and application of mind, to be a spiritual action, (though conversant
about material things and accompanied with oral manduca-

[s] [See p. 458.]

CHAP.
II.

tion,) but I now speak according to the sentiments of Dr. Clagett, expressed in his Discourse on John vi. 51. And it is to be noted, that Dr. Whitby falls in with him thus far, that he asserts the eating and drinking Christ's Flesh and Blood to be "doing it spiritually by faith in His Blood;" which he elsewhere explains by "receiving or believing Christ's doctrine," exclusive of oral manducation. All the difference seems to be this, that Dr. Clagett, by this phrase, understands all spiritual actions; Dr. Whitby, one spiritual action or habit, viz., believing in Christ, particularly in His Death: and therefore I conceive that these opinions are so far one, that the same arguments will confute both, especially if it be considered, that though Dr. Clagett does generally speak of spiritual actions, yet in his paraphrase of ver. 51 he supposes our Saviour's meaning to be this, "When I tell you that I am the Living Bread, &c., as you are to understand this with respect to all the doctrine which I deliver; so especially with respect to that part of it, that I am come into the world to lay down My life for the salvation of mankind." So that by 'spiritual actions,' Dr. Clagett must have meant actions proceeding from, and consequent upon, a true faith in Christ and His doctrine; and Dr. Whitby cannot mean a barren dead faith, for he makes eternal Life the reward of it; so that, as to this particular, there is little or no difference in their opinion, though in paraphrasing ver. 63, they depart widely from each other. Now against this opinion I thus argue,

First argument against Dr. C. and Dr. W.'s sense of John vi.

First, if our Saviour do make a plain distinction, a very observable difference between believing Him or His doctrine, and the meat which He promises to give, and which He declares afterward to be His Flesh and Blood; then He cannot by His Flesh and Blood mean believing His doctrine, and the spiritual actions proceeding from that faith; but He makes a clear distinction betwixt the believing Him or His doctrine, and the meat which He promises to give them; therefore the one cannot be the other. Now He clearly

ver. 27.

makes this distinction in His entrance on this discourse, in those words, "Labour not for the meat that perisheth, but for the meat that endureth to everlasting Life, which the Son of Man shall give you." Here He speaks of a labour or

is the condition, the meat is the wages or reward; which are SECT.
two things as clearly distinct from each other, as any two V.
things in nature. So again, "He that cometh to Me" or believeth in Me, (which is the labour or condition) "shall never
hunger or thirst," (which is the reward or wages;) for 'not to
hunger and thirst' doth not here signify 'to want an appetite
or stomach,' but 'to want food for the supply of that appetite'; there must always be a holy hunger and thirst in Christ's
disciples; and here, as elsewhere, He promises to fill or satisfy
it. So again, "He that believeth on Me," or performs the ver. 47.
labour of faith, "hath" for his wages "eternal Life" or maintenance by virtue of this food; "For I" Myself "am" mys- ver. 48.
teriously that food, "the Bread of" eternal "Life," to be
eaten in a Sacramental manner. It is very evident then,
that here are two things very different from each other; and
what the labour is, Jesus Christ has expressly told us, namely,
faith in Him; for "This," says He, "is the work of God,
that ye believe in Him Whom God hath sent;" and what
the meat is, He fully declares in the sequel of this chapter.
Sometimes He says it is He Himself; at other times, His
Flesh and Blood. As sure therefore as the labour is a distinct thing from the meat or wages; so sure is it, that believing in Him or His doctrine is one thing, and the "meat"
He promises to them who believe is another. And I humbly
offer it to Dr. W.'s consideration, whether his overlooking
this distinction were not the fundamental mistake of his
paraphrase and annotations on this context; for nothing
can be more apparent than that he confounds the end and
the means, the "work" and the "meat." Thus in his second
note on ver. 53, 54, p. 489, he asserts, that "It is the same
thing in this chapter to eat of the Bread which came down
from heaven, and to believe in Christ breaking the Bread of
eternal Life to us by His doctrine;" and to prove this, he
adds, "When He had exhorted them to labour for the meat
that did not perish," He tells them, "that this was to believe ver. 29.
on Him Whom God had sent;" whereas the Doctor might
have remembered, that our Saviour speaks not one word of
the "meat" or wages, in the twenty-ninth verse, but only
tells the Jews what the work was; and that was the only
thing which the Jews had mentioned in their question; they

inquire not of the "meat," but "what they should do, that
they might work the work of God." So in his note on ver.
51, by the Bread which Christ promises to give, and which
He calls His Flesh, he understands "faith in Christ as
suffering and shedding His Blood;" but more apparently
in his paraphrase of ver. 55, "My Flesh is meat indeed,
and My Blood is drink indeed;" that is, says the Doctor,
"Faith in Me giving up My Body to the death, and shedding My Blood for the remission of sins, is the true meat
and drink which nourisheth to eternal Life." In which
places he evidently supposes the "work" and the "meat" to be
all one; nay, he makes no manner of difference between the
hand whereby we receive the meat, which is faith, and the
meat thereby received, which is the Flesh and Blood. But
it is very clear to any one that reads this context with attention, that faith, which if true and lively is attended with
pious and devout affections of all sorts, and which Dr. Clagett calls 'spiritual actions,' is the labour or work by which
the meat or wages is obtained; and that therefore the latter
must be something clearly distinguished from the former.
And it is further evident, that doctrine or precepts cannot
be the meat or wages; for that is the object or matter, on
which we labour or on which our faith is employed. For
faith[t] is an assent to the doctrine revealed by Christ; if
therefore this faith be the work or labour, then the meat
must be somewhat distinct both from that assent and
that doctrine, to which the assent is given. It is certain,
that this work or labour is not only a condition necessary
in order to obtain the meat, but it is a preparation for the
profitable receiving of it; it quickens the appetite, and
strengthens the digestion, and converts the meat into solid
food; but still it is an action or habit, attended with variety
of other good spiritual actions or dispositions: whereas the
meat itself is neither action nor habit, but some refreshment
or alimony, intended as a present reward for our labour and
for our support in the performance of it. Therefore I conclude, that the Bread, Meat, or Flesh and Blood promised in

---

[t] [" Fides est habitus mentis, quo
assentimus dictis Scripturæ, propter
authoritatem Dei revelantis." See Du-
randus, *apud* Pearson, on the Creed,
Notes, p. 5.]

this chapter, cannot primarily denote either faith or any spiritual action attending our faith, nor the doctrine received by
faith; for that Christ made a clear distinction between them.

2. If to eat Christ's Flesh and to drink His Blood signify
no more than to believe Him or His doctrine, and to lead a
moral holy life; and if this may be relied on; then it ought
to appear, that these phrases have been used by some other
great master of religion or philosophy in this sense; or that
Christ Jesus did Himself, at some other time or place, so use
them; but no such instance has been yet produced, and therefore this sense is perfectly precarious. Dr. Whitby on this
occasion produces several passages from Scripture and the
Rabbies, where meat and drink, bread and wine, seem to signify instruction or precepts of wisdom, or religion; but this
does not come home to his purpose, unless some Prophet or
great Doctor had been produced by him, inviting his disciples
to eat of his flesh and drink of his blood, and explaining his
words as meant of nothing but hearing or reading his lectures
and endeavouring to practise them. The phrases are singular,
and never used by any other but Christ, in a religious sense;
and therefore the signification of them must be singular too.
The most that any who are of this opinion undertake to prove
is, that these words are capable of this sense; it is impossible they should prove that this and no other is the first
and proper meaning of them, because the phrases were
never used by any but our blessed Saviour; and there are
no parallel expressions of any other great man, by which we
can make a judgment of the sense of them. But suppose
that they may be so understood; it does not follow that they
were actually so meant by our blessed Master; and the affair
He treats of is of the greatest moment, in which we ought not
to take up with a 'may be;' for eternal Life is that which
depends upon it. And certainly it is most enormously improbable to suppose, that so very extraordinary a phrase as
eating the flesh and drinking the blood of a Doctor or master
of religion should signify no more than so common a thing
as receiving his instruction; and therefore if it do so signify,
it ought to be soundly proved: whereas I must profess, I
cannot feel the force of any of the arguments, which I have
yet met withal on this head.

3. If to eat Christ's Flesh and to drink His Blood were phrases primarily and directly intended by our Saviour to denote believing His doctrine or practising it; then Flesh and Blood must signify doctrine in this place; but Flesh and Blood do not here signify doctrine; for it is said of the Flesh and Blood here spoken of by Christ, that they were "to be given or offered for the Life of the world." Now not His doctrine but His personal Flesh and Blood were actually given or offered for the sins of the world, Sacramentally in the institution of the Eucharist, substantially on the Cross: therefore these words cannot directly and primarily be understood of doctrine, but either of His Sacramental or natural Flesh and Blood. I do not dispute but that Origen and some others did give this sense to the phrases of eating Christ's Flesh and drinking His Blood; and I have shewed, that eating Christ's Sacramental Flesh and drinking His Sacramental Blood does implicitly and by consequence import a reception of His doctrine; but the question now is not, whether this may remotely and by implication be meant by our Saviour; much less, whether an allegorist may not put this sense upon them; but the question is, what our Saviour did primarily and directly mean by these phrases; and I think it very evident by what is said, that He could not mean 'spiritual actions' in Dr. Clagett's sense, or 'believing in Christ and particularly in His Death,' which is Dr. W.'s gloss.

[But I find some Divines of name and worth in an opinion, that those words of Christ, "He that believeth on Me hath everlasting Life," contain the same sense with those in the 54th verse, viz., "He that eateth My Flesh and drinketh My Blood hath everlasting Life;" and that therefore 'to believe in Christ,' and 'to eat of His Flesh and to drink His Blood,' are phrases of the same signification.

But this is a mere supposition; it will, I humbly conceive, be impossible to advance it into so much as a fair probability.

I have already proved, that there is as much difference between 'believing' and 'eating Christ's Flesh,' as between 'labour' and the 'reward' of that labour; and that this distinction is made by Christ Himself; and that therefore 'faith,' which is the labour, cannot be the same with 'eating Christ's Flesh,' which is the reward. And farther, I have just above

shewed, that we have no authority to prove that the eating
the flesh of any master of religion does ever signify to receive or believe his doctrine.]

(2.) Our Saviour cannot rationally be understood of eating
and drinking His natural Flesh and Blood by faith.   For,

1. Eating and drinking, whether naturally or morally, cannot be performed, except the things eaten and drunk be present first before us, and then within us.   What we eat and
drink, in a natural sense, must first be placed within our reach,
and then must be taken in by our mouths.   What we eat
or what we drink, in a moral sense, must first be present to
our eyes by reading, or to our ears by hearing, and then to
our understandings by which we apprehend it, and to our
memories by which we retain it; but the natural Body and
Blood of Christ cannot be present to us here on earth, so
as to be first before us and then within us, and therefore is
not capable of manducation : and this I hope need not be
proved to Protestants of the Church of England.   It may
indeed be pretended that the natural Body and Blood may
be present by virtue of our faith; but this is all mere shift;
for faith can make nothing present, which is in fact absent,
but only teaches us to apprehend what is invisibly present
and which is imperceptible by our external senses.   "Christ
dwells in our heart by faith;" not that faith can bring our
Saviour's Body down from heaven, but because His Divine
Nature is omnipresent, and our faith when it duly operates
makes Him graciously present to us; or rather, He dwells
in us by His proxy, the Holy Spirit, Which is ordinarily received by the Sacraments only.

2. We cannot eat Christ's natural Flesh and drink His
natural Blood by faith, because drinking His natural Blood
necessarily supposes this Blood of His separated from His
Flesh; but His natural Blood separated from His Flesh is
not now *in rerum natura;* for this supposes Christ again crucified and dead, which is absurd; and His Blood can in no
sense be said to be drunk, but only as actually separated
from His Body.

It may be said that we eat and drink Christ's natural
Flesh and Blood spiritually, by a sincere belief in His
Death; but then the meaning of it can be only this, that

SECT.
V.

John vi.
cannot
rationally
be under-
stood of
eating
Christ's
natural
Body by
faith.
First
argument.

Second
argument.

CHAP.
II.

we eat and drink Christ's Body and Blood by believing in His Death and the merits of it: and this is no more but what was contained in the proposition before confuted, viz., that our Saviour, by His Flesh and Blood, meant nothing but spiritual actions, and particularly a belief in Him, and the merits of His Death. Now to believe in Christ or His Death is only to consent to the doctrines revealed in Scripture concerning His Person and sufferings for us; and I presume it has been already proved that Flesh and Blood do not signify doctrine in that text.

Further disproof of both these opinions.

But further I apprehend that there are several arguments which are equally valid against both these two manners of eating Christ's Flesh and Blood, which I have now been confuting, viz.,

First argument.

1. The assertors of these two opinions do both take that for granted, which is I think improbable to the last degree, viz., that our Saviour here speaks metaphorically, and even catachrestically. The first opinion supposes, that both the eating and drinking is merely figurative and notional; and that the Flesh and Blood eaten and drunk denote no more than bare doctrine and precepts. The other opinion supposes indeed the things eaten and drunk to be real material things, but to be swallowed, masticated, and digested by mere mental actions; which is therefore, of the two, I think, more incongruous and unnatural; but both agree in putting a very harsh and most remote sense upon our Saviour's words; and if it were only for this reason, I should never be able to reconcile myself to either of them: for no man can believe either of these senses to be the true one, but that he must suppose that our blessed Saviour affected such metaphors and catachreses to such a degree as designedly to amuse and give offence to his hearers, by inculcating and insisting upon these excessively figurative expressions with a most extraordinary degree of zeal and vehemence. It must be owned that if our Saviour, by men's eating His Flesh and drinking His Blood, meant nothing but so obvious a thing as receiving Him and His doctrine by faith and obedience, He clothed His thoughts in most unnatural language, (for what is more unnatural to civilized men than to eat a man's flesh and drink his blood?) and yet He laid so great stress on

these words, that He never appears, in the whole course of SECT.
His life, to have spoken with more warmth and solemnity. ——V.——
Some suppose that the repeated *Amen* is a positive oath; ver. 53.
but however that be, it is certainly a word importing a very
high degree of asseveration; and to suppose that our Saviour
used it only to justify a very catachrestical expression is, to
suppose that a wise and humble Teacher was so fond of a
figure, as for the sake of it to give occasion to His hearers to
desert Him. Dr. Clagett found himself pinched with this difficulty; and he attempts to answer it by saying [u], " Sometimes
it becomes a man of wisdom and authority, when he finds his
words perverted, to repeat them again, and thereby speak his
own assurance." But the Doctor does not so much as offer in
this place, at any reason, why our Saviour chose this way of expressing Himself, which is so very singular and extraordinary;
and in this consists the main force of the objection; and as to
the rest, I do not believe that any man raises his reputation or
authority, or is thought the wiser or greater by men of competent sense, merely for repeating his words again, and thereby speaking his own assurance; especially when the dispute
is concerning nothing else but only the aptness of a word or
phrase. For, according to the sentiments of these learned
men, our Saviour's discourse here was not intended to
instruct His hearers in any duty which He had not taught
them before or to inform them in any Divine truth, but only
to tell them in a very dark and obscure way, what He had
formerly taught them very plainly, viz., that " He who be- John iii. 36.
lieveth on the Son hath everlasting Life." And it is not
consistent with the character, which I think all good Christians have of their great Master, to suppose, that He would
so earnestly contend for the justness of a metaphorical and
exceedingly remote way of expression; for so it must be
owned to be, if it import no more than receiving His doctrine.
At another place Dr. Clagett would have it thought that
" our Lord did not think fit to foretell the ignominious death
He was to suffer, or the reasons and ends of His Passion [v].
And yet in his paraphrase of ver. 51. he supposes our Saviour
says, " You are to understand Me to be the Living Bread,
with respect to all the doctrine I deliver, but especially with

[u] [Preface, p. v.]　　　　　　　　　　[v] pp. 39, 40.

CHAP.
II.

respect to that part of it, that I am to lay down My life for the salvation of mankind[x]." And therefore here he takes that for granted, which afterwards he denies. And indeed it is very evident, that our Saviour never made His Death or the end of it a secret. The Capernaites themselves could not be so stupid as to believe that He was to remain alive, when His Flesh was eaten and His Blood drunk in that literal manner that they understood Him. Soon after this, He informed them concerning the manner and instruments of His Death; but as to His Death itself and the design of it, He in this context clearly enough foretells it to the multitude. And nothing could have driven a person of so clear a head and so penetrating a judgment as Dr. Clagett upon such inconsistencies as these, but a misplaced zeal for a popular error: for so, I hope, I may by this time have leave to call it.

Second
argument.

2. If either of the senses, against which I am now arguing, be the true one, then all good communicants are to receive more than one Body or Flesh, more than one Blood, in the holy Sacrament. Dr. Clagett and Dr. Whitby by Flesh and Blood here understand doctrine; the Calvinists, the natural Flesh and Blood of Christ; and I conceive all that are in the sentiments of these Doctors, or of the Calvinists, will allow, that pious communicants may and do receive the Flesh and Blood meant in John vi. as well as the Body and Blood mentioned in the words of institution. All, at least, that I have read, do confess so much; and the necessary consequence of this is, that all believers do in the Sacrament receive two Bodies and Bloods of Christ, the typical or symbolical and the spiritual Flesh and Blood (which is, in the sense of the two Doctors, His doctrine), or the natural, according to the hypothesis of the Calvinists. Nay, it from hence follows, that communicants are in duty bound to receive both; because it is the duty of all to receive with faith. And therefore, according to these suppositions, our Saviour should have said, " Take My Bodies, My Bloods:" for no one can suppose that our Saviour designed to bid His disciples receive but one, when it was their duty to receive both.

Now I conceive, that that bids fairest for the most proper

[x] p. 32.

sense and meaning of this context, which is not attended with any of those inconveniences or inconsistences to which these opinions are liable; nor to those greater absurdities, with which the doctrines of Transubstantiation or Consubstantiation are attended. These latter are so gross and incredible, that I cannot conceive I have any occasion to argue against them. Nor can the primitive doctrine, which I am now defending, be justly charged with any such consequences as have made the two doctrines last mentioned so universally abhorred amongst us. I shall therefore only observe, that if we believe our Saviour to speak of His Eucharistical Flesh and Blood in John vi. we shall avoid all those difficulties and objections, with which the hypothesis of Dr. Clagett and Dr. Whitby, and that of the Calvinists are pressed.

1. The doctrine of the primitive Church, viz., that John vi. is to be understood of the Eucharist, is not liable to those objections which are brought against the opinion of Dr. Whitby and Dr. Clagett, and which now seem to prevail among us. For, 1. taking St. John's context to be meant primarily of the Eucharist, there is a clear distinction between the labour and the meat; the labour is faith, the meat is the Sacramental Flesh of Christ; and this is, as it were, an earnest of eternal Life to come. It is the wages paid us in hand; our present refreshment, whereby we have a supply of whatever is necessary for us during our present pilgrimage. It is to be given only to believers, as Justin Martyr[y] observes; and he who comes to Christ or believes in Him can never suffer for want of spiritual food, can never have a starving hunger or thirst. 2. The primitive Fathers did not take the sixth of John to be primarily understood in a precarious arbitrary sense; but in that very sense, which they believed our Saviour to have stamped upon the phrases of eating His Flesh and drinking His Blood, in the words of institution. And since they did not find, that any other person had ever used these expressions in a religious sense but only Christ Jesus; therefore they judged it safest, to take them according to the same meaning that Christ elsewhere had given them.

Some of the Fathers did indeed use the same liberty with

SECT. V.

None of these absurdities follow, if John vi. be understood of the Eucharist.

[y] a. p. 2, 3. Ap. l. 12.

CHAP.
II.

By Flesh
John vi.
and by
Body Matt.
xxvi. 26.
is meant
the same
thing.

both these contexts, which they do with other the plainest texts of Scripture; that is, they do suppose that they were capable of an anagogical, as well as a proper sense; but they never took the liberty to suppose, that Flesh and Blood in John vi. meant one thing, and Body and Blood in the institution meant quite another.

They thought it unreasonable to suppose, that our Saviour in John vi. by the word 'Flesh,' should mean any other thing than what He called His 'Body' in the words of institution. Flesh indeed sometimes signifies human nature; but when Flesh and Blood are spoken of, as separated from each other, as they are John vi. 51, 53, there Flesh can import no more than Body. Therefore as three of the most ancient writers of the Church, Ignatius, Justin, and Clement of Alexandria, do expressly call the Eucharistical Bread, " the Flesh of Christ;" so all the following writers do indifferently call it, Flesh or Body. And I believe I may safely challenge the greatest critic to shew any difference between them. And 3. by these means they avoided the inconvenience of asserting, as the moderns do, that Flesh and Blood signify in this context (primarily and directly) doctrine; for though it might be thought tolerable for Origen and the allegorists, when they did not desire to have the texts they were speaking of too well understood, to speak of doctrine and precepts as meant by those expressions; yet certainly this latitude is not to be allowed to those, who undertake to give us the most proper and direct signification of these texts.

2. The inconveniences of the Calvinistical doctrine do not at all affect the judgment of the ancient Church. For, 1st, the primitive Fathers did not believe that any Body and Blood were eaten or drunk in the Sacrament but only the Eucharistical Bread and Wine, consecrated into the Body and Blood of Christ, by the especial presence and power of the Spirit. And 2ndly, they believed no Blood of Christ as separated from His Body to be anywhere else but in the Sacrament, and that it was there not in substance but in power and effect.

3. The doctrine of the primitive Fathers, who understood John vi. of the Eucharist, was free from the inconveniences and inconsistencies with which both the hypotheses above

mentioned, are justly chargeable. For first, they were far
from thinking that the words there spoken by Christ were
merely figurative or catachrestical; they knew that our
Saviour there spoke of the Eucharist; and they did by no
means believe that Christ in that holy Sacrament feeds the
souls of men with mere dry metaphors or catachreses.
Though they did not understand Christ in a literal sense,
as the Capernaites did; yet neither on the other side did
they suppose that it was the intention of Christ to puzzle
His auditors, and even to stagger His own disciples with
strained enigmatical sayings; for they believed He spoke of
a real mystery, and therefore spoke in a manner very agreeable to the subject of which He was treating. They conceived
He was now opening His intention of establishing the most
Divine Sacrament of His Flesh and Blood; and to raise in
them just thoughts and apprehensions of that heavenly mystery, He speaks of it in the most elevated words, and represents the benefits of it in terms befitting so admirable an
institution. If He had begun by speaking to them of the
outward symbols, they might have been apt from thence to
conceive a very little and unworthy opinion of it; they could
scarce have believed it equal to the manna with which their
fathers were fed for forty years together in the wilderness;
and since, as has been shewed, He performed the Melchisedecian oblation of His Body and Blood in Bread and Wine,
He had not done justice to His subject, if He had not called
the former 'the Bread of God' and the 'Flesh,' the Sacramental Flesh, which He was "to give to God" as an earnest of
His natural Flesh, "for the Life of the world." And this is
the mystical sense of these words; for they were never intended by Christ either in a literal or merely figurative sense.
It was our Saviour's design to speak of a mystery as such;
and the mystical is therefore in this case the primary and
direct sense. And, secondly, it needs no proof, that the
ancients believed but one Body and Blood of Christ to be
received in the Eucharist, viz., the Sacramental Bread and
Wine, which was, as they believed, made the Body and Blood
by the enlivening power of the Spirit, according to the doctrine of Christ taught them in this very chapter.

They did indeed justly suppose, that it was by virtue of

the Word, that the elements became Christ's Body and Blood; and that none did beneficially partake of the Sacrament with their mouths, who did not receive the Word with their hearts; nay, they looked on the Eucharist to be an ordinance, which implied the reception of the whole revealed will of God, as it certainly is by virtue of its representing the crucified Body of Christ Jesus, which is indeed the substance of Christianity; but they did by no means think His Flesh in St. John to be one thing, and His Body in St. Matthew to be another.

Positive proof that John vi. is meant of the Eucharist.

2. I proceed to give some positive proofs, that John vi. is to be understood most properly of eating and drinking Christ's Sacramental Body and Blood.

Now by His Flesh and Blood we must either understand His natural substantial Flesh and Blood; and that this is not capable of manducation has been so often and so largely proved by many Protestant Divines, especially of the Church of England, that I think my reader will gladly spare me the pains of a recital of the arguments and authorities produced by them upon this head: or else, secondly, by the Flesh and Blood we must understand the natural Body received by faith and spiritually, which I have just now refuted: or, thirdly, the imaginary spiritual Body spoken of by one or two of our Divines, and which is by Robert Barclay said to be the spiritual Seed or Light within; which is a notion, that I have sufficiently confuted in the foregoing treatise: or, fourthly, we must take it for doctrine and precepts, which is a notion that I have just before considered and disproved: or else, fifthly, we must take it in the only remaining sense, for which I am now contending; I mean, for the Eucharistical Body and Blood, which appears to have been the general sense of antiquity, and for which cause I should prefer it to all other opinions whatever, if there were no violent reason to the contrary. And I am fully convinced, that it is not only the opinion or rather universal judgment and doctrine of the primitive Church, but that it is in itself most agreeable to the words and intentions of our Blessed Lord and Master in this place.

I have already shewed, that there is no ground for making any difference between the word 'Body' in the history of institution, and 'Flesh' in St. John's context; and that they are words of the very same import and signification.   And I cannot but be of opinion, that any man of middling judgment, who reads the Holy Scriptures without prejudice or prepossession, will, by comparing the context now in dispute with the history of institution recorded by the three other Evangelists and St. Paul, be naturally led into this opinion, without any laborious proof or argumentation.   This has been the case in relation to myself.   For it is now almost or altogether twenty years, that I have been fully persuaded in my own judgment, that John vi. was so to be understood; though I can truly declare, that I never to this hour have met with any book but the Scriptures themselves and the ancients above cited, that could in the least dispose me to be of this sentiment; all the modern books that I have ever read on this subject, being directly against me in this particular.   And I was fully fixed in this judgment, before I could have an opportunity of consulting many of the ancients on this head.   Origen, whom I first consulted on this occasion, seemed to me at first sight rather an adversary than a friend, until upon a more full scrutiny I found myself mistaken in my man; which was a good encouragement to me to proceed in examining others.   And I am now come to a perfect conviction, that I have both reason and authority on my side.   My authorities for this sense, which I now maintain, have already been presented to my reader, and my reasons against those other senses, which now prevail amongst us. And the positive proofs now follow.

This the most obvious sense.

1. It is incredible, that our Saviour should all at once make known, and administer so very solemn and mysterious an institution, considering that the Apostles, to whom He administered it, were slow in understanding and believing spiritual things.   I am very sure, that Priest, who in this degenerate age, should frequently administer this Sacrament to the people, but never take any care to let them into the knowledge of the mystery, any further than by rehearsing the words of institution as often as he celebrated, would be thought very notoriously defective in his duty.   And shall we permit our Saviour to lie under such an imputation, as would be thought criminous in one of His inferior Ministers?

First argument.

CHAP.
II.

Nay, I am bold to say, that upon this supposition our Saviour would appear more culpable than any of us in this case. For the Eucharist is now become an ancient ordinance, of many hundred years' standing; the history of it's institution is well known to all, if it be not absolutely their own fault; and no man can wholly be ignorant of the nature of it, who has lived in a Christian Church to the age of twenty or thirty, except his ignorance be affected. But the Sacrament was an institution perfectly new and unheard of before, when our Saviour first administered it, in the opinion of those who deny John vi. to relate to this matter. It therefore must be supposed, that our Saviour did *extempore* institute and oblige His Apostles to receive the Sacrament, without giving them any previous notice or information, whereby they might be prepared for it; unless it be acknowledged, that here in this context He did give them this notice and information; for we have not the least intimation of His doing it in any other place of the histories of the Evangelists. And therefore to acquit our Saviour from this imputation, it ought in reason to be acknowledged that He did it here; and that St. John, observing that the other Evangelists had omitted this discourse, thought it necessary to be inserted in his Gospel; whereas, the history of the institution being related by the other three, there was no occasion for him to repeat it.

Second
argument.

2. It is very evident, that no Flesh and Blood of Christ can be eaten and drunk, but the Eucharistical only; and that no other Body of Christ is capable of oral or bodily manducation, will be readily granted: and we may as properly be said to eat and drink the Trinity by believing in It, as to eat the Body of Christ by bare faith or any actions purely mental or intellectual; much less can we drink the Blood of Christ apart from the Body, anywhere but in the Eucharist. The natural extravasated Blood of Christ can be drunk in imagination only, for it is not *in rerum natura*; the spiritual Body of Dr. More and some others is a mere airy speculation. Christ's Body and Blood were never designed by Christ directly to denote mere doctrine and precepts; this is only an anagogical construction of some commentators both ancient and modern; but with this difference, the ancients used it as an improper and secondary exposition, and chiefly applied it

to the catechumens; the modern, as the prime and sole inten- SECT. V.
tion of our blessed Saviour in these words, and as a more
perfect way of eating Christ's Flesh and drinking His Blood
than that in the Eucharist; but that Flesh and Blood do in
this context primarily denote doctrine, can neither be proved
by authority, nor as I believe by any good and solid reason.
I conclude, that therefore no Body or Blood can be properly
received, eaten, or drunk by us, but the Sacramental only.

3. It is a fixed rule, with all good interpreters, to prefer Third
the literal sense before any other, when there is no violent argument.
reason to the contrary. It is allowed that in this case we
have a violent and irresistible reason against understanding
John vi. in the literal sense; for nothing can be more absurd
than to suppose, that Christ intended literally to feast His
disciples with the natural Flesh, to be eaten with the teeth
and swallowed by the throat. And I have already shewed
that His natural Flesh and Blood cannot be said to be eaten
and drunk by faith.

Now I submit it to my reader, whether it be not as just
and reasonable a rule in interpreting Scripture, that when
the literal sense cannot be allowed, we should in the next
place prefer that sense which is nearest to the literal. For
I conceive this rule is built upon the same reason and grounds
that the former is; and sure it will not bear a dispute, whether receiving the Sacrament or believing and obeying Christ
do come nearest to the literal sense of eating Christ's Flesh
and drinking His Blood. I suppose I have sufficiently proved
that to receive the Sacrament is verily and indeed to eat
Christ's Flesh and drink His Blood in power and effect,
though not in substance; whereas it yet remains to be proved
that to believe in Christ is ever denoted by eating Christ's
Flesh and drinking His Blood, except perhaps in three or
four places of the ancients, when they were speaking allegories.

4. That which seems to me to be decisive, and of itself suffi- Fourth
cient to determine the sense of John vi. to the Eucharist, is argument.
this, that the same phrases used by the same person, though
in several places, ought to be taken in the same sense, if
there be no cogent reason to the contrary. Now I suppose
it very evident from what has been said, that 'to eat Christ's

CHAP.
II.

Body' and 'to eat His Flesh' are the very same phrase, though not the same words; and it is evident that St. Ignatius and Justin Martyr and Clemens Alexandrinus thought them so; and therefore to suppose that two different things are to be understood by this phrase, is to talk precariously; it is to say, that our Saviour's discourses were not all of a piece, and that we cannot enter into His meaning at one place, by what He has expressed in the same phrase at another.   And this argument will be of greater force, if it be considered that this phrase is very singular and extraordinary, never used by any person in a religious sense but by our blessed Saviour, and by Him but twice in the whole course of His life and ministry, so far as appears to us.   What legislators would they be thought, who should take this course in forming human laws? Who would think them worthy of the names of lawyers or lawyer's clerks, who should take this liberty; I mean, in the same law or instrument, or even in two several laws or instruments, to use the same phrase in two different meanings? Especially if this phrase were peculiar to these legislators or lawyers, and used by none else, which is the present case?   And by consequence, what interpreters are they who will pawn that on our Saviour, when He was instructing us in the way to eternal happiness, which would be thought intolerable in men of common sense, in things that relate only to civil rights and the concerns of human government? I am pretty sure, that such glosses as these do very much undervalue the Gospel and the Divine Author of it, and expose it to the bold conjectures of enthusiasts and to the scoffs of atheists and infidels.   It was this method of expounding John vi. which gave a handle to the Quakers, to interpret it of the Light within.   And while the generality of Divines give up this context, as they have done of late ages, for a passage of Scripture not primarily meant of the Eucharist, we can neither effectually confute this wild conceit of the Quakers, nor any other, which the glaring fancy of any man of new light may hereafter produce.   When Origen gave an anagogical turn to John vi., he did the same to the history of institution; for he could not but be sensible, that all discerning men who understood Christianity in any tolerable measure, would from hence infallibly conclude, that he could

not intend this to be the direct primary meaning of our
Saviour in the first place of Scripture, any more than in the
second.   And it is observable, that even from this anagogical
exposition of both these places, he gives us to understand,
that he took the phrases of eating Christ's Flesh and eating
His Body to be the same, and therefore treats them in the
same manner.   And though I am not over much in love with
this way of expounding Holy Scripture, yet if our modern interpreters would be content to follow Origen's example, thus
much at least would have remained clear and indisputable,
viz., that John vi. is a context meant of the Eucharist, as
well as the history of the institution; and that the phrases
of eating Christ's Flesh and eating His Body are parallel,
or rather are the very same.

If indeed there were any violent reason for taking this
phrase in two distinct senses in these two several places; if
any absurdity or inconsistence were by this means to be
avoided, I should readily grant, that they who were for
taking the phrase in two several senses, might do it out of
a pious design to secure the honour of our blessed Master;
though I think he would much better consult the reputation
of Christ Jesus and His religion, who could reconcile those
seeming absurdities and inconsistences in such a manner as
to leave the same phrase to be meant in both places of the
same thing.   But in this case I cannot discern any appearance of difficulty or inconvenience that follows upon taking
the phrase in both places to signify receiving the Sacramental Body and Blood.

I know it is commonly thought a sufficient objection against The objec-
understanding John vi. of the Eucharist, that our Saviour as- tion of
eternal Life
serts eternal Life to be settled as a reward upon them who eat being annexed to
His Flesh and drink His Blood; and it seems incredible to eating of
Christ's
many modern Divines, that so ample a reward should be pro- Flesh, is of
mised to them who receive the Sacrament.   And so should I no force.
too, if by receiving the Sacrament I understood nothing but
an external eating and drinking of the Eucharistical Body and
Blood; but I suppose I have sufficiently guarded my reader
against any such misapprehension.   For I have all along
argued upon this principle, that it is our Saviour's intention,
both in John vi. and in the other Evangelists, to oblige His

disciples to an internal as well as external manducation; that to eat His Flesh in John vi., and to eat His Body according to the institution, are words of the very same import; and that they who make those words imply two several actions or duties, proceed upon a precarious and false supposition. And certainly they who receive the Eucharist with faithful, humble, penitent, and obedient hearts, do all that Dr. W. or Dr. Clagett mean by faith and spiritual actions; and therefore may reasonably be presumed to have a right to eternal Life. Nay, they do something more, they receive the Sacrament of Christ's Body and Blood: [that is, they fulfil a positive command of Christ, and use a necessary means of salvation instituted by Him.]

What is our Saviour's meaning, when He says, "Take, eat," in the institution.
And that I may convince my reader that there is no ill consequence attending this interpretation, I shall desire him to consider what is the certain and infallible meaning of our Saviour, when He said (after He had blessed the Bread) "Take, eat, This is My Body." That He bade His disciples eat the consecrated Bread with their mouths, will be readily agreed by all. What I further insist upon, and what I think no man can in justice deny, is, that He did not only bid them eat with their mouths but with their minds; for He assures them that it was His Body, and yet they saw it to be Bread; and therefore they could not receive or eat it with their mouths as His natural Body; but at the same time they did outwardly eat the Bread, they could by their understandings apprehend it as a full and perfect representation of that natural Body of His. The Apostles indeed might have rather been startled than instructed by what our Saviour now did, if He had not long before warned and advertised them of this His intention, as He did in John vi.; but being so long before apprised that He would give them something to eat under the title and character of His Flesh, they were by this means prepared to eat it as a mystery; which though it was to the sight and in gross substance but Bread, yet by His appointment and the Divine benediction was to them the Flesh of their Master. It could not indeed be perceived to be so by their outward senses; and this therefore necessarily supposes, that they could not receive it as the Body of Christ without the as-

sistance of their faith, and the inward faculties of their
minds; and that therefore they must not rest in the outward
action, but "eat it rationally," as Clemens Alex.[z] expresses
it, like men and Christians, not like brutes and infidels.
And indeed it is strange and unaccountable to me, how the
same phrase in John vi. should be supposed to carry a more
perfect and sublime meaning than in the words of institution.
To eat Christ's Flesh and Body in St. John is such a duty,
as has eternal Life and all evangelical blessings annexed to it;
and that in such strong words, that it is impossible for interpreters to stifle or abate the signification and power of them.
And the most plausible reason which modern writers have to
suppose, that eating Christ's Body in the words of institution
is to have another sense given it, is this, viz., that eternal
Life is too great a promise to be annexed to Sacramental
eating; and indeed this is true, if by Sacramental eating be
meant no more than by communicating *Sacramento tenus*, as
St. Augustine just now expressed it. But can any man believe, that when Christ Jesus says, "Take, eat, This is My
Body," He means no more than that they should press the
symbol of His Body with their teeth, and swallow it with the
organs of deglutition? I am persuaded, that all honest
Christians, whether learned or unlearned, will readily acknowledge that, when Christ bade His Apostles to eat His
Body in the Eucharist, He invited and exhorted them to
perform it as a mystery; and therefore internally as well as
externally to believe, that He had already in the intention of
His will and by the Sacramental Bread and Wine, given
His Body and Blood for them; and that they were to receive it with such dispositions of mind as became men, when
they came to drink the Blood of the Covenant for remission
of sins, that is, with sincere faith and repentance and other
holy affections.

And I cannot conceive, that eating and drinking Christ's
Flesh and Blood in St. John can import more than it necessarily must in the words of institution. It is true, our Saviour
in the words of institution does more strongly imply external
or oral manducation than he does in John vi., for then He
shewed them what the external substance of this Sacrament

Eating Christ's Flesh can import no more in John vi.

[z] d. p. 7. Ap.

was, which He had not expressly done in John vi.; but sure
none will from thence infer, that He excludes the inward or
intellectual part.   And I hope no one can think the inward
or intellectual part of the duty of a communicant the less
valuable or considerable, because it is attended with external
manducation.   Why our Saviour thought it more proper to
make external manducation necessary, I shall have occasion
to shew in the second Part.   In the meantime we certainly
know the meaning of these phrases, "Eat My Body," "Drink
My Blood," in the words of institution: and I affirm that,
taking these phrases in the same sense in John vi. all runs
clear, and there is no manner of difficulty, nor any thing
that looks like it.   For in both places we understand eating,
not only externally with the mouth, but internally with faith
and a sense of the duty we are performing, and with all such
dispositions as are required in people that come to receive
so great favours from the hand of God.   And if eternal Life
do not belong to such communicants, it is certain, that promise cannot of right be applied to any Christians on this
side of heaven.   And I shall hereafter prove, that we are to
continue our claim to this right by a constant and sincere
use of the means.

Though I conceive, if we would speak strictly and precisely, our Saviour does not say, that he who feeds upon His
Flesh has thereby a right to eternal Life; but that he who
having performed the labour of faith receives his present
wages in hand, that is, the Sacrament, has in that Sacrament such a spiritual maintenance or subsistence, as will
supply him with constant strength and ability to perform
his duty, and give him such a gradual growth in virtue and
grace, as knows no bounds or limits; and will, if it be not
his own fault, convey to him the principles of a resurrection
to that state of blessedness, which shall have no end.   For I
take $Z\omega\grave{\eta}$ to denote, not so directly life itself, as the means
or provision by which life is maintained, as I may have occasion hereafter to shew more at large.

And they that use the means outwardly and in appearance
only, that eat, as Judas is by many supposed to have done,
with malicious intentions, or for an hypocritical disguise;
they are so far from performing the duty required by Christ,

that they eat and drink their own damnation. Nay, they
who perform this duty carelessly, without a sincere faith,
love, humility, &c., they do but one part of the duty, and
that the least valuable; they do not come to the Lord's
Table with such good affections and desires, as are necessary
in order to receive the spiritual blessings there reached out
to all worthy communicants.

I know some think it an objection against taking John vi. How eter-
in this sense, that our Saviour makes the eating His Flesh nal salva-
tion de-
and drinking His Blood a necessary condition of eternal pends on
eating
Life; but this objection seemed none in the judgment of the Christ's
Flesh.
primitive Church, who did always believe that without this
none is capable of eternal Life, as will be shewed in the second
Part. I am sensible some Divines, in order to represent the
absurdity of the doctrine which I now defend, aggravate
this necessity to such a degree, as to suppose that even the
Patriarchs and others who lived before Christ were not capable of future happiness, without eating Christ's Flesh and
drinking His Blood in the sense here intended. But they
have no grounds for this, in the words used by our blessed
Saviour. He says indeed, "Except ye," that are My disciples
and hearers, who may, if you think fit, be members of My
Church, and live in constant communion with it; except ye,
I say, that are capable of this blessing, if it be not your own
fault, do "eat My Flesh and drink My Blood, ye have no
Life in you:" for our Saviour spake to none but Jews, who
dwelt in the Holy Land, where His Church was first erected,
and who might become members of it, if their own obstinacy
and perverseness did not prevent: and I suppose our Saviour's
laws are to be understood in the same sense with the laws of
all wise governors, and therefore with this tacit reserve,
Nemo tenetur ad impossibile.

I am not ignorant, that many of the ancients did from Whether
hence conclude, and some Christians do to this day believe, communi-
cating in-
that by virtue of this declaration of Jesus Christ, even infants fants can be
inferred
are under an obligation of eating and drinking the Sacra- from hence.
mental Body and Blood; but I must profess that I cannot
see that this is fairly deducible from the words; for our
Saviour speaks to grown persons, such as were capable of
'labouring or doing the work of God,' that is, 'believing,'

CHAP.
II.
ver. 27—29.
ver. 36. 64.

as He Himself explains it, to such as were culpable for not believing, and therefore not to children; nor indeed was the communicating of children ever the universal practice of the Church; but I believe withal, that the giving the Sacramental Body and Blood to infants was a much more excusable practice than that contempt or neglect of it, which now so much prevails. God grant that what I have written may serve for the cure of this great evil.

How the
Bread
in the
Eucharist
is from
heaven.

If any shall think it an objection against this sense of the words, that it is said of this Bread that it "comes down from heaven," or that it "came down from heaven" (for Christ indifferently useth either the present or the aorist), it is to be observed, that this is as hard to be understood of His natural Body as of His Sacramental; for it is certain that His human Nature was "conceived of the Virgin Mary," and therefore was not from heaven as His Divine Nature was; and it is evident to a demonstration, that this must be understood of His natural Body, or of His Sacramental Body, or

ver. 50, 51.

of both; for thus the words stand, " I am the Living Bread which cometh down from heaven, that a man may eat thereof and not die. I am the Living Bread which came down from heaven; if any man eat of this Bread, he shall live for ever; and the Bread which I will give is My Flesh, which I will give for the Life of the world." And certainly it may as well be said of His Sacramental Body as of His doctrine, that It came down from heaven; because both of them are from God; and if our Saviour speak of the baptism of John as a

Matt. xxi.
25.

thing "from heaven," much more might He say so of the Sacrament of His own Body and Blood. The truth is, as His human personal Body was from heaven, by reason of It's being conceived of the Holy Ghost, for the same reason is His Sacramental Body from heaven, as being made what It is by the secret operation of the same Divine Person; both the one and the other are so "from heaven," that they are "not of men;" the Divine power of the Spirit is to be considered as the principal agent, both in forming Christ's natural Body, and consecrating the Eucharistical.

The first
Reformed
Church of
Bohemia so

And I must own that it is a great satisfaction to me, that I have the first Reformed Church of the world on my side in this particular. Dr. Clagett observes, in his Discourse on

John vi.[a] that Cardinal Cajetan says of the Bohemians, that
"They argued, that if our Lord had not treated in John vi. concerning the Sacrament, He would not have distinguished between eating and drinking, least of all between eating His Flesh and drinking His Blood." By this I have the confession of two learned adversaries at once, that I have the Bohemians with me as to this point. The Cardinal supposed, that if John vi. were understood of the Eucharist, "it would imply a necessity of communicating children," which I have shewed to be a groundless supposition; but that which I believe weighed most with the Cardinal was the other reason mentioned in the same place, viz., that if this text be understood of the Eucharist, it will follow that there is a necessity of the Cup as well as of the Host. And indeed the words of Christ are very emphatical, "Except ye eat the Flesh of the Son of Man and drink His Blood, ye have no Life in you." No wonder therefore that Dr. Clagett justly boasts[b], that "he had Popes, Cardinals, Bishops, and Doctors, before the Council of Trent, for number as well as quality not inferior to those who maintained the contrary side;" and it is probable that this was the main motive for so many Divines of the Church of Rome to assert, that John vi. was not to be understood of Sacramental manducation, viz., because if this were allowed, they thought the practice of that Church in denying the Cup to the laity to be indefensible, as without doubt it is; and therefore the Council of Trent would by no means determine that John vi. was to be understood of the Sacrament; for they were not insensible that the principal ground of the Bohemians demanding the Eucharist in both kinds for the laity as well as Priests, and of the absolute necessity of it, was this text in John vi. I am further informed by my reverend and learned neighbour Mr. Dorrington, (who will ere long oblige the world with a more particular account of the most early Reformers,) that while they went under the name of Taborites (from the chief place of their residence) they presented to the States of Bohemia a Confession of their faith, in which the article of the Eucharist runs thus[c]; "Now after the Sacrament

---

[a] [Preface, p. xix.]
[b] [p. xxi.]

[c] [Johnson has omitted the verification of these passages in his 2nd Ed.]

CHAP.
II.

of Baptism, and imposition of hands, it remains, that we speak of the third Sacrament of the Body and Blood of the Lord or of the Lord's Supper; because these three Sacraments follow after one another; for by the grace of Christ we are cleansed from our sins, by the grace of imposition of hands we are confirmed in what is good for the [spiritual] conflict; but this grace of the Sacrament of the Body and Blood of the Lord cherishes and increases the grace of Baptism, and of imposition of hands; since the Sacrament of the Body and Blood of the Lord is a sign deputed by Divine institution to signify the spiritual nourishment of a man in God, by the assistance of which the spiritual Life is preserved, and by the want of which it fails. He that is Truth itself saying, 'Except ye eat the Flesh of the Son of Man and drink His Blood, ye have no Life in you.'" In a Confession of their faith sent to Vladislaus, king of Bohemia and Hungary, about the year 1508, they speak of the Eucharist in the following manner[d]. " By that faith, which we have

Because the Latin used by these Bohemians is somewhat singular, I will therefore give it my reader here in the margin, that he may judge whether I attain it or not. " Jam post Sacramentum Baptismi, et manus impositionem, restat de tertio Sacramento, sc. Dominici Corporis et Sanguinis, seu Cœnæ Dominicæ pertractandum, quia illa tria Sacramenta sunt continua. Nam per gratiam Baptismi a peccato mundamur, per gratiam manus impositionis in bono ad pugnam roboramur. Ipsa autem gratia Sacramenti Dominici Corporis et Sanguinis gratiam Baptismi et manus impositionis nutrit et augmentat: cum Sacramentum Dominici Corporis et Sanguinis sit signum ex Divina institutione deputatum ad significandum efficaciter spiritualem nutritionem hominis in Deo, qua assistente vita spiritualis conservatur, et qua deficiente deficit, dicente Veritate, Joh. vi. ' Nisi manducaveritis Carnem Filii hominis, &c." [Confessio Waldensium, p. 18. Ed. Basil. 1568. BS. 8vo. D. 284. Bodl.]

[d] Fide ipsa, quam Scripturarum sanctarum ministerio hausimus, credimus, lingua quoque nostra resonamus. Ubicunque dignus Sacerdos cum fido populo juxta sensum et Christi intentionem Ecclesiæque ordinationem orationem faciens, hujusmodi verbis videlicet, *Hoc est Corpus Meum, Hic est Sanguis Meus*, testificatus fuerit: confestim præsens panis est Corpus Christi in mortem pro nobis oblatum. Vinum similiter præsens est Sanguis Ejus pro nobis effusus in peccatorum remissionem. Hæc fidei nostræ professio verbis Christi firmatur ab Evangelistis, et a S. Paulo conscriptis. Ad hanc professionem etiam istud accedat hoc Corpus Christi et Sanguis Ejus, juxta Christi et Ecclesiæ quoque Ejus institutionem, sub panis vinique speciebus utrisque in commemorationem Ejus mortis, Sanguinis etiam effusionem Ipsius, quemadmodum ait, *Hoc facite in Meam commemorationem*, sumi debet. Deinde mors Christi, verbo Evangelii, atque bona utilia morte Ejus disposita, annuntianda sunt; similiter spes fusi Sanguinis, ut Apostolus testatur: *Quotiescunque* (ait) *manducabitis panem hunc, et calicem Domini bibetis, mortem Domini annuntiabitis donec veniat.* Tertio, pro veritatis spiritalis notitia, de qua Joh. Evangelista scribit: in certificationem similiter donationis, sumptionis, usus, acceptionis, veritatis, per fidem in spe, sicut ait Dominus, *Accipite et comedite : Accipite et bibite.*—[Fasciculus Rerum, p. 165. Ed. Brown.]

imbibed by the ministry of the Holy Scriptures, we believe and declare with our tongues, wherever a worthy Priest, with a faithful people, offering prayer according to the sense and intention of Christ and the ordination of the Church, has solemnly used these words, 'This is My Body, This is My Blood,' forthwith the Bread there present is the Body of Christ offered for us, and the Wine there present is likewise His Blood, shed for the remission of sins; this profession of our faith is confirmed by the words of Christ, written by the Evangelists and St. Paul. It may further be added to this profession, that this Body and Blood of His, according to the institution of Christ and His Church, ought to be received under both species of Bread and Wine, in commemoration of His Death and shedding of His Blood, as He says, 'Do ye this in remembrance of Me.' Further, the Death of Christ, according to the word of the Gospel, and the advantageous benefits bestowed by His Death, are to be set forth, as likewise the hope of His Blood, as the Apostle testifies; 'As often,' says he, 'as ye eat this Bread and drink this Cup of the Lord, ye do shew forth the Death of the Lord, until He come.' Thirdly, for [setting forth] the knowledge of spiritual truth, concerning which John the Evangelist [speaks]; as likewise for the assurance of the giving, receiving, use, acceptance of the truth by faith in hope, as the Lord says, 'Take, eat,' 'Take, drink.'" Together with this Confession, they sent to the king an Apology, in answer to a famous Doctor, who was a notable adversary to them and their doctrine; in which they argue against him to this effect, viz., that what is received in the Sacrament is either distinct from that Christ, Who is at God's right hand; and then why do men worship Him at all? Or else it is the same Christ; and then, why do not they worship Him, after He has been received by the Priest or by any faithful men, as well as before? And they add[e], "Certainly they ought rather to do this according to the precept of faith; for Christ is in a more

---

[e] "Et certe deberent hoc facere ex præcepto fidei plus, quia digniore modo est in homine quam in Sacramento: quia propter hoc est in Sacramento ad tempus, ut Eum homines sumant cum reverentia, non solum ad tempus, sed in perpetuum, sicut potest dici et confirmari ex verbis Christi, ubi dicit, *Qui manducat hunc panem vivet in æternum.*"—[Responsio Excusatoria Fratrum Waldensium; Fascicul. Rerum, vol. i. p. 185.]

worthy manner in the man, than in the Sacrament; for He is in the Sacrament for a while to this end, that men may receive Him with reverence, not only for a time, but for ever; as may be affirmed and proved from the words of Christ, where He says, ' He that eateth of this Bread shall live for ever.' " Now this authority is of greater weight with me, than that of any other Church now in the world, except our own, would be; not only because they were the first-fruits of the Reformation, but because their constitution was episcopal, and they retained confirmation, as we also do; and it is very evident, as Mr. Dorrington observes to me, that in the passage above cited they are declaring or arguing against transubstantiation, and I may add, the Communion in one kind only. And it is not unworthy our notice, that though they do expressly apply John vi. to the Eucharist in all three citations, yet they do in the second passage suppose that our Saviour intended in this context to represent Divine Truth as well as His Body and Blood; nay, in the last words of that passage they clearly take the words of institution in the same manner. They who penned the Confession, [were] more probably well versed in the writings of Origen and St. Jerome, from whence they took these hints.

It is true, that these confessions are found in the FASCICU-LUS RERUM, (published first by Orthuinus Gratius, A.D. 1535, and here in England by Mr. Brown about the year 1690,) and are there said to have been drawn and presented by the Waldenses; but the Rev. Mr. Dorrington assures me that this is only by a vulgar mistake, whereby it often happens, that things done or said in reality by the Bohemians are attributed to the Waldenses; they being two several bodies of men that joined in the same cause against the Church of Rome. I shall say no more of this matter, since Mr. Dorrington gives the world leave to expect a very full and perfect account of the Churches of the Bohemian brethren, if it please God to favour his studies.

[He never lived to accomplish this work.]

A PARAPHRASE

ON JOHN vi. 26—36, 47—64.

IN WHICH I HAVE TAKEN THE LIBERTY OF TRANSLATING SOME WORDS OTHERWISE THAN THEY ARE TURNED BY OUR ENGLISH TRANSLATORS.

VER. 26.—*Amen, Amen I say unto you,* and it concerns you greatly to consider and understand what I tell you, *ye seek Me, not because ye saw the miracles,* and from thence conclude, as ye ought to do, that I am the Messias; *but because ye did eat of the loaves* and fishes multiplied miraculously by Me, *and were filled;* and so expect, that I should ver. 9. maintain you in the same manner for the future.

Ver. 27. I advise you, that you *labour not for the meat that perisheth,* such as I lately gave you; *but for that* mysterious *meat that endureth,* in it's effects at least, *to everlasting life,* or so as to become an eternal maintenance; *which the Son of Man,* Who lately gave you that plentiful entertainment, *shall* hereafter *give unto* as many of *you,* as are willing and fit to receive it; *for Him hath God the Father sealed,* or commissioned to promise such maintenance.

N.B. That ζωὴ signifies 'maintenance,' and ζᾶν 'to be subsisted' or 'maintained,' is a thing of which learned men want no proof.

Ver. 28. Now because Christ had spoken of labouring, *therefore they said unto Him, what shall we do, that we may do* ver. 27. *the work of God;* and so procure this eternal maintenance, of which Thou speakest?

Ver. 29. In answer to this question, *Jesus said unto them, this is the work of God,* meant by Me, *that ye believe in Him,* ver. 27. *Whom He hath sent,* that is, in Me [and particularly as to what I am now going to say concerning the Meat which endureth to everlasting Life;] and this is really a work or labour of the mind; it consists not in following Me with a bodily fatigue, in getting boats, and rowing, and sailing after Me, as you have now done, but in submitting to Me, as [to ver. 24, 25.

what I am now going to teach you:] and this is a work very hard to be done by men of your temper.

Ver. 30. *They said therefore unto Him, what sign shewest Thou, that we may see it, and believe* that Thou art the Messias? *what* miracle *dost Thou work?* as to Thy giving us one meal's meat by unknown means, that is not to be compared to what was done by Moses:

Ver. 31. *For our Fathers did feed upon manna in the wilderness* for forty years together, *as it is written, He gave them food from heaven.*

N.B. I turn φαγεῖν here and throughout this discourse, as likewise τρώγειν, not "eat," but "feed upon," as implying not the act of eating once and away, sometimes or occasionally; but a constant daily supplying our natural wants; such was the manducation of the Israelites, who fed upon manna for forty years, during the whole time of their pilgrimage in the desert; and it is very evident, that the people followed Him in expectation, that He would maintain them in some such manner. We find, that when they had been witnesses to the miracle of multiplying the loaves,

ver. 15. they were endeavouring "by force to make Him a king," they thought Him the only person fit to be a king or general, when they found that He was able to subsist an army by His miracles; they therefore, beyond all doubt, hoped to have a constant provision furnished by Him, and followed

ver. 34.
1 Cor. x. 3. Him on this presumption. And in correspondence to this I suppose St. Paul's words should thus be rendered, "Our fathers did all feed upon the same spiritual meat, and they all made the same spiritual liquor their drink" (they in type, we in verity), "for they all made" the stream which

Exod. xvii.
Numb. xx. issued from "the Rock, their drink;" which stream "followed them" for thirty-eight years together, from Rephidim to Cades Barnea. In both places a constant daily eating and drinking is meant.

Ver. 32. *Jesus said unto them* by way of reply, Amen, Amen I say unto you, and it is what particularly deserves your consideration; *Moses gave you not that* mysterious *Bread from heaven,* of which I have now been speaking; *but My Father*[a] *is now about to give you the true* mysterious *Bread from heaven.*

Ver. 33. *For the Bread of God is that* Bread *which cometh down from heaven and giveth life* or *maintenance to* that part *of the world* which labours for it.

N.B. "The Bread of God" signifies, in Scripture language, any sacri-

[a] The present indicative often stands for the future participle and the substantive verb. See Matt. ii. 4; iii. 10; xx. 22; 1 Cor. xvi. 5. How the Eucharist is 'Bread from heaven,' I have shewed in my Discourse on John vi. which immediately precedes this Paraphrase.

fice, whether animate or inanimate, which was offered to God.   It is said
of the priests, "The offerings of the Lord made by fire, the Bread of God Lev. xxi. 6.
they do offer."   'The offerings of the Lord' in this text are the same with
'the Bread of God.'   Our translators have supplied 'and;' but that is
superfluous.   'To offer the Bread of God' is a phrase denoting the whole Lev. xxi. 8.
sacrificial office of the priest.   And the Law speaking of maimed animals 17.
says, "Neither of these shall ye [priests] offer the Bread of your God." Lev. xxii.
["Neither from a stranger's hand shall ye offer the Bread of your God of 25.
any of these; because their corruption is in them, and blemishes be in
them: they shall not be accepted for you."]   The kidneys, fat, and caul of
the beast offered as a peace-offering, are expressly called "the Bread of the Lev. iii. 11.
offering made by fire unto the Lord."   Our translators do indeed there
render the word, 'food;' and so they might have done in the other places
before cited, for לחם in Hebrew, ἄρτος in the Hellenistic tongue, signify
all manner of victuals.   Sometimes those portions of the sacrifice, which
were eaten by the priests or their families, are called "the Bread of God;"
for it is said of the maimed priest, that though he may not officiate, "yet Lev. xxi.22.
he shall eat the Bread of His God," "both of the most holy," (that is, the
remnant of the meal-offering and the sin-offering, of the trespass-offering,) Lev. ii. 5;
"and of the holy" (that is, the peace-offering.)   Our Saviour therefore calls vi. 25. 29,
Himself "the Bread of God," as He was a Sacrifice for the sins of the &c.; vii. 6;
world, and mysteriously to be eaten as such; and every animal sacrificed xix. 8.
for sin or as a peace-offering under the Law might, if it could have spoke,
have called itself "the Bread of God."—Further, I turn the article ὁ not
"he" but "that," as if ἄρτος had been repeated; it is certain the hearers
did not yet apprehend that Christ meant Himself; for they desire that
this Bread might be given to them in the next verse; whereas, when they
apprehended that He spake of Himself, they were offended and forsook
Him.

Ver. 34. *They said unto Him, Lord give us this Bread,* and
that not for one meal, but *for a perpetuity.*   See ver. 31.

Ver. 35. *Jesus said unto them, I am the Bread of Life* or
spiritual *maintenance; he that cometh to Me* [out of a desire
of this spiritual Bread (not as you do for the sake of temporal food)], *shall never suffer* starving spiritual *hunger; and
he that believeth on Me* [when I promise him My Blood to
drink, as well as in all other particulars] *shall never suffer*
killing spiritual *thirst;* [for I will give him an ample supply
of My Body and Blood.]

N.B. Our Saviour gives a direct answer to His hearers, who desired this
Bread 'for a perpetuity;' He assures them that if they come to Him, or
believe on Him, they shall not want this mysterious Bread; or as it is
ver. 27, if they laboured, they should have the meat that endureth to everlasting Life.   It seems absurd to suppose, that our Saviour here promises
that His disciples should not hunger and thirst (that is, have an appetite)

after this mysterious meat; what He promises is, that they should never die of hunger and thirst for want of it. An appetite after this meat is a blessing; the withholding of it is destructive. Our Saviour calls Himself the " Bread of life," or maintenance, in allusion to the sin-offerings of the Jews, which were the chief maintenance of the priests during the time of their attendance; for the whole sin-offering and trespass-offering belonged to the priest, and was to be eaten by him and his family, except the rump and the fat and the kidneys and the caul, whereas only the breast and shoulder of the peace-offering was the priests'. Therefore it is said of the priests, that " they fed on the sin-offerings of the people."

Lev. vii. 1—7. and 28—34. Hos. iv. 8.

Ver. 36. *But I said unto you, that ye also have seen Me* doing miracles, *and yet believe not* [what I am now saying of giving men My Flesh to eat, and My Blood to drink;] or that ye followed Me, because ye had eaten of the loaves and hoped to do so again (ver. 26), not because ye from thence concluded Me to be [a veracious infallible Master.] Ye do not perform the labour of faith, and so the promise of eternal maintenance does not belong to you.

Ver. 47. *Amen, Amen, I say unto you,* and it is a matter of the greatest consequence, *he that believeth on Me,* and so performeth the labour or work of God, *hath* for his reward or wages in hand, *eternal life* or *maintenance.*

Ver. 48. And *I Myself am that Bread of eternal life* or *maintenance.* I Myself am to be eaten in a mysterious manner.

Ver. 49. *Your fathers did feed upon manna in the wilderness* for forty years together, *and* yet *are dead;*

Ver. 50. But the excellency of this Bread, which I now promise, is, that *this is the Bread which comes down from heaven, that a man may feed upon it, and not die* the death of a sinner.

Ver. 51. " *I myself am the living* or *life-giving Bread, which came down from heaven; if any man feed on this Bread* in the mysterious manner, which I will hereafter discover, *he shall live for ever* or be maintained to an eternal duration.—

N.B. Some of the ancients seem to suppose, that these and the foregoing words may be understood either of the Sacrament, or of the Holy Ghost, or of Christ's doctrine. I have above given instances of this from St. Augustine, who yet perpetually understands the following verses of the Eucharist only, and rather mentions this as a gloss on the foregoing words than insists upon it as the primary sense; and indeed I can see no reason to believe that our Saviour meant one thing in the foregoing words, another in the following. It may be allowed that our Saviour in the foregoing words speaks of Himself only as potential food; just as the animal sacrifice for the sins of private persons might, if it could have spoke, have said, while it was yet alive, to the Jewish priests, " I am the Bread of God, the Bread of life or maintenance for you." Not that it had been possible for the priests to eat every part of such animal sacrifice, though it had been allowed them to do it; but by a usual synecdoche of the part for the whole, in the following words He lets them know, that not His whole Person but His Flesh only was actually to become their food. And it is evident that our Saviour uses the phrases of ' eating Me,' and ' eating My Flesh,' in the same sense, as may be seen by comparing this verse with the 57th; and that therefore to make our Saviour intend two several things in what goes before and in what follows, is only a conjectural gloss.

Ver. 51.—*And the Bread which I will give, is* not My entire Person, but *My Flesh, Which I will give for the life* or maintenance *of* the *world,* on condition that it do believe in Me.

N.B. I have before shewed, how Christ gave His natural Body to God by the pledge of His Sacramental Body; therefore here He makes no distinction; because in giving one He did in effect give the other, first to God, and then to men.

Ver. 52. *The Jews therefore strove among themselves, saying, How can this man give us His Flesh to feed upon?* It is evident one carcase can never maintain so great a multitude, much less the whole world, if we could find in our hearts to eat it.

Ver. 53. Then *Jesus said unto them, Except ye,* who now hear Me, *do feed upon the Flesh of the Son of Man and make His Blood your drink, ye have no* spiritual *life in you,* or ye cannot have any thing in you, whereby to support your spiritual life.

Ver. 54. *Whoso feedeth on My Flesh and maketh My Blood his drink, hath eternal life* or *maintenance, and I will raise him up at the last day,* to an endless state of happiness.

Ver. 55. *For My Flesh is indeed* spiritual life-giving *meat;* and *My Blood is indeed* spiritual life-giving *drink.*

Ver. 56. *He that feedeth on My Flesh, and maketh My Blood his drink, he dwelleth in Me, and I in him,* by means of the one Spirit thereby communicated to him. See ver. 63.

Ver. 57. *As the Father, Who lives,* that is, is the fountain of Life, *sent Me, and I live by the Father; so he who feedeth on Me* in the mysterious manner, which I will hereafter discover, *even he shall live* or *be maintained by Me.*

Ver. 58. *This is the Bread which is come down from heaven* to be fed upon, *not as your fathers fed upon manna in the wilderness* with unbelieving hearts, and so are dead in their sins ; *he that feedeth on this Bread shall live* or *be maintained for ever.*

Ver. 59. *These things said He in the synagogue, as He taught in Capernaum.*

Ver. 60. *Many therefore of His disciples, when they had heard this* discourse of His feeding them with His Flesh and making His Blood their drink, *said, This is a hard saying,* See ch. viii. *who can hear* or *believe it ?*
47.

Ver. 61. *When Jesus knew in Himself, that His disciples murmured at it, He said unto them, Doth this cause you to be offended,* or *to stumble ?*

Ver. 62. *What, and if you shall see the Son of Man to ascend up* into heaven, *where He was before ?* Will ye not then think what I now say of feeding men with My Flesh to be more incredible than it can seem at present? And yet He will certainly ascend thither clothed with His Flesh, and will as certainly give His Flesh to be fed upon by men.

Ver. 63. *It is the* Divine *Spirit, that giveth life ;* and therefore, when I promised My Flesh as an eternal maintenance to them who eat and drink it, you ought so to understand Me, as if I intended, together with My Flesh and Blood, to convey to men the power of the Spirit : for *the Flesh* of itself *profiteth not at all* to the end, which I propose, of giving you an eternal Life or maintenance, whether by *Flesh* you understand My natural Body, or any other material thing dignified with that character ; *the words which I speak* or *the promises which I pronounce,* when I mentioned My Flesh and Blood, *are* not only material visible things, but they likewise contain an assurance of *spirit and life* or eternal *maintenance.*

Ver. 64. *But there are some of you who believe not,* or put no trust in Me, as to the promise I have been now making of giving My Flesh to be eat, and My Blood to be drunk. You will not perform the labour, and so cannot receive the wages in hand, which I promise to all that submit to the condition.

*A very learned friend having several times hinted to me his
dislike of the explication given by me of this context in
John vi., I desired him to draw up in writing his objections
against me on this head; he complied with my request; and
here I present my reader with his objections, and my
answers to them, paragraph by paragraph.*

FIRST PARAGRAPH.

'Our Saviour, in the sixth of St. John, from ver. 27 to
ver. 51, so often speaks of coming to and believing on Him
as a person sent from God, that there is to me no appearance that He intended any thing more. Nor is it, I think,
reasonable to believe, that He spake of a different thing in
the following part of His discourse.'

ANSWER.

There was good reason, and even a necessity, that Christ
should often speak of believing and coming to Him, when
He was teaching such a doctrine as He found so disagreeable
to His hearers, that they seemed one and all to be disposed
to abandon Him: and especially, because at the beginning
of His discourse He had declared faith to be that "work," ver. 27.
or labour, which alone could qualify men "to eat His Flesh,"
or "that meat which endured to everlasting Life."

I am persuaded that in this first paragraph I can discern
the principal occasion of your mistake in this point; namely,
that you suppose our Saviour to speak of "coming to," and
"believing" on Himself as a person sent from God only.
For you say, there is "no appearance that he intended any
thing more." But now it appears evident to me, that He
here speaks of believing in Himself not only as a person sent
from God, but as one that also promised His Flesh to be eat,
and His Blood to be drunk in a mysterious manner. And
it was the want of this faith chiefly, which Christ resented in
His hearers. For,

1. It is so far from being true, that a general faith in

Christ, as sent from God, was the only thing required by our Saviour in this context, that so far as appears, all His present hearers did already actually believe Him to be such a person. For all that murmured, all that went back from ver. 60, 61. walking any more with Him, are expressly called "disciples;" and it is not credible that they should be so styled, 66. except they had believed in Christ as the Messias. The very worst of His present hearers, except Judas, were they who had seen the miracle of the loaves and fishes. And yet ver. 14. even these were believers in Christ at large; for "the men who had seen the miracle which Jesus did, said, This is of a truth that Prophet that should come into the world." And therefore, if to "believe in Christ," and "eat His Flesh," were phrases of the same signification, then all these murmurers, even they that could not bear to hear of eating Christ's Flesh, had yet done that which they could not endure to hear of: they had eat His Flesh in your sense of these words, they had owned Christ the great Prophet, and had been His disciples, and were so until they were told of the necessity of eating of their Master's Flesh. I call them who had seen the miracle of the loaves and fishes the worst of Christ's present hearers, except Judas; because they followed Him rather for the sake of the loaves than on account of the ver. 26. miracle, as they are told by Christ Himself: they had a greater regard to things temporal than spiritual; a thing too incident to them that believe in Christ, as we find by daily experience.

2. However it is certain that eleven of the Apostles had now for many months, not to say years, believed in Christ as a person sent from God, and did at this time continue so to do; therefore they must certainly have eat Christ's Flesh all this time, and did so now, according to your opinion. Yet if they had, or did eat His Flesh, it was more than they knew; for they also were so shocked with what He had said concerning the eating of His Flesh, that our Saviour saw ver. 67. occasion to ask them, "Will ye also go away?" Therefore it is certain, that in the judgment of these Apostles, Christ in this place, under the phrase of eating His Flesh, had taught them some new doctrine. For if they had believed that He required them only to acknowledge Him as a person sent

from God, this was no more than what they had long since been convinced of; and Christ, by explaining this dark phrase according to your meaning, might presently have set them right. And God forbid that any man should suppose that our Divine Master caused some to apostatize, and shook the faith of His own good Apostles, rather than He would explain to them a very singular phrase that no man had ever used before Him, when it imported no more as you would have it than a persuasion of His Divine mission, which they would have acknowledged without hesitation.

3. The sacred text doth clearly teach us that the doctrine here taught contained very considerable difficulties, and was hard to be digested. The main body of the hearers found no such difficulties in owning Him to be that great Prophet that should come into the world; and they thus express their unbelief, "How can this Man give us His Flesh to eat?" And ver. 52. when our Saviour had said, "This is that Bread which came ver. 58. down from heaven," ... they presently reply, "This is an hard ver. 60. saying, who can hear it?" And it was "at this," that "Jesus ver. 61. knew in Himself, His disciples murmured." Nay farther, our Saviour in His preface to this discourse plainly intimates that what He was now going to say required a very laborious ver. 27. 29. faith in His hearers, and at the same time hints to us the sum of that doctrine which He was going to inculcate, namely, that He would hereafter give His disciples "Bread which should endure to everlasting life." And when they murmured at it, He says, "doth this offend you?" that is, ver. 61. does it cause you to stumble into unbelief? I know it does. He adds, "What, and if ye shall see the Son of Man ascend up" into heaven, "where He was before?" If you cannot believe Me now, how will you be able to believe that you can eat My Flesh, when I shall be removed wholly out of your sight as far as heaven is from earth? He not only acknowledges that the point He was now pressing was hard to be believed, but that it would hereafter be harder still. It therefore could not be His mission from God. For that was never hard to them who saw and considered His miracles. And His resurrection and ascension into heaven would make it more easy still, because by this means His Divine power was still made more manifest. It was therefore the mysterious

or Sacramental eating of His Flesh which He here taught; which is a thing very different from believing Him to be a person sent from God, though this belief was a necessary qualification for the internal and beneficial eating Christ's mystical Flesh.

4. I have shewed in the foregoing Discourse on John vi. that faith is the work or labour; eating Christ's Flesh and drinking His Blood the reward of that labour; and this dis- ver. 27. 29. tinction is made by Christ Himself.   And the labour and reward cannot in the nature of things be the same.   Yet they must be the same, if, as you say, 'to believe in Christ' and 'to eat His Flesh' are but two expressions without any difference in true sense and meaning.

Whereas you say our Saviour " so often" speaks of coming to Him and believing on Him, I cannot find that He speaks of coming to Him, or believing on Him, from ver. 27 to ver. 64 above eight times; whereas He nine times speaks of eating or drinking, and seven times of the meat or drink.

SECOND PARAGRAPH.

'Indeed He there (viz., in the following part of His dis- course) expresses Himself more obscurely, because He saw that the plainest instructions and even miracles would not convince many of His followers.'

ANSWER.

I have shewed, in answer to the first paragraph, that most of His hearers were actually convinced that He was a person sent from God, until they drew back because they could not believe His doctrine of the Sacrament. Will you say He involved His meaning in obscure expressions on purpose to harden them that were already hardened? Is it not more just to say, that the nature of the mystery of which He was speaking, could be expressed in no other words but what must seem obscure to them and all others unto the end of the world?

THIRD PARAGRAPH.

'Perhaps, by "eating His Flesh" He might mean believing on Him when crucified, since ver. 51 He seems to speak of His Death.'

ANSWER.

Your expression shews that you are not clear in the point. I cannot wonder at this. For we must all be at uncertainties in expounding Scripture, if we set on this work without having a just regard to the analogy of the words and phrases used in that sacred Book, and rather attend to our own fancies and conjectures than to the use of the same expressions in other texts. It is clear from my answer to the first paragraph, No. 3, that what Christ here demanded of them to believe had some considerable difficulty in it. But there was no difficulty in believing that He was to die. If indeed they had believed Him to be the Messiah, they would, according to the vulgar notion of the Jews, have expected that John xii.34. He should have abode on earth for ever. But since they did not, according to you, esteem Him a person sent from God, what should make His Death, or the manner of it, seem incredible? But I see no occasion to enlarge on this head, since you are pleased in effect to revoke this in paragraph 6 and 8 below.

FOURTH PARAGRAPH.

'However, when they understood Him in a gross, literal sense, he adds, ver. 63, "It is the Spirit that quickeneth," &c. *q. d.* I speak not unto you of oral eating, but of such a mental eating of Me, as will produce in you a spiritual life, and bring you to an eternal Life hereafter.'

ANSWER.

When you deny that our Saviour did intend oral manducation, you allege no reason for your opinion. I readily own, and earnestly contend, that He meant not such an oral manducation as excluded what is mental; nay, I assert that the

mental manducation is the main point. And every good
communicant is a full evidence that these two manducations
are perfectly consistent with each other, and ought not to be
separated. Yet literal bodily eating cannot be excluded, except you can shew some absurdity implied in this sense of
the word. I have at large explained this text in the foregoing book, when I shew on what texts of Scripture the
ancients grounded their doctrine, that "the Holy Ghost made
the symbols the Body and Blood" of Christ.

FIFTH PARAGRAPH.

' "But there are some of you," says He, "that believe
not," viz., that I am a person sent from God, as in ver. 36.

ANSWER.

I find no such explanation in ver. 36. I must observe,
that here you depart from your notion mentioned in paragraph 3, and reassume your former supposition, that to eat
Christ's Flesh is to believe Him a person sent from God,
which I have fully disproved in the answer to paragraph
the first.

SIXTH PARAGRAPH.

' If He had been speaking of believing the mystery of the
Eucharist, He might rather have said, "There are none of
you that believe," since the sum total of the belief, even of
His Apostles, was but this, ver. 69, "We believe and are
sure that Thou art Christ, the Son of the living God;" which
yet He never charges with any defect, and doubtless was
therefore all that He then required of His followers.'

ANSWER.

You forget, dear Sir, the words which are the first and
principal in St. Peter's confession, viz., "Lord, to whom
shall we go, Thou hast the words of eternal life." For by
this St. Peter declares his assent to all that Christ had said,
but especially to His doctrine of attaining eternal Life by

eating His Flesh. He acknowledges eternal Life to be at His disposal, and to be had by such means as He had been expressing. It is true, Christ had not here fully opened the nature of eating His Flesh and Blood, but only hinted what hereafter He designed more perfectly to reveal. Nor on the other side had He yet fully performed the office of the Messiah; He had not yet died, nor rose again, nor ascended into heaven. Until all this was done they could not believe in Him, as one that had wholly discharged His Messiahship, nor as one that had yet actually given His Flesh to be eat. It was sufficient in both points to believe in what He had hitherto said or done, and to rely on His promise, that the rest should hereafter be accomplished in its season.

SEVENTH PARAGRAPH.

'I think it must be taken for granted, that our Saviour in this discourse speaks of what all His followers might have done, if they had not been of an obstinate and unteachable temper; otherwise it would reflect upon His wisdom and goodness. But if He speaks of eating Sacramentally, this could not be performed by any of them before the institution of the Eucharist.'

ANSWER.

It would indeed have been a reflection upon His wisdom and goodness, if He had commanded them to do that out of hand, which could not possibly have been done until some time after. But He requires nothing to be done out of hand, but to believe in the promise which He gave them of making His Flesh to be meat indeed, His Blood drink indeed. Nay, He expresses Himself in the future tense when He speaks of the Sacrament, as of "Bread, which the Son of Man shall ver. 27. give:" and says, "The Bread which I shall give is My Flesh." This is a demonstration that He did not speak of eating His Flesh, as of a thing to be done out of hand. The rest is answered, in what I have said to the sixth paragraph.

EIGHTH PARAGRAPH.

'Nor could they understand Him in such a sense, when His Death, which this [Sacrament] was to represent, was

not then manifested even to His Apostles; but we find them
after this startled, and offended at the mention of it. For
they, as well as other of the Jews, were a long time before
they could be cured of their fond opinion, that their Messiah
was to be a temporal prince.'

ANSWER.

As they could believe His Death yet to come, so they
could believe His Sacrament, though not yet instituted; and
this was all that Christ now required of them. I desire you
to compare this paragraph with paragraph 3.

NINTH PARAGRAPH.

' As to your laying so great a stress upon the necessity of
understanding the same phrase (used but twice by our
Saviour) in the same sense; it may be answered, that our
Saviour might speak with allusion to the Sacrament, though
not directly of it.'

ANSWER.

To speak in allusion to a thing utterly unknown before,
is a figure of speech not to be met with in any book of
rhetoric. I can at present remember nothing like to it,
except it be proving or illustrating a thing unknown by a
thing less known. But what is the thing of which He intended to speak, when He speaks in allusion to the Sacrament? Your answer must be according to your opinion here
laid down, that He either speaks of Himself, as a person
sent from God, or as a person that was to suffer death. But
I should rather choose to say, that the Sacrament was an
allusion to Christ's Person, especially as put to death, than
that His Person, particularly as crucified, was an allusion to
the Sacrament; which is what you here seem to say.

TENTH PARAGRAPH.

' And so eating of His Flesh, and drinking of His Blood
may signify the same here as in the Sacrament, excepting
only the oral manducation, which the context will by no
means bear.'

ANSWER.

This is, in effect, to confess that this phrase is used in two senses, and in next paragraph you expressly own it.

ELEVENTH PARAGRAPH.

'But after all, the words of institution, and the words of St. John seem to me not to be the same phrases. One mentions a proper subject of oral manducation, and expressly requires it, the other does neither. One may be understood of eating and drinking literally, the other cannot.'

ANSWER.

How far you have proved that the Bread or Flesh in St. John is not capable of oral manducation, I must leave to your own reflection. You allow that to " eat Christ's Flesh," and to " eat His Body" are two several phrases, and mean two different things; therefore I have no more to say, but that you have laid yourself open to the consequences of this opinion, which have sufficiently, I think, been shewed in my Discourse on this context, and toward the latter end of it. Pray, why is not Christ's ' Flesh' as capable of oral manducation as His ' Body?' If Christ's Body signifies not His natural but Sacramental Body, why may not and ought not His Flesh to denote, not His natural, but Sacramental Flesh ?

END OF VOL. I.

CORRIGENDA.

In the Prefatory Epistle, p. 41. the reference to Cardinal Bona's work *De Rebus Liturgicis* should be, [cap. x. p. 362. Ed. Antverp. 1677.]
In p. 48. for "Frontanellense" read 'Fontanellense.'

APPENDIX.

Ed. Hefele, 1842.

(a) *Epist. ad Corinth.* cap. 35, 36. "Θυσία αἰνέσεως δοξάσει με, καὶ ἐκεῖ ὁδὸς ἣν δείξω αὐτῷ τὸ σωτήριον τοῦ Θεοῦ." Αὕτη ἡ ὁδός, ἀγαπητοί, ἐν ᾗ εὕρομεν τὸ σωτήριον ἡμῶν, Ἰησοῦν Χριστόν, τὸν Ἀρχιερέα τῶν προσφορῶν ἡμῶν.

(b) *Ibid.* cap. 40, 41. Πάντα τάξει ποιεῖν ὀφείλομεν, ὅσα ὁ Δεσπότης ἐπιτελεῖν ἐκέλευσεν κατὰ καιροὺς τεταγμένους. Τάς τε προσφορὰς καὶ λειτουργίας ἐπιτελεῖσθαι, καὶ οὐκ εἰκῇ ἢ ἀτάκτως ἐκέλευσεν γίνεσθαι, ἀλλ' ὡρισμένοις καιροῖς καὶ ὥραις. Ποῦ τε καὶ διὰ τίνων ἐπιτελεῖσθαι θέλει, Αὐτὸς ὥρισεν τῇ ὑπερτάτῃ Αὐτοῦ βουλήσει, ἵν' ὁσίως πάντα τὰ γινόμενα ἐν εὐδοκήσει εὐπρόσδεκτα εἴη τῷ θελήματι Αὐτοῦ. Οἱ οὖν τοῖς προστεταγμένοις καιροῖς ποιοῦντες τὰς προσφορὰς αὐτῶν εὐπρόσδεκτοί τε καὶ μακάριοι· τοῖς γὰρ νομίμοις τοῦ Δεσπότου ἀκολουθοῦντες οὐ διαμαρτάνουσιν. Τῷ γὰρ Ἀρχιερεῖ ἴδιαι Λειτουργίαι δεδομέναι εἰσίν, καὶ τοῖς Ἱερεῦσιν ἴδιος ὁ τόπος προστέτακται, καὶ Λευΐταις ἴδιαι διακονίαι ἐπίκεινται· ὁ Λαϊκὸς ἄνθρωπος τοῖς λαϊκοῖς προστάγμασι δέδεται. Ἕκαστος ὑμῶν, Ἀδελφοί, ἐν τῷ ἰδίῳ τάγματι εὐχαριστείτω Θεῷ. ἐν ἀγαθῇ συνειδήσει ὑπάρχων, μὴ παρεκβαίνων τὸν ὡρισμένον τῆς λειτουργίας αὐτοῦ κανόνα, ἐν σεμνότητι. Οὐ πανταχοῦ, Ἀδελφοί, προσφέρονται θυσίαι ἐνδελεχισμοῦ, ἢ εὐχῶν, ἢ περὶ ἁμαρτίας, καὶ πλημμελείας, ἀλλ' ἢ ἐν Ἱερουσαλὴμ μόνῃ· κἀκεῖ δὲ οὐκ ἐν παντὶ τόπῳ προσφέρεται, ἀλλ' ἔμπροσθεν τοῦ ναοῦ πρὸς τὸ θυσιαστήριον, μωμοσκοπηθὲν τὸ προσφερόμενον διὰ τοῦ Ἀρχιερέως καὶ τῶν προειρημένων Λειτουργῶν. Οἱ οὖν παρὰ τὸ καθῆκον τῆς βουλήσεως αὐτοῦ ποιοῦντές τι, θάνατον τὸ πρόστιμον ἔχουσιν.

(c) *Ibid.* cap. 44. Ἁμαρτία γὰρ οὐ μικρὰ ἡμῖν ἔσται, ἐὰν τοὺς ἀμέμπτως καὶ ὁσίως προσενέγκοντας τὰ δῶρα τῆς Ἐπισκοπῆς ἀποβάλωμεν.

S. Ignatius floruit A.D. 101.

(a) *Epist. ad Ephes.* cap. 5. Μηδεὶς πλανάσθω· ἐὰν μή τις ᾖ ἐντὸς τοῦ θυσιαστηρίου, ὑστερεῖται τοῦ ἄρτου τοῦ Θεοῦ.

(b) *Ibid.* cap. 20. Ὅτι οἱ κατ' ἄνδρα κοινῇ πάντες ἐν χάριτι ἐξ ὀνόματος συντρέχεσθε ἐν Ἰησοῦ Χριστῷ—εἰς τὸ ὑπακούειν ὑμᾶς τῷ Ἐπισκόπῳ καὶ τῷ Πρεσβυτερίῳ ἀπερισπάστῳ διανοία, ἕνα ἄρτον κλῶντες, ὅς ἐστι φάρμακον ἀθανασίας, ἀντίδοτος τοῦ μὴ ἀποθανεῖν, ἀλλὰ ζῆν ἐν Ἰησοῦ Χριστῷ διὰ παντός.

(c) *Epist. ad Magnesios*, cap. 1. Ἄιδω τὰς Ἐκκλησίας, ἐν αἷς ἕνωσιν εὔχομαι σαρκὸς καὶ πνεύματος Ἰησοῦ Χριστοῦ.

a

(d) *Ibid.* cap. 7. Πάντες οὖν ὡς εἰς ἕνα ναὸν συνέρχεσθε Θεοῦ, ὡς ἐπὶ ἕν θυσιαστήριον, ὡς ἐπὶ ἕνα Ἰησοῦν Χριστόν.

(e) *Epist. ad Trallian.* cap. 7. Ὁ ἐντὸς Θυσιαστηρίου ὢν καθαρός ἐστιν.

(f) *Epist. ad Roman.* cap. 7. Οὐχ ἥδομαι τροφῇ φθορᾶς, οὐδὲ ἡδοναῖς τοῦ βίου τούτου· ἄρτον Θεοῦ θέλω, ὅς ἐστι σὰρξ Ἰησοῦ Χριστοῦ τοῦ ἐκ σπέρματος Δαβὶδ· καὶ πόμα Θεοῦ θέλω τὸ Αἷμα Αὐτοῦ, ὅ ἐστιν Ἀγάπη ἄφθαρτος.

(g) *Epist. ad Philadelphen.* cap. 4. Σπουδάζετε οὖν μιᾷ Εὐχαριστίᾳ χρῆσθαι· μία γὰρ σὰρξ τοῦ Κυρίου ἡμῶν Ἰησοῦ Χριστοῦ, καὶ ἓν ποτήριον εἰς ἕνωσιν τοῦ αἵματος Αὐτοῦ, ἓν θυσιαστήριον, ὡς εἷς Ἐπίσκοπος, ἅμα τῷ πρεσβυτερίῳ, καὶ διακόνοις, τοῖς συνδούλοις μου.

(h) *Epist. ad Smyrn.* cap. 7. Εὐχαριστίας καὶ προσευχῆς ἀπέχονται, διὰ τὸ μὴ ὁμολογεῖν, τὴν Εὐχαριστίαν σάρκα εἶναι τοῦ Σωτῆρος ἡμῶν Ἰησοῦ Χριστοῦ, τὴν ὑπὲρ ἁμαρτιῶν ἡμῶν παθοῦσαν, ἣν χρηστότητι ὁ Πατὴρ ἤγειρεν. Οἱ οὖν ἀντιλέγοντες τῇ δωρεᾷ τοῦ Θεοῦ, συζητοῦντες ἀποθνήσκουσιν. Συνέφερεν δὲ αὐτοῖς ἀγαπᾶν, ἵνα καὶ ἀναστῶσιν.

(i) *Ibid.* cap. 8. Ἐκείνη βεβαία Εὐχαριστία ἡγείσθω, ἡ ὑπὸ τὸν Ἐπίσκοπον οὖσα, ἢ ᾧ ἂν αὐτὸς ἐπιτρέψῃ.

S. JUSTINUS MARTYR. floruit A.D. 140.

Edit. Parisiis, A.D. 1742.

(a) *Apologia prima*, pp. 82-3. quondam *secunda* dicta, cap. 65, 66. Προσφέρεται τῷ προεστῶτι τῶν Ἀδελφῶν ἄρτος, καὶ ποτήριον ὕδατος, καὶ κράματος, καὶ οὗτος λαβὼν, αἶνον καὶ δόξαν τῷ Πατρὶ τῶν ὅλων διὰ τοῦ ὀνόματος τοῦ Ὑιοῦ, καὶ τοῦ Πνεύματος τοῦ Ἁγίου, ἀναπέμπει· καὶ Εὐχαριστίαν ὑπὲρ τοῦ κατηξιῶσθαι τούτων παρ' αὐτοῦ ἐπὶ πολὺ ποιεῖται· οὗ συντελέσαντος τὰς εὐχὰς, καὶ τὴν Εὐχαριστίαν, πᾶς ὁ παρὼν λαὸς ἐπευφημεῖ λέγων, Ἀμήν.—Εὐχαριστήσαντος δὲ τοῦ Προεστῶτος, καὶ ἐπευφημήσαντος παντὸς τοῦ λαοῦ, οἱ καλούμενοι παρ' ἡμῶν διάκονοι, διδόασιν ἑκάστῳ τῶν παρόντων μεταλαβεῖν ἀπὸ τοῦ Εὐχαριστηθέντος ἄρτου καὶ οἴνου, καὶ ὕδατος, καὶ τοῖς οὐ παροῦσιν ἀποφέρουσιν· καὶ ἡ τροφὴ αὕτη καλεῖται παρ' ἡμῶν Εὐχαριστία, ἧς οὐδενὶ ἄλλῳ μετασχεῖν ἐξόν ἐστιν, ἢ τῷ πιστεύοντι ἀληθῆ εἶναι τὰ δεδιδαγμένα ὑφ' ἡμῶν, καὶ λουσαμένῳ τὸ ὑπὲρ ἀφέσεως ἁμαρτιῶν καὶ εἰς ἀναγέννησιν λουτρὸν, καὶ οὕτως βιώσαντι, ὡς Χριστὸς παρέδωκεν· οὐ γὰρ ὡς κοινὸν ἄρτον, οὐδὲ κοινὸν πόμα, ταῦτα λαμβάνομεν· ἀλλ' ὃν τρόπον διὰ λόγου Θεοῦ σαρκοποιηθεὶς Ἰησοῦς Χριστός, ὁ Σωτὴρ ἡμῶν, καὶ σάρκα καὶ αἷμα ὑπὲρ σωτηρίας ἡμῶν ἔσχεν· οὕτως καὶ τὴν δι' εὐχῆς λόγου τοῦ παρ' αὐτοῦ εὐχαριστηθεῖσαν τροφὴν, ἐξ ἧς σάρκες καὶ αἷμα κατὰ μεταβολὴν τρέφονται ἡμῶν, ἐκείνου τοῦ σαρκοποιηθέντος Ἰησοῦ καὶ σάρκα καὶ αἷμα ἐδιδάχθημεν εἶναι. Οἱ γὰρ Ἀπόστολοι ἐν τοῖς γινομένοις ἀπ' αὐτῶν ἀπομνημονεύμασιν, ἃ καλεῖται Εὐαγγέλια, οὕτως παρέδωκαν ἐντετάλθαι αὐτοῖς τὸν Ἰησοῦν, λαβόντα ἄρτον, εὐχαριστήσαντα εἰπεῖν, τοῦτο ποιεῖτε εἰς τὴν ἀνάμνησίν μου. τουτέστι τὸ Σῶμά μου· καὶ τὸ ποτήριον ὡμοίως λαβόντα, καὶ εὐχαριστήσαντα εἰπεῖν, τοῦτό ἐστι τὸ αἷμά μου, καὶ μόνοις αὐτοῖς μεταδοῦναι.

(b) *Dialog. cum Tryphone*, p. 137. Ἡ τῆς σεμιδάλεως προσφορὰ ἡ ὑπὲρ τῶν καθαριζομένων ἀπὸ τῆς λέπρας προσφέρεσθαι παραδοθεῖσα, τύπος ἦν τοῦ ἄρτου τῆς Εὐχαριστίας, ὃν εἰς ἀνάμνησιν τοῦ πάθους Ἰησοῦς Χριστὸς Κύριος ἡμῶν παρέδωκε ποιεῖν.

(c) *Mox post.* Περὶ τῶν ἐν παντὶ τόπῳ ὑφ' ἡμῶν τῶν ἐθνῶν προσφερομένων αὐτῷ (Θεῷ) θυσιῶν, τουτέστι τοῦ ἄρτου τῆς Εὐχαριστίας, καὶ τοῦ ποτηρίου ὁμοίως τῆς Εὐχαριστίας, προλέγει τότε εἰπὼν, καὶ τὸ ὄνομα αὐτοῦ δοξάζειν ἡμᾶς. Indicat *Malach.* cap. i. 10, 11.

(d) *Ibid.* pp. 168-9. Ἐν ταύτῃ τῇ προφητείᾳ (viz. Isai. xxxiii. 16.) περὶ τοῦ ἄρτου ὃν παρέδωκεν ἡμῖν ὁ ἡμέτερος Χριστὸς ποιεῖν εἰς ἀνάμνησιν τοῦ τε σωματοποιήσασθαι διὰ τοὺς πιστεύοντας εἰς Αὐτὸν, δι' οὓς καὶ παθητὸς γέγονε· καὶ περὶ τοῦ ποτηρίου, ὃ εἰς ἀνάμνησιν τοῦ αἵματος Αὐτοῦ παρέδωκεν εὐχαριστοῦντας ποιεῖν, φαίνεται.

(e) *Ibid.* pp. 209-10. Πάντας οὖν, οἱ διὰ τοῦ ὀνόματος τούτου θυσίας [a] ἃς παρέδωκεν Ἰησοῦς ὁ Χριστὸς γίνεσθαι, τουτέστιν ἐπὶ τῇ Εὐχαριστίᾳ τοῦ ἄρτου καὶ τοῦ ποτηρίου, τὰς ἐν παντὶ τόπῳ τῆς γῆς γινομένας ὑπὸ τῶν Χριστιανῶν, προλαβὼν ὁ Θεὸς, μαρτυρεῖ εὐαρέστους ὑπάρχειν Αὐτῷ· τὰς δὲ ὑφ' ὑμῶν, καὶ δι' ἐκείνων ὑμῶν τῶν Ἱερέων γινομένας ἀπαναίνεται, λέγων, καὶ τὰς θυσίας ὑμῶν οὐ προσδέξομαι ἐκ τῶν χειρῶν ὑμῶν· διότι ἀπὸ ἀνατολῆς ἡλίου ἕως δυσμῶν, τὸ ὄνομά Μου δεδόξασται, λέγει, ἐν τοῖς ἔθνεσιν. ὑμεῖς δὲ βεβηλοῦτε αὐτὸ καὶ μέχρι νῦν φιλονεικοῦντες λέγετε, ὅτι τὰς μὲν ἐν Ἱερουσαλὴμ ἐπὶ τῶν ἐκεῖ τότε οἰκούντων Ἰσραηλιτῶν καλουμένων, θυσίας οὐ προσδέχεται ὁ Θεὸς, τὰς δὲ διὰ τῶν ἐν τῇ διασπορᾷ τότε δὴ ὄντων ἀπὸ τοῦ γένους ἐκείνου ἀνθρώπων εὐχὰς προσίεσθαι Αὐτὸν εἰρηκέναι, καὶ τὰς εὐχὰς αὐτῶν θυσίας καλεῖν. Ὅτι μὲν οὖν καὶ εὐχαὶ, καὶ εὐχαριστίαι ὑπὸ τῶν ἀξίων γινόμεναι, τέλειαι μόναι, καὶ εὐάρεστοί εἰσιν τῷ Θεῷ θυσίαι, καὶ αὐτός φημι· ταῦτα γὰρ μόνα καὶ Χριστιανοὶ παρέλαβον ποιεῖν, καὶ ἐπ' ἀναμνήσει τῆς τροφῆς αὐτῶν, ξηρᾶς τε, καὶ ὑγρᾶς, ἐν ᾗ καὶ τοῦ πάθους ὃ πέπονθε— μέμνηται.

S. IRENÆUS floruit A.D. 167.

Ed. Paris. 1710.

(a) Lib. i. cap. 13. p. 60. Ποτήρια οἴνῳ κεκραμένα προσποιούμενος εὐχαριστεῖν, καὶ ἐπὶ πλέον ἐκτείνων τὸν λόγον τῆς ἐπικλήσεως, πορφύρεα καὶ ἐρυθρὰ ἀναφαίνεσθαι ποιεῖ· ὡς δοκεῖν τὴν ἀπὸ τῶν ὑπὲρ τὰ ὅλα χάριν τὸ αἷμα τὸ ἑαυτῆς στάζειν ἐν τῷ ἐκείνῳ ποτηρίῳ, διὰ τῆς ἐπικλήσεως αὐτοῦ,

---

[a] It is evident that προσφέροντας, or some such word, is here wanting, or else for πάντας we must read πάσας.

καὶ ὑπεριμείρεσθαι τοὺς παρόντας ἐξ ἐκείνου γεύσασθαι τοῦ πόματος, ἵνα καὶ εἰς αὐτοὺς ἐπομβρήσῃ ἡ διὰ τοῦ μάγου τούτου καλουμένη χάρις.

(b) Lib. iv. cap. 8. p. 237. Sacerdotes autem sunt omnes Domini Apostoli, qui neque agros, neque domos hæreditant hic, sed semper altari et Deo serviunt, de quibus, et Moyses in Deuteronomio, in Benedictione Levi : *Qui dicit patri suo, et matri suæ : non novi te ; et fratres suos non agnovit.*

(c) Lib. iv. cap. 17. p. 247. Quoniam autem non indigens Deus servitute eorum, sed propter ipsos quasdam observantias in Lege præceperit, plenissime Prophetæ indicant. Et rursus quoniam non indiget Deus oblatione hominum, sed propter ipsum qui offerat hominem, manifeste Dominus docuit—si quando enim negligentes eos justitiam, et abstinentes a dilectione Dei videbat, per sacrificia autem et reliquas typicas observantias putantes propitiari Deum, dicebat iis Samuel quidem sic, *Non vult Deus Holocausta, &c.* *Then he cites* Psalm xl. 1 ; Isaiah i. 11, 16—18, *and many other places, and then proceeds,* Ex quibus omnibus manifestum est, quia non sacrificia et holocaustomata quærebat ab iis Deus, sed fidem, et obedientiam, et justitiam propter illorum salutem : *then he cites* Hos. vi. 6, et Dominus noster quidem eadem monebat eos, dicens, *si enim cognovissetis, quid est: Misericordiam volo, et non sacrificium ; nunquam condemnassetis innocentes.* Testimonium quidem reddens (Christus) prophetis, quoniam veritatem prædicabant ; illos autem arguens sua culpa insipientes. Sed et suis discipulis dans consilium, primitias Deo offerre ex suis creaturis, non quasi indigenti, sed ut ipsi nec infructuosi, nec ingrati sint, eum qui ex creatura est panis, accepit, et gratias egit, dicens, *Hoc est corpus meum.* Et calicem similiter, qui est ex ea creatura, quæ est secundum nos, suum sanguinem confessus est, et Novi Testamenti novam docuit oblationem, quam Ecclesia ab Apostolis accipiens, in universo mundo offert Deo, Ei qui alimenta nobis præstat, primitias suorum munerum in Novo Testamento, de quo in duodecim Prophetis Malachias sic præsignificavit ; *he cites* Malachi, i. 10, 11. *and adds,* manifestissime significans per hæc, quoniam prior quidem populus cessabit offerre Deo, omni autem loco sacrificium offeretur Ei, et hoc purum : *Nomen autem ejus glorificatur in Gentibus.*

(d) Lib. iv. cap. 17. p. 249. Quoniam ergo nomen Filii proprium Patris est, et Deo Omnipotenti per Jesum Christum offert Ecclesia, bene ait secundum utraque, *et in omni loco incensum offeretur Nomini meo. Incensum* autem Joannes in Apocalypsi *orationes,* ait, *esse sanctorum.*

(e) Lib. iv. cap. 18. p. 250. Igitur Ecclesiæ oblatio, quam Dominus docuit offerri in universo mundo, purum sacrificium reputatum est apud Deum, et acceptum est Ei : non quod indigeat a nobis sacrificium, sed quoniam is qui offert glorificatur ipse in eo quod offert, si acceptetur munus ejus. Per munus enim erga regem, et honos et affectio ostenditur : quod in omni simplicitate et innocentia Dominus volens nos offerre, prædicavit dicens, *Cum igitur offers munus tuum ad altare, &c. he recites* Matt. v. 23, 24. *and then goes on;* offerre igitur oportet Deo primitias Ejus creaturæ—et non genus oblationum reprobatum est, oblationes enim et illic, oblationes autem et hic : sacrificia in populo, sacrificia et in ecclesia, sed species immutata est tantum, quippe cum jam non a servis, sed a filiis offerantur.—ab initio enim respexit Deus ad munera Abel, quoniam cum simplicitate et justitia offerebat ; super sacrificium autem Cain non respexit, quoniam cum zelo et malitia quæ erat adversus fratrem divisionem habebat in corde.

(f) *Ibid.* Igitur non sacrificia sanctificant hominem, non enim indiget sacrificio Deus ; sed conscientia ejus qui offert sanctificat sacrificium pura existens, et præstat acceptare Deum quasi ab amico —Quoniam igitur cum simplicitate offert Ecclesia, juste munus ejus purum sacrificium apud Deum deputatum est, quemadmodum et Paulus Philippensibus ait, (*he cites* Phil. iv. 18.) Oportet enim nos oblationem Deo facere, et in omnibus gratos inveniri fabricatori Deo, in sententia pura, et fide sine hypocrisi, in spe firma, in dilectione ferventi, primitias earum, quæ sunt Ejus, creaturarum offerentes. Hanc oblationem Ecclesia sola puram offert fabricatori, offerens Ei cum gratiarum actione ex creatura Ejus. Judæi autem jam non offerunt : manus enim eorum sanguine plenæ sunt : non enim receperunt Verbum per quod offertur Deo ; sed neque omnes Hæreticorum Synagogæ. Alii enim alterum præter fabricatorem dicentes Patrem, ideo quæ secundum nos, creaturæ sunt, offerentes Ei, cupidum alieni ostendunt Eum.

Quomodo autem constabit eis, eum panem in quo gratiæ actæ sint corpus esse Domini sui, et calicem sanguinis Ejus, si non ipsum fabricatoris mundi Filium dicant, id est, Verbum Ejus, per quod lignum fructificat, &c.

Quomodo autem rursus dicunt carnem, &c. Gr. Πῶς τὴν σάρκα λέγουσιν εἰς φθορὰν χωρεῖν, καὶ μὴ μετέχειν τῆς ζωῆς, τὴν ἀπὸ τοῦ σώματος τοῦ Κυρίου, καὶ αἵματος Αὐτοῦ τρεφομένην ; ἢ τὴν γνώμην ἀλλαξάτωσαν, ἢ τὸ προσφέρειν τὰ εἰρημένα παραιτείσθωσαν· ἡμῶν σύμφωνος ἡ γνώμη τῇ Εὐχαριστίᾳ, καὶ ἡ Εὐχαριστία βεβαιοῖ τὴν γνώμην (nostram, addit Interpres) προσφέρομεν δὲ Αὐτῷ τὰ ἴδια—ὡς γὰρ ἀπὸ γῆς ἄρτος προσλαμβανόμενος τὴν ἐπίκλησιν τοῦ Θεοῦ, οὐκέτι κοινὸς ἄρτος ἐστὶν, ἀλλ Εὐχαριστία ἐκ δύο πραγμάτων συνεστηκυῖα, ἐπιγείου τε, καὶ οὐρανίου· οὕτως καὶ τὰ σώματα ἡμῶν μεταλαμβάνοντα Εὐχαριστίας μηκέτι εἶναι φθαρτὰ τὴν ἐλπίδα τῆς εἰς αἰῶνας ἀναστάσεως ἔχοντα.—Offerimus autem Ei, non quasi indigenti, sed gratias agentes Dominationi Ejus, et sanctificantes creaturam : quemadmodum enim Deus non indiget eorum quæ a nobis sunt, sic nos indigemus offerre aliquid Deo— Sicut igitur non his indigens, attamen a nobis propter nos fieri vult, ne simus infructuosi ; ita id ipsum Verbum dedit populo præceptum faciendarum oblationum, quamvis non indigeret eis, ut discerent Deo servire ; sic et ideo nos offerre vult munus ad altare frequenter, sine intermissione. Est ergo altare in cœlis (illuc enim preces nostræ, et oblationes nostræ diriguntur) et templum, quemadmodum Joannes in Apocalypsi ait, (*he cites*, Rev. xxi. 3.)

(f) Lib. iv. cap. 33. p. 270. Quomodo autem juste Dominus, si alterius Patris existit, hujus conditionis, quæ est secundum nos, accipiens panem, suum corpus esse confitebatur, et temperamentum calicis suum sanguinem confirmavit ?

(g) Lib. v. cap. 2. Vani autem omni modo, qui universam dispositionem Dei contemnunt, et carnis salutem negant, et regenerationem ejus spernunt, dicentes, non eam capacem esse incorruptibilitatis : si autem non salvetur hæc, videlicet, nec Dominus sanguine suo redemit nos, neque calix Eucharistiæ communicatio sanguinis Ejus est, neque panis, quem frangimus, communicatio corporis Ejus est.

Μέλη αὐτοῦ ἐσμὲν, καὶ διὰ τῆς κτίσεως τρεφόμεθα, τὴν δὲ κτίσιν ἡμῖν Αὐτὸς παρέχει—τὸ ἀπὸ τῆς κτίσεως ποτήριον αἷμα ἴδιον ὡμολόγησε, ἐξ οὗ τὸ ἡμέτερον δεύει αἷμα, καὶ τὸν ἀπὸ τῆς κτίσεως ἄρτον ἴδιον σῶμα διεβεβαιώσατο, ἀφ' οὗ τὰ ἡμέτερα αὔξει σώματα. Ὁπότε οὖν καὶ τὸ κεκραμένον ποτήριον, καὶ ὁ γεγονὼς ἄρτος ἐπιδέχεται τὸν λόγον τοῦ Θεοῦ, καὶ γίνεται ἡ Εὐχαριστία σῶμα Χριστοῦ, ἐκ τούτων δὲ αὔξει, καὶ συνίσταται ἡ τῆς σαρκὸς ἡμῶν ὑπόστασις· πῶς δεκτικὴν μὴ εἶναι λέγουσι τὴν σάρκα τῆς δωρεᾶς τοῦ Θεοῦ, ἥτις ἐςτὶ ζωὴ αἰώνιος, τὴν ἀπὸ τοῦ σώματος καὶ αἵματος τοῦ Κυρίου τρεφομένην, καὶ μέλος Αὐτοῦ ὑπάρχουσαν·—καὶ ὅνπερ τρόπον τὸ ξύλον τῆς ἀμπέλου κλιθὲν εἰς τὴν γῆν τῷ ἰδίῳ καιρῷ ἐκαρποφόρησε, καὶ ὁ κόκκος τοῦ σίτου πεσὼν εἰς τὴν γῆν, καὶ διαλυθεὶς, πολλοστὸς ἐγέρθη διὰ τοῦ Πνεύματος τοῦ Θεοῦ, ἔπειτα δὲ διὰ τῆς σοφίας τοῦ Θεοῦ εἰς χρῆσιν ἐλθόντα ἀνθρώπων, καὶ προσλαμβανόμενα τὸν λόγον τοῦ Θεοῦ Εὐχαριστία γίνεται, ὅπερ ἐστὶ σῶμα καὶ αἷμα τοῦ Χριστοῦ· οὕτως καὶ τὰ ἡμέτερα σώματα ἐξ αὐτῆς τρεφόμενα, καὶ τεθέντα εἰς τὴν γῆν, καὶ διαλυθέντα ἐν αὐτῇ ἀναστήσεται ἐν τῷ ἰδίῳ καιρῷ, τοῦ λόγου τοῦ Θεοῦ τὴν ἔγερσιν αὐτοῖς χαριζομένου εἰς δόξαν Θεοῦ καὶ Πατρός.

CLEMENS ALEXANDRINUS floruit A.D. 192.

Ed. Oxon. 1715.

(a) *Pædagog.* lib. i. cap. 6. p. 123. Ὁ λόγος τὰ πάντα τῷ νηπίῳ, καὶ πατήρ, καὶ μήτηρ, καὶ παιδαγωγὸς, καὶ τροφεύς. Φάγεσθε μοῦ, φησὶ, τὴν σάρκα, καὶ πίεσθε μοῦ τὸ αἷμα. [ἐναργὲς τῆς πίστεως, καὶ τῆς ἐπαγγελίας τὸ πότιμον ἀλληγορῶν[b]] ἀποδύσασθαι ἡμῖν τὴν παλαιὰν καὶ σαρκικὴν ἐγκελεύεται φθορὰν, ὥσπερ καὶ τὴν παλαιὰν τροφήν· καινῆς δὲ ἄλλης τοῦ Χριστοῦ διαίτης μεταλαμβάνοντας, ἐκεῖνον, εἰ δυνατὸν, ἀναλαμβάνοντας, ἐν ἑαυτοῖς ἀποτίθεσθαι, καὶ τὸν Σωτῆρα ἐνστερνίζεσθαι.

(b) *Ibid.* lib. ii. cap. 2. p. 177. Διττὸν δὲ τὸ αἷμα τοῦ Κυρίου· τὸ μὲν γάρ ἐστιν αὐτοῦ σαρκικὸν, ᾧ τῆς φθορᾶς λελυτρώμεθα· τὸ δὲ, πνευματικὸν, τουτεστιν ᾧ κεχρίσμεθα· καὶ τοῦτεστι πιεῖν τὸ αἷμα τοῦ Ἰησοῦ, τῆς κυριακῆς μεταλαμβάνειν ἀφθαρσίας· ἰσχὺς δὲ τοῦ λόγου τό πνεῦμα, ὡς αἷμα σαρκὸς· ἀναλόγως τοίνυν κίρναται ὁ μὲν οἶνος τῷ ὕδατι, τῷ δὲ ἀνθρώπῳ τὸ πνεῦμα. καὶ τὸ μὲν εἰς πίστιν (lege πόσιν) εὐωχεῖ τὸ κρᾶμα, τὸ δὲ εἰς ἀφθαρσίαν ὁδηγεῖ τὸ πνεῦμα· ἡ δὲ ἀμφοῖν αὖθις κρᾶσις, ποτοῦ τε καὶ λόγου, Εὐχαριστία κέκληται, χάρις ἐπαινουμένη καὶ καλή· ἧς οἱ κατὰ πίστιν μεταλαμβάνοντες, ἁγιάζονται καὶ σῶμα καὶ ψυχήν.

(c) *Ibid.* p. 186. Εὖ γὰρ ἴστε, μετέλαβεν οἴνου καὶ Αὐτὸς (Χριστὸς)· καὶ γὰρ ἄνθρωπος καὶ Αὐτὸς καὶ εὐλόγησέν γε τὸν οἶνον, εἰπὼν, λάβετε, πίετε, τοῦτό Μου ἐστὶ τὸ αἷμα, αἷμα τῆς ἀμπέλου· τὸν λόγον τὸν περὶ πολλῶν ἐκχεόμενον εἰς ἄφεσιν ἁμαρτιῶν, εὐφροσύνης ἅγιον ἀλληγορεῖ νᾶμα.

(d) *Stromat.* lib. i. p. 343. Ἄρτον λαβὼν (Χριστὸς) πρῶτον ἐλάλησε, καὶ εὐχαρίστησεν· εἶτα κλάσας τὸν ἄρτον προέθηκεν, ἵνα δὴ φάγωμεν λογικῶς.

(e) *Ibid.* lib. iv. p. 637. Μελχισεδὲκ, βασιλεὺς Σαλὴμ, ὁ ἱερεὺς τοῦ Θεοῦ τοῦ ὑψίστου ὁ τὸν οἶνον καὶ τὸν ἄρτον, τὴν ἡγιασμένην διδοὺς τροφὴν, εἰς τύπον Εὐχαριστίας.

(f) *Ibid.* lib. vii. p. 848. Καὶ γάρ ἐστιν ἡ θυσία τῆς Ἐκκλησίας, λόγος ἀπὸ τῶν ἁγίων ψυχῶν ἀναθυμιώμενος, ἐκκαλυπτομένης ἅμα τῆς θυσίας, καὶ τῆς διανοίας ἁπάσης τῷ Θεῷ.

(g) In *Quis Dives salvetur*, p. 956. Καὶ μέλλων σπένδεσθαι, καὶ λύτρον Ἑαυτὸν ἐπιδιδοὺς, καινὴν ἡμῖν Διαθήκην καταλιμπάνει.

TERTULLIANUS floruit A.D. 192.

Ed. Paris. 1664.

(a) *Apologet.* cap. 39. p. 31. Modicam unusquisque stipem menstrua die, vel cum velit, et si modo velit, et si modo possit, apponit, nam nemo compellitur, sed sponte confert. Hæc quasi deposita pietatis sunt.

(b) *De Spectaculis*, xxv. p. 83. Quale est ex ore, quo Amen in Sanctum protuleris, gladiatori testimonium reddere?

---

[b] [The words inclosed in brackets are found in Heinsius' edition.]

(c) *De Corona Militis*, cap. 3. p. 102. Oblationes pro defunctis, pro natalitiis annua die facimus.

(d) *De Exhortatione Castitatis*, cap. 11. p. 523. Pro cujus spiritu postulas, pro qua oblationes reddis—et offeres pro duabus? et commendabis illas duas per sacerdotem?

(e) *De Cultu Fœminarum*, lib. ii. cap. 11. p. 159. Vobis autem (mulieribus) nulla procedendi causa non tetrica; aut imbecillus aliqui e fratribus visitandus; aut sacrificium offertur, aut Dei sermo administratur.

(f) *De velandis Virginibus*, cap. 9. p. 178. Non permittitur mulieri in Ecclesia loqui, sed nec docere, nec tinguere, nec offerre, neque ullius virilis muneris, nedum sacerdotalis officii sortem sibi vindicare.

(g) *De Oratione*, cap. 6. p. 131. Quam eleganter divina sapientia ordinem orationis instruxit, ut post cœlestia, id est, post Dei nomen, Dei voluntatem, et Dei regnum, terrenis quoque necessitatibus petitioni locum faceret?—Quanquam *panem nostrum quotidianum da nobis hodie*, spiritaliter potius intelligamus. Christus enim panis noster est—tum quod et corpus Ejus in pane censetur, *hoc est corpus meum*. Itaque petendo panem quotidianum, perpetuitatem postulamus in Christo, et individuitatem a corpore Ejus.

(h) *Ibid.* cap. 10. p. 133. Ne prius ascendamus ad Dei altare, quam si quid discordiæ vel offensæ cum fratribus contraxerimus, resolvamus.

(i) *Ibid.* cap. 14. p. 135. Stationum diebus, non putant plerique sacrificiorum orationibus interveniendum, quod statio solvenda sit accepto corpore Domini: ergo devotum Deo obsequium Eucharistia resolvit? an magis Deo obligat? Nonne solennior erit statio tua, si ad aram Dei steteris? Accepto corpore Domini, et reservato, utrumque salvum est, et participatio sacrificii, et executio officii.

(k) *De Patientia*, cap. 12. p. 147. Nemo convulsus animum in fratrem suum, munus apud altare perficiet, nisi prius reconciliando fratri reversus ad patientiam fuerit.

(l) *Adversus Judæos*, cap. 5. p. 187. Sacrificia terrenarum oblationum, et spiritualium sacrificiorum prædicta ostendimus. Et quidem a primordio majoris filii, id est Israel, terrena fuisse in Cain præostensa sacrificia: et minoris filii Abel, id est, populi nostri, sacrificia diversa monstrata; namque major natu Cain de fructu terræ obtulit munera Deo; minor vero filius Abel de fructu ovium suarum. Respexit Deus in Abel et in munera ejus; in Cain autem et in munera ejus non respexit.—Ex hoc igitur duplicia duorum populorum sacrificia præostensa jam tunc a primordio animadvertimus.

(m) *De Resurrectione Carnis*, cap. 8. p. 330. Caro abluitur, ut anima emaculetur; caro ungitur, ut anima consecretur; caro signatur, ut et anima muniatur; caro manus impositione adumbratur, ut et anima spiritu illuminetur; caro corpore et sanguine Christi vescitur, ut et anima de Deo saginetur. Non possunt ergo separari in mercede, quas opera conjungit.

(n) *Adversus Marcion.* lib. i. cap. 14. p. 372. Usque nunc nec aquam reprobavit Creatoris, qua suos abluit; nec oleum, quo suos ungit; nec mellis et lactis societatem, qua suos infantat; nec panem, quo ipsum corpus suum repræsentat; etiam in sacramentis propriis egens mendicitatibus Creatoris.

(o) *Ibid.* lib. iv. c. 40. p. 457-8. Acceptum panem et distributum discipulis, corpus illum suum fecit, hoc est, Corpus Meum dicendo, id est, figura Corporis Mei.

(p) *Ibid. He cites* Genesis xlix. 11. Lavabit in vino stolam suam —ita et nunc sanguinem suum in vino consecravit, qui tunc vinum in sanguine figuravit.

(q) *Ad Scapulam,* cap. 2. p. 69. Sacrificamus pro salute imperatoris sed Deo nostro et ipsius, sed quo modo præcepit Deus, pura prece. Non enim eget Deus, conditor universitatis, odoris aut sanguinis alicujus.

(r) *De Præscriptione,* cap. 40. p. 216. Qui (diabolus) ipsas quoque res sacramentorum divinorum, idolorum mysteriis æmulatur. Tinguit et ipse quosdam, utique credentes, et fideles suos: expositionem peccatorum de lavacro repromittit; et si adhuc memini, Mithra signat illic in fronte milites suos; celebrat et panis oblationem.

AMMONIUS ALEXANDRINUS floruit A.D. 220.

Apud Catenam PP. Græcorum, Ed. Corderio, p. 89, in Joan. iii. 5.

(a) Τὸ αἰσθητὸν ὕδωρ πρὸς θείαν ἀναστοιχειοῦται δύναμιν, καὶ ἁγιάζει τοὺς ἐν οἷς ἂν γένηται· τὸ ὕδωρ ἐπινοίᾳ μόνον διαφορὰν ἔχει πρὸς τὸ Πνεῦμα, ἐπεὶ ταὐτόν ἐστι τῇ ἐνεργείᾳ.

(b) In Catena in Joan. vi. 64. p. 200. Πνεῦμα ὧδε καλεῖ τὴν σάρκα πεπληρωμένην τῆς ζωοποιοῦ Πνεύματος ἐνεργείας.

ORIGENES floruit A.D. 230.

Ed. Paris. 1733.

(a) *Contra Celsum,* lib. viii. cap. 33. tom. i. p. 766. Κέλσος μὲν, ὡς ἀγνοῶν Θεὸν, τὰ χαριστήρια Δαίμοσιν ἀποδιδότω· ἡμεῖς δὲ, τῷ τοῦ πάντος Δημιουργῷ εὐχαριστοῦντες, καὶ τοὺς μετ' εὐχαριστίας καὶ εὐχῆς ἐπὶ τοῖς δοθεῖσι προσαγομένους ἄρτους ἐσθίομεν, σῶμα γενομένους διὰ τὴν εὐχὴν ἅγιόν τι, καὶ ἁγιάζον τοὺς μεθ' ὑγιοῦς προθέσεως αὐτῷ χρωμένους. Ἀλλὰ δὲ ἀπαρχὰς Κέλσος μὲν Δαιμονίοις ἀνατιθέναι βούλεται· ἡμεῖς δὲ τῷ εἰπόντι, βλαστησάτω ἡ γῆ (he cites Gen. i. 11.) Ὧι δὲ τὰς ἀπαρχὰς ἀποδίδομεν,

b

Τούτῳ καὶ τὰς εὐχὰς ἀναπέμπομεν ἔχοντες Ἀρχιερέα μέγαν—καὶ κρατοῦμεν τῆς ὁμολογίας, ἕως ἂν ζῶμεν.

(aa) *In Exod. Homil.* 13. tom. ii. p. 176. Cum suscipitis corpus Domini, cum omni cautela et veneratione servatis, ne ex eo parum quid decidat, ne consecrati muneris aliquid dilabatur.

(b) *In Leviticum Homil.* 13. tom. ii. p. 255. Sed si referantur hæc ad mysterii magnitudinem, invenies commemorationem istam habere ingentis repropitiationis effectum. Si redeas ad illum panem, qui de cœlo descendit, et dat huic mundo vitam ; illum panem propositionis, quem proposuit Deus propitiationem per fidem in sanguine Ejus ; et si respicias ad illam commemorationem, de qua dicit Dominus, *Hoc facite in meam commemorationem ;* invenies quod ista est commemoratio sola, quæ propitium facit hominibus Deum.

(c) *In Numeros,* Homil. 7. tom. ii. p. 290. Antea in ænigmate fuit Baptismus in nube, et in mari, nunc autem in specie regeneratio est in aqua, et in Spiritu Sancto : tunc in ænigmate erat Manna cibus ; nunc autem in specie caro Verbi Dei est verus cibus, sicut et Ipse dixit, quia *Caro mea est vere cibus, et sanguis meus vere est potus.*

(d) *Ibid.* Homil. 11. tom. ii. p. 303. Deo offerri dicit quod sacerdotibus datur. Et hoc est quod docemur ex lege, quia nemo licite nec legitime utatur fructibus quos terra produxit—nisi ex singulis quibusque Deo primitiæ, id est, sacerdotibus offerantur ; hanc ergo legem observari etiam secundum literam, sicut et alia nonnulla, necessarium puto.

(e) *Ibid.* p. 305. Decet, et utile est etiam sacerdotibus Evangelii offerri primitias : ita enim et Dominus disposuit, ut qui Evangelium annunciant de Evangelio vivant, et qui altari deserviunt, de altari participent. Et sicut hoc dignum et decens est, sic e contrario et indecens et indignum existimo et impium, ut is qui Deum colit, et ingreditur Ecclesiam Dei, qui scit sacerdotes et ministros adsistere altari—de fructibus terræ quos dat Deus, non offerat primitias sacerdotibus.

(f) *In Matthæum,* tom. iii. p. 498. Οὐ τὸ εἰσερχόμενον εἰς τὸ στόμα ἁγιάζει τὸν ἄνθρωπον, κἂν ὑπὸ τῶν ἀκεραιοτέρων νομίζηται ἁγιάζειν ὁ ὀνομαζόμενος ἄρτος τοῦ Κυρίου.

p. 499. Τὸ ἁγιαζόμενον βρῶμα κατὰ τὴν ἐπιγενομένην αὐτῷ εὐχὴν αὐτῷ, κατὰ τὴν ἀναλογίαν τῆς πίστεως, ὠφέλιμον γίνεται, καὶ τῆς τοῦ νοῦ αἴτιον διαλάμψεως—καὶ οὐχ ἡ ὕλη τοῦ ἄρτου, ἀλλ᾽ ὁ ἐπ᾽ αὐτῷ εἰρημένος λόγος ἐστὶν ὁ ὠφελῶν τὸν μὴ ἀναξίως τοῦ Κυρίου ἐσθίοντα αὐτόν.

(g) *Apud Bulenger. contra Casaubon.* Diatribe iii. p. 177. Ed. Lugdun. 1617. Καὶ γὰρ ὁ τοῦ ἄρτου μετέχων, τοῦ Σώματος τοῦ Κυρίου μεταλαμβάνει· οὐ γὰρ προσέχομεν τῇ φύσει τῶν αἰσθητῶν προκειμένων, ἀλλ᾽

ἀνάγομεν τὴν ψυχὴν διὰ πίστεως ἐπὶ τὸ τοῦ Λόγου Σῶμα· οὐ γὰρ εἶπε, τοῦτο
ἐστι σύμβολον, ἀλλὰ τοῦτό ἐστι τὸ Σῶμα· δεικτικῶς, ἵνα μὴ νομίσῃ τὶς τύπον
εἶναι τὰ φαινόμενα.

S. CYPRIANUS floruit A.D. 248.

Ed. Paris. 1726.

(a) *Testimoniorum adversus Judæos*, lib. i. cap. 16. p. 280. Quod
sacrificium vetus evacuaretur, et novum celebraretur [legitur] apud
Malachiam, *Non est mihi voluntas circa vos*, &c.

(b) *De Unitate Ecclesiæ*, p. 196. *In domo una comedetur, non eji-
cietis de domo carnem foras.* Caro Christi, et sanctum Domini ejici
foras non potest, nec alia ulla credentibus præter unam Ecclesiam
domus est.

(c) *Ibid.* p. 198. Ad sacrificium cum dissensione venientem revocat
[Christus] ab altari, et jubet prius concordare cum fratre, tunc cum
pace redeuntem Deo munus offerre.—Quam sibi igitur pacem pro-
mittunt inimici fratrum se credunt, quæ sacrificia celebrare æmuli
sacerdotum? An secum esse Christum, cum collecti fuerint, opinantur,
qui extra Christi ecclesiam colliguntur?

(d) *Ibid.* p. 200. Hostis altaris, adversus sacrificium Christi
rebellis—contemptis episcopis, et Dei sacerdotibus derelictis, consti-
tuere audet aliud altare, precem alteram illicitis vocibus facere,
Dominicæ hostiæ veritatem per falsa sacrificia profanare.

(e) *De Lapsis*, p. 186. A diaboli aris revertentes ad sanctum
Domini sordidis et infectis nidore manibus accedunt. Mortiferos
idolorum cibos adhuc pene ructantes, exhalantibus etiam nunc scelus
suum faucibus et contagia funesta redolentibus, Domini corpus inva-
dunt. (*He cites* Levit. vi. 20; xxii. 3. 1 Cor. x. 21; xi. 27.)
Spretis his omnibus atque contemptis; ante expiata delicta, ante
exomologesin factam criminis, ante purgatam conscientiam sacrificio
et manu sacerdotis, ante offensam placatam indignantis Domini et
minantis, vis infertur corpori Ejus et sanguini, atque plus modo in
Dominum manibus atque ore delinquunt, quam cum Dominum nega-
verunt: pacem putant esse, quam quidam verbis fallacibus venditant.

(f) *Ibid.* p. 189. Et quidem alius, quia et ipse maculatus sacrificio
a sacerdote celebrato partem cum cæteris ausus est latenter accipere,
sanctum Domini edere et contrectare non potuit: cinerem ferre se,
apertis manibus, invenit. Documento unius ostensum est Dominum
recedere cum negatur, nec immerentibus ad salutem prodesse quod
sumitur, quando gratia salutaris in cinerem, sanctitate fugiente, mutatur.

(g) *De Oratione Dominica*, p. 209. *Panem nostrum quotidianum da nobis hodie.* Quod potest et spiritaliter et simpliciter intelligi—nam panis vitæ Christus est; et panis hic omnium non est, sed noster est; et quo modo dicimus *Pater noster,* quia intelligentium et credentium Pater est, sic et panem *nostrum* vocamus, quia Christus eorum, qui corpus Ejus contingunt, panis est. Hunc autem panem dari nobis quotidie postulamus, ne qui in Christo sumus, et Eucharistiam quotidie ad cibum salutis accipimus, intercedente aliquo graviore delicto, dum abstenti et non communicantes a cœlesti pane prohibemur, a Christi corpore separemur, Ipso prædicante et monente, *Ego sum panis vitæ, &c., siquis ederit de meo pane, &c. Panis autem quem Ego dedero caro mea est pro sæculi vita.* Quando ergo dicit, *in æternum vivere siquis ederit de Ejus pane,* ut manifestum est eos vivere, qui corpus Ejus attingunt et Eucharistiam jure communicationis accipiunt; ita contra timendum est, et orandum, ne dum quis abstentus separatur a Christi corpore, procul remaneat a salute, comminante Ipso, et dicente; *nisi ederitis carnem Filii Hominis,* &c. et ideo panem nostrum, id est, Christum, dari nobis quotidie petimus, ut qui in Christo manemus, et vivimus, a sanctificatione Ejus et corpore non recedamus: potest vero et sic intelligi, ut cibum nobis tantum petamus, et victum.

(h) *De Opere et Eleemosynis,* p. 242. Locuples et dives es, et Dominicum celebrare te credis, quæ corban omnino non respicis, quæ in Dominicum sine sacrificio venis, quæ partem de sacrificio quod pauper obtulit, sumis?

(i) *Epistola* lxvi. p. 114. Singuli divino sacerdotio honorati et in clerico ministerio constituti non nisi altari et sacrificiis deservire, et precibus atque orationibus vacare debent. (*et pag. proxima.*) Episcopi antecessores nostri (hoc) salubriter providentes censuerunt, ne quis frater excedens ad tutelam vel curam clericum nominaret, ac siquis hoc fecisset, non offerretur pro eo, nec sacrificium pro dormitione ejus celebraretur.

(kk) *Epist. Ibid.* p. 114. Neque enim apud altare Dei meretur nominari in sacerdotum prece, qui ab altari sacerdotes et ministros voluit avocare.

(k) *Epist.* iv. p. 9.—ita ut presbyteri quoque, qui illic apud confessores offerunt, singuli cum singulis diaconis per vices alternent; quia et personarum mutatio, et vicissitudo convenientium minuit invidiam.

(l) *Epist.* liv. p. 78. Episcopatus nostri honor grandis et gloria est, pacem dedisse martyribus, ut sacerdotes, qui sacrificia Dei quotidie celebramus, hostias Deo et victimas præparemus.—ut quos excitamus, et hortamur ad prælium, non inermes et nudos relinquamus, sed protectione corporis et sanguinis Christi muniamus; et cum ad hoc fiat Eucharistia, ut possit accipientibus esse tutela.—nam quomodo docemus aut provocamus eos in confessione Nominis sanguinem suum fundere, si eis militaturis Christi sanguinem denegamus?

(m) *Epist.* lxiii. p. 104. Quidam vel ignoranter vel simpliciter in calice Dominico sanctificando et plebi ministrando non hoc faciunt, quod Jesus Christus Dominus et Deus noster sacrificii hujus auctor et doctor fecit et docuit.—Quando aliquid, Deo inspirante et mandante præcipitur, necesse est Domino servus fidelis obtemperet. Admonitos autem nos scias, ut in calice offerendo Dominica traditio servetur, neque aliud fiat a nobis, quam quod pro nobis Dominus prior fecerit, ut calix, qui in commemoratione Ejus offertur, mixtus vino offeratur.—Nec potest videri sanguis Ejus, quo redempti et vivificati sumus, esse in calice, quando vinum desit calici.—In sacerdote Melchisedec sacrificii Dominici sacramentum præfiguratum videmus, secundum quod Scriptura divina testatur et dicit ; *et Melchisedec rex Salem protulit panem et vinum, fuit autem sacerdos Dei summi, et benedixit Abraham ;* quod autem Melchisedec typum Christi portaret, declarat in Psalmis Spiritus Sanctus, ex persona Patris ad Filium dicens, *Tu es sacerdos in æternum secundum ordinem Melchisedec.* Qui ordo utique hic est de sacrificio illo veniens et inde descendens, quod Melchisedec sacerdos Dei summi fuit, quod panem et vinum obtulit, quod Abraham benedixit. Nam quis magis sacerdos Dei summi, quam Dominus noster Jesus Christus, qui sacrificium Deo Patri obtulit, et obtulit hoc idem quod Melchisedec obtulerat, id est, panem et vinum, suum scilicet corpus et sanguinem ? et circa Abraham benedictio illa præcedens ad nostrum populum pertinebat.—Ut ergo in Genesi per Melchisedec sacerdotem benedictio circa Abraham posset rite celebrari, præcedit ante imago sacrificii Christi, in pane et vino scilicet constituta ; quam rem perficiens et adimplens Dominus, panem et calicem mixtum vino obtulit, et Qui est plenitudo veritatis veritatem præfiguratæ imaginis adimplevit. Sed et per Salomonem Spritus Sanctus typum Dominici sacrificii ante præmonstrat immolatæ hostiæ panis et vini, sed et altaris, et apostolorum faciens mentionem : *Sapientia,* inquit, *ædificavit sibi domum,* (*he cites the five first verses of the ninth chapter of Proverbs.*) Vinum *mixtum* declarat, id est, calicem Domini aqua et vino mixtum prophetica voce prænuntiat, ut appareat in passione Dominica id esse gestum, quod fuerat ante prædictum.—*In the next page he cites the words of the institution of the Eucharist, and adds,* Unde apparet sanguinem Christi non offerri, si desit vinum calici, nec sacrificium dominicum legitima sanctificatione celebrari, nisi oblatio et sacrificium nostrum respondeat passioni. Quomodo autem de creatura vitis novum vinum cum Christo in regno Patris bibemus, si in sacrificio Dei Patris et Christi vinum non offerimus ?—Cujus rei sacramentum nec in Psalmis tacet Spiritus Sanctus faciens mentionem Dominici calicis, et dicens, *calix tuus inebrians, perquam optimus:* calix autem qui *inebriat* vino utique mixtus est—addidit *perquam optimus,* quod scilicet calix Dominicus sic bibentes inebriat, ut sobrios faciat, ut mentes ad spiritalem sapientiam redigat—ut mæstum pectus, ac triste, quod prius peccatis augentibus premebatur, divinæ indulgentiæ lætitia resolvatur ; quod tunc demum potest lætificare in ecclesia Domini bibentem, si quod bibitur Dominicam teneat veritatem.— Videmus in aqua populum intelligi, in vino verò ostendi sanguinem Christi ; quando autem in calice vino aqua miscetur, Christo populus adunatur.—Sic autem in sanctificando calice Domini offerri aqua sola non potest, quomodo nec vinum solum potest. Nam si vinum tantum quis offerat, sanguis Christi incipit esse sine nobis ; si vero aqua sit sola, plebs incipit esse sine Christo.—Si in sacrificio quod Christus obtulit, non nisi Christus sequendus est, utique id nos obaudire et facere oportet, quod Christus fecit, et quod faciendum esse mandavit : —quod si nec minima de mandatis Dominicis licet solvere, quanto magis tam magna, tam grandia, tam ad ipsum Dominicæ passionis et nostræ redemptionis sacramentum pertinentia fas non est infringere, aut in aliud quam quod divinitus institutum sit, humana traditione mutare. Nam si Jesus Christus Dominus et Deus noster Ipse est summus sacerdos Dei Patris, et sacrificium Patri Seipsum primus obtulit, et hoc fieri in sui commemorationem præcepit, utique ille sacerdos vice Christi vere fungitur, qui id quod Christus fecit, imitatur ; et *sacrificium verum et plenum* tunc offert in ecclesia Deo Patri, si sic incipiat offerre, secundum quod Ipsum Christum videat obtulisse. Cæterum omnis religionis et veritatis disciplina subvertitur, nisi id quod spiritaliter præcipitur fideliter reservetur, nisi si in sacrificiis matutinis hoc quis veretur, ne per saporem vini redoleat sanguinem Christi. Sic ergo incipit et a passione Christi in persecutionibus fraternitas retardari, dum in oblationibus discit de sanguine Ejus et cruore confundi.—At enim non mane sed post cœnam, mixtum calicem obtulit Dominus. Numquid ergo Dominicum post cœnam celebrare debemus, ut sic mixtum calicem frequentandis Dominicis offeramus? Christum offerre oportebat circa vesperam diei, ut hora ipsa sacrificii ostenderet occasum, et vesperam mundi, sicut in Exodo scriptum est, (*he cites* Exod. xii. 6.) Nos autem resurrectionem Domini mane celebramus ; et quia passionis Ejus mentionem in sacrificiis omnibus facimus (passio est enim Domini sacrificium quod offerimus) nihil aliud quam quod Ille fecit, facere debemus, (*he cites* 1 Cor. xi. 26.) Quotiescunque ergo calicem in commemorationem Domini et passionis Ejus offerimus, id quod constat Dominum fecisse faciamus.—Nobis vero non poterit ignosci, qui nunc a Domino admoniti et instructi sumus, ut calicem Dominicum vino mixtum, secundum quod Dominus obtulit, offeramus.—Religioni igitur nostræ congruit, et timori, et ipsi loco, atque officio sacerdotii nostri—in Dominico calice miscendo et offerendo custodire traditionis Dominicæ veritatem.

(n) *Epist.* lxviii. p. 115. A concilio plurimorum sacerdotum qui præsentes eramus sententiam retulerit (legatus) non posse a quoquam nostrûm sibi communicari qui, episcopo Cornelio in Catholica Ecclesia de Dei judicio, et cleri ac plebis suffragio ordinato, profanum altare erigere, et adulteram cathedram collocare, et sacrilega contra verum sacerdotem sacrificia offerre tentaverit.

(o) *Epist.* lxxiii. p. 130. Quid ergo—quia Novatianus altare collocare, et sacrificia offerre contra fas nititur, ab altari et sacrificiis cessare nos oportet, ne paria et similia cum illo celebrare videamur? vanum prorsus, et stultum est, ut quia Novatianus éxtra Ecclesiam vindicat sibi veritatis imaginem, relinquamus Ecclesiæ veritatem.

MAGNES floruit A.D. 350.

Apud Bibliothecam Vett. PP. Ed. Galland. tom. iii. p. 541.

Adversus Theosthenem, οὐκ ἐστὶν Εὐχαριστία τύπος τοῦ σώματος καὶ τοῦ αἵματος, ὥσπερ τίνες ἐρραψώδησαν πεπηρωμένοι τὸν νοῦν, μᾶλλον δὲ σῶμα καὶ αἷμα.

EUSEBIUS CÆSARIENSIS floruit A.D. 315.

Ed. Zimmerman, 1822.

(a) *Histor. Eccl.* lib. vi. cap. 43. p. 471. Ποιήσας γὰρ τὰς προσφορὰς, καὶ διανέμων ἑκάστῳ τὸ μέρος—ἀντὶ τοῦ εἰπεῖν λαμβάνοντα τὸν ἄρτον ἐκεῖνον τὸ 'Αμὴν, οὐκέτι ἀνήξω πρὸς Κορνήλιον λέγει.

(b) *De Laudibus Constantini,* p. 1221. 'Αναίμους δὲ καὶ λογικὰς θυσίας τὰς δι' εὐχῶν καὶ ἀπορρήτου θεολογίας τοῖς αὐτοῦ θιασώταις, τὶς ἐπιτελεῖν παρέδωκεν ἄλλος, ἢ μόνος ὁ ἡμέτερος Σωτὴρ ; διὸ ἐπὶ τῆς καθ' ὅλης ἀνθρώπων οἰκουμένης, θυσιαστήρια συνέστη, 'Εκκλησιῶν τε ἀφιερώματα, νοερῶν τε καὶ λογικῶν θυσιῶν ἱεροπρεπεῖς λειτουργίαι.

(c) *De vita Constantini,* lib. iv. cap. 45. p. 1022. Οἱ δὲ μὴ διὰ τούτων χωρεῖν οἷοί τε, θυσίαις ἀναίμοις καὶ μυστικαῖς ἱερουργίαις τὸ θεῖον ἱλάσκοντο, ὑπὲρ τῆς κοινῆς εἰρήνης, ὑπὲρ τῆς 'Εκκλησίας τοῦ Θεοῦ, αὐτοῦ δὲ βασιλέως, παιδῶν τ' αὐτοῦ θεοφιλῶν, ἱκετηρίους εὐχὰς τῷ Θεῷ, προσαναφέροντες.

(d) *Demonstratio Evangelica,* lib. i. cap. 6. Ed. Paris. p. 20. Μετατιθεμένου δὲ τοῦ θυσιαστηρίου παρὰ τὰ τῷ Μωϋσεῖ δοκοῦντα, ἀνάγκη πᾶσα καὶ τοῦ Μωϋσέως νόμου μεταβολὴν γενέσθαι—ἑνὶ δὲ τῷ μόνῳ Κυρίῳ θυσιαστήριον ἀναίμων καὶ λογικῶν θυσιῶν, κατὰ τὰ καινὰ μυστήρια τῆς νέας καὶ καινῆς Διαθήκης, καθ' ὅλης τῶν ἀνθρώπων οἰκουμένης ἀνεγηγέρθαι.

(e) *Ibid.* cap. 10. p. 37. Εἰκότως τὴν τοῦ σώματος Αὐτοῦ καὶ τοῦ αἵματος τὴν ὑπόμνησιν ὁσημέραι ἐπιτελοῦντες, καὶ τῆς κρείττονος ἢ κατὰ τοὺς παλαιοὺς, θυσίας τε καὶ ἱερουργίας ἠξιωμένοι, οὐκέτι ὅσιον ἡγούμεθα καταπίπτειν ἐπὶ τὰ πρῶτα καὶ ἀσθενῆ στοιχεῖα, σύμβολα καὶ εἰκόνας, ἀλλ' οὐκ αὐτὴν ἀλήθειαν περιέχοντα. He cites Psalm xxxix. (nobis xl.) ver. 7, 8, 9. and goes on ; Μετὰ δὴ πάντα οἷον τι θαυμάσιον θῦμα, καὶ σφαγίον ἐξαίρετον τῷ Πατρὶ καλλιερησάμενος, ὑπὲρ τῶν ἁπάντων ἡμῶν ἀνήνεγκε σωτηρίας, μνήμην καὶ ἡμῖν παραδοὺς, ἀντὶ θυσίας.

(f) *Ibid.* In the next page he adds, τούτου δῆτα τοῦ θύματος τὴν μνήμην ἐπὶ τραπέζης ἐκτελεῖν διὰ συμβόλων, τοῦ τε σώματος Αὐτοῦ, καὶ τοῦ σωτηρίου αἵματος, κατὰ θεσμοὺς τῆς καινῆς Διαθήκης παρειληφότες, πάλιν ὑπὸ τοῦ προφήτου Δαβὶδ παιδευόμεθα λέγειν, Ἡτοίμασας ἐνώπιόν Μου τράπεζαν, ἐλίπανας ἐν ἐλαίῳ τὴν κεφαλήν Μου· διαρρήδην γοῦν ἐν τούτοις καὶ τὸ μυστικὸν σημαίνεται χρίσμα, καὶ τὰ σεμνὰ τῆς Χριστοῦ τραπέζης θύματα, δι' ὧν καλλιεροῦντες, τὰς ἀναίμους καὶ λογικὰς Αὐτῷ τε προσηνεῖς θυσίας διὰ παντὸς βίου τῷ ἐπὶ πάντων προσφέρειν Θεῷ, διὰ τοῦ πάντων ἀνωτάτου Ἀρχιερέως Αὐτοῦ δεδιδάγμεθα.

(g) *Ibid.* After citing Malach. i. 10, 11. p. 40. Θύομεν δῆτα τοιγαροῦν τῷ ἐπὶ πάντων Θεῷ θυσίαν αἰνέσεως· θύομεν τὸ ἔνθεον καὶ σέμνον καὶ ἱεροπρεπὲς θῦμα, θύομεν καινῶς, κατὰ τὴν καινὴν Διαθήκην, τὴν καθαρὰν θυσίαν, he cites Psalm l. (nobis li. ver. 17.) and proceeds thus : καὶ δὴ καὶ θυμιῶμεν τὸ προφητικὸν θυμίαμα, ἐν παντὶ τόπῳ προσκομίζοντες Αὐτῷ τὸν εὐώδη καρπὸν τῆς παναρέτου θεολογίας, διὰ τῶν πρὸς Αὐτὸν εὐχῶν ἀναφέροντες·—οὐκοῦν καὶ θύομεν, καὶ θυμιῶμεν· τότε μὲν τὴν μνήμην τοῦ μεγάλου θύματος, κατὰ τὰ πρὸς Αὐτοῦ παραδοθέντα μυστήρια ἐπιτελοῦντες, καὶ τὴν ὑπὲρ σωτηρίας ἡμῶν Εὐχαριστίαν δι' εὐσεβῶν ὕμνων τε, καὶ εὐχῶν τῷ Θεῷ προσκομίζοντες· τότε δὲ σφᾶς αὐτοὺς ὅλως καθιεροῦντες Αὐτῷ, καὶ τῷ γε Ἀρχιερεῖ Αὐτοῦ Λόγῳ, αὐτῷ σώματι καὶ ψυχῇ ἀνακείμενοι.

(h) *Ibid.* lib. v. cap. 3. p. 223. Ὁ Σωτὴρ ἡμῶν Ἰησοῦς, ὁ Χριστὸς τοῦ Θεοῦ, τῷ τοῦ Μελχισεδὲκ τρόπῳ, τὰ τῆς ἐν ἀνθρώποις ἱερουργίας εἰσέτι καὶ νῦν διὰ τῶν Αὐτοῦ θεραπευτῶν ἐπιτελεῖ· ὥσπερ γὰρ ἐκεῖνος ἱερεὺς ἐθνῶν τυγχάνων, οὐδαμοῦ φαίνεται θυσίαις σωματικαῖς κεχρημένος, οἴνῳ δὲ μόνῳ καὶ ἄρτῳ τὸν Ἀβραὰμ εὐλογῶν· τὸν αὐτὸν δὴ τρόπον πρῶτος μὲν Αὐτὸς ὁ Σωτὴρ καὶ Κύριος ἡμῶν, ἔπειτα οἱ ἐξ Αὐτοῦ πάντες ἱερεῖς ἀνὰ πάντα τὰ ἔθνη τὴν πνευματικὴν ἐπιτελοῦντες κατὰ τοὺς Ἐκκλησιαστικοὺς θεσμοὺς ἱερουργίαν, οἴνῳ καὶ ἄρτῳ, τοῦ τε σώματος Αὐτοῦ καὶ τοῦ σωτηρίου αἵματος αἰνίττονται τὰ μυστήρια, τοῦ Μελχισεδὲκ ταῦτα πνεύματι θείῳ προτεθεωρηκότος, καὶ τῶν μελλόντων ταῖς εἰκόσι προκεχρημένου.

(i) *Ibid.* lib. viii. in Genes. xlix. 12. p. 380. Καὶ τὸ, λευκοὶ οἱ ὀδόντες αὐτοῦ ἢ γάλα, τὸ λαμπρὸν καὶ κάθαρον τῆς μυστηριώδους τροφῆς [δοκεῖ μοι σημαίνειν·] αὐτὸς γὰρ τὰ σύμβολα τῆς ἐνθέου οἰκονομίας τοῖς Αὐτοῦ παρεδίδου μαθηταῖς, τὴν εἰκόνα τοῦ ἰδίου σώματος ποιεῖσθαι παρακελεύομενος· ἐπειδὴ γὰρ οὐκέτι τὰς δι' αἱμάτων θυσίας, οὐδὲ τὰς παρὰ Μωϋσεῖ ἐν διαφόρων ζώων σφαγαῖς νενομοθετημένας προσίετο, ἄρτῳ δὲ χρῆσθαι συμβόλῳ τοῦ ἰδίου σώματος παρεδίδου, εἰκότως τὸ λαμπρὸν καὶ καθαρὸν ἠνίξατο τῆς τροφῆς, εἰπὼν, καὶ λευκοὶ οἱ ὀδόντες αὐτοῦ ἢ γάλα. Τούτου καὶ ἄλλος ἐμνημόνευσε Προφήτης, φήσας, θυσίαν καὶ προσφορὰν οὐκ ἠθέλησας, σῶμα δὲ κατηρτίσω μοι.

(k) In Psalm xci. p. 608. Ed. Montfaucon, 1707. Ἀλλὰ καὶ τοὺς ἄρτους τῆς προθέσεως προσφέρομεν, τὴν σωτήριον μνήμην ἀναζωπυροῦντες, τό τε τοῦ ῥαντισμοῦ αἷμα τοῦ Ἀμνοῦ τοῦ Θεοῦ, τοῦ περιελόντος τὴν ἁμαρτίαν τοῦ κόσμου, καθάρσιον τῶν ἡμετέρων ψυχῶν.

S. ATHANASIUS floruit A.D. 326.

Ed. Paris. 1698.

(a) Epist. iv. ad Serapionem, tom. i. par. ii. p. 710. Ἀμφότερα περὶ Ἑαυτοῦ εἴρηκε, σάρκα καὶ πνεῦμα· καὶ τὸ πνεῦμα, πρὸς τὸ κατὰ σάρκα διέστειλεν, ἵνα μὴ μόνον τὸ φαινόμενον, ἀλλὰ καὶ τὸ ἀορατὸν αὐτοῦ πιστεύσαντες μάθωσιν, ὅτι καὶ ἃ λέγει, οὐκ ἐστὶν σαρκικὰ, ἀλλὰ πνευματικὰ· πόσοις γὰρ ἦρκει τὸ σῶμα πρὸς βρῶσιν, ἵνα καὶ τοῦ κόσμου παντὸς τοῦτο τροφὴ γένηται, ἀλλὰ διὰ τοῦτο τῆς εἰς οὐρανοὺς ἀναβάσεως ἐμνημόνευσε τοῦ υἱοῦ τοῦ ἀνθρώπου, ἵνα τῆς σωματικῆς ἐννοίας αὐτοὺς ἀφελκύσῃ, καὶ λοιπὸν τὴν εἰρημένην σάρκα βρῶσιν ἄνωθεν οὐράνιον καὶ πνευματικὴν τροφὴν παρ' Αὐτοῦ διδομένην μάθωσιν· ἃ γὰρ λελάληκα, φησὶν, ὑμῖν, πνεῦμά ἐστι, καὶ ζωή· ἴσον τῷ εἰπεῖν, τὸ μὲν δεικνύμενον καὶ διδόμενον ὑπὲρ τῆς τοῦ κόσμου σωτηρίας δοθήσεται τροφή, ὥστε πνευματικῶς ἐν ἑκάστῳ ταύτην ἀναδίδοσθαι καὶ γίνεσθαι πᾶσι φυλακτήριον εἰς ἀνάστασιν ζωῆς αἰωνίου.

(b) De Incarnatione, tom. i. par. ii. p. 883. Ἀλλαχοῦ τὸ Ἅγιον Πνεῦμα καλεῖ ἄρτον οὐράνιον, λέγων· τὸν ἄρτον ἡμῶν τὸν ἐπιούσιον δὸς ἡμῖν σήμερον· ἐδίδαξε γὰρ ἡμᾶς ἐν τῇ εὐχῇ ἐν τῷ νῦν αἰῶνι αἰτεῖν τὸν ἐπιούσιον ἄρτον, τουτέστι, τὸν μέλλοντα, οὗ ἀπαρχὴν ἔχομεν ἐν τῇ νῦν ζωῇ, τῆς σαρκὸς τοῦ Κυρίου μεταλαμβάνοντες, καθὼς Αὐτὸς εἶπε· ὁ ἄρτος δὲ ὅν Ἐγὼ δώσω ἡ σάρξ μου ἐστὶν ὑπὲρ τῆς τοῦ κόσμου ζωῆς· πνεῦμα γὰρ ζωοποιοῦν ἡ σάρξ ἐστι τοῦ Κυρίου, διότι ἐκ Πνεύματος τοῦ ζωοποιοῦ συνελήφθη· τὸ γὰρ γεγεννημένον ἐκ τοῦ Πνεύματος πνεῦμά ἐστι.

(c) Historia de Melchisedec, tom. ii. p. 241. Καὶ οὕτως (Μελχισεδὲκ) πρῶτος τύπος ἐγένετο, τῆς ἀναίμακτου θυσίας τοῦ Σωτῆρος φέρων εἰς τὴν ἁγίαν προσφοράν. διὸ λέγει· σὺ ἱερεὺς εἰς τὸν αἰῶνα κατὰ τάξιν Μελχισεδὲκ· ἐπειδὴ τύπος ἐγένετο τῆς ἁγίας προσφορᾶς.

(d) Ex opere Athanasii quodam deperdito fragmentum apud Theodoritum Dialog. 2. p. 92. vol. iv. Edit. Lutetiæ, 1642. Τὸ σῶμα τοίνυν ἐστὶν, ᾧ λέγει, κάθου ἐκ δεξιῶν μου. οὗ καὶ γέγονεν ἔχθρος ὁ Διάβολος σὺν ταῖς πονηραῖς δυνάμεσι, καὶ Ἰουδαῖοι, καὶ Ἕλληνες· δι' οὗ σώματος Ἀρχιερεὺς καὶ Ἀπόστολος γέγονε, καὶ ἐχρημάτισε· δι' οὗ παρέδωκεν ἡμῖν μυστηρίου, λέγων, τοῦτό ἐστι τὸ σῶμά μου τὸ ὑπὲρ ὑμῶν, καὶ, τὸ αἷμα τῆς καινῆς Δια-

c

θήκης, οὐ τῆς παλαιᾶς, τὸ ὑπὲρ ὑμῶν ἐκχυνόμενον· θεότης δὲ οὔτε σῶμα ἔχει, οὔτε αἷμα ἔχει.

JULIUS FIRMICUS floruit A.D. 340.

De Errore profanarum Religionum in Bibliotheca PP. Edit. anno 1718, tom. iv. p. 114. Alius est cibus, qui languentes relevat, errantes revocat, lapsos erigit, qui morientibus æternæ immortalitatis largitur insignia. Christi panem, Christi poculum quære, ut terrena fragilitate contempta, substantia hominis immortali pabulo saginetur. Quis est autem hic panis, vel quod poculum? De quo in libris Salomonis sapientia præclamat; ait enim, *venite*, &c. (ut Prov. ix. 1—5.) Melchisedec rex Salem, et sacerdos summi Dei, revertenti Abrahæ cum pane et vino benedictionis obtulit gratiam.—ut autem manifestius diceretur quinam ille esset panis, per quem miseræ mortis vincuntur exitia, Ipse Dominus sancto ac venerando ore signavit, ne per diversos tractatus spes hominum pravis interpretationibus fallerentur. Dicit enim in Evangelio Joannis, *Ego sum panis vitæ; qui venerit ad Me non esuriet, et qui in Me crediderit non sitiet unquam.* Item in sequentibus hoc idem simili modo significat; ait enim, *siquis sitit, veniat, et bibat, qui credit in Me.* Et rursus Ipse, ut majestatis suæ substantiam credentibus traderet, ait, *Nisi ederitis carnem Filii Hominis, &c.*, quare nihil vobis cum tympanis, cibo odii, miseri mortales; salutaris cibi gratiam quærite, et immortale poculum bibite.

CYRILLUS HIEROSOLYMITANUS floruit A.D. 350.

Edit. Paris. 1720.

(a) *Catechism. Mystagog.* i. p. 308. Ὥσπερ ὁ ἄρτος, καὶ ὁ οἶνος τῆς Εὐχαριστίας, πρὸ τῆς ἁγίας ἐπικλήσεως τῆς προσκυνητῆς Τριάδος, ἄρτος ἦν, καὶ οἶνος λιτός· ἐπικλήσεως δὲ γινομένης, ὁ μὲν ἄρτος γίνεται σῶμα Χριστοῦ, ὁ δὲ οἶνος αἷμα Χριστοῦ· τὸν αὐτὸν δὴ τρόπον, τὰ τοιαῦτα βρώματα τῆς πομπῆς τοῦ Σατανᾶ, τῇ ἰδίᾳ φύσει λιτὰ ὄντα, τῇ ἐπικλήσει τῶν Δαιμόνων βέβηλα γίνεται.

(aa) *Catech. Mystag.* iii. p. 317. Ὁ ἄρτος τῆς Εὐχαριστίας, μετὰ τὴν ἐπίκλησιν τοῦ ἁγίου Πνεύματος, οὐκ ἔτι ἄρτος λιτός, ἀλλὰ σῶμα Χριστοῦ.

(b) *Catech. Mystag.* iv. p. 320. Αὐτοῦ οὖν ἀποφηναμένου, καὶ εἰπόντος περὶ τοῦ ἄρτου, Τοῦτό μου ἐστὶ τὸ σῶμα· τὶς τολμήσει ἀμφιβάλλειν λοιπόν, καὶ Αὐτοῦ βεβαιωσαμένου καὶ εἰρηκότος, Τοῦτό μου ἐστὶ τὸ αἷμα· τὶς ἐνδοιάσει ποτέ, λέγων μὴ εἶναι Αὐτοῦ τὸ αἷμα; τὸ ὕδωρ ποτὲ εἰς οἶνον μεταβέβληκεν, οἰκεῖον αἵματι, ἐν Κανᾷ τῆς Γαλιλαίας· καὶ οὐκ ἀξιόπιστός ἐστιν, οἶνον μεταβαλὼν εἰς αἷμα;—καὶ τοῖς υἱοῖς τοῦ νυμφῶνος οὐ πολλῷ μᾶλλον τὴν ἀπόλαυσιν τοῦ σώματος Αὐτοῦ καὶ τοῦ αἵματος, δωρησάμενος ὁμολογηθήσεται.

(c) *Ibid.* et eadem pagina. Μετὰ πάσης πληροφορίας, ὡς σώματος καὶ αἵματος μεταλαμβάνωμεν Χριστοῦ· ἐν τύπῳ γὰρ ἄρτου, δίδοται σοι τὸ σῶμα·

καὶ ἐν τύπῳ οἴνου, δίδοταί σοι τὸ αἷμα, ἵνα γένῃ—σύσσωμος καὶ σύναιμος Αὐτοῦ.

(d) *Ibid.*—ποτὲ Χριστὸς τοῖς Ἰουδαίοις διαλεγόμενος, ἔλεγεν, Ἐὰν μὴ φαγῆτε Μοῦ τὴν σάρκα, κ.τ.λ. (as John vi. 53.) ἐκεῖνοι μὴ ἀκηκοότες πνευματικῶς τῶν λεγομένων, σκανδαλισθέντες ἀπῆλθον εἰς τὰ ὀπίσω, νομίζοντες ὅτι ἐπὶ σαρκοφαγίαν αὐτοὺς προτρέπεται· ἦσαν δὲ ἐν παλαιᾷ διαθήκῃ ἄρτοι προθέσεως· ἀλλ' ἐκεῖνοι παλαιᾶς ὄντες διαθήκης, τελὸς εἰλήφασιν. ἐν δὲ τῇ καινῇ διαθήκῃ, ἄρτος οὐράνιος καὶ ποτήριον σωτηρίου, ψυχὴν καὶ σῶμα ἁγιάζοντα. ὥσπερ γὰρ ὁ ἄρτος σώματι κατάλληλος, οὕτω καὶ ὁ Λόγος τῇ ψυχῇ ἁρμόδιος. μὴ προσέχε οὖν ὡς ψιλοῖς τῷ ἄρτῳ καὶ τῷ οἴνῳ· σῶμα γὰρ καὶ αἷμα Χριστοῦ, κατὰ τὴν Δεσποτικὴν τυγχάνει ἀπόφασιν. εἰ γὰρ καὶ ἡ αἴσθησίς σοι τοῦτο ὑποβάλλει, ἀλλ' ἡ πίστις σε βεβαιούτω· μὴ ἀπὸ τῆς γεύσεως κρίνῃς τὸ πρᾶγμα, ἀλλ' ἀπὸ τῆς πίστεως πληροφοροῦ ἀνενδοιάστως, σώματος καὶ αἵματος Χριστοῦ καταξιωθείς.

(e) *Ibid.* pag. proxima. Ὁ Σολομὼν ταύτην αἰνιττόμενος τὴν χάριν, ἐν τῷ Ἐκκλησιάστῃ (he means Eccl. ix. 7.) λέγει· Δεῦρο, φάγε ἐν εὐφρο-σύνῃ τὸν ἄρτον σοῦ, τὸν πνευματικὸν,—καὶ πίε τὸν οἶνον σου, τὸν πνευμα-τικὸν οἶνον.

(f) *Catechism. Mystag.* v. p. 327. Παρακαλοῦμεν τὸν φιλάνθρωπον Θεὸν, τὸ ἅγιον Πνεῦμα ἐξαποστεῖλαι ἐπὶ τὰ προκείμενα· ἵνα ποιήσῃ τὸν μὲν ἄρτον σῶμα Χριστοῦ, τὸν δὲ οἶνον αἷμα Χριστοῦ. πάντως γὰρ οὗ ἐὰν ἐφάψαιτο τὸ Ἅγιον Πνεῦμα, τοῦτο ἡγίασται καὶ μεταβέβληται. εἶτα, μετὰ τὸ ἀπαρτισθῆναι τὴν πνευματικὴν θυσίαν, τὴν ἀναίμακτον λατρείαν, ἐπὶ τῆς θυσίας ἐκείνης τοῦ ἱλασμοῦ παρακαλοῦμεν τὸν Θεὸν, ὑπὲρ κοινῆς τῶν ἐκκλησιῶν εἰρήνης· ὑπὲρ τῆς τοῦ κόσμου εὐσταθείας· ὑπὲρ βασιλέων· ὑπὲρ στρατιωτῶν καὶ συμμά-χων· ὑπὲρ τῶν ἐν ἀσθενείαις· ὑπὲρ τῶν καταπονουμένων· καὶ ἁπαξαπλῶς, ὑπὲρ πάντων βοηθείας δεομένων δεόμεθα πάντες ἡμεῖς, καὶ ταύτην προσφέ-ρομέν τὴν θυσίαν. Εἶτα μνημονεύομεν καὶ τῶν προκεκοιμημένων, πρῶτον πατριαρχῶν, προφητῶν, ἀποστόλων, μαρτύρων· ὅπως ὁ Θεὸς ταῖς εὐχαῖς αὐτῶν καὶ πρεσβείαις προσδέξηται ἡμῶν τὴν δέησιν. εἶται καὶ ὑπὲρ τῶν προκεκοιμημένων ἁγίων πατέρων, καὶ ἐπισκόπων, καὶ πάντων ἁπλῶς τῶν ἐν ἡμῖν προκεκοιμημένων· μεγίστην ὄνησιν πιστεύοντες ἔσεσθαι ταῖς ψυχαῖς, ὑπὲρ ὧν ἡ δέησις ἀναφέρεται, τῆς ἁγίας καὶ φρικωδεστάτης προκειμένης θυσίας.

(g) *Ibid.* Χριστὸν ἐσφαγιασμένον, ὑπὲρ τῶν ἡμετέρων ἁμαρτημάτων προσφέρομεν, ἐξιλεούμενοι ὑπὲρ αὐτῶν τε καὶ ἡμῶν τὸν φιλάνθρωπον Θεόν.

(h) *Ibid.* Panem supersubstantialem in Oratione Dominica de pane Eucharistica interpretans, p. 329. Ἄρτος οὗτος ὁ κοινὸς οὐκ ἐστὶν ἐπιούσιος. ἄρτος δὲ οὗτος ὁ ἅγιος ἐπιούσιός ἐστιν·—οὗτος ὁ ἄρτος οὐκ εἰς κοιλίαν χωρεῖ καὶ εἰς ἀφεδρῶνα ἐκβάλλεται· ἀλλ' εἰς πᾶσαν σοῦ τὴν σύστα-σιν ἀναδίδοται, εἰς ὠφέλειαν σώματος καὶ ψυχῆς.

(i) *Ibid.* p. 331. Τὴν ἀριστερὰν θρόνον ποιήσας τῇ δεξιᾷ, ὡς μελλούσῃ Βασιλέα ὑποδέχεσθαι, καὶ κοιλάνας τὴν παλάμην, δέχου τὸ σῶμα τοῦ Χριστοῦ, ἐπιλέγων τὸ, ᾽Αμήν. εἶτα προσέρχου καὶ τῷ ποτηρίῳ—κύπτων, καὶ τρόπῳ προσκυνήσεως καὶ σεβάσματος λέγων τὸ, ᾽Αμήν.

HILARIUS PICTAVIENSIS floruit A.D. 354.

Ed. Paris. 1693.

(a) *De Trinitate*, lib. viii. p. 954. Si enim vere Verbum caro factum est, et nos vere Verbum carnem cibo Dominico sumimus; quomodo non naturalitér in nobis manere existimandus est, qui et naturam carnis nostræ jam inseparabilem sibi homo natus assumpsit, et naturam carnis suæ ad naturam æternitatis sub sacramento nobis communicandæ carnis admiscuit?—Si vere igitur carnem corporis nostri Christus assumpsit, et vere homo ille, quia ex Maria natus fuit, Christus est, nosque vere sub mysterio carnem corporis sui sumimus; (et per hoc unum erimus, quia Pater in Eo est, et Ille in nobis)—Ipse enim ait, *Caro mea vere est esca, et sanguis meus vere est potus. Qui edit carnem meam, et bibit sanguinem meum, in Me manet, et Ego in eo.*—Nunc enim et ipsius Domini professione, et fide nostra vere caro est, et vere sanguis est: et hæc accepta atque hausta id efficiunt, ut et nos in Christo, et Christus in nobis sit.—quam autem in Eo per sacramentum communicatæ carnis et sanguinis simus, Ipse testatur dicens, *et hic mundus jam Me non videt; vos autem Me videbitis,* &c.—Hæc ergo vitæ nostræ causa est, quod in nobis carnalibus manentem per carnem Christum habemus:—si ergo nos naturaliter secundum carnem per Eum vivimus, id est, naturam carnis suæ adepti, quomodo non naturaliter secundum Spiritum in Se Patrem habeat, cum vivat Ipse per Patrem?

(b) *Commentar.* in Matth. cap. 31. p. 743. Quî autem, *ut a se transeat* rogat? Numquid possibile erat non pati Christum? atquin jam a constitutione mundi sacramentum hoc in Eo erat nostræ salutis ostensum: numquid pati Ipse nolebat? atquin superius fundendum in remissionem peccatorum corporis sui sanguinem consecraverat.

HILARIUS DIACONUS floruit A.D. 354.

Inter opera S. Ambrosii. Ed. Paris. 1690-1.

(a) *In* 1 *Epistol. ad Corinth.* cap. xi. p. 149. Quia enim morte Domini liberati sumus, hujus rei memores, in edendo et potando carnem et sanguinem, quæ pro nobis oblata sunt, significamus.

(b) *In primam Epistolam ad Timoth.* cap. iv. p. 298. Prophetia est, qua eligitur quasi doctor futurus idoneus: manus vero impositiones verba sunt mystica, quibus confirmatur ad hoc opus electus, accipiens auctoritatem, teste conscientia sua; ut audeat vice Domini sacrificium Deo offerre.

S. Gregorius Nazianzenus floruit A.D. 370.

Ed. Paris. 1778.

(a) *Orat.* 2. *Apolog.* p. 56. Εἰδὼς, ὅτι μηδεὶς ἄξιος τοῦ μεγάλου καὶ Θεοῦ καὶ θύματος καὶ Ἀρχιερέως, ὅστις μὴ πρότερον ἑαυτὸν παρέστησε τῷ Θεῷ θυσίαν ζῶσαν, ἁγίαν, μηδὲ τὴν λογικὴν λατρείαν εὐάρεστον ἐπεδείξατο, μηδὲ ἔθυσε τῷ Θεῷ θυσίαν αἰνέσεως καὶ πνεῦμα συντετριμμένον, ἣν μόνην Ὁ πάντα δοὺς ἀπαιτεῖ παρ' ἡμῶν θυσίαν, πῶς ἔμελλον θαρρῆσαι προσφέρειν Αὐτῷ τὴν ἔξωθεν τὴν τῶν μεγάλων μυστηρίων ἀντίτυπον· ἢ πῶς ἱερέως σχῆμα καὶ ὄνομα ὑποδύεσθαι.

(b) *Orat.* 4. *quæ est* στηλιτευτικὴ *in Julianum* i. p. 101. Καὶ τὰς χεῖρας ἀφαγνίζεται τῆς ἀναιμάκτου θυσίας ἀποκαθαίρων, δι' ἧς ἡμεῖς Χριστῷ κοινωνοῦμεν, καὶ τῶν παθημάτων καὶ τῆς Θεότητος· ἐντόμοις δὲ καὶ θυσίαις, καθιστᾷ τὰ Βασίλεια.

(c) *Orat.* 5. *quæ est in Julianum,* ii. p. 166. Οὐκ ἔτι τοῖς ἱεροῖς οἴκοις ἡμῶν πονηρὸν ἐμβλέψουσιν· οὐκ ἔτι μιανοῦσιν αἵματι μιαρῷ τὰ τῆς καθαρωτάτης καὶ ἀναιμάκτου θυσίας ἐπώνυμα θυσιαστήρια.

(d) *Orat. Funebris in Basilium Magnum,* 43. p. 805. Θυσιαστηρίων κατορχούμενοι, καὶ τὰς ἀναιμάκτους θυσίας ἀνθρώπων καὶ θυσιῶν αἵμασι χραίνοντες (Ἀριανοὶ.)

(e) *Orat.* 26. *contra Maximum,* p. 483. Θυσιαστηρίων εἴρξουσιν ; ἀλλ' οἶδα καὶ ἄλλο θυσιαστήριον, ἐφ' ὃ λαξευτήριον οὐκ ἀναβέβηκεν οὐδὲ χεὶρ, οὐδὲ ἠκούσθη σίδηρος, ἤ τι τῶν τεχνιτῶν καὶ ποικίλων, ἀλλ' ὅλον τοῦ νοῦ τὸ ἔργον, καὶ διὰ θεωρίας ἡ ἀνάβασις. τούτῳ παραστήσομαι, τούτῳ θύσω δεκτὰ, θυσίαν καὶ προσφορὰν καὶ ὁλοκαυτώματα κρείττονα τῶν νῦν προσαγομένων, ὅσῳ κρείττον σκιᾶς ἡ ἀλήθεια· περὶ οὗ μοι δοκεῖ καὶ Δαβὶδ ὁ μέγας φιλοσοφεῖν, λέγων· καὶ εἰσελεύσομαι πρὸς τὸ θυσιαστήριον κ. τ. λ.

(f) *Orat.* 45. *quæ est in Pascha,* 2da p. 863. Μεταληψόμεθα δὲ τοῦ Πάσχα, νῦν μὲν τυπικῶς ἔτι, καὶ εἰ τοῦ παλαιοῦ γυμνότερον· τὸ γὰρ νομικὸν Πάσχα, τολμῶ καὶ λέγω, τύπου τύπος ἦν ἀμυδρότερος.

(g) *Carmen Iambic.* 34. tom. ii. p. 622. Θεῷ δὲ δῶρον, θυσίαι, καθάρσιοι, Δώρων δοχεῖον ἁγνὸν, ἡ θεηδόχος Τράπεζ'—.

(h) *Εἰς Ἐπισκόπους.* Tom. ii. p. 824. Ὦ θυσίας πέμποντες ἀναιμάκτους, Ἱερῆες.

Epiphanius floruit A.D. 368.

(a) *Advers. Hæres.* 55. Num. ii. p. 470. Edit. Parisiis, 1622. Μετατιθεμένης δὲ εἰς τὴν πρὸ τοῦ Λευῒ καὶ πρὸ Ἀαρὼν κατὰ τὴν τάξιν Μελχισεδὲκ τῆς ἱερωσύνης· ὅπερ νυνὶ ἐν τῇ Ἐκκλησίᾳ πολιτεύεται, ἀπὸ Χριστοῦ καὶ δεῦρο, μηκέτι τοῦ σπέρματος κατὰ διαδοχὴν ἐκλεγομένου, ἀλλὰ τοῦ κατὰ ἀρετὴν τύπου ζητουμένου.

(b) *Ibid.* Numb. 6. p. 472. Ὁ Μελχισεδὲκ αὐτῷ (Ἀβραὰμ) ἀπήντα

τότε, καὶ ἐξέβαλεν αὐτῷ ἄρτον καὶ οἶνον, προτυπῶν τῶν Μυστηρίων τὰ αἰνίγ-
ματα, ἀντίτυπα τοῦ Κυρίου ἡμῶν, λέγοντος· ὅτι Ἐγώ εἶμι ὁ ἄρτος ὁ ζῶν. καὶ
ἀντίτυπα τοῦ αἵματος τοῦ ἐκ τῆς πλευρᾶς Αὐτοῦ νυχθέντος, καὶ ῥεύσαντος
εἰς κάθαρσιν τῶν κεκοινωμένων, καὶ ῥαντισμὸν, καὶ σωτηρίαν τῶν ἡμετέρων
ψυχῶν.

(c) *Anchorat.* 57. p. 60. Ὁρῶμεν γὰρ ὅτι ἔλαβεν ὁ Σωτὴρ εἰς τὰς
χεῖρας Αὐτοῦ, ὡς ἔχει ἐν τῷ Εὐαγγελίῳ, ὅτι ἀνέστη ἐν τῷ δείπνῳ, καὶ ἔλαβε
τάδε, καὶ εὐχαριστήσας εἶπε, Τοῦτό μου ἐστὶ τόδε, καὶ ὁρῶμεν ὅτι οὐκ ἴσόν
ἐστιν, οὐδὲ ὅμοιον, οὐ τῇ ἐνσάρκῳ εἰκόνι, οὐ τῇ ἀοράτῳ Θεότητι, οὐ τοῖς
χαρακτῆρσι τῶν μελῶν· τὸ μὲν γάρ ἐστι στρογγυλοειδὲς καὶ ἀναίσθητον, ὡς
πρὸς τὴν δύναμιν. καὶ ἠθέλησεν χάριτι εἰπεῖν, Τοῦτό μου ἐστὶ τόδε, καὶ οὐδεὶς
ἀπιστεῖ τῷ λόγῳ. ὁ γὰρ μὴ πιστεύων εἶναι Αὐτὸν ἀληθινὸν, ὡς εἶπεν, ἐκπίπ-
τει τῆς χάριτος, καὶ τῆς σωτηρίας. ὅ τι δὲ ἠκούσαμεν, πιστεύομεν ὅτι ἐστιν
Αὐτοῦ.

(d) *Anacephalæosis,* p. 154. Ἰσχυροποιουμένων τῆς δυνάμεως τοῦ
ἄρτου, καὶ τῆς τοῦ ὕδατος ἰσχύος· ἵνα οὐκ ἄρτος ἡμῖν γένηται δύναμις, ἀλλὰ
δύναμις ἄρτου· καὶ βρῶσις μὲν ὁ ἄρτος, ἡ δὲ δύναμις ἐν αὐτῷ εἰς ζωογόν-
ησιν.

OPTATUS MILEVITANUS floruit A.D. 368.

Ed. Paris. 1679.

(a) *Advers. Parmenianum,* lib. vi. p. 111. Quid enim est tam
sacrilegum, quam altaria Dei (in quibus aliquando et vos obtulistis)
frangere, radere, removere? in quibus vota populi, et membra Christi
portata sunt; quo Deus Omnipotens invocatus sit; quo postulatus
descendit Spiritus Sanctus; unde a multis pignus salutis æternæ, et
tutela fidei, et spes resurrectionis accepta est.

(aa) *Ibid.* p. 112. Cur vota et desideria hominum cum ipsis altaribus evertistis? Illac ad aures Dei ascendere populi solebat oratio.
Cur concidistis precibus viam? et ne ad Deum supplicatio de more
solito ascensum haberet, impia manu quodammodo scalas subducere
laborastis?

(b) *Ibid.* p. 111. Altaria, inquam, in quibus fraternitatis munera
non jussit Salvator poni, nisi quæ essent de pace condita. *Depone,*
inquit, *munus tuum ante altare,* &c. (ut in Matth. v. 23.) ut possit pro
te sacerdos offerre.

(c) *Ibid.* p. 111. Quid est enim altare, nisi sedes et corporis et
sanguinis Christi? Quid vos offenderat Christus, cujus illic per certa
momenta corpus et sanguis habitabat? Quid vos offendistis etiam
vos ipsi, ut illa altaria frangeretis, in quibus ante nos per longa temporis spatia sancte (ut arbitramini) obtulistis? (p. 113.) Hoc tamen

immane facinus geminatum est, dum fregistis etiam calices, sanguinis Christi portatores.

S. Basilius Magnus floruit A.D. 370.

Edit. Paris. 1721.

(a) *De Baptismo*, lib. ii. q. 2. tom. ii. p. 653. Ὁ δὲ Κύριος λέγων· μείζων τοῦ ἱεροῦ ὧδε, παιδεύει ἡμᾶς, ὅτι τοσοῦτον ἀσεβέστερός ἐστιν ὁ τολμῶν [ἐν μολυσμῷ ψυχῆς] ἱερατεύειν τὸ σῶμα τοῦ Κυρίου τοῦ δόντος Ἑαυτὸν ὑπὲρ ἡμῶν προσφορὰν καὶ θυσίαν τῷ Θεῷ, ὅσον τὸ σῶμα τοῦ Μονογενοῦς Υἱοῦ τοῦ Θεοῦ ὑπερέχει κριῶν καὶ ταύρων.

(b) *Ibid.* q. 3. pag. proxima. Ὅσῳ γὰρ πλεῖον τοῦ ἱεροῦ ὧδε κατὰ τὴν τοῦ Κυρίου φωνήν, τοσούτῳ δεινότερον καὶ φοβερώτερον τὸ ἐν μολυσμῷ ψυχῆς τολμῆσαι ἅψασθαι τοῦ σώματος τοῦ Χριστοῦ, παρὰ τὸ ἅψασθαι κριῶν ἢ ταύρων.

(c) *Epistola* 93. tom. iii. p. 186. Τὸ κοινωνεῖν κάθ᾽ ἑκάστην ἡμέραν, καὶ μεταλαμβάνειν τοῦ ἁγίου σώματος καὶ αἵματος τοῦ Χριστοῦ, καλὸν καὶ ἐπωφελές· Αὐτοῦ σαφῶς λέγοντος, Ὁ τρώγων μου τὴν σάρκα, καὶ πίνων μου τὸ αἷμα, ἔχει ζωὴν αἰώνιον· τίς γὰρ ἀμφιβάλλει, ὅτι τὸ μετέχειν συνεχῶς τῆς ζωῆς, οὐδὲν ἄλλο ἐστὶν ἢ ζῆν πολλαχῶς;

(d) *Ibid.* pag. proxima. Ἐν Ἀλεξανδρείᾳ δὲ, καὶ ἐν Αἰγύπτῳ, ἕκαστος καὶ τῶν ἐν λαῷ τελούντων, ὡς ἐπὶ τὸ πλεῖστον, ἔχει κοινωνίαν ἐν τῷ οἴκῳ αὐτοῦ· ἅπαξ γὰρ τὴν θυσίαν τοῦ ἱερέως τελειώσαντος καὶ δεδωκότος, ὁ λαβὼν αὐτὴν ὡς ὅλην ὁμοῦ, καθ᾽ ἑκάστην μεταλαμβάνων, παρὰ τοῦ δεδωκότος εἰκότως μεταλαμβάνειν καὶ ὑποδέχεσθαι πιστεύειν ὀφείλει.

(e) *De Spiritu Sancto*, cap. 27. tom. iii. p. 55. Τὰ τῆς ἐπικλήσεως ῥήματα ἐπὶ τῇ ἀναδείξει τοῦ ἄρτου τῆς Εὐχαριστίας καὶ τοῦ ποτηρίου τῆς εὐλογίας, τίς τῶν ἁγίων ἐγγράφως ἡμῖν καταλέλοιπεν; οὐ γὰρ δὴ τούτοις ἀρκούμεθα, ὧν ὁ Ἀπόστολος ἢ τὸ Εὐαγγέλιον ἐπεμνήσθη, ἀλλὰ καὶ προλέγομεν καὶ ἐπιλέγομεν ἕτερα, ὡς μεγάλην ἔχοντα πρὸς τὸ μυστήριον τὴν ἰσχύν, ἐκ τῆς ἀγράφου διδασκαλίας παραλαβόντες.

Gregorius Nyssenus floruit A.D. 370.

Ed. Paris. 1638.

(a) *Oratio Magna Catechetica*, cap. 37. tom. iii. p. 102. Ἐπειδὴ διπλοῦν τὸ ἀνθρώπινον, ψυχῇ τε καὶ σώματι συγκεκραμένον, ἀνάγκη τῷ πρὸς τὴν ζωὴν καθηγουμένῳ, δι᾽ ἀμφοτέρων, τοῖς σωζομένοις ἐφέπεσθαι· οὐκοῦν ἡ ψυχὴ μὲν διὰ πίστεως πρὸς αὐτὸν ἀνακραθεῖσα τὰς ἀφορμὰς ἐντεῦθεν τῆς σωτηρίας ἔχει·—τὸ δὲ σῶμα ἕτερον τρόπον ἐν μετουσίᾳ τε καὶ ἀνακράσει τοῦ Σώζοντος γίνεται.—ἀναγκαῖον—ὡς ἂν ἐν ἡμῖν γινόμενον ἀλεξιτήριον τὴν προεντεθεῖσαν τῷ σώματι τοῦ δηλητηρίου βλάβην διὰ τῆς οἰκείας ἀντιπαθείας ἀπώσοιτο. τί οὖν ἐστι τοῦτο; οὐδὲν ἕτερον ἢ ἐκεῖνο τὸ Σῶμα, ὃ τοῦ τε θανάτοῦ κρεῖττον ἐδείχθη, καὶ τῆς ζωῆς ἡμῶν κατήρξατο. καθάπερ γὰρ μικρὰ ζύμη, καθὼς φησὶν ὁ Ἀπόστολος, ὅλον τὸ φύραμα πρὸς ἑαυτὴν συνεξομοιοῖ, οὕτως τὸ θανατίσθεν ὑπὸ τοῦ Θεοῦ σῶμα ἐν τῷ ἡμετέρῳ γινόμενον, ὅλον πρὸς ἑαυτὸ μεταποιεῖ καὶ μετατίθησι.—Ἀλλὰ μὲν οὐκ ἔστιν ἄλλως ἐντός τι γίγνεσθαι τοῦ σώματος, μὴ διὰ βρώσεως καὶ πόσεως τοῖς σπλάγχνοις καταμιγνύμενον· οὐκοῦν ἐπαναγκὲς κατὰ τὸν δυνατὸν τῇ φύσει τρόπον τὴν ζωοποιὸν δύναμιν τοῦ Πνεύματος δέξασθαι· μόνον δὲ τοῦ Θεοδόχου σώματος ἐκείνου ταύτην δεξαμένου τὴν χάριν,—σκοπῆσαι προσήκει, πῶς ἐγένετο δυνατὸν τὸ ἐν ἐκείνῳ σῶμα ταῖς τοσαύταις τῶν πιστῶν μυριάσι κατὰ πᾶσαν τὴν οἰκουμένην εἰσαεὶ καταμεριζόμενον, ὅλον ἐν ἑκάστῳ διὰ τοῦ μέρους γενέσθαι, καὶ αὐτὸ μένειν ἐφ' ἑαυτοῦ ὅλον. In order to solve this difficulty, he discourses at large of bread and wine by digestion turned into human flesh; and that our Saviour's body, while on earth, was nourished in this manner; and then he adds, ὥσπερ τοίνυν ἐφ' ἡμῶν, ὁ τὸν ἄρτον ἰδὼν, τρόπον τινὰ τὸ ἀνθρώπινον βλέπει σῶμα, ὅτι ἐν τούτῳ ἐκεῖνο γινόμενον, τοῦτο γίνεται· οὕτω κἀκεῖ τὸ Θεοδόχον σῶμα τὴν τροφὴν ἄρτου παραδεξάμενον, λόγῳ τινὶ ταὐτὸν ἦν ἐκείνῳ—τὸ δὲ σῶμα τῇ ἐνοικήσει τοῦ Θεοῦ Λόγου πρὸς τὴν Θεϊκὴν ἀξίαν μετεποιήθη. καλῶς οὖν καὶ νῦν τὸν τῷ λόγῳ τοῦ Θεοῦ ἁγιαζόμενον ἄρτον εἰς σῶμα τοῦ Θεοῦ Λόγου μεταποιεῖσθαι πιστεύομαι. Καὶ γὰρ ἐκεῖνο τὸ σῶμα ἄρτος τῇ δυνάμει ἦν, ἡγιάσθη δὲ τῇ ἐπισκηνώσει τοῦ Λόγου τοῦ σκηνώσαντος ἐν τῇ σαρκὶ—καὶ νῦν τὸ ἴσον γίνεται. Ἐκεῖ γὰρ ἡ τοῦ Λόγου χάρις ἅγιον ἐποιεῖτο σῶμα, ᾧ ἐκ τοῦ ἄρτου ἡ σύστασις ἦν, καὶ τρόπον τινὰ καὶ αὐτὸ ἄρτος ἦν· ἐνταῦθά τε ὡσαύτως ὁ ἄρτος ἁγιάζεται διὰ λόγου Θεοῦ καὶ ἐντεύξεως, οὐ διὰ βρώσεως καὶ πόσεως προϊὼν εἰς τὸ σῶμα τοῦ Λόγου, ἀλλ' εὐθὺς πρὸς τὸ σῶμα τοῦ Λόγου μεταποιούμενος, καθὼς εἴρηται ὑπὸ τοῦ λόγου, ὅτι Τοῦτό ἐστι τὸ σῶμά μου. Then he speaks to the same purpose of wine being turned into blood, and subjoins : Πᾶσι τοῖς πεπιστευκόσι τῇ οἰκονομίᾳ τῆς χάριτος Ἑαυτὸν ἐνσπείρει διὰ τῆς σαρκὸς, οἷς ἡ σύστασις ἐξ οἴνου τε καὶ ἄρτου ἐστὶ, τοῖς σώμασι τῶν πεπιστευκότων κατακιρνάμενος, ὡς ἂν τῇ πρὸς τὸ ἀθάνατον ἑνώσει, καὶ ἄνθρωπος τῆς ἀφθαρσίας μέτοχος γένοιτο. ταῦτα δὲ δίδωσι, τῇ τῆς εὐλογίας δυνάμει πρὸς ἐκεῖνο μεταστοιχειώσας τῶν φαινομένων τὴν φύσιν.

(b) *Oratio de Resurrectione Christi, sive in Pascha prima*, tom. iii. p. 389. Ὁ γὰρ πάντα κατὰ τὴν δεσποτικὴν αὐθεντίαν οἰκονομῶν, οὐκ ἀναμένει τὴν ἐκ τῆς προδοσίας ἀνάγκην, καὶ τὴν λῃστρικὴν ἔφοδον τῶν Ἰουδαίων, καὶ τὴν τοῦ Πιλάτου παράνομον κρίσιν, ὥστε τὴν ἐκείνων κακίαν, ἀρχηγὸν καὶ αἰτίαν τῆς κοινῆς τῶν ἀνθρώπων σωτηρίας γενέσθαι· ἀλλὰ προλαμβάνει τῇ οἰκονομίᾳ τὴν ἔφοδον, κατὰ τὸν ἄρρητον τῆς ἱερουργίας τρόπον καὶ τοῖς ἀνθρώποις ἀόρατον, καὶ Ἑαυτὸν προσήνεγκε προσφορὰν καὶ θυσίαν ὑπὲρ ἡμῶν, ὁ ἱερεὺς ἅμα καὶ ὁ ἀμνὸς τοῦ Θεοῦ, ὁ αἴρων τὴν ἁμαρτίαν τοῦ κόσμου· πότε τοῦτο ; ὅτε βρωτὸν Ἑαυτοῦ τὸ σῶμα, [καὶ πότιμον τὸ αἷμα τοῖς συνοῦσιν ἐποίησε. πάντι γὰρ τοῦτο δῆλόν ἐστιν, ὅτι οὐκ ἂν βρωθείη παρὰ ἀνθρώπων πρόβατον, εἰ μὴ τῆς βρώσεως ἡ σφαγὴ καθηγήσαιτο· ὁ τοίνυν δοὺς τὸ σῶμα τοῖς μαθηταῖς Αὐτοῦ] εἰς βρῶσιν, σαφῶς ἐνδείκνυται τῷ ἤδη τοῦ ἀμνοῦ τὴν θυσίαν ἐντελῆ γεγεννῆσθαι· οὐ γὰρ ἂν ἦν τὸ σῶμα τοῦ ἱερείου πρὸς ἐδωδὴν ἐπιτήδειον, εἴπερ ἔμψυχον ἦν. οὐκοῦν ὅτε παρέσχε τοῖς μαθηταῖς ἐμφαγεῖν τοῦ σώματος, καὶ τοῦ αἵματος ἐμπιεῖν, ἤδη κατὰ τὸ θέλητον τοῦ τὸ μυστήριον οἰκονομοῦντος ἀρρήτως τε καὶ ἀοράτως τὸ σῶμα ἐτέθυτο.

(c) Orat. in Baptism. Christi, p. 370. Ἄρτος ἐστὶ τέως κοινός· ἀλλ᾽ ὅταν αὐτὸν τὸ μυστήριον ἱερουργήσῃ, σῶμα Χριστοῦ λέγεταί τε καὶ γίνεται.

EPHRÆM. SYRUS floruit A.D. 370.

Ed. Romæ, 1732.

(a) De Sacerdotio, tom. iii. p. 1, 2, 3. Dignitas sacerdotalis mysteriis, sacrificiis, peccatorum remissioni per manuum impositionem dicata.—Sacerdotium cœlum volitans ascendit ad Deum, procidensque [ante excelsum thronum] instanter pro servis orat Dominum—ut Spiritus Sanctus pariter descendat, sanctificetque dona in terris proposita; cumque oblata fuerint tremenda mysteria immortalitate plena, præside sacerdote orationem pro cunctis faciente, tunc animæ accedentes, per illa tremenda mysteria macularum purificationem accipiunt.

(b) De Iis, qui Filii Dei Naturam scrutantur, tom. iii. p. 423. Diligenter intuere, quomodo in manibus panem accipiens benedixit, ac fregit in figuram immaculati sui corporis, calicemque in figuram pretiosi sanguinis sui benedixit, deditque discipulis suis.

(c) Ibid. p. 682. Participa immaculatum corpus, et sanguinem Domini tui fide plenissima, certus, quod agnum ipsum integre comedas. Ignis immortalis sunt mysteria Christi. Cave ea temere scruteris, ne in ipsorum participatione comburaris. Abraham patriarcha cœlestibus angelis terrenos cibos apposuit, illique eos comederunt. Ingens sane miraculum est cernere spiritus incorporeos, in terris carnium cibos manducantes; sed hoc profecto excedit [omnem admirationem,] omnem mentem, omnemque sermonem, quod nobis fecit unigenitus Christus Salvator noster. Ignem quippe et Spiritum manducandum atque bibendum præstitit nobis carne vestitis, corpus videlicet, et sanguinem suum.

MACARIUS ÆGYPTIACUS SENIOR floruit A.D. 373.

Apud Bibliothecam Vett. P.P. Ed. Galland. 1770.

(a) Homil. iv. p. 16. Σωματοποιεῖ Ἑαυτὸν καὶ εἰς βρῶσιν καὶ πόσιν ὁ Κύριος, καθὼς γέγραπται ἐν τῷ Εὐαγγελίῳ· ὁ τρώγων τὸν ἄρτον τοῦτον, ζήσεται εἰς τὸν αἰῶνα· ἵνα ἀναπαύσῃ ἀνεκλαλήτως, καὶ ἐμπλήσῃ εὐφροσύνης πνευματικῆς τὴν ψυχήν.

d

(b) *Homil.* 27. p. 108. Κατ᾽ ἐκεῖνον τὸν καιρὸν οἱ μεγάλοι, καὶ δίκαιοι, καὶ προφῆται, ὅτι μὲν ἔρχεται ὁ Λυτρωτὴς, ᾔδεισαν· ὅτι δὲ πάσχει, καὶ σταυροῦται, καὶ αἷμα ἐκχεῖται ἐπὶ τοῦ σταυροῦ, οὔτε ᾔδεισαν, οὔτε ἤκουσαν· οὔτε ἀνέβη αὐτῶν ἐπὶ τὴν καρδίαν, ὅτι ἔσται βάπτισμα πυρὸς καὶ Πνεύματος Ἁγίου· καὶ ὅτι ἐν τῇ Ἐκκλησίᾳ προσφέρεται ἄρτος καὶ οἶνος, ἀντίτυπον τῆς σαρκὸς Αὐτοῦ καὶ τοῦ αἵματος· καὶ ὅτι οἱ μεταλαμβάνοντες ἐκ τοῦ φαινομένου ἄρτου, πνευματικῶς τὴν σάρκα τοῦ Κυρίου ἐσθίουσι.

S. Ambrosius floruit A.D. 374.

Edit. Parisiis, A.D. 1686.

(a) *De Benedictione Patriarcharum*, cap. 9. tom. i. p. 525. Hunc panem dedit (Christus) Apostolis, ut dividerent populo credentium; hodieque dat nobis eum, quem ipse quotidie sacerdos consecrat suis verbis. Hic ergo panis factus est esca sanctorum. Possumus et ipsum Dominum accipere, qui suam carnem nobis dedit, sicut Ipse ait, *Ego sum panis vitæ, &c.*—Etiamsi quis mortuus fuerit, tamen si panem meum acceperit, vivet in æternum. Ille enim accipit, qui seipsum *probat.* Qui autem accipit, non morietur peccatoris morte, quia panis hic remissio peccatorum est.

(c) *In Psalm. trigesimum octavum*, p. 853. Vidimus Principem sacerdotum, vidimus et audivimus offerentem pro nobis sanguinem suum : sequimur ut possumus sacerdotes ; ut offeramus pro populo sacrificium ; etsi infirmi merito, tamen honorabiles sacrificio—quia etsi nunc Christus non videtur offerre, tamen Ipse offertur in terris, quando Christi corpus offertur ; immo Ipse offerre manifestatur in nobis, cujus sermo sanctificat sacrificium quod offertur.

(d) *Comment. in Lucam*, lib. i. tom. i. p. 1275. Atque utinam nobis quoque adolentibus altaria, sacrificium deferentibus adsistat angelus, immo se præbeat vïdendum : non enim dubites adsistere angelum, quando Christus adsistit, quando Christus immolatur.

(e) *De Fide ad Gratianum*, lib. iv. cap. 10. tom. ii. p. 543. Nos autem quotiescunque sacramenta sumimus, quæ per sacræ orationis mysterium in carnem transfigurantur et sanguinem, mortem Domini annunciamus.

(f) *De Mysteriis Pasch.* cap. i. p. 293. edit. 1586. Pascha enim passio Salvatoris est, sicuti beatus Apostolus dicit : *Pascha enim nostrum immolatus est Christus.* Ad hoc enim humanum corpus Christus accipiens, se in passionem Paschæ mysterio consecravit.

(g) *De Mysteriis*, cap. 8. tom. ii. p. 337. Ista autem esca, quam accipis, iste panis vivus qui de cœlo descendit, vitæ æternæ substantiam subministrat ; et quicunque hunc non manducaverit, morietur in æternum.

(h) *Ibid.* Abraham vero cum potiretur victoria, tunc illi occurrit Melchisedec, et protulit ea quæ Abraham veneratus accepit.

(i) *Ibid.* cap. 9. p. 338, 339. Forte dicas: aliud video, quomodo tu mihi asseris, quod corpus Christi accipiam? Et hoc nobis adhuc superest ut probemus—probemus non hoc esse quod natura formavit, sed quod benedictio consecravit; majoremque esse vim benedictionis quam naturæ; quia benedictione etiam natura mutatur. [He speaks of Moses's rod being changed into a serpent, and the waters of Egypt being turned into blood, &c.]—quod si tantum valuit sermo Eliæ, ut ignem de cœlo deponeret; non valebit Christi sermo, ut species mutet elementorum? [He afterwards adds,] Præter naturæ ordinem generavit. Et hoc quod conficimus corpus, ex Virgine est,—vera utique caro Christi, quæ crucifixa est, quæ sepulta est: vere ergo carnis Illius sacramentum est. Ipse clamat Dominus Jesus; *hoc est corpus meum.* Ante benedictionem verborum cœlestium alia species nominatur, post consecrationem corpus significatur. Ipse dicit sanguinem suum. Ante consecrationem aliud dicitur, post consecrationem sanguis nuncupatur. Et tu dicis: Amen, hoc est, verum est. Quod os loquitur, mens interna fateatur; quod sermo sonat, affectus sentiat.

(k) *Ibid.* p. 341. In illo sacramento Christus est; quia corpus est Christi: non ergo corporalis esca, sed spiritalis est. Unde Apostolus de typo Ejus ait; quia *Patres nostri escam spiritalem manducaverunt, et potum spiritalem biberunt;* corpus enim Dei corpus est spiritale: corpus Christi corpus est divini Spiritus; quia Spiritus est Christus.

(l) *De Officiis,* lib. i. cap. 41. tom. ii. p. 54. Cum videret (Laurentius) Xystum episcopum suum ad martyrium duci, flere cœpit, non passionem illius, sed suam remansionem. Itaque his verbis appellare cœpit: quo progrederis sine filio, pater; quo, sacerdos sancte, sine diacono properas? nunquam sacrificium sine ministro offerre consueveras. Quid in me ergo displicuit, pater? num degenerem probasti? experire certe, utrum idoneum ministrum elegeris? cui commisisti Dominici sanguinis consecrationem, cui consummandorum consortium sacramentorum, huic consortium tui sanguinis negas?

(m) *Ibid.* cap. 48. p. 63. Umbra in lege, imago in evangelio, veritas in cœlestibus. Ante agnus offerebatur, offerebatur et vitulus; nunc Christus offertur—et offert se Ipse quasi sacerdos, ut peccata nostra dimittat. Hic in imagine, ibi in veritate, ubi apud Patrem pro nobis quasi advocatus intervenit.

(n) *De Incarnationis Dominicæ Sacramento,* cap. 4. p. 708. Nam etsi credas a Christo veram carnem esse susceptam, et offeras transfigurandum corpus altaribus; non distinguas tamen naturam divinitatis et corporis, et tibi dicitur; *si recte offeras, non recte autem dividas, peccasti.*

S. Hieronymus floruit A.D. 378.

Edit. Paris. 1706.

(a) *Ad Heliodorum*, tom. iv. pars ii. p. 10. Absit ut de his quidquam sinistrum loquar, quia Apostolico gradui succedentes, Christi corpus sacro ore conficiunt.

(b) *Ad Marcellam, ib.* p. 547. Recurre ad Genesin, et Melchisedec regem Salem, hujus principem invenies civitatis : qui jam tunc in typo Christi panem et vinum obtulit, et mysterium Christianum in salvatoris corpore et sanguine dedicavit.

(c) *Adversus Jovinianum*, tom. iv. pars ii. p. 198. [Dominus] in typo sanguinis sui non obtulit aquam, sed vinum, (*they are the words of Jovinian allowed by St. Hierome.*)

(d) *Ibid.* p. 218. Quasi non et nos Christi corpus æqualiter accipiamus. Una est in mysteriis sanctificatio, Domini et servi, nobilis et ignobilis—quanquam pro accipientium meritis diversum fiat quod unum est.

(e) *Adversus Vigilantium, ibid.* p. 284. Male facit ergo Romanus episcopus, qui super mortuorum hominum Petri et Pauli, secundum nos ossa veneranda, secundum te vilem pulvisculum, offert Domino sacrificia, et tumulos eorum Christi arbitratur altaria.

(f) *Ad Theophilum, ibid.* p. 335. *He cites* Matt. v. 23. *and adds,* Si munera nostra absque pace offerre non possumus, quanto magis et Christi corpus accipere? Qua conscientia ad Eucharistiam Christi accedam, et respondebo Amen, cum de caritate dubitem porrigentis?

(g) *Advers. Pelagianos, ibid.* lib. iii. p. 543. Sic docuit [Christus] Apostolos suos, ut quotidie in corporis illius sacrificio credentes audeant loqui ; *Pater Noster, qui es in cœlis, &c.*

(h) *Ad Evangelum*, tom. ii. p. 571. Neque carnis et sanguinis victimas immolaverit (Melchisedec), et brutorum sanguinem animalium, dextra susceperit : sed pane et vino, simplici puroque sacrificio, Christi dedicaverit sacramentum.

(i) *Ibid.* p. 572. *He points at* Heb. v. 11. Difficultatem rei procemio exaggerat, dicens ; *super quo multus est nobis sermo, et in interpretabilis :* non quia Apostolus id non potuerit interpretari, sed quia illius temporis non fuerit. Hebræis enim, id est, Judæis persuadebat, non jam fidelibus, quibus passim proderet sacramentum.

(k) *Ad Hedibiam*, tom. iv. p. 171. Nos autem audiamus panem, quem fregit Dominus, deditque discipulis suis, esse corpus Domini Salvatoris, Ipso dicente ad eos : *accipite, et comedite, hoc est corpus meum :* et calicem illum esse, de quo iterum locutus est : *Bibite ex hoc omnes : hic est sanguis, &c.*—Si ergo *panis qui de cœlo descendit*, corpus est Domini ; et vinum quod discipulis dedit, *sanguis, qui pro mul-*

tis effusus est,—ascendamus cum Domino *cœnaculum magnum, stratum, atque mundatum:* et accipiamus ab Eo sursum calicem Novi Testamenti; ibique cum Eo Pascha celebrantes, inebriemur ab eo vino sobrietatis. *Non enim est regnum Dei cibus et potus; sed justitia, et gaudium, et pax in Spiritu Sancto.* Nec Moyses dedit nobis panem verum; sed Dominus Jesus: Ipse conviva et convivium, Ipse comedens et Qui comeditur. Illius bibimus sanguinem, et sine Ipso potare non possumus, et quotidie in sacrificiis Ejus de genimine vitis veræ, et vineæ Sorec, quæ interpretatur, *electa,* rubentia musta calcamus; et novum ex his *vinum* bibimus *de regno Patris,* nequaquam *in vetustate literæ, sed in novitate Spiritus.*

(l) *Quæstiones in Genesin,* tom. ii. p. 520. (Exponens verba Davidis Psalm. (nobis) cx. ver. 4.) Mysterium nostrum in verbo *ordinis* significatur: nequaquam per Aaron irrationalibus victimis immolandis, sed oblato pane et vino, id est, corpore et sanguine Domini Jesu.

(m) *In Esaiam,* cap. 62. tom. iii. p. 462. Triticum quoque, de quo panis cœlestis efficitur, illud est, de quo loquitur Dominus: *caro mea vere est cibus;* rursumque de vino: *Et sanguis meus vere est potus.*

(n) *In Ezechiel.,* cap. 44. p. 1026. *Offertis panes meos,* panes videlicet propositionis in cunctis ecclesiis, et orbe terrarum, de uno pane pullulantes.

(o) *In Malach.,* p. 1811. *Polluimus panem,* id est, corpus Christi, quando indigni accedimus ad altare, et sordidi mundum sanguinem bibimus, et dicimus, *mensa Domini despecta est:* non quod hoc aliquis audeat dicere; *sed opera peccatorum* despiciunt mensam Dei.

(p) *Ibid.* p. 1813. Sciant carnalibus victimis spirituales victimas successuras. Et nequaquam taurorum hircorumque sanguinem, sed θυμίαμα, id est, sanctorum orationes Domino offerendas, et non in una orbis provincia Judæa; nec in una Judææ urbe Hierusalem: sed in omni loco offerri oblationem, nequaquam immundam, ut a populo Israel; sed mundam, ut in ceremoniis Christianorum.

(q) *Comment. in Matth.,* cap. 26. tom. iv. p. 128. Postquam typicum Pascha fuerat impletum, et agni carnes cum Apostolis comederat, assumit panem, qui confortat cor hominis, et ad verum Paschæ transgreditur sacramentum; ut quo modo in præfiguratione Ejus Melchisedec, summi Dei sacerdos, panem et vinum offerens fecerat, Ipse quoque veritatem sui corporis et sanguinis repræsentaret.

(r) *In Epistolam ad Titum,* cap. 1. p. 418. Tantum interest inter panes propositionis et corpus Christi, quantum inter imaginem et veritatem; inter exemplaria futurorum, et ea ipsa quæ per exemplaria præfigurabantur. (*He is speaking of the purity that is necessary for them who celebrate the Eucharist.*)

(s) *Ad Fabiolam,* tom. ii. p. 577. Pontifex et episcopus—ut semper moretur in Sanctis: et paratus sit victimas offerre pro populo, sequester Dei et hominum, et carnes agni sacro ore conficiens.

GAUDENTIUS BRIXIENSIS floruit A.D. 387.

Extat in Biblioth. PP. Tom. iv. edit. Coloniæ A.D. 1618.

(a) *Tractat. in Exod.* ii. p. 806. In umbra illius legalis Paschæ non unus agnus occidebatur, sed plures. Singuli enim occidebantur per domos: nam sufficere unus non poterat universis; quoniam figura erat, non proprietas Dominicæ passionis: figura enim non est veritas, sed imitatio veritatis: ergo in hac veritate qua sumus, unus pro omnibus mortuus est, et idem per singulas ecclesiarum domos in mysterio panis et vini reficit immolatus, vivificat creditus, consecrantes sanctificat consecratus. Recte etiam vini specie tum sanguis Ejus exprimitur, quia cum Ipse dicit in Evangelio, *Ego sum vitis vera;* satis declarat sanguinem suum esse omne vinum, quod in figura passionis Ejus offertur—Ipse igitur naturarum Creator et Dominus, qui producit de terra panem, de pane rursus (quia potest, et promisit,) efficit proprium corpus; et qui de aqua vinum fecit, et de vino sanguinem suum.

(b) *Ibid.* p. 807. Quod annunciatum est, credas; quia quod accipis, corpus est illius panis cœlestis, et sanguis est illius veræ vitis. Nam cum panem consecratum, et vinum discipulis suis porrigeret, sic ait; *Hoc est corpus meum, hic est sanguis meus.* Credamus, quæso, cui credidimus. Nescit mendacium Veritas.—Non infringentes illud os Ipsius solidissimum, *Hoc est corpus meum, hic est sanguis meus.* Siquid autem superfuerit etiam nunc in uniuscujusque sensu, quod expositione ista non ceperit, ardore fidei concrematur.

(c) *Ibid.* Vere istud hæreditarium munus Testamenti Ejus Novi, quod nobis ea nocte qua tradebatur crucifigendus, tanquam pignus suæ præsentiæ dereliquit. Hoc illud est viaticum nostri itineris, quo in hac via vitæ alimur ac nutrimur, donec ad Ipsum pergamus de hoc sæculo recedentes, unde dicebat Idem Dominus: *Nisi manducaveritis carnem Filii hominis, et biberitis sanguinem Ejus, non habebitis vitam in vobis ipsis.* Voluit enim beneficia sua permanere apud nos, voluit animas pretioso sanguine suo semper sanctificari per imaginem propriæ passionis, et ideo discipulis fidelibus mandat, quos primos et Ecclesiæ suæ constituit sacerdotes, ut indesinenter ista vitæ æternæ mysteria exercerent, quæ necesse est a cunctis sacerdotibus per singulas totius orbis ecclesias celebrari, usque quo iterum Christus de cœlis adveniat, quo et ipsi sacerdotes, et omnes pariter fidelium populi exemplar passionis Christi ante oculos habentes quotidie, et gerentes in manibus, ore etiam sumentes et pectore, redemptionis nostræ [pretium vel gratiam] indelebili memoria teneamus, et contra venena diaboli dulcem medicinam sempiterni tutaminis consequamur.

(d) *Ibid.* Quod autem sacramenta corporis sui et sanguinis in specie panis et vini offerenda constituit, duplex ratio est. Primum, ut immaculatus Dei Agnus hostiam mundam mundato populo traderet celebrandam, sine ustione, sine sanguine, sine brodio, id est, jure carnium, et quæ omnibus ad offerendum prompta esset ac facilis. Deinde quomodo panem de multis tritici granis in pollinem redactis per aquam confici, et per ignem necesse est consummari; rationabiliter in eo figura accipitur corporis Christi, quia novimus ex multitudine totius generis humani unum esse corpus effectum, per ignem Sancti Spiritus consummatum. Natus est enim de Spiritu Sancto—.

S. Augustinus floruit A.D. 396.

Ed. Benedictinorum, A.D. 1679.

(a) *Confessionum*, lib. ix. cap. 13. tom. i. p. 170. Memoriam sui ad altare tuum, [Deus,] fieri, desideravit (Monica), cui nullius diei prætermissione servierat, unde sciret dispensari victimam sanctam, qua deletum est chirographum, quod erat contrarium nobis.

(b) *Epistol.* 149. *ad Paulinum*, tom. ii. p. 509. Voventur autem omnia quæ Deo offeruntur, maxime sancti altaris oblatio.

(c) *Ibid.* (*in verba* 1 *Epistol. ad Timoth.* ii. ver. 1.) Sed eligo in his verbis hoc intelligere, quod omnis vel pene omnis frequentat ecclesia, ut *precationes* accipiamus dictas, quas facimus in celebrationem sacramentorum, antequam illud, quod est in mensa Domini, incipiat benedici; *orationes* cum benedicitur et sanctificatur, et ad distribuendum comminuitur, quam totam petitionem fere omnis ecclesia Dominica oratione concludit.—In hujus sanctificationis præparatione, existimo Apostolum jussisse proprie fieri προσευχὰς,—*interpellationes* autem, cum populus benedicitur.

(d) *Epistol. ad Bonifacium* 185, *ibid.* p. 653. Convivium Domini, unitas est corporis Christi, non solum in sacramento altaris sed etiam in vinculo pacis.

(e) *De Doctrina Christiana*, lib. iii. cap. 16. tom. iii. pars 1. p. 52. (in Joan. vi. 53. Nisi manducaveritis carnem Filii hominis, &c.) Facinus vel flagitium videtur jubere; figura ergo est, præcipiens passioni Dominicæ communicandum, et suaviter atque utiliter in memoria recondendum, quod caro Ejus pro nobis crucifixa et vulnerata sit.

(f) *In Leviticum, ibid.* p. 516, 517. Cum Dominus dicat, *Nisi manducaveritis carnem meam*, &c., quid sibi vult, quod a sanguine sacrificiorum, quæ pro peccatis offerebantur, tantopere populus pro-

hibetur, si illis sacrificiis hoc unum sacrificium significabatur, in quo
vera fit remissio peccatorum : a cujus tamen sacrificii sanguine in
alimentum sumendo, non solum nemo prohibetur, sed ad bibendum
potius omnes exhortantur, qui volunt habere vitam ?

(g) *De sermone Domini in Monte,* lib. ii. cap. 7. tom. iii. pars 2.
p. 209. Panis quotidianus, aut pro iis omnibus dictus est, quæ hujus
vitæ necessitatem sustentant, aut pro sacramento Corporis Christi,
quod quotidie accipimus : aut pro spiritali cibo, de quo idem Dominus
dicit, *Ego sum panis,* &c.

(h) *Tract. in Joannem* xi. *ibid.* p. 376. *Jesus non se credebat eis.*
Tales sunt omnes catechumeni ; ipsi jam credunt in nomine Christi,
sed Jesus non se credit eis. Si dixerimus catechumeno, Credis in
Christum ? respondet, Credo, et signat se (cruce Christi): jam crucem
Christi portat in fronte, et non erubescit de cruce Domini sui. Inter-
rogemus eum, Manducas carnem Filii hominis, et bibis sanguinem ?
Nescit quid dicimus, quia Jesus non se credidit ei—Nesciunt cate-
chumeni quid accipiant Christiani.

(i) *Tract. in Joannem* xxvi. *ibid.* p. 494. Credere enim in Eum, hoc
est manducare panem vivum. Qui credit, manducat ; invisibiliter
saginatur quia invisibiliter renascitur ; intrare quisquam potest nolens,
accedere ad altare potest nolens, accipere sacramentum potest nolens,
credere non potest nisi volens.

(k) *Ibid.* p. 498. Aliud est Sacramentum, aliud virtus Sacramenti.

Ibid. p. 499. *Hic est panis de cœlo descendens*—Sed quod pertinet
ad virtutem Sacramenti, non quod pertinet ad visibile Sacramentum :
qui manducat intus, non foris ; qui manducat in corde, non qui premit
dente.

(l) *Ibid.* p. 500. Hujus rei Sacramentum, id est, unitatis corporis
et sanguinis Christi alicubi quotidie, alicubi certis intervallis dierum in
Dominica mensa præparatur, et de mensa Dominica sumitur ; quibusdam ad vitam, quibusdam ad exitium : res vero Ipsa cujus Sacramentum est, omni homini ad vitam, nulli ad exitium, quicumque Ejus
particeps fuerit.

(m) *Ibid.* p. 501. Qui non manet in Christo, et in quo non
manet Christus, proculdubio nec manducat [spiritaliter] carnem Ejus,
nec bibit Ejus sanguinem, [licet carnaliter et visibiliter premat
dentibus Sacramentum corporis et sanguinis Christi ;] sed magis
tantæ rei Sacramentum ad judicium sibi manducat et bibit.

(n) *Tract. in Joan.* xxvii. *ibid.* p. 502. *Si ergo videritis Filium
hominis ascendentem ubi erat prius ;* certe vel tunc videbitis, quia non
eo modo quo putatis erogat corpus suum ; certe vel tunc intelligetis,
quia gratia Ejus non consumitur morsibus.

(o) *Ibid.* p. 506. Ut carnem Christi et sanguinem Christi non edamus tantum in sacramento, quod et multi mali; sed usque ad Spiritus participationem manducemus et bibamus, ut in Domini corpore tanquam membra maneamus, ut Ejus spiritu vegetemur.

(p) *Ibid. Tract. in Joan.* 80. p. 703. Accedit verbum ad elementum, et fit sacramentum.

(q) *In Psalm.* xxxiii. tom. iv. p. 210, 211. Erat autem, ut nostis, sacrificium Judæorum antea secundum ordinem Aaron in victimis pecorum, et hoc in mysterio: nondum erat sacrificium corporis et sanguinis Domini, quod fideles norunt,—quod sacrificium nunc diffusum est toto orbe terrarum,—sublatum est ergo sacrificium Aaron, et cœpit esse sacrificium secundum ordinem Melchisedec.

(r) *In Psalm.* xxxix. (*nobis* xl.) Ibid. p. 334. Sacrificia ergo illa, tamquam verba promissiva, ablata sunt, [data sunt completiva]. Quid est, quod datum est completivum? corpus quod nostis, quod non omnes nostis; quod utinam qui nostis, omnes ad judicium non noveritis. Videte, quando dictum est. Christus enim Ille est Dominus noster, modo loquens ex membris suis, modo loquens ex persona sua. *Sacrificium*, inquit, *et oblationem noluisti.* Quid ergo? Nos jam hoc tempore sine sacrificio dimissi sumus? Absit: *corpus autem perfecisti mihi.* Ideo illa noluisti, ut hoc perficeres; illa voluisti, antequam hoc perficeres. Perfectio promissorum abstulit verba promittentia. Nam si adhuc sunt promittentia, nondum impletum est, quod promissum est. Hoc promittebatur quibusdam signis: ablata sunt signa promittentia, quia exhibita est veritas promissa. In hoc corpore sumus, hujus corporis participes sumus: et qui non nostis noveritis, et cum didiceritis, utinam non ad judicium accipiatis. Qui enim manducat et bibit indigne, judicium sibi manducat et bibit. Perfectum nobis est corpus, perficiamur in corpore.

(s) *In Psalm.* xcviii. (*nobis* xcix.) Ibid. p. 1065. Timeo adorare terram, ne damnet me Qui fecit cœlum et terram: rursum timeo non adorare scabellum pedum Ejus—et dicit mihi Scriptura, *Terra scabellum pedum meorum.* Fluctuans converto me ad Christum, quia Ipsum quæro hic; et invenio quomodo sine impietate adoretur terra, sine impietate adoretur scabellum pedum Ejus. Suscepit enim de terra terram: quia caro de terra est, et de carne Mariæ carnem accepit. Et quia in ipsa carne hîc ambulavit, et ipsam carnem nobis manducandam ad salutem dedit; nemo autem illam carnem manducat, nisi prius adoraverit: inventum est, quemadmodum adoretur tale scabellum pedum Domini, et non solum non peccemus adorando, sed peccemus non adorando. Numquid autem caro vivificat? Ipse Dominus dixit, cum de ipsa commendatione ejusdem terræ loqueretur, *Spiritus est Qui vivificat, caro autem nihil prodest.* Ideo et ad terram quamlibet cum te inclinas atque prosternis, non quasi terram intuearis, sed Illum Sanctum, Cujus pedum scabellum est quod adoras ; propter Ipsum enim adoras : ideo et hic subjecit, *Adorate scabellum pedum Ejus, quoniam sanctus est.* Quis sanctus est ? In Cujus honore adoras scabellum pedum Ejus. Et cum adoras Illum, ne cogitatione remaneas in carne, et ab Spiritu non vivificeris : *Spiritus est enim* inquit, *Qui vivificat ; caro autem nihil prodest.*—Et mox p. 1066, *he introduceth Christ pronouncing these words*, Jo. vi. 53. 63, *and thus explaining them*, spiritaliter intelligite quod locutus sum : non hoc corpus quod videtis, manducaturi estis ;—sacramentum aliquod vobis commendavi, spiritaliter intellectum vivificabit vos. Etsi necesse est illud visibiliter celebrari, oportet tamen invisibiliter intelligi.

(t) *Sermo* lxxi. *de verbis Domini*, tom. v. pars i. p. 391. Illud etiam [*siquis manducaverit ex hoc pane vivet in æternnm*] quomodo intellecturi sumus ? Numquid etiam illos hîc poterimus accipere, de quibus dicit Apostolus, quod judicium sibi manducent et bibant ; cum ipsam carnem manducent, et ipsum sanguinem bibant ? Numquid et Judas magistri venditor et traditor impius, (quamvis primum ipsum manibus Ipsius confectum sacramentum carnis et sanguinis Ejus cum cæteris discipulis, sicut apertius Lucas Evangelista declarat, manducaret et biberet) mansit in Christo, aut Christus in eo ? Jam multi denique, qui vel corde ficto carnem illam manducant et sanguinem bibunt, vel cum manducaverint et biberint, apostatæ fiunt, numquid manent in Christo, aut Christus in eis ? sed profecto est quidam modus manducandi illam carnem, et bibendi illum sanguinem, quo modo qui manducaverit et biberit, in Christo manet, et Christus in eo.

(tt) *S. Ambros. De Sacrament.*, lib. v. cap. 4. p. 378. Ed. Par. Dixi vobis, quod ante verba Christi quod offertur, panis dicatur ; ubi Christi verba deprompta fuerint, jam non panis dicitur, sed corpus appellatur.

(u) *Serm.* cxii. Ibid. Quis est panis de regno Dei, nisi Qui dicit, *Ego sum panis vivus, qui de cœlo descendi?* noli parare fauces, sed cor. Inde commendata est ista cœna. Ecce credimus in Christum, cum fide accipimus. In accipiendo novimus quid cogitemus. Modicum accipimus, et in corde saginamur. Non ergo quod videtur, sed quod creditur, pascit.

(w) *De verbis Apostoli, Serm.* cxxxi. Ibid. p. 640, 641. Audivimus veracem Magistrum, Divinum Redemptorem, humanum Salvatorem, commendantem nobis pretium nostrum, sanguinem suam. Locutus est enim nobis de corpore et sanguine suo : corpus dixit escam, sanguinem potum, sacramentum fidelium agnoscunt Fideles. —Tunc autem hoc erit, id est, vita erit unicuique corpus et sanguis Christi ; si quod in sacramento visibiliter sumitur, in ipsa veritate spiritaliter manducetur, spiritaliter bibatur. Audivimus enim Ipsum Dominum dicentem, *Spiritus est, qui vivificat.*

(x) *Enchiridion,* tom. vi. pars i. p. 238. Neque negandum est, defunctorum animas pietate suorum viventium relevari, cum pro illis sacrificium Mediatoris offertur, vel eleemosynæ in ecclesia fiunt. Sed iis hæc prosunt, qui cum viverent, ut hæc sibi postea prodesse possent, meruerunt.—Est enim quidam vivendi modus, nec tam bonus ut non requirat ista post mortem, nec tam malus ut ei non prosint ista post mortem—Quocirca hîc omne meritum comparatur, quo possit post hanc vitam relevari quispiam vel gravari.

(y) *De civitate Dei,* lib. x. cap. 5. tom. vii. p. 241. Sacrificium ergo visibile invisibilis sacrificii sacramentum, id est, sacrum signum est.

(z) *Ibid.* cap. 6. Hoc est sacrificium Christianorum : *multi unum corpus in Christo.* Quod etiam sacramento altaris fidelibus noto frequentat Ecclesia, ubi ei demonstratur, quod in ea re quam offert, ipsa offeratur.

[A] *Ibid.* lib. x. cap. 20. p. 256. Jesus Christus sacrificium maluit esse quam sumere—per hoc et sacerdos est, Ipse offerens, Ipse et oblatio. Cujus rei sacramentum quotidianum esse voluit Ecclesiæ sacrificium : quæ cum Ipsius capitis corpus sit, seipsam per Ipsum discit offerre. Hujus veri sacrificii multiplicia variaque signa erant sacrificia prisca sanctorum.

(B) *Ibid.* lib. xvi. cap. 22. p. 435. [Cum Melchisedec Abrahæ benediceret] ibi primum apparuit sacrificium, quod nunc a Christianis offertur toto terrarum orbe.

(C) *Ibid.* lib. xvii. cap. 5. p. 467. *Manducare panem ;* quod est, est in Novo Testamento sacrificium Christianorum.—p. 466. *He produces the words of God to Eli,* 1 Sam. ii. 36, *and adds,* Quod ergo addidit, *manducare panem,* etiam ipsum sacrificii genus eleganter expressit, de quo dicit sacerdos Ipse, *Panis, quem Ego dedero, caro mea est pro seculi vita.* Ipsum est sacrificium, non secundum ordinem Aaron, sed secundum ordinem Melchisedec : qui legit, intelligat.

(D) *Ibid.* lib. xvii. cap. 17. p. 480. *Tu es sacerdos in æternum,* ex eo quod jam nusquam est sacerdotium et sacrificium secundum ordinem Aaron, et ubique offertur sub sacerdote Christo, quod protulit Melchisedec, quando benedixit Abraham.

(E) *Ibid.* cap. 20. p. 484. *Non est bonum homini, nisi quod manducabit, et bibet.* Quid credibilius dicere intelligitur, quam quod ad participationem mensæ hujus pertinet, quam sacerdos Ipse Mediator Testamenti Novi exhibet secundum ordinem Melchisedec de corpore et sanguine suo ? Id enim sacrificium successit omnibus illis sacrificiis Veteris Testamenti, quæ immolabantur in umbra futuri : propter quod etiam vocem illam in Psalmo xxxix. [*nobis* xl.] Ejusdem Mediatoris per prophetiam loquentis agnoscimus : *sacrificium et oblationem noluisti, corpus autem perfecisti mihi.* Quia pro omnibus illis sacrificiis et oblationibus corpus Ejus offertur, et participantibus ministratur.

(F) Lib. xxi. cap. 25. p. 646, 647.   Non sacramento tenus, sed revera corpus Christi manducare, [id est] in Christo manere, ut in illo maneat et Christus.

[G] *Contra Faustum*, lib. xix. cap. 13. tom. viii. p. 320.   Prima sacramenta ablata sunt—et alia sunt instituta virtute majora, utilitate meliora, actu faciliora, numero pauciora.

(H) *Ibid.* lib. xx. cap. 18.   Christiani peracti ejusdem sacrificii memoriam celebrant, sacrosancta oblatione et participatione corporis et sanguinis Christi.

(I) *Ibid.* cap. 21. p. 348.   Sacrificare Deo in memoriis martyrum, quod frequentissime facimus, illo duntaxat ritu, quo Sibi sacrificari Novi Testamenti manifestatione præcepit : quod pertinet ad illum cultum, qui *latria* dicitur, et Uni Deo debetur.

(K) *Ibid.* p. 348.   Hujus sacrificii caro et sanguis ante adventum Christi per victimas similitudinum promittebatur ; in passione Christi per ipsam veritatem reddebatur ; post ascensum Christi per sacramentum memoriæ celebratur.

(L) *Ibid. Contra adversarium Legis et Prophetarum,* lib. i. cap. 20. p. 571. *Mentioning* Malachi i. 11, *he says,* Incensum enim, quod est Græce θυμίαμα, sicut exponit Johannes in Apocalypsi, orationes sunt sanctorum.

(M) *Ibid.* lib. ii. cap. 9. p. 599.   Mediatorem Dei et hominum, hominem Christum Jesum, carnem suam nobis manducandam bibendumque sanguinem dantem, fideli corde atque ore suscipimus.

(N) *Contra Cresconium*, lib. i. cap. 25. tom. ix. p. 403.   Quid, de ipso corpore et sanguine Domini, unico sacrificio pro salute nostra? Quamvis Ipse Dominus dicat, *Nisi quis manducaverit carnem Filii hominis, et biberit Ejus sanguinem, non habebit vitam,* &c., nonne idem Apostolus docet etiam hoc perniciosum male utentibus fieri? Ait enim : *Quicumque manducaverit panem, et biberit calicem Domini indigne, reus erit corporis et sanguinis Domini.*

(O) *De spiritu et litera,* cap. 11. tom. x. pars i. p. 94. Θεοσέβεια —Dei cultus dici poterat, qui in hoc maxime constitutus est, ut anima Ei non sit ingrata. Unde et in ipso verissimo et singulari sacrificio, Domino Deo nostro gratias agere admonemur.

(P) *De Meritis ac Remissione peccatorum,* lib. i. cap. 24. Ibid. p. 19. Optime Punici Christiani baptismum ipsum nihil aliud quam *salutem,* et sacramentum corporis Christi nihil aliud quam *vitam* vocant.

Unde, nisi ex antiqua, ut existimo, et apostolica traditione, qua ecclesiæ Christi institutum tenent, præter baptismum et participationem
mensæ Dominicæ, non solum ad regnum Dei, sed nec ad salutem et
vitam æternam posse quemquam hominum pervenire?—Quid aliud
[tenent] etiam, qui sacramentum mensæ Dominicæ *vitam* vocant, nisi
quod dictum est, *Ego sum panis.*

(Q) *De Peccatorum meritis, ac remissione*, lib. ii. cap. 26. Ibid.
p. 62, 63. Quod accipiunt [*Catechumeni*], quamvis non sit corpus
Christi, sanctum est tamen, et sanctius quam cibi quibus alimur,
quoniam sacramentum est. Verum et ipsos cibos, quibus ad necessitatem sustentandæ hujus vitæ alimur, sanctificari idem Apostolus
dixit, per verbum Dei et orationem, qua oramus, utique nostra cor-
puscula refecturi. Sicut ergo ista ciborum sanctificatio non efficit, ut
quod in os intraverit non in ventrem vadat et in secessum emittatur
per corruptionem, qua terrena omnia solvuntur, unde et ad aliam
escam nos Dominus hortatur ; ita sanctificatio catechumeni, si non
fuerit baptizatus, non ei valet ad intrandum in regnum cœlorum, aut
ad peccatorum remissionem.

(R) *De Trinitate*, lib. iii. cap. 4. tom. viii. p. 798. Nec linguam
quippe ejus, nec membranas, nec atramentum, nec significantes sonos
linguæ editos, nec signa literarum conscripta pelliculis, corpus Christi
et sanguinem dicimus ; sed illud tantum, quod ex frugibus terræ acceptum et prece mystica consecratum rite sumimus ad salutem spiritalem in memoriam pro nobis Dominicæ passionis : quod cum per
manus hominum ad illam visibilem speciem perducatur, non sanctificatur, ut sit tam magnum sacramentum, nisi operante invisibiliter
Spiritu Dei.

N. B. *This is misplaced, but cannot now be removed, because the
reader is directed to it by the letter* R.

S. JOANNES CHRYSOSTOMUS floruit A.D. 398.

Ed. Savile, 1612.

(a) *Homil. ad populum Antioch.*, tom. vi. p. 605. Ἔχεις τράπεζαν
πνευματικὴν ―― βούλει μαθεῖν, πῶς καὶ τράπεζά σοι γίνεται ; ―― ὁ
τρώγων Μοῦ τὴν σάρκα ἐν Ἐμοὶ μένει.

(b) *De Incomprehensibili Dei natura.* Ibid. p. 407. Σφόδρα ἐστέ-
ναξα, ὅτι τοῦ μὲν συνδούλου διαλεγομένου, πολλὴ ἡ σπουδὴ, ἐπιτεταμένη ἡ
προθυμία συνωθούντων ἀλλήλους καὶ μέχρι τέλους παραμένοντων. τοῦ δὲ
Χριστοῦ φαίνεσθαι μέλλοντος ἐπὶ τῶν ἱερῶν Μυστηρίων, κένη καὶ ἔρημος ἡ
ἐκκλησία γίνεται.

De Beato Philogonio, tom. v. p. 509. Ἡ γὰρ τράπεζα αὕτη τάξιν
τῆς φάτνης πληροῖ. καὶ γὰρ καὶ ἐνταῦθα κείσεται τὸ Σῶμα τὸ Δεσποτικὸν, οὐχὶ

ἐσπαργανωμένον, καθάπερ τότε, ἀλλὰ Πνεύματι πανταχόθεν Ἁγίῳ περιστελλόμενον. ἴσασιν οἱ μεμνημένοι τὰ λεγόμενα. οἱ μὲν οὖν μάγοι προσεκύνησαν μόνον· σὺ δε, ἂν μετὰ καθαροῦ προσέλθῃς συνειδότος, καὶ λαβεῖν σοι Αὐτὸ συγχωρήσομεν, καὶ ἀπελθεῖν οἴκαδε.

(d) *In Psalm.* cix. tom. i. p. 731. Καὶ διὰ τί εἶπε, κατὰ τὴν τάξιν Μελχισεδὲκ; καὶ διὰ τὰ Μυστήρια, ὅτι κἀκεῖνος ἄρτον καὶ οἶνον προσήνεγκε τῷ Ἀβραάμ· καὶ διὰ τὸ ἐλεύθεραν εἶναι ἀπὸ τοῦ νόμου ταύτην τὴν ἱερωσύνην.

(e) *In Psalm.* cxxxiii. Ibid. p. 821. Πόσης ἐννόησον ἁγιωσύνης σοι δεῖ τῷ πολλῷ μείζονα σύμβολα δεξαμένῳ, ὧν ἐδέξατο τὰ ἅγια τῶν ἁγίων τότε. οὐ γὰρ χερουβὶμ ἔχεις, ἀλλ᾽ Αὐτὸν τῶν χερουβὶμ Δεσπότην ἐνοικοῦντα· οὐδὲ σταμνὸν καὶ μαννὰ καὶ πλάκας λιθίνας, καὶ τὴν ῥάβδον τὴν Ἀαρὼν, ἀλλὰ Σῶμα καὶ Αἷμα Δεσποτικὸν, καὶ Πνεῦμα ἀντὶ γράμματος, καὶ χάριν ὑπερβαίνουσαν λογισμὸν ἀνθρώπινον, καὶ δωρεὰν ἀνεκδιήγητον. ὅσῳ μειζόνων ἠξιώθης συμβόλων, καὶ φρικτῶν μυστηρίων, τοσούτῳ μείζονος ὑπεύθυνος εἶ τῆς ἁγιωσύνης, καὶ πλείονος κολάσεως, εἰ παραβαίνῃς τὰ ἐπιτεταγμένα.

(f) *In Psalm.* xcv. (*citans verba Malachiæ.*) Ibid. p. 918. Ὅρα πῶς λαμπρῶς καὶ περιφανῶς τὴν μυστικὴν ἡρμήνευσε τράπεζαν, τὴν ἀναίμακτον θυσίαν; θυμίαμα δὲ λέγει καθαρὸν, τὴν προσευχὴν τὴν ἁγίαν τὴν μετὰ τῆς θυσίας ἀναφερομένην. ἐστὶ μὲν οὖν θυσία καθαρὰ, πρώτη μὲν ἡ μυστικὴ τράπεζα, τὸ οὐράνιον, τὸ ὑπερκόσμιον θῦμα.

(g) Ibid. p. 919. Ἔχεις οὖν πρώτην θυσίαν, τὸ Σωτήριον Δῶρον· δευτέραν, τὴν τῶν Μαρτύρων· τρίτην, τὴν τῆς προσευχῆς· τετάρτην, τὴν τοῦ ἀλαλαγμοῦ· πέμπτην, τὴν τῆς δικαιοσύνης· ἕκτην, τὴν τῆς ἐλεημοσύνης· ἑβδόμην, τὴν τῆς αἰνέσεως· ὀγδόην, τὴν τῆς κατανύξεως· ἐννάτην, τὴν τῆς ταπεινοφροσύνης· δεκάτην, τὴν τοῦ κηρύγματος.

(h) *De Sacerdotio,* lib. iii. tom. vi. p. 16. Ἔστηκε γὰρ ὁ ἱερεὺς, οὐ πῦρ καταφέρων, ἀλλὰ τὸ Πνεῦμα τὸ Ἅγιον, καὶ τὴν ἱκετηρίαν ἐπὶ πολὺ ποιεῖται, οὐχ ἵνα τὶς λαμπὰς ἄνωθεν ἀφθεῖσα καταναλώσῃ τὰ προκείμενα, ἀλλ᾽ ἵνα ἡ χάρις ἐπιπεσοῦσα τῇ θυσίᾳ, δι᾽ ἐκείνης τὰς ἁπάντων ἀνάψῃ ψυχὰς.

(i) Lib. vi. Ibid. p. 46. Ὅταν δὲ καὶ τὸ Πνεῦμα τὸ Ἅγιον καλῇ, καὶ τὴν φρικωδεστάτην ἐπιτελῇ Θυσίαν, καὶ τοῦ κοινοῦ πάντων συνεχῶς ἐφάπτεται Δεσπότου, ποῦ τάξομεν αὐτὸν;

(k) *De proditione Judæ,* tom. v. p. 557. Ἐν αὐτῇ τῇ τραπέζῃ ἑκάτερον γίνεται Πάσχα, καὶ τὸ τοῦ τύπου, καὶ τὸ τῆς ἀληθείας. καθάπερ γὰρ οἱ ζωγράφοι ἐν αὐτῷ τῷ πίνακι καὶ τὰς γράμμας περιάγουσι, καὶ τὴν σκιὰν γράφουσι, καὶ τότε τὴν ἀλήθειαν τῶν χρωμάτων αὐτῷ ἐπιτεθέασιν· οὕτω καὶ ὁ Χριστὸς ἐποίησεν, ἐπ᾽ αὐτῆς τῆς τραπέζης καὶ τὸ τυπικὸν Πάσχα ὑπέγραψε, καὶ τὸ ἀληθινὸν προσέθηκε.

(l) Ibid. p. 559. Οὐδὲ γὰρ ἄνθρωπός ἐστιν Ὁ ποιῶν τὰ προκείμενα γενέσθαι Σῶμα καὶ Αἷμα Χριστοῦ· ἀλλ᾽ Αὐτὸς ὁ σταυρωθεὶς ὑπὲρ ἡμῶν Χριστὸς· σχῆμα πληρῶν ἔστηκεν ὁ ἱερεὺς, τὰ ῥήματα φθεγγόμενος ἐκεῖνα· ἡ δὲ δύναμις καὶ ἡ χάρις, τοῦ Θεοῦ ἐστι. Τοῦτό Μου ἐστὶ τὸ Σῶμά, φησι, τοῦτο τὸ ῥῆμα μεταρρυθμίζει τὰ προκείμενα. καὶ καθάπερ ἡ φωνὴ ἐκείνη ἡ λέγουσα· αὐξάνεσθε, καὶ πληθύνεσθε, &c. ἐρρέθη μὲν ἅπαξ, διὰ πάντος δὲ τοῦ χρόνου γίνεται ἔργῳ ἐνδυναμοῦσα τὴν φύσιν τὴν ἡμέτεραν πρὸς παιδοποιίαν· οὕτω καὶ φωνὴ αὕτη ἅπαξ λεχθεῖσα καθ᾽ ἑκάστην τράπεζαν ἐν ταῖς ἐκκλησίαις, ἐξ ἐκείνου μέχρι σήμερον, καὶ μέχρι τῆς Αὐτοῦ παρουσίας, τὴν θυσίαν ἀπηρτισμένην ἐργάζεται.

(m) *Homil. in Cœmeterii appellationem,* Ibid. p. 566. Ὅταν ἐστήκῃ πρὸ τῆς τραπέζης ὁ ἱερεὺς, τὰς χεῖρας ἀνατείνων εἰς τὸν οὐρανὸν, καλῶν τὸ Πνεῦμα τὸ Ἅγιον, τοῦ παραγενέσθαι καὶ ἅψασθαι τῶν προκειμένων, πολλὴ ἡσυχία, πολλὴ σιγή. ὅταν διδῷ τὴν χάριν τὸ Πνεῦμα, ὅταν κατέλθῃ, ὅταν ἅψηται τῶν προκειμένων, ὅταν ἴδῃς τὸ πρόβατον ἐσφαγιασμένον καὶ ἀπηρτισμένον, τότε θόρυβον, τότε ταραχὴν, τότε φιλονεικίαν, τότε λοιδορίαν ἐπεισάγεις;

(n) *De Resurrectione mortuorum,* tom. vi. p. 713. Εἰ γὰρ μὴ ἦν ἀρραβὼν τοῦ Πνεύματος καὶ νῦν, οὐκ ἂν συνέστη τὸ βάπτισμα, οὐκ ἂν ἁμαρτημάτων ἄφεσις ἐγένετο, οὐκ ἂν δικαιοσύνη καὶ ἁγιασμός, οὐκ ἂν υἱοθεσίαν ἐλάβομεν, οὐκ ἂν Μυστηρίων ἀπελαύσαμεν (Σῶμα γὰρ καὶ Αἷμα Μυστικὸν οὐκ ἂν πότε γένοιτο τῆς τοῦ Πνεύματος χάριτος χωρὶς) οὐκ ἂν ἱερέας ἐσχήκαμεν· οὐδὲ γὰρ ταύτας δυνατὸν τὰς χειροτονίας ἄνευ ἐκείνης τῆς ἐπιφοιτήσεως γίνεσθαι.

(o) *Homil. de Pœnitentia,* or, *de Eucharistia in Encœniis.* Ibid. p. 791. Μὴ ὅτι ἄρτος ἐστὶν ἴδῃς, μηδ᾽ ὅτι οἶνός ἐστι νομίσῃς· οὐ γὰρ ὡς αἱ λοιπαὶ βρώσεις εἰς ἀφεδρῶνα χωρεῖ. ἄπαγε, μὴ τοῦτο νόει. ἀλλ᾽ ὥσπερ κηρὸς πυρὶ προσομιλήσας οὐδὲν ἀπουσιάζει, οὐδὲν περισσεύει· οὕτω καὶ ὧδε νόμιζε συναλίσκεσθαι τὰ Μυστήρια τῇ τοῦ Σώματος οὐσίᾳ. *A little before this citation are these words,* πυρὸς πνευματικοῦ ἐκ τῆς ἀχράντου ἀναβλύζοντος τραπέζης.

(oo) *Hom. de filio prodigo,* post medium, tom. vii. p. 543. Μή τις τῶν κατηχουμένων, μή τις τῶν μὴ ἐσθιόντων, μή τις τῶν κατασκόπων, μή τις τῶν μὴ δυναμένων θεάσασθαι τὸν μόσχον ἐσθιόμενον, μή τις τῶν μὴ δυναμένων θεάσασθαι τὸ οὐράνιον Αἷμα τὸ ἐκχυνόμενον εἰς ἄφεσιν ἁμαρτιῶν, μή τις ἀνάξιος τῆς ζώσης Θυσίας, μή τις ἀμύητος, μή τις μὴ δυνάμενος ἀκαθάρτοις χείλεσι προσψαύσασθαι τῶν φρικτῶν Μυστηρίων.

(p) *Homil. 7. In Matthæum,* tom. ii. p. 48. Οὐδὲ γὰρ ὕδωρ ἀπὸ ταύτης ἡμῖν παρέχει τῆς πηγῆς, ἀλλ᾽ Αἷμα ζῶν, καὶ μὴν θανάτου ἐστὶ σύμβολον, ἀλλὰ ζωῆς γέγονεν αἴτιον.

(q) *Homil. 25. In Matthæum.* Ibid. pp. 178-9. Καὶ τὰ φρικώδη μυστήρια καὶ πολλῆς γέμοντα τῆς σωτηρίας, τὰ καθ᾽ ἑκάστην τελούμενα σύναξιν, Εὐχαριστία καλεῖται, ὅτι πολλῶν ἐστιν εὐεργετημάτων ἀνάμνησις— διὸ δὴ καὶ ὁ ἱερεὺς ὑπὲρ τῆς οἰκουμένης, ὑπὲρ τῶν προτέρων, ὑπὲρ τῶν νῦν, ὑπὲρ τῶν γεννηθέντων ἔμπροσθεν, ὑπὲρ τῶν μετὰ ταῦτα ἐσομένων [εἰς] ἡμᾶς εὐχαριστεῖν κελεύει, τῆς θυσίας προκειμένης ἐκείνης.

(r) *Homil. 50. In Matthæum.* Ibid. p. 332. Τὸ δὲ προσελθεῖν μετὰ πίστεως, οὐ τὸ λαβεῖν ἐστὶ μόνον τὸ προκείμενον, ἀλλὰ καὶ τὸ μετὰ καθαρᾶς καρδίας ἅψασθαι, τὸ οὕτω διακεῖσθαι, ὡς Αὐτῷ προσίοντας τῷ Χριστῷ. Τί γὰρ εἰ μὴ φωνῆς ἀκούεις; φθεγγομένου Αὐτοῦ [ἀκούεις] διὰ τῶν Εὐαγγελιστῶν. πιστεύσατε τοίνυν, ὅτι καὶ νῦν ἐκεῖνο τὸ δεῖπνόν ἐστιν, ἐν ᾧ Αὐτὸς ἀνέκειτο· οὐδὲν γὰρ ἐκεῖνο τούτου διενήνοχεν. οὐδὲ γὰρ τοῦτο μὲν ἄνθρωπος ἐργάζεται· ἐκεῖνο δὲ Αὐτός· ἀλλὰ καὶ τοῦτο κἀκεῖνο Αὐτός· ὅταν τοίνυν τὸν ἱερέα ἐπιδιδοῦντά σοι ἴδῃς, μὴ τὸν ἱερέα νόμιζε τὸν τοῦτο ποιοῦντα, ἀλλὰ τὴν τοῦ Χριστοῦ χεῖρα εἶναι ἐκτεινομένην.

(s) *Homil. in Matth.* 82. Ibid. p. 510. Καὶ Αὐτὸς οὖν ἔπιεν ἐξ αὐτοῦ, ἵνα μὴ ταῦτα ἀκούοντες εἴπωσι, τί οὖν, αἷμα πίνομεν, καὶ σάρκα ἐσθίομεν; καὶ τότε θορυβηθῶσιν ἐντεῦθεν. καὶ γὰρ ὅτε τοὺς περὶ τούτων ἐκίνει λόγους, καὶ πρὸς τὰ ῥήματα ταῦτα πολλοὶ ἐσκανδαλίζοντο· ἵνα οὖν μὴ καὶ τότε ταραχθῶσι, πρῶτος Αὐτὸς τοῦτο ἐποίησεν ἐνάγων αὐτοὺς ἀταράχως εἰς τὴν κοινωνίαν τῶν Μυστηρίων.

(t) Ibid. p. 513. Οὕτω καὶ ἐπὶ τῶν μυστηρίων ποιῶμεν, οὐ τοῖς κειμένοις μόνον ἐμβλέποντες, ἀλλὰ τὰ ῥήματα Αὐτοῦ κατέχοντες. ὁ μὲν γὰρ λόγος Αὐτοῦ ἀπαραλόγιστος, ἡ δὲ αἴσθησις ἡμῶν εὐεξαπάτητος· οὗτος οὐδέποτε διέπεσεν, αὐτή δὲ τὰ πλείονα σφάλλεται. ἐπεὶ οὖν ὁ Λόγος φησὶ, Τοῦτό ἐστι τὸ Σῶμά Μου, καὶ πειθώμεθα, καὶ πιστεύωμεν, καὶ νοητοῖς Αὐτὸ βλέπωμεν ὀφθαλμοῖς. οὐδὲν γὰρ αἰσθητὸν παρέδωκεν ἡμῖν ὁ Χριστός· ἀλλ' αἰσθητοῖς μὲν πράγμασι, πάντα δὲ νοητά.

(u) Ibid. p. 514. Σκόπει τοίνυν, μὴ καὶ αὐτὸς ἔνοχος γένῃ τοῦ σώματος καὶ τοῦ αἵματος τοῦ Χριστοῦ. ἐκεῖνοι κατέσφαξαν τὸ Πανάγιον Σῶμα· σὺ δὲ ῥυπαρᾷ ὑποδέχῃ ψυχῇ.—καὶ ἀναφύρει Ἑαυτὸν ἡμῖν. καὶ οὐ τῇ πίστει μόνον, ἀλλὰ καὶ αὐτῷ τῷ πράγματι Σῶμα Αὐτοῦ ἡμᾶς κατασκευάζει· τίνος οὖν οὐκ ἔδει καθαρώτερον εἶναι ταύτης ἀπολαύοντα τῆς θυσίας;

(w) Ibid. p. 515. Κἂν στρατηγὸς τὶς ᾖ, κἂν ὕπαρχος, κἂν αὐτὸς ὁ τὸ διάδημα περικείμενος, ἀναξίως δὲ προσίῃ, κώλυσον. μείζονα ἐκείνου τὴν ἐξουσίαν ἔχεις.—εἰ δὲ αὐτὸς οὐ τολμᾷς, ἐμοὶ πρόσαγε, καὶ οὐ συγχωρήσω ταῦτα τολμᾶσθαι. καὶ τὸ αἷμα τὸ ἐμαυτοῦ προήσομαι πρότερον, ἢ τοῦ Αἵματος μεταδώσω οὕτω φρικώδους παρὰ τὸ προσῆκον.

(x) *Homil. in Joannem* xiv. tom. ii. p. 609. Καὶ ἁγιασμὸς καὶ ἁγιασμὸς, καὶ βάπτισμα καὶ βάπτισμα, καὶ θυσία καὶ θυσία, καὶ ναὸς καὶ ναὸς, καὶ περιτομὴ καὶ περιτομή· οὕτω καὶ χάρις καὶ χάρις· ἀλλ' ἐκεῖνα μὲν ὡς τύποι, ταῦτα δὲ ὡς ἀλήθεια.

(y) *Hom.* 47. Ibid. p. 750. Ταῦτα πάντα ἔδει μυστικῶς νοεῖν καὶ πνευματικῶς—πνεῦμά ἐστι, καὶ ζωή· τουτέστι, θεῖα καὶ πνευματικά ἐστι. τί οὖν; οὐκ ἔστιν ἡ σὰρξ Αὐτοῦ σάρξ; καὶ σφόδρα μὲν οὖν. καὶ πῶς εἶπεν, ἡ σὰρξ οὐκ ὠφελεῖ οὐδὲν; οὐ περὶ τῆς Ἑαυτοῦ σαρκὸς λέγων, [μὴ γένοιτο] ἀλλὰ περὶ τῶν σαρκικῶς ἐκλαμβανόντων τὰ λεγόμενα. τί δέ ἐστι τὸ σαρκικῶς νοῆσαι; τὸ ἁπλῶς εἰς τὰ προκείμενα ὁρᾶν.—Χρὴ δὴ μὴ οὕτω κρίνειν τοῖς ὁρωμένοις, ἀλλὰ πάντα τὰ μυστήρια τοῖς ἔνδον ὀφθαλμοῖς κατοπτεύειν. ταῦτα γάρ ἐστι πνευματικῶς.

(z) *Hom.* 46. Ibid. p. 746. Ἵνα οὖν μὴ μόνον κατὰ τὴν ἀγάπην τοῦτο [ἓν] γενώμεθα, ἀλλὰ καὶ κατ' αὐτὸ τὸ πρᾶγμα εἰς ἐκείνην ἀνακερασθῶμεν τὴν σάρκα. διὰ τῆς τροφῆς τοῦτο γίνεται, ἧς ἐχαρίσατο, βουλόμενος ἡμῖν δεῖξαι τὸν πόθον, ὃν ἔχει περὶ ἡμᾶς. διὰ τοῦτο ἀνέμιξεν Ἑαυτὸν ἡμῖν, καὶ ἀνέφυρε τὸ Σῶμα Αὐτοῦ εἰς ἡμᾶς, ἵνα ἕν τι γενώμεθα, καθάπερ σῶμα κεφαλῇ συνημμένον.

(A) Ibid. p. 747. Τοῦτο τὸ Αἷμα ἀξίως λαμβανόμενον ἐλαύνει μὲν δαίμονας καὶ πόρρωθεν εἶναι ποιεῖ, καλεῖ δὲ ἀγγέλους πρὸς ἡμᾶς, καὶ τὸν Δεσπότην τῶν ἀγγέλων· —— Τούτου χωρὶς οὐκ ἐτόλμα ὁ ἀρχιερεὺς εἰς τὰ ἄδυτα εἰσιέναι· Τοῦτο τὸ Αἷμα ἱερέας ἐχειροτόνει· Τοῦτο ἐκάθηρεν ἁμαρτίας ἐν τοῖς τύποις· εἰ δὲ ἐν τοῖς τύποις τοσαύτην ἔσχεν ἰσχὺν, εἰ τὴν σκιὰν οὕτως ὁ θάνατος ἔφριξε, τὴν Ἀλήθειαν Αὐτὴν, εἰπέ μοι, πῶς οὐκ ἂν ἐφοβήθη ; —— Τοῦτο ἐξεχύθη τὸ Αἷμα, καὶ τὸν οὐρανὸν ἐποίησε βατόν. φρικτὰ ὄντως τὰ μυστήρια τῆς ἐκκλησίας, φρικτὸν ὄντως τὸ θυσιαστήριον· then he compares the Eucharist to the tree of life.

(B) Ibid. Εἰ γὰρ οἱ ῥυποῦντες τὴν πορφύραν τὴν βασιλικὴν κολάζονται ὁμοίως, ὥσπερ οἱ διαρρήγνυντες· τί ἀπεικὸς καὶ τοὺς ἀκαθάρτῳ διανοίᾳ δεχομένους τὸ Σῶμα, τὴν αὐτὴν ὑπομεῖναι τιμωρίαν τοῖς Αὐτὸ διαρρήξασι διὰ τῶν ἥλων.

(C) *In Acta Apostolorum, Hom.* 21. tom. iv. p. 735. Ἐν χερσὶν ἡ θυσία, καὶ πάντα πρόκειται ηὐτρεπισμένα· πάρεισιν Ἄγγελοι, Ἀρχάγγελοι· πάρεστιν ὁ Υἱὸς τοῦ Θεοῦ· μετὰ τοσαύτης φρίκης ἑστήκασιν ἅπαντες· παρεστήκασιν ἐκεῖνοι [Διάκονοι] βοῶντες, πάντων σιγώντων, καὶ ἡγῇ ἁπλῶς γίνεσθαι τὰ γινόμενα ; οὐκοῦν καὶ τὰ ἄλλα ἁπλῶς, καὶ τὰ ὑπὲρ τῆς Ἐκκλησίας, καὶ τὰ ὑπὲρ τῶν ἱερέων προσφερόμενα, καὶ τὰ ὑπὲρ τοῦ πληρώματος ; μὴ γένοιτο· ἀλλὰ πάντα μετὰ πίστεως γίνεται· τί οἴει τὸ ὑπὲρ Μαρτύρων προσφέρεσθαι· τὸ κληθῆναι ἐν ἐκείνῃ τῇ ὥρᾳ ; κἂν μάρτυρες ὦσι, κἂν ὑπὲρ μαρτύρων, μεγάλη τιμή, τὸ ὀνομασθῆναι, τοῦ Δεσπότου παρόντος, τοῦ θανάτου ἐπιτελουμένου ἐκείνου, τῆς φρικτῆς θυσίας, τῶν ἀφάτων Μυστηρίων.

(D) *Homil.* 7. *In primam Epistolam ad Corinth.*, tom. iii. p. 280. Μυστήριον καλεῖται, ὅτε οὐχ ἅπερ ὁρῶμεν πιστεύομεν ἀλλ' ἕτερα ὁρῶμεν, καὶ ἕτερα πιστεύομεν. τοιαύτη γὰρ ἡ τῶν μυστηρίων ἡμῶν φύσις. ἑτέρως γοῦν ἐγὼ, καὶ ἑτέρως ὁ ἄπιστος περὶ τούτων διακείμεθα.—ἀκούων λουτρὸν ἐκεῖνος, ἁπλῶς ὕδωρ νομίζει· ἐγὼ δὲ οὐ τὸ ὁρώμενον ἁπλῶς βλέπω, ἀλλὰ τὸν τῆς ψυχῆς καθαρμὸν τὸν διὰ τοῦ Πνεύματος.—ἀκούω σῶμα Χριστοῦ· ἑτέρως ἐγὼ νοῶ τὸ εἰρημένον, ἑτέρως ὁ ἄπιστος. κ. τ. λ.

(E) *Homil.* 18. *in secundam Epistolam ad Corinth.* Ibid. p. 647. Ἔστι δὲ ὅπου οὐδὲ διέστηκεν ὁ ἱερεὺς τοῦ ἀρχομένου· οἷον, ὅταν ἀπολαύειν δέῃ τῶν φρικτῶν μυστηρίων· ὁμοίως γὰρ πάντες ἀξιούμεθα τῶν αὐτῶν— πᾶσιν ἓν Σῶμα πρόκειται, καὶ Ποτήριον ἕν·

N. B. This is misplaced, but cannot now be removed, because the reader is directed to it by the letter E.

(F) *Hom.* 24. *in Epistolam primam ad Corinth.*, tom. iii. p. 396.

Τὸ ποτήριον τῆς εὐλογίας, ὃ εὐλογοῦμεν, οὐχὶ κοινωνία τοῦ Αἵματος τοῦ Χριστοῦ ἐστι; σφόδρα πιστῶς καὶ φοβερῶς εἴρηκεν. ὃ γὰρ λέγει, τοῦτο ἔστιν· ὅτι τοῦτο τὸ ἐν ποτηρίῳ ὄν, Ἐκεῖνό ἐστι τὸ ἀπὸ τῆς πλευρᾶς ῥεῦσαν, καὶ Ἐκείνου μετέχομεν. (G) Ibid. p. 397. Ἐνταῦθα δὲ ἐπὶ τὸ πολλῷ φρικωδέστερον καὶ μεγαλοπρεπέστερον τὴν ἱερουργίαν μετεσκεύασε, καὶ τὴν θυσίαν αὐτὴν ἀμείψας, καὶ ἀντὶ τῆς τῶν ἀλόγων σφαγῆς Ἑαυτὸν προσφέρειν κελεύσας.

(H) Ibid. Ὁ ἄρτος, ὃν κλῶμεν, οὐχὶ κοινωνία τοῦ Σώματος τοῦ Χριστοῦ ἐστι; διατὶ μὴ εἶπε, μετοχή ; ὅτι πλέον τι δηλῶσαι ἠβουλήθη, καὶ πολλὴν ἐνδείξασθαι τὴν συνάφειαν. οὐ γὰρ τῷ μετέχειν μόνον καὶ μεταλαμβάνειν, ἀλλὰ καὶ τῷ ἑνοῦσθαι κοινωνοῦμεν. Καθάπερ γὰρ τὸ Σῶμα Ἐκεῖνο ἥνωται τῷ Χριστῷ, οὕτω καὶ ἡμεῖς Αὐτῷ διὰ τοῦ ἄρτου τούτου ἑνούμεθα. διὰ τί δὲ προσέθηκεν, ὃν κλῶμεν ; τοῦτο γὰρ ἐπὶ μὲν τῆς Εὐχαριστίας ἐστὶν ἰδεῖν γινόμενον· ἐπὶ δὲ τοῦ σταυροῦ οὐκέτι, ἀλλὰ καὶ τοὐναντίον τούτῳ· he refers to John xix. 36.

(I) Ibid. Εἶτα ἐπειδὰν εἶπε, κοινωνία τοῦ Σώματος, τό δὲ κοινωνοῦν ἕτερόν ἐστιν ἐκείνου, οὗ κοινωνεῖ, καὶ ταύτην τὴν δοκοῦσαν εἶναι μικρὰν διαφορὰν ἀνεῖλεν. εἴπων γὰρ, κοινωνία τοῦ Σώματος ἐζήτησε πάλιν ἐγγύτερόν τι εἰπεῖν· διὸ καὶ ἐπήγαγεν, Ὅτι εἷς ἄρτος, ἐν σῶμά ἐσμεν οἱ πολλοί. Τί γὰρ λέγω κοινωνίαν, φησὶν ; αὐτό ἐσμεν ἐκεῖνο τὸ σῶμα. τί γὰρ ἐστιν ὁ ἄρτος ; Σῶμα Χριστοῦ. τί δὲ γένονται οἱ μεταλαμβάνοντες ; σῶμα Χριστοῦ. οὐχὶ σώματα πολλὰ, ἀλλὰ σῶμα ἕν. καθάπερ γὰρ ἄρτος ἐκ πολλῶν συγκείμενος κόκκων ἥνωται, κ. τ. λ.

(K) Ibid. Ἐπειδὴ ἡ προτέρα τῆς σαρκὸς φύσις ἡ ἀπὸ γῆς διαπλασθεῖσα ἀπὸ τῆς ἁμαρτίας ἔφθασε νεκρωθῆναι, καὶ ζωῆς γενέσθαι ἔρημος, ἑτέραν, ὡς ἂν εἴποι τὶς, μάζαν καὶ ζύμην ἐπεισήγαγε, τὴν Ἑαυτοῦ Σάρκα, φύσει μὲν οὖσαν τὴν αὐτὴν, ἁμαρτίας δὲ ἀπηλλαγμένην καὶ ζωῆς γέμουσαν· καὶ πᾶσιν ἔδωκεν αὐτῆς μεταλαμβάνειν, ἵνα ταύτῃ τρεφόμενοι, καὶ τὴν προτέραν ἀποθέμενοι τὴν νεκρὰν, εἰς τὴν ζωὴν τὴν ἀθάνατον διὰ τῆς τραπέζης ἀνακερασθῶμεν ταύτης.

(L) Ibid. p. 399. Πῶς τὸ Σῶμα τοῦ ἐπὶ πάντων Θεοῦ, τὸ ἄμωμον, τὸ καθαρὸν, τὸ τῇ θείᾳ ἐκείνῃ φύσει ὁμιλῆσαν, δι᾽ ὃ ἐσμεν καὶ ζῶμεν, δι᾽ οὗ πύλαι θανάτου κατεκλάσθησαν, καὶ οὐρανοῦ ἁψίδες ἀνεῴχθησαν, Τοῦτο μετὰ τοσαύτης ὕβρεως ληψόμεθα ;

(M) Ibid. p. 400. Σὺ δὲ οὐκ ἐν φάτνῃ ὁρᾷς, ἀλλ᾽ ἐν θυσιαστηρίῳ, οὐ γυναῖκα κατέχουσαν, ἀλλ᾽ ἱερέα παρεστῶτα, καὶ Πνεῦμα μετὰ πολλῆς τῆς δαψιλείας τοῖς προκειμένοις ἐφιπτάμενον.

(N) Ibid. p. 401. Ὥσπερ γὰρ τὸ ὡς ἔτυχε προσιέναι, κίνδυνος, οὕτω τὸ μὴ κοινωνεῖν τῶν Μυστικῶν Δείπνων ἐκείνων, λιμὸς καὶ θάνατος.

(O) Homil. 3. In Epistolam ad Philippenses, tom. iv. p. 20. Οὐκ εἰκῇ ταῦτα ἐνομοθετήθη ὑπὸ τῶν Ἀποστόλων, τὸ ἐπὶ τῶν φρικτῶν Μυστηρίων μνήμην γίνεσθαι τῶν ἀπελθόντων. ἴσασιν αὐτοῖς πολὺ κέρδος γινόμενον, πολλὴν τὴν ὠφέλειαν. ὅταν γὰρ ἑστήκῃ λαὸς ὁλόκληρος χεῖρας ἀνατείνοντες, πλήρωμα ἱερατικὸν, καὶ πρόκειται ἡ φρικτὴ Θυσία, πῶς οὐ δυσωπήσομεν ὑπὲρ τούτων τὸν Θεὸν παρακαλοῦντες ;

(P) *In Epistolam ad Hebræos. Homil.* 17. Ibid. p. 523. Προσφέρομεν μὲν, ἀλλ᾽ ἀνάμνησιν ποιούμενοι τοῦ θανάτου Αὐτοῦ.——τὴν αὐτὴν [θυσίαν] αἰεὶ ποιοῦμεν· μᾶλλόν δε ἀνάμνησιν ἐργαζόμεθα θυσίας.

(Q) 1 *Epistol. ad Cæsarium,* tom. iii. p. 22. ed. Paris. p. 744. ed. Traj. 1687. Antequam sanctificetur panis, panem quidem nominamus, divina autem illum sanctificante gratia, mediante sacerdote, liberatus est quidem ab appellatione panis, etiamsi natura panis in ipso permansit, et non duo corpora sed unum Filii corpus prædicatur.

VICTOR ANTIOCHENUS in Biblioth. P.P. Col. AGRIP. A.D. 1610, floruit circa Ann. Dom. 401.

In S. Marci Evangelium, cap. xiv. tom. iv. p. 330. Cum autem [Dominus] ad apostolos dicit, Hoc est Corpus Meum. Item : Hic est Sanguis Meus ; certo apud se statuant vult, posteaquam benedictio et gratiarum actio, ad panem, vel calicem propositam accesserit, per panis quidem symbolum, corporis Christi ; per calicem vero, Ejusdem sanguinis participes se fieri.

CYRILLUS ALEXANDRINUS floruit A.D. 412.
Edit. Lutetiæ, A.D. 1638.

(a) *Glaphyra in Gen.,* lib. ii. tom. 1. p. 61. Δέχεται δὲ τῆς ὑπὲρ νόμον ἱερωσύνης σύμβολον, τὸ κατευλογῆσαι τὸν Ἀβραὰμ, οἰνόν τε καὶ ἄρτους αὐτῷ παρασχεῖν, εὐλογούμεθα γὰρ οὐχ ἑτέρως παρὰ Χριστοῦ.

(aa) *Ibid.* Αὐτὸν δὲ τῆς ἱερωσύνης τὸν τρόπον, εἰς παράδειξιν τοῦ πράγματος ἐποιεῖτο σαφῆ. ἄρτους γὰρ καὶ οἶνον ἐξεκόμιζεν ὁ Μελχισεδέκ.

(b) *De adoratione in Spiritu, &c.* Lib. x. p. 355. (Hæreticos describens.) Παρὰ τὴν οὖσαν ἀληθῶς ἁγίαν σκηνήν, ἑαυτοῖς ἑτέραν διαπήγνυντες, καὶ ἔξω θύοντες τὸν ἀμνὸν, καὶ ἀπωτάτω που τῆς μιᾶς ἀποφέροντες οἰκίας, καὶ μερίζοντες τὸν ἀμέριστον.

(c) *Ibid.* lib. xiii. p. 457. Σημαίνει μὲν ἡ τράπεζα, τὴν πρόθεσιν ἔχουσα τῶν ἄρτων, τὴν ἀναίμακτον θυσίαν, δι᾽ ἧς εὐλογούμεθα τὸν ἄρτον ἐσθίοντες τὸν ἐξ οὐρανοῦ, τουτέστι, Χριστόν.

(d) *Ibid.* lib. xvii. p. 605, 606. Μυρίαις μὲν γὰρ ὅσαις πόλεσί τε καὶ κώμαις ἡ τῶν Ἰουδαίων ἐπεπλήθη χώρα, τελεῖν δὲ καὶ τὰ ἱερὰ καὶ τὸν ἐπὶ τῷ Πάσχα νόμον, ἐν μόνῃ δὲ χρῆναι τῇ ἁγίᾳ πόλει διετύπου Θεὸς——ὡς οὐκ ἂν εἴη θέμις τὸ ἐπὶ Χριστῷ μυστήριον, καθ᾽ ὃν ἂν ἕλοιτο τρόπον, ἤγουν ἐν τόπῳ παντὶ δύνασθαι πληροῦν. χῶρος γὰρ μόνος ὁ πρέπων αὐτῷ, καὶ οἰκειότατος ἀληθῶς, ἡ ἁγία πόλις, τουτέστιν, ἡ Ἐκκλησία, ἐν ᾗ καὶ νομιμὸς ἱερεὺς, καὶ διὰ χειρῶν ἡγιασμένων τελεῖται τὰ ἱερὰ, καὶ θυμίαμα προσφέρεται τῷ πάντων κρατοῦντι Θεῷ, καὶ θυσία καθαρὰ, κατὰ τὴν τοῦ Προφήτου φωνήν.

(e) *In Malachiam*, tom. iii. p. 830. Προαγορεύει δὲ, ὅτι μέγα καὶ ἐπιφανὲς ἔσται τὸ ὄνομα Αὐτοῦ παρὰ τοῖς ἀνὰ πᾶσαν τὴν ὑπ᾽ οὐρανὸν, καὶ ἐν παντὶ τόπῳ τε καὶ ἔθνει θυσίαι καθαραὶ καὶ ἀναίμακτοι προσκομισθήσονται τῷ ὀνόματι Αὐτοῦ, κατασμικρυνόντων Αὐτὸν οὐκέτι τῶν ἱερουργῶν, οὔτε μὴν ῥᾳθύμως προσκομιζόντων Αὐτῷ τὰς πνευματικὰς λατρείας· ἀλλ᾽ ἐν σπουδῇ, καὶ ἐπιεικείᾳ, καὶ ἁγιασμῷ τὰς τῶν νοητῶν θυμιαμάτων εὐωδίας ἀνακομίζειν ἐσπουδακότων, τουτέστι, πίστιν, ἐλπίδα, ἀγάπην, καὶ τὰ ἐξ ἔργων ἀγαθῶν αὐχήματα, προστεταγμένης δηλονότι τῆς Χριστοῦ θυσίας τῆς οὐρανίου καὶ ζωοποιοῦ, δι᾽ ἧς κατήργηται θάνατος, καὶ ἡ φθαρτὴ δὴ αὕτη καὶ ἀπὸ γῆς σὰρξ ἀμφιέννυται τὴν ἀφθαρσίαν.

(f) *In Johannem*, lib. iv. cap. 2. tom. 4. p. 360. Treating on John vi. 53, "Except ye eat the flesh of," &c., and having shewed in many words that Christ did not here shew the manner, how His flesh was to be eaten, but the advantage of eating It, and required them to believe, rather than to be inquisitive ; he adds, τοῖς γὰρ ἤδη πεπιστευκόσι, διακλάσας τὸν ἄρτον ἐδίδου, λέγων· λάβετε, φάγετε· Τοῦτι ἔστι τὸ Σῶμά Μου.—ὁρᾷς ὅπως τοῖς μὲν ἀνοηταίνουσιν ἔτι, καὶ τὸ πιστεύειν ἀζητήτως ἐξωθουμένοις, οὐκ ἐξηγεῖται τοῦ μυστηρίου τὸν τρόπον, τοῖς δὲ ἤδη πεπιστευκόσι σαφέστατα διεπὼν εὑρίσκεται. and then repeating John vi. 53, he immediately subjoins, ἀμέτοχοι γὰρ παντελῶς, καὶ ἄγευστοι μένουσι τῆς ἐν ἁγιασμῷ καὶ μακαριότητι ζωῆς, οἱ διὰ τῆς μυστικῆς εὐλογίας οὐ παραδεξάμενοι τὸν Υἱόν.

(g) Ibid. p. 365. Ὥσπερ οὖν ὁ Παῦλος φησὶν, ὅτι μικρὰ ζύμη ὅλον τὸ φύραμα ζυμοῖ, οὕτως ὀλιγίστη πάλιν εὐλογία, σύμπαν ἡμῶν εἰς ἑαυτὴν ἀναφύρει τὸ σῶμα, καὶ τῆς ἰδίας ἐνεργείας ἀναπληροῖ, οὕτω τὲ ἐν ἡμῖν γίνεται Χριστὸς, καὶ ἡμεῖς αὖ πάλιν ἐν Αὐτῷ.

(h) Ibid. p. 377. Ὅλον ἤδη τῇ ζωοποιῷ τοῦ Πνεύματος ἐνεργείᾳ τὸ ἴδιον σῶμα πληροῖ· Πνεῦμα γὰρ λοιπὸν τὴν σάρκα καλεῖ, καὶ οὐκ ἀνατρέπων τὸ εἶναι σάρκα αὐτήν· διὰ δὲ τὸ ἀκρῶς ἡνῶσθαί τε Αὐτῷ, καὶ ὅλην τὴν Αὐτοῦ τὴν ζωογόνον ἐνδύσασθαι δύναμιν, ὀφείλουσαν ἤδη καλεῖσθαι τὸ Πνεῦμα.

(i) *Contra Nestorium*, lib. v. tom. 6. p. 123. Ἐν ἡμῖν ἐστι [Χριστὸς], διὰ τῆς ἰδίας σαρκὸς ζηνοποιούσης ἡμᾶς ἐν Πνεύματι· οὐ γὰρ ἐπειδήπερ οὐκ ἐσθίεται θεότητος φύσις, διὰ τοῦτο κοινὸν εἶναι φαίη τὶς ἂν τὸ ἅγιον σῶμα Χριστοῦ· εἰδέναι δὲ ἀναγκαῖον ὅτι ἴδιόν ἐστι σῶμα τοῦ πάντα ζωοποιοῦντος Λόγου.

(l) *Cyrilli et Synodi Alexandrinæ Epistol. in Act. Synodi Ephesinæ Œcumenicæ.* apud Binium, edit. Lutetiæ, A.D. 1636, vol. ii. p. 210, 211. Τὴν ἀναίμακτον ἐν ταῖς Ἐκκλησίαις τελοῦμεν θυσίαν· προσίμεν τε οὕτω ταῖς μυστικαῖς εὐλογίαις, καὶ ἁγιαζόμεθα, μέτοχοι γενόμενοι τῆς τε ἁγίας σαρκὸς, καὶ τοῦ τιμίου αἵματος τοῦ πάντων ἡμῶν Σωτῆρος Χριστοῦ.— οὐχ ὡς ἀνθρώπου τῶν καθ᾽ ἡμᾶς ἑνὸς, καὶ αὐτὴν εἶναι λογιούμεθα. πῶς γὰρ ἡ ἀνθρώπου σὰρξ ζωοποιὸς ἔσται, κατὰ φύσιν τὴν ἑαυτῆς ; ἀλλ᾽ ὡς ἰδίαν ἀληθῶς γενομένην τοῦ δι' ἡμᾶς καὶ υἱοῦ καὶ ἀνθρώπου γεγονότος, καὶ χρηματίσαντος·—[κοινὴ γὰρ σὰρξ οὐ ζωοποιεῖν δύναται. καὶ τούτου μαρτὺς Αὐτὸς ὁ Σωτὴρ, λέγων· ἡ σὰρξ οὐκ ὠφελεῖ οὐδὲν· τὸ πνεῦμά ἐστι τὸ ζωοποιοῦν· ἐπειδὴ γὰρ ἰδία γέγονε τοῦ λόγου, ταύτη τοὶ νοεῖται, καὶ ἔστι ζωοποιός[c].]

(m) *Apud Victorem Antiochen. Marc.* 14. MS. in Biblioth. Regis Galliæ. *Thomam de Aquino in Latina Catena P.P. in Lucæ* 22. nec non in *Nicetæ Catena Græca in Matthæum, a Balth. Corderio edita,* inquit D. Grabe *in Notis ad Irenæum,* p. 397. Ἵνα μὴ ἀποναρκήσωμεν σάρκα τε καὶ αἷμα προκείμενα βλέποντες ἐν ἁγίαις τραπέζαις τῶν ἐκκλησιῶν, συγκαθιστάμενος ὡς Θεὸς ταῖς ἡμετέραις ἀσθενείαις, ἐνίησι τοῖς προκειμένοις δύναμιν ζωῆς, καὶ μεθίστησιν αὐτὰ πρὸς ἐνεργεῖαν τῆς Ἑαυτοῦ σαρκὸς, ἵνα εἰς μέθεξιν ζωοποιὸν ἔχωμεν αὐτὰ, καὶ οἷον σπέρμα ζωοποιὸν ἐν ἡμῖν εὑρεθῇ τὸ σῶμα τῆς ζωῆς.

THEODORITUS floruit A.D. 423.

Edit. Lutetiæ, A.D. 1642.

(a) *In Genesin, Interrog.* 55. tom. i. p. 44. Ἀβελτηρίας γὰρ ἐσχάτης προσκυνεῖν τὸ ἐσθιόμενον.

(b) *In Exodum, Interrog.* 24. p. 90. Κἀκείνους ἔδει μαθεῖν διὰ τοῦ συμβόλου τὴν τοῦ Θεοῦ κηδεμονίαν· καὶ ἡμᾶς τοὺς τὸν ἄμωμον ἀμνὸν θυόντας γνῶναι προδιαγραφέντα τὸν τύπον.

(c) *In Leviticum, Interrog.* 11. p. 124. Πῶς γὰρ ἂν τὶς σωφρονῶν, ἢ τὸ ἀκάθαρτον ὀνομάσαι Θεὸν, ὁ μυσαττόμενος ἀποστρέφεται, ἢ τὸ τῷ ἀληθινῷ Θεῷ προσφερόμενον, καὶ παρ' αὐτοῦ ἐσθιόμενον ;

(d) *In Psalm.* cix. (nobis cx.) p. 852. Ἄρχεται δὲ τῆς ἱερωσύνης ἐν τῇ νυκτὶ, μεθ' ἣν τὸ πάθος ὑπέμεινεν· ἡνίκα λαβὼν ἄρτον, καὶ εὐχαριστήσας, ἔκλασε καὶ εἶπε (he recites Matt. xxvi. 26 &c.) εὑρίσκομεν δὲ τὸν Μελχισεδὲκ, καὶ ἱερέα ὄντα καὶ βασιλέα· τύπος γὰρ ἦν τοῦ ἀληθινοῦ ἱερέως καὶ βασιλέως· καὶ προσφέροντα τῷ Θεῷ οὐκ ἄλογα θύματα, ἀλλ' ἄρτους καὶ οἶνον·—ἱερατεύει δὲ νῦν ὁ ἐξ Ἰούδα κατὰ σάρκα βλαστήσας Χριστὸς, οὐκ Αὐτὸς τὶ προσφέρων, ἀλλὰ τῶν προσφερόντων κεφαλὴ χρηματίζων· σῶμα γὰρ Αὐτοῦ τὴν Ἐκκλησίαν καλεῖ, καὶ διὰ ταύτης ἱερατεύει ὡς ἄνθρωπος, δέχεται δὲ τὰ προσφερομένα ὡς Θεὸς· προσφέρει δὲ ἡ Ἐκκλησία τὰ τοῦ σώματος Αὐτοῦ καὶ τοῦ αἵματος σύμβολα.

(dd) *In Malach.* tom. ii. p. 935. Πέπαυται μὲν γὰρ ἡ περιγεγραμμένη τῶν ἱερέων λατρεία, πᾶς δὲ τόπος ἐπιτήδειος εἰς τὴν τοῦ Θεοῦ θεραπείαν νενόμισται· καὶ τῶν μὲν ἀλόγων θυμάτων τέλος ἔλαβεν ἡ σφαγὴ, μόνος δὲ ὁ ἄμωμος ἀμνὸς ἱερεύεται, ὁ αἴρων τὴν ἁμαρτίαν τοῦ κόσμου.

(e) *In primam Epistolam ad Corinth.* cap. xi. tom. 3. p. 175.

[c] [The passage in brackets alone answers to the reference given by Johnson in the text.]

Ἀνέμνησεν αὐτοὺς τῆς ἱερᾶς ἐκείνης καὶ παναγίας νυκτὸς, ἐν ᾗ καὶ τῷ τυπικῷ Πάσχα τὸ τέλος ἐπέθηκε, καὶ τοῦ τύπου τὸ ἀρχέτυπον ἔδειξε, καὶ τοῦ σωτηρίου μυστηρίου τὰς θύρας ἀνέῳξε. (f) *In Epistol. ad Hebræos*, cap. ix. v. 23. p. 437. [αὐτὰ δὲ τὰ ἐπουράνια κρείττοσι θυσίαις παρὰ ταύτας.] τουτέστι τῇ λογικῇ, καὶ ἀμώμῳ, καὶ ἁγίᾳ θυσίᾳ· οὐράνια δὲ τὰ πνευματικὰ κέκληκεν, οἷς ἡ Ἐκκλησία καθαίρεται.

(g) *Ibid*. cap. x. v. 9. p. 439. [ἀναιρεῖ τὸ πρῶτον, ἵνα τὸ δεύτερον στήσῃ.] πρῶτον εἶπε, τὴν τῶν ἀλόγων θυσίαν· δεύτερον δὲ τὴν λογικὴν, τὴν ὑπ' Αὐτοῦ προσενεχθεῖσαν.

(h) *Epistola* 130 *ad Timotheum quendam*, p. 1003. Αὐτὸς δὲ ὁ Κύριος, οὐ τὴν ἀόρατον φύσιν, ἀλλὰ τὸ σῶμα δώσειν ὑπέσχετο ὑπὲρ τῆς τοῦ κόσμου ζωῆς. ὁ γὰρ ἄρτος, φησὶν, (he cites John vi. 51.) κἂν τῇ τῶν θείων μυστηρίων παραδόσει λαβὼν τὸ σύμβολον ἔφη, Τοῦτο ἔστι τὸ Σῶμά Μου.

(i) *Dialog*. 1. tom. iv. p. 18. Ἐν δὲ γὲ τῇ τῶν μυστηρίων παραδόσει, σῶμα τὸν ἄρτον ἐκάλεσε, καὶ αἷμα τὸ κρᾶμα—Ἠβουλήθη γὰρ (ὁ Χριστὸς) τοὺς τῶν θείων μυστηρίων μεταλαγχάνοντας, μὴ τῇ φύσει τῶν βλεπομένων προσέχειν, ἀλλὰ διὰ τῆς τῶν ὀνομάτων ἐναλλαγῆς πιστεύειν τῇ ἐκ τῆς χάριτος γεγεννημένῃ μεταβολῇ. ὁ γὰρ δὴ τὸ φύσει σῶμα σῖτον καὶ ἄρτον προσαγορεύσας, καὶ αὖ πάλιν Ἑαυτὸν ἄμπελον ὀνομάσας, Αὐτὸς τὰ ὁρώμενα σύμβολα τῇ τοῦ Σώματος καὶ Αἵματος προσηγορίᾳ τετίμηκεν, οὐ τὴν φύσιν μεταβαλὼν, ἀλλὰ τῇ φύσει τὴν χάριν προστεθεικώς.

(k) *Ibid*.—Ὁ Κύριος τὸ σύμβολον λαβὼν, οὐκ εἶπε, Τοῦτο ἔστιν ἡ Θεότης Μου, ἀλλὰ, Τοῦτο ἔστι τὸ Σῶμά Μου. καὶ ἑτέρωθι, ὁ δὲ ἄρτος ὃν Ἐγὼ δώσω, ἡ σάρξ Μού ἐστιν, ἣν Ἐγὼ δώσω ὑπὲρ τῆς τοῦ κόσμου ζωῆς.

(l) *Dialog*. 2. p. 84. Ο. τὰ μυστικὰ σύμβολα παρὰ τῶν ἱερωμένων τῷ Θεῷ προσφερόμενα τίνων ἐστὶ σύμβολα ; Ε. τοῦ δεσποτικοῦ Σώματός τε, καὶ Αἵματος.

(m) *Ibid*. p. 84, 85. Ε. τί καλεῖς τὸ προσφερόμενον δῶρον πρὸ τῆς ἱερατικῆς ἐπικλήσεως ;—Ο.—τὴν ἐκ τοιῶνδε σπερμάτων τροφήν. Ε. τό δε ἔτερον σύμβολον πῶς ὀνομάζομεν ; Ο. κοινὸν καὶ τοῦτο ὄνομα, πόματος εἶδος σήμαινον· Ε. Μετά δὲ τὸν ἁγιασμὸν, πῶς ταῦτα προσαγορεύεις ; Ο. Σῶμα Χριστοῦ, καὶ Αἷμα Χριστοῦ. Ε. Καὶ πιστεύεις γὲ σώματος Χριστοῦ μεταλαμβάνειν, καὶ αἵματος ; Ο. οὕτω πιστεύω· Ε. Ὥσπερ τοίνυν τὰ σύμβολα τοῦ δεσποτικοῦ σώματος τὲ καὶ αἵματος ἄλλα μέν εἰσι πρὸ τῆς ἱερατικῆς ἐπικλήσεως, μετά δε γὲ τὴν ἐπίκλησιν μεταβάλλεται, καὶ ἔτερα γίνεται· οὕτω τὸ δεσποτικὸν σῶμα μετὰ τὸν ἀνάληψιν εἰς τὴν οὐσίαν μετεβλήθη τὴν θείαν· Ο. Ἑάλως οἷς ὕφηνες ἄρκυσιν· οὐδὲ γὰρ μετὰ τὸν ἁγιασμὸν τὰ μυστικὰ σύμβολα τῆς οἰκείας ἐξίσταται φύσεως· μένει γὰρ ἐπὶ τῆς προτέρας οὐσίας, καὶ τοῦ σχήματος καὶ τοῦ εἴδους, καὶ ὁρατά ἐστι καὶ ἅπτα, οἷα καὶ πρότερον ἦν· νοεῖται δὲ ἅπερ ἐγένετο, καὶ πιστεύεται, καὶ προσκυνεῖται, ὡς ἐκεῖνα ὄντα ἅπερ πιστεύεται.

AUCTOR CONSTITUTIONUM APOSTOLICARUM.

Ed. Labbe and Cossart.

(a) Lib. ii. cap. 34. p. 271. Διὸ τὸν ἐπίσκοπον στέργειν ὀφείλετε ὡς πατέρα, φοβεῖσθαι ὡς βασιλέα, τιμᾶν ὡς κύριον, τοὺς καρποὺς ὑμῶν καὶ τὰ ἔργα τῶν χειρῶν ὑμῶν εἰς εὐλογίαν ὑμῶν προσφέροντες αὐτῷ τὰς ἀπαρχὰς ὑμῶν, καὶ τὰς δεκάτας ὑμῶν καὶ τὰ ἀφαιρέματα ὑμῶν καὶ τὰ δῶρα ὑμῶν διδόντες αὐτῷ ὡς ἱερεῖ Θεοῦ, ἀπαρχὴν σίτου, οἴνου, ἐλαίου, ὀπώρας, ἐρέας, καὶ πάντων ὧν Κύριος ὁ Θεὸς ἐπιχορηγεῖ ὑμῖν, καὶ ἔσται σοι ἡ προσφορά σου δεκτὴ εἰς ὀσμὴν εὐωδίας Κυρίῳ τῷ Θεῷ σου—c. 35. χρὴ δὲ ὑμᾶς γινώσκειν, ὅτι εἰ καὶ ἐῤῥύσατο ὑμᾶς Κύριος τῆς δουλείας τῶν ἐπεισάκτων δεσμῶν, καὶ ἐξήγαγεν ὑμᾶς εἰς ἀνάψυξιν, μηκέτι ἐάσας ὑμᾶς θύειν ἄλογα ζῶα περὶ ἁμαρτιῶν, καὶ καθαρισμοῦ, καὶ ἀποπομπαίων, καὶ λουτρῶν συνεχῶν, καὶ περιῤῥαντηρίων, οὐ δήπου καὶ τῶν εἰσφορῶν ὑμᾶς ἐλευθέρωσεν.

(b) Lib. ii. cap. 59. ad calcem, p. 302. Ἐν ᾗ (κυριακῇ) προφητῶν ἀνάγνωσις, καὶ εὐαγγελίου κηρυκία, καὶ θυσίας ἀνάφορα, καὶ τροφῆς ἱερᾶς δωρεά.

(bb) Lib. v. c. 18. p. 367. Καὶ ὑμεῖς, ἀναστάντος τοῦ Κυρίου, προσενέγκατε τὴν θυσίαν ὑμῶν περὶ ἧς ὑμῖν διετάξατο δι' ἡμῶν, λέγων, Τοῦτο ποιεῖτε εἰς τὴν ἐμὴν ἀνάμνησιν.

(c) Lib. vi. c. 23. p. 403. Ἀντὶ μὲν καθημερινοῦ ἓν μόνον δοὺς βάπτισμα, τὸ εἰς τὸν Αὐτοῦ θάνατον· ἀντὶ δὲ μιᾶς φυλῆς, ἀφ' ἑκάστου ἔθνους προστάξας τοὺς ἀρίστους εἰς ἱερωσύνην προχειρίζεσθαι, καὶ οὐ τὰ σώματα μωμοσκοπεῖσθαι ἀλλὰ θρησκείαν καὶ βίους· ἀντὶ θυσίας τῆς δι' αἱμάτων, λογικὴν καὶ ἀναίμακτον καὶ τὴν μυστικὴν εἰς τὸν θάνατον τοῦ Κυρίου συμβόλων χάριν ἐπιτελεῖσθαι, τοῦ σώματος Αὐτοῦ καὶ τοῦ αἵματος.

(d) Ibid. c. 29. p. 411. (ad Laicos loquitur.) Καὶ τὴν ἀντίτυπον τοῦ βασιλείου σώματος Χριστοῦ δεκτὴν Εὐχαριστίαν προσφέρετε ἔν τε ταῖς ἐκκλησίαις ὑμῶν, καὶ ἐν τοῖς κοιμητηρίοις, καὶ ἐν ταῖς ἐξόδοις τῶν κεκοιμημένων.

(e) Lib. viii. c. 46. p. 507. Εἰκότως τὸν ἐπηρτημένον κίνδυνον τοῖς τὰ τοιαῦτα πράττουσι προειδόμενοι, καὶ τὴν εἰς τὰς θυσίας καὶ εὐχαριστίας ἀμέλειαν ἐκ τοῦ ὑφ' ὧν μὴ χρὴ προσαγομένας ἀσεβῶς, παιδίαν ἡγουμένων τὴν ἀρχιερατικὴν τιμήν, ἥτις μίμησιν περιέχει τῆς μεγάλου Ἀρχιερέως Ἰησοῦ Χριστοῦ βασιλέως ἡμῶν, ἀνάγκην ἔσχομεν καὶ τοῦτο παραινέσαι·—οὔ τε γὰρ διακόνῳ προσφέρειν θυσίαν θεμιτόν.

(f) Ibid. Pagina proxima. Πρῶτος τοίνυν τῇ φύσει Ἀρχιερεὺς ὁ μονογενὴς Χριστὸς οὐχ' Ἑαυτῷ τὴν τιμὴν ἁρπάσας, ἀλλὰ παρὰ τοῦ Πατρὸς κατασταθεὶς· ὃς γινόμενος ἄνθρωπος δι' ἡμᾶς, καὶ τὴν πνευματικὴν θυσίαν προσφέρων τῷ Θεῷ Αὐτοῦ καὶ Πατρὶ πρὸ τοῦ πάθους, ἡμῖν [ἀποστόλοις] διετάξατο μόνοις τοῦτο ποιεῖν.

(g) Ibid. Μετὰ δὲ τὴν ἀνάληψιν Αὐτοῦ ἡμεῖς [οἱ ἀπόστολοι] προσενέγκοντες κατὰ τὴν διάταξιν Αὐτοῦ θυσίαν καθαρὰν καὶ ἀναίμακτον, προεχειρίσαμεθα ἐπισκόπους, καὶ πρεσβυτέρους, καὶ διακόνους, κ.τ.λ.

CANONES APOSTOLICI.

Ed. Labbe and Cossart, 1728.

Can. 3. tom. i. p. 26. Εἴ τις ἐπίσκοπος ἢ πρεσβύτερος 'παρὰ τὴν ὑπὸ Κυρίου διάταξιν τὴν ἐπὶ τῇ θυσίᾳ, προσενέγκῃ ἕτερά τινα ἐπὶ τὸ τοῦ Θεοῦ θυσιαστήριον, ἢ μέλι, ἢ γάλα, ὡς παρὰ τὴν διάταξιν Κυρίου ποιῶν καθαιρείσθω.

Μὴ ἐξὸν δὲ ἔστω προσάγεσθαι τι ἕτερον πρὸς τὸ θυσιαστήριον, πλὴν νέων χίδρων, ἢ στάχυος σίτου, ἢ σταφυλῆς, τῷ καιρῷ τῷ δέοντι κ.τ.λ.

Can. 4. Ἡ ἄλλη πᾶσα ὀπώρα εἰς οἶκον ἀποστελλέσθω, ἀπαρχὴ τῷ ἐπισκόπῳ καὶ τοῖς πρεσβυτέροις, ἀλλὰ μὴ πρὸς θυσιαστήριον· δῆλον δὲ, ὡς ὁ ἐπίσκοπος καὶ οἱ πρεσβύτεροι ἐπιμερίζουσι τοῖς διακόνοις, καὶ τοῖς λοιποῖς κληρικοῖς.

Can. 8. Εἴ τις ἐπίσκοπος, ἢ πρεσβύτερος, ἢ διάκονος, ἢ ἐκ τοῦ καταλόγου τοῦ ἱερατικοῦ, προσφορᾶς γενομένης μὴ μεταλάβοι, τὴν αἰτίαν εἰπάτω· καὶ ἐὰν εὔλογος ᾖ, συγγνώμης τυγχανέτω, εἰ δὲ μὴ λέγει, ἀφοριζέσθω, ὡς αἴτιος βλάβης γενηθεὶς τῷ λαῷ, καὶ ὑπόνοιαν ἐμποιήσας κατὰ τοῦ προσενέγκαντος, ὡς μὴ ὑγιῶς ἀνενέγκοντος.

Can. 9. p. 27. Πάντας τοὺς εἰσίοντας πιστοὺς, εἰς τὴν ἁγίαν τοῦ Θεοῦ ἐκκλησίαν, καὶ τῶν ἱερῶν γραφῶν ἀκούοντας, μὴ παραμένοντας δὲ τῇ προσευχῇ, καὶ τῇ ἁγίᾳ μεταλήψει, ὡς ἀταξίαν ἐμποιοῦντας τῇ ἐκκλησίᾳ, ἀφορίζεσθαι χρή.

Can. 45. p. 35. Ἐπίσκοπον, ἢ πρεσβύτερον, ἢ διάκονον αἱρετικῶν δεξαμένους βάπτισμα, ἢ θυσίαν, καθαιρεῖσθαι προστάσσομεν· τίς γὰρ συμφώνησις Χριστῷ πρὸς Βελίαλ; ἢ τίς μέρις πιστῷ μετὰ ἀπίστου;

DIONYSII ALEXANDRINI. A.D. 247.

Ed. Labbe and Cossart.

Canon secundus, tom. i. p. 857. Περί δε τῶν ἐν ἀφέδρῳ γυναικῶν. —— οὐδὲ γὰρ αὐτὰς οἶμαι πιστὰς, οὔσας καὶ εὐλαβεῖς τολμήσειν —— τοῦ σώματος καὶ τοῦ αἵματος τοῦ Χριστοῦ προσάψασθαι. —— εἰς δὲ τὰ ἅγια τῶν ἁγίων ὁ μὴ πάντῃ καθαρὸς καὶ ψυχῇ καὶ σώματι, προσιέναι κωλυθήσεται.

CONCILIUM ELIBERITANUM. A.D. 305.

Ed. Labbe and Cossart.

Can. 28. p. 995. Episcopos placuit ab eo qui non communicat, munera accipere non debere.

Can. 29. Energumenus, qui ab erratico spiritu exagitatur —
hujus nomen neque ad altare cum oblatione recitandum, neque permittendum, ut sua manu in ecclesia ministret.

CONCILIUM ARELATENSE. A.D. 314.

Can. 15. p. 1452. De diaconibus quos cognovimus multis locis
offerre, placuit minime fieri debere.

CONCILIUM ANCYRANUM. A.D. 315.

Can. 1. p. 1485. Πρεσβυτέρους τοὺς ἐπιθύσαντας — τούτους ἔδοξε
τῆς μὲν τιμῆς τῆς κατὰ τὴν καθέδραν μετέχειν, προσφέρειν δὲ αὐτούς, ἢ
ὁμιλεῖν, ἢ ὅλως λειτουργεῖν τὶ τῶν ἱερατικῶν λειτουργιῶν, μὴ ἐξεῖναι.

Can. 2. Διακόνους ὁμοίως θύσαντας — πεπαῦσθαι δὲ αὐτοὺς τῆς
ἱερᾶς λειτουργίας, τῆς τε τοῦ ἄρτον ἢ ποτήριον ἀναφέρειν, ἢ κηρύσσειν.

Can. 5. Ὅσοι δὲ — ἔφαγον — δακρύοντες, εἰ ἐπλήρωσαν τὸν τῆς
ὑποπτώσεως τριετῆ χρόνον, χωρὶς προσφορᾶς δεχθήτωσαν· εἰ δὲ μὴ ἔφαγον,
δύο ὑποπεσόντες ἔτη, τῷ τρίτῳ κοινωνησάτωσαν χωρὶς προσφορᾶς, ἵνα τὸ
τέλειον ἐν τετραετίᾳ λάβωσιν.

Can. 6. Περὶ τῆς τῶν ἀπειλῇ μόνον εἰξάντων — ἔδοξε μέχρι μεγάλης
ἡμέρας εἰς ἀκρόασιν δεχθῆναι,—καὶ ὑποπεσεῖν τρία ἔτη, καὶ μετὰ ἄλλα δύο
ἔτη, κοινωνῆσαι χωρὶς προσφορᾶς, καὶ οὕτως ἐλθεῖν ἐπὶ τὸ τέλειον.

Can. 7. Ἔδοξε διετίαν ὑποπεσόντας δεχθῆναι· τὸ δὲ εἰ χρὴ μετὰ τῆς
προσφορᾶς, ἕκαστον τῶν ἐπισκόπων δοκιμάσαι.

Can. 8. Οἱ δὲ δεύτερον καὶ τρίτον θύσαντες μετὰ βίας, τετραετίαν ὑποπεσέτωσαν, δύο δὲ ἔτη χωρὶς προσφορᾶς κοινωνησάτωσαν, καὶ τῷ ἑβδόμῳ
τελείως δεχθήτωσαν.

Can. 9. Ὅσοι δὲ ἠνάγκασαν τοὺς ἀδελφοὺς — οὗτοι ἔτη μὲν τρία τὸν
τῆς ἀκροάσεως δεξάσθωσαν, τόπον, ἐν δὲ ἄλλῃ ἐξαετίᾳ τὸν τῆς ὑποπτώσεως,
ἄλλον δὲ ἐνιαυτὸν κοινωνησάτωσαν χωρὶς προσφορᾶς, ἵνα τὴν δεκαετίαν πλη-
ρώσαντες τοῦ τελείου μετάσχωσιν.

Can. 16. Ὅσοι πρὶν εἰκοσαετεῖς γενέσθαι, ἥμαρτον, πέντε καὶ δέκα
ἔτεσιν ὑποπεσόντες, κοινωνίας τυγχανέτωσαν τῆς εἰς τὰς προσευχάς· εἶτα ἐν
τῇ κοινωνίᾳ διατελέσαντες ἔτη πέντε, τότε καὶ τῆς προσφορᾶς ἐφαπτέσθωσαν.
— ὅσοι δὲ ὑπερβάντες τὴν ἡλικίαν ταύτην — περιπεπτώκασι τῷ ἁμαρ-
τήματι, πέντε καὶ εἴκοσι ἔτη ὑποπεσέτωσαν, καὶ κοινωνίας τυγχανέτωσαν τῆς
εἰς τὰς προσευχάς. εἶτα ἐκτελέσαντες πέντε ἔτη ἐν τῇ κοινωνίῳ τῶν εὐχῶν
τυγχανέτωσαν τῆς προσφορᾶς.

Can. 24. Οἱ καταμαντευόμενοι — τρία ἔτη ὑποπτώσεως, καὶ δύο ἔτη
εὐχῆς χωρὶς προσφορᾶς.

CONCILIUM NEOCÆSARIENSE. A.D. 315.

Can. 9. p. 1512. Πρεσβύτερος, ἐὰν προημαρτηκὼς σώματι προαχθῇ
— μὴ προσφερέτω, μένων ἐν τοῖς λοιποῖς.

g

Can. 13. Ἐπιχώριοι πρεσβύτεροι ἐν τῷ κυριακῷ τῆς πόλεως προσφέρειν οὐ δύνανται.

Can. 14. Οἱ δὲ χωρεπίσκοποι προσφέρουσι τιμώμενοι.

Concilium Nicænum Œcumenicum Primum. A.D. 325.

Can. 5. tom. ii. p. 36. Μία μὲν [σύνοδος γινέσθω] πρὸ τῆς τεσσαρακοστῆς, ἵνα πάσης μικροψυχίας ἀναιρουμένης, τὸ δῶρον καθαρὸν προσφέρηται τῷ Θεῷ.

Can. 11. Περὶ τῶν παραβάντων χωρὶς ἀνάγκης — τρία ἔτη ἐν ἀκροωμένοις ποιήσουσιν οἱ πιστοί, καὶ ἑπτὰ ἔτη ὑποπεσοῦνται, δύο δὲ ἔτη χωρὶς προσφορᾶς κοινωνήσουσι τῷ λαῷ τῶν προσευχῶν.

Can. 13. Εἰ τὶς ἐξοδεύοι, τοῦ τελευταίου — ἐφοδίου μὴ ἀποστερεῖσθαι· εἰ δὲ πάλιν ἐν τοῖς ζῶσιν ἐξετασθῇ, μετὰ τῶν κοινωνούντων τῆς εὐχῆς μόνης ἔστω.

Can. 18. Ἦλθεν εἰς τὴν ἁγίαν καὶ μεγάλην σύνοδον, ὅτι ἔν τίσι τόποις, τοῖς πρεσβυτέροις τὴν εὐχαριστίαν οἱ διάκονοι διδόασιν· ὅπερ οὔτε ὁ κανὼν, οὔτε ἡ συνήθεια παρέδωκε, τοὺς ἐξουσίαν μὴ ἔχοντας προσφέρειν, τοῖς προσφέρουσι διδόναι τὸ σῶμα τοῦ Χριστοῦ.

Concilium Gangrense. A.D. 340.

Can. 4. p. 428. Εἰ τὶς διακρίνοιτο παρὰ πρεσβυτέρου γεγαμηκότος, ὡς μὴ χρῆναι, λειτουργήσαντος αὐτοῦ προσφορᾶς μεταλαμβάνειν, ἀνάθεμα ἔστω.

Concilium Laodicenum. A.D. 367.

Can. 14. tom. i. p. 1533. Περὶ τοῦ, μὴ ἅγια εἰς λόγον εὐλογιῶν εἰς ἑτέρας παροικίας διαπέμπεσθαι.

Can. 19. Καὶ μετὰ τὸ πρεσβυτέρους δοῦναι τῷ ἐπισκόπῳ τὴν εἰρήνην, τότε τοὺς λαϊκοὺς τὴν εἰρήνην διδόναι, καὶ οὕτω τὴν ἁγίαν προσφορὰν ἐπιτελεῖσθαι, καὶ μόνοις ἐξὸν εἶναι τοῖς ἱερατικοῖς εἰσιέναι εἰς τὸ θυσιαστήριον, καὶ κοινωνεῖν.

Can. 49. Οὐ δεῖ τῇ τεσσαρακοστῇ ἄρτον προσφέρειν, εἰ μὴ ἐν σαββάτῳ καὶ κυριακῇ μόνον.

Can. 58. Οὐ δεῖ ἐν τοῖς οἴκοις προσφορὰς γίνεσθαι παρὰ ἐπισκόπων, ἢ πρεσβυτέρων.

Concilium Carthaginense secundum, aliter quintum. A.D. 390.

Can. 2. tom. ii. p. 1391. Ut ab omnibus pudicitia custodiatur, qui altari deserviunt.

Can. 4. Si quisquam in periculo fuerit constitutus, et se reconciliari divinis altaribus petierit, si episcopus absens fuerit, debet utique presbyter consulere episcopum, &c.

Can. 8. Si quis forte presbyter ab episcopo suo correptus — putaverit separatim Deo sacrificia offerenda, vel aliud erigendum altare contra ecclesiasticam fidem disciplinamque crediderit, non exeat impunitus — Si quis presbyter a præposito suo excommunicatus, vel correptus fuerit — [et] superbia inflatus secernendum se ab episcopi sui communione duxerit, ac separatim cum aliquibus schisma faciens sacrificium Dei obtulerit, anathema habeatur, et locum amittat.

CONCILIUM CARTHAGINENSE TERTIUM, *aliter* SEXTUM. A.D. 397.

Can. 24. tom. ii. p. 1403. Et in sacramentis corporis et sanguinis Domini nihil amplius offeratur, quam Ipse Dominus tradidit, hoc est, panis et vinum aqua mixtum.

Can. 29. Ut sacramenta altaris non nisi a jejunis hominibus celebrentur, excepto uno die anniversario, quo cæna Domini celebratur. Si episcoporum — defunctorum commendatio facienda est, solis orationibus fiat, si illi qui faciunt jam pransi inveniantur.

Can. 48. Honoratus et Urbanus dixerunt — Verùm et de sacrificiis inhibendis post prandium, ut a jejunis, sicut dignum est, offerantur, et tunc et nunc confirmatum est.

CONCILIUM CARTHAGINENSE QUARTUM, *aliter* SEPTIMUM. A.D. 378.

Can. 33. p. 1440. Episcopi vel presbyteri, si causa visitandæ ecclesiæ ad alterius ecclesiam venerint — ad oblationem consecrandam invitentur.

Can. 79. Pœnitentes, qui attente leges pœnitentiæ exequuntur, si casu in itinere vel in mari mortui fuerint, ubi eis subveniri non possit, memoria eorum et orationibus, et oblationibus commendetur.

Can. 93. Oblationes dissidentium fratrum neque in sacrario neque in gazophylacio recipiantur.

Can. 94. Eorum qui pauperes opprimunt, dona a sacerdotibus refutanda.

CONCIL. TOLETANUM primum, A.D. 400.

Can. 5. Clericus si ad ecclesiam ad sacrificium quotidianum non accesserit, clericus non habeatur.

CONCIL. CONSTANTINOP. 28. ŒCUM. 8. A.D. 754.

In Actis Concilii Nicæni secundi, tom. iii. versus finem. tom. viii. p. 1097. Εὐφρανθήτωσαν, καὶ ἀγαλλιάσθωσαν, καὶ παρρησιαζέσθωσαν οἱ τὴν ἀληθῆ τοῦ Χριστοῦ εἰκόνα εἰλικρινεστάτῃ ψυχῇ ποιοῦντες καὶ ποθοῦντες καὶ σεβόμενοι, καὶ εἰς σωτηρίαν ψυχῆς καὶ σώματος προσφερόμενοι· ἣν Αὐτὸς ὁ Ἱεροτελεστὴς καὶ Θεός, τὸ ἡμῶν ἐξ ἡμῶν ὁλικῶς ἀναλαβόμενος φύραμα, κατὰ τὸν καιρὸν τοῦ ἑκουσίου πάθους εἰς τύπον καὶ ἀνάμνησιν ἐναργεστάτην τοῖς Αὐτοῦ μύσταις παραδέδωκε. Μέλλων γὰρ Αὐτὸν ἑκουσίως ἐκδιδόναι τῷ ἀοιδίμῳ καὶ ζωοποιῷ θανάτῳ Αὐτοῦ, λαβὼν τὸν ἄρτον εὐλόγησε, καὶ εὐχαριστήσας ἔκλασε, καὶ μεταδοὺς εἶπε· λάβετε, φάγετε εἰς ἄφεσιν ἁμαρτιῶν· Τοῦτό Μου ἔστι τὸ Σῶμα. ὁμοίως καὶ τὸ ποτήριον μεταδοὺς εἶπε· Τοῦτό Μου ἔστι τὸ αἷμα· τοῦτο ποιεῖτε εἰς τὴν ἐμὴν ἀνάμνησιν· ὡς οὐκ ἄλλου εἴδους ἐπιλεχθέντος παρ' Αὐτοῦ ἐν τῇ ὑπ' οὐρανὸν, ἢ τύπου, εἰκονίσαι τὴν Αὐτοῦ σάρκωσιν δυναμένου. Ἰδοὺ οὖν ἡ εἰκὼν τοῦ ζωοποιοῦ Σώματος Αὐτοῦ, ἡ ἐντίμως καὶ τετιμημένως πραττομένη. τί γὰρ ἐμηχανήσατο ἐν τούτῳ ὁ πάνσοφος Θεός ; οὐχ ἕτερόν τι, ἢ δεῖξαι καὶ τρανῶσαι φανερῶς ἡμῖν τοῖς ἀνθρώποις τὸ πραγματευθὲν μυστήριον ἐν τῇ κατ' Αὐτὸν οἰκονομίᾳ· ὅτι ὥσπερ ὁ ἐξ ἡμῶν ἀνελάβετο, ὕλη μόνη ἐστὶν ἀνθρωπίνης οὐσίας κατὰ πάντα τελείας, μὴ χαρακτηριζούσης ἰδιοσύστατον πρόσωπον, ἵνα μὴ προσθήκη προσώπου ἐν τῇ Θεότητι παρεμπέσῃ· οὕτω καὶ τὴν εἰκόνα ὕλην ἐξαίρετον, ἤγουν ἄρτου οὐσίαν προσέταξε προσφέρεσθαι, μὴ σχηματίζουσαν ἀνθρώπου μορφὴν, ἵνα μὴ εἰδωλολατρεία παρεισαχθῇ. ὥσπερ οὖν τὸ κατὰ φύσιν τοῦ Χριστοῦ Σῶμα ἅγιον, ὡς θεωθέν· οὕτως δῆλον καὶ τὸ θέσει, ἤτοι ἡ εἰκὼν Αὐτοῦ ἁγία, ὡς διά τινος ἁγιασμοῦ χάριτι θεουμένη. τοῦτο γὰρ καὶ ἐπραγματεύσατο, ὡς ἔφημεν, ὁ Δεσπότης Χριστός, ὅπως καθάπερ τὴν σάρκα, ἣν ἀνέλαβε, τῷ οἰκείῳ κατὰ φύσιν ἁγιασμῷ ἐξ αὐτῆς ἑνώσεως ἐθέωσεν, ὁμοίως καὶ τὸν τῆς εὐχαριστίας ἄρτον, ὡς ἀψευδῆ εἰκόνα τῆς φυσικῆς σαρκὸς διὰ τῆς τοῦ Ἁγίου Πνεύματος ἐπιφοιτήσεως ἁγιαζόμενον, θεῖον Σῶμα εὐδόκησε γίνεσθαι, μεσιτεύοντος τοῦ ἐν μετενέξει ἐκ τοῦ κοινοῦ πρὸς τὸ ἅγιον τὴν ἀναφορὰν ποιουμένου Ἱερέως. Λοιπὸν ἡ κατὰ φύσιν ἔμψυχος καὶ νοερὰ σὰρξ τοῦ Κυρίου ἐχρίσθη Πνεύματι Ἁγίῳ [τὴν Θεότητα]. ὡσαύτως καὶ ἡ Θεοπαράδοτος εἰκὼν τῆς σαρκὸς Αὐτοῦ, ὁ θεῖος ἄρτος ἐπληρώθη Πνεύματος Ἁγίου σὺν τῷ ποτηρίῳ τοῦ ζωηφόρου αἵματος τῆς πλευρᾶς Αὐτοῦ. Αὕτη οὖν ἀποδέδεικται ἀψευδὴς εἰκὼν τῆς ἐνσάρκου οἰκονομίας Χριστοῦ τοῦ Θεοῦ ἡμῶν, καθὼς προλέλεκται· ἣν Αὐτὸς ἡμῖν ὁ ἀληθινὸς τῆς φύσεως Ζωοπλάστης οἰκειοφώνως παραδέδωκεν.

LITURGIA CLEMENTINA *in Constitutionibus Apostolicis vulgo dictis.*

(a) Lib. viii. cap. 5. tom. i. p. 462. Δὸς ἐν τῷ ὀνόματί σου, καρδιογνῶστα Θεέ, ἐπὶ τὸν δοῦλόν σου τόνδε, ὃν ἐξελέξω εἰς ἐπίσκοπον — ἀρχιερατεύειν σοι ἀμέμπτως λειτουργοῦντα νυκτὸς καὶ ἡμέρας· καὶ ἐξιλασκόμενόν σου τὸ πρόσωπον, ἐπισυναγαγεῖν τὸν ἀριθμὸν τῶν σωζομένων, καὶ προσφέρειν σοι τὰ δῶρα τῆς ἁγίας σου Ἐκκλησίας. — εὐαρέστειν δέ σοι ἐν πραότητι καὶ καθαρᾷ καρδίᾳ, ἀτρέπτως, ἀμέμπτως, ἀνεγκλήτως· προσφέροντά σοι καθαρὰν καὶ ἀναίμακτον θυσίαν, ἣν διὰ Χριστοῦ διετάξω, τὸ μυστήριον τῆς καινῆς διαθήκης — Εἷς τῶν ἐπισκόπων ἀναφερέτω τὴν θυσίαν ἐπὶ τῶν χειρῶν τοῦ χειροτονηθέντος.

(aa) *Ibid.* cap. 16. Περὶ χειροτονίας πρεσβυτέρων. In oratione super electum. καὶ τὰς ὑπὲρ τοῦ λαοῦ ἱερουργίας ἀμώμους ἐκτελῇ διὰ τοῦ Χριστοῦ σου.

(b) *Ibid.* cap. 10. Δεηθῶμεν — ὑπὲρ τῶν τὰς θυσίας καὶ τὰς ἀπαρχὰς προσφερόντων Κυρίῳ τῷ Θεῷ ἡμῶν, ὅπως ὁ παναγαθὸς Θεὸς ἀμείψηται αὐτοὺς ταῖς ἐπουρανίοις Αὐτοῦ δωρεαῖς.

(c) *Ibid.* cap. 12. — ἵν᾽ εὐθὺς ὁ διάκονος λέγῃ· μή τις τῶν κατηχουμένων· μή τις τῶν ἀκροωμένων· μή τις τῶν ἀπίστων· μή τις τῶν ἑτεροδόξων. — μή τις κατά τινος· μή τις ἐν ὑποκρίσει· Ὀρθοὶ πρὸς Κύριον μετὰ φόβου καὶ τρόμου ἑστῶτες ὦμεν προσφέρειν. ὧν γενομένων οἱ διάκονοι προσαγέτωσαν τὰ δῶρα τῷ ἐπισκόπῳ πρὸς τὸ θυσιαστήριον. — εὐξάμενος οὖν καθ᾽ ἑαυτὸν ὁ ἀρχιερεὺς ἅμα τοῖς ἱερεῦσι, καὶ λαμπρὰν ἐσθῆτα μετενδὺς, καὶ στὰς πρὸς τῷ θυσιαστηρίῳ — εἰπάτω· ἡ χάρις τοῦ παντοκράτορος Θεοῦ, καὶ ἡ ἀγάπη τοῦ Κυρίου, κ.τ.λ. — καὶ ὁ ἀρχιερεύς· Ἄνω τὸν νοῦν· καὶ πάντες· Ἔχομεν πρὸς τὸν Κύριον. καὶ ὁ ἀρχιερεύς, Εὐχαριστήσωμεν τῷ Κυρίῳ· καὶ πάντες· Ἄξιον καὶ δίκαιον· καὶ ὁ ἀρχιερεὺς εἰπάτω, Ἄξιον ὡς ἀληθῶς καὶ δίκαιον πρὸ πάντων ἀνυμνεῖν σε τὸν ὄντως ὄντα Θεόν, κ.τ.λ. The bishop proceeds to acknowledge God as the First Cause and Author of all things, and Father of our Lord Jesus Christ, as Maker and Governor of angels and men, and all creatures; and to rehearse the history of all the great providences from the creation of Adam down to the delivery of the people of Israel from the Egyptian bondage, and ends with the words of the prophet Daniel, chap. vii. ver. 10. ἅμα χιλίαις χιλιάσιν ἀρχαγγέλων, καὶ μυρίαις μυριάσιν ἀγγέλων ἀκαταπαύστως καὶ ἀσιγήτως βοώσαις· καὶ πᾶς ὁ λαὸς ἅμα εἰπάτω· Ἅγιος, ἅγιος, ἅγιος Κύριος σαβαώθ. καὶ ὁ ἀρχιερεὺς ἑξῆς λεγέτω· Ἅγιος γὰρ εἶ ὡς ἀληθῶς, καὶ πανάγιος· — ἅγιός δὲ καὶ ὁ μονογενὴς σοῦ Ὑιὸς, κ.τ.λ. He recites our Saviour's incarnation, miracles, death, resurrection, and ascension; and adds, Μεμνημένοι οὖν ὧν δι᾽ ἡμᾶς ὑπέμεινεν, εὐχαριστοῦμεν σοι — καὶ τὴν διάταξιν Αὐτοῦ πληροῦμεν. Ἐν ᾗ γὰρ νυκτὶ παρεδίδοτο λαβὼν ἄρτον — ὡσαύτως καὶ τὸ ποτήριον κεράσας ἐξ οἴνου καὶ ὕδατος, κ.τ.λ. as in the institution : and then proceeds, Μεμνημένοι τοίνυν τοῦ πάθους Αὐτοῦ, καὶ τοῦ θανάτου, καὶ τῆς ἐκ νεκρῶν ἀναστάσεως, καὶ τῆς εἰς οὐρανοὺς ἐπανόδου, καὶ τῆς μελλούσης Αὐτοῦ δευτέρας παρουσίας, προσφέρομέν σοι τῷ βασιλεῖ καὶ Θεῷ κατὰ τὴν Αὐτοῦ διάταξιν τὸν ἄρτον τοῦτον καὶ τὸ ποτήριον τοῦτο, εὐχαριστοῦντες σοι δι᾽ Αὐτοῦ, ἐφ᾽ οἷς κατηξίωσας ἡμᾶς ἑστάναι ἐνώπιόν σου, καὶ ἱερατεύειν σοι· καὶ ἀξιοῦμεν σε, ὅπως εὐμενῶς ἐπιβλέψῃς ἐπὶ τὰ προκείμενα δῶρα ταῦτα ἐνώπιόν σου, σὺ ὁ ἀνενδεὴς Θεός· καὶ εὐδοκήσῃς ἐπ᾽ αὐτοῖς εἰς τιμὴν τοῦ Χριστοῦ σου· καὶ καταπέμψῃς τὸ Ἅγιόν σου Πνεῦμα ἐπὶ τὴν θυσίαν ταύτην τὸν Μάρτυρα τῶν παθημάτων τοῦ Κυρίου Ἰησοῦ, ὅπως ἀποφήνῃ τὸν ἄρτον τοῦτόν σῶμα τοῦ Χριστοῦ σου, καὶ τὸ ποτήριον τοῦτο αἷμα τοῦ Χριστοῦ σου· ἵνα οἱ μεταλαβόντες αὐτοῦ βεβαιωθῶσι πρὸς εὐσέβειαν, ἀφέσεως ἁμαρτημάτων τύχωσι, τοῦ διαβόλου καὶ τῆς πλάνης αὐτοῦ ῥυσθῶσι, Πνεύματος Ἁγίου πληρωθῶσιν, ἄξιοι τοῦ Χριστοῦ σου γένωνται, ζωῆς αἰωνίου τύχωσι, σοῦ καταλλαγέντος αὐτοῖς, Δεσπότα παντοκράτορ· ἔτι δεόμεθά σου, Κύριε, καὶ ὑπὲρ τῆς ἁγίας σου Ἐκκλησίας — ὑπὲρ τῆς ἐμῆς τοῦ προσφέροντός σοι οὐδενίας· καὶ ὑπὲρ παντὸς τοῦ πρεσβυτερίου, ὑπὲρ τῶν διακόνων καὶ παντὸς κλήρου — ὑπὲρ τοῦ βασιλέως καὶ τῶν ἐν ὑπεροχῇ — ἔτι προσφέρομέν σοι καὶ ὑπὲρ πάντων τῶν ἀπ᾽ αἰῶνος εὐαρεστησάντων σοι ἁγίων, πατριαρχῶν, προφητῶν, κ.τ.λ. — ἔτι προσφέρομέν σοι ὑπὲρ τοῦ λαοῦ τούτου — ἔτι ἀξιοῦμέν σε καὶ ὑπὲρ τῆς πόλεως ταύτης — ἔτι παρακαλοῦμέν σε ὑπὲρ τῶν μισούντων ἡμᾶς — ὑπὲρ τῶν κατηχουμένων — ὑπὲρ τῶν χειμαζομένων ὑπὸ τοῦ ἀλλοτρίου, καὶ ὑπὲρ τῶν ἐν μετανοίᾳ — ἔτι προσφέρομέν σοι ὑπὲρ εὐκρασίας τοῦ ἀέρος, καὶ τῆς εὐφορίας τῶν καρπῶν· — ἔτι παρακαλοῦμέν σε καὶ ὑπὲρ τῶν δι᾽ εὔλογον αἰτίαν ἀπόντων — καὶ ὁ διάκονος κηρυσσέτω πάλιν.

(d) *Ibid.* cap. 13. ἔτι καὶ ἔτι δεηθῶμεν τοῦ Θεοῦ διὰ τοῦ Χριστοῦ Αὐτοῦ ὑπὲρ τοῦ δώρου τοῦ προσκομισθέντος Κυρίῳ τῷ Θεῷ· ὅπως ὁ ἀγαθὸς Θεὸς προσδέξηται αὐτὸ διὰ τῆς μεσιτείας τοῦ Χριστοῦ Αὐτοῦ εἰς τὸ ἐπουράνιον Αὐτοῦ θυσιαστήριον εἰς ὀσμὴν εὐωδίας· ὑπὲρ τῆς ἐκκλησίας ταύτης, καὶ τοῦ λαοῦ δεηθῶμεν· ὑπὲρ πάσης ἐπισκοπῆς, κ.τ.λ. — καὶ ὁ ἐπίσκοπος εἰπάτω, ὁ Θεὸς ὁ μέγας — ἐπίβλεψον ἐφ᾽ ἡμᾶς — καὶ ἁγιάσας ἡμῶν τὸ σῶμα καὶ τὴν ψυχήν, καταξίωσον καθαροὺς γενομένους ἀπὸ παντὸς μολυσμοῦ σαρκὸς καὶ πνεύματος τυχεῖν τῶν προκειμένων ἀγαθῶν, καὶ μηδένα ἡμῶν ἀνάξιον κρίνῃς — καὶ ὁ ἐπίσκοπος προσφωνησάτω τῷ λαῷ οὕτω· Τὰ ἅγια τοῖς ἁγίοις· καὶ ὁ λαὸς ὑπακουέτω· Εἷς Ἅγιος, εἷς Κύριος, εἷς Ἰησοῦς Χριστός. — Ὡσαννὰ ἐν τοῖς ὑψίστοις· καὶ μετὰ τοῦτο μεταλαμβανέτω ὁ ἐπίσκοπος· ἔπειτα οἱ πρεσβύτεροι, καὶ οἱ διάκονοι — καὶ τότε πᾶς ὁ λαὸς κατὰ τάξιν μετὰ αἰδοῦς καὶ εὐλαβείας [d] ἄνευ θορύβου· καὶ ὁ μὲν ἐπίσκοπος διδότω τὴν προσφοράν, λέγων, Σῶμα Χριστοῦ· καὶ ὁ δεχόμενος λεγέτω, Ἀμήν· ὁ δὲ διάκονος κατεχέτω τὸ ποτήριον, καὶ ἐπιδιδοὺς λεγέτω, Αἷμα Χριστοῦ ποτήριον ζωῆς· καὶ ὁ πίνων λεγέτω, Ἀμήν. — καὶ ὅταν πάντες μεταλάβωσι καὶ πᾶσαι, λαβόντες οἱ διάκονοι τὰ περισσεύσαντα εἰσφερέτωσαν εἰς τὰ παστοφόρια.

LITURGIA S. JACOBI, ex Biblioth. Patrum. Tom. ii.

Edit. Parisiis, 1624.

(a) P. 1. Sacerdos ait pro mensa propositionis, οὐκ εἰμὶ ἄξιος ἀντοφθαλμῆσαι τῇ ἱερᾷ σου ταύτῃ καὶ πνευματικῇ τραπέζῃ.

(b) P. 7. Sacerdos adferens dona dicit, Ὁ Θεὸς — εὐλόγησον τὴν πρόθεσιν ταύτην, καὶ πρόσδεξαι αὐτὴν εἰς τὸ ὑπερουράνιόν σου θυσιαστήριον.

(c) P. 10. Sacerdos in transitu a mensa propositionis versus altare dicit, Δεσπότα Κύριε, καὶ χαρισάμενος παρρησίαν ἡμῖν — προσφέρειν σοι

---

[d] Lib. ii. cap. 57. p. 297. These very words are used on the same occasion, and the following words are added, ὡς βασιλέως προσερχόμενοι σώματι.

τὴν φοβερὰν ταύτην καὶ ἀναίμακτον θυσίαν ὑπὲρ τῶν ἡμετέρων ἁμαρτημάτων, καὶ τῶν τοῦ λαοῦ ἀγνοημάτων — εὐδόκησον δεκτὰ γίνεσθαι τὰ προσαγόμενα ταῦτα δῶρα διὰ τῶν ἡμετέρων χειρῶν.

(d) P. 11. — ἵνα ἄξιοι γενώμεθα τοῦ προσφέρειν σοι δῶρά τε καὶ θυσίας ὑπέρ τε ἑαυτῶν, καὶ τῶν τοῦ λαοῦ ἀγνοημάτων — καὶ δὸς ἡμῖν, Κύριε, μετὰ παντὸς φόβου — προσκομίσαι σοι τὴν πνευματικὴν ταύτην καὶ ἀναίμακτον θυσίαν, ἣν προσδεξάμενος εἰς τὸ ὑπερουράνιόν — σου θυσιαστήριον — ἀντικατάπεμψον ἡμῖν τὴν χάριν τοῦ παναγίου σου Πνεύματος — πρόσδεξαι καὶ ἐκ χειρῶν ἡμῶν τῶν ἁμαρτωλῶν τὰ προκείμενα δῶρα ταῦτα — εἰς ἐξίλασμα τῶν ἡμετέρων πλημμελημάτων καὶ τῶν τοῦ λαοῦ ἀγνοημάτων, καὶ εἰς ἀνάπαυσιν τῶν προκεκοιμημένων ψυχῶν.

(e) Ibid. Εὐχὴ τοῦ καταπετάσματος. When the priest enters within the veil. Εὐχαριστοῦμέν σοι, Κύριε ὁ Θεὸς — ὅτι ἔδωκας ἡμῖν παρρησίαν εἰς τὴν εἴσοδον τῶν ἁγίων σου· ἣν ἐνεκαίνισας ἡμῖν ὁδὸν, κ.τ.λ. as Heb. x. 19 —22.

(f) P. 12. Ὁ διάκονος. — πρόσχωμεν τῇ ἁγίᾳ ἀναφορᾷ.

P. 13. Sacerdos recitat verba institutionis primo super panem, usque ad verba, ἔδωκεν ἡμῖν τοῖς Αὐτοῦ μαθηταῖς καὶ ἀποστόλοις, deinde λέγουσιν οἱ διάκονοι. Εἰς ἄφεσιν ἁμαρτιῶν, καὶ εἰς ζωὴν αἰώνιον. Εἶτα ἐκφωνεῖ [ἱερεὺς]. Λάβετε, φάγετε, κ.τ.λ.

(g) Inter verba institutionis, λαβών τὸ ποτήριον, καὶ κεράσας ἐξ οἴνου καὶ ὕδατος — εὐχαριστήσας, ἁγιάσας, πλήσας Πνεύματος Ἁγίου. — Post verba institutionis, addit sacerdos, Μεμνήμενοι οὖν καὶ ἡμεῖς οἱ ἁμαρτωλοὶ τῶν ζωοποιῶν Αὐτοῦ παθημάτων — προσφέρομέν σοι, Δεσπότα, τὴν φοβερὰν ταύτην καὶ ἀναίμακτον θυσίαν, δεόμενοι, ἵνα κ.τ.λ. Deprecatur peccatorum merita.

(h) Καὶ ἐξαπόστειλον ἐφ᾽ ἡμᾶς, καὶ ἐπὶ τὰ προκείμενα δῶρα ταυτα τὸ Πνεῦμά σου τὸ πανάγιον — P. 15. Αὐτὸ τὸ Πνεῦμά σου τὸ πανάγιον κατάπεμψον, Δεσπότα, ἐφ᾽ ἡμᾶς, καὶ ἐπὶ τὰ προκείμενα ἅγια δῶρα ταῦτα — ἵνα ποιήσῃ τὸν μὲν ἄρτον τοῦτον, σῶμα ἅγιον τοῦ Χριστοῦ σοῦ· καὶ τὸ ποτήριον τοῦτο, αἷμα τίμιον τοῦ Χριστοῦ σου.

(i) P. 17. Diaconus loquitur, Ἔτι καὶ ἔτι δεηθῶμεν ὑπὲρ τῶν προσκομισθέντων καὶ ἁγιασθέντων — θείων δώρων — ὅπως Κύριος ὁ Θεὸς ἡμῶν προσδεξάμενος αὐτὰ εἰς τὸ ὑπερουράνιον θυσιαστήριον, — ἀντικαταπέμψῃ ἡμῖν — τὴν δωρεὰν τοῦ παναγίου Πνεύματος.

LITURGIA S. MARCI, ex Biblioth. Patrum, mox post Liturgiam S. Jacobi.

(a) In Prothesi, p. 32. Ἐπίφανον τὸ πρόσωπόν Σου ἐπὶ τὸν ἄρτον τοῦτον, καὶ ἐπὶ τὰ ποτήρια ταῦτα.

(b) Ibid. Ὁ ἱερεὺς ἄρχεται τῆς ἀναφορᾶς. Ἀληθῶς γὰρ ἄξιόν ἐστι καὶ δίκαιον — δι᾽ οὗ (Χριστοῦ) Σοὶ σὺν Αὐτῷ, καὶ Ἁγίῳ Πνεύματι, εὐχαριστοῦντες προσφέρομεν τὴν λογικὴν καὶ ἀναίμακτον λατρείαν ταύτην, ἣν προσφέρει σοι, Κύριε, πάντα τὰ ἔθνη, κ.τ.λ. as Mal. i. 10, 11. — P. 35. τὰ εὐχαριστήρια πρόσδεξαι, ὁ Θεός, εἰς τὸ ἅγιον, καὶ ἐπουράνιον, καὶ νοερόν σου θυσιαστήριον — τῶν τὸ πολὺ καὶ ὀλίγον, κρύφα, καὶ παρρησίᾳ βουλομένων, καὶ οὐκ ἐχόντων· καὶ τῶν ἐν τῇ σήμερον ἡμέρᾳ τὰς προσφορὰς προσενεγκάντων, ὡς προσεδέξω τὰ δῶρα τοῦ δικαίου σου Ἀβέλ.

(c) P. 36. Πλήρης γάρ ἐστιν ὡς ἀληθῶς ὁ οὐρανὸς καὶ ἡ γῆ τῆς ἁγίας σου δόξης — πλήρωσον, ὁ Θεός, καὶ ταύτην τὴν θυσίαν τῆς παρὰ σου εὐλογίας διὰ τῆς ἐπιφοιτήσεως τοῦ παναγίου σου Πνεύματος — Deinde, p. 37, sacerdos profert verba institutionis. Inter verba institutionis, καὶ τὸ ποτήριον μετὰ τὸ δειπνῆσαι λαβὼν, καὶ κεράσας ἐξ οἴνου καὶ ὕδατος, εὐχαριστήσας, εὐλογήσας, πλήσας Πνεύματος Ἁγίου, τὸν θάνατον, Δεσπότα Κύριε·— τοῦ μονογενοῦς σου Υἱοῦ — καταγγέλλοντες — καὶ ἀνάστασιν — καὶ ἀνάληψιν — καὶ τὴν δευτέραν Αὐτοῦ παρουσίαν — τὰ σὰ ἐκ τῶν σῶν δώρων προεθήκαμεν ἐνώπιόν σου· καὶ δεόμεθα — ἐξαπόστειλον — τὸ Πνεῦμά σου τὸ Ἅγιον, ἵνα αὐτὰ ἁγιάσῃ καὶ τελειώσῃ — καὶ ποιήσῃ τὸν μὲν ἄρτον Σῶμα — τὸ δὲ ποτήριον Αἷμα τῆς καινῆς διαθήκης Αὐτοῦ τοῦ Κυρίου. κ.τ.λ.

LITURGIA S. BASILII M. ex Biblioth. Patrum. Tom. ii.

Edit. Paris. 1624. mox post LITURGIAM S. MARCI.

(a) P. 42. In Oratione propositionis. Εὐλόγησον τὴν πρόθεσιν ταύτην, καὶ πρόσδεξαι αὐτὴν εἰς τὸ ὑπερουράνιόν σου θυσιαστήριον.

(b) P. 46. Εὐχὴ πιστῶν πρώτη, ἣν ὁ ἱερεὺς λέγει μυστικῶς — Σύ, [Κύριε] ἱκάνωσον ἡμᾶς — ἵνα ἀκατακρίτως προσάγωμέν σοι θυσίαν αἰνέσεως· σὺ γὰρ εἶ ὁ ἐνεργῶν τὰ πάντα ἐν πᾶσι· δὸς, Κύριε, καὶ ὑπὲρ τῶν ἡμετέρων ἁμαρτημάτων, καὶ τῶν τοῦ λαοῦ ἀγνοημάτων, δεκτὴν γενέσθαι τὴν θυσίαν ἡμῶν.

(c) P. 46, 47. Εὐχὴ ἥν λέγει ὁ ἱερεὺς μυστικῶς, καὶ ἄχραντον τοῦ Χερουβικοῦ ᾀδομένου — Βασιλεῦ τῆς δόξης — ἱκάνωσόν με — ἱερουργῆσαι τὸ ἅγιόν σου Σῶμα, καὶ τίμιον Αἷμα — ἀξίωσον προσενεχθῆναι σοι ὑπ᾽ ἐμοῦ ἁμαρτωλοῦ — τὰ δῶρα ταῦτα· Σὺ γὰρ εἶ ὁ προσφέρων, καὶ ὁ προσφερόμενος, καὶ προσδεχόμενος, καὶ διαδιδόμενος.

(d) P. 47. Εὐχὴ προσκομιδῆς — Πρόσδεξαι ἡμᾶς, ἵνα γινώμεθα ἄξιοι τοῦ προσφέρειν σοι τὴν λογικὴν ταύτην καὶ ἀναίμακτον θυσίαν ὑπὲρ τῶν ἡμετέρων ἁμαρτημάτων, καὶ τῶν τοῦ λαοῦ ἀγνοημάτων· ἣν προσδεξάμενος εἰς τὸν ἅγιον καὶ νοερόν σου θυσιαστήριον, ἀντικατάπεμψον ἡμῖν τὴν χάριν τοῦ Ἁγίου σου Πνεύματος.

(e) P. 84. Στῶμεν μετὰ φόβου, πρόσχωμεν τὴν ἁγίαν ἀναφορὰν ἐν εἰρήνῃ προσφέρειν.

(f) P. 50, 51. Incipit recitare verba institutionis, usque ad verba λαβὼν ἄρτον — εὐχαριστήσας, κλάσας, deinde ὁ ἱερεὺς — αἴρων τὴν δεξιὰν αὐτοῦ — εὐλογεῖ τὸν ἅγιον ἄρτον, ἐκφώνως λέγων· Ἔδωκε τοῖς ἁγίοις

Αὐτοῦ μαθηταῖς — εἰπὼν, λάβετε, φάγετε, τοῦτό Μου ἐστὶ τὸ Σῶμα. Idem facit super poculum in hæc verba, Ὁμοίως καὶ τὸ ποτήριον ἐκ τοῦ γεννήματος τοῦ ἀμπέλου λαβὼν, κεράσας, εὐχαριστήσας, κ.τ.λ. Deinde Μεμνημένοι οὖν, Δεσπότα, καὶ ἡμεῖς τῶν σωτηρίων Αὐτοῦ παθημάτων — ἀναστάσεως — εἰς οὐρανοὺς ἀνόδου — καὶ φοβερᾶς Αὐτοῦ παρουσίας (ἐκφώνως ὁ ἱερεὺς) Τὰ σὰ ἐκ τῶν σῶν σοι προσφέροντες, κατὰ πάντα καὶ διὰ πάντα (ὁ χορὸς ψάλλει τὸ) Σὲ ὑμνοῦμεν, σὲ εὐλογοῦμεν, σοὶ εὐχαριστοῦμεν— κ.τ.λ.

(g) *Ibid.* Ὁ ἱερεὺς — εὔχεται. Δεσπότα πανάγιε — προσεγγίζομεν τῷ ἁγίῳ σου θυσιαστηρίῳ, καὶ προσθέντες τὰ ἀντίτυπα τοῦ Ἁγίου Σώματος καὶ Αἵματος τοῦ Χριστοῦ σου, σοῦ δεόμεθα — ἐλθεῖν τὸ Πνεῦμά σου τὸ Ἅγιον ἐφ' ἡμᾶς, καὶ ἐπὶ τὰ προκείμενα δῶρα ταῦτα, καὶ εὐλογῆσαι αὐτὰ, καὶ ἁγιάσαι, καὶ ἀναδείξαι — τόν μεν ἄρτον τοῦτον αὐτὸ τὸ τίμιον Σῶμα τοῦ — Ἰησοῦ Χριστοῦ — καὶ τὸ ποτήριον τοῦτο κ.τ.λ. Ὁ δὲ ἱερεὺς εὐλογῶν μετὰ τῆς χειρὸς ἀμφότερα τὰ ἅγια, λέγει· Μεταβαλὼν τῷ Πνεύματί σου τῷ Ἁγίῳ.

(h) P. 52. Ὁ ἱερεὺς ἐπεύχεται — Ἡμᾶς δὲ πάντας τοὺς ἐκ τοῦ ἑνὸς ἄρτου καὶ τοῦ ποτηρίου μετέχοντας, ἑνῶσαι ἀλλήλοις — καὶ μηδένα ἡμῶν εἰς κρίμα ἢ εἰς κατάκριμα ποιῆσαι μετασχεῖν τοῦ Ἁγίου Σώματος καὶ Αἵματος τοῦ Χριστοῦ σου. Deinde post quasdam laudes et preces pro populo communicaturo, pergit sacerdos ut in Liturgia Chrysostomi.

Liturgia S. JOANNIS CHRYSOSTOMI. Ex Biblioth. prædict. mox post Liturgiam S. BASILII.

(a) P. 64. Εὐχὴ προθέσεως. Ὁ Θεὸς, εὐλόγησον τὴν πρόθεσιν ταύτην, καὶ πρόσδεξαι αὐτὴν εἰς τὸ ὑπερουράνιόν σου θυσιαστήριον· — μνημόνευσον— προσενεγκάντων, καὶ δι' οὕς προσήγαγον.

(b) P. 73. Εὐχὴ ἥν λέγει ὁ ἱερεὺς μυστικῶς τοῦ Χερουβικοῦ ᾳδομένου· — ἱκάνωσον — μὲ παραστῆναι τῇ ἁγίᾳ σου ταύτῃ τραπέζῃ, καὶ ἱερουργῆσαι τὸ Ἅγιόν — σου Σῶμα, καὶ τὸ Τίμιόν σου Αἷμα· ἀξίωσον προσενεχθῆναι σοι ὑπ' ἐμοῦ — τὰ δῶρα ταῦτα· Σὺ γὰρ εἶ ὁ προσφέρων καὶ ὁ προσφερόμενος, κ. τ. λ. ut supra in Liturgia S. Basilii.

(c) P. 76. Εὐχὴ προσκομιδῆς — Ἱκάνωσον ἡμᾶς προσενέγκειν σοι δῶρά τε καὶ θυσίας πνευματικὰς ὑπὲρ τῶν ἡμετέρων ἁμαρτημάτων, καὶ τῶν τοῦ λαοῦ ἀγνοημάτων· καὶ καταξίωσον ἐπισκηνῶσαι τὸ Πνεῦμα τῆς χάριτος σου τὸ Ἀγαθὸν ἐφ' ἡμᾶς, καὶ ἐπὶ τὰ προκείμενα δῶρα, καὶ ἐπὶ πάντα τὸν λαόν σου.

(d) P. 77—79. Ὁ Διάκονος λέγει ἐκφώνως, Στῶμεν μετὰ φοβόυ, πρόσχωμεν τὴν ἁγίαν ἀναφορὰν ἐν εἰρήνῃ προσφέρειν· καὶ ἱερεὺς, Ἄξιον καὶ δίκαιον — et sic pergit verba Institutionis proferre ut supra in Liturgia S. Basilii, et per eadem verba dicitur εὐλογεῖν τὸν ἄρτον, καὶ τὸ ποτήριον.

Deinde Μεμνημένοι τοίνυν τῆς σωτηρίου ταύτης ἐντολῆς, καὶ — τοῦ

h

σταυρού, τοῦ τάφου — ἀναστάσεως, κ. τ. λ. Τὰ σὰ ἐκ τῶν σῶν σοι προσφέρομεν — ὁ χορὸς, Σὲ ὑμνοῦμεν, σὲ εὐλογοῦμεν, κ. τ. λ. Deinde ᾿Ἔτι προσφέρομέν — (inquit sacerdos) σοι τὴν λογικὴν ταύτην καὶ ἀναίμακτον λατρείαν, καὶ παρακαλοῦμεν — κατάπεμψον τὸ Πνεῦμά σου τὸ ῞Αγιον ἐφ᾿ ἡμᾶς καὶ ἐπὶ τὰ προκείμενα δῶρα ταῦτα. Et ποίησον τὸν μὲν ἄρτον τοῦτον, Τίμιον Σῶμα τοῦ Χριστοῦ, — τὸ δὲ ἐν τῷ ποτηρίῳ τούτῳ, Τίμιον Αἷμα τοῦ Χριστοῦ — μεταβαλὼν τῷ Πνεύματι σοῦ τῷ ῾Αγίῳ — ὥστε γενέσθαι τοῖς μεταλαμβάνουσιν εἰς νῆψιν ψυχῆς, εἰς ἄφεσιν ἁμαρτιῶν, εἰς κοινωνίαν τοῦ ῾Αγίου Πνεύματος, εἰς βασιλείας οὐρανῶν πλήρωμα.

(e) P. 80. ᾿Ἔτι προσφέρομέν σοι τὴν λογικὴν ταύτην λατρείαν ὑπὲρ τῶν ἐν πίστει ἀναπαυομένων προπατόρων, πατέρων, πατριαρχῶν, κ. τ. λ.

(f) P. 81. ῾Υπὲρ τῶν — τιμίων δώρων, τοῦ Κυρίου δεηθῶμεν — ὅπως ὁ Θεὸς, ὁ προσδεξάμενος αὐτὰ εἰς ὑπερουράνιον Αὐτοῦ θυσιαστήριον ἀντικαταπέμψῃ ἡμῖν — τὴν δωρεὰν τοῦ Παναγίου Πνεύματος — hæc diaconus.

(g) P. 83. Αὐτὸς, Δεσπότα, οὐρανόθεν ἔπιδε ἐπὶ τοὺς ὑποκεκλικότας σοι τὰς ἑαυτῶν κεφαλὰς· οὐ γὰρ ἔκλιναν σαρκὶ καὶ αἵματι, ἀλλά σοι τῷ φοβερῷ Θεῷ.

Liturgia S. PETRI, ex Biblioth. prædict. mox post
Liturg. S. CHRYSOSTOMI.

(a) P. 116. Εὐχὴ προθέσεως — ᾿Ἔπιδε ἐφ᾿ ἡμᾶς, καὶ ἐπὶ τὸν ἄρτον τοῦτον, καὶ ἐπὶ τὸ ποτήριον τοῦτο, καὶ ποίησον αὐτὸ ἄχραντόν σου Σῶμα, καὶ Τίμιον Αἷμα εἰς μετάληψιν ψυχῶν τε, καὶ σωμάτων. P. 118. Θυσίαν, Κύριέ, σοι προορισθεῖσαν προσφορὰν ἁγίασον, καὶ δι᾿ αὐτῆς ἡμᾶς ἀσμένως πρόσδεξαι διὰ τοῦ Κυρίου ἡμῶν ᾿Ἰησοῦ, κ. τ. λ. Sursum corda, Trisagium.

(b) P. 119. Σὲ τοίνυν, ἐπιεικέστατε Πάτερ, — δεόμεθα, ἵνα προσδεκταῖα σχῇς, καὶ εὐλογήσῃς ταῦτα τὰ δῶρα, ταύτην τὴν προσφορὰν, ταύτην τὴν ἁγίαν θυσίαν — ἅπερ σοι προσφέρομεν ὑπὲρ τῆς ῾Αγίας σου Καθολικῆς καὶ ᾿Αποστολικῆς ᾿Εκκλησίας — ἅμα τῷ δούλῳ σου τῷ πάπᾳ, κ.τ.λ. Deinde, ταύτην τοίνυν τὴν προσφορὰν — προσδεκταῖα ποιῆσαι καταξιώσῃς, ἵνα ἡμῖν Σῶμα καὶ Αἷμα γένηται — ᾿Ἰησοῦ Χριστοῦ, ὃς πρὸ μιᾶς ἡμέρας τοῦ πάθους Αὐτοῦ λαβὼν ἄρτον, κ.τ.λ. Recitat verba Institutionis, deinde.

(c) P. 121. Μνημονεύοντες, Κύριε, ἡμεῖς — τοῦ Χριστοῦ σου — πάθους — ἐγέρσεως — ἀναβάσεως, τὰ σὰ ἐκ τῶν σοι προσφέροντες (ὁ λαὸς) Σὲ ὑμνοῦμεν, σὲ εὐλογοῦμεν. ῾Ο ἱερεὺς ἐπεύχεται repetens verba, τὰ σὰ κ.τ.λ. Θυσίαν καθαρὰν, θυσίαν ἁγίαν, θυσίαν ἄμωμον, ἄρτον ἅγιον ζωῆς αἰωνίου, καὶ ποτήριον σωτηρίας ἀεννάου· ὑπὲρ ὧν ἵλεῳ καὶ εὐιλάτῳ προσώπῳ ἐπισκέψαι καταξιώσῃς, καὶ προσδεκτὰ σχεῖν, καθὰ κατηξίωσας τὰ δῶρα τοῦ — ᾿Αβὲλ, καὶ τὴν θυσίαν τοῦ — ᾿Αβραάμ· καὶ ὥσπερ σοι προσήγαγεν ὁ πρῶτος ἱερεύς σου Μελχισεδὲκ ἁγίαν θυσίαν, ἄμωμον προσφορὰν, ἱκετεύοντές Σε δεόμεθα, Παντοδύναμε Θεέ, κέλευσον τοῦτο διακονηθῆναι διὰ χειρὸς ἁγίου ἀγγέλου σου εἰς τὸ ὑψηλόν σου θυσιαστήριον — ἵνα οἵαν δήποτε ἐκ τούτου τοῦ θυσιαστηρίου μερίδα ἁγίαν τοῦ Σώματος τοῦ Ὑιοῦ, ἢ καὶ τοῦ Αἵματος ληψώμεθα, πάσης ἐπουρανίου εὐλογίας καὶ χάριτος ἐμπλησθῶμεν· — ἐν πρώτοις μνήσθητι κυρίου τοῦ ἀρχιεπισκόπου — pergit commemorare vivos, deinde Apostolos, Martyres, &c. μεθ' ὧν ἡμᾶς σύνταξον, μὴ ἐπισκέπτων τὰς πράξεις, κ.τ.λ.

S. Gregorii Lib. Sacramentorum.

Ed. Paris. 1642.

(a) P. 1. *Antiphona. Kyrie Eleison.* Gloria in excelsis, sive Litania. Oratio. Apostolus. Gradale, sive Alleluja. Postmodum legitur Evangelium, deinde Offertorium, et dicitur Oratio super Oblata. Dominus vobiscum. Sursum corda. Trisagium.

(b) P. 2. Deinde sacerdos. Te igitur, clementissime Pater, per Jesum Christum — rogamus et petimus, uti accepta habeas et benedicas hæc dona, hæc munera, hæc sancta sacrificia illibata : inprimis quæ Tibi offerimus pro Ecclesia, — una cum famulo tuo Papa nostro, Ill. et rege nostro Ill. et omnibus orthodoxis, atque Catholicæ et Apostolicæ fidei cultoribus.—Memento, Domine, famulorum, famularumque tuarum, Ill. et Ill. et omnium circumadstantium, quorum Tibi fides cognita est, et nota devotio ; qui Tibi offerunt hoc sacrificium laudis pro se suisque omnibus, pro redemptione animarum suarum, pro spe salutis et incolumitatis suæ, Tibi reddunt vota sua, æterno Deo, vivo, et vero. Commemoratio B. Mariæ Virginis, Apostolorum, et omnium Sanctorum.

(c) Quam oblationem Tu, Deus, in omnibus, quæsumus, benedictam, adscriptam, ratam, rationabilem, acceptabilemque facere digneris, ut nobis cor✠pus, et san✠guis fiat dilectissimi Filii Tui Domini Dei nostri Jesu Christi. Qui pridie quam pateretur (sequuntur verba Institutionis.) Unde et memores sumus, Domine, nos Tui servi, sed et plebs Tua sancta, Christi Filii Tui Dei nostri tam beatæ passionis, necnon et ab inferis resurrectionis, sed et in cœlos gloriosæ ascensionis. Offerimus præclaræ majestati Tuæ de Tuis donis ac datis, hostiam✠puram, hostiam✠sanctam, hostiam✠immaculatam, panem ✠sanctum vitæ æternæ, et calicem✠salutis perpetuæ. Super quæ, propitio ac sereno vultu respicere digneris, et accepta habere, sicuti accepta habere dignatus es munera pueri tui justi Abel, et sacrificium patriarchæ nostri Abrahæ, et quod Tibi obtulit summus sacerdos tuus Melchisedec sanctum sacrificium, immaculatam hostiam — Jube hæc perferri per manus angeli Tui in sublime altare Tuum,—ut quotquot ex hac altaris participatione sacro-sanctum Filii Tui ✠ Corpus, et ✠ Sanguinem sumpserimus, omni benedictione cœlesti, et gratia repleamur.

(d) *Super Diptycha.* Memento etiam, Domine, famulorum, famularumque tuarum Ill. qui nos præcesserunt cum signo fidei, et dormiunt in somno pacis. Ipsis, Domine, et omnibus in Christo quiescentibus locum refrigerii, lucis, et pacis, ut indulgeas, deprecamur.

Made in the USA
Columbia, SC
01 October 2022

68393072R00335